Rock Climbing
Yosemite Free Climbs

CHOCKSTONE

FALCON®

Rock Climbing Yosemite Free Climbs (2nd Edition)
© 1994 and 1998   Don Reid and George Meyers. All rights reserved. This book or any part rtherof may not be reproduced in any form whatsoever, whether by graphic, visual, electronic, or any other means other than for brief passages embodied in critical reviews and articles, without the written permission of the publisher.

Published and Distributed by
Falcon Press Publishing Co., Inc.
PO Box 1718
Helena, Montana 59624

Developed by
Chockstone Press

ISBN 0-934641-59-5

Front cover
Daniela Massetti on Cookie Monster, 5.12a, The Cookie Cliff. Photo by Chris Falkenstein. All uncredited photos by George Meyers.

Corrections
Please send corrections as well as new-route information to the author in care of Falcon Press Publishing Co., Inc.

In memory of Ferdinando Castillo, longtime gatekeeper to Yosemite.

WARNING: **CLIMBING IS A SPORT WHERE YOU MAY BE SERIOUSLY INJURED OR DIE. READ THIS BEFORE YOU USE THIS BOOK.**

This guidebook is a compilation of unverified information gathered from many different climbers. The author cannot assure the accuracy of any of the information in this book, including the topos and route descriptions, the difficulty ratings, and the protection ratings. These may be incorrect or misleading and it is impossible for any one author to climb all the routes to confirm the information about each route. Also, ratings of climbing difficulty and danger are always subjective and depend on the physical characteristics (for example, height), experience, technical ability, confidence and physical fitness of the climber who supplied the rating. Additionally, climbers who achieve first ascents sometimes underrate the difficulty or danger of the climbing route out of fear of being ridiculed if a climb is later down-rated by subsequent ascents. Therefore, be warned that you must exercise your own judgment on where a climbing route goes, its difficulty and your ability to safely protect yourself from the risks of rock climbing. Examples of some of these risks are: falling due to technical difficulty or due to natural hazards such as holds breaking, falling rock, climbing equipment dropped by other climbers, hazards of weather and lightning, your own equipment failure, and failure or absence of fixed protection.

You should not depend on any information gleaned from this book for your personal safety; your safety depends on your own good judgment, based on experience and a realistic assessment of your climbing ability. If you have any doubt as to your ability to safely climb a route described in this book, do not attempt it.

The following are some ways to make your use of this book safer:

1. **CONSULTATION:** You should consult with other climbers about the difficulty and danger of a particular climb prior to attempting it. Most local climbers are glad to give advice on routes in their area and we suggest that you contact locals to confirm ratings and safety of particular routes and to obtain first-hand information about a route chosen from this book.
2. **INSTRUCTION:** Most climbing areas have local climbing instructors and guides available. We recommend that you engage an instructor or guide to learn safety techniques and to become familiar with the routes and hazards of the areas described in this book. Even after you are proficient in climbing safely, occasional use of a guide is a safe way to raise your climbing standard and learn advanced techniques.
3. **FIXED PROTECTION:** Many of the routes in this book use bolts and pitons which are permanently placed in the rock. Because of variances in the manner of placement, weathering, metal fatigue, the quality of the metal used, and many other factors, these fixed protection pieces should always be considered suspect and should always be backed up by equipment that you place yourself. Never depend for your safety on a single piece of fixed protection because you never can tell whether it will hold weight, and in some cases, fixed protection may have been removed or is now absent.

Be aware of the following specific potential hazards which could arise in using this book:

1. **MISDESCRIPTIONS OF ROUTES:** If you climb a route and you have a doubt as to where the route may go, you should not go on unless you are sure that you can go that way safely. Route descriptions and topos in this book may be inaccurate or misleading.
2. **INCORRECT DIFFICULTY RATING:** A route may, in fact, be more difficult than the rating indicates. Do not be lulled into a false sense of security by the difficulty rating.
3. **INCORRECT PROTECTION RATING:** If you climb a route and you are unable to arrange adequate protection from the risk of falling through the use of fixed pitons or bolts and by placing your own protection devices, do not assume that there is adequate protection available higher just because the route protection rating indicates the route is not an "X" or an "R" rating. Every route is potentially an "X" (a fall may be deadly), due to the inherent hazards of climbing – including, for example, failure or absence of fixed protection, your own equipment's failure, or improper use of climbing equipment.

THERE ARE NO WARRANTIES, WHETHER EXPRESS OR IMPLIED, THAT THIS GUIDEBOOK IS ACCURATE OR THAT THE INFORMATION CONTAINED IN IT IS RELIABLE. THERE ARE NO WARRANTIES OF FITNESS FOR A PARTICULAR PURPOSE OR THAT THIS GUIDE IS MERCHANTABLE. YOUR USE OF THIS BOOK INDICATES YOUR ASSUMPTION OF THE RISK THAT IT MAY CONTAIN ERRORS AND IS AN ACKNOWLEDGEMENT OF YOUR OWN SOLE RESPONSIBILITY FOR YOUR CLIMBING SAFETY.

CONTENTS

Preface 1998..vii
Preface to the First Edition........................ix

Introduction
General Information 1
Environmental Issues 4
Staying Alive, By John Dill 8
Other Notes 22
Yosemite Valley Overview Map 23
Topo Key 24
How to Use this Book 25

Routes
Lower Merced Canyon: North 26
Ribbon Falls 86
El Capitan 94
Three Brothers 124
Yosemite Falls 140
Royal Arches 165
Washington Column 183
Tenaya Canyon 197
Little Yosemite 214
Glacier Point 228
Sentinel Rock 244
Cathedral 265
Leaning Tower 309
Lower Merced Canyon: South 318

Appendix and Index
First Ascents..349
Rated Route Index 385
Routes 401
US Geological Maps 414

PREFACE 1998

The ongoing forces of man and nature have been active in shaping the landscape of Yosemite since *Yosemite Free Climbs* came into print four years ago. The most dramatic of these was a major rockfall in the summer of 1996 which decimated the eastern portion of the Glacier Point Apron. Although the real impact area was east or left of the Cow and the Grack, these climbs lie on the fringe of a bona fide death zone. Future catastrophic events of this nature can not be predicted, therefore the utmost discretion must be used when considering these climbs. Happy Isles and the old approach are wiped out so the only thinkable approach would be from the west, closer to Curry Village. In the Mirror Lake area of Tenaya Canyon a recent gravity check has transformed Werner's Crack into a mere pile of talus. This rock debris has smothered the beginnings of the neighboring climbs as well. Immediately right of pitches 4 through 7 on the regular North Face Route of East Quarter Dome a rockfall occurring in 1997 appears to have showered debris on the lower portion of this route. The great flood of January 1997 had no direct impact on the cliffs of Yosemite. However, new public works projects and replacement structures prompted by the flood should cause climbers to take notice. The proposed encroachment of Camp 4 and Swan Slab have already seen much public debate. Hwy. 140, which accesses climbing in the Lower Merced Canyon, is being stabilized and widened. It is also possible that mileage references used for existing turnouts may be relocated in the future. One of the more noticeable manmade changes has been the removal of the gas station adjacent to Camp 4 (AKA Sunnyside Campground). Besides being more conscious of one's fuel consumption, the user of this book will have to substitute "Camp 4" for "the gas station" when used in approach information as a mileage reference for areas extending west of El Capitan (pages 114-133 are affected). In the years to come, the National Park Service will attempt to resolve some of the issues of automobile traffic within Yosemite Valley. Attemps to mitigate other resourse impacts are also in the works. In the end the natural spirit of the Valley inspires and dominates.

—D.R., 1998

PREFACE TO THE FIRST EDITION

The discovery of Yosemite Valley continues. Experiencing the natural beauty of this valley is timeless and has inspired generations. Each generation has found new facets of exploration within this incomparable valley.

The number of climbing routes has once again expanded significantly since the last edition of *Yosemite Climbs*. In an effort to maintain a guidebook of practical size for both the user and publisher, the information is now being presented in two volumes: *Yosemite Big Walls* and *Yosemite Free Climbs*. Although each book will be more focused and manageable, categorizing climbing routes in this manner has some shortcomings. For example, on the West Face of El Capitan or the Chouinard-Herbert on Sentinel Rock, where once big-wall technique was the norm, contemporary mainstream climbers are more often dealing with a chalkbag rather than a haulbag. Although other big routes such as Lurking Fear, The Nose, and Zodiac on El Capitan; the South Face Route and The Prow of Washington Column; the Regular Northwest Face route on Half Dome, etc., are now climbed in a day with increasing regularity, most parties still pursue a multi-day, haul and jümar, traditional big-wall game plan. Conversely, free or mostly free routes that are particularly long, involved, and difficult, such as Escape from Freedom on Mt. Watkins and Southern Belle and Karma on Half Dome may require days. On these routes, bivys, haulbags and an atmosphere of big-wall logistics intercedes. In the end, the individual climber, and not a big-wall or free-climbing guidebook, will determine the most realistic format of ascent.

As in previous editions of *Yosemite Climbs*, a number of the valley's climbs have been excluded, mostly pre-1970 in origin and of dubious interest to contemporary climbers. The 1971 *Climber's Guide to Yosemite Valley*, written by Steve Roper and published by the Sierra Club, is a valuable archive of information for these routes. Other established routes do not appear because of confusing or questionable information. Still other areas have been omitted beacuse of aesthetic, resource, or public safety issues.

John Dill again provides a valuable and illuminating analysis of the serious climbing accidents that have occurred in the Park since 1970.

There is no historical perspective provided here. Several books are planned that will deal with the rich and extensive history that climbing and Yosemite share. This guidebook is big and expensive enough without dealing with such a complex subject.

The topos are the result of compiling route information from many sources. Those climbers who provided information for previous editions of this guide are to be thanked again; they helped build the framework for this book. Once again, many people were generous with their time by providing detailed lists of corrections to the previous work, and many others unselfishly shared with the authors information about their new routes. This guide is clearly the result of a group effort. Of particular note are the following people who devoted an extraordinary amount of time and effort to ensure that this guide is as accurate as possible: Jerry Anderson, Brian Bennett, Dave Bengston, Clint Cummins, Dan and Sue McDevitt, Kevin Fosburg, Jim Howard, Eric Kohl, Greg Murphy, Bill Russell, Jeff Schoen, Ron Skelton, Jonny Woodward, and Brad Young. Thanks to the many others which contributed to this project.

Special thanks to Tucker Tech for sharing his extensive log of new and corrected route information. My appreciation too, goes to Walt Shipley for providing substantial as well as vivid route information. The continued support and assistance of Susan Lilly-Reid has contributed greatly to this and past works; I deeply thank her. Thanks to Chris Falkenstein for his help, and particularly the use of his excellent photos.

The authors wishes to acknowledge and thank the United States Geological Survey for the map of Yosemite Valley (1:24,000 scale) that has been reproduced at the back of this book.

The author wishes to thank the National Park Service for the use of photos, some taken from perspectives impossible to duplicate without a helicopter. Special thanks to John Dill and Gary Colliver for their contributions to the environmental and safety sections of the introductory.

Several environmental/climber use issues are just now being actively examined by the National Park Service. Dealing with these issues, particularly at this stage, is an evolving process. In order to ensure continued climbing access, as well as promoting natural resource protection, climbers are urged to stay informed through the Visitors Center, the Sunnyside Campground Bulletin Board (Camp 4), and any posting at specific climbing or approach/descent localities.

—D.R., 1994

INTRODUCTION

Yosemite Valley continues to reveal itself as an incomparably beautiful and vast rock-sculptured wonder. Decade after decade, it has been an inspiring dream for climbers, and has also provided the fulfilling reality of a supreme granite-climbing experience. The number of climbers attracted to Yosemite, and the level of drama played out in this arena, is testimony to Yosemite's allure, as is the sheer number of routes established by these climbers.

Hundreds of rock climbing areas have been developed around the world in the last 100 years, yet none have so fired the imagination of climbers, or meant so much to the high standards of contemporary mountaineering, as Yosemite Valley. As a result, the Valley has taken on an increasingly international flavor as thousands of climbers from around the world have traveled here to climb. Fun-in-the-sun rock climbing is what Yosemite is all about, but it is more than just a crag area; it is a complicated valley, with the many cliff formations placed in such a way as to require of the climber some greater mountaineering skills.

Located 150 miles east of San Francisco, Yosemite Valley is the dramatic centerpoint of Yosemite National Park. Although only seven square miles in area, it contains some of North America's most exquisite scenery and is popular with tourists: millions of people visit the Park each year, though primarily in summer. While the Valley remains the traffic center of this 1,200-square-mile Park for both tourist and climber alike, the intricate terrain provides adequate cover for the rock climber wishing to lose sight of the tourists and gain some sense of a wilderness experience. Not all climbers adopt this option, of course, and in full season roadside crags are often crowded.

Direct flights can be taken to Los Angeles or San Francisco from most major cities of the world. Buses travel regularly to the nearby cities of Fresno and Merced, and on to Yosemite, albeit somewhat inconveniently. Hitchhiking is commonly successful in California, especially for those prepared with destination signs and interesting-looking climbing paraphernalia.

GENERAL INFORMATION:
When to Come

The best time to climb in Yosemite is during the months of April and May, September and October. Pleasant temperatures, lack of summertime tourist crowds, and the fact that the waterfalls are in their full glory make the spring the most popular time for climbers. April can be pretty rainy, however. Autumn is usually quieter and normally has great climbing weather, but the days are short and it can storm just about any time. Summer sees most of the local climbers heading to Yosemite's high-country domes at Tuolumne Meadows to escape the heat. In spite of occasional 100°F temperatures in summer, climbing can still be comfortable on the shady south side of the Valley. The first snowfall of the season usually comes to Yosemite

INTRODUCTION

Valley sometime after November 15th; the last snows fall sometime before April 15. Only during the dead of winter will the snow remain unmelted in the shade. Winter climbing activity is usually slow, although there can be long periods of clear, dry, mild weather.

The main information office for Yosemite National Park can be reached at PO Box 577, Yosemite, California 95389, or by calling (209)372-0264 for a recording, or (209)372-0265 during business hours. A road, weather, and camping recording is available at (209)372-0209. The Public Information office can be reached at (209)372-0529 for current information on peregrine falcon closures and other climbing concerns.

Staying in the Park

An entrance fee must be paid upon entering the park, which can be dealt with in one of three ways. Visitors can purchase a $20 one-week pass per car; a $40 Yosemite Pass, which allows yearly access to Yosemite only; or a $50 Golden Eagle Pass, which allows annual passage into national parks and monuments throughout the country. During the summer season, from June 1 to September 15, there is a seven-day camping limit in the valley. There is a 30-day limit the rest of the year.

The National Park Service is the governing authority within Yosemite, and the park service's obligation is the preservation of this national resource. Thus, the service is responsible for law enforcement, ambulance service, roads, campgrounds (although the reservation system is handled by Destinet), water, sewage, trash, etc. It also conducts search and rescue operations when necessary. Also, and not to be eclipsed by the above-mentioned, the park service also handles resource management and interpretive programs.

The concessionaire in Yosemite is the Yosemite Concession Services. It offers and operates virtually all of the goods and services within the park. The medical clinic, Ansel Adams Studio and an automatic teller machine are a few exceptions. A general store, post office, medical clinic, visitor center, garage and delicatessen are located in Yosemite Village. Curry Village, Yosemite Lodge and Ahwahnee Hotel provide accommodations ranging from modest tent-cabins to fairly luxurious hotel rooms. Additional public facilities can be found at these locations as well. At Yosemite Lodge, for instance, there is a year-round cafeteria, restaurant, bar and gift shop/convenience store. Of special interest, there are showers at Curry Village ($2.00, soap and towel provided). Also at Curry Village, there is a mountain shop, the Yosemite Mountaineering School and Guide Service, and the usual cafeteria, convenience store, fast food, etc. The laundromat can be found at Curry Housekeeping Camp. The only gas station currently in the valley is adjacent to Sunnyside Campground. However, there are plans to remove the gas station in the near future.

Four campgrounds are located in the valley. Sunnyside Campground (AKA Camp 4) is the place with the most atmosphere, and is the popular choice among climbers. In this boulder-strewn, walk-in campground, individuals are charged $3 per night for shared sites, with up to six people allowed in each site. It can be overflowing or deserted, depending on the time of year and weather conditions. Most of the other campgrounds provide conventional car camping, with sites going for $15 per night with a six-person,

INTRODUCTION

two-car maximum. Advance reservations for car camping are necessary from spring to mid-fall, particularly on weekends. Reservations may be made up to five months in advance, starting on the fifthteenth of each month. The mailing address for Destinet is 9450 Carroll Park Drive, San Diego, California 92121, or call Destinet toll-free at (800) 436-7275. From outside the U.S., call Destinet at 1(619) 452-8787. Mindful of the great demand for campsites in Yosemite Valley, callers are advised that the phone numbers become operational starting at 7:00 am Pacific Standard Time. Reservations also may be made in person at the campground Reservation Office in Curry Village. Pets are permitted in designated campgrounds (Upper Pines) only and must be leashed at all times. Pets are not allowed on any park trails.

A free shuttle bus system runs between the Lodge, Village, Ahwahnee and Curry, which provides easy access to climbs within the east end of the valley. Bicycles work well in the main valley, but for climbers without cars, arranging rides with other climbers may be necessary to get to cliffs in the lower valley.

Suggestions and Precautions

For the climber interested in bouldering, an excellent bouldering circuit extends from the western end of Camp 4 east to Swan Slab. Other prime bouldering spots are the start of the Four-Mile Trail, below Sentinel Rock, and near the Curry Housekeeping Camp.

Poison oak is found throughout the Valley, although it grows most abundantly west of the Pohono Bridge and throughout Lower Merced Canyon. Rattlesnakes may be encountered during warm weather months basking in the sun along the base of cliffs. Rarely do they provide more than just a notable nuisance on an approach to a climb.

Yosemite Valley is no wilderness, and the climber must share the relatively small space with thousands of other visitors. It is still possible for the imaginative climber to find a quiet day, alone with the cliffs and the swallows. While the crowded camping experience may leave some climbers cold, those who complain of the crowded climbing experience are simply unimaginative in their route-finding abilities. Nighttime is a different story; Yosemite is known among the regulars for its boring nights as much as its exciting days. The options are limited: the Lodge-wandering circuit with bar or restaurant, or back to camp. Books help, but it's difficult to find a place to read. Solution? There is no solution, but you will have lots of company.

Yosemite Valley has all the ingredients of a small town, and it does not revolve around the world of the climber. About 1,200 people live or work throughout the year in the Park, mostly in Yosemite Valley; the number rises to perhaps 2,200 during the height of the tourist season. These residents all fall into various social groups but, except for a minute percentage, share a total lack of interest in climbing or climbers. Curry employees, both career professionals and the incredibly temporary juveniles, form the bulk of the work force. Then there is the Park Service employee, from the dedicated naturalist to the law enforcement officer. It is the latter group that spells trouble for anyone who loves to climb a lot in Yosemite, but also needs to be loud about it. Keeping in mind that to most of the residents of Yosemite, climbers are merely tourists who spend little money, can be disorderly, and

INTRODUCTION

try to stay as long as possible, it is not difficult to understand why some law enforcement rangers see their job as challenged by those who bend the rules. There are rangers who climb very actively, however, and since the mandate of the Park Service is to protect the natural resource, most rangers will be found to be very helpful.

Interaction between the Park Service and the climbing community is bridged in one other way. With a couple of sites in Camp 4 reserved for the free use of the most experienced Yosemite climbers, the Park has a competent and obligated source of paid help for technical searches and rescues. The experience of the Yosemite Search and Rescue Team is invaluable to all climbers by providing feedback on the prevention of major accidents.

Free Climbing in Yosemite

Yosemite is known for cliffs that are clean and beautifully sheer, big and plentiful. El Capitan and Half Dome are familiar to climbers the world over for their sculptured and dramatic rises of 3,000 and 2,000 feet respectively. Throughout the Valley are dozens of sheer faces that rise over 1,200 vertical feet, some, in fact, still unclimbed. Ascents of these big walls usually involve aid techniques, methods that are neither fast nor uncomplicated. No one appreciates the size of El Cap more than one who has spent days climbing it. Nonetheless, most climbers who come to Yosemite come to free climb.

The classic free climbs of Yosemite – the steepest, cleanest lines – are crack climbs. They require specialized crack climbing techniques and stamina not easily practiced at most other climbing areas. This state of affairs breeds several results: newcomers to Yosemite rarely succeed on long, difficult crack climbs, and the face climbs that are found in Yosemite attract a disproportionate amount of nonresident traffic. That said, with conditioning and practice, all well-traveled climbers can enjoy Yosemite's incomparable concentration of long, free routes. In addition, Yosemite is home for many long face climbs that are exposed, bold, and exciting. And, in stride with a trend that is well-established throughout the world, short, intense sport routes are found in Yosemite, many in excitingly exposed situations unique to a 3,000-foot-deep valley.

From the standpoint of fighting litter, it is imperative to carry down what is carried up. Old slings, wads of tape, and assorted trash found at the base of obscure and remote cliffs discredit the notion that climbers are actively respectful of the natural environment. Few issues threaten the climber's freedom as seriously as littering. Officially, Park Service policy says that anything above 4,200 feet is wilderness and everything that is carried in should be packed out.

ENVIRONMENTAL ISSUES:
The National Park Service Perspective

The National Park Service was created in 1916 to "provide for the enjoyment of the visitor" and to "leave the park unimpaired for future generations." Unfortunately, these two goals often conflict, and balancing the immediate demands of visitors with the long-term health of the Park is a task that often generates controversy. Climbers and non-climbers alike affect, and are affected by, Park Service land use policy.

INTRODUCTION

Climbing is one of the oldest recreational uses in Yosemite, predating the establishment of the Park in 1890. James Hutchings, John Muir, and Clarence King had little impact on the mountains they climbed, using no equipment that marred the rock and leaving nothing behind. With the exception of George Anderson's bolt route on the Northeast Face of Half Dome in 1875, this benign relationship prevailed until the 1930s, when the use of pitons, bolts, and other modern climbing methods became popular. The increasing number of climbers through the 1940s, '50s, and '60s led to noticeable rock damage and the clean climbing revolution of the '70s.

Given the large number of climbers and the nature of the damage they cause, the Park Service has enacted surprisingly little regulation of the sport. This is partly because of the historic use of the Park for climbing and partly because climbers have traditionally policed themselves. Indeed, for many years climbing and environmentalism were seen as close partners; until recently, the *Sierra Club Bulletin* published climbing stories and route descriptions next to articles on preserving wilderness areas. Many of the outstanding conservationists in American history were climbers, notably Muir and David Brower. To Muir, the term "mountaineer" implied that one not only climbed and felt at home in the high country, but loved and cared for mountains as well.

This perception, however, has changed. Climbing is now seen by some people as just one more destructive use of the land. In several areas of the country, both private landowners and public land agencies have responded to climber-caused environmental damage by restricting climbing. The list of problems caused by climbers is lengthy: multiple approach trails and the subsequent erosion, disturbance of cliff-dwelling animals, destruction of American Indian rock art, litter, chalk marks, pin scars, bolts, chopped holds and aid placements, glued-on artificial holds, gardening (an ironic euphemism for destroying vegetation), "trails" of lichen-free rock that can be seen from miles away, bivy ledges that reek of urine and feces, chopping down trees close to a route, bright-colored rappel slings, etc. Virtually all of these impacts have occurred in Yosemite in the last few years. Some of these impacts are reversible (litter, feces, chalk) while some are permanent (bolts, chopped holds, pin scars).

No other users of the Park are permitted to cause such damage. These practices not only degrade the natural environment and diminish the climbing experience, but are also noticed by the nonclimbing public. The average visitor to Yosemite expects to view the Park's famous cliffs without seeing chalk marks, bolts, and rappel slings. Visitor complaints (from nonclimbers and climbers) about this damage are common.

Look around you when you go climbing. Erosion turning that approach trail into a gully? Is there a maze of trails where one would do? Is your climbing route visible from across the valley as a white scar up the lichen-covered rock? Note the absence of small trees, bushes, and flowering plants that were there a few years ago. None of that will regrow overnight. (Soil formation and lichen growth can take hundreds of years.) Now extend the damage you've identified ahead a decade, a generation, several generations. What will it look like then? (How many new routes will have gone up in that time?) Compare that future with what you think the Park should look like.

INTRODUCTION

For how long do you think the Park should be maintained in its natural state? Do your wishes match the changes you see around you?

Clearly, some limitations are necessary. Currently, motorized drilling, cutting trees, attaching artificial holds, and littering are illegal in the Park. If present trends continue, more control of climbing activity may be required to protect the natural environment. If climbers undertake reforms themselves, additional regulations may not be necessary.

What can you do to protect the environment while preserving your climbing freedom? First, climb in an environmentally responsible manner. Minimize your impact. Follow the Climber's Code, recently published by the Access Fund. Second, get involved. Write the park superintendent (NPS, PO Box 577, Yosemite, CA 95389) and express your opinions on climbing issues. Contact the Access Fund (PO Box 17010, Boulder, Colorado 80308) and local climbing groups. Third, exercise restraint. Just because a route *can* be climbed doesn't mean it *should* be climbed. Does El Cap really need another route with pitch after pitch of chiselled copperhead placements? Is it worth destroying hundreds of square feet of cliffside vegetation for yet another 5.11 face climb? Is it worth incurring public complaints for putting up *another* bolted route in Lower Falls amphitheater? Is it really necessary to place bolts up a route that can easily be top-roped? Only by seriously considering such questions can Yosemite's walls, and your climbing freedom, be preserved.

Areas Not Included in this Guide

Climbs in several areas have not been included in this edition of *Yosemite Climbs*. The reasons vary from area to area, but center around aesthetic, resource, or public safety issues.

Several areas in the Lower Merced River Canyon Wild and Scenic River corridor have been excluded due to of their high visibility, the potential for lichen scraping scars and/or chalk marks to detract from the aesthetics of the canyon, and because of the potential traffic hazard of climbs readily visible from the narrow and curvy Highway 140.

Numerous climbs in the Upper and Lower Yosemite Falls corridors and along the Upper Yosemite Falls Trail are not listed. Overall this corridor is one of the most scenic areas of the whole Yosemite Valley area, the destination of a high percentage of Park visitors. The NPS has received numerous complaints about climbers in this area, especially in the Lower Falls Amphitheater. The presence of large numbers of climbers and/or climbing equipment in these areas is viewed as an unacceptable conflict with the aesthetics of the area, the protection of which was one of the major purposes for the creation of Yosemite National Park. Certain climbs along the Upper Falls Trail, in addition to detracting from the wilderness atmosphere of the Falls corridor, create both an attractive nuisance and, potentially, a direct hazard to hikers on the Trail. Climbs in the vicinity of Vernal and Nevada Falls are likewise seen as conflicting with the aesthetics of those areas.

The short span of rock and talus below the Lower Royal Arch between the popular climbing areas of the Royal Arches and Washington Column is readily accessible, yet relatively pristine. It will be managed to maintain that condition.

INTRODUCTION

The area between Public Sanitation Wall and Chapel Wall harbors a relatively uncommon talus-riparian community. Characterized by a very unstable sand and scree slope, the area is dominated by mature big-leaf maples, and a unique assemblage of shrub species, including wild mock orange, American dogwood, willow and gooseberry. Additionally, the rock in the area tends to be heavily covered with lichen and moss. Because of the unstable slopes, unacceptable, unmitigable environmental degradation is virtually inevitable from any heavy use of this area.

The voluntary "delisting" of certain climbs or areas is being tried as an initial means of reducing use and mitigating impacts in sensitive areas, an alternative to their begin officially closed by the NPS. Climbing in officially closed areas would be illegal and subject to citation. We hope that climbers will voluntarily cooperate in this effort at self-regulation by the climbing community, in an effort to reduce impacts, share Yosemite's resources with other user groups, and, hopefully, forestall the need for more forceful NPS action.

Code of Conduct

Awareness, accountability, and self-restraint are what will preserve the right to climb in Yosemite.

- Stay current with issues and regulations (peregrine falcon closures, etc.). Current climber-related information can be found posted on the bulletin boards at Sunnyside, at Curry Village, and (in Tuolumne Meadows), at the Mountain School.
- Climb in a safe and responsible manner. Rescue helicopters in a meadow and an army of rescuers on the summit make for big-time environmental impact.
- Use established approach/descent trails whenever possible.
- Above 4,200 feet of elevation is designated wilderness. This includes all the wall routes of Yosemite.
- Camping at the base of routes and cliffs is considered out-of-bounds, and is illegal.
- The Park Service considers equipment that has been in place for 24 hours to be abandoned. Fixed ropes and "high-point" gear caches are high-profile actions to be avoided.
- Don't throw haulbags–or anything–else off cliffs.
- Don't litter. Pack all trash out.
- Dispose of human waste properly. Ejecting garbage and waste, then returning to the base to pick-up is illegal and no solution to waste disposal. Contain it. A PVC 'pipe-bomb' or other bombproof container will help keep routes and bivy spots from being gross-out health hazards. Current Park Service Regulations require containerization of human waste. The Park Service suggests that climbers initially defecate into a small paper bag. Small amounts of kitty litter and/or slack lime may be used to stabilize moisture and odors if desired. The paper bag can then be safely and conveniently stored and transported in a sturdy plastic container with a tight fitting lid. This outer container can either be placed into a pack or haulbag, or suspended below the haulbag. Upon returning to the ground, the paper bags containing human waste must be disposed of in one of the vault toilets located in the Park. Pumped vault toilets are the only facilities capable of handling the

INTRODUCTION

disposal of paper bags containing waste. Please do not dispose of any other type of trash in the vaults, place bags of feces in flush toilets, or use plastic bags instead of paper..With ascents almost always in progress (especially on El Capitan), deposit of dumpage at the base is unacceptable.

- Car pool or ride a bicycle when possible. Cutting down on overnight parking at El Capitan would be particularly helpful.

STAYING ALIVE:
by John Dill, NPS Search and Rescue

Most climbers do a good job coping with the hazards of their sport, yet more than 100 climbing accidents occur in the Park every year. What factors contribute to them? What, if anything, can climbers do to avoid them? And just how dangerous *is* climbing, anyway? With these questions in mind, the National Park Service (NPS) recently examined most of the serious accidents that occurred in the Park during the years from 1970 through 1990. The conclusions provide interesting reading for those wishing to stay alive.

Fifty-one climbers died from traumatic injuries in that period. A dozen more, critically hurt, would have died without rapid transport and medical treatment. In addition, there were many serious, but survivable, injuries, from fractured skulls to broken legs (at least 50 fractures per year), and a much larger number of cuts, bruises, and sprains.

Not surprisingly, most injuries occurred during leader falls and involved feet, ankles, or lower legs; for many, these are the accepted risks of climbing. However, leader falls accounted for only 25% of the fatal and near-fatal traumatic injuries; roughly 10% were from rockfall, 25% from being deliberately unroped, and 40% from simple mistakes with gear. Many cases are not clear cut; several factors may share the credit, and it is sometimes hard to quantify the weird adventures climbers have.

Not to be overlooked in the body count are environmental injuries. Inadequately equipped for the weather, four climbers died of hypothermia and perhaps 45 more would have died of the cold or the heat if not rescued.

Fifteen to 25 parties require an NPS rescue each year. Sixty more climbers stagger into Yosemite's medical clinic on their own, and an unknown number escape statistical immortality by seeking treatment outside the Park (or at the Mountain Room Bar).

Most Yosemite victims are experienced climbers: 60% have been climbing for three years or more, lead at least 5.10, are in good condition, and climb frequently. Short climbs and big walls, easy routes and desperate ones — all get their share of the accidents.

The NPS keeps no statistics on how many climbers use the park, but 25,000 to 50,000 climber-days annually is a fair estimate. With this in mind, 2.5 deaths and a few serious injuries per year may seem a pretty low rate. It's much too high, however, if your climbing career is cut short by a broken hip, or worse. It's also too high when you consider that at least 80% of the fatalities, and many injuries, were easily preventable. In case after case, igno-

INTRODUCTION

rance, a casual attitude, and/or some form of distraction proved to be the most dangerous aspects of the sport.

As the saying goes, "good judgement comes from bad experience." In the pages that follow are condensed 21 years of bad experience — the situations Yosemite climbers faced, the mistakes they made, and some recommendations for avoiding bad experiences of your own. This information comes, in many cases, from the victims' own analysis, or from that of their peers.

Environmental Dangers

On October 11, 1983, a climber on El Cap collapsed from heat exhaustion. On October 11, 1984, a party on Washington Column was immobilized by hypothermia. You can expect this range of weather year-'round.

Heat No Yosemite climber has died from the heat, but a half-dozen parties have come close. Too exhausted to move, they survived only because death by drying-up is a relatively slow process, allowing rescuers time to get there.

Temperatures on the sunny walls often exceed 100°F, but even in cool weather, climbing all day requires lots of water. The generally accepted minimum, two quarts per person per day, is just that — a minimum. It may not replace what you use, so don't let the desire for a light haulbag be your overriding concern–and take extra water–for unanticipated delays. Do not put all your water in a single container, and watch out for leaks.

If you find yourself rationing water, remember that dehydration will seriously sap your strength, slowing you even further. It's not uncommon to go from mere thirst to a complete standstill in a single day. Continuing up may be the right choice, but several climbers have said, "I should have gone down while I could."

Storms We still hear climbers say, "It never rains in Yosemite." In fact, there are serious storms year-'round. Four climbers have died of hypothermia and almost 50 have been rescued, most of whom would not have survived otherwise. Several were very experienced, with winter alpine routes, Yosemite walls, and stormy bivouacs to their credit — experts, by most measures. In many cases they took substandard gear, added another mistake or two, and couldn't deal with the weather.

Mountain thunderstorms are common in spring, summer, and fall. They may appear suddenly out of a clear blue sky and rapidly shift position, their approach concealed by the route you are on. A few minutes' warning may be all that you get. Thunderstorms may last only a couple of hours, but they are very intense, with huge amounts of near-freezing water often mixed with hail, strong winds, and lightning. The runoff can be a foot deep and fast enough to cause rockfall. A common result is a panicky retreat, a jammed rope, and cries for help. (The standard joke is that someone will drown on a Tuolumne climb one of these days. It's actually possible.)

No climber has died in such a storm yet, because rescuers were able to respond. No climbers have died from lightning either, but there have been several near-misses, and hikers on Half Dome and elsewhere have been killed. Get out of the way of a thunderstorm as fast as you can, and avoid summits and projections.

INTRODUCTION

The big Pacific storm systems have proven more dangerous. They sweep through the Sierra at any time of year, most frequently from September through May. They are unpredictable, often appearing back-to-back after several weeks of gorgeous, mind-numbing weather. It may rain on Half Dome in January and snow there in July. These Pacific storms are dangerous because they are usually warm enough to be wet, even in winter, yet always cold enough to kill an unprotected climber. They last from one to several days, offering little respite if you can't escape.

With no soil to absorb it, rain on the walls quickly collects into streams and waterfalls, pouring off overhangs and down the corner you're trying to climb up or sleep in. Wind blows the water in all directions, including straight up. It may rip apart a plastic tube tent or blow a portaledge up and down until the tubing breaks or the fly rips. Overhanging faces and other "sheltered" spots are not always immune—rain and waterfalls several yards away may be blown directly onto your bivy, and runoff will wick down your anchor rope. Even a slow but steady leak into your shelter can defeat you. Temperatures may drop, freezing solid the next pitch, your ropes, and your wet sleeping bag.

Once cold and wet, you are in real trouble and your options run out. If you leave your shelter to climb or rappel, you deteriorate more rapidly from the wind and water. Even with good gear, water runs down your sleeve every time you reach up. As your body temperature drops, you begin making dumb mistakes, such as clipping in wrong or dropping your rack. You are seriously hypothermic and soon you will just hang there, no longer caring. It happens quickly. In two separate incidents, climbers on the last pitch of The Nose left what protection they had to make a run for the top. They all died on that pitch.

Staying put may be no better. If you need help, no one may see you or hear you, and reaching you may take days longer than it would in good weather. Survivors say they had no idea how helpless they'd be until it happened to them. To find out for yourself, stand in the spray of a garden hose on a cold, windy night. How long will you last?

Big Wall Bivouacs

Despite this grim scenario, reasonable precautions will turn stormy big-wall bivouacs into mere annoyances:

- Check the forecast just before you start up but don't rely on it. For several parties, the weather forecast provided no warning whatsoever.
- Assume you'll be hit by a storm, and that you'll not have a choice of bivies.
- Ask friends to check on you if the weather or the forecast turns bad.
- Evaluate ahead of time the problems of retreat from any point on the route. Did you bring a bolt kit? How about a "cheater stick" for clipping into bolt hangers and stuffing cams into out-of-reach cracks as you flee down an overhanging pitch?
- If it's starting to rain, think twice about climbing "just one more pitch"—once wet, you won't dry out. It's better to set up your bivy while you're still dry.
- Frozen ropes are useless for climbing or retreating, as several parties

INTRODUCTION

found out. Put them away early.

All such hints and tricks aside, the bottom line is your ability to sit out the storm. Your first priority is to keep the wind and outside water away. Secondly, you must be insulated enough to stay warm, even though you are wet from your own condensation.

- Stick with high-quality gear in good condition, and don't leave key items behind to ease the hauling. Don't go up with a poorly equipped partner: it will be your neck as well.
- For insulation, never rely on cotton or down (even if it's covered with one of the waterproof/breathable fabrics). Even nylon absorbs water. Wool, polypropylene, and polyester insulators stay relatively warm when wet, and the synthetics dry fastest. Take along long underwear, warm pants, sweater, jacket, balaclava/hat, gloves, sleeping bag, insulating pad, extra socks or booties, and plenty of food and water—dehydration hastens hypothermia.
- For rain, use coated nylon, sailors' oilskins, or the waterproof/breathable fabrics. Take rain pants and jacket, overmitts, bivy bag, and hammock or portaledge with waterproof fly. The fly is critical — it must overlap your hammock generously and be of heavy material, in excellent condition, with strong, well-sealed seams. For sleeping on ledges, take a big tent fly or a piece of heavy-duty, reinforced plastic and the means to pitch it. Then hope that your ledge doesn't turn into a lake. Do you know how to run your anchor through the fly without making a hole? Did you spend more for lycra than rainwear?
- **Warning:** Several climbers have blamed the waterproof/breathable fabrics for their close calls. They claim that no version of it can take the punishment of a storm on the walls. Whether true or not, you must be the judge; test all of your gear ahead of time under miserable conditions, but where your exit is an easy one.

For more information on bad weather, including a description of the waterproof anchor, see "Surviving Big Walls," by Brian Bennett, *Climbing*, February/March 1990.

Unplanned Bivouacs Getting caught by darkness is common, especially on the longer one-day climbs and descent routes, e.g., Royal Arches and Cathedral Rocks. It happens easily—a late start, a slow partner, off-route, a jammed or dropped rope, or a sprained ankle. Usually it's nothing to get upset about, but if you are unprepared, even a cold wind or a mild storm becomes serious. One death and several close calls occurred this way. To avoid becoming a statistic:

- Consider the following gear for each person's day pack: long underwear, gloves, balaclava, rain jacket and pants (which double as wind protection). In warmer weather, all can be of the lightweight variety. If that's too heavy for you, at least take one of those disposable plastic rainsuits or tube tents that occupy virtually no space. Take more warm clothes in colder weather. A headlamp with spare bulb and new batteries is very important for finding safe anchors, signaling for help, or avoiding that bivy altogether. Matches and heat-tabs will light wet wood. Food and water increase your safety after a night of shivering.
- Keep your survival gear with you not with your partner, whenever practical, not with your partner—climbers get separated from their gear and each other in imaginative ways, sometimes with serious consequences.

- Standing in slings on poor anchors is not the way to spend a night. If a bivy is inevitable, don't climb until the last moment; find a safe, sheltered, and/or comfortable spot while you've got enough light.

Descents Consult the guidebook and your friends, but be wary of advice that the way down is obvious; look the route over ahead of time. If you carry a topo of the way up, consider a topo a photograph for the way down. Your ultimate protection is route-finding ability, and that takes experience. Some trouble spots: North Dome Gully, the Kat Walk, Michael's Ledge.

- Many rappel epics are born when an easy descent, often a walk-off, is missed. Search for it thoroughly before you commit to a big drop — it may be well worth the effort.
- Conversely, footprints and rappel anchors often lead nowhere — they were someone else's mistake. Be willing and able to retrace your steps, and remember that the crux may not be at the top.
- To further evaluate an uncertain descent, consider rappelling a single line as far as possible (160 feet if one rope, 320 feet if two). Learn to be comfortable on the rope and be willing to swing around a corner to look for the next anchor. Carry enough gear to go back up your rope —and know how to use it.
- Any time you can't see anchors all the way to the ground, take the gear to set your own. That includes established descents, since ice and rockfall frequently destroy anchors. It sometimes means carrying a bolt kit.
- Consider taking a second (7-9mm) rope, even for one-rope descents and walk-offs. You'll save time, depend on fewer anchors, leave less gear, and more easily reverse the climbing route in an emergency. This is one advantage of leading on double ropes. But don't forget that thinner ropes are more vulnerable to sharp edges.
- Friction from wet or twisted ropes, slings, ledges, cracks and flakes may jam your rope. Plan ahead when you rig the anchor and be willing to leave gear behind to avoid friction. You can retrieve the gear tomorrow.
- Rappelling through trees? Consider short rappels, from tree to tree. It's slow but avoids irretrievable snarls.
- Is your rope jammed? You can go back up and re-rig if you still have both ends, so keep them until you're sure it will pull or you have to let go. If you do have to climb that rope, be careful that it isn't jammed by a sharp edge. Don't forget to untie the knots in the ends of the rope before you pull.
- Dropped ropes and gear can be more than just embarrassing; without a rescue, a stranded climber is a dead climber, even in good weather. When transferring gear, clip it to its next anchor before unclipping it from the current one.

Loose Rock There's plenty of it in Yosemite. Ten percent of all injuries are associated with rockfall, including six deaths and one permanent disability. In several other deaths, loose rock was implicated but not confirmed, e.g., possible broken handholds and failed placements. Spontaneous rockfall is not the problem — all the fatal and serious accidents were triggered by the victim, the rope, or by climbers above.

Rocks lying on ledges and in steep gullies are obviously dangerous. Not so obvious is that old, reliable mantel block, five times your weight, wedged in place, and worn smooth by previous climbers. Yet with distressing regularity, "bombproof" blocks, flakes, and even ledges collapse under body weight, spit out cams, or fracture from the pressure of a piton. The forces placed on anchors and protection, even from rappelling, may be far higher than you generate in a test. Handholds may pass your scrutiny, then fail in mid-move. The rock you pull off can break your leg after falling only a couple of feet. Finally, watch out for rotten rock, responsible for at least two of these fatalities. It's common on the last couple of pitches of climbs that go to the rim of the Valley, e.g., Yosemite Point Buttress and Washington Column.

The East Buttress of Middle Cathedral Rock is a well-known bowling alley, the site of many rockfall injuries. The Northwest Face of Half Dome is another, with the added excitement of tourist "firing squads" on the summit. But the most dangerous, surprisingly, may be El Cap; on rock so steep, loose blocks balance precariously and big flakes wait for an unlucky hand to trigger the final fracture.

Some rockfall accidents may not be preventable (short of staying home) but being alert to the hazard and following a few guidelines will cut the injury rate:

- Consider a helmet for loose routes. (See "Helmets," page 19.)
- Throw in an occasional piece on long, easy runouts, as insurance against the unpredictability of the medium.
- Avoid rotten rock as protection, even if you can back it up. When it fails it endangers everyone below.
- Ropes launch almost as many missiles as climbers do. Watch where you run your lead rope. Use directionals to keep it away from loose — and sharp — stuff, and check it frequently. Keep in mind that your bag or pack, when hauled, may dislodge everything in its path. When you pull your rappel ropes, stand to one side, look up, and watch out for delayed rockfall.
- You have no control over a party above you, and by being below, you accept the risk. If you are catching up, don't crowd— ask for permission to pass. You can probably get by safely, but remember that climbers have been killed or hurt by rocks dislodged by parties above, including those they allowed to pass. The party you want to pass may have gotten an early start to avoid that risk, and they have no obligation to let you by. When you are above someone else, including your partner, put yourself in their shoes. Slow down, watch your feet and the rope.

Climbing Unroped

Everybody does it, to some extent. There's no reason to stop, but good reason to be cautious: 14 climbers were killed and two critically injured while deliberately climbing unroped. At least eight of these people climbed 5.10 or better. Most, if not all, of those accidents were avoidable. You may find yourself unroped in several situations—on third-class terrain, spontaneously on fifth-class, or while deliberately free-soloing a route.

Third-class terrain may be easy, but add a bit of sand, loose or wet rock, darkness, a moment of distraction, and the rating becomes meaningless. Four climbers have died this way, typically on approach and descent routes such as North Dome Gully, all in spots that did not demand a rope.

Sometimes you lose the way on the approach, or unrope at what you thought was the top of the climb, only to find a few feet of "easy" fifth-class blocking your way. Your rope is tucked away in your pack, and you're in a hurry. Before you go on, remember that you didn't plan to free-solo an unknown quantity today. Four people died this way, falling from fifth-class terrain that they were climbing on the spur of the moment.

Seven of the 14 killed were rappelling or otherwise tied in. They unroped while still on fifth-class rock, for various reasons of convenience, without clipping into a nearby anchor. Three slipped off their stances, a ledge collapsed under another, one decided to downclimb the last few feet, and two tried to climb their rappel ropes hand-over-hand to attend to some problem. Like the previous group, they all went unroped onto fifth-class terrain on the spur of the moment. In addition, they all had a belay immediately available. Did its nearness give them a false sense of security?

At least one true free-soloer has been killed, and one, critically hurt, survived only by the speed of his rescue. Are most free-soloers more alert to the task, having planned it in advance, than those who unrope on the spur of the moment? Were the unlucky 14 still relaxed in their minds, not quite attuned to their new situation? We can only speculate.

Keep these cases and the hidden hazards in mind as you travel through any steep terrain. Be aware of what is underfoot, and in hand, at each moment. Be patient enough to retrace your steps, to find the easy way, and, if there's a belay hanging in front of you, to think twice before rejecting it. Finally, remember that your climbing ability has probably been measured on clean, rated routes, not on unpredictable sand and wet moss. Being a 5.11 climber does not mean you can fly.

Leading

Nine climbers died and six were critically injured in leader-fall accidents involving inadequate protection. Most fell simply because the moves were hard, and several were victims of broken holds. They were all injured because they hit something before their protection stopped them. Either they did not place enough protection (one-third of the cases) or it failed under the force of the fall (the remaining two-thirds). In every case, their injuries were serious because they fell headfirst or on their sides — the head, neck, or trunk took a lethal blow. Half fell 50 feet or less. The climber who fell the shortest distance (25 feet) died, and the longest distance (270 feet!) survived.

Were these catastrophes avoidable? It's sometimes hard to tell, but the answer is often yes. Here are a few lessons frequently learned the hard way:

- Climbers frequently describe the belaying habits they see on Yosemite routes as "frightening." Before you start up, how frightening is your belay? Can the anchor withstand pulls in all directions? Is there more than one piece, with the load shared? Is the tie-in snug and in line with the fall force? Is your belayer experienced with that belay gadget and in position to operate it effectively when you fall? (You'd be surprised.) Will you clip through a bombproof directional as you start up, even on an easy pitch?

INTRODUCTION

- Don't cheat on your groundfall calculations. (A good belayer will keep you honest.) With rope stretch and slack in the system, you may fall twice as far below your last protection as you are above it — if it holds.
- Nuts want to fall out. One that self-cleans below you may turn a comfortable lead into a groundfall situation. Or, during a fall, the top piece may hold just long enough for the rope to yank the lower nuts out sideways, then also fail. For more reliable placements, set those nuts with a tug and sling them generously. A tug on a marginal nut, however, is worthless as a test. Tiny nubbins may hold a nut firmly under those conditions, but give way in a fall. Be especially cautious about placements you can't see. Back them up.
- Camming devices "fail" regularly, but it's seldom the fault of the device. It's more likely due to haste, coupled with undeserved faith in technology. As with nuts, a blind placement — often in a layback crack — may feel solid, but be worthless.
- Fixed pitons loosen from freeze-thaw cycles and repeated use. They may not have been installed well to begin with. A hammer is the only reliable way to test and reset them, but you don't see many hammers on free routes these days. You don't see them on rappel routes, either, but you may find yourself hanging from anchors that belong in a museum. If you don't test pitons properly, do not depend on them — routinely back them up.
- There is no reliable way to test bolts, but plenty of reasons to want to. For example, the common 1/4" split-shaft type was not designed or intended for life support, let alone for rock climbing. Bolt quality varies; several have broken under body weight, and others like them await you. Reliability also depends on the quality of the rock and the skill of the bolter. Add years of weathering and mistreatment by climbers and the result is that many bolts can easily be pulled out by fingers or a sharp yank with a sling. Several bolt hangers have cracked as well, with one fatal accident so far.
- Never test a bolt with a hammer. Instead, examine the surrounding rock, the bolt, and the hanger for cracks, and hope they are large enough to see. Is the bolt tight and fully seated in the hole? Is the nut snug? Good luck.
- Back up all untested fixed protection.
- Okay. So you know this stuff. You're a little shaky on the lead right now and you've had some trouble getting your pro to stick, but the book said this was 5.10a, and besides, two teenage girls just walked up this pitch. It's only 20 feet more and one of those pieces is bound to hold. Think for a minute. Are you willing to free-solo this pitch? Keep your answer in mind as you climb, because poorly placed protection amounts to just that — you may not be deliberately unroped, but you might as well be.

About Falling There's an art to falling safely — like a cat. Bouldering helps build the alertness required. Controlling your fall may be out of the question on those 200-foot screamers, but it will reduce the risk of injury. Whenever possible, land on your feet — even if you break your leg. Absorbing the shock this way may save your life. Laybacks and underclings hold special risks in this regard — you are already leaning back, and if you lose your grip the friction of your feet on the rock may rotate you into a head-first — and backward — dive.

INTRODUCTION

- A chest harness will not keep you from tumbling as you free-fall, but it will turn you upright as the rope comes tight. This reduces the chance of serious injury during the braking phase and may be life-saving if you hang there for long, already seriously hurt.
- The wall may look vertical below you, but even glancing off a steep slab can be fatal. Three climbers died this way.
- Pendulum falls are particularly dangerous. If you swing into a corner from 20 feet to one side of your protection, you will hit with the same bone-breaking speed as when striking a ledge in a 20-foot vertical fall. The crucial difference is that you are "landing" on your side, exposing vital organs to the impact. Two climbers died this way, and others suffered serious injuries. Even small projections are dangerous: a 20-foot swing on Glacier Point Apron fractured a skull, and another smashed a pelvis. In a pendulum, there is no difference between a leader and a follower fall; don't forget to protect your second from this fate as you lead a hard traverse.

Learning to Lead Four of the 15 killed or critically injured in leader falls were good climbers on well-defined routes, but the majority were intermediates, often off-route. There may be a couple of lessons in that.

- Don't get cocky because you just led your first 5.8 or your protection held on your first fall. Experienced climbers have died from errors "only a beginner would make," so you have plenty of time left in your career to screw up.
- Climbing and protecting are separate skills, but both keep you alive. Don't challenge yourself in both at the same time — you may not have the skill and presence of mind to get out of a tight spot. If you're out to push your limits, pick a route that's well-defined and easy to protect, place extra pieces for practice, and be willing and equipped to back off.
- Route-finding is another survival skill. A mistake here can quickly put you over your head in climbing, protecting, or both. Learn to look ahead and recognize what you want to avoid. Climb it mentally before you climb it physically.
- Some "easy" terrain in the valley is actually pretty dangerous. Low-angle gullies are often full of loose blocks cemented together with moss. Opportunities for protection may be scarce and route-finding subtle. These routes are not usually cataloged. Three or four climbers have been killed, or nearly so, on such terrain while looking for easy routes to climb.
- **A Leading Problem:** The last pitch of The Nutcracker provides a subtle challenge for the fledgling 5.8 leader. Once over the mantel, you may relax as you contemplate the easy climb to the top. But if you forget about your protection, a slip in the next few moves may send you back over the side to crash into the slab below. This pitch has scored several broken ankles when the fall was longer than expected, and a more serious injury is possible. There are many such situations in the Valley, and one key to safety is to look below you while you plan ahead.

INTRODUCTION

The Belay Chain

Whether you are climbing, rappelling, or just sitting on a ledge, the belay chain is what connects you to the rock. There are many links, and mistakes with almost every one have killed 22 climbers, 40% of all Yosemite climbing fatalities. In every case the cause was human error. In every case the death was completely preventable, not by the subtle skills of placing protection on the lead, but by some simple precaution to keep the belay chain intact. Experienced climbers outnumbered the inexperienced in this category, two to one.

Mistakes with the belay chain can occur at any time. Make one and you'll fall to the end of the rope . . . or farther. Minor injuries are rare. Here are some key points to remember:

- Before you commit yourself to a system, always apply a few pounds of tension in the directions in which it will be loaded, analyzing it like an engineer: what if this happens . . . or that? Check every link, from the buckle of your harness to the rock around your anchor. You would be amazed at the inadequate systems often used by experienced climbers, even though it takes only a few seconds to run a proper check.
- Both lives depend on that system, so go through it with your partner. Nine climbers have died in multi-victim accidents.
- Check the system periodically while you're using it. Forces may change direction (two died when their anchors failed for this reason), ropes and slings can wear through (serious injuries and one death), and gear can come undone (two died when a wiggling bolt hanger unscrewed its nut — they were relying on a single bolt).
- Are you about to rappel? Stay clipped to the anchor for a few seconds. Check both the anchor and your brake system, as above. If one anchor point fails, will you remain attached to others? Are the knots in your rappel slings secure? Did you check every inch of those fixed slings for damage? Skipping these precautions cost eight lives, plus serious injuries, from poorly tied slings, partially dismantled anchors (a simple misunderstanding), relying on single carabiners, and other reasons. The next accident may be caused by something new, but it will have been preventable by double-checking.
- Two climbers died by rappelling off the ends of their ropes, even though both had tied knots in the ends as a safety measure. In one case, the knots pulled through the brake. In the second, the victim forgot to double-check the ropes after a knot had been untied to deal with a problem. Knots are still a recommended safety procedure, but do not take anything for granted. Tie both strands into one knot or knot each separately—(there are pros and cons to each method).
- When rappelling in unpredictable circumstances—dark, windy, poor communications, unknown anchors below—consider a Prusik Hitch or a mechanical ascender for safety. If improperly handled, neither one may stop you if you fall; they are primarily for quickly, but deliberately, stopping yourself to deal with other emergencies. Both of those who rappelled off their ropes would have survived with safeties.
- In separate incidents, five climbers somehow became detached from their ropes while climbing with mechanical ascenders — not the fault of the devices. Only three were tied to their ropes at all, at the lower ends. All five died because they had not tied in "short," leaving themselves open to a long fall. To tie in short, tie a loop in the rope a few

feet below your ascenders and clip it to your harness. As you climb, repeat the process often enough to limit your fall should you come off your rope. At the very least, do this when you must pass one ascender around protection, traverse (three deaths), or change to another rope. (Is that other rope well anchored? One climber died partly because his wasn't. Ask your partner first.) In addition, always be tied into both of your ascenders.

- Self-belayers should also tie in short — one died when his Prusik belay melted during a fall (a Prusik cord too large for the rope). At least two were treated to close calls when other types of self-belay systems jammed open.
- Clip into a new belay point before unclipping from the old one. During those few vulnerable seconds, pitons have pulled, hero loops have broken, rocks have struck, and feet have slipped.
- Three climbers were killed and one critically injured by "failures" of single-carabiner tie-ins and rappel anchors. Be careful of relying on a single nonlocking carabiner for any link in the chain. The rope or sling may flip over the gate and unclip itself, especially if it is slack or shock-loaded. Even if you watch it carefully and/or it is "safely" under tension, you may become distracted. One climber died when his figure eight descender unclipped while he was busy passing a knot on rappel. (He should have tied in short.) For those critical points, use either two nonlocking carabiners with gates opposed and reversed, or a locking carabiner. Don't forget to lock it! For many applications the two-carabiner method is safer and faster to operate.
- Ropes have been cut in three fatal accidents. They did not break, but were stressed over sharp edges, a condition never intended by the manufacturer. Two of these accidents were avoidable: one climber should have tied in short to prevent a 100-foot fall that cut the rope; the other should have protected a fixed rope from a well-defined sharp edge. Ascending a rope produces a weighted, seesawing action that can destroy it, even over a rounded, moderately rough edge.
- As with ropes, most gear failure falls into the misuse category. Failure from a design or manufacturing flaw is rare. It was the initiating factor in one fatal accident — three climbers died when a bolt hanger broke at a two-bolt rappel anchor. The tragic outcome would have been avoided, however, had the climbers noticed they were not properly backed up to the second bolt.

These cases illustrate one of the rules most commonly overlooked: BACK YOURSELF UP. No matter what initially pulled, broke, slipped, jammed, or cut, the incident became an accident because the climber did not carefully ask himself, "What if. . . ?" By leaving yourself open, you are betting against a variety of unpredictable events. You don't lose very often, but when you do, you may lose very big.

Beginners! From your first day on the rock, you have the right to inspect— and ask questions about—any system to which you're committing your life. It's a good way to learn, and a good way to stay alive. If your partner or instructor is offended, find someone else to climb with. Never change the system or the plan, however, without your partner's knowledge.

INTRODUCTION

Helmets

While we can never know for certain, helmets might have made a difference in roughly 25% of the fatal and critical trauma cases. They would have significantly increased — but not guaranteed — the survival chances for five of those fatalities. Furthermore, helmets would have offered excellent protection against less serious fractures, concussions, and lacerations.

Most deaths, however, involved impacts of overwhelming force or mortal wounds other than to the head, i.e., beyond the protection offered by a helmet. This is not an argument against helmets; the point is, a helmet doesn't make you invincible. What goes on inside your head is more important than what you wear on it.

When to wear a helmet is a personal choice, but it is especially recommended for the following: beginners pushing their skills, roped-solo climbing, whenevers there's a high risk of a bad fall or of ice fall (several El Cap routes in winter and spring), and for all approaches, descents, and climbing routes that are crowded and/or particularly loose. (See "Loose Rock," page 12.)

States of Mind

This is the key to safety. It's impossible to know how many climbers were killed by haste or overconfidence, but many survivors will tell you that they somehow lost their good judgment long enough to get hurt. It's a complex subject and sometimes a touchy one. Nevertheless, at least three states of mind frequently contribute to accidents: ignorance, casualness, and distraction.

Ignorance There is always more to learn, and even the most conscientious climber can get into trouble if unaware of the danger ("I thought it never rained . . . .") Here are some ways to fight ignorance:

- Look in the mirror. Are you the stubborn type? Do you resist suggestions? Could you be a bit overconfident? (Ask your friends.) Several partners have said of a dead friend, "I wanted to give him advice, but he always got mad when I did that. I didn't realize he was about to die."
- Read. The climbing magazines are full of good recommendations. Case histories in the American Alpine Club's *Accidents in North American Mountaineering*, a yearly compilation of accident reports, will show you how subtle factors may combine to catch you unaware. Such accounts are the next best (or worst?) thing to being there.
- Practice. Reading may make you aware, but not competent. In fact, you can be dangerously misled by what you read, including this report. Important details are often left out, the advice may be incorrect, and in the long run, you must think and act for yourself. Several climbers, for example, waited to learn Prusiking until it was dark, raining, overhanging and they were actually in trouble. They had read about it, but they had to be rescued despite having the gear to improvise their own solutions. Book-learning alone gave them a complacency that could have proved fatal.

INTRODUCTION

Casualness "I just didn't take it seriously" is a common lament. It's often correct, but it's more a symptom than a cause — there may be deeper reasons for underestimating your risk. Ignorance is one, and here are some more:

- Habit reinforcement. The more often you get away with risky business, the more entrenched your lazy habits become. Have you unconsciously dropped items from your safety checklists since you were a chicken-hearted (or hare-brained) beginner?
- Your attitudes and habits can be reinforced by the experiences (and states of mind) of others. The sense of awe and commitment of the 1960s is gone from the big-wall trade routes, and young aspirants with no Grade VIs, or even Vs, to their credit speak casually about them. Even for experts, most accidents on El Cap occur on the easier pitches, where their guard is down.
- Memory Decay. "I'm not going up again without raingear — I thought I would die!" A week later this climber had forgotten how scared he had been in that thunderstorm. Raingear was now too heavy and besides, he was sure he'd be able to rap off the next time. Many of us tend to forget the bad parts. We have to be hit again.
- Civilization. With fixed anchors marking the way up and ghetto blasters echoing behind, it may be hard to realize that the potential for trouble is as high in Yosemite as anywhere. Some say the possibility of fast rescue added to their casualness. Maybe, but who wants a broken leg, or worse, in the first place?

Distraction It is caused by whatever takes your mind off your work: anxiety, sore feet, skinny-dippers below — the list is endless. Being in a hurry is one of the most common distractions. Here are two ways it has happened:

- Experienced climbers were often hurt after making "beginner errors" (their words) to get somewhere quickly. There was no emergency or panic, but their minds were elsewhere — on a cold beer, a good bivy, or just on being sick of being on that route for a week. (It's often called "summit fever.") Their mistakes were usually shortcuts in protecting easy pitches, on both walls and shorter climbs. As one put it, "We were climbing as though we were on top."
- Darkness had caught two day-climbers for the first time. Unprepared, upset, and off-route, they rushed to get down, arguing with each other about what to do. After several errors—which they knew how to avoid—one died rappelling off the end of his rope.

An adequate state of mind is like good physical conditioning. It doesn't happen overnight, and it takes constant practice, but the payoff in both safety and fun is well worth it. Stay aware of your mental state: Are you uneasy before this climb? Learn to recognize that, then ask yourself why, and deal with it. Are you taking shortcuts on this pitch? Could it be you're distracted? Stop, get your act together, then go.

Rescue Despite the best of attitudes, an accident can happen to anyone. Self-rescue is often the fastest and safest way out, but whether it's the wise course of action depends on the injury and how well-prepared you are. Combining resources with a nearby party will often give you the margin of safety you need, but do not risk aggravating an injury or getting yourself into a more serious predicament. Ask for help if you need it. Sometimes a bit of advice, delivered by loudspeaker, is all that's required. In making your

INTRODUCTION

decision, keep an eye on weather and darkness — call for help early.

- If you don't have formal first-aid training (which is strongly recommended), at least know how to keep an unconscious patient's airway open, how to protect a possible broken neck or back, and how to deal with external bleeding and serious blood loss. These procedures are lifesaving, do not require fancy gear, and are easy to learn.
- Head-injury victims, even when unconscious, may try to untie themselves. If you have to leave one alone, make escape impossible.
- If ropes are lowered to you from a helicopter for any purpose, do not attach them to your anchors unless you are specifically instructed to do so. If the helicopter has to leave suddenly, it could pull you off the wall. If you are told to anchor a rope, rescuers will be using a system that does not expose you to that risk. Anchor that rope securely — it may be a rescuer's lifeline. Follow instructions exactly.

Who Pays for Rescues? The taxpayer does. The NPS does not charge for the cost of rescues, except for any ambulance services required. This is true even if you are fined by the courts for negligence, which is a separate charge altogether (see below). But rescues can be expensive and what the future holds is anybody's guess. The NPS is examining the possibility of charging all victims for the full cost of their rescues, and partial costs are currently charged in some parks now. This issue is complex, but it is clear that responsible behavior by those who use the Park will minimize the threat.

Risk, Responsibility, and the Limits to Climbing

The NPS has no regulations specifying how you must climb. There is one regulation, however, requiring that all park users act responsibly. This applies to climbers, in that the consequences of your actions put rescuers and other climbers at risk. So far, one rescuer has been killed in the Park. Thus, if your own negligence got you into trouble, you may be charged with "creating a hazardous condition" for others. As an example, a climber was fined because he became stranded by a hailstorm while attempting to free-solo the Steck-Salathé on Sentinel Rock. Storms had been predicted, and his rescue should not have been necessary.

Even avoidable accidents are understandable, and, consequently, legal charges are not often filed. Of all park users, however, climbers should be particularly aware — they know that their sport is dangerous, that safety lies in education and training, and that there is an information network available.

So take what you'll need with you on the climb, or have competent friends ready to back you up. The climber stranded on Sentinel, for example, could have been rescued by friends without NPS participation or knowledge, the way it must often be done on expeditions. Freedom of expression and responsibility need not be incompatible.

Climbing will always be risky. It should be clear, however, that a reduced accident rate is possible without seriously restricting the sport. The party in its fifth day on The Nose and the party passing them in its fifth hour may each be climbing safely, or each be blindly out of control. You have a right to choose your own climbing style and level of risk, but you owe it to yourself and everyone else to make that choice with your eyes wide open.

INTRODUCTION

OTHER NOTES

Voluntary Registration System If you wish, you may register at the Valley Visitor Center before your climb. However, the NPS does not monitor your progress at any time; the registration information you provide is used only if someone reports that you are overdue. Your best insurance is a friend who checks on you frequently.

To Report An Emergency From a public phone, dial 911. No money is needed to make the call. Stay at the phone until a ranger arrives, unless you are specifically given other instructions.

Accident/Hazard Reporting If you know of dangerous route conditions such as loose rock or bad anchors, consider posting the information on the bulletin board at Camp 4 (irreverently called Sunnyside by the NPS). Your information will help other climbers.

Fixed Gear Warning The park is a Wilderness Area, not an urban climbing wall. The NPS does not inspect or maintain climbing or descent routes, including fixed anchors, loose rock, or any other feature. You are strictly on your own. Recently, there have been several individuals involved in upgrading the quality of the fixed anchors (some of which are 30 years old) that are found on many climbs. A selfless act and an incredible amount of work and expense, the result of their effort benefits all climbers. In addition, the removal of old gear has demonstrated just how unreliable fixed anchors can be. Some examples: fixed slings on Half Dome (clearly having seen repeated use as rappel anchors) were found to be simply jammed in a crack, not actually attached to anything! Relatively new ⅜-inch bolts on Middle Cathedral were found to be placed in a hole drilled too big, and held in place merely with latex caulk! Not specifically mentioned are the many old ¼-inch bolts that failed with a simple pull. If you *do* replace old bolts, use the same hole, and be certain of your ability to place lasting anchors.

Fixed pins should be replaced or removed before the eyes are broken.

Many lone ¼-inch bolts have been placed off-route as emergency rappel anchors over the years. They may falsely entice the novice off-route and/or provide the false presumption that they provide a safe way down. These bolts should not be trusted for anything!

A great habit is to carry spare slings to replace the old ones at rappel stations which will help amortize route maintenance throughout the climbing community.

Tossing Haulbags Do not throw your haulbag off a wall. The bag will drift in the wind and you cannot always be sure the coast is clear. No one has been hurt yet, but it will happen — there have been a few close calls. Bag-tossing also creates a carnival atmosphere, a big mess (of your gear), and lots of false alarms for rescuers. (Tourists usually think it's a body.)

Sources of Information Try the local climbers (found in the parking lot at Camp 4), the bulletin board at the Camp 4 kiosk, the Mountain Shop in Curry Village, the Visitor Center at Yosemite Village, any ranger, or the NPS library (next to the Visitor Center). The library is the home of the American Alpine Club's Sierra Nevada Branch Library. It carries magazines, journals, and books on all aspects of climbing, mountaineering, and natural history.

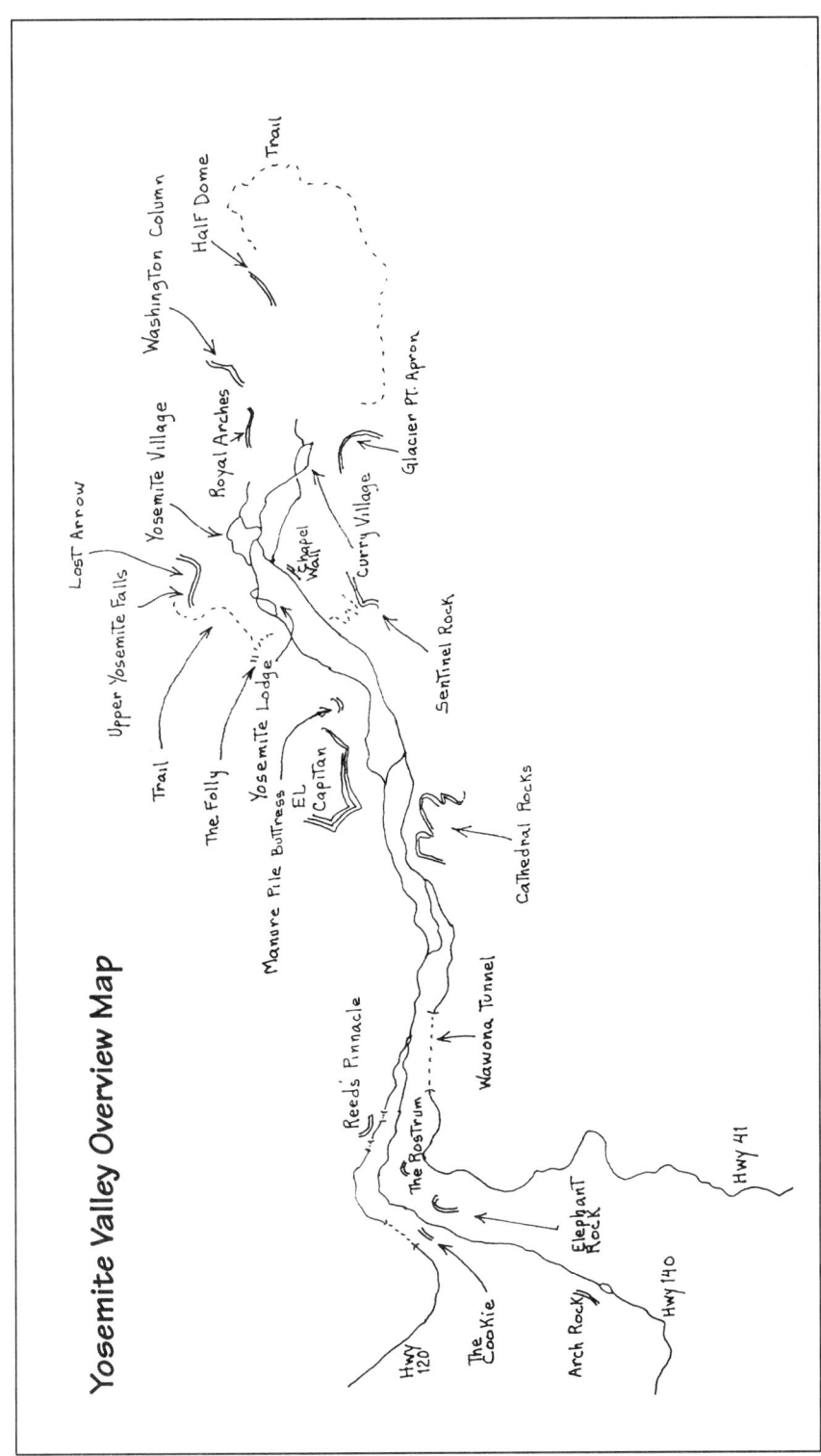

INTRODUCTION

Topo Key

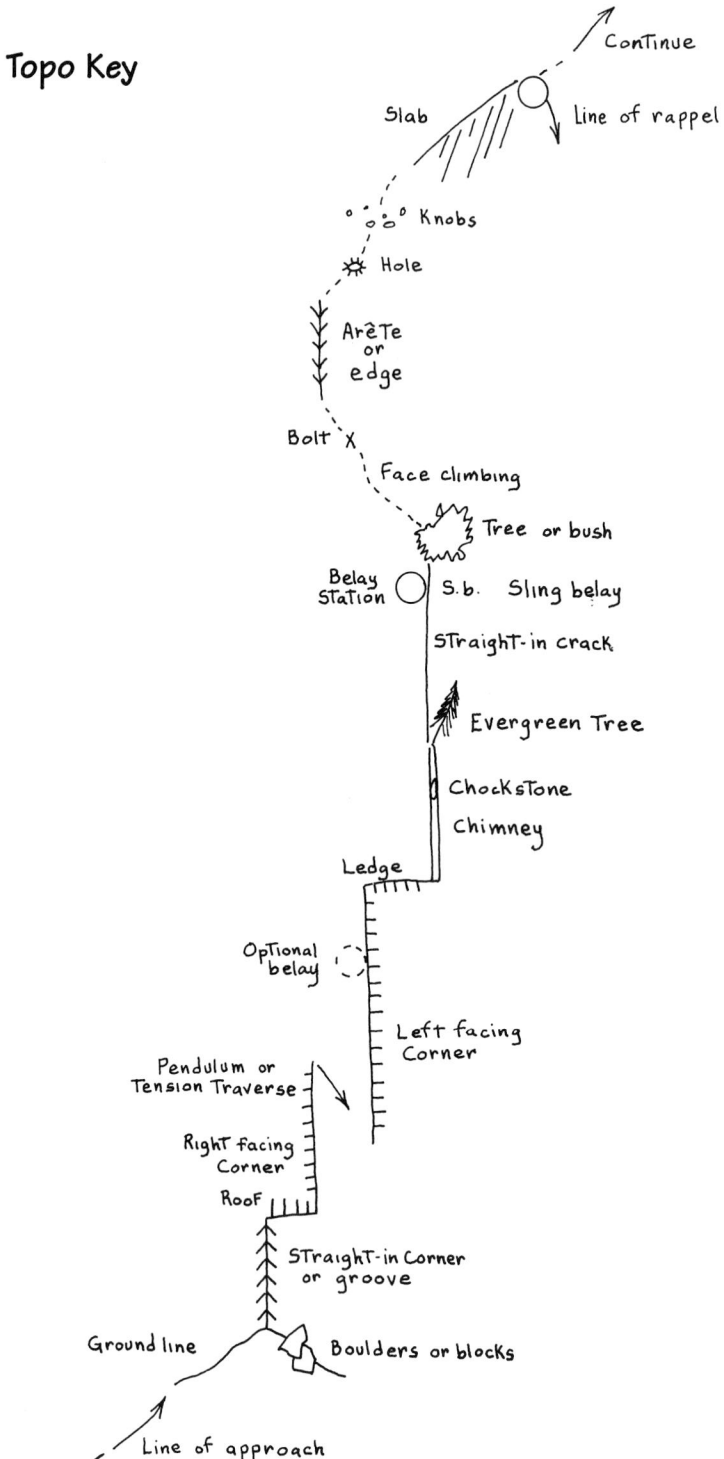

INTRODUCTION

HOW TO USE THIS BOOK

Confusion could arise from the existence of other routes not presented in this selected guide. Often, bolts on adjacent, unlisted routes are shown simply as landmarks of the area.

The term arête is stretched far beyond its true definition. In this book it means any edge formed by two planes of rock, regardless of the mechanics of creation.

Free Ratings The Yosemite Decimal System is used throughout this guide. Developed at Tahquitz Rock in the early 1950s and applied to a great extent in Yosemite, the decimal ratings found in the Valley represent the standards by which climbs throughout the country are compared. With the continuing rise of free climbing standards, the Decimal System has ceased to be strictly decimal, and instead reflects the open-ended nature of free climbing possibilities. Today there are routes of 5.10, 5.11, 5.12 and so on, but in the early '70s, the top grade—5.10—was considered by many to be too broad in scope, describing routes that were as varied in difficulty as 5.7 is from 5.9. Consequently, Jim Bridwell promoted a "sub-grading" system to further define the "easiest" and "hardest" 5.10. This system was widely accepted and today the upper rock climbing grades will often show an a, b, c, or d suffix that further defines the difficulty. An effort was also made at that time to establish a standard for the various grades.

The Decimal System gives no information on the protection possibilities for a climb. This is left to the leader to ascertain on the lead. As a rule, on the crack climbs you are climbing your source of protection. On the face and slab routes, you must rely more on your ability to judge the terrain ahead of you.

Aid Ratings This complex and subjective rating system is beyond the scope of this book, devoted to free climbs. Refer to the companion book, *Yosemite Climbs: Big Walls* for a detailing of ratings relevent to scaling the big walls of Yosmite.

The Arrangement of the Book The routes in this book are arranged in geographical order, starting from the west end of the north side of the Valley. The south side follows, from east to west. The Overview Map of the Valley locates all the cliff formations. To assist in identifying the climbs on the cliffs, photos identify the major routes. Occasionally, the photo pages may provide the sole description for obscure routes. In this case the caption will include the rating. Also, some routes that do not have topo information are included in the First Ascent appendix. The topo page will include the route name, its grade, and any unusual protection needs for the climb. It is assumed that a selection of nuts, from wired stoppers to something for a 3½-inch crack, is usually carried, and that special requirements for particular climbs were provided to the guidebook author.

Parkline Slab

A. **Hayley Anna** 5.8★ This and the following route are located a few hundred feet left of The Cockshead, near a prominent right facing corner. **Hayley Anna** starts thirty feet left of the edge of this corner and climbs a straight-up hand crack to a ledge with a rappel tree 150 feet up. Turn a roof about a third of the way up.

B. **Dressed to Kill** 5.10b R From the prominent right facing corner left of The Cockshead, climb up and left on a ramp to the edge of the corner, runout 5.10b, and belay. Runout 5.8 continues up the edge and leads to the same ledge and rappel tree as **Hayley Anna**.

The Cockshead

C. **Woody Woodpecker** 5.9
D. **Sawyer Crack** 5.9
E. **Eagle's Eyrie** 5.9 (Only three of this route's ten pitches are shown. Please leave the nesting site higher up undisturbed.)
F. **Crossover** 5.9★
G. **Color Me Gone** 5.9★
H. **The Hawaiian** 5.10a
I. **Fly By** 5.11a
J. **Too High** 5.6
K. **Farm Alarm** 5.7

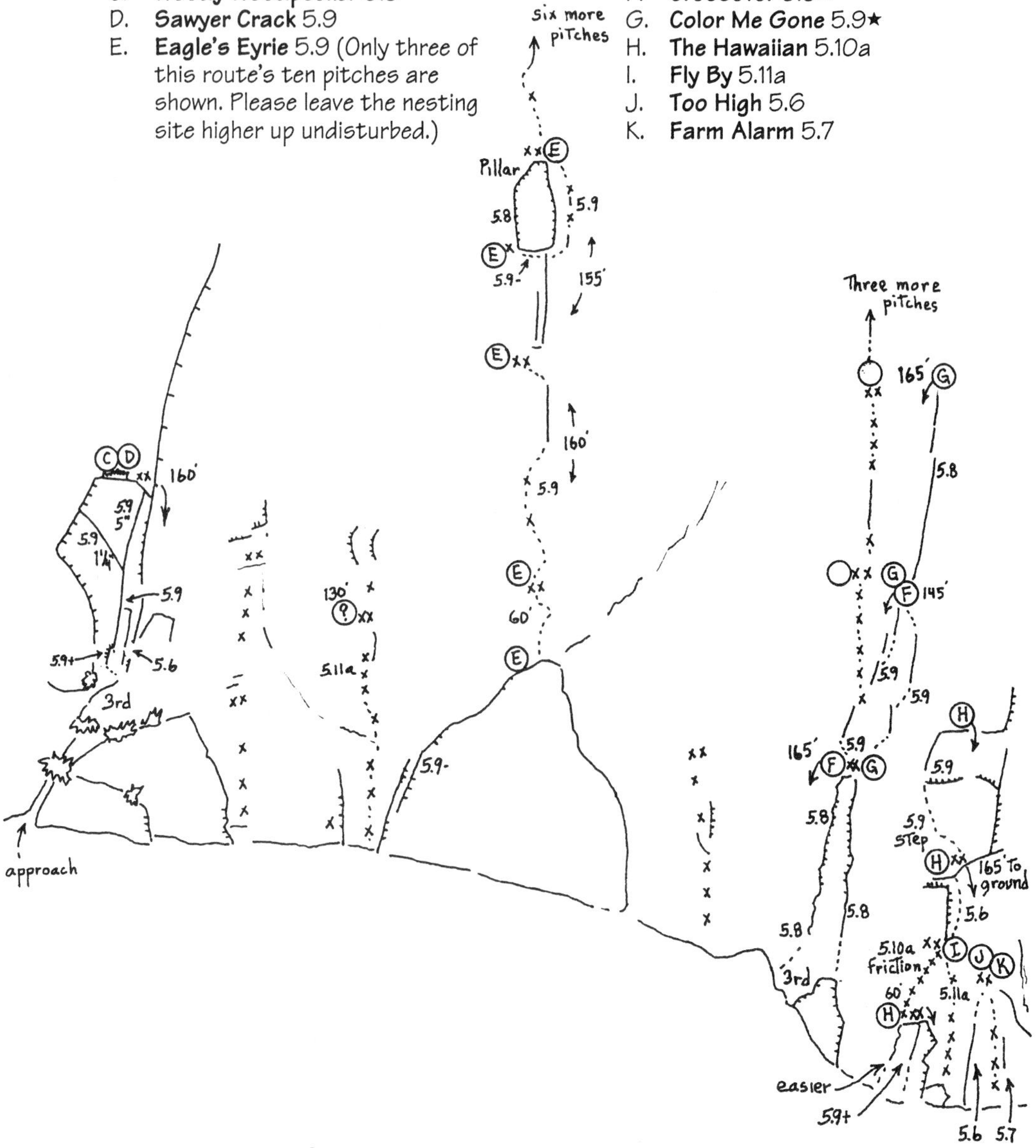

Parkline Slab

Approach: This is the large cliff readily visible from the Park boundary on Hwy. 140 and the community of El Portal. Park roughly beneath Parkline Pinnacle. A nearby streambed provides brush-free access up to munge covered ledges. Work right, then back left along the base of Parkline Pinnacle.

Parkline Pinnacle
- L. Cool Cliff 170 5.8
- M. Stonequest 5.8+★★ R
- N. Center Route 5.9 (A2 ?)
- O. Aids Curve 5.10
- P. The Chase 5.9+★★ R
- Q. Right Side 5.7
- R. The Soloist 5.10★ R
- S. The Perpetrator 5.10+
- T. Costa Rica 5.9★ R?

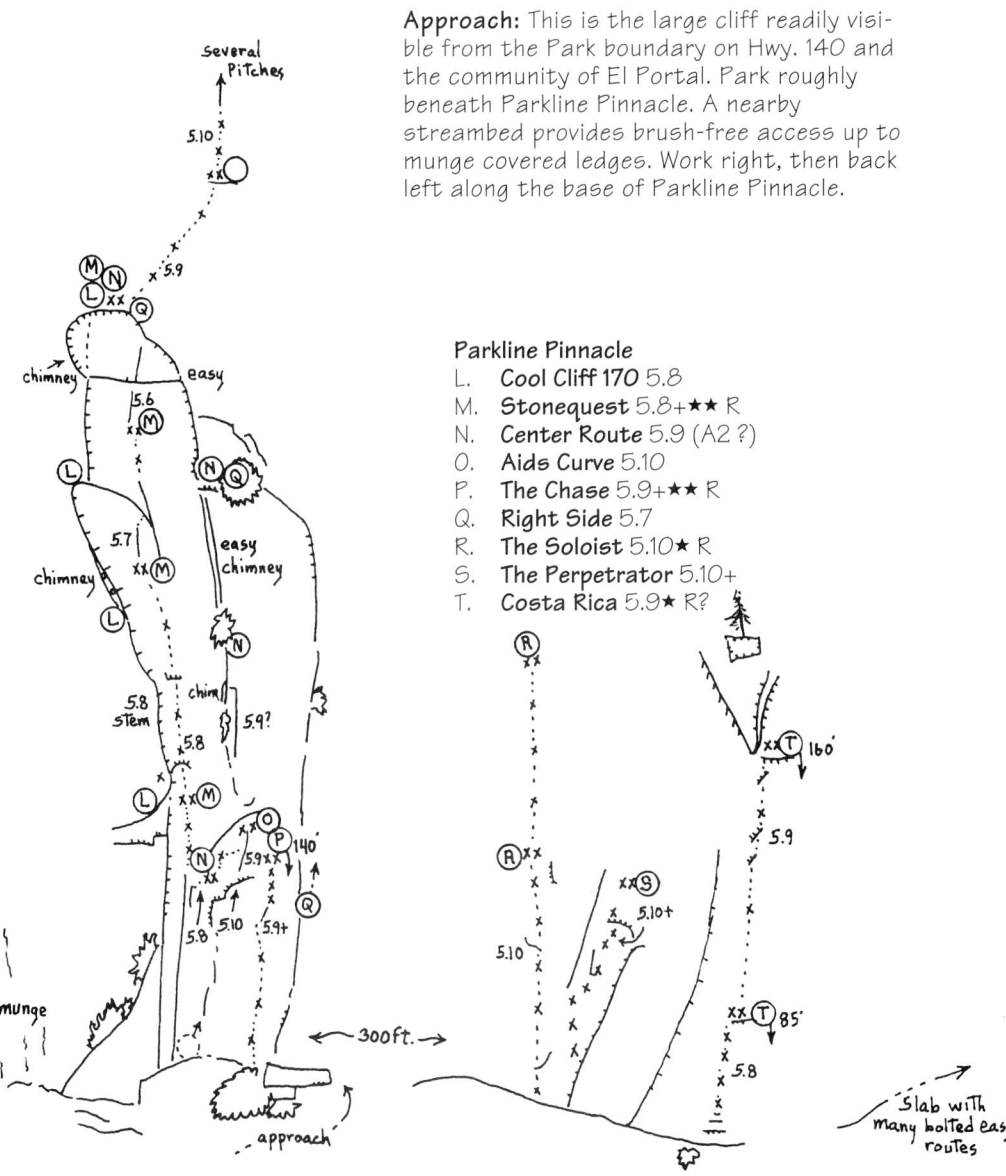

LOWER MERCED CANYON: NORTH

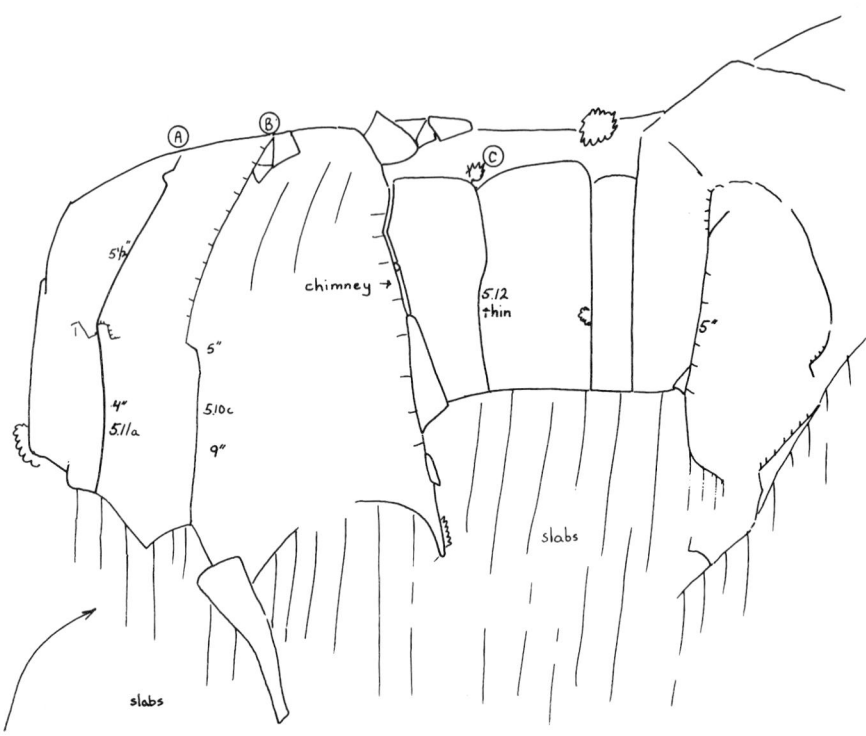

Narrow Escape Cliff

Approach: This little cliff lies outside the Park entrance station at Arch Rock. Perhaps because this lump of rock is in an area of limited turnouts and viewing possibilities, it remains somewhat obscure. Approach from directly below, where the cliff can be seen clearly, just uphill from a prominent prow of rock that juts out over the road. Be careful of the poison oak. There are dirt parking turnouts nearby.

A. **A Desperate Kneed** 5.11a★
B. **Narrow Escape** 5.10c
C. **Remember Ribbon Falls** 5.12

Nic Taylor does an early ascent of Short Circuit

Arch Rock Area

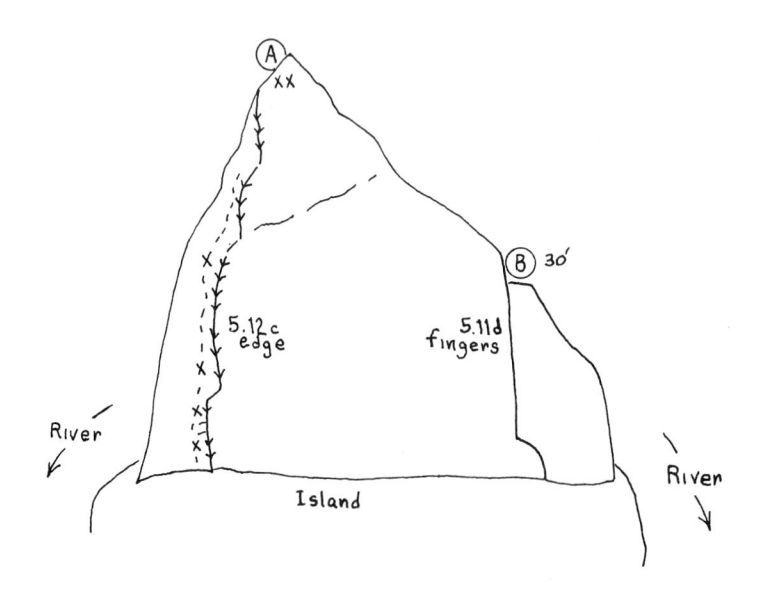

Short Circuit Boulder

Approach: This huge, split boulder lies on an island 0.1 mile upriver from the Arch Rock parking area. The routes face downriver.

Photo on page 29.

- A. **666** 5.12c★ Pro: QDs. This features one really wicked section.
- B. **Short Circuit** 5.11d★★ Pro: ⅝" to 1½". Although usually top-roped, this climb is sometimes soloed and rarely led. Slightly-overhanging, tight hand-to finger-sized fracture. A must on the crack-climbing training circuit.

Arch Rock Area

1. Anticipation 5.11b
2. Entrance Exam 5.9
3. English Breakfast Crack 5.10c
4. Midterm 5.10b
5. New Dimensions 5.11a
6. Cross Country Crack 5.9
7. Kindergarten Crack 5.8
8. Nerf Test 5.8
9. Quickie Quizzes 5.10a

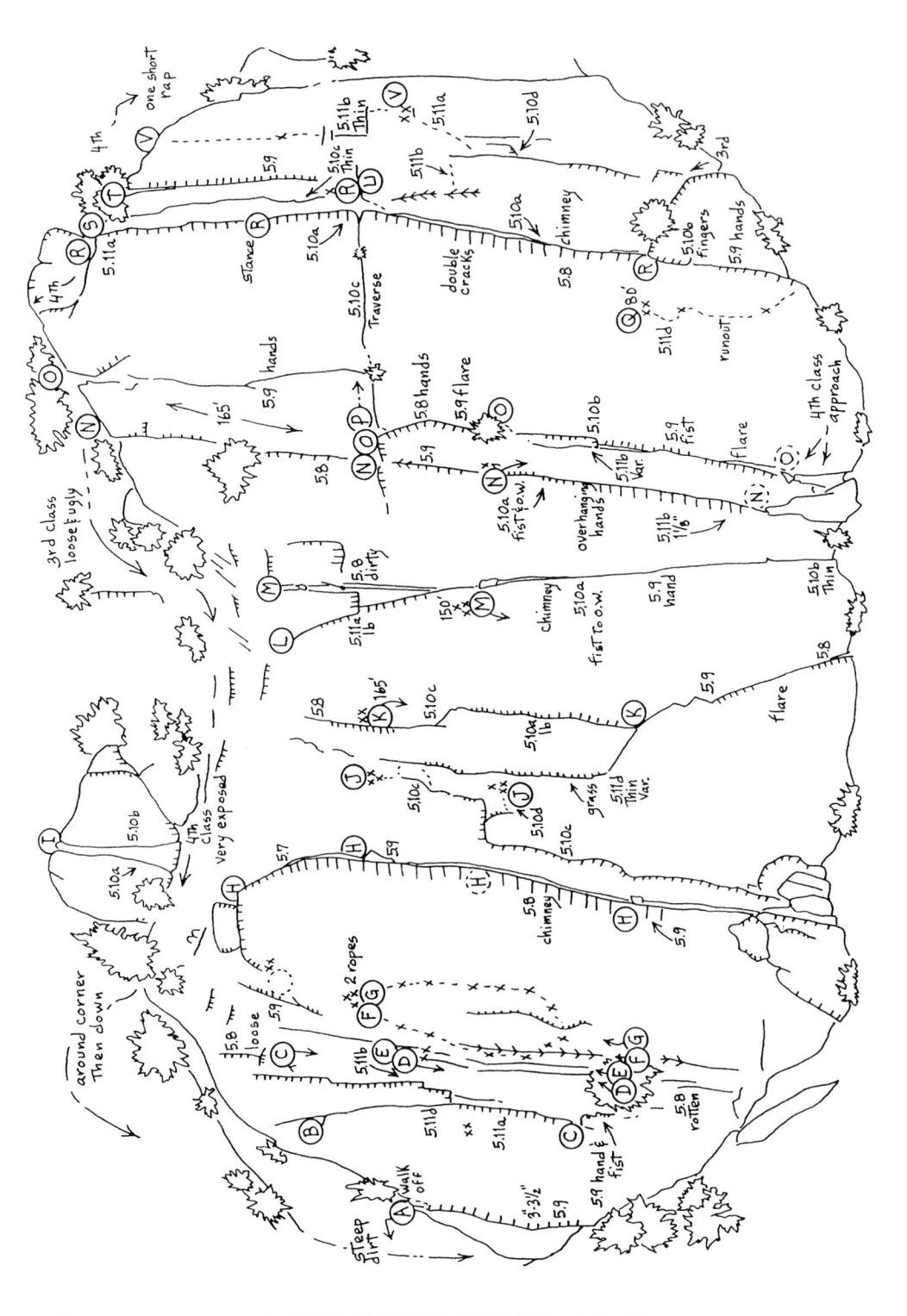

Arch Rock

Arch Rock

Approach: From the parking area at the entrance station, walk up the road to a clearing adjacent to the power lines. Class 2 talus leads directly up to the base of **Midterm**.

Photo on page 31.

A. **Dirty Little Secret** 5.9 Pro: To 4".
B. **Constipation** 5.11d★ Pro: To 3".
C. **Anticipation** 5.11b★★ Pro: To 3½", including two each ⅛" to ¾", 3" to 3½" useful at the crux.
D. **Supplication** 5.10c★ Pro: To 3", extra ⅝" to 1½".
E. **Application** 5.9 Pro: Many large to 3½".
F. **TKO** 5.11c★★ Pro: QDs and a few pieces, including a #3.5 Friend.
G. **Punchline** 5.12c★★ Pro: QDs and a few pieces including a #3.5 Friend. Both **TKO** and **Punchline** step out of the fist crack above the tree onto the sublimely featured arête. Heated controversy surrounding these rap routes has resulted in smashed bolt hangers that have since been straightened. This is the case on **TKO** at least.
H. **Entrance Exam** 5.9★ Pro: To 3".
I. **Quickie Quizzes** 5.10a/b★ Pro: To 3¾".
J. **Blotto aka Axis** 5.10d★ Pro: To 3", including many ¾" to 1¾".
K. **English Breakfast Crack** 5.10c★ Pro: To 2½".
L. **Sidetrack** 5.11a Pro: To 3½".
M. **Midterm** 5.10b★★★ Pro: ⅝" to 3½". An ever-widening polished crack.
N. **Leanie Meanie** 5.11b★★★ Pro: ¾" to 3½", especially 1" to 2½". A #11 hex is useful. Ever-widening leaning crack. Steep and clean.
O. **Gripper** 5.10b★★★ Pro: ⅜" to 3½". Varied crack climbing with an emphasis on handjamming. The third pitch is amazing.
P. **Two "D"** 5.10c
Q. **John's Ring Job** 5.11d★ R/X
R. **New Dimensions** 5.11a★★★ Pro: ⅜" to 3". The second and third pitches each have a section of awkward, physical climbing. A superb crack system with a climactic final move.
S. **Voyage** 5.10c★ Pro: To 3".
T. **Klemens' Escape** 5.9★ Pro: To 3".
U. **Inchworm** 5.11b R
V. **Grokin'** 5.11b★ R

LOWER MERCED CANYON: NORTH — 33

Arch Rock Area

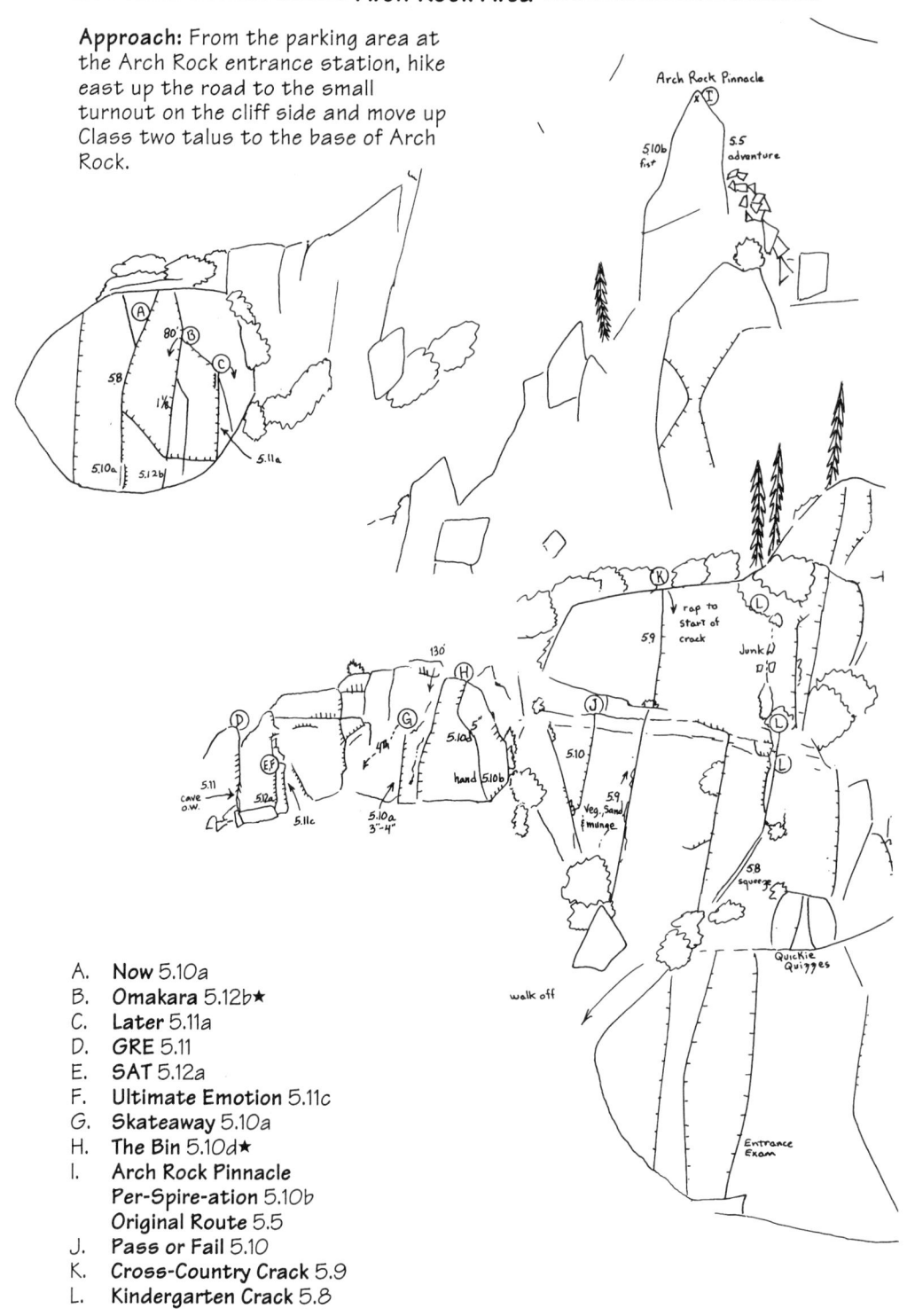

Approach: From the parking area at the Arch Rock entrance station, hike east up the road to the small turnout on the cliff side and move up Class two talus to the base of Arch Rock.

- A. **Now** 5.10a
- B. **Omakara** 5.12b★
- C. **Later** 5.11a
- D. **GRE** 5.11
- E. **SAT** 5.12a
- F. **Ultimate Emotion** 5.11c
- G. **Skateaway** 5.10a
- H. **The Bin** 5.10d★
- I. **Arch Rock Pinnacle**
  Per-Spire-ation 5.10b
  Original Route 5.5
- J. **Pass or Fail** 5.10
- K. **Cross-Country Crack** 5.9
- L. **Kindergarten Crack** 5.8

Arch Rock Area

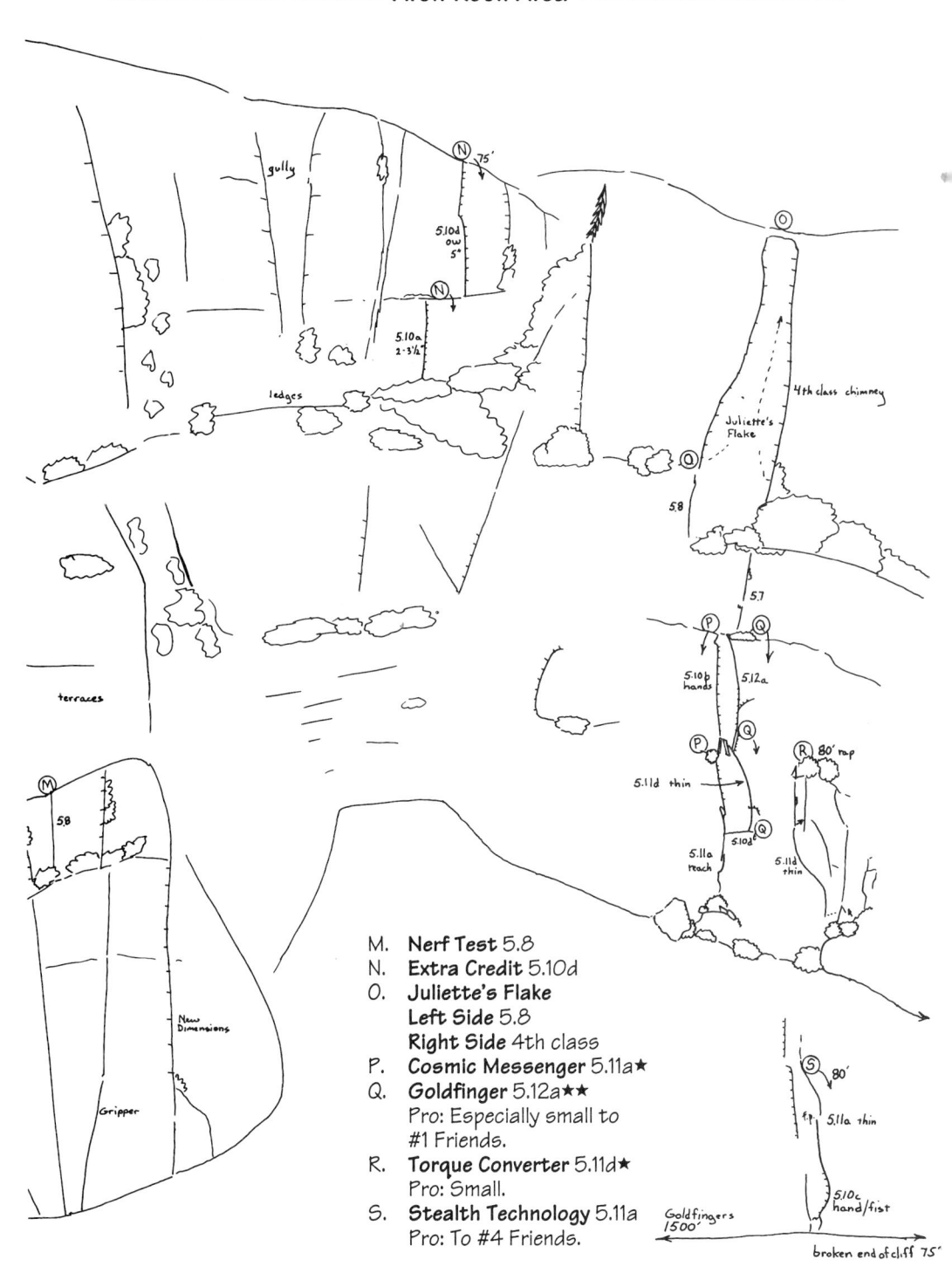

M. **Nerf Test** 5.8
N. **Extra Credit** 5.10d
O. **Juliette's Flake**
   Left Side 5.8
   Right Side 4th class
P. **Cosmic Messenger** 5.11a ★
Q. **Goldfinger** 5.12a ★★
   Pro: Especially small to #1 Friends.
R. **Torque Converter** 5.11d ★
   Pro: Small.
S. **Stealth Technology** 5.11a
   Pro: To #4 Friends.

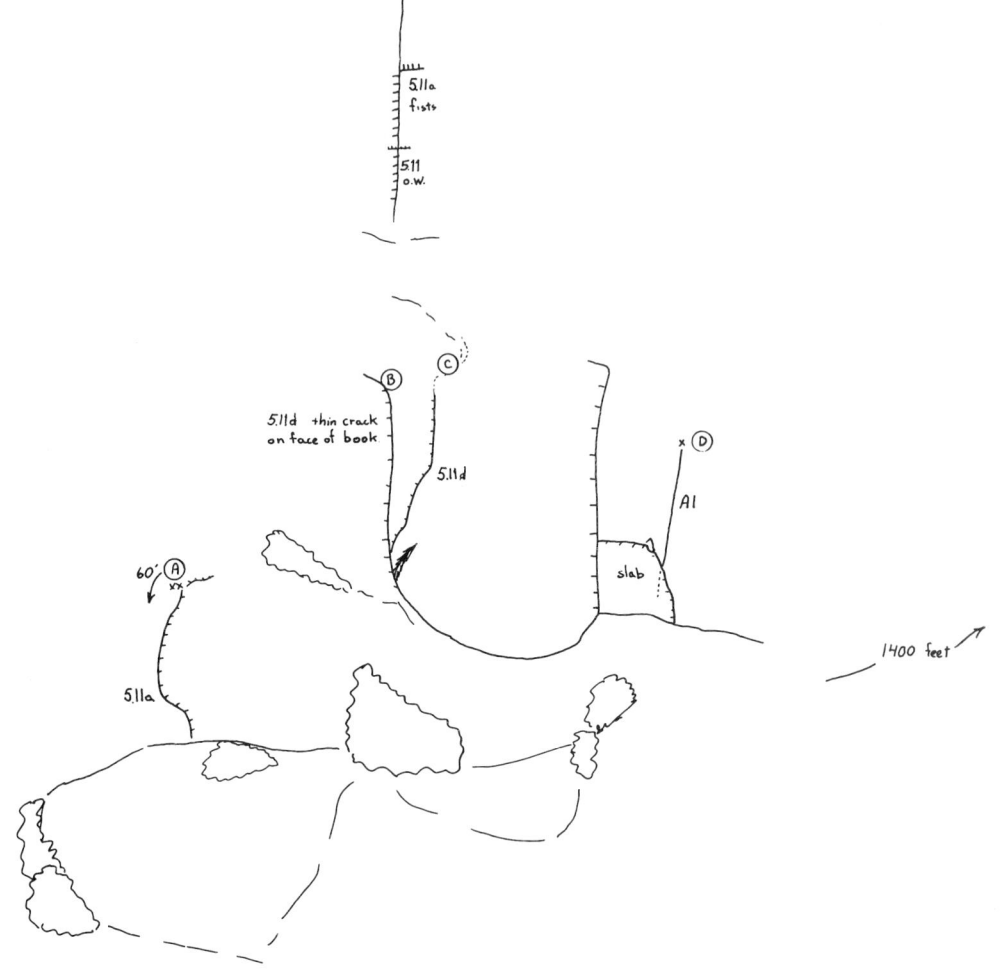

Dog Dik Cliff

Approach: From the turnout 0.8 mile east from the Arch Rock parking area walk downriver to brush-free talus. Hike up, skirting the first cliff on its right. For **Short but Thick** go a bit higher, then follow a 2nd and 3rd class ledge system that diagonals up and left. For **Opposition, Happy Days**, etc. continue up and right on steep dirt and brush slopes. **Fist Puppet** is reached from above after circuitous easy 5th class and a rappel.

- A. **Short but Thick** 5.11a★
- B. **Opposition** 5.11d★
- C. **Happy Days** 5.11d★★
- D. **Pink Pussycat** A1★ Pro: Needs many baby angles.
- E. **Fist Puppet** 5.11a

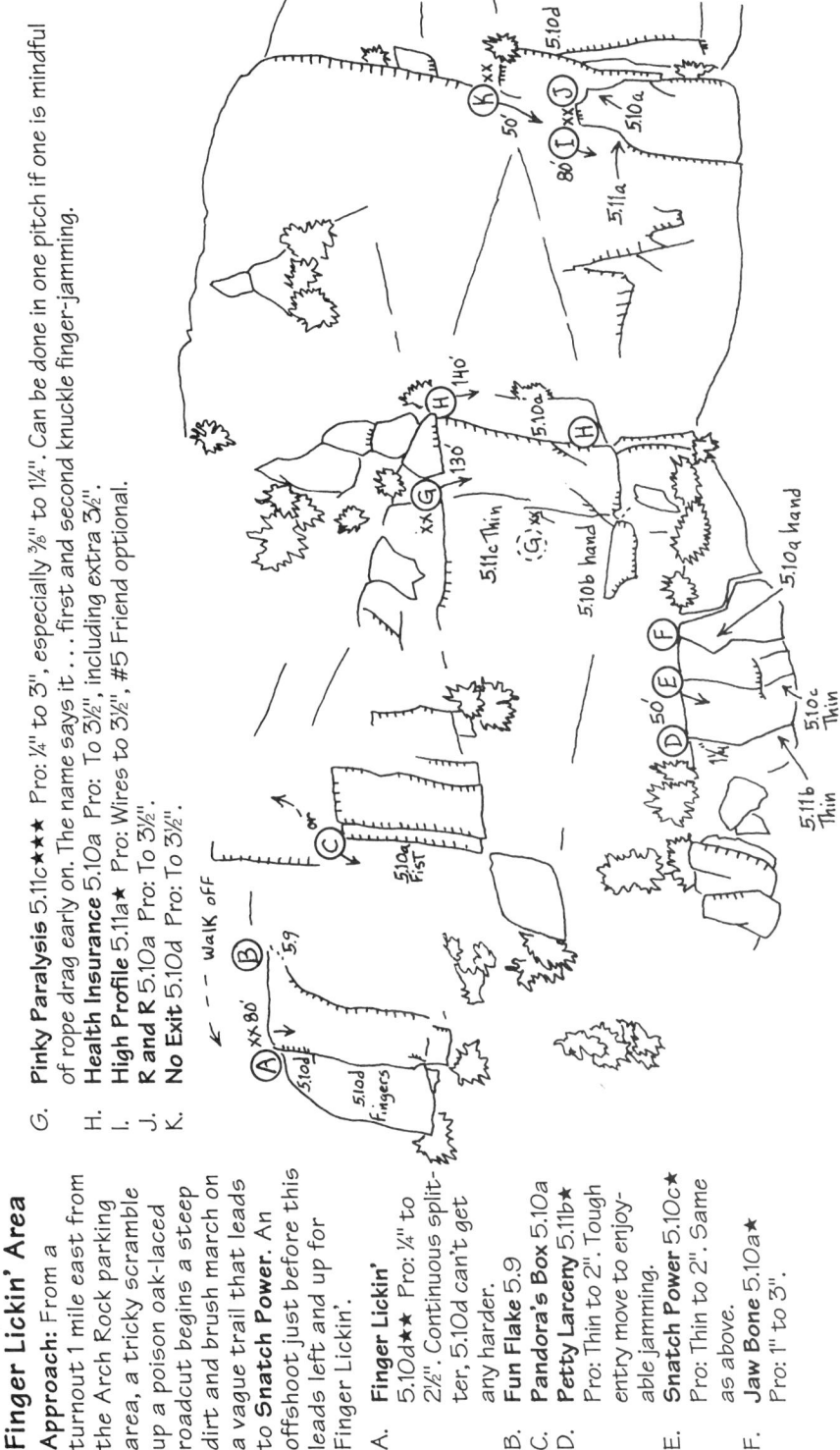

Finger Lickin' Area

Approach: From a turnout 1 mile east from the Arch Rock parking area, a tricky scramble up a poison oak-laced roadcut begins a steep dirt and brush march on a vague trail that leads to **Snatch Power**. An offshoot just before this leads left and up for Finger Lickin'.

A. **Finger Lickin'** 5.10d★★ Pro: ¼" to 2½". Continuous splitter, 5.10d can't get any harder.
B. **Fun Flake** 5.9
C. **Pandora's Box** 5.10a
D. **Petty Larceny** 5.11b★ Pro: Thin to 2". Tough entry move to enjoyable jamming.
E. **Snatch Power** 5.10c★ Pro: Thin to 2". Same as above.
F. **Jaw Bone** 5.10a★ Pro: 1" to 3".
G. **Pinky Paralysis** 5.11c★★★ Pro: ¼" to 3", especially ⅜" to 1¼". Can be done in one pitch if one is mindful of rope drag early on. The name says it ... first and second knuckle finger-jamming.
H. **Health Insurance** 5.10a Pro: To 3½", including extra 3½".
I. **High Profile** 5.11a★ Pro: Wires to 3½", #5 Friend optional.
J. **R and R** 5.10a Pro: To 3½".
K. **No Exit** 5.10d Pro: To 3½".

LOWER MERCED CANYON: NORTH

Roadside Attraction Area

Roadside Attraction Area

Approach: Parking for the various cliffs in this area is located 3.5 miles west from the Hwy 120/Hwy 140 junction.

A. **River Boulder** 5.11d★ TR
B. **Roadside Attraction** 5.12a★★ Though usually toproped, this has been soloed once. Slightly overhanging. A leg pump, then an arm pump.
C. **Roadside Infraction** 5.12b TR

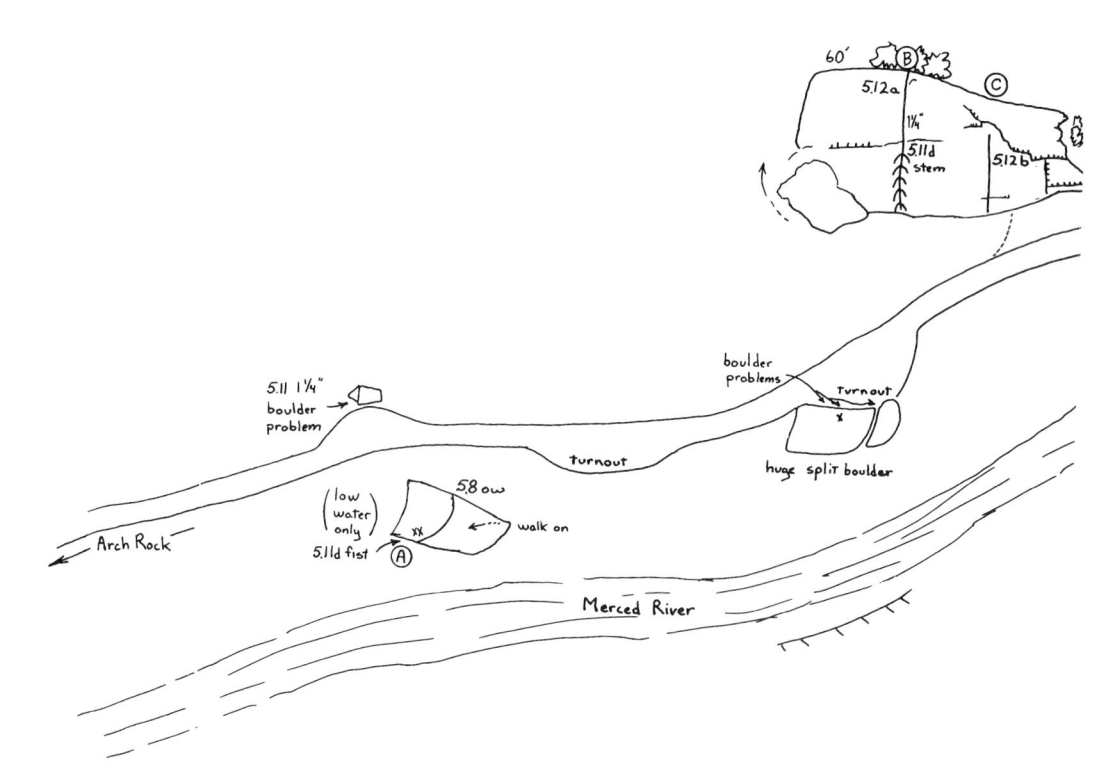

Roadside Attraction Area

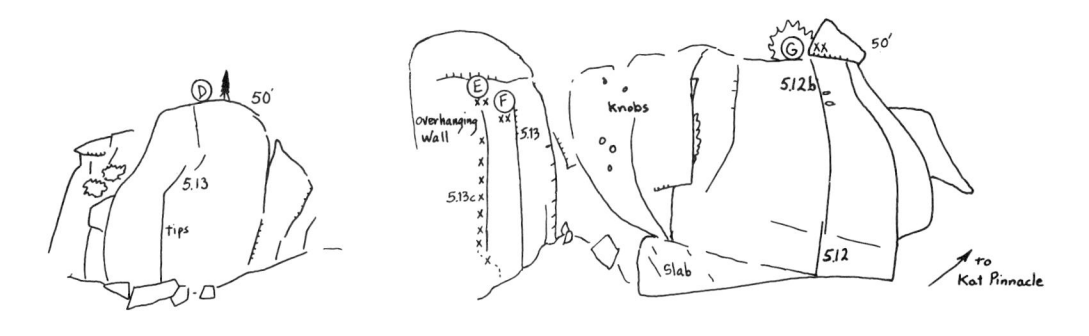

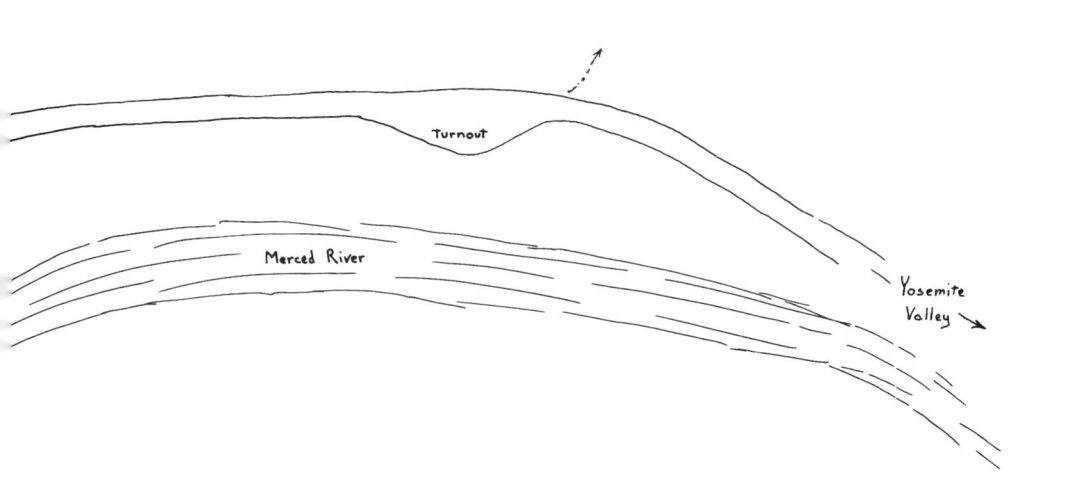

Approach: From a dirt (riverside) turnout just upriver from **Roadside Attraction**, the obvious cliff just above the road is a useful landmark. **Dale's Pin Job** is at the extreme downriver end of the cliff; **Back to the Future** is at the extreme upriver end. A pair of leaning cedars marks the start of the rough approach trail (also useful for the tramp up to Kat Pinnacle).

- D. **Dale's Pin Job** 5.13
- E. **Van Belle O Drome** 5.13c★
- F. **Van Belle Syndrome** 5.13★
- G. **Back to the Future** 5.12b

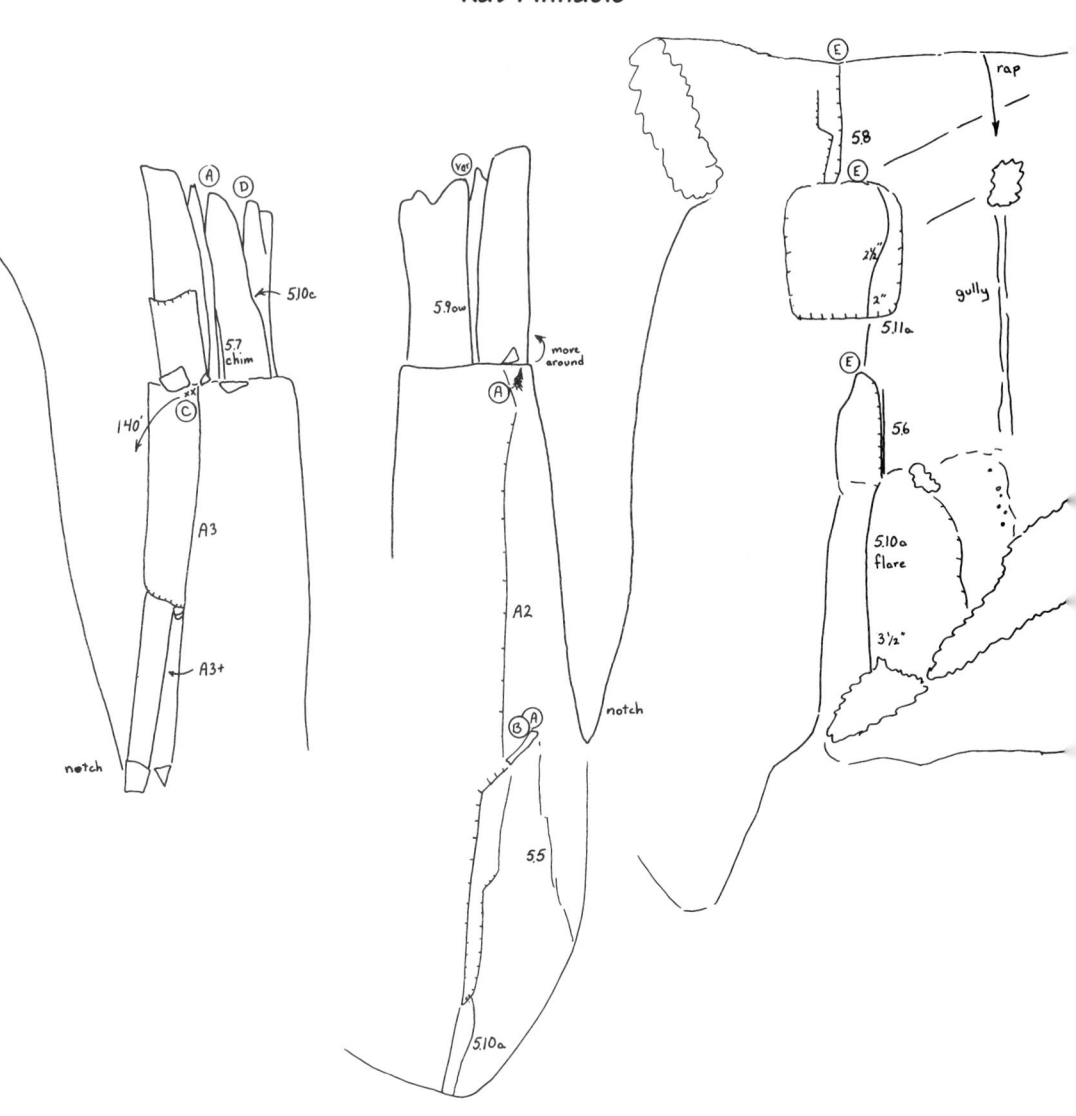

Kat Pinnacle

Approach: From a dirt (riverside) turnout just upriver from **Roadside Attraction**, the obvious cliff just above the road is a useful landmark. A pair of leaning cedars marks the start of the rough approach trail. Only **A la Moana** is approached from above. Walk up the Cookie Road about a mile to a broad, flat, pine tree area (near the Dynamite Crack). **A la Moana** is down below in the brush.

- A. **Northwest Corner** 5.7 A2★
- B. **Katchup** 5.10a
- C. **Southwest Corner** 5.7 A3+★
- D. **Compass** 5.10c
- E. **A la Moana** 5.11a

Bobcat Buttress

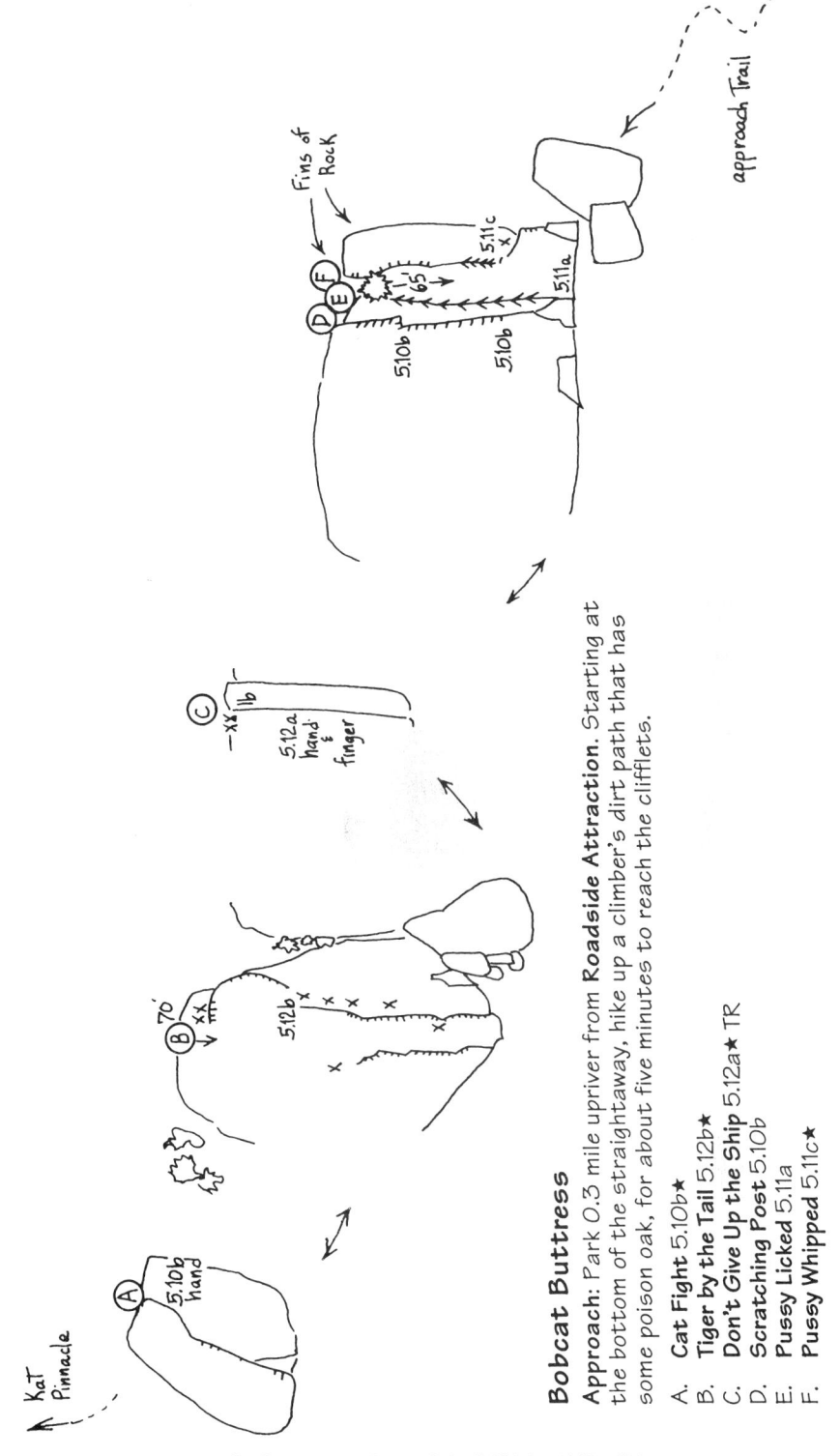

Approach: Park 0.3 mile upriver from **Roadside Attraction**. Starting at the bottom of the straightaway, hike up a climber's dirt path that has some poison oak, for about five minutes to reach the clifflets.

A. **Cat Fight** 5.10b ★
B. **Tiger by the Tail** 5.12b ★
C. **Don't Give Up the Ship** 5.12a ★ TR
D. **Scratching Post** 5.10b
E. **Pussy Licked** 5.11a
F. **Pussy Whipped** 5.11c ★

LOWER MERCED CANYON: NORTH — 41

Cookie Cliff Area

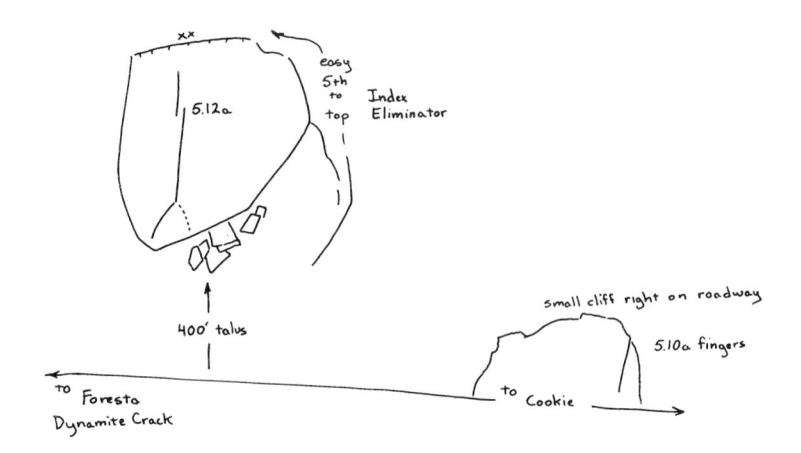

Boulder Cracks

Approach: Approximately one mile further up the Cookie Road, at a level area that is characterized by a large, open pine forest, is an explosion-fractured 20'-high boulder. A 5.10 finger crack is located on the west side.

Index Eliminator 5.12a
Dynamite Crack 5.10

Oreo Cliff

Approach: Can be reached by hiking up from the left side of the Cookie Cliff.

A. **Animal Crackers** 5.11c This climbs a 70-foot thin crack on the left side of the cliff. It is about 100 feet left of the Ninja Flake, a 45-foot high detached plate of rock, and ends at a two-bolt rappel/belay anchor.
B. **Original Chips Ahoy** 5.10c Steep knobs and edging lead to a two-bolt rappel/belay anchor 60 feet up. This route is about 40 feet left of **Ninja Flake**.
C. **Ninja Flake** 5.11 On the inside of the Ninja Flake, a face gains a one-inch splitter crack.
D. **Fig Neutron** 5.11b A crack and steep knobs on the outside of the Ninja Flake lead to the two-bolt rappel/belay anchor on top.
E. **Spuds McKenzie** 5.10d A thin crack followed with steep face climbing past one bolt arrives at the two-bolt anchor.
F. **What's your Fantasy** 5.11b This is located 30 feet right of **Spuds McKenzie**. It ascends steep knobs (5.11b) past three bolts and a fixed pin to a two-bolt belay station 60 feet up. From here move left then climb up (5.11a) passing three more bolts and a fixed pin to a two bolt rappel/belay anchor 165 feet up.
G. **Snap, Crackle, and Pop** 5.10c This 50-foot route climbs a thin crack and steep knobs on a small section of crag 100 feet right of the previous climbs.

The Cookie Cliff and Above

1. Capital Punishment 5.8
2. Hobknob 5.8
3. Gait of Power 5.11d
4. Separate Reality 5.12a

The Cookie Cliff

Approach: Park at the turnout adjacent to the river (0.5 mile down from the Cascade Falls Bridge) amid giant white talus boulders. Follow a climber's trail somewhat left of the talus field to meet the old road at the base of the cliff.

Descent: Contour left (downriver). Near the margin of the cliff, angle down steep dirt, skirting short walls. One third-class move near the bottom of this section leads to the ground a short distance west of **Twinkie**.

Photo on page 43.

- A. **Mystic Mint** 5.11b★
- B. **Twinkie** 5.10c Pro: To 6".
- C. **Nutter Butter** 5.12b★
- D. **Tennessee Strings** 5.12a★ Pro: Small, HBs and Tricams.
- E. **Coffin Nail** A3+★
- F. **Banana Dreams** 5.10a Pro: 3" to 6".
- G. **Hardd** 5.11b★★★ Pro: ¼" to 2", especially ½" to 1½" pieces. First pitch: Staying fresh is helpful through the final moves. Second pitch: The finger crack is a bit harder than it first appears.
- H. **Crack-a-Go-Go** 5.11c ★★★ Pro: ½" to 2", especially ¼" to 1¼". It is standard to rappel after the first pitch. Fine technique and using both cracks saves energy on this continuous pitch. Somewhat difficult to see the placements.
- I. **Outer Limits** 5.10c★★★ Pro: ½" to 3½", especially ¾" to 2½". First pitch: This is strangely off-balance for a straight-in crack. Staying power is put to the test. Second pitch: Excellent hands to a boulder-type traverse. TCUs are helpful here.
- J. **Satanic Mechanic** 5.12c R? Pro: Small TCUs.
- K. **Orangutan Arch** 5.11b★ Pro: To 3½".
- L. **Elevator Shaft** 5.8★ R
- M. **Cookie Monster** (Second pitch/upper section aka Cookie Cutter) 5.12a/5.13b★★★ Pro: QDs. The route has been done free in one pitch, though when first freed it was done in two pitches. The first half involved lie backing a shallow, arching crack. The second half cranks on flat edges up a wildly steep orange wall.
- N. **Twilight Zone** 5.10d★★ Pro: To 6".
- O. **Chips Ahoy** 5.12b★★ Pro: QDs. Climb the right side of the arête.
- P. **Ginger Snap** 5.12b★
- Q. **America's Cup** 5.12b★ R
- R. **Red Zinger** 5.11d★★★ Pro: To 2". This route breaks away from, then comes close to rejoining, **Meat Grinder**. First knuckle jams to a widening finger crack.
- S. **Meat Grinder** 5.10c★★ Pro: To 3½". This follows the huge corner. Finish the second pitch by stepping into a belay alcove out left or continuing the off-width above to a belay, then a 5.8 hand pitch off.
- T. **Meat Grinder Arête** 5.13b★★★ Pro: Mostly QDs.
- U. **Beverly's Tower** 5.10a★★ Pro: ¼" to 2½", mainly small. Provides an easier way onto the Nabisco Wall.
- V. **Aftershock** 5.11b★★ Pro: Many small.
- W. **Waverly Wafer** 5.10c★★★ Pro: ½" to 2½". A burning 1¼" jam/lieback above the rest alcove.

X. **Butterballs** 5.11c★★★ Pro: ⅜" to 1¼", with extra ¾" to 1¼" pieces. Continuous all-time finger crack.
Y. **Wheat Thin** 5.10c★★★ Pro: To 2", especially ½" to 1¼" pieces. Move right, then an off-balance lieback gains a spectacular lieback flake. Very airy.
Z. **Butterfingers** 5.11a★★ Pro: Mainly ⅜" to 1½". A foothold appears as the crack diminishes. Then reach right. Tight hands to the top.
Ladyfingers 5.11a★★ (right-side start) Pro: ¼" to 1½". Move right from the belay, then follow discontinuous finger cracks up to a reach left—tight hands to the top.

The Cookie

AA. **Left Side** 5.10a Pro: To 3½".
BB. **Center Route** 5.9★ (R–depending on body size) Pro: To 2½".
CC. **Right Side** 5.9 ★★ Pro: To 2½".
DD. **Vendetta** 5.10b★ Pro: To 5".
EE. **Infraction** 5.9
FF. **Anathema** 5.10b★★ Pro: To 4".
GG. **Last in Line** 5.11b
HH. **Jardine's Hand** 5.11a★
II. **The Cleft** 5.9★ R A caving adventure.
JJ. **Catchy** 5.10d★★★ Pro: ¼" to 2". Span past a thin section at the top.
KK. **Catchy Corner** 5.11a ★★★ Pro: To 2½", extra ½" to ¾".
LL. **Pringles** 5.11a/b★★
MM. **Zipperhead** 5.12c
NN. **The Void** 5.11b★ R Pro: To 3".
OO. **Void Continuation** 5.10d★ R/X
PP. **The Stigma** (aka The Renegade) 5.13 A3★★ Pro: Thin and high tech.
QQ. **The Enigma** 5.10a ★★ Pro: To 2 1/2".
Last pitch variations, from left:
Ramp of Deception 5.10a ★★
Abstract Corner 5.11d★★
Escape 5.8
Shortcake 5.11b★★★ Pro: To 3½".
RR. **The Enema** 5.11b ★★★ Pro: To 3". Climb a wildly overhanging hand crack, then saddle a rest knob. Continue up the flared vertical crack crux via thin or fist jams.
SS. **Ray's Pin Job** 5.12b★ Pro. Thin.
TT. **Something for Nothing** 5.11d★
UU. **Gunning for Buddha** 5.11c★
VV. **Terminator**
Left 5.11b★
Right 5.10d★

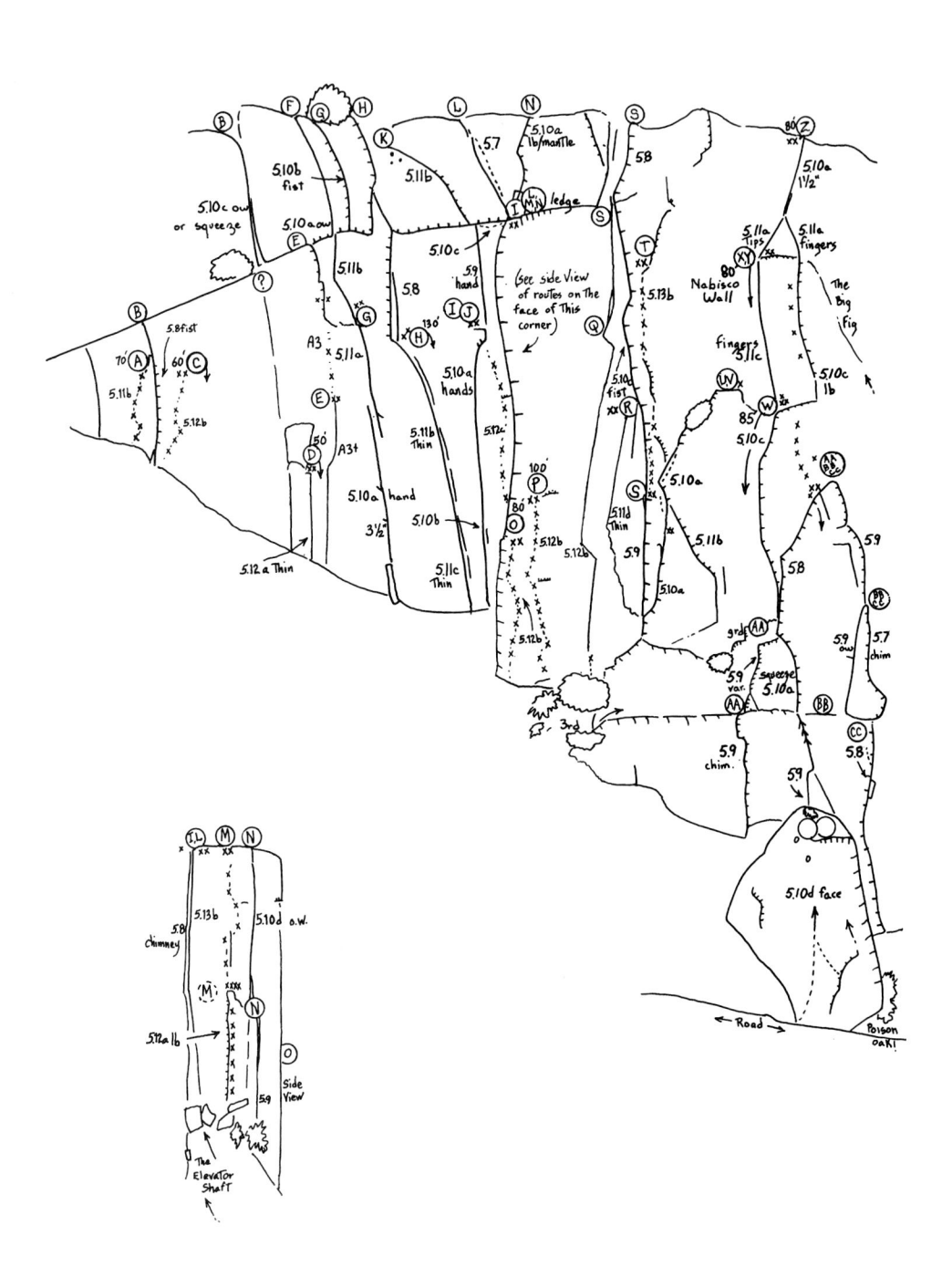

The Cookie Cliff

LOWER MERCED CANYON: NORTH

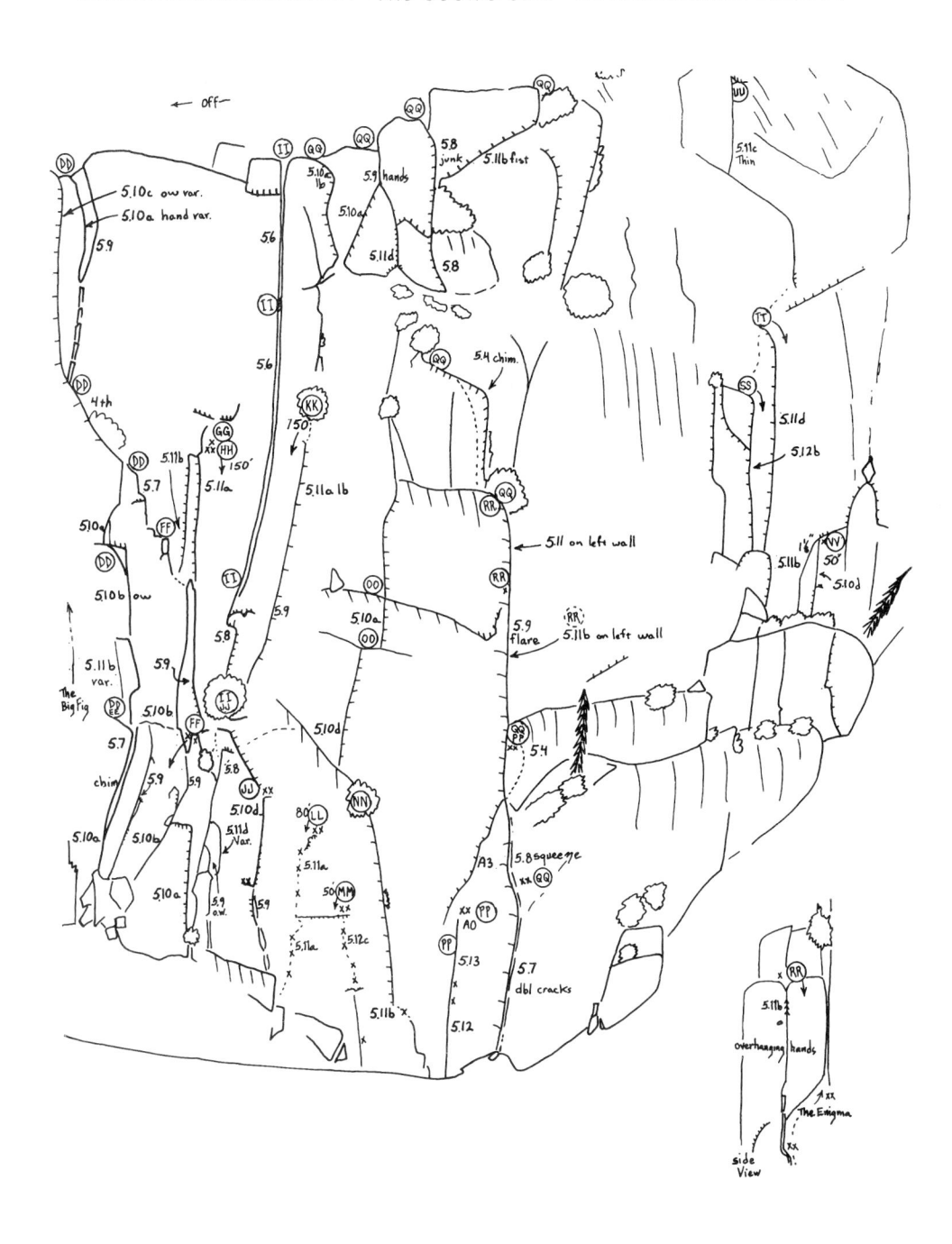

The Cookie Cliff

LOWER MERCED CANYON: NORTH

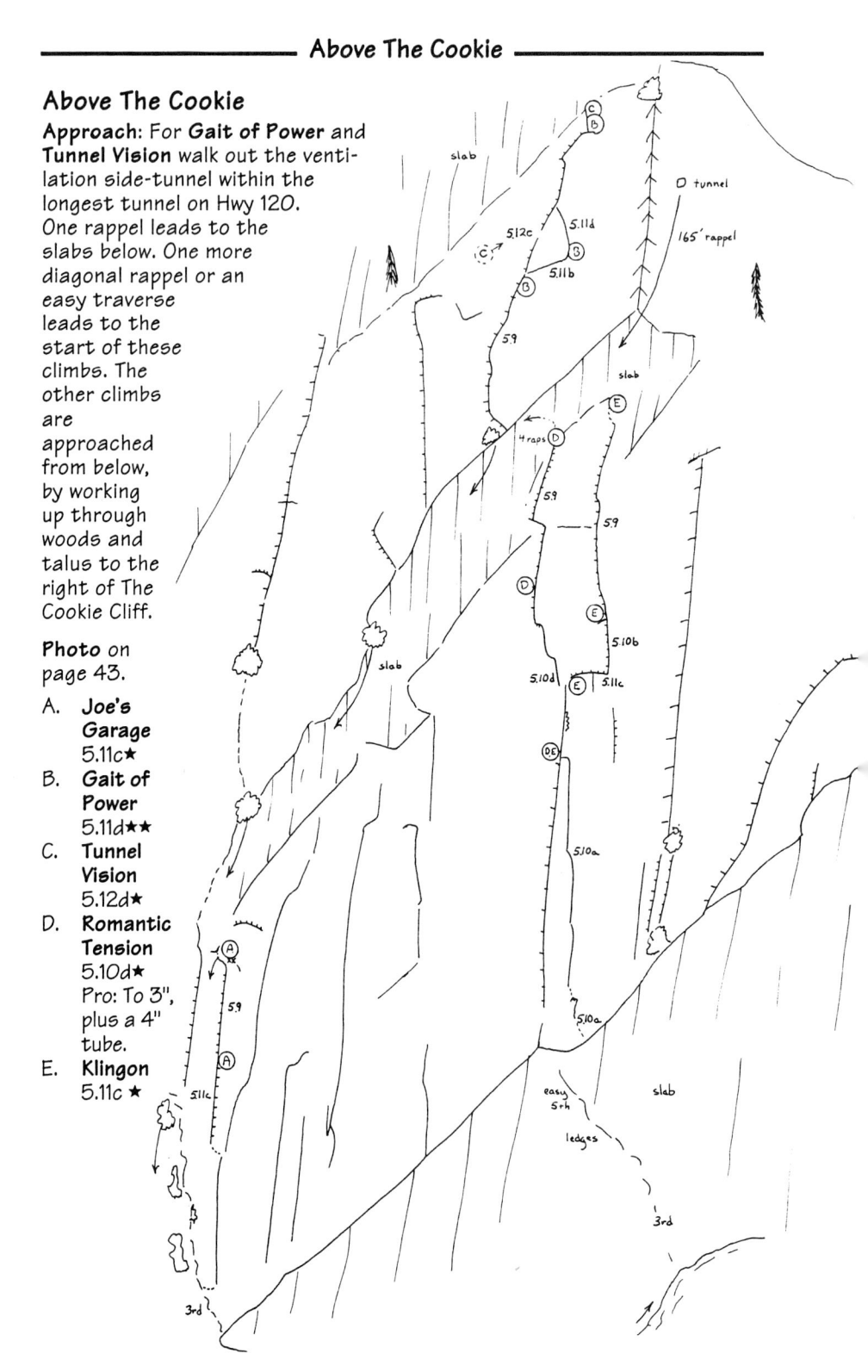

Above The Cookie

Approach: For **Gait of Power** and **Tunnel Vision** walk out the ventilation side-tunnel within the longest tunnel on Hwy 120. One rappel leads to the slabs below. One more diagonal rappel or an easy traverse leads to the start of these climbs. The other climbs are approached from below, by working up through woods and talus to the right of The Cookie Cliff.

Photo on page 43.

A. **Joe's Garage** 5.11c★
B. **Gait of Power** 5.11d★★
C. **Tunnel Vision** 5.12d★
D. **Romantic Tension** 5.10d★
   Pro: To 3", plus a 4" tube.
E. **Klingon** 5.11c ★

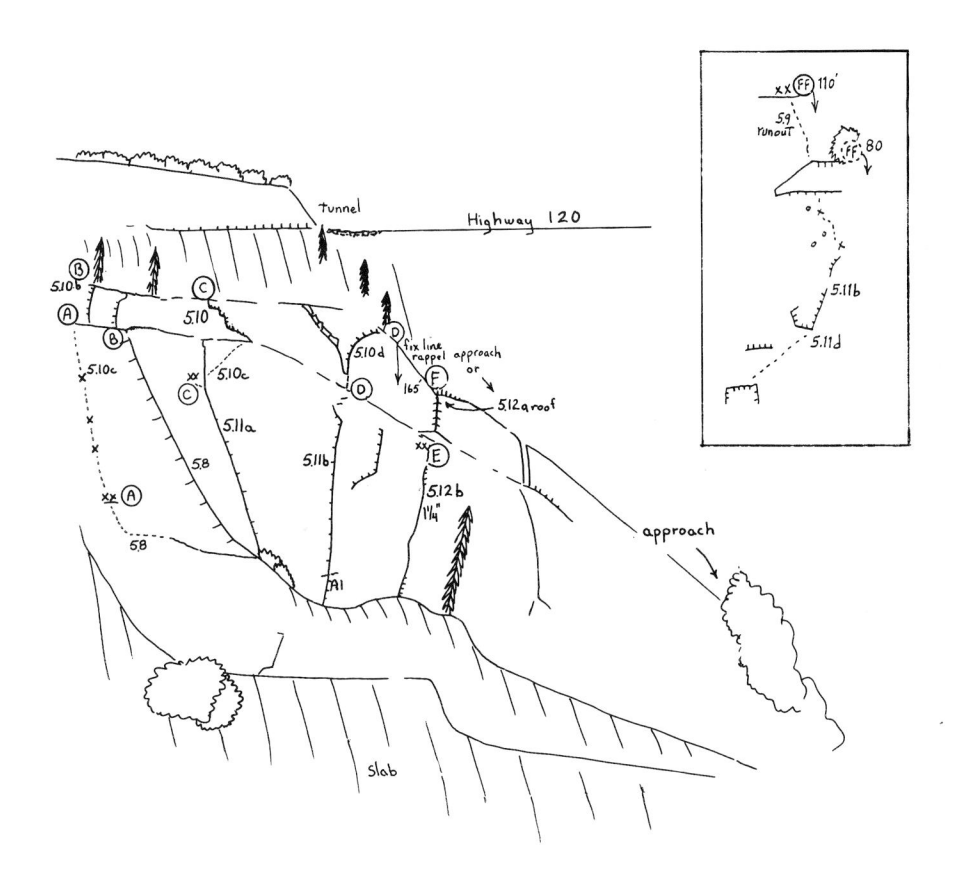

Above The Cookie

Approach: From the eastern end of the longest tunnel on Hwy 120 scramble down brush and slabs to the edge. Rappel 165 feet from a cedar between **Skunk Crack** and **Tales of Power**.

Photo on page 43.
- A. **Miramonte** 5.10c
- B. **Uncertain Ending** 5.10b★
- C. **Obscure Destiny** 5.11a★
- D. **Skunk Crack** 5.11b A1★
- E. **Tales of Power** 5.12b★★★ Pro: ¾" to 2½" (also a fixed rappel line). Beautiful straight-in off-hand jamming on an overhanging wall.
- F. **Separate Reality** 5.12a★★★ Pro: ¾" to 3½" (also a fixed rappel line). Airy roof from hand to fingers. At the lip, flip around.

Approach: **Guillotine** is below **Separate Reality** and immediately west of Wildcat Creek. Hike up talus from Hwy 140.

- FF. **Guillotine** 5.11d

Wildcat Falls Area

Through Bein' Cool

Approach: Park at a spring beside a long paved turnout just west of the Cascade Creek Bridge on Hwy 120. Trace the watercourse toward the canyon (still somewhat east of Tamarack Creek). Skirt a 50-foot wall near the rim via Class 2 chutes to a flat grove beside a minor waterfall. Rappel 80 feet from there.

G. **Through Bein' Cool** 5.10c★
H. **Meatheads** 5.10d TR
I. **Prime Time** 5.9

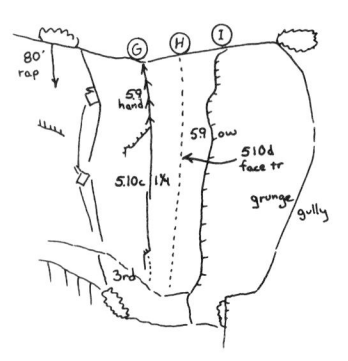

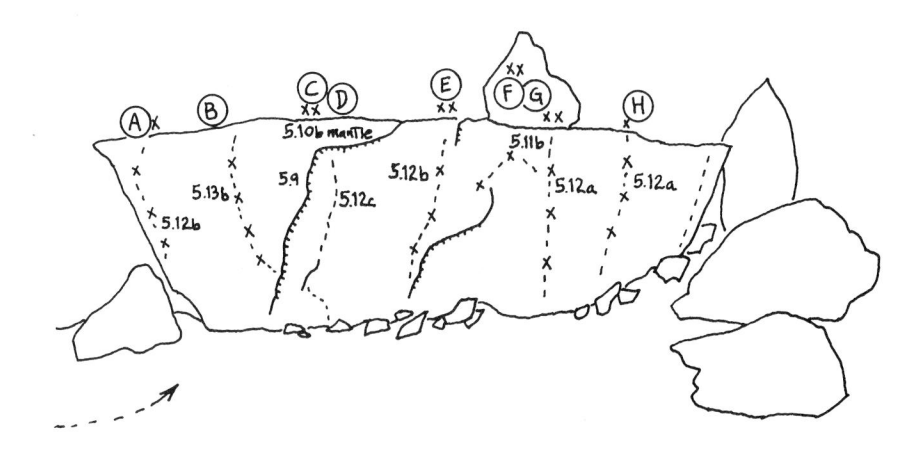

Knobby Wall

Approach: This small but incredibly steep toprope boulder is located 20 yards to the north of Hwy 140, 0.3 mile west of the Cascade Creek Bridge, 0.4 mile east of The Cookie Cliff parking area.

A. **Portside** (aka Roland's Hole Route) 5.12b★★
B. **Keep the Muscle, Lose the Fat** 5.13b★★
C. The Flake 5.10b
D. **Meltdown** 5.12c★★
E. **Changos Cabrones** 5.12b★★
F. **Unnamed** 5.11b★★
G. **Shaft of the Penetrator** 5.12a★★
H. **Unnamed** 5.12a★★
I. **Pumping Hate** 5.12a Not shown. This climb is located just right of the Knobby Wall Boulder, and traverses right along the lip of an overhang past four bolts.

Photo by Chris Falkenstein

Sue McDevitt on Crimson Cringe

Cascade Area

1. Pat and Jack Pinnacle
2. My-Toe-Sis 5.11b
3. The Wedge 5.11a
4. The Tube 5.11a
5. Golden Needles 5.8
6. Phoenix 5.13a

Pat and Jack Pinnacle

Approach: Park at the broad turnout just west of the Cascade Creek Bridge on Hwy 140. Find the climber's trail that goes straight up to **Trough of Justice**. Follow along the wall to the other routes.

Descent: To descend routes including and between **Gilligan's Chicken** and **Desperate Straights**, negotiate 3rd and 4th class left (west) to the top of **Gilligan's Chicken**. Head down 3rd class chimneys on the left side of the buttress. Almost all of these routes offer rappel options as well.

Topos on pages 54 and 55.

Pat Pinnacle 5.7

Jack Pinnacle
    Left 5.9
    Right 5.7

- A. **Domehead** 5.10b Hangerless bolt.
- B. **Scorpion Man** 5.10d
- C. **Stinger** 5.11a ★
- D. **Stand and Quiver** 5.11a ★ Pro: Tiny wires to #4 Friend.
- E. **Hat Pin** 5.11d ★
- F. **The Knife** 5.11b
- G. **Flailing Dog** 5.11a ★ Pro: To 3".
- H. **Gilligan's Chicken** 5.7
- I. **Chicken Fever** 5.10b
- J. **Sherrie's Crack** 5.10c ★★ Pro: ⅜" to 2½", TCUs. Finger cranks to enjoyable jamming.
- K. **Nurdle** 5.8 ★
- L. **Knob Job** 5.10b ★ Pro: ¼" to 3". Crack switch and reach for jug.
- M. **G-Man** 5.11b R
- N. **Book 'em, Dano** 5.10d
- O. **Trough of Justice** 5.10b ★ Pro: QDs. Balance face and mantels on knobs. Moves around arête.
- P. **Knuckleheads** 5.10b ★★
- Q. **People's Court** 5.10d
- R. **Desperado** 5.11d ★★
- S. **Desperate Straights** 5.10a ★ Pro: To 3".
- T. **Cat's Squirrel** 5.12a ★
- U. **Cat's Squirrel Continuation** 5.12b ★
- V. **Nine Lives** 5.11b
- W. **Black Heads** 5.11b
- X. **Skinheads** 5.10d ★★★
- Y. **Underclingon** 5.12a ★★ Pro: QDs, piece up high optional. Delicate endurance arch. An interesting face above.
- Z. **The Tube** 5.11a ★★ Pro: ⅛" to 2½". Appealing corner with abstract lieback and wedging at the crux.
- AA. **Guardian Angel** 5.11b R
- BB. **Gay Bob's** 5.10b
- CC. **Tricky Fingers** 5.10c Pro: To 3", extra ⅛" to ¾".
- DD. **Brainbucket** 5.10d
- EE. **Babble On** 5.10a Pro: To 3".
- FF. **Showtime** 5.11c ★ R
- GG. **Rocky Horror Show** 5.12a ★★
- HH. **Wart Hog** 5.8
- II. **My-Toe-Sis** 5.11b ★ Pro: To 3½".
- JJ. **Eraser Flake** 5.11a R Pro: Including two #0.5 Friends.
- KK. **Sunblast** 5.13a/A2+ Pro: Rurps, KBs, LAs, nuts to 2½".
- LL. **The Wedge** 5.11b Pro: Small to an 8" tube.

Photo on page 52.

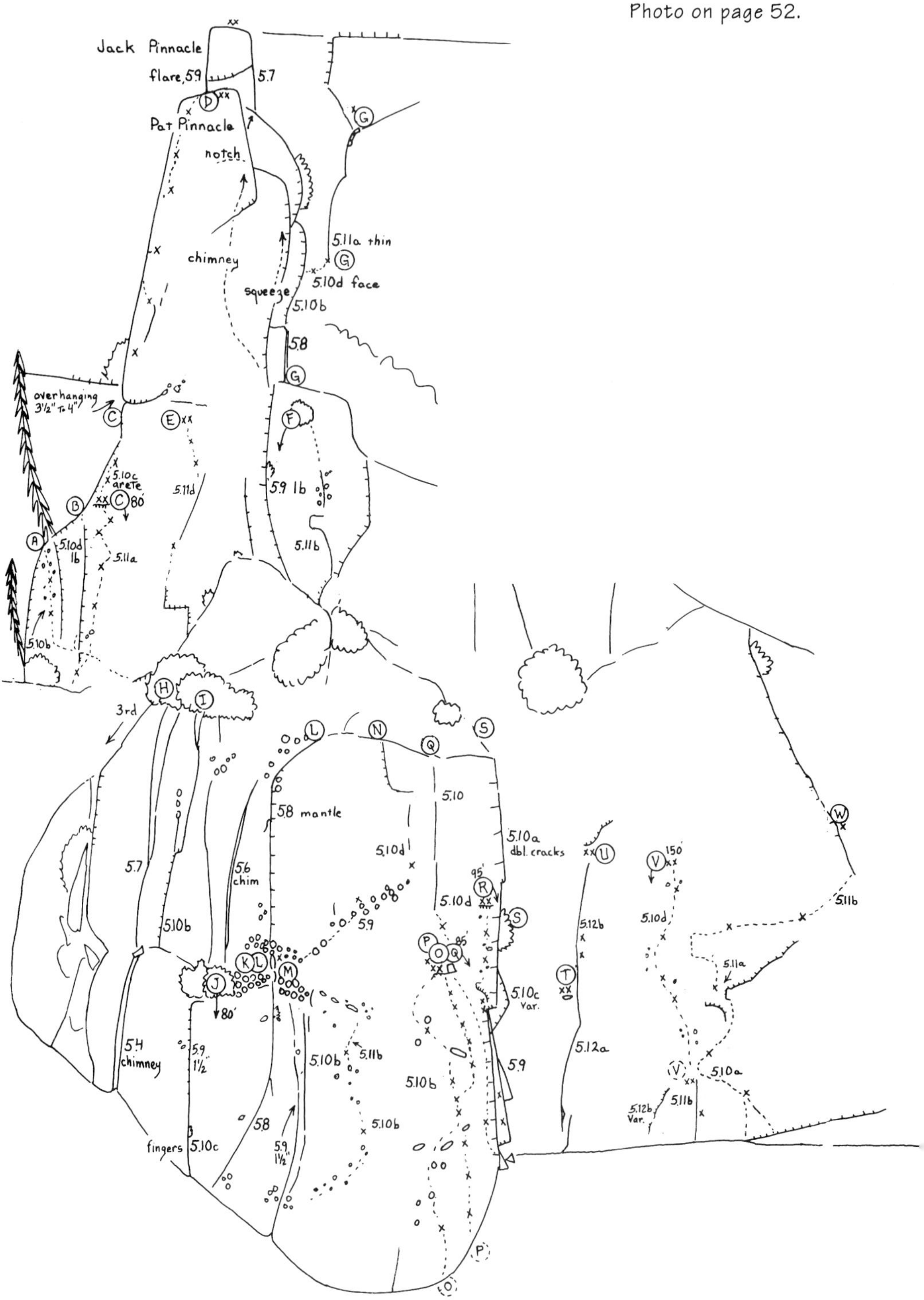

Photo on page 52.

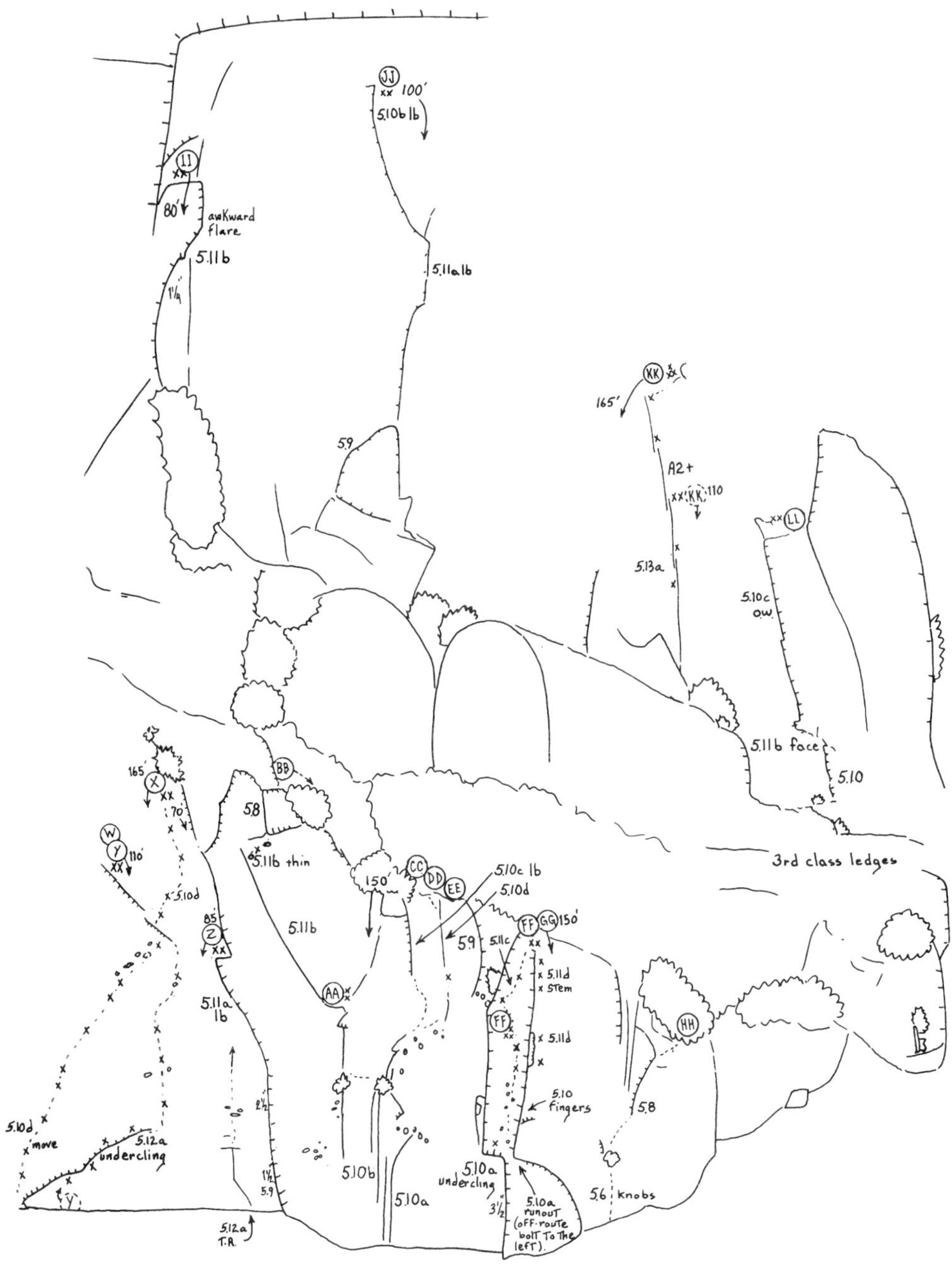

Cascade Falls: Left

LOWER MERCED CANYON: NORTH

Cascade Falls, Left

Approach: This area is located immediately to the west of Cascade Creek, behind the large parking area 1.8 miles down Hwy 140 from the Hwy 120/Hwy 140 junction. Some of the routes are blocked by water in the spring.

- A. **Law of Tools** 5.11a★
- B. **Bolt Adventures** 5.11a★
- C. **Psychological Warfare** 5.12c★★ Pro: Small selection of TCUs to #3.5 Friend.
- D. **Flary Tales** 5.10a
- E. **Toxic Avenger** 5.11c
- F. **Maltese Falcon** 5.11a★ Pro: To #3.5 Friend.
- G. **Eraser Head** 5.10d R/X Pro: #0.4 TCU to #1.5 Friend.
- H. **White Cloud** 5.10d
- I. **A Boy and his Knob** 5.11c Pro: Including #3 Friend.
- J. **Filthy Rich** 5.9
- K. **Wicked Arêtation** 5.10d Pro: Including long runners.
- L. **Golden Needles** 5.8★
- M. **Scurv** 5.9
- N. **Opposite World** 5.10 R/X
- O. **Jug Monkey** 5.9★ Pro: TCU and knob tie-offs.
- P. **Mud Shark** 5.8
- Q. **Fish Crack** 5.12b★★ Pro: Wireds and #0.4 to #1.5 TCUs; also, one 3½" piece for the start. Slightly flared fingers.
- R. **Free Press** 5.10a★★ Pro: To 3½". One grunt section—use your fingers in the back of a body-sized flare.
- S. **Crimson Cringe** 5.12a★★★ Pro: ½" to 3" wireds, with extra 1¼" to 2" pieces. Cranking reaches to solid fingers, continuing to off-hand endurance climbing. Finally, sporty moves take you out a lieback/undercling.

Cascade Falls: Upper

Cascade Falls, Upper

Approach: Phoenix is located on the upper west side of Cascade Falls. It is approached from above via Hwy 120 and two rappels. From the west end of the Tamarack Creek Bridge (2.0 miles west of the Hwy 120/Hwy 140 junction) walk down to an open, flat area. Cross the brook and contour to the brink of the cliff. At a faint arête make a short rappel from small trees to a one-bolt, two-piton station. From here a 140 foot rappel leads to the bottom of the crack.

A. **The Phoenix** 5.13a★★★
   Pro: Small to 2¼". This is an incredible splitter.

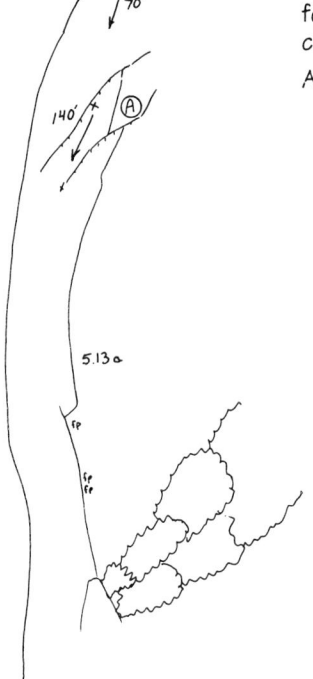

Cascade Falls: Upper

Cascade Falls, Right

False Verde is located just above Hwy 140 on the right side of Cascade Creek and is reached with a simple walk from the Cascade Falls parking lot.

A. **False Verde** 5.9 Pro: 3½"
B. **The Gerbil Launcher** 5.10d Pro: One each 2½" to 7".
C. **Notably Knobular** 5.8 Pro: Slings on knobs only.
D. **Just Scraping By** 5.8
E. **On the Wedge** 5.10a Pro: To 2½".
F. **Solo Crack** 5.9

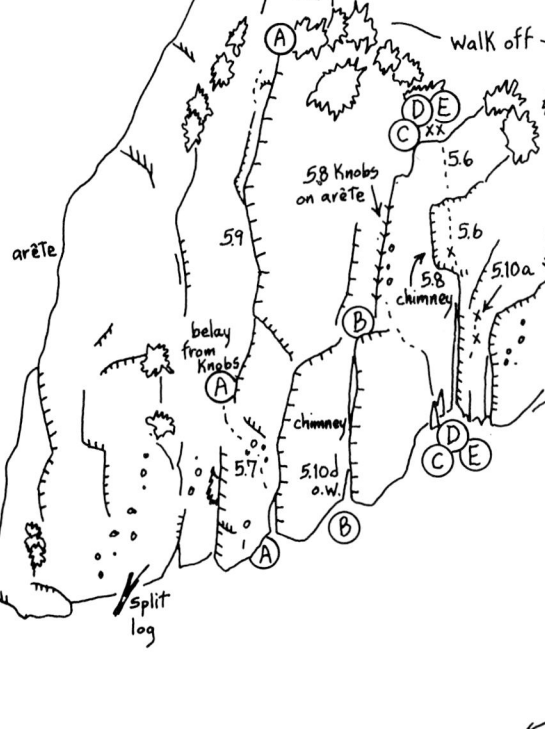

Cascade Falls, Upper

These climbs are visible from the Cascade Bridge on Hwy 120 looking upstream.

A. **On the Spot** 5.11b
B. **Cascade Crack** 5.10b Usually top-roped.

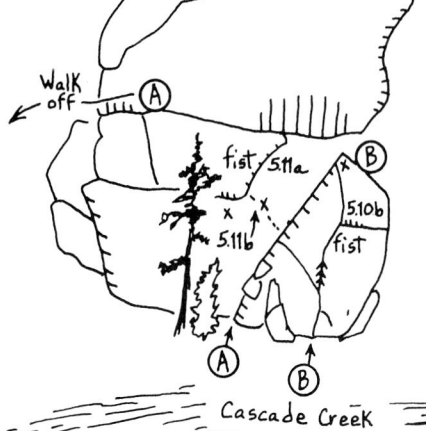

LOWER MERCED CANYON: NORTH

Lower Merced Canyon

1. Cramming 5.10d
2. Scram 5.12a

Lower Merced Canyon

3. The Iota
4. REED'S PINNACLE
5. Lunatic Fringe 5.10c
6. Stone Groove 5.10b
7. INDEPENDENCE PINNACLE
8. Fasten Your Seatbelts

LOWER MERCED CANYON: NORTH

This and That Cliff

This and That Cliff

Approach: The upper routes (**Weird Scenes** through **Blame it on 800**) are approached from above. Park at the Owl Roof turnout on Hwy 120. Locate the B-1 marker beside the road and hike down to the edge of the cliff. Bring one rope for the rappel approach and one rope with which to climb out. The other routes are approached from Hwy 140, starting from a gravel parking area across from some houses, 1.5 miles west of the Hwy 120/Hwy 140 junction. Two main climber's trails access the cliff. One goes straight up to **Tips**; the eastern one heads for **Cramming**.

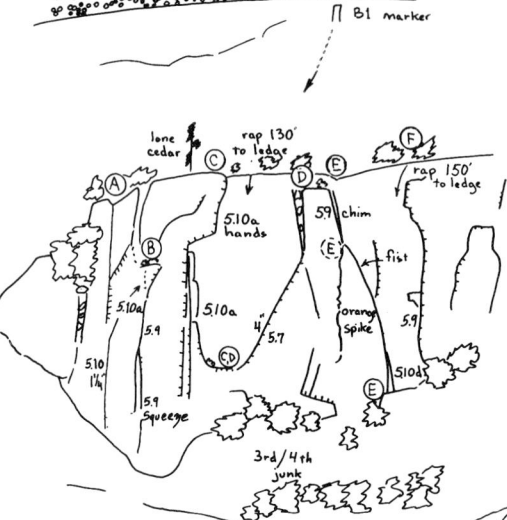

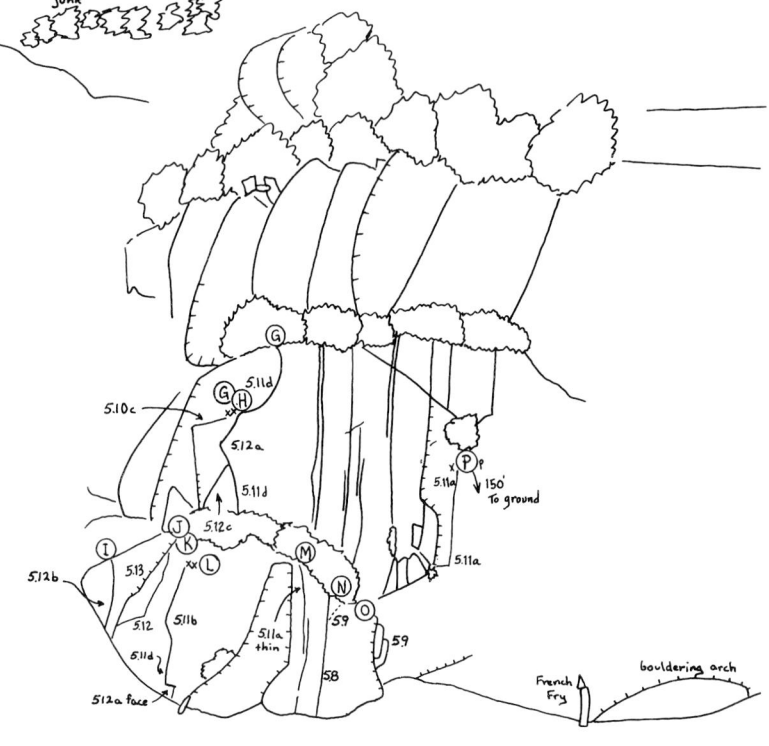

LOWER MERCED CANYON: NORTH

This and That Cliff

- A. **Meat Puppet** 5.10
- B. **Weird Scenes in the Gold Mine** 5.10a
- C. **King Cobra** 5.10a
- D. **Psuedo Desperation** 5.7
  Pro: To 4"
- E. **Agent Orange** 5.10d ★
  Pro: Extra 3½".
- F. **Blame it on 800**
- G. **Gotham City** 5.11d ★
- H. **Robin** 5.12a/c ★★
- I. **Stubs** 5.12a
- J. **Title Fight** 5.13
- K. **Master Lock** 5.12
- L. **Tips** 5.12a ★★
- M. **Back in the Saddle** 5.11a
- N. **Whim** 5.9
- O. **Said and Done** 5.9
- P. **Grateful Pinheads** 5.11a ★
- Q. **Slamming Left** 5.11b ★
  Pro to 1½". Double rope useful.
  Slamming Right 5.10d
  Pro: To 1½".
- R. **Stumped Ray** 5.11
- S. **This and That** 5.10a ★
  (Star rating for the first pitch only.)
  Pro: To 4".
- T. **Slap that Bitch** 5.10d
- U. **Summary Judgment** 5.11a
- V. **Humdinger** 5.10d ★
- W. **Humdinger Continuation** 5.11b
- X. **Pink Banana** 5.10d A1
- Y. **Cramming** 5.10d ★★★
  Pro: ¾" to 2½", especially ¾" to 1½" pieces. A short yet appealing fracture—conducive to doing laps. It is warm in winter.
- Z. **Scram** 5.12a ★★★
  Pro: QDs. Absorbing moves on fascinating rock.
- AA. **Secret Agent** 5.10c
- BB. **Cleaver** 5.11d

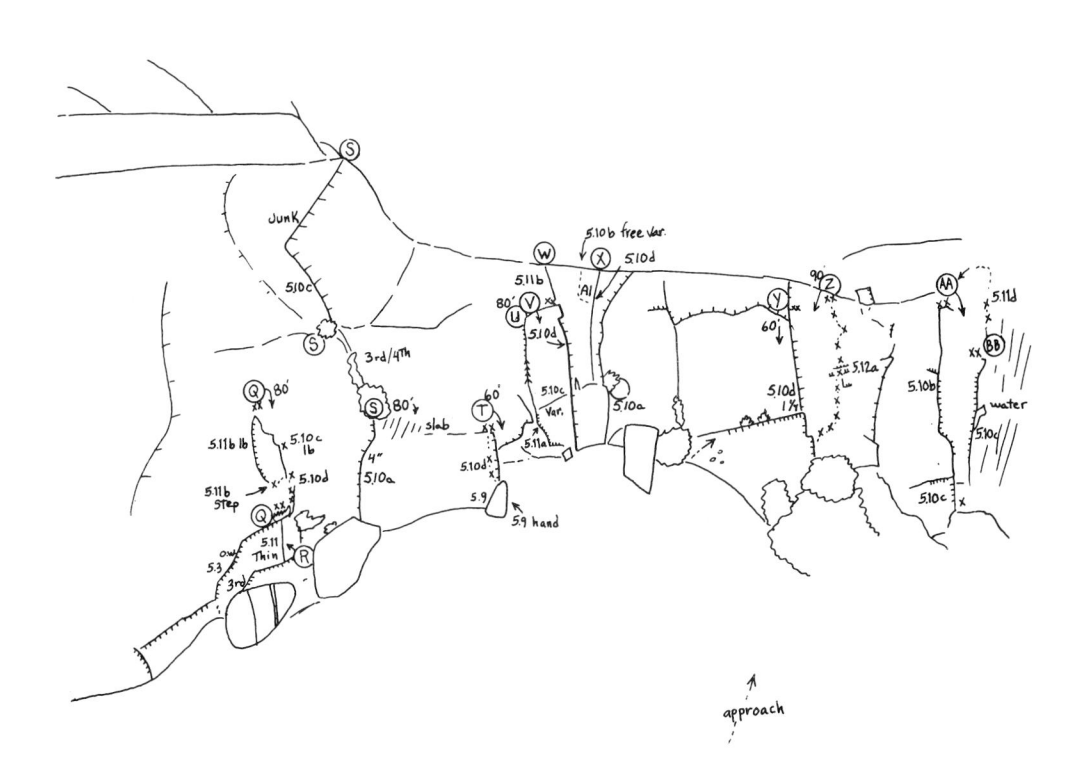

LOWER MERCED CANYON: NORTH

Generator Station

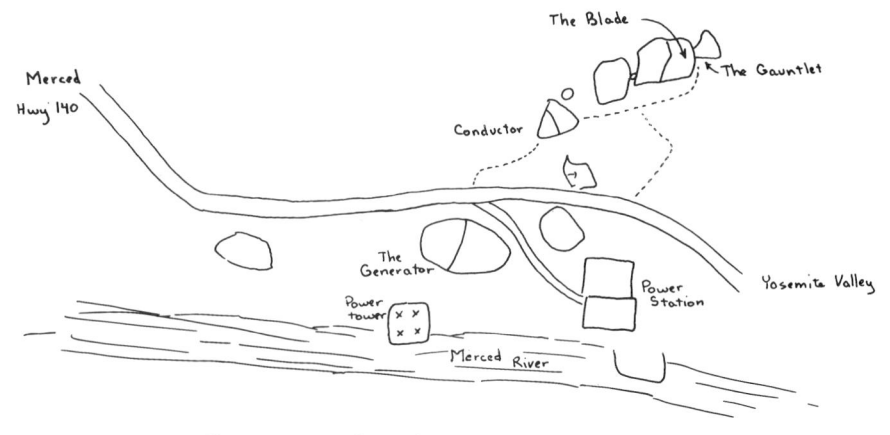

Generator Station

Approach: These various top-rope problems are located near the old generator station off Hwy 140, 1.2 miles west of the Hwy 120/Hwy 140 junction.

- A. **Conductor Crack** 5.10d TR
- B. **Generator Crack** 5.10c★ TR
- C. **The Blade** 5.12 TR
- D. **The Gauntlet** 5.11c TR

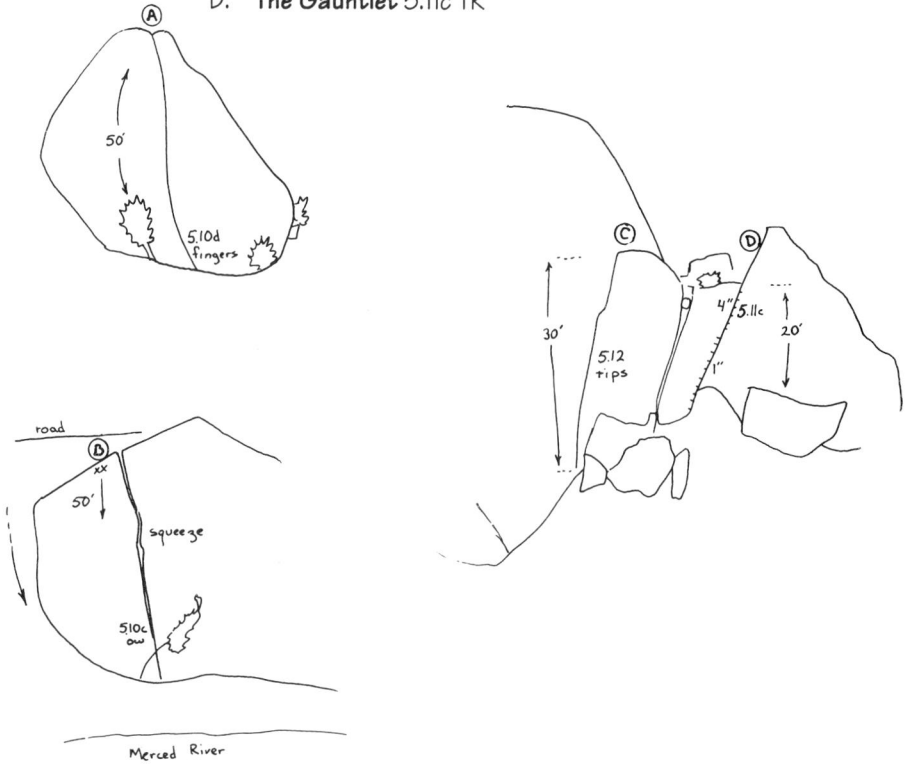

LOWER MERCED CANYON: NORTH

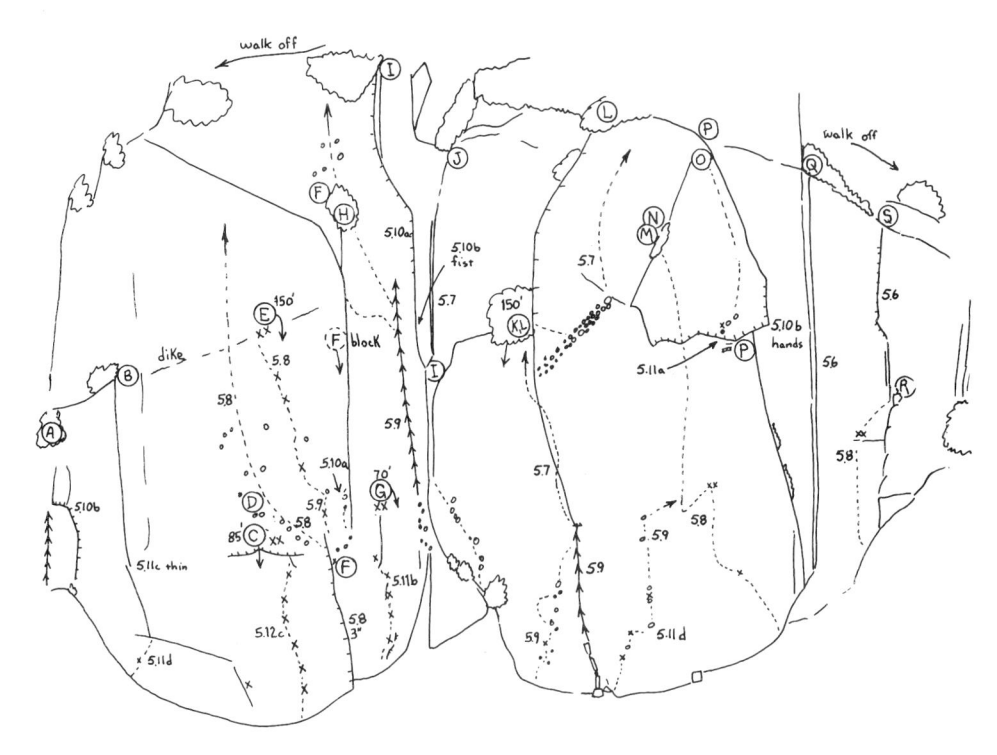

New Diversions Cliff

Approach: From the old generator station off Hwy 140, 1.2 miles west of the Hwy 120/Hwy 140 junction, walk up the hydro-line ditch about 200 feet. The climber's trail begins to the left, and leads up to the base of the wall.

- A. **Falcon** 5.10b
- B. **Rocket Man** 5.11d★
- C. **Highlander** 5.12c Pro: Including #4 Rock.
- D. **Chicken Pox** 5.8
- E. **New Deviations** 5.9★★ Pro: To 3¼".
- F. **New Diversions** 5.10a★★★ Pro: To 3¼", including long runners (knob tie-offs). This is hair-raising, featuring big knobs on a steep wall.
- G. **Burst of Brilliance** 5.11b★
- H. **Wasp** 5.9+
- I. **Strangers in the Night** 5.10b
- J. **Electric Gully** 5.7
- K. **Radical Chic** 5.9 R
- L. **Chicken Pie** 5.9★★ Pro: To 2½", especially ½" to 1¾" pieces; optional pieces to 3½" and knob tie-offs.
- M. **Catch a Wave** 5.11d
- N. **Jugs** 5.8 R/X
- O. **Spring Chicken** 5.11a
- P. **Shake, Rattle, and Drop** 5.10b★
- Q. **Chimney for Two** 5.6
- R. **Holidays** 5.8 R/X
- S. **Tail End** 5.6

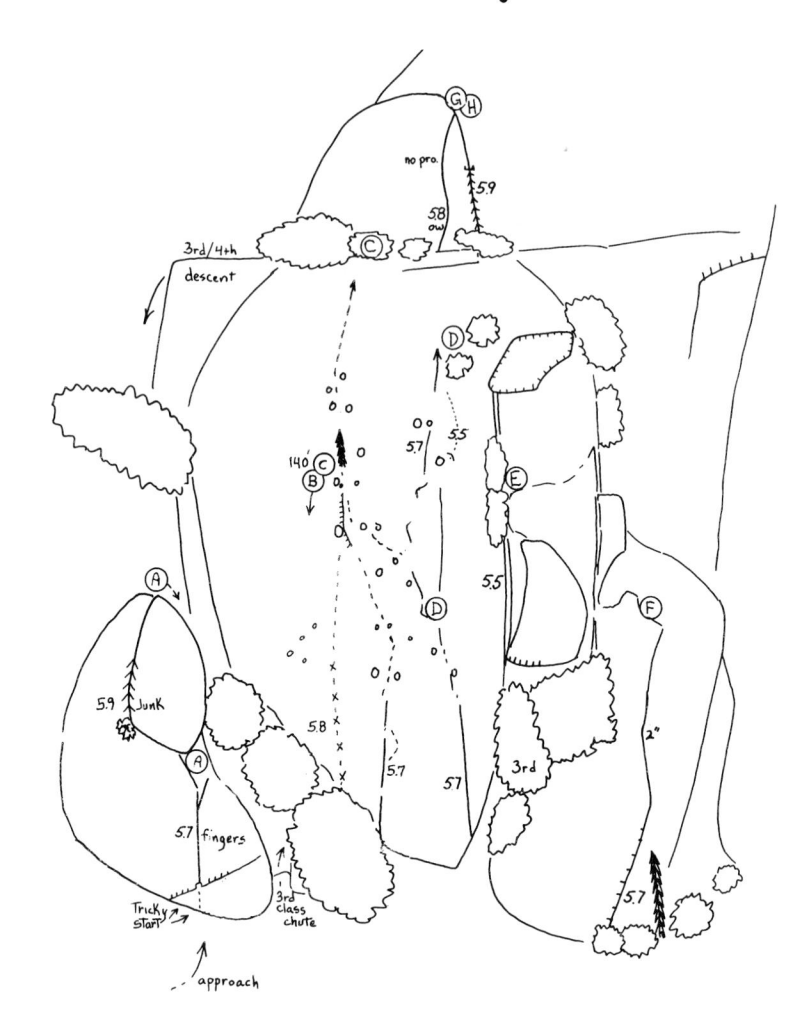

Knob Hill

Approach: This bluff is located above Hwy 120 immediately to the east of Cascade Creek. Park across the road in a paved parking area and scramble steeply up and right to the base of the cliff.

Descent: Scramble off the top of Knob Hill to the west, encountering steep and dirty 3rd class chimneys and gullies.

- A. **Pot Belly** 5.7★ Pro: To 2", especially ½" to 1¼" pieces.
- B. **Movin' to Montana** 5.8★
- C. **Sloth Wall** 5.7★ Pro: To 2½".
- D. **Anti-Ego Crack** 5.7★ Pro: To 2½".
- E. **Sloppy Seconds** 5.5
- F. **Turkey Pie** (aka Chicken Pie) 5.7★ Pro: To 2½".
- G. **Knob Hill Rapist** 5.8 R/X
- H. **Deception Gully** 5.9

Photo by Chris Falkenstein

The Owl Roof

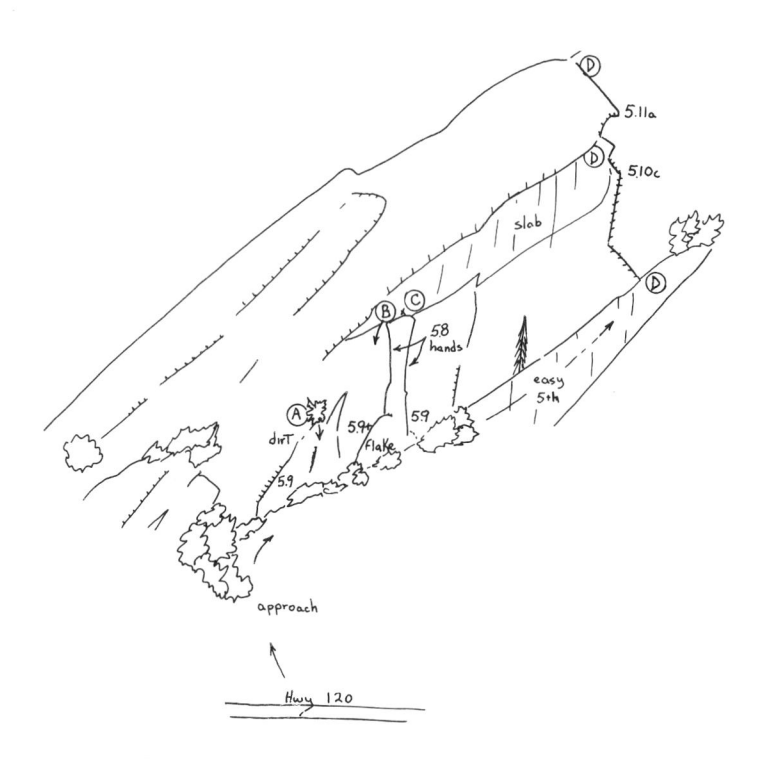

Trix Area

Approach: The climbs **Arlington Heights** through **Trix** lie on the steep east wall of Knob Hill, and are approached from directly below via steep scrambling. **Pimper's Paradise** lies well to the right. **White Owl** lies on the furthest left of the columns that comprise The Owl Area.

Photo on page 67.

- A. **Wrong Address** 5.9
- B. **Arlington Heights** 5.9★
- C. **Hampton Estates** 5.9
- D. **Trix** 5.11a Pro: To 6".

Owl Roof Area

Photo on page 67.

E. **Pimper's Paradise** 5.11d
F. **White Owl** 5.11d
G. **Loose Tooth City** 5.10a
H. **Block Horror Picture Show** 5.9
I. **Teenage Warning** 5.10d
   Pro: To 3", including one #5 Friend.

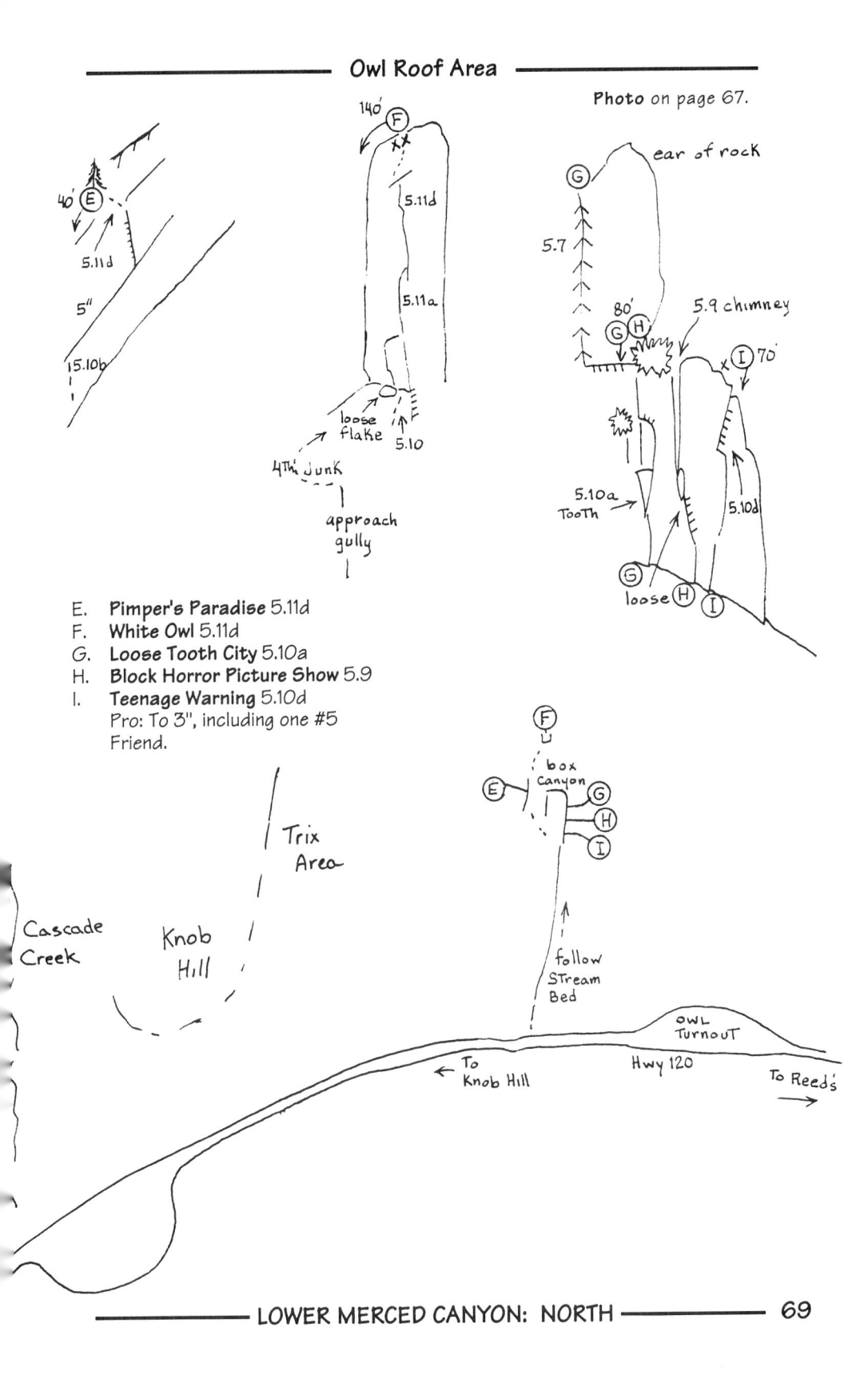

LOWER MERCED CANYON: NORTH

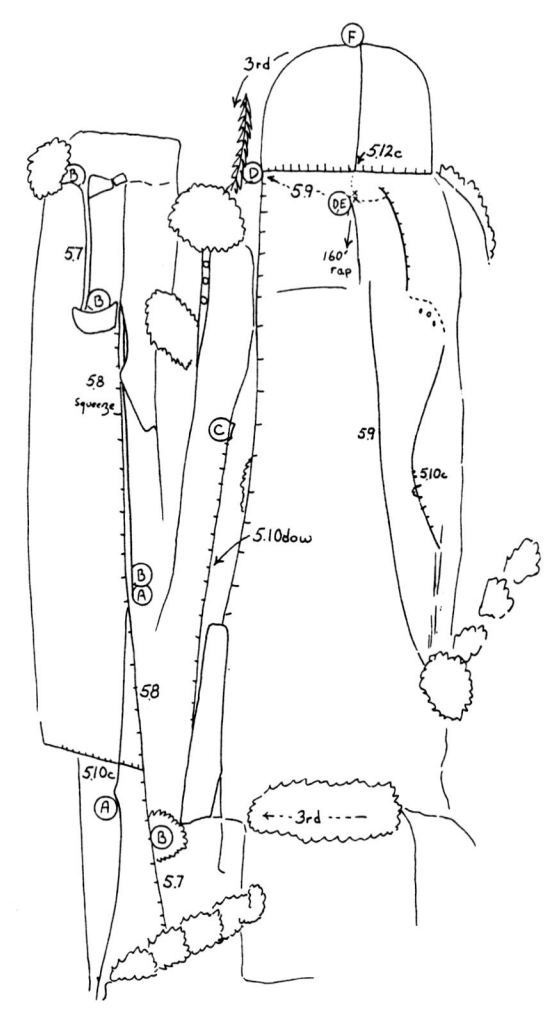

The Owl Area

Approach: A paved turnout is found directly below The Owl on Hwy 120, a bit west of Reed's Pinnacle Area. Scramble up a short roadcut, then approach the formation somewhat from the right.

Photo on page 67.
- A. **Dromedary Direct** 5.10c Pro: To 2½", extra ¾" to 2".
- B. **Dromedary** 5.8+
- C. **The Shaft** 5.10d Pro: To 2½" to 6".
- D. **The Owl Bypass** 5.9★
- E. **Stroke (My Erect Ear Tufts)** 5.10c R Pro: Two each Friends to #3.
- F. **Owl Roof** 5.12c Pro: To 6".

The Owl Area

The Owl Area, Far Right
G. **Floating Lama** 5.11c A1★ Pro: Including many to 3¾".
H. **Mirage** 5.12a★ Pro: Extra ½" to 1".
I. **Color Purple** 5.11b
J. **Pygmy Sex Circus** 5.10b Pro: Wires to #3.5 Friend
K. **Wicked Jones Crusher** 5.10b Note: Poor rappel bolts.
L. **Walrus** 5.9
M. **Traffic Jam** 5.9 Not shown. This right slanting, straight-in, two-inch crack is one-tenth of a mile east of the Owl Roof turnout and immediately above the road. The crux is at the top where the beautiful crack turns into a rotten lieback. (Be careful of cars!)

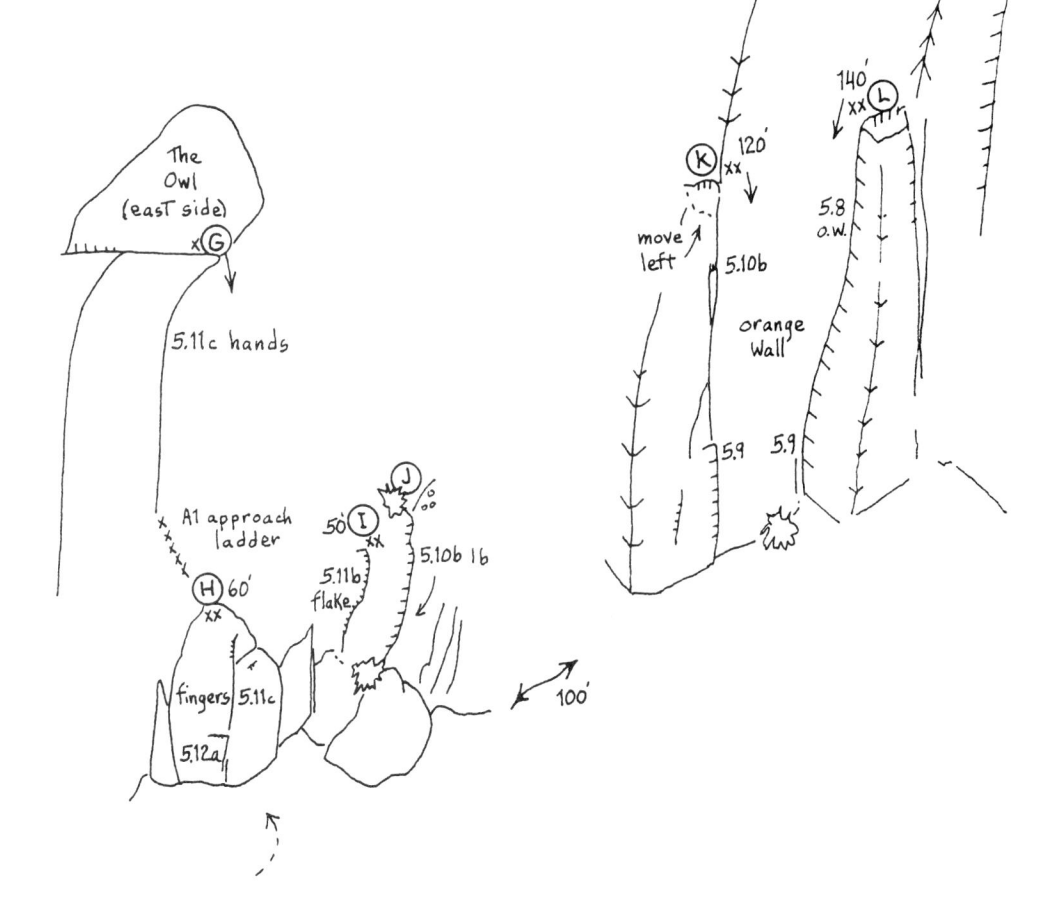

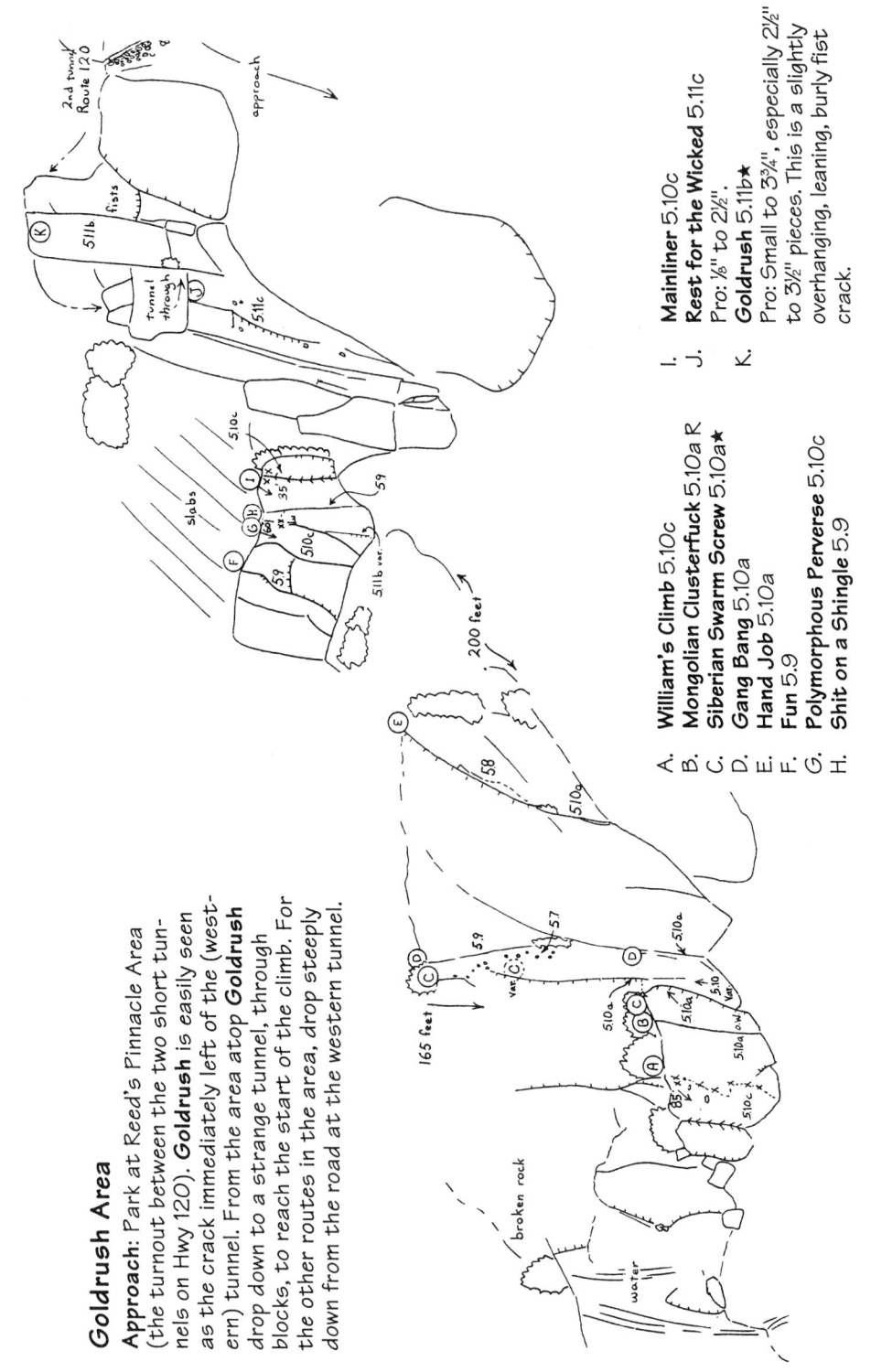

Reed's Pinnacle Area

Goldrush Area

Approach: Park at Reed's Pinnacle Area (the turnout between the two short tunnels on Hwy 120). **Goldrush** is easily seen as the crack immediately left of the (western) tunnel. From the area atop **Goldrush** drop down to a strange tunnel, through blocks, to reach the start of the climb. For the other routes in the area, drop steeply down from the road at the western tunnel.

A. **William's Climb** 5.10c
B. **Mongolian Clusterfuck** 5.10a R
C. **Siberian Swarm Screw** 5.10a ★
D. **Gang Bang** 5.10a
E. **Hand Job** 5.10a
F. **Fun** 5.9
G. **Polymorphous Perverse** 5.10c
H. **Shit on a Shingle** 5.9
I. **Mainliner** 5.10c
J. **Rest for the Wicked** 5.11c
   Pro: ½" to 2½"
K. **Goldrush** 5.11b ★
   Pro: Small to 3¾", especially 2½" to 3½" pieces. This is a slightly overhanging, leaning, burly fist crack.

LOWER MERCED CANYON: NORTH

Photo by Chris Falkenstein

Karine Nissen on Reed's Direct

LOWER MERCED CANYON: NORTH

Reed's Pinnacle Area

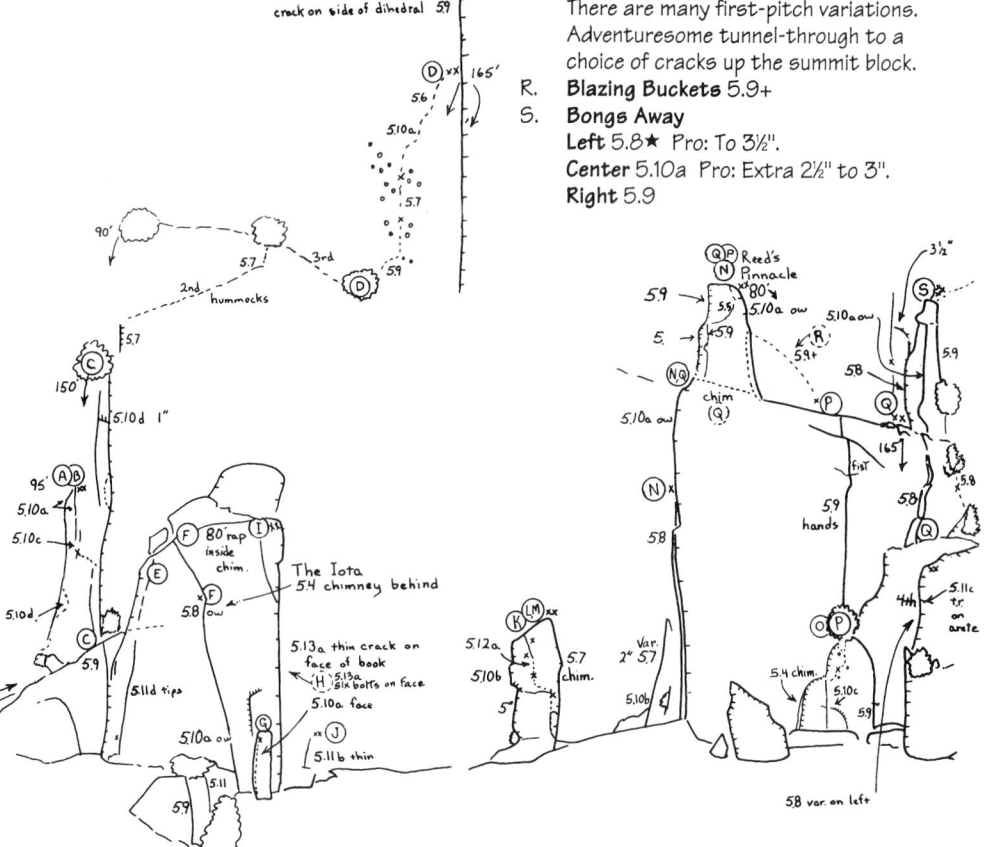

Reed's Pinnacle Area

Approach: Park between the two short tunnels on Hwy 120 in a paved turnout that overlooks the lower canyon. Access that avoids steep road-cuts is made by walking 100 feet (west) up the road before cutting up to the cliff. For **The Iota** and the routes left of it, walk (west) up the road nearly to the mouth of the western tunnel. Follow the Class 2 gully above, until an inobvious access right leads to the massive chamber of **The Iota**. **Photo** on page 73.

- A. **Danger Will Robinson** 5.10d
- B. **Anal Tongue Darts** 5.10c
- C. **Olga's Trick** 5.10d★ Pro: To 3".
- D. **Crazy Train** 5.10c
- E. **Isotope** 5.11d
- F. **Chingando** 5.10a★ Pro: 2" to 6". Part of the Hardman Offwidth Training Circuit.

The Iota leads up a 5.4 chimney behind Chingando. It is approached from the ledges below **Olga's Trick**.

- G. **The Tooth** 5.10a
- H. **Crossroads** 5.13a★ Pro: Include small stopper.
- I. **Phantom** 5.13a★ R
- J. **Micron** 5.11b

The Remnant
- K. **Left Side** 5.10b Pro: To 3½".
- L. **Center Route** 5.12a
- M. **Right Side** 5.7

Reed's Pinnacle
- N. **Left Side** 5.10a Pro: To 4".
- O. **Goosebumps** 5.10c (Direct finish 5.11a.)
- P. **Direct** 5.10a★★★ Pro: To 3½".
- Q. **Regular Route** 5.9★★★ Pro: To 3½". There are many first-pitch variations. Adventuresome tunnel-through to a choice of cracks up the summit block.
- R. **Blazing Buckets** 5.9+
- S. **Bongs Away**
  Left 5.8★ Pro: To 3½".
  Center 5.10a Pro: Extra 2½" to 3".
  Right 5.9

LOWER MERCED CANYON: NORTH

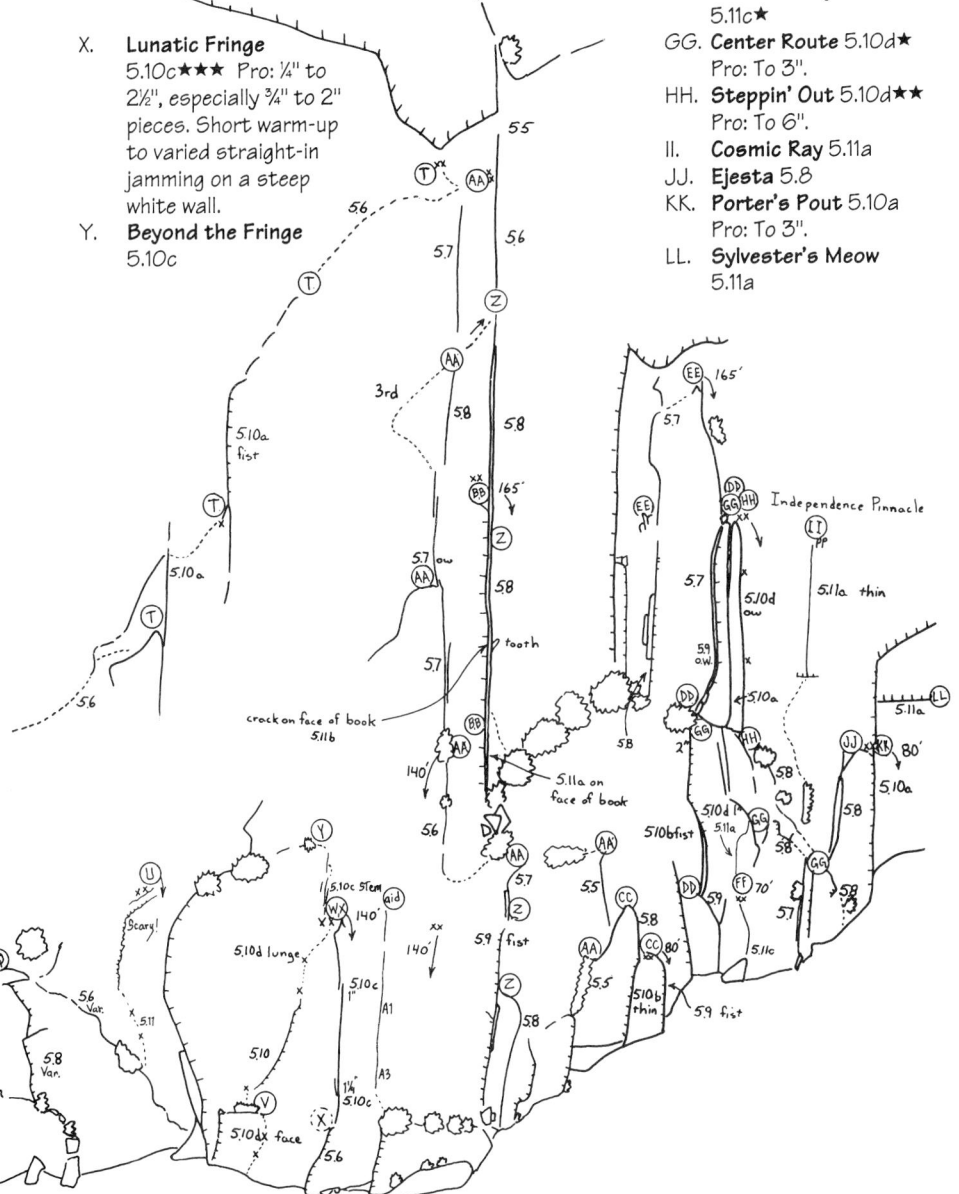

Reed's Pinnacle Area

- T. **Magical Mystery Tour** 5.10a★ Pro: To 3".
- U. **Duck and Cover** 5.11 R/X
- V. **Old Five Ten** 5.10d★ R
- W. **Midnight Rampest** 5.10d R
- X. **Lunatic Fringe** 5.10c★★★ Pro: ¼" to 2½", especially ¾" to 2" pieces. Short warm-up to varied straight-in jamming on a steep white wall.
- Y. **Beyond the Fringe** 5.10c
- Z. **Flatus** 5.9 (Star rating applies to first two pitches only.) Pro: Extra 2½" to 3".
- AA. **The Rorp** 5.7★
- BB. **Tooth or Consequences** 5.11b★ Pro: To 3½", especially 1½" to 3½".
- CC. **Stone Groove** 5.10b★★ Pro: ⅜" to 2½", especially ¾" to 1½" pieces. Cranker finger/tight hands to crux 30 feet up.

Independence Pinnacle
- DD. **Independent Route** 5.10b★ Pro: To 4".
- EE. **The Gray Bullet** 5.8
- FF. **Rocket in my Pocket** 5.11c★
- GG. **Center Route** 5.10d★ Pro: To 3".
- HH. **Steppin' Out** 5.10d★★ Pro: To 6".
- II. **Cosmic Ray** 5.11a
- JJ. **Ejesta** 5.8
- KK. **Porter's Pout** 5.10a Pro: To 3".
- LL. **Sylvester's Meow** 5.11a

LOWER MERCED CANYON: NORTH

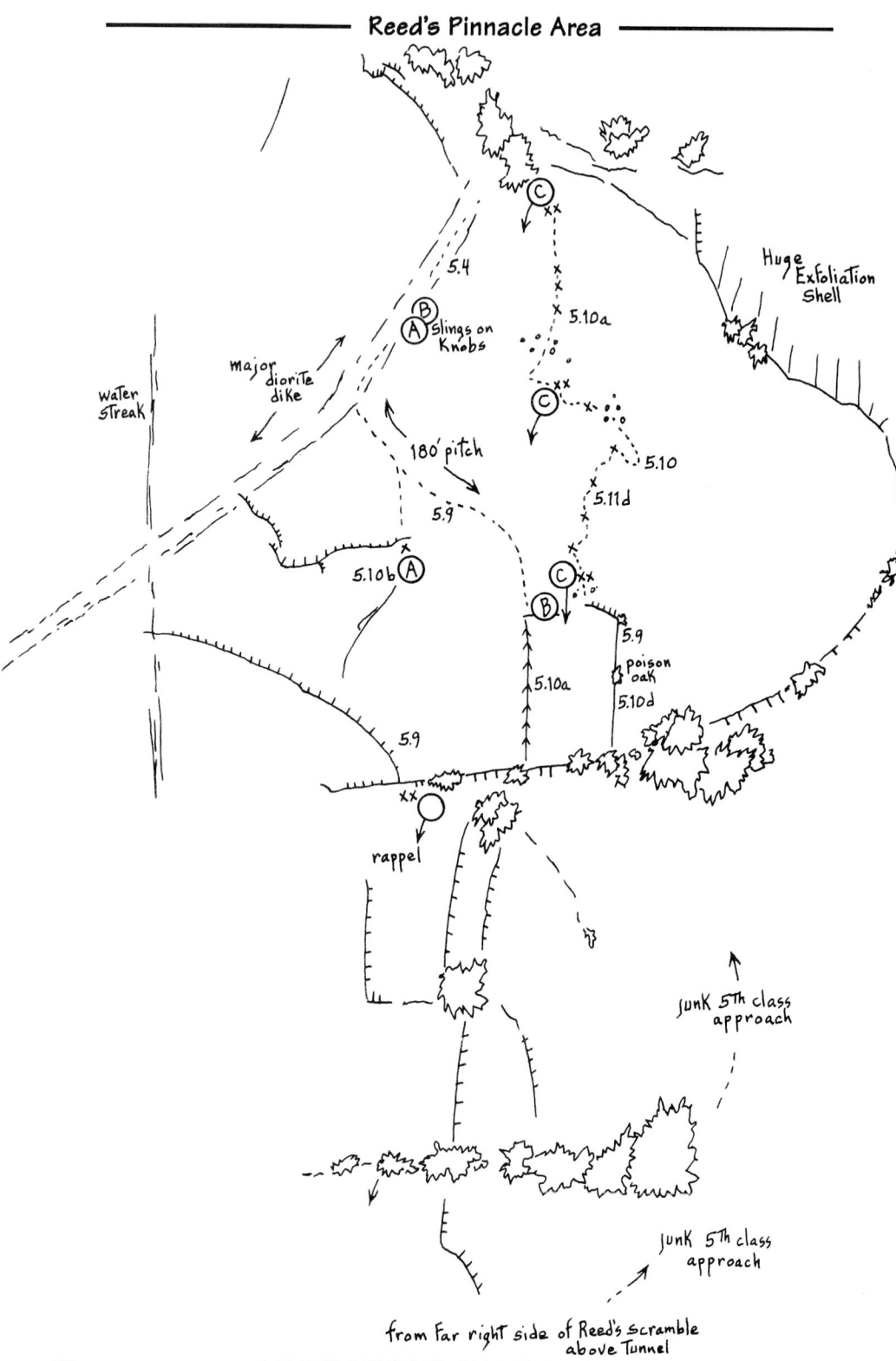

Reed's Pinnacle Area

(topo diagram with the following labels)

- Huge Exfoliation Shell
- 5.4
- Slings on Knobs
- Major diorite dike
- Water streak
- 180' pitch
- 5.10a
- 5.10
- 5.11d
- 5.9
- 5.10b
- 5.10a
- 5.9
- poison oak
- 5.10d
- 5.9
- rappel
- Junk 5th class approach
- Junk 5th class approach
- from far right side of Reed's Scramble above Tunnel

LOWER MERCED CANYON: NORTH

Reed's Pinnacle Area
Upper Right
Approach: From **Porter's Pout** (see page 75) walk up and right; start atop the buttress above the tunnel.

- A. **Fasten your Seat Belts** 5.10b★ R/X
- B. **Free Ride** 5.10a★ R/X Pro: Especially tiny to small.
- C. **Magic Carpet** 5.11d★ R

These areas are isolated crags above Hwy 120.

Approach: Park at Reed's and walk down Hwy 120 through the tunnel and approximately 0.25 mile further. Ten minutes up a steep dirt slope leads to a minor buttress. Climbs are on the right (east-facing) wall. (The top part of **Cro-Magnon Capers** can be seen on the drive up to Reed's, as an orange wall split by a crack.)

- D. **Cro-Magnon Capers** 5.11b★
- E. **Nothing Good Ever Lasts** 5.10d

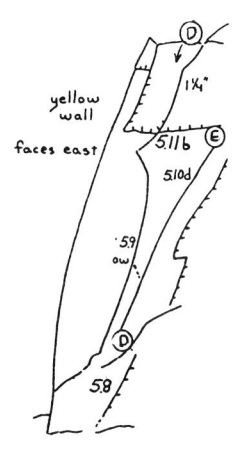

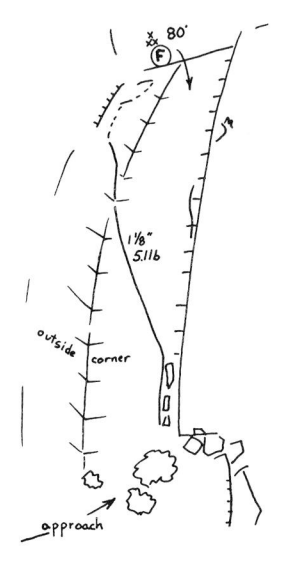

Approach: Park in the first paved turnout on the right, west of the Hwy 120/Hwy 140 junction. Walk up the road another 0.4 mile. The climb can be seen from the road as a left-slanting crack that crosses a yellow east-facing corner. Hike up the dirt slope (past poison oak) and enter onto the perch from where the climb starts.

- F. **Spring Fever** 5.11b★ Pro: Small 2½", especially ¾" to 1¼".

Five and Dime Cliff

Approach: Park at Reed's Pinnacle Area (between the two short tunnels on Hwy 120) and walk to the mouth of the eastern tunnel. A climber's trail leads first to the top of the cliff, then drops down circuitously to the base.

A. Bijou 5.10c ★
B. Chump Change 5.12a
C. Keystone Corner 5.8 ★ Pro: To 2½". Jamming and stemming in a steep corner.
D. Copper Penny 5.10a ★ Pro: To 6". The crux is the entry to the off-width. Inside edge for long arms—steep and wild.
E. Five and Dime 5.10d ★★★ Pro: To 2½". Slightly overhanging, straight-in. A range of sizes...beautiful.
F. Whack and Dangle 5.11a Pro: To 2½".
G. Penny Ante 5.11 TR
H. Ride the Lightning 5.12a ★★
I. The Anti-Christ 5.11d ★★
J. The Reception 5.10a
K. Inner Reaches 5.7
L. Crack 'n Face 5.10b

LOWER MERCED CANYON: NORTH

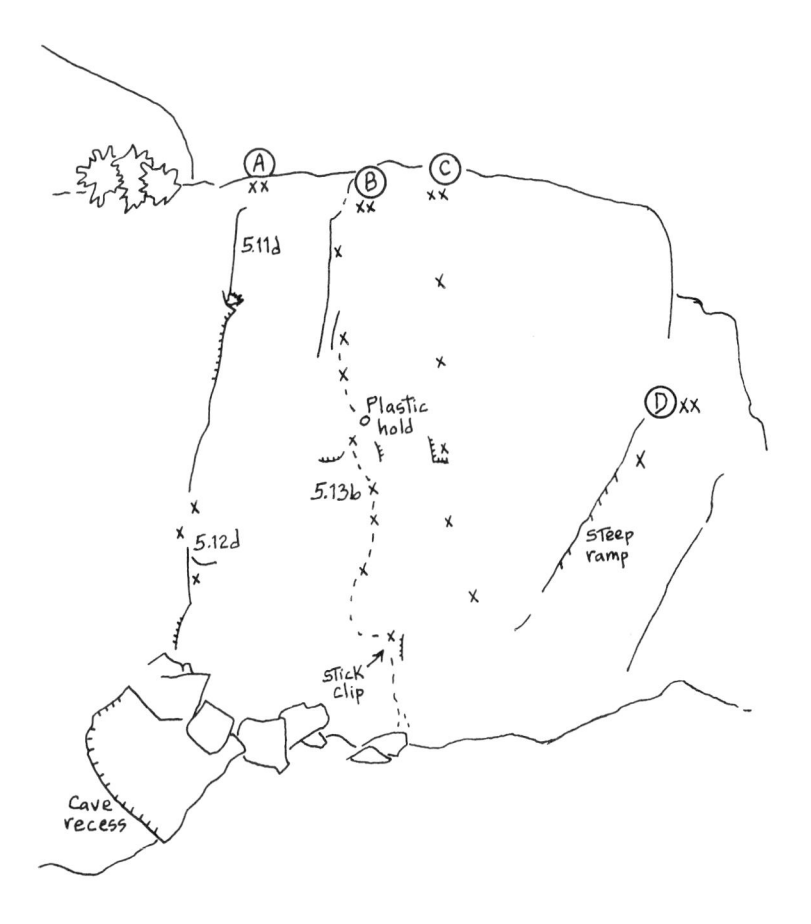

Fantasy Island

Approach: Park at the Hwy 140/Hwy 120 junction and walk west up Hwy 120 about 100 yards. Hike up the boulderfield to the cliff. (Hot area, best in winter.)

A. **Jupiter** 5.12d★ Pro: To 3".
B. **Fantasy Island** 5.13b★★ A0 (Artifical hold.) Pro: Including medium Rocks.
C. **Project**
D. **Project**

The Mojo Tooth

The Mojo Tooth: Left

Approach: The parking area at the Hwy 120/Hwy 140 junction lies directly below this formation. For the regular **Mojo Tooth** and routes left, head up steep dirt slopes. For those climbs to the right, sloppy dirt and talus leads up and right. Move left where one can contour onto a sloping ledge—the starting point for the other routes.

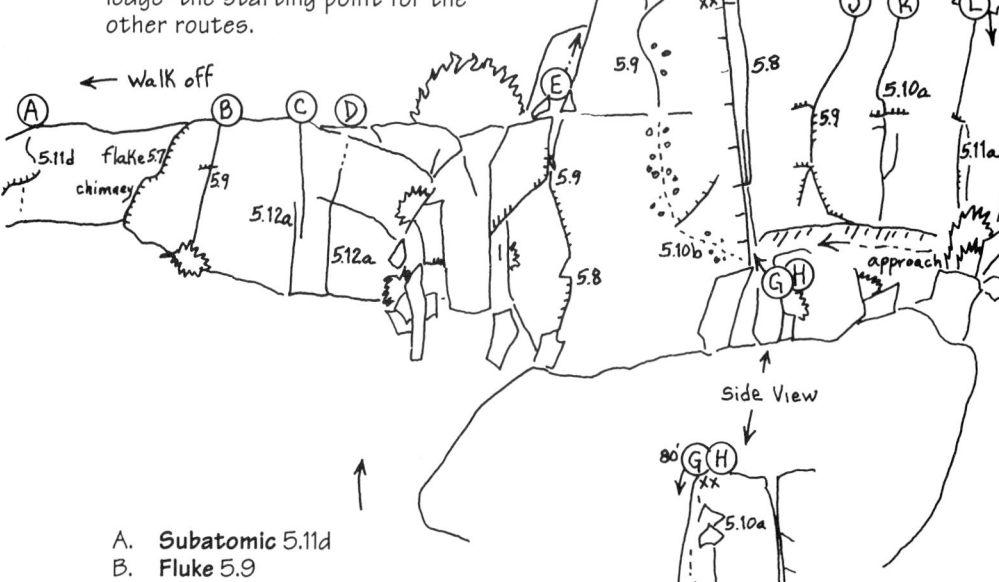

A. **Subatomic** 5.11d
B. **Fluke** 5.9
C. **Tongue and Groove** 5.12a
D. **Scratch and Sniff** 5.12a★
E. **Mojo Tooth** 5.8
F. **New Traditionalists** 5.10b★ R
G. **Yankee Clipper** 5.11b★ Pro: #0.5 TCU to #2 Friend.
H. **Cereal Killer** 5.10a Pro: Small to 4".
I. **Figment** 5.8
J. **Grape Nuts** 5.9★
K. **Euellogy** 5.10a★
L. **Mighty Crunchy** 5.10d★
M. **Bad News Bombers** 5.10a
N. **Deception** 5.11
O. **Jomo** 5.11d★
P. **Natural End** 5.9
Q. **Golden Shower** 5.12a★
R. **Yellow Peril** 5.11b★

LOWER MERCED CANYON: NORTH

The Mojo Tooth

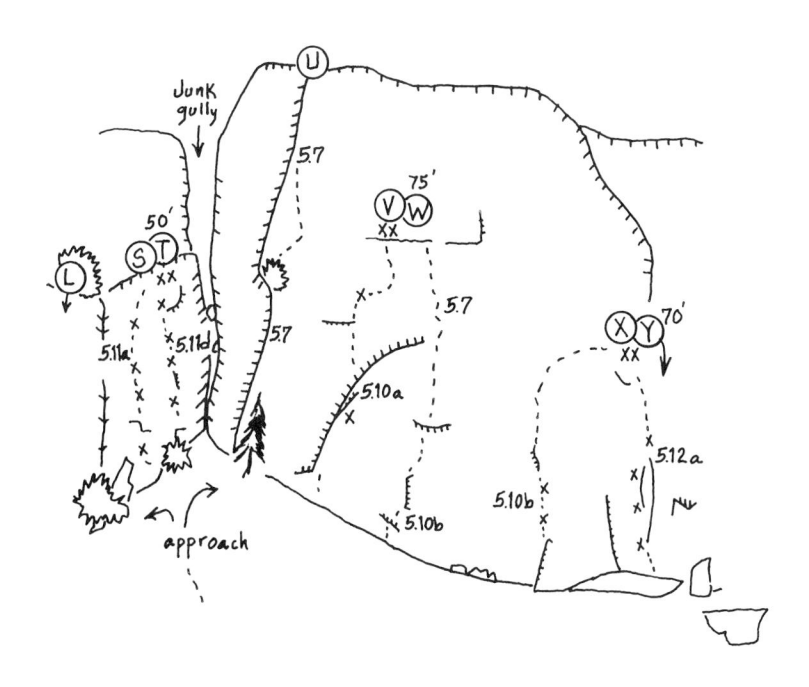

The Mojo Tooth: Right
L. Mighty Crunchy 5.10d★
S. Motor Drive 5.11a
T. Vibrator 5.11d
U. Yuk 5.7
V. Rehab Doll 5.10a
W. Skid Roper 5.10b
X. Tooth Fairy 5.10b
Y. Old 5.11 5.12a★

Highway Star Bluff

Highway Star Bluff

Approach: This bluff cannot be seen from the road, yet is only two minutes away. Park at the first large dirt turnout east of the Hwy 120/Hwy 140 junction. A 25 mph sign is a useful marker for the start of the uphill hike.

Highway Star 5.10a★ Pro: ¾" to 2½". Steep hand-jamming—great for doing laps.

Last Resort Cliff

1. Plumkin 5.10a
2. Ready or Not 5.11a

Last Resort Cliff

Approach: Park at the first turnout east of the Hwy 120/Hwy 140 junction. A large flat boulder in the Merced River marks the spot. Head up and slightly right. About halfway to the cliff, house-sized boulders (at the right margin of a talus field) mark a traverse left through the talus and up to the toe of the cliff.

A. **Turning Point** 5.10c★ Pro: To 2½".
B. **Side Kick** 5.9
C. **Tiger's Paw** 5.10a A1
D. **Plumkin** 5.10a
E. **Moon Age Daydream** 5.11a★
F. **The Steal** 5.10a
G. **Sex, Drugs and Violence** 5.10a
H. **PMS** 5.11a
I. **B & B** 5.10a★ (Star rating for first pitch only.)
J. **No Falls Wall** 5.10b
K. **Black Sunday** 5.10a
L. **Shattered** 5.10d
M. **Ready or Not** 5.11a★
N. **Slumgullion** 5.10
O. **Neutron Escape** 5.10a
P. **Radioactive** 5.11a
Q. **Atomic Finger Crack** 5.12b★

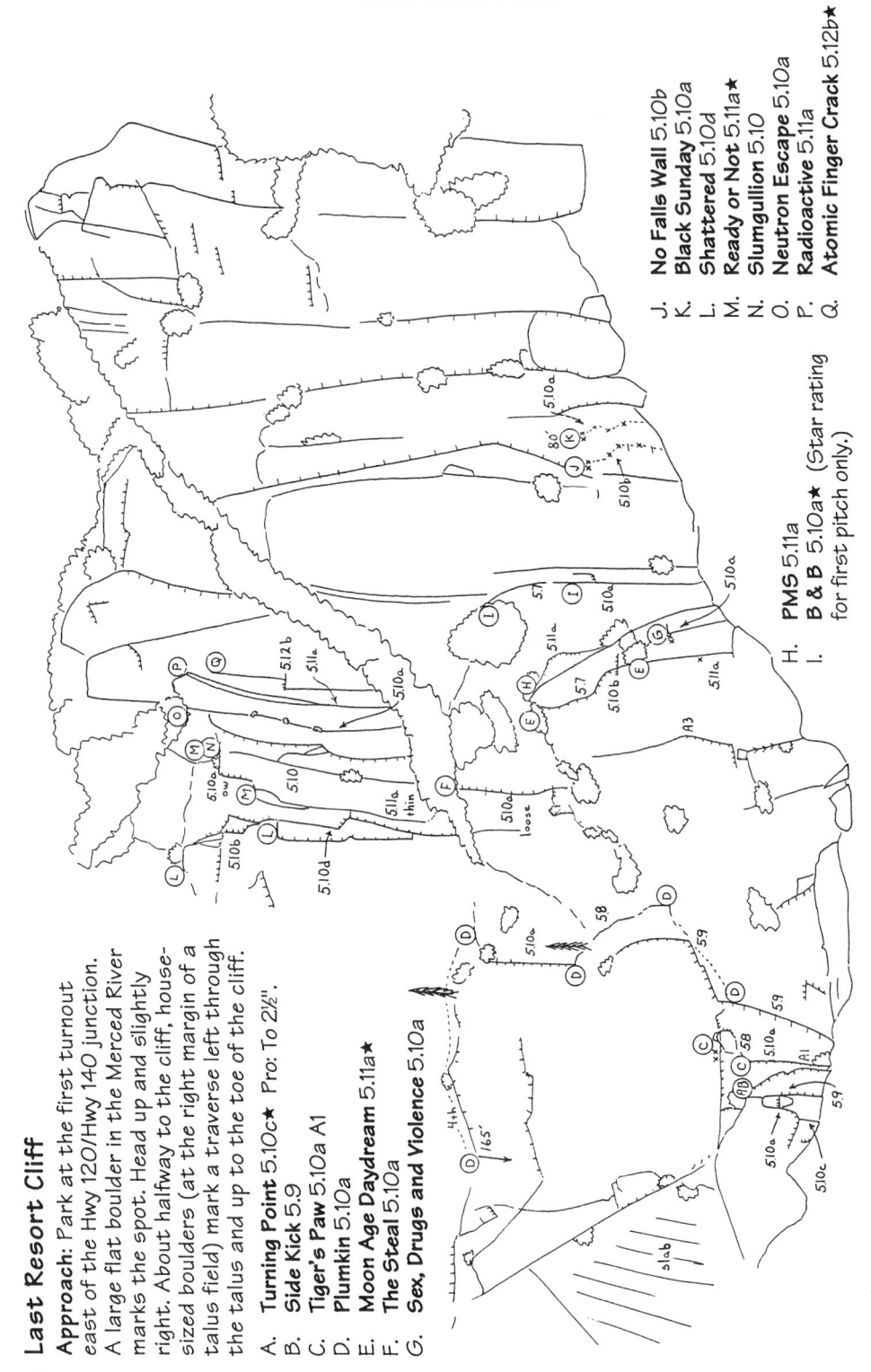

LOWER MERCED CANYON: NORTH

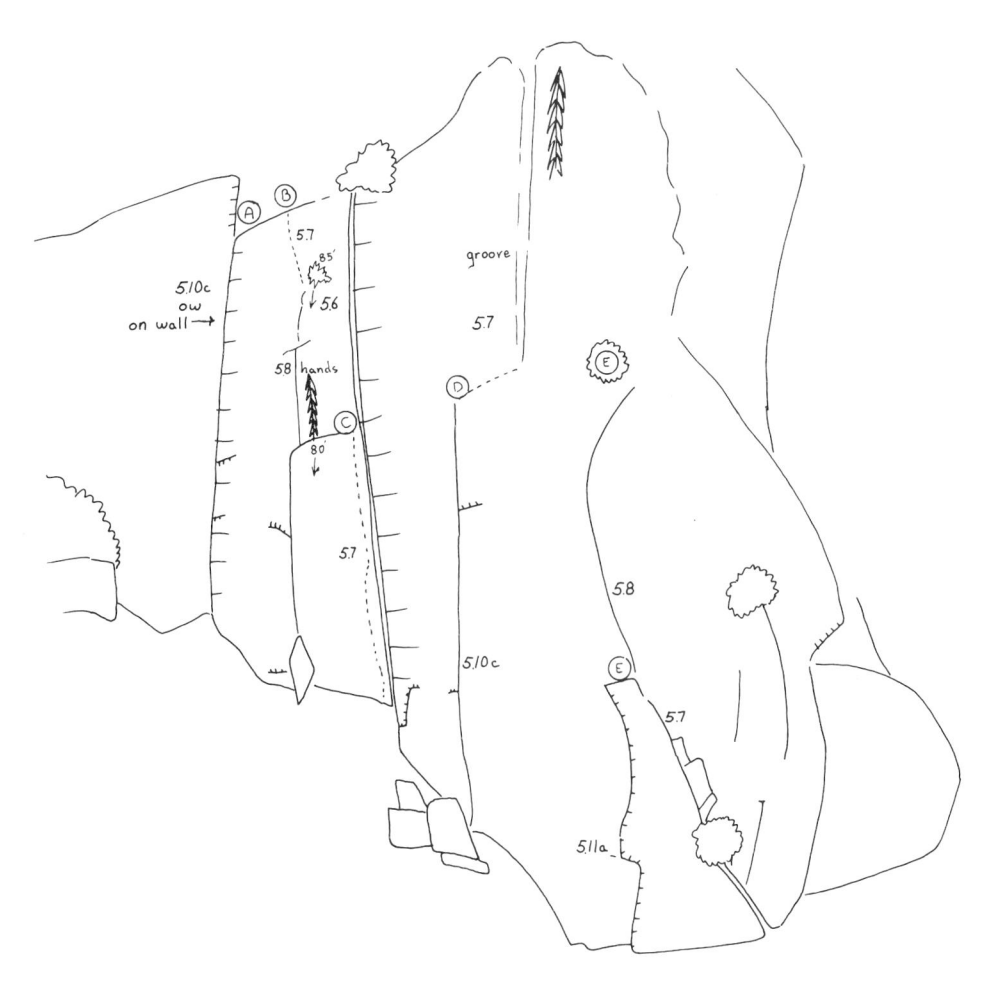

Audubon Buttress

Approach: This small cliff, as well as the Nuts Only Cliff and Little Wing Area, is approached from the Old Big Oak Flat Road, the head of which is located as a service road to a wood yard, 0.2 mile west of El Cap Meadow. Walk straight north up the hill before finding the main roadbed that angles gently up to the west. Ten or fifteen minutes of hiking, sometimes past rock slides, leads to open talus slopes below the Nuts Only Wall. A few minutes further on leads to the roadside Little Wing Cliff. After 45 minutes of hiking, a railing that overlooks the Last Resort Cliff is reached. To find the Audubon Buttress, hike an additional ten minutes from this point. The cliff lies hidden in the woods directly above. (The hike-up point is a bit before the road curves gently right, then left, moving past a spring area.)

A. **Wild Turkey** 5.10c★ Pro: To 6".
B. **The Dove** 5.8
C. **Birds of a Feather** 5.7
D. **Eagle Feather** 5.10c★
E. **Duncan Imperial** 5.11a

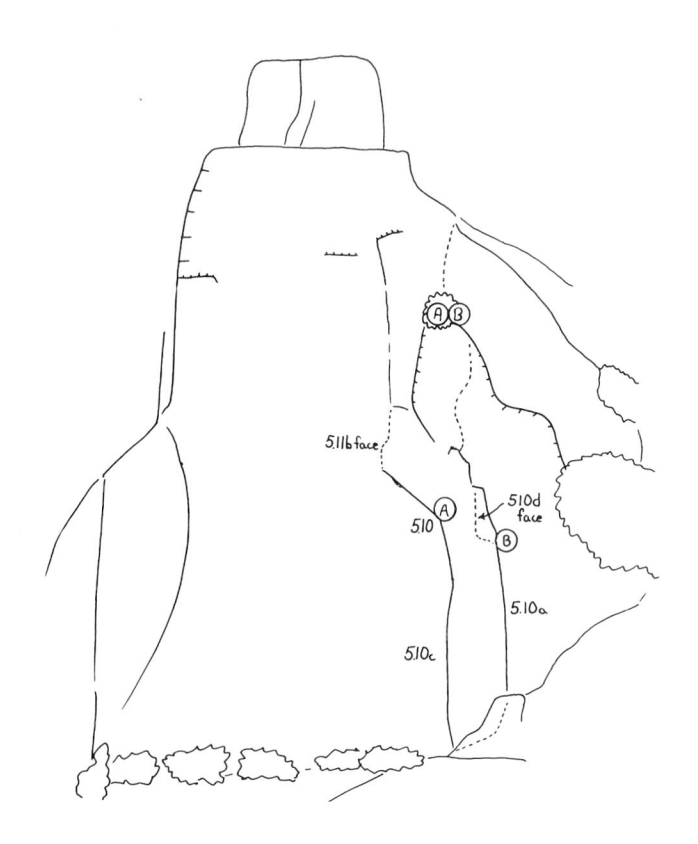

Nuts Only Cliff

Approach: Hike to this cliff as described on page 85

A. **Catch-U** 5.11b★ R Pro: Double nuts to 3½".
B. **W'allnuts** 5.10d Pro: To 3", extra 1¼".

Little Wing Area

Approach: Hike to this cliff along the Old Big Oak Flat Road, as described on page 85.

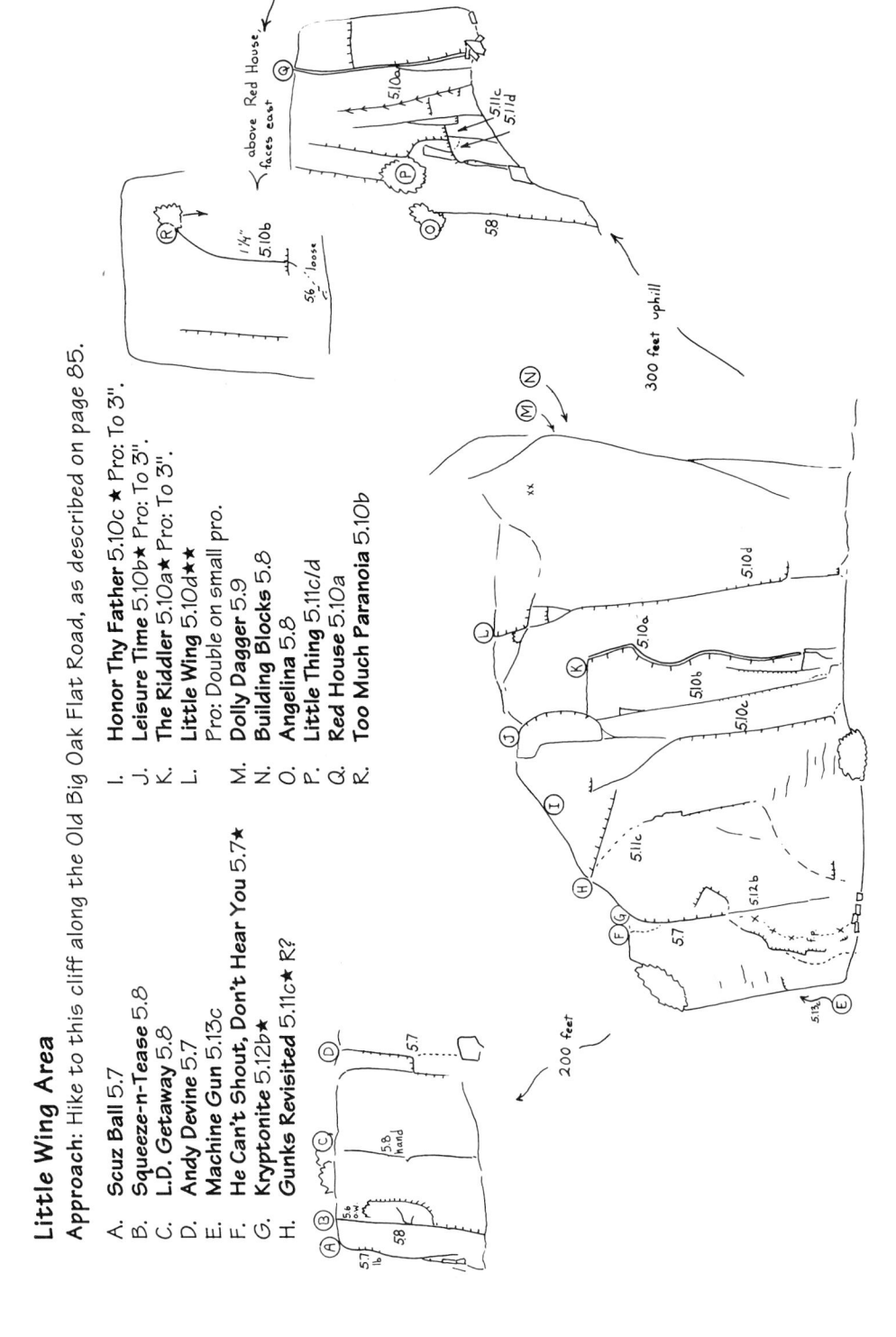

A. Scuz Ball 5.7
B. Squeeze-n-Tease 5.8
C. L.D. Getaway 5.8
D. Andy Devine 5.7
E. Machine Gun 5.13c
F. He Can't Shout, Don't Hear You 5.7 ★
G. Kryptonite 5.12b ★
H. Gunks Revisited 5.11c ★ R?
I. Honor Thy Father 5.10c ★ Pro: To 3".
J. Leisure Time 5.10b ★ Pro: To 3".
K. The Riddler 5.10a ★ Pro: To 3".
L. Little Wing 5.10d ★★
   Pro: Double on small pro.
M. Dolly Dagger 5.9
N. Building Blocks 5.8
O. Angelina 5.8
P. Little Thing 5.11c/d
Q. Red House 5.10a
R. Too Much Paranoia 5.10b

RIBBON FALLS — 87

Ribbon Falls Amphitheatre

1. Golden Bough 5.10a
2. Silent Line 5.10 A1
3. Fool's Gold 5.10a
4. Chockstone Chimney 5.9
5. The Lionheart 5.10b
6. Nottingham 5.10a
7. THE HOURGLASS

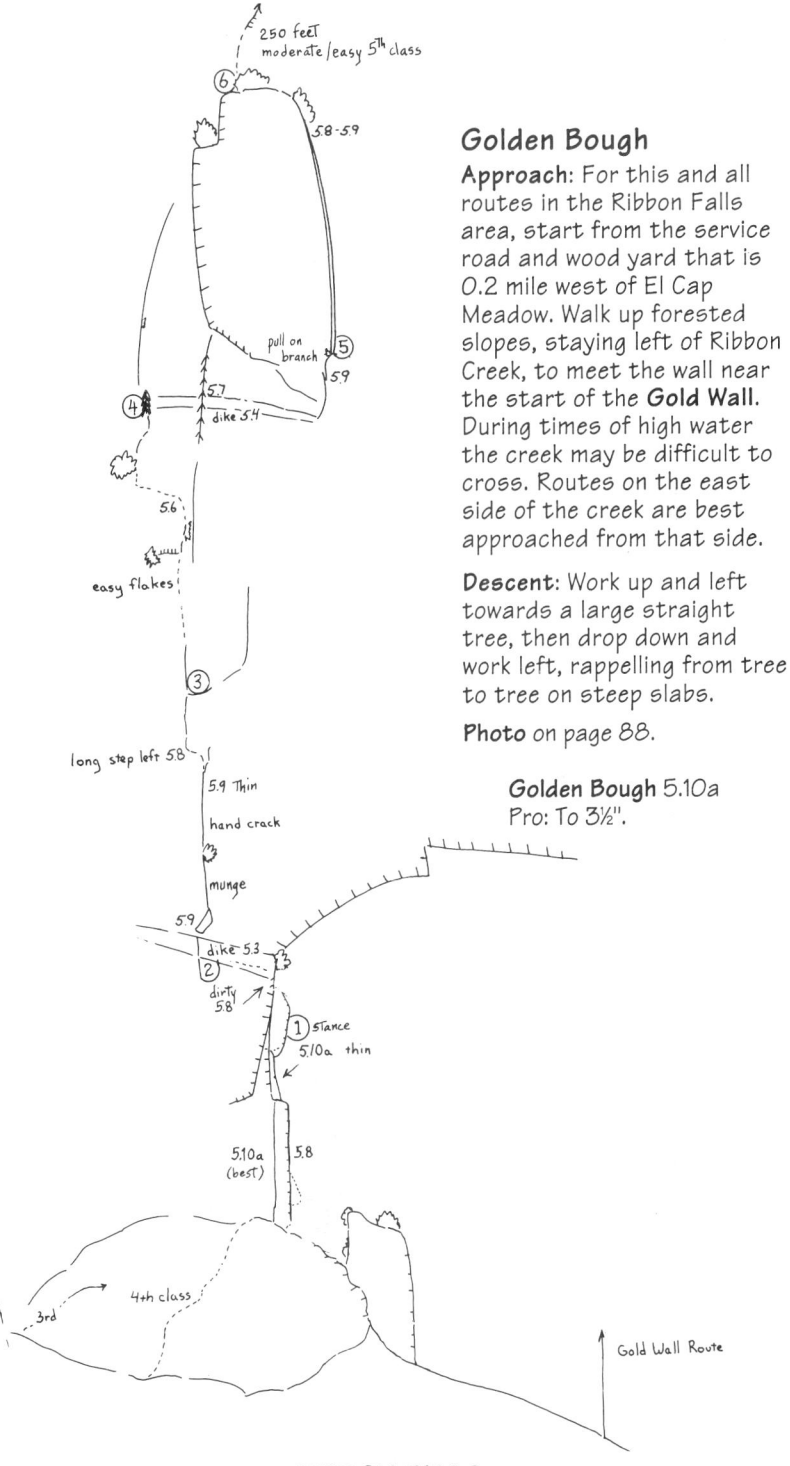

Ribbon Falls Area

Golden Bough

Approach: For this and all routes in the Ribbon Falls area, start from the service road and wood yard that is 0.2 mile west of El Cap Meadow. Walk up forested slopes, staying left of Ribbon Creek, to meet the wall near the start of the **Gold Wall**. During times of high water the creek may be difficult to cross. Routes on the east side of the creek are best approached from that side.

Descent: Work up and left towards a large straight tree, then drop down and work left, rappelling from tree to tree on steep slabs.

Photo on page 88.

Golden Bough 5.10a
Pro: To 3½".

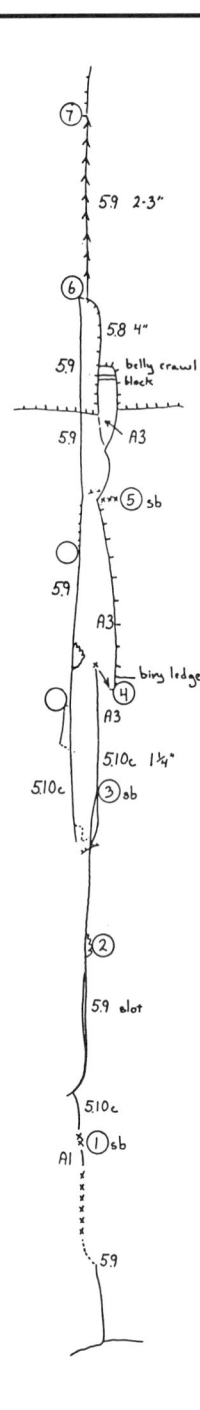

Ribbon Falls, Gold Wall

Approach: See page 89.

Descent: From the top of the last pitch, walk left on ledges to a gully that leads to the top. Walk up and left to ramps that lead down. Keep to the west until the ledge runs out to two pitons that provide the anchor for the first of three rappels to trees and eventually to the final descent ledges.

Photo on page 88.

Silent Line V 5.10 A1
Pro: small nuts,;
3 ea. Friend to #3, 1 ea. #4

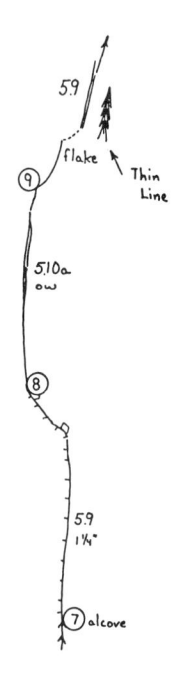

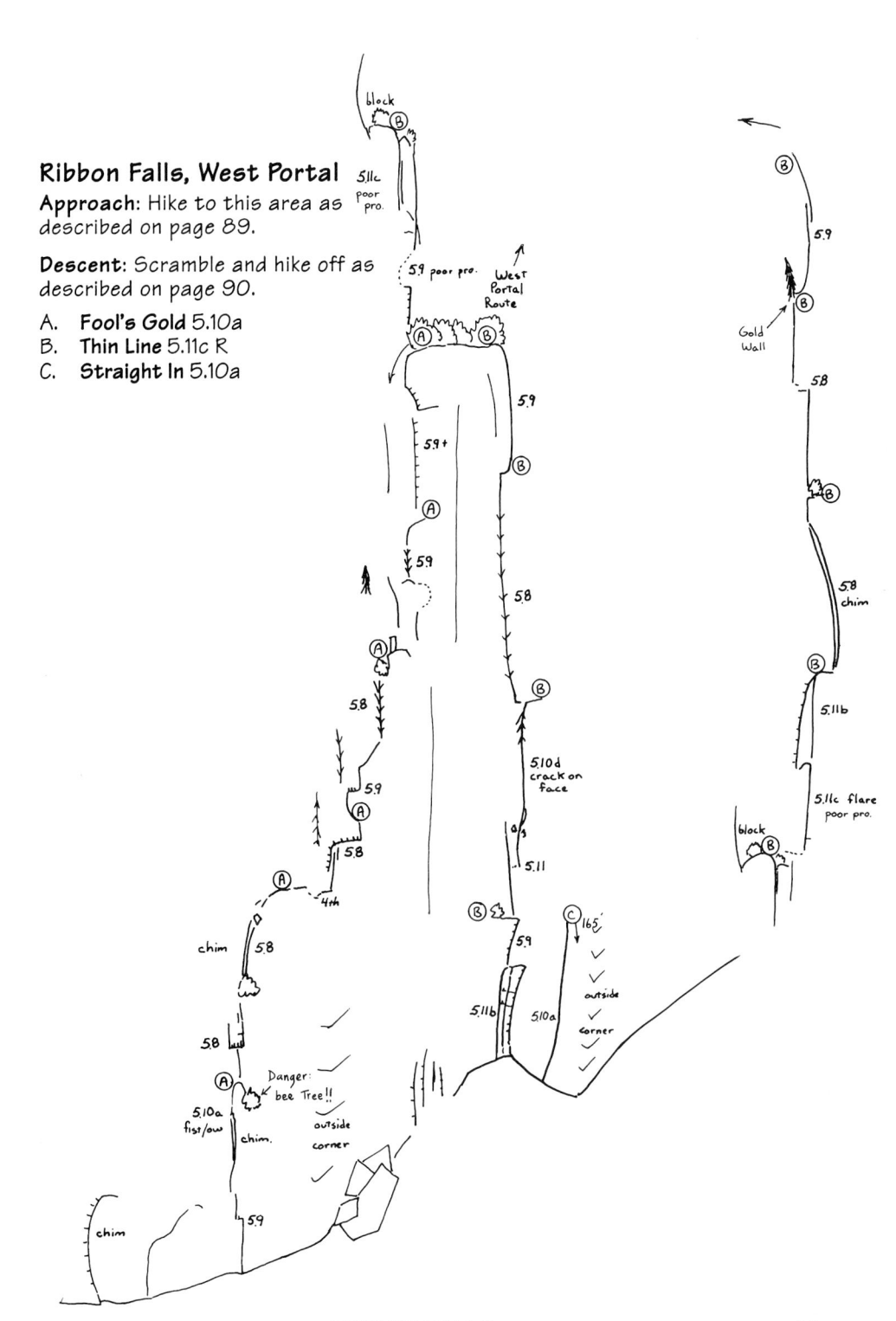

Ribbon Falls, West Portal

Approach: Hike to this area as described on page 89.

Descent: Scramble and hike off as described on page 90.

A. **Fool's Gold** 5.10a
B. **Thin Line** 5.11c R
C. **Straight In** 5.10a

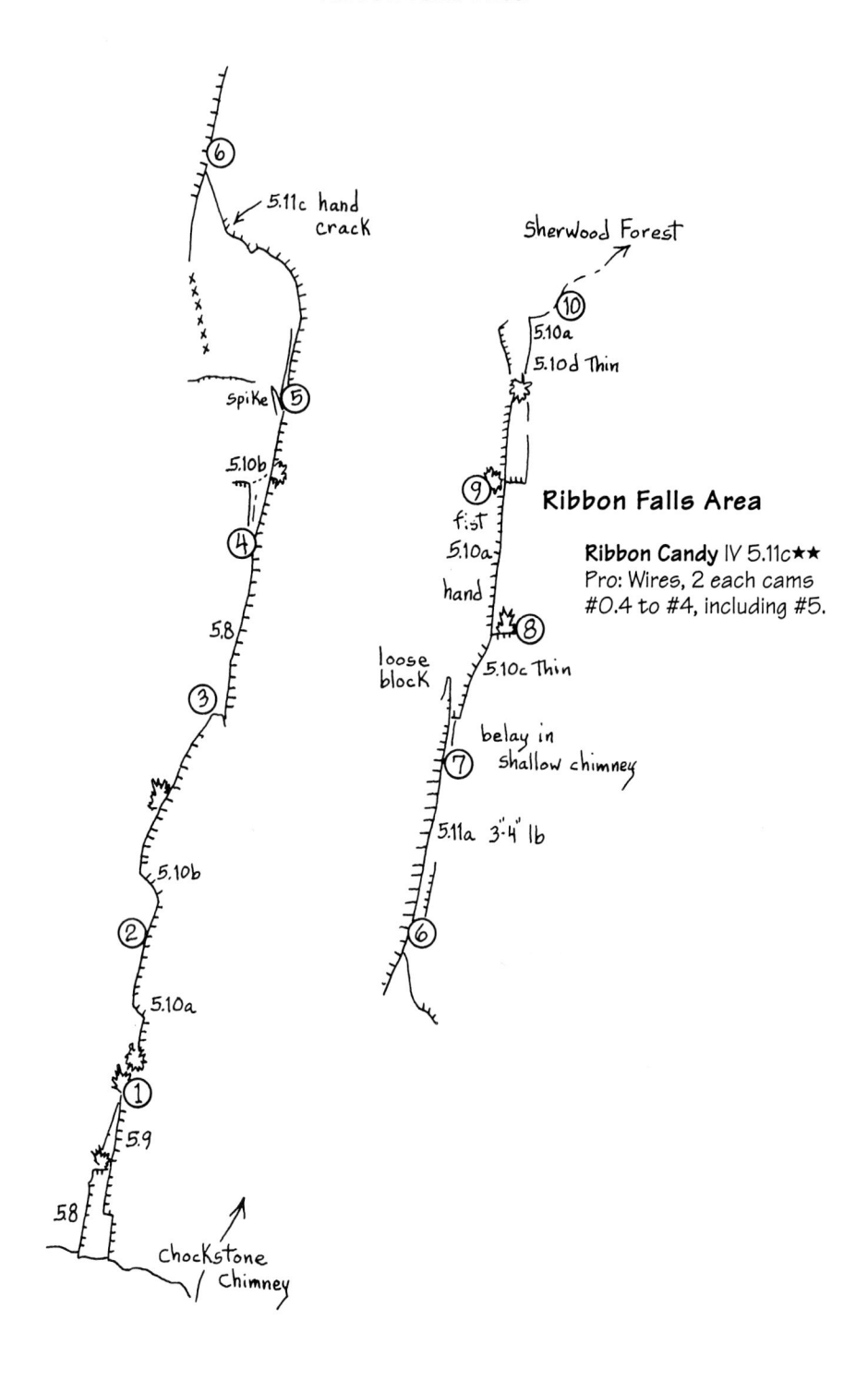

Ribbon Falls Area

Ribbon Falls Area

Ribbon Candy IV 5.11c★★
Pro: Wires, 2 each cams #0.4 to #4, including #5.

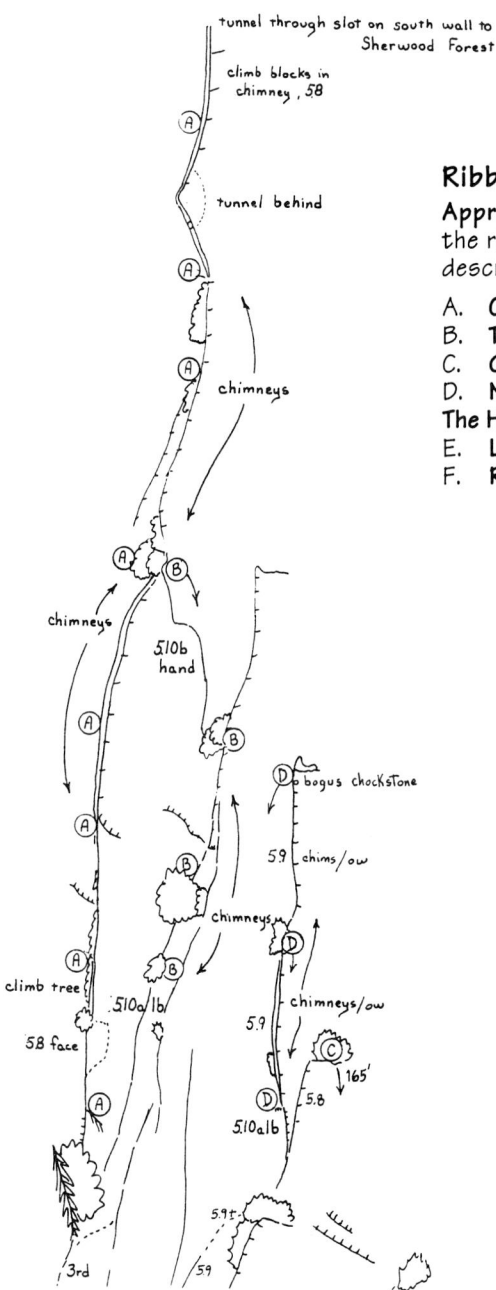

Ribbon Creek Area

Approach: Hike up to this area along the right side of Ribbon Creek, as described on page 89.

A. **Chockstone Chimney** 5.9
B. **The Lionheart** 5.10b
C. **Gold Leaf** 5.9+
D. **Nottingham** 5.10a

The Hourglass
E. **Left Side** 5.11a★ R
F. **Right Side** 5.10a

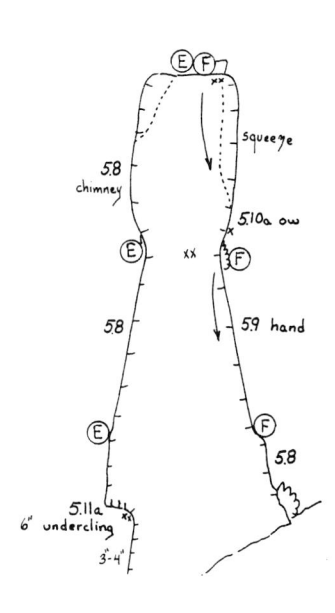

El Capitan, West Face

El Capitan

The following pages describe short routes that climb to exfoliated "summits" that sit just above the base of El Capitan. Park 0.1 mile west of the El Cap Bridge. Take the climber's trail that heads back through the woods directly toward The Nose. Beneath that route, the trail divides, leading along both sides of the cliff. The southwest side is described first, from furthest up the hill by the West Buttress down along the wall to The Nose and then eastward along the base of the southeast face.

As one walks up and left from The Nose, the major formations are encountered in the following order: Pterodactyl Terrace, Moby Dick, Little John, La Cosita, The Slack, La Escuela, Delectable Pinnacle, Captain Hook and Peter Pan. Walking up and right from The Nose is Negative Pinnacle, the slab routes below the obvious amphitheater, Gollum, The Footstool and finally the orange-striped slab located at the far west end of the wall.

West of El Capitan are two prominent gullies separated by a long, brushy, serrated ridge. The left gully is El Capitan Gully. It is in large part a talus slope, although exposed 3rd class slabs must be negotiated before the rim can be reached. Among the many pinnacles of the ridge to the east, one spire stands out most prominently. This is K-P Pinnacle. Its summit is reached with easy 5th class climbing from the east. The gully/chimney that lies immediately below the West Face of El Cap is the West Chimney. Most of the large chockstones that occasionally block the gully can be avoided with circuitous and exposed scrambling. The West Chimney ends atop the K-P Pinnacle ridge, where a short rappel leads west into El Capitan Gully.

Descent: Most climbers descend from the top of El Cap to the Valley floor by one of the following methods: 1. Hike up several hundred yards to the rounded summit knoll and pick up the trail that heads back into the woods. The campground off Tuolumne Road at Tamarack Flat can be reached after about eight miles of rolling, but mostly gentle, downhill hiking. Consult a map. 2. From the woods behind El Cap a trail can be taken east along the rim past Eagle Peak to the Yosemite Falls Trail for a descent directly to Camp 4. The Falls Trail part of this eight-mile alternative is grueling in its continuous steepness. 3. The East Ledges Descent requires some 3rd class scrambling and some rappels, but does offer the advantage of being snow-free in the early season and it only takes about 2½ hours to reach the Valley floor. See page 122 for more exact information.

West Face

El Capitan, Salami Ledge

Approach: This route starts from a low-angle talus area in the West Chimney, just before the final steep part.

Salami Ledge IV 5.10

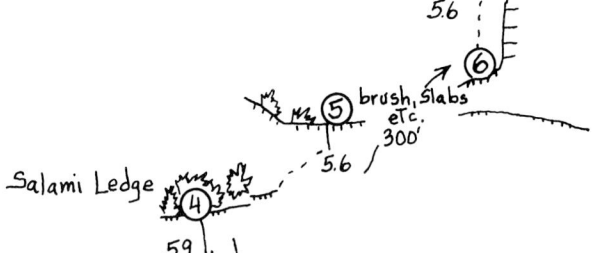

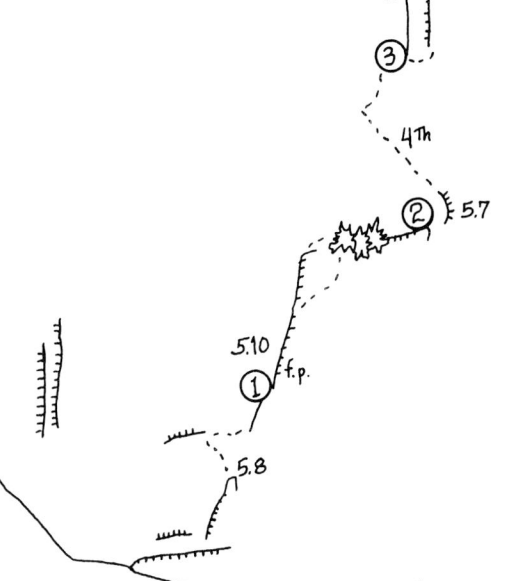

West Face

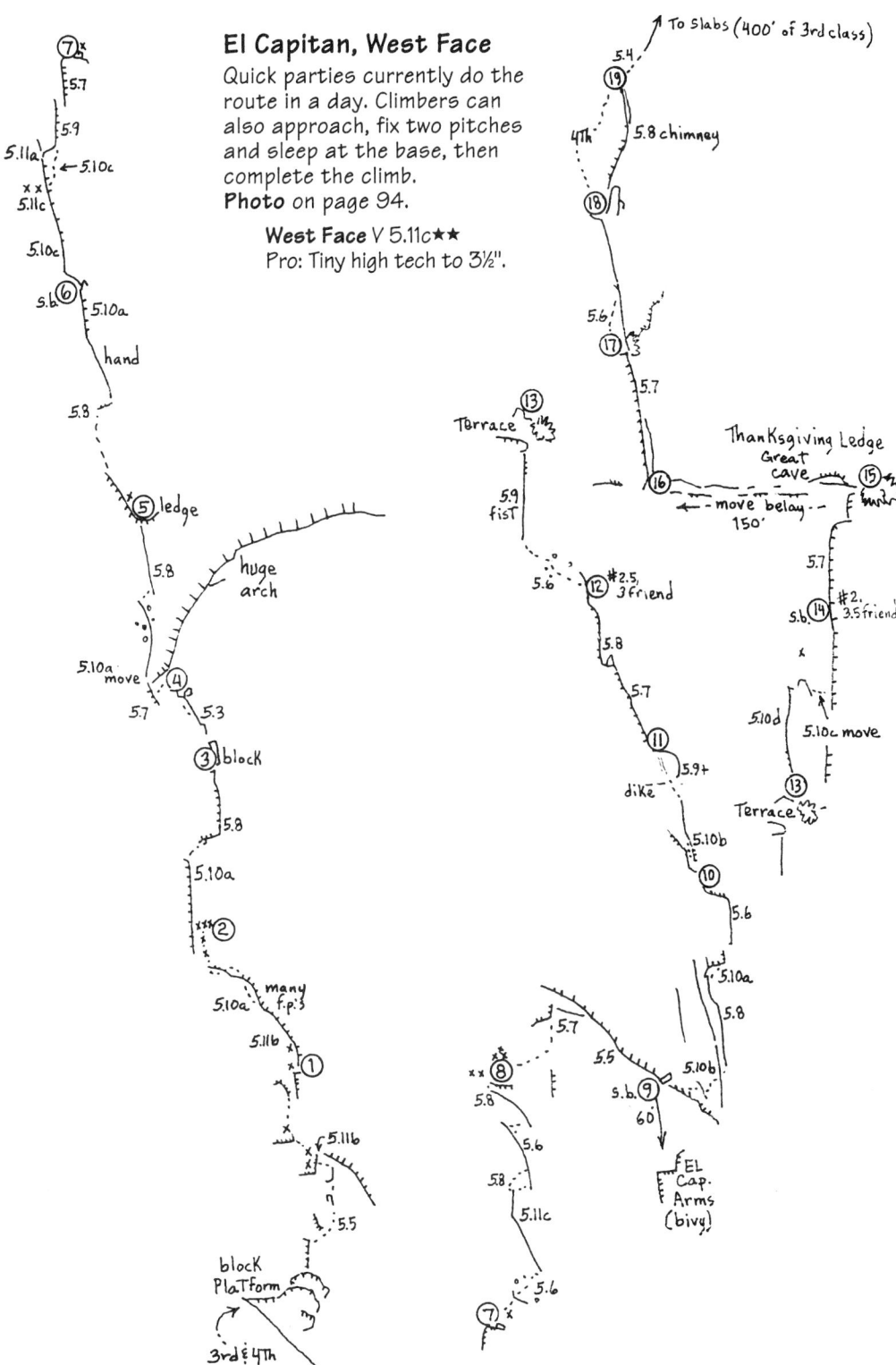

El Capitan, West Face

Quick parties currently do the route in a day. Climbers can also approach, fix two pitches and sleep at the base, then complete the climb.
Photo on page 94.

West Face V 5.11c ★★
Pro: Tiny high tech to 3½".

West Buttress

West Buttress, Base Area

Approach: Park 0.1 mile west of the El Cap Bridge. Take the climber's trail that heads back through the woods directly toward **The Nose**. Beneath that route, the trail divides, leading along both sides of the cliff.

For the climbs beyond **Captain Hook**, skirt the scruffy gray barrier by dropping down and around the corner to a 3rd class path that leads up. To proceed further up the West Chimney for the West Face, stay left of the main chimney on a 3rd class rib until above the chockstone.

A. **West Buttress** 5.10a★★ (Star rating for initial pitches only.)
B. **Peter Pan** 5.9+★ Pro: To 6".
C. **Cuthulu** 5.10d R Pro: Extra 1" to 2".
D. **Indubious Battle** 5.11a★
E. **Peter Left** 5.10c★ Pro: To 3½".
F. **Tinkerbell**
   Left 5.7
   Right 5.9 Pro: To 3½".
G. **Lost Boys** 5.9
H. **Wendy** 5.9
I. **Smee's Come-on** 5.11a
J. **Captain Hook**
   Left 5.7+
   Right 5.9
K. **Captain Crunch** 5.11b★

EL CAPITAN

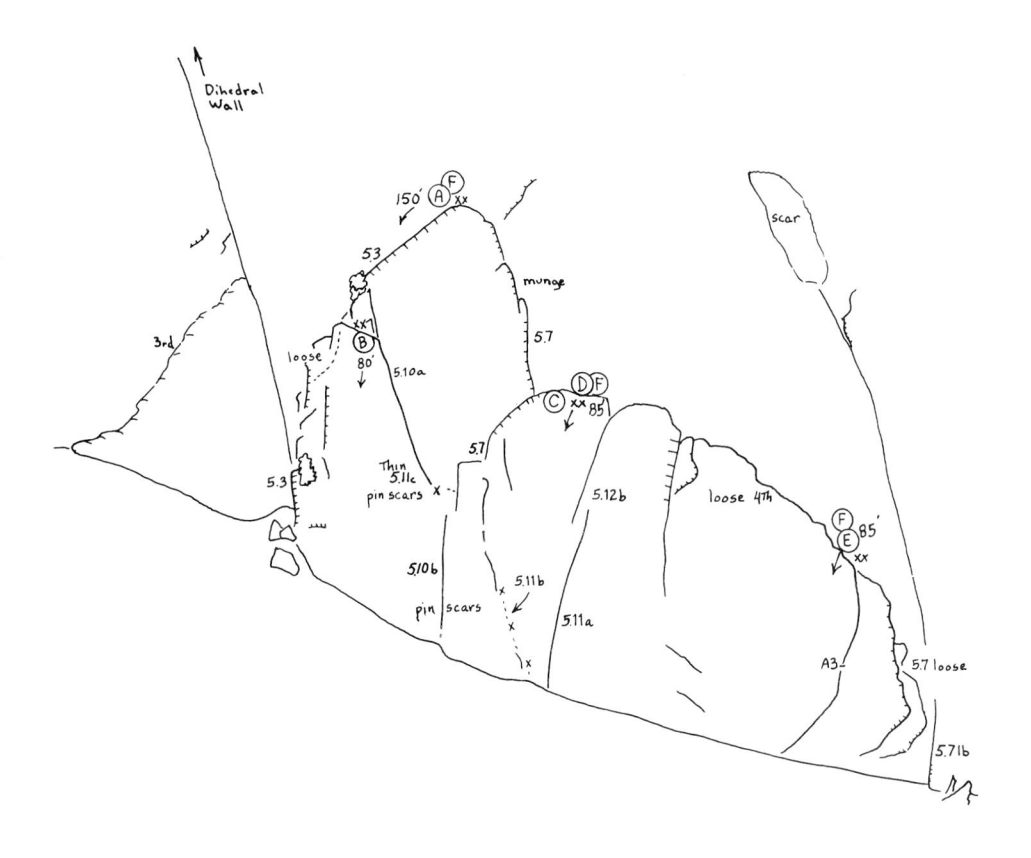

Delectable Pinnacle

Approach: Described on page 98.

A. **Left Side** 5.3★
B. **Center Route** 5.11c★ R Pro: H.B. brass nuts to #2.5 Friend.
C. **Cosmic Charley** 5.11b
D. **Meteorite** 5.12b TR
E. **Aid Route** A3-★ Pro: Include small selection of pitons.
F. **Right Side** 5.7

West Face
Approach

El Capitan, Southwest Face

1. La Escuela 5.11b
2. The Slack 5.10b,d
3. La Cosita 5.9
4. Little John 5.8
5. Moby Dick 5.9, 5.10a, 5.10b
6. Salathé Wall 5.13b
7. Pine Line 5.7
8. The Nose 5.13b

Southwest Base Area, La Escuela and The Slack

Photo on page 101.

A. **La Escuela** 5.11b★★★
   Pro: Many small pieces to 2½".
B. **La Escula Direct** A4
C. **The Slack, Left Side** 5.10b
D. **The Slack, Center Route** 5.10d
   Pro: To 3½"
E. **Sacherer Cracker** 5.10a★★★
   Pro: To 3½".
F. **The Mark of Art** 5.10d★★
   Pro: To 2½", with extra ¾" to 1½".
G. **Short but Thin** 5.11b★
   Pro: Small. This is most often toproped.
H **Fifteen Seconds of Fame** 5.9
   Pro: To 4".

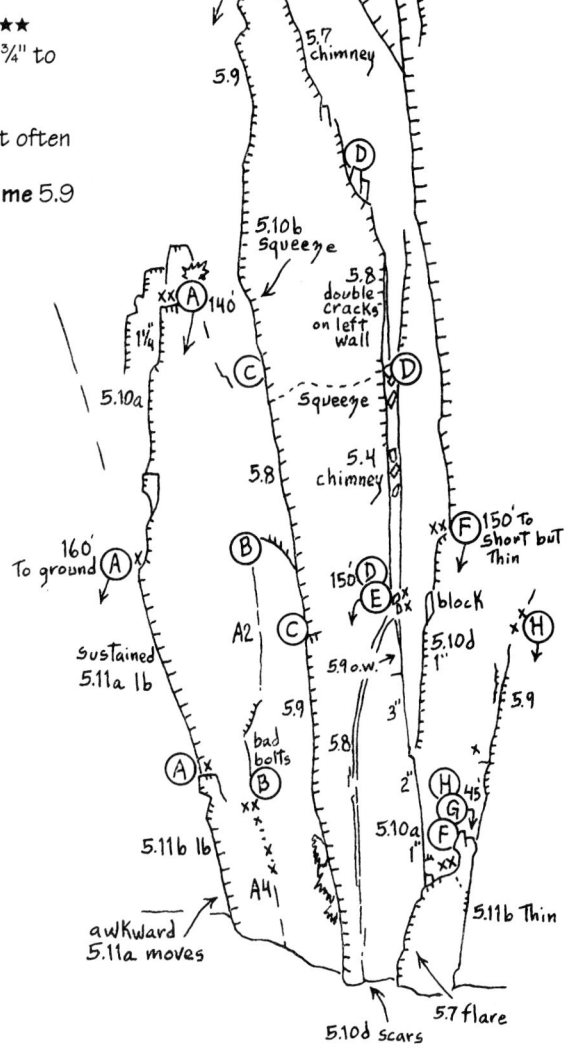

Southwest Base Area, La Cosita and Little John

Photo on page 101.

- I. **La Cosita, Left** 5.9★ Spooky.
- J. **Sparkling Give-away** 5.11a
- K. **La Arista** 5.10c
- L. **La Cosita, Right** 5.9★★★ Pro: To 2¼", especially ⅝" to 1½". Smooth, thin jam and lieback.
- M. **Little John, Left** 5.8★ Pro: To 3½". Robust and smooth.
- N. **Hardly Pinnacle** 5.10d★
- O. **Little John, Center** 5.10d A3-
- P. **Moonchild** 5.10 R
- Q. **Little John, Right** 5.8★★★ Pro: From ¼" to 3". A stiff adventure over three pitches.
- R. **Sunday Driver** 5.10b

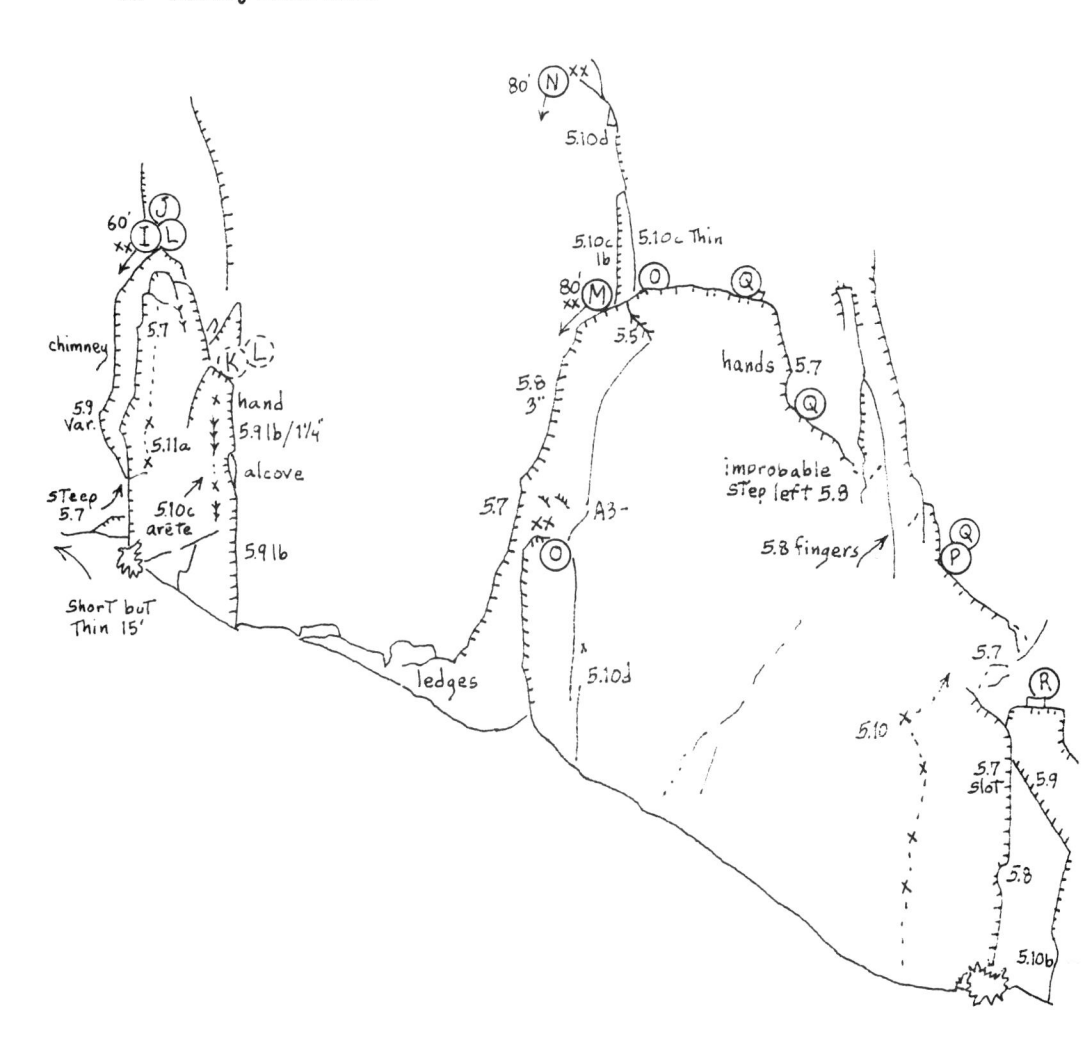

Southwest Base, Moby Dick to The Nose

Approach: Described on page 98.

Photo on page 101.

A. **Moby Dick, Left** 5.9 ★ Pro: To 3½"
B. **Moby Dick, Center** 5.10a ★★★ Pro: To 3½", especially 2" to 3" pieces. Torturous finger locks to start. Physically sustained jamming above.
C. **Moby Dick, Ahab** 5.10b ★ Pro: To 3". V-shaped leaning slot...a struggle for security and upward progress.
D. **Masquerade** 5.11d R
E. **Reed's Leads** 5.10b
F. **Seedy Leads** 5.11a
G. **Thread of Life** 5.11a
H. **Dust in the Wind** 5.10a
I. **Pterodactyl Terrace, Left** 5.10a R Poor rap bolts.
J. **Pterodactyl Terrace, Right** 5.11b Pro: RPs up.
K. **Pine Line** 5.7 ★★ Pro: From ¼" to 1½".

Southwest Face

Southwest Face, Salathé Wall

Photo on page 100.

Salathé Wall VI 5.13b

EL CAPITAN — 105

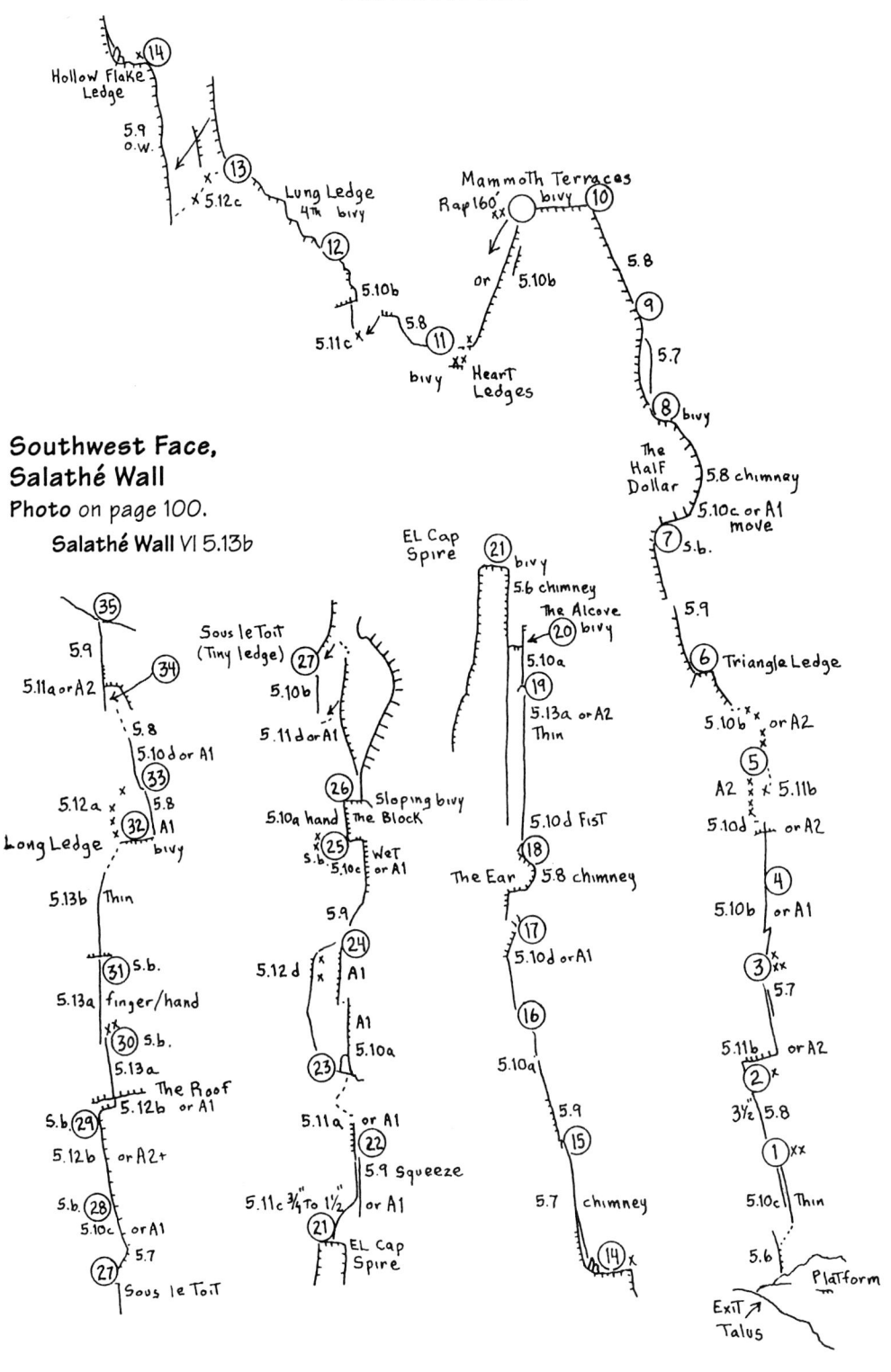

South Buttress

South Buttress, The Nose
Photo on page 100.

Note: Parties often fix to Sickle Ledge. Speed ascents work different strategies with regard to maximum pitch height and belay locations.

The Nose VI 5.13b
Bring wireds, Friends (two each) to #4, nuts to 3½ inch

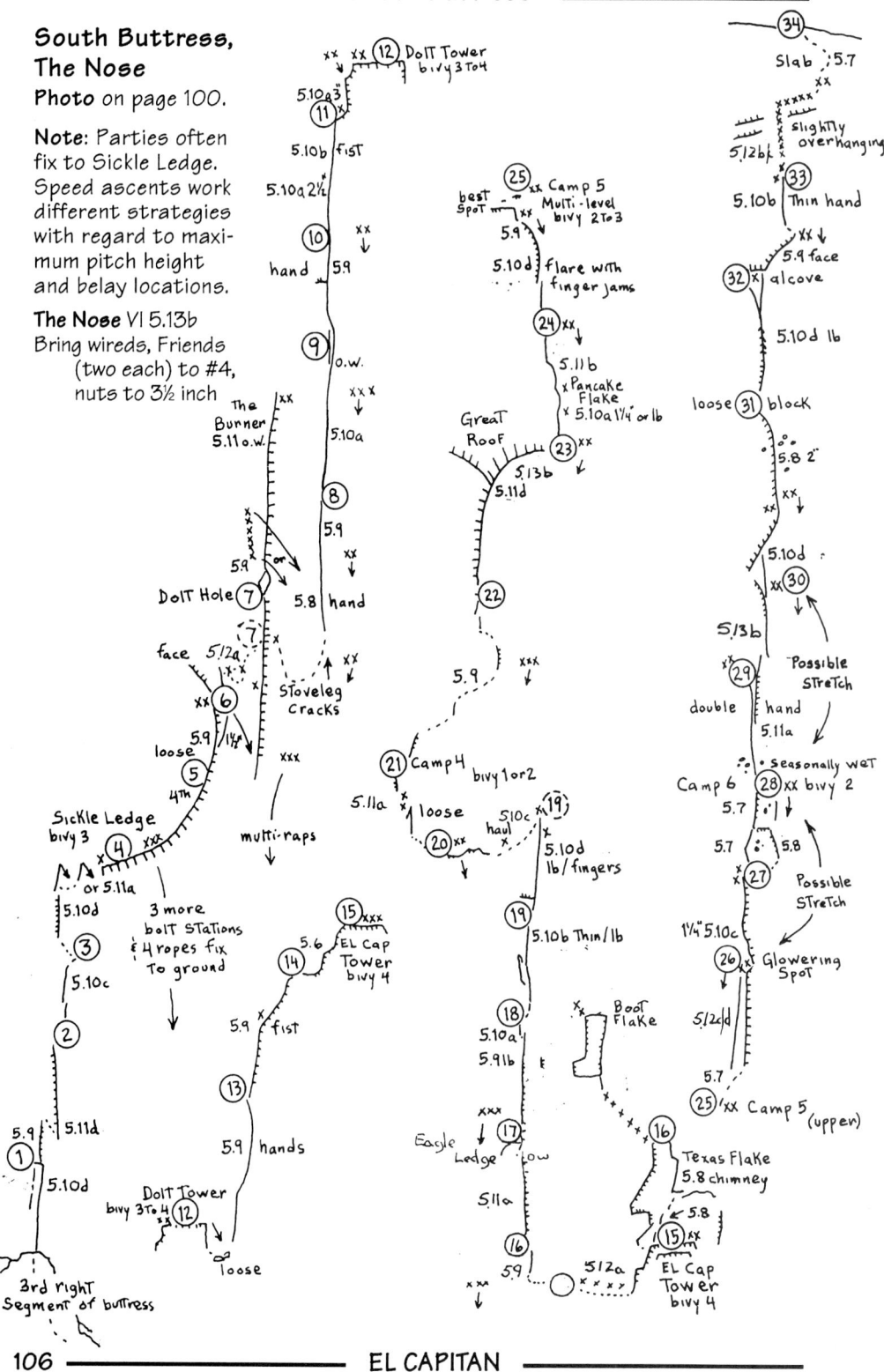

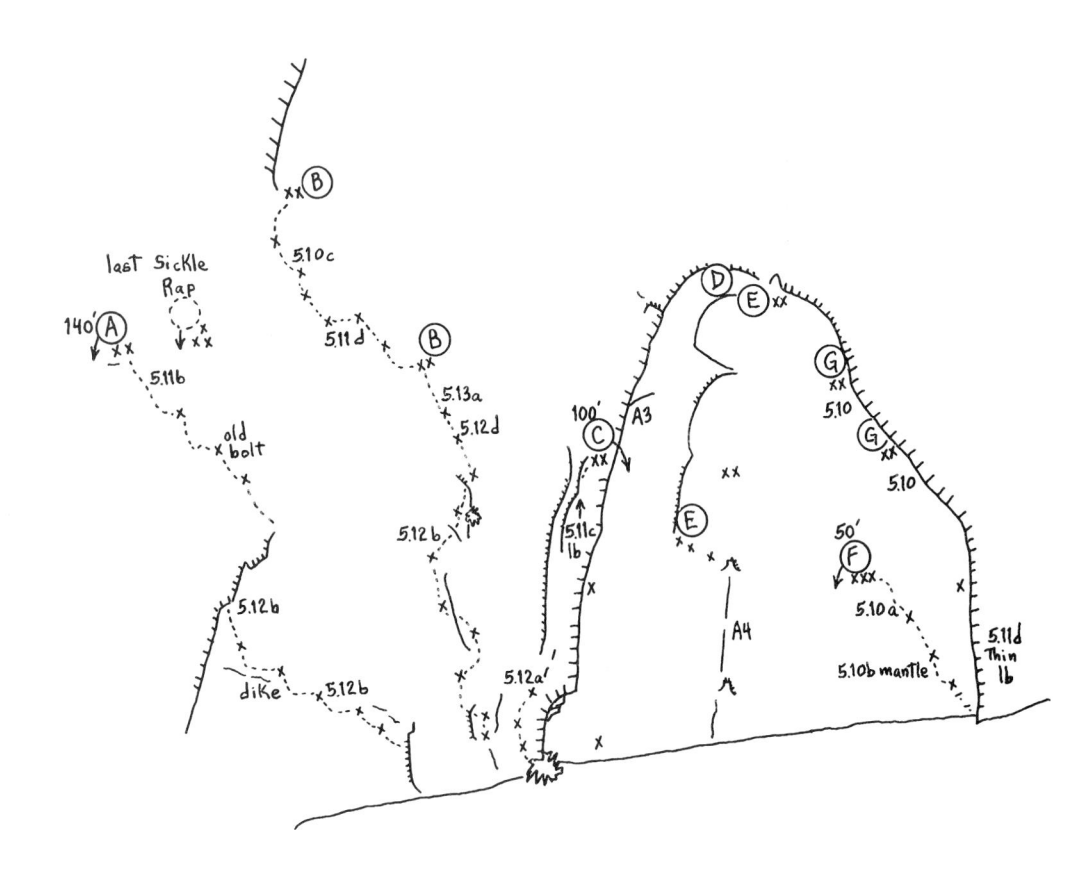

Southeast Base, Negative Pinnacle
Approach: Described on page 98.
- A. **Duty Now For the Future** 5.12b★ R Use double-rope technique.
- B. **General Dynamics** 5.13a★★ R Use double rope technique.
- C. **Base Hits** 5.12a★ Pro: Small to 1½".
- D. **Negative Pinnacle, Left** A3
- E. **Negative Pinnacle, Center** A4
- F. **Party Mix** 5.10b★ Pro: Three QDs. Quality rock with fair-sized holds. A steep balance challenge.
- G. **The High Arc** 5.11d★ Pro: Bring many tiny pieces.

El Capitan Base, Rock Neurotic to Gollum
Approach: Described on page 98.
- A. **Rock Neurotic** 5.11b R
- B. **Armageddon** 5.10d R
- C. **Say Mama, Say Daddy** 5.10a R
- D. **Lunar Landscape** 5.10b R Pro: #0.4 TCU to #3 Friend.
- E. **Simulkrime** 5.9 R/X
- F. **Blazo** 5.8 X

Gollum
- G. **Left Side** 5.10a Pro: To 6".
- H. **Right Side** 5.8 ★

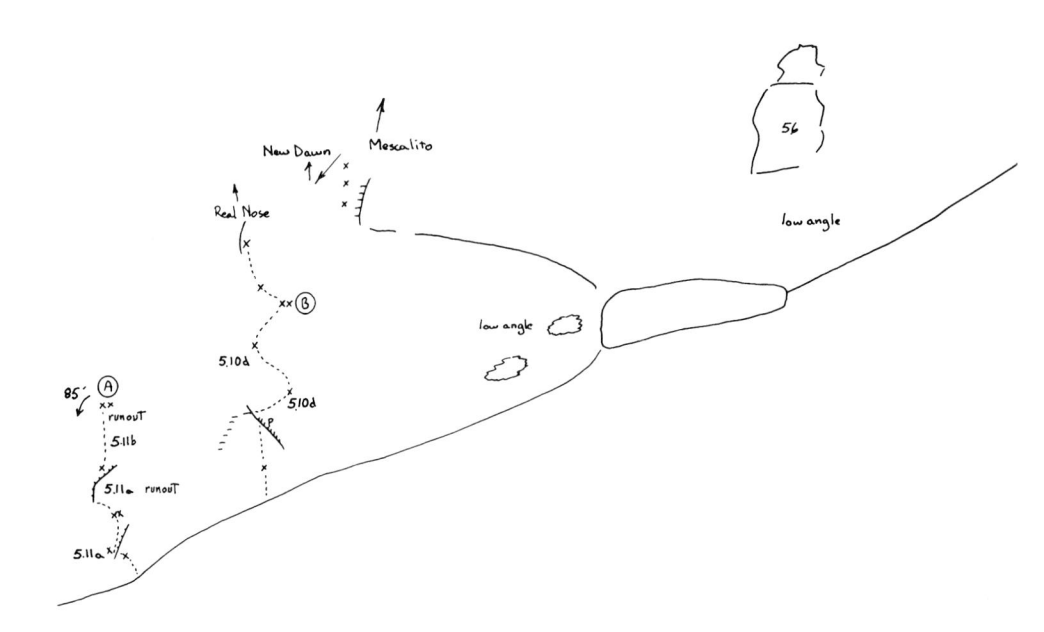

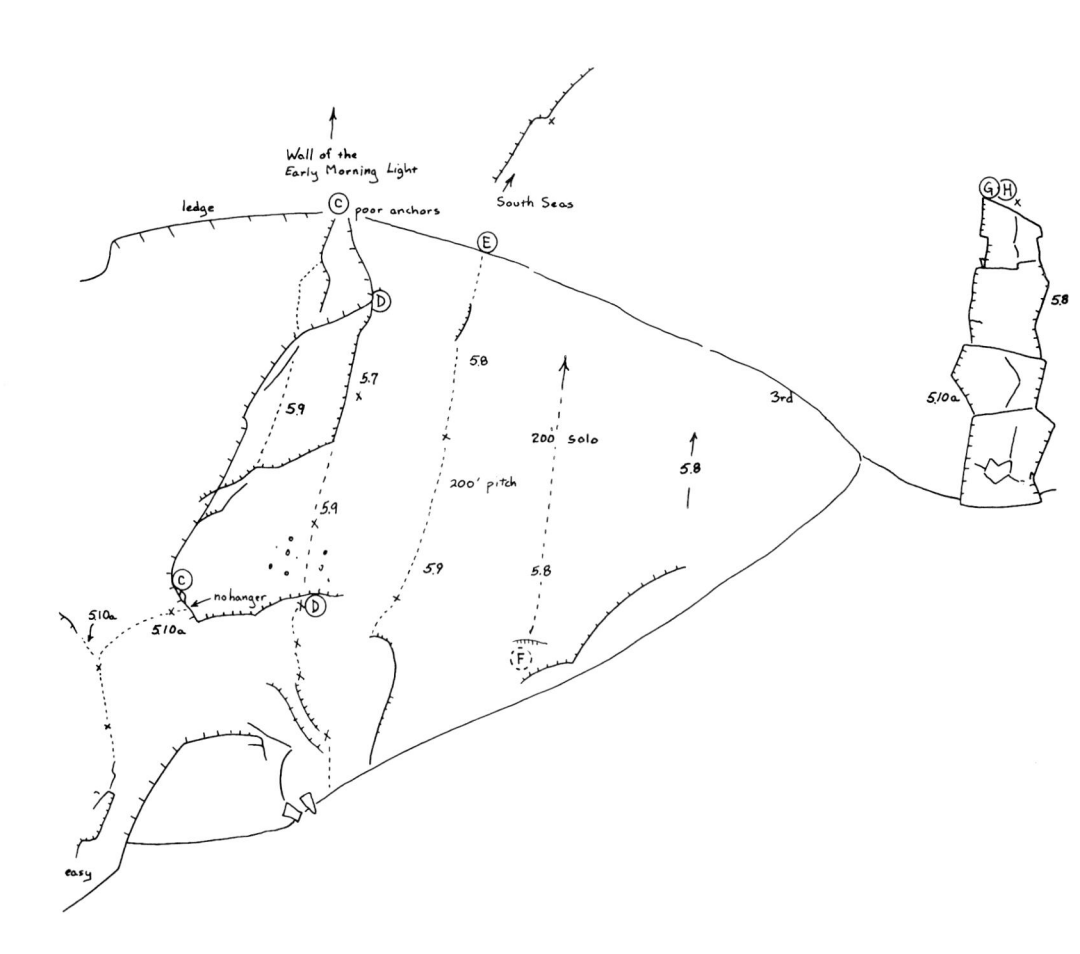

Southeast Base

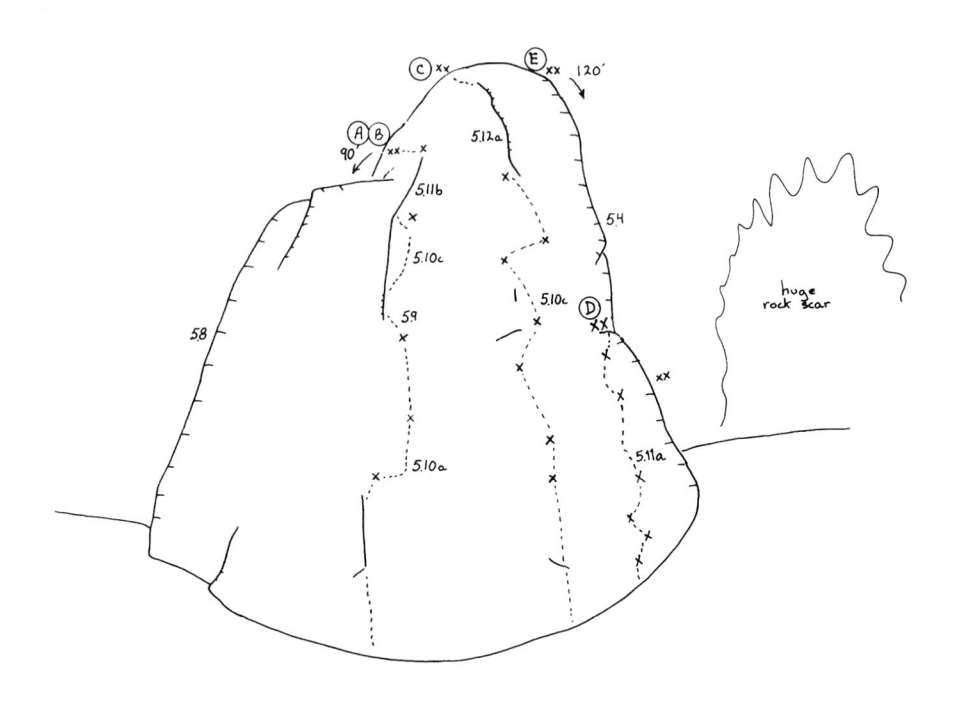

Southeast Base, The Footstool
Approach: Described on page 98.
- A. **Left Side** 5.8
- B. **The Promise** 5.11b★ R Rock-fall damaged hangers.
- C. **The Believer** 5.12a★ R
- D. **The Bluffer** 5.11a★
- E. **Right Side** 5.4★ R

Southeast Base

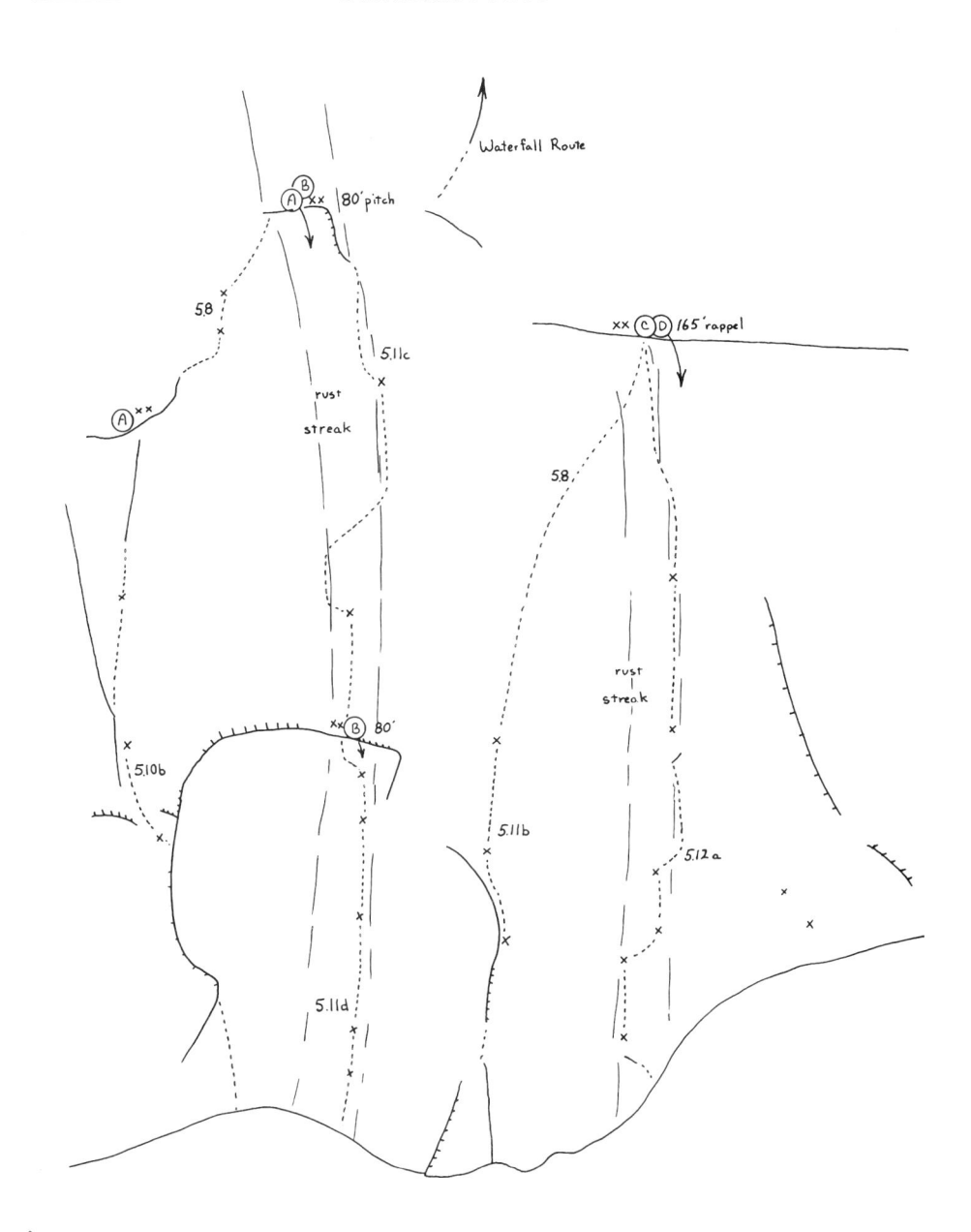

Southeast Base, Base of Horsetail Fall
Approach: Described on page 98.
- A. **Waterfall Route** start 5.10b R
- B. **Champagne on Ice** 5.11d★★ R
- C. **Submen** 5.11b★ R
- D. **El Matador** 5.12a★★ R

El Capitan, Southeast Face

1. The Nose 5.13b
2. NEGATIVE PINNACLE
3. GOLLUM
4. THE FOOTSTOOL
5. East Buttress 5.10b
6. SLAB HAPPY PINNACLE

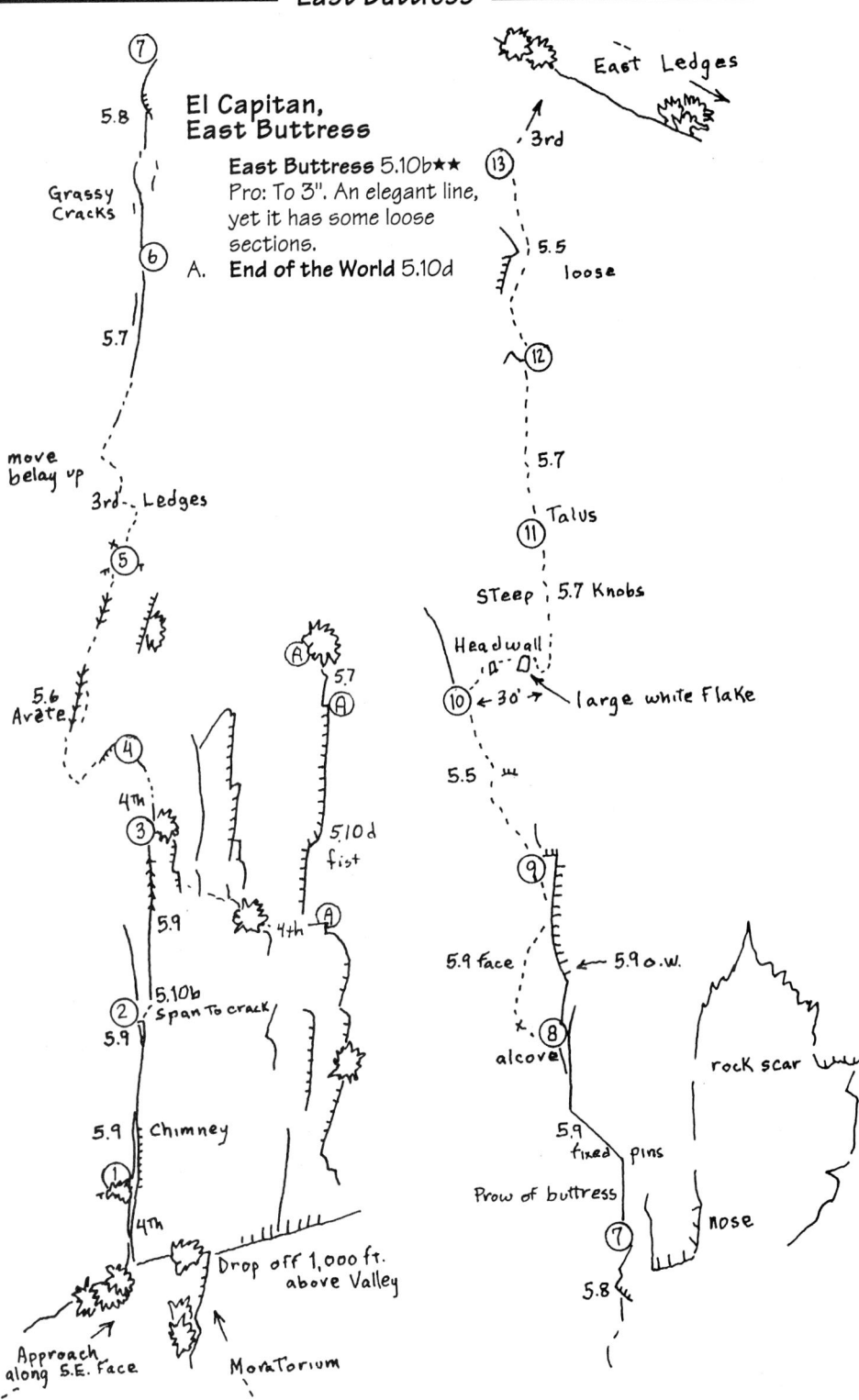

East Buttress

El Capitan, East Buttress

East Buttress 5.10b★★
Pro: To 3". An elegant line, yet it has some loose sections.

A. **End of the World** 5.10d

Schultz's Ridge: West Side

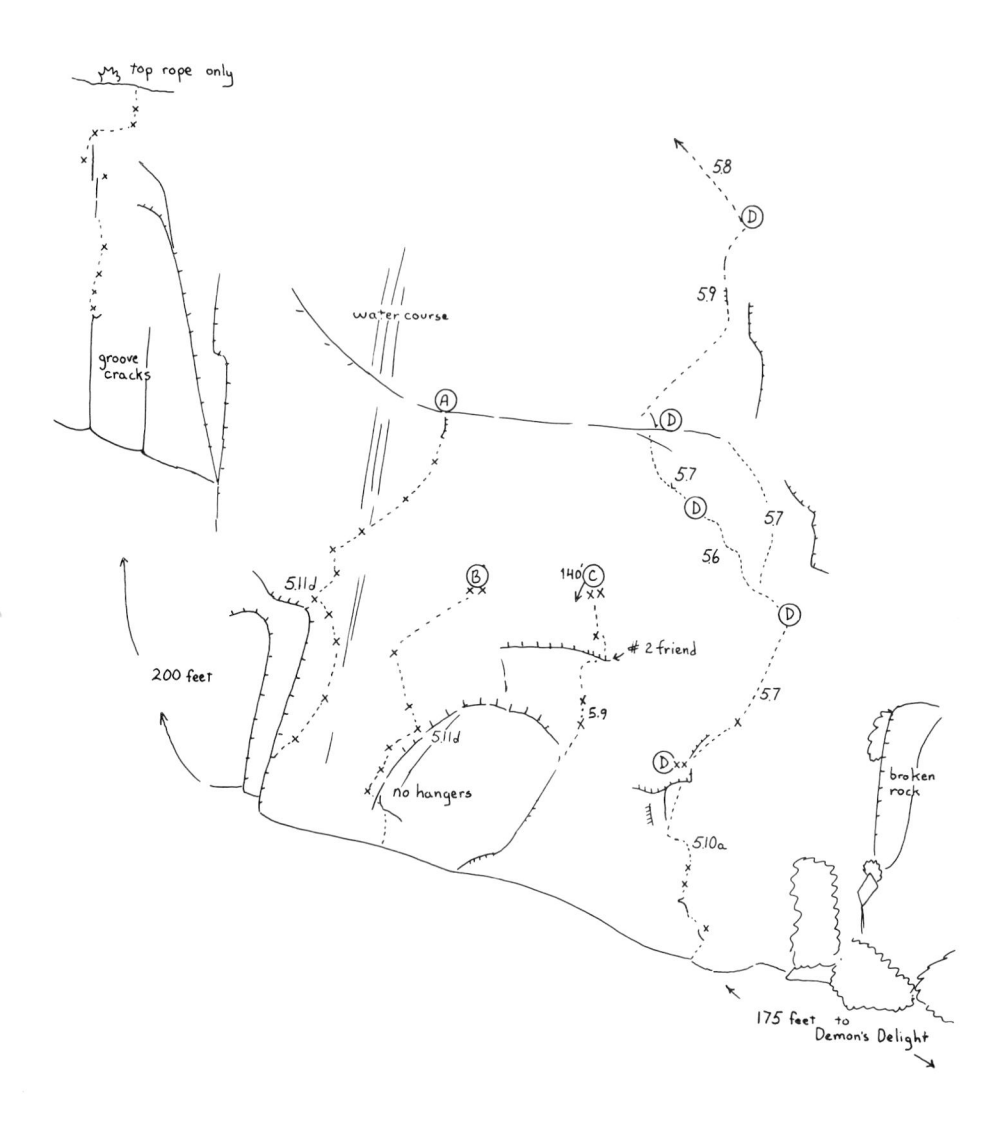

Schultz's Ridge, West Side

Approach: Park in the dirt turnout just past the "S" curve, 1.9 miles west of the gas station, or in the picnic pullout located 2.1 miles beyond the station. A short walk leads to the routes.

A. **The White Zone** 5.11d
B. **Annette Funicello** 5.11d
C. **Gidget Goes to Yosemite** 5.9 ★
D. **Bikini Beach Party** 5.10a

Shultz's Ridge, West Side
A. **Demon's Delight** 5.11a★★★ Pro: Brass nuts to 3½", especially ¾" to 1½".
B. **Supertoe** 5.10d
C. **Superstem** 5.11a Pro: Hi-tech thin.
D. **Rectum Ranch** 5.8
E. **Brown Sugar** 5.10a R
F. **Free Bong** 5.11a
G. **Deucey's Elbow** 5.10d
H. **Deucey's Nose** 5.11 Pro: To 4", 5" optional.

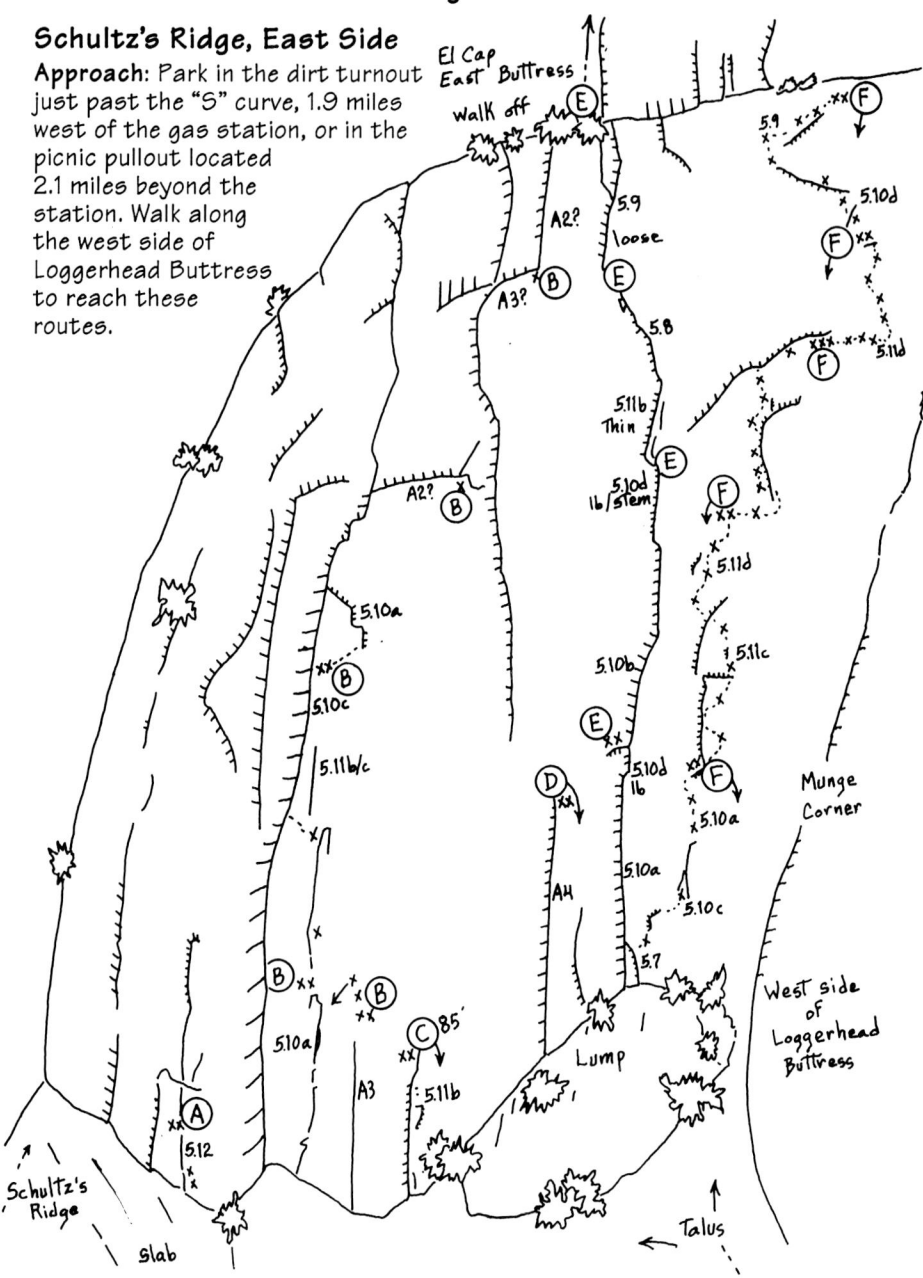

Schultz's Ridge: East Side

Schultz's Ridge, East Side

Approach: Park in the dirt turnout just past the "S" curve, 1.9 miles west of the gas station, or in the picnic pullout located 2.1 miles beyond the station. Walk along the west side of Loggerhead Buttress to reach these routes.

A. **Ain't That a Bitch** 5.12
B. **Abazaba** 5.11b/c A3
C. **End Game** 5.11b Pro: #1 to #3.5 Friends.
D. **Creamatorium** A4
E. **The Moratorium** 5.11b★★ Pro: To 2½". Features some long endurance sections lower down, with creative technical moves higher up. The **East Buttress/Moratorium** combination provides even greater length and challenge.
F. **Burden of Dreams** IV 5.12b★★ Pro: Wires, TCUs and Friends to #2.5.

Eagle Creek Area

1. El Capitan East Buttress 5.10b
2. The Moratorium 5.11b
3. SLAB HAPPY PINNACLE
4. East Ledges Descent
5. After Six 5.6
6. The Nutcracker 5.8
7. Commissioner Buttress 5.9
8. Split Pinnacle 5.10c or 5.8 A1+
9. Essence 5.11b

Loggerhead Buttress

Approach: Park in a dirt turnout 1.7 miles west of the gas station and 0.1 mile past the El Cap Picnic Area. Hike up the hill to the toe of the buttress and trend along its base foot for the various routes.

Photo on page 117.

- A. **Orange Juice Avenue** 5.10a★ Pro: To 5".
- B. **Chester the Molester** 5.11b★★ Pro: A few small to 2".
- C. **Yeast Infection** 5.10c
- D. **Sink Like a Stone** 5.11d★★ Pro: Optional, #1 Friend useful.
- E. **Lycra Virgin** 5.11d★★ Pro: Many small.
- F. **Material Girl** 5.12b ★★
- G. **Goodhead** 5.11d
- H. **Hammerhead** 5.11b
- I. **Lagerhead** 5.11a★
- J. **Head Banger** 5.11b
- K. **Loggerhead Ledge Route** 5.7
- L. **Log Jam** 5.11b
- M. **Simian Sex** 5.10d★★
- N. **Dick Wrenching Classic** 5.10b Pro: To 5½".

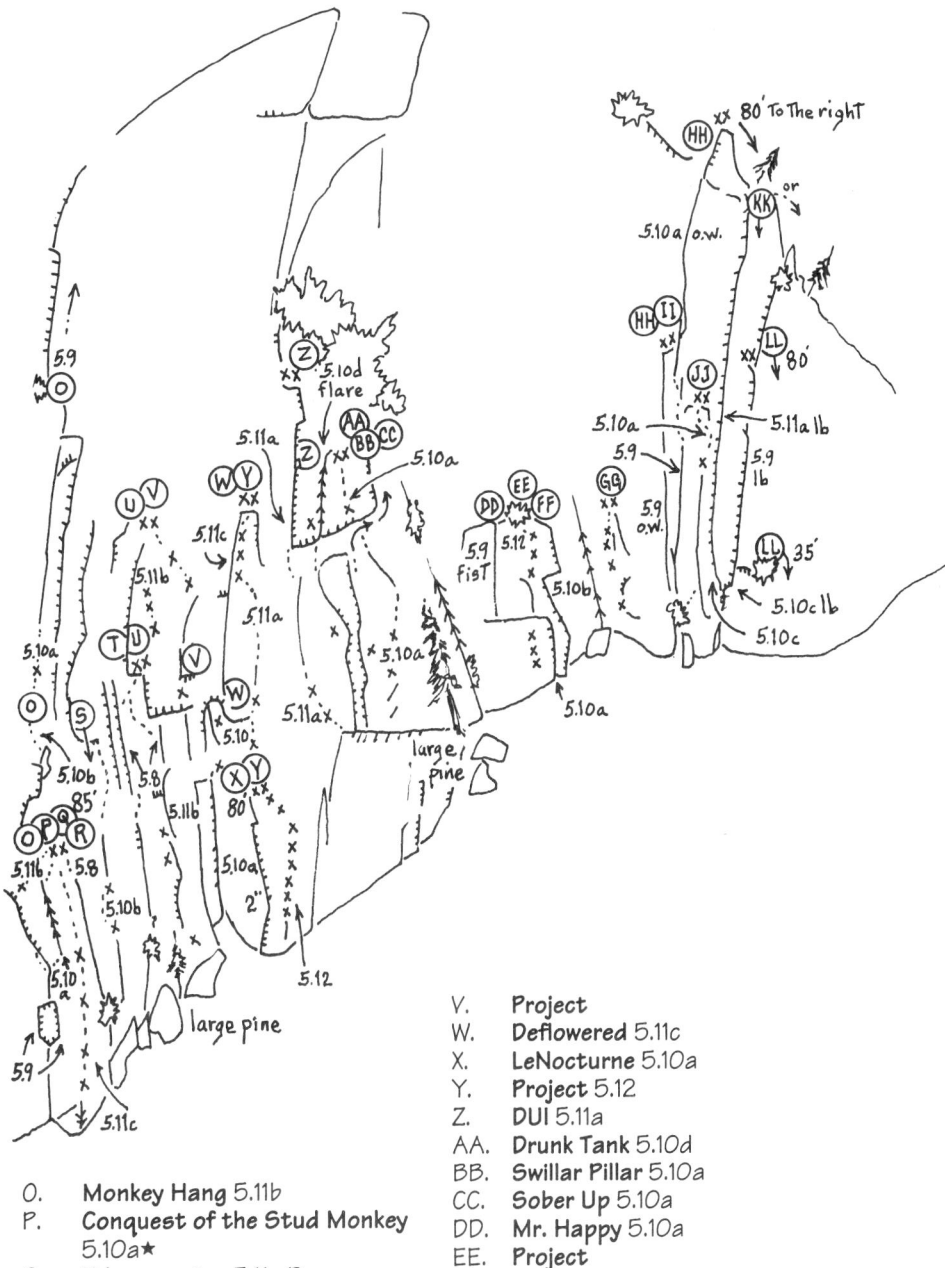

Loggerhead Buttress

O. Monkey Hang 5.11b
P. Conquest of the Stud Monkey 5.10a★
Q. Edge-u-cator 5.11c R
R. Sorry Poopsie 5.8★
S. Teenage Mutant Blowjobs 5.10b
T. Agricultural Manuvers in the Dark 5.8
U. Cherry Picker 5.11b
V. Project
W. Deflowered 5.11c
X. LeNocturne 5.10a
Y. Project 5.12
Z. DUI 5.11a
AA. Drunk Tank 5.10d
BB. Swillar Pillar 5.10a
CC. Sober Up 5.10a
DD. Mr. Happy 5.10a
EE. Project
FF. Happy's Favorite 5.10b
GG. Project
HH. Sow Sow Sow 5.10a
II. Brown-Eyed Girl 5.9
JJ. Stay Lady Stay Back 5.10a
KK. Here on the Inside 5.11a★
LL. Chow Chow Chow 5.10c★

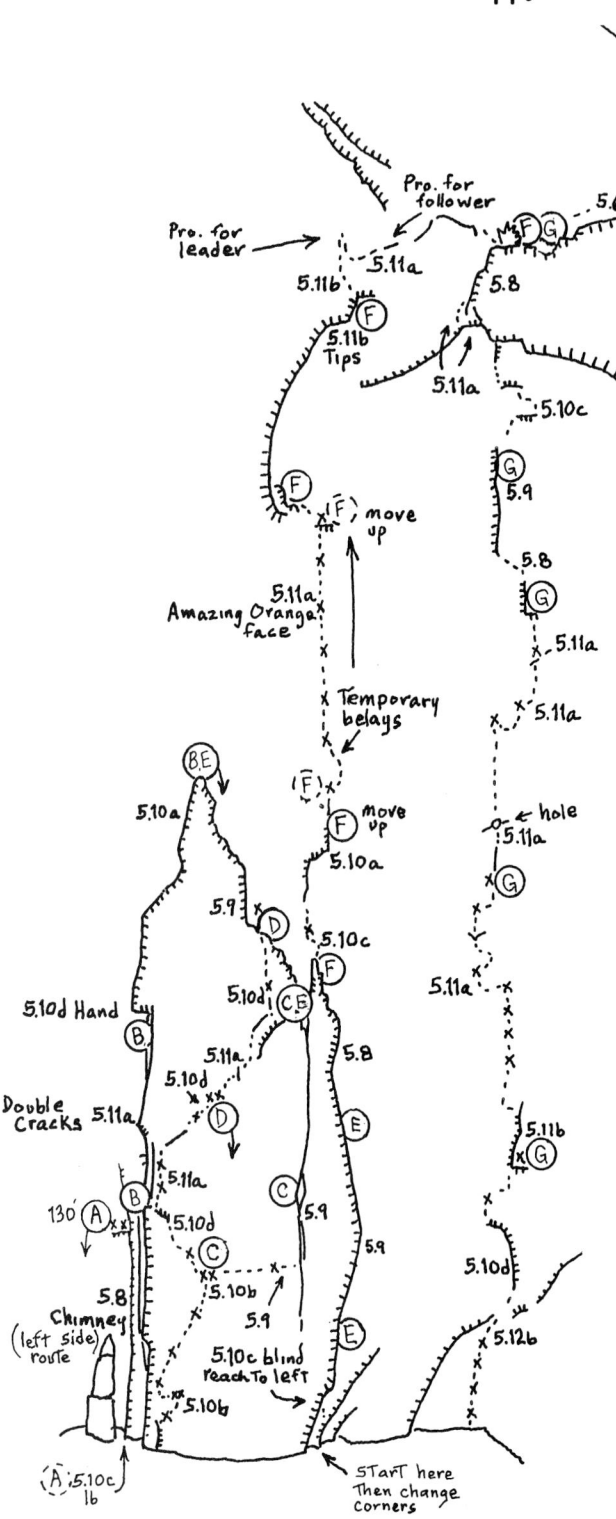

Slab Happy

Approach: Park in the dirt turnout 1.7 miles west of the gas station and 0.2 mile past the El Cap picnic area. Hike up the hill, skirting the east side of Loggerhead Buttress. Traverse right along a barrier until 3rd class passage can be made to the main wall. Slab Happy is out to the left along a broad ledge system. Nearby Horsetail Falls and afternoon winds can affect climbing conditions in this area.
Photo on page 117.

A. **The Silent Freeway** 5.10c★
   Pro: Friends to #3.
B. **Left Side** 5.11a★
   Pro: To 3".
C. **Center Route** 5.10b★
   Pro: To 3½".
D. **The Happy Ending** 5.11a★
   Pro: To 2½".
E. **The Dihardral** 5.10c★
   Pro: To 3".
F. **Never Say Dog** 5.11b★★
   Pro: To 3", extra to 2".
   Bold and beautiful.
G. **The Big Juan** 5.12b★★
   Pro: Many to 2". Also bold and beautiful.

East Ledges Area

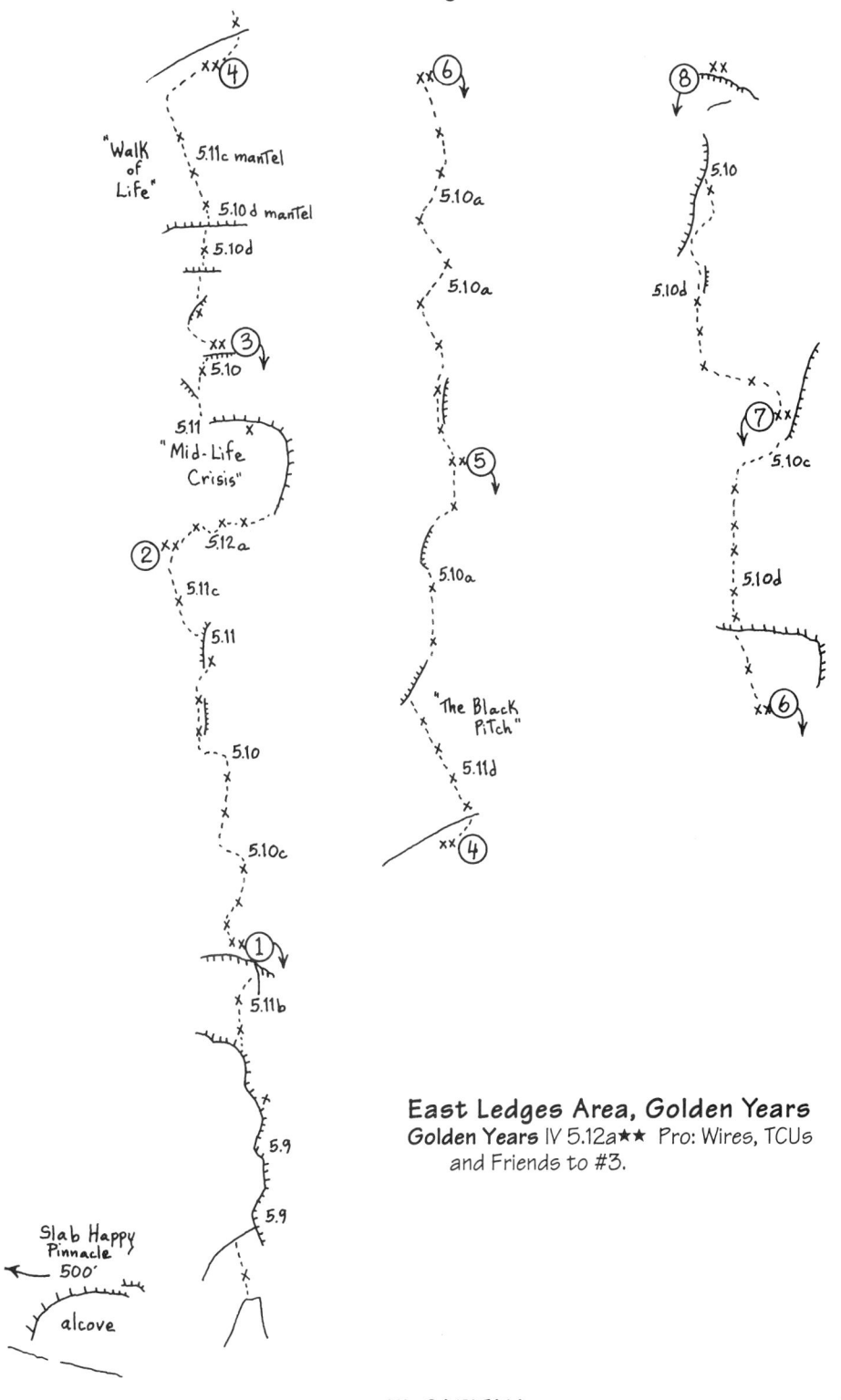

East Ledges Area, Golden Years
Golden Years IV 5.12a★★ Pro: Wires, TCUs and Friends to #3.

EL CAPITAN

East Ledges Area

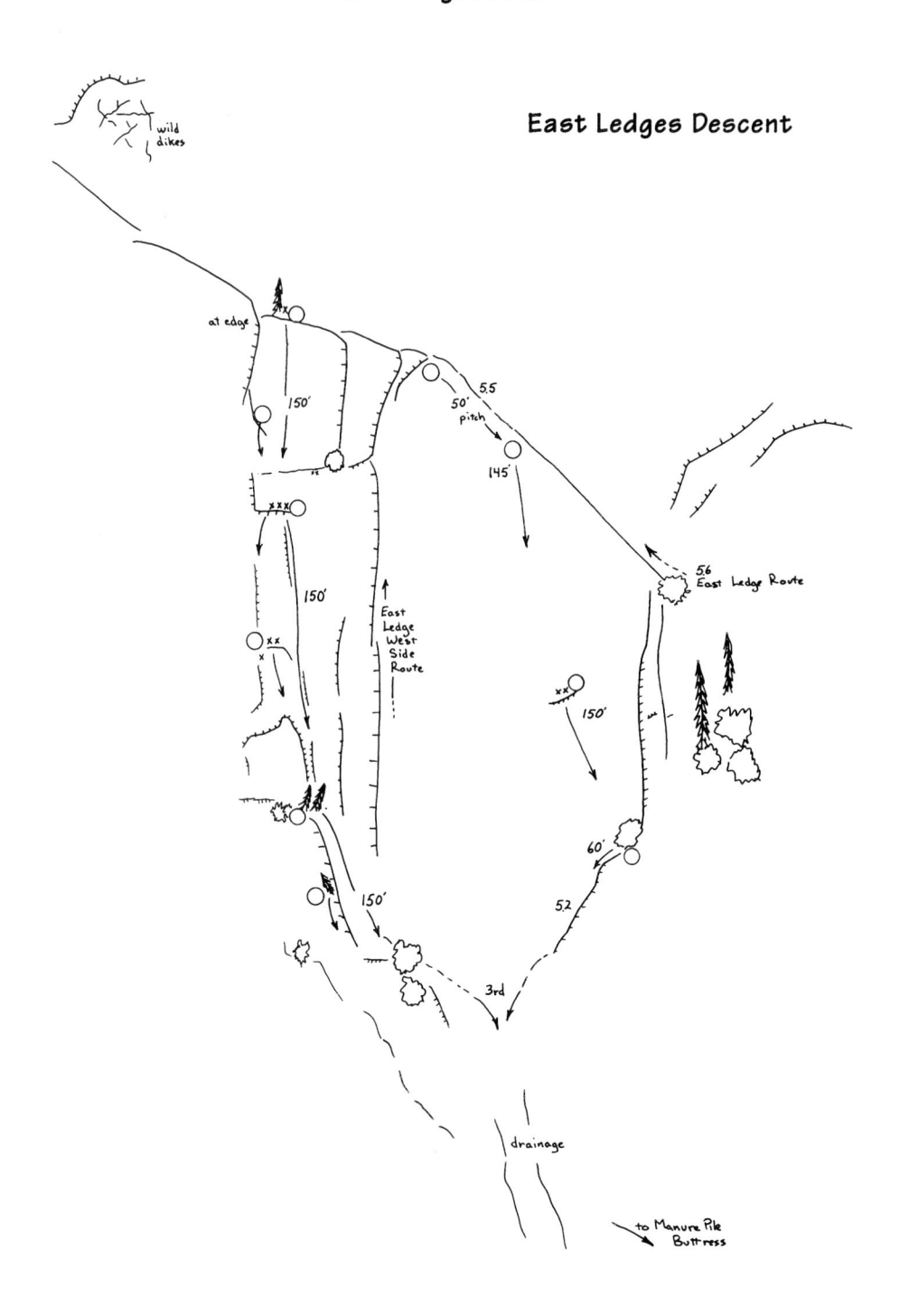

East Ledges Descent

wild dikes

at edge

150'

50' pitch
5.5

145'

5.6
East Ledge Route

East Ledge West Side Route

150'

150'

150'

60'

5.2

150'

3rd

drainage

to Manure Pile Buttress

EL CAPITAN

Photo by Allen Steck

Willi Unsoeld on El Capitan, East Buttress, 1953

Manure Pile Buttress

Approach: Park at an area on the right side of the road 1.6 miles west of the gas station. A short walk up the remaining section of dirt road leads to the formation.

Descent: Scramble off the top of the formation to the west to gain a steep, dirty descent gully.

A. **Chairman Ted Scraps the Time Machine** 5.10a
B. **God's Creation** 5.9 Pro: To 3".
C. **Jump for Joy** 5.9★ Pro: A few pieces to 2". Reachy moves up and left to slick, positive edges allows escape from the initial bowl/depression.
D. **Beer Pressure** 5.10a R
E. **After Six** 5.6★★ Pro: To 2½". The crux is found on the first pitch and many parties escape after that. Moderate to easy climbing with big ledges and superior views found above.
F. **After Seven** 5.8★ Pro: To 2½". Jamming leads to face moves that are not obvious. The face moves lead right, then up.
G. **Just Do-Do It** 5.10a Pro: A few small pieces.
H. **C.S. Concerto** 5.8★ Pro: To 2½". Varied climbing that is somewhat runout on the first and third pitches.
I. **Fecophilia** 5.9★ R
J. **Easy Wind** 5.9 R Pro: Many small nuts.
K. **The Mouse King** 5.9 R
L. **Nutcracker** 5.8★★★ Pro: To 2½", especially small to medium pieces. Intriguing climbing, clean rock. A number of starting variations exist.
M. **Renus Wrinkle** 5.10a★ Pro: Brass nuts to #2.5 Friend.
N. **Dynamic Doubles** 5.9★
O. **Flexible Flyer** 5.10d

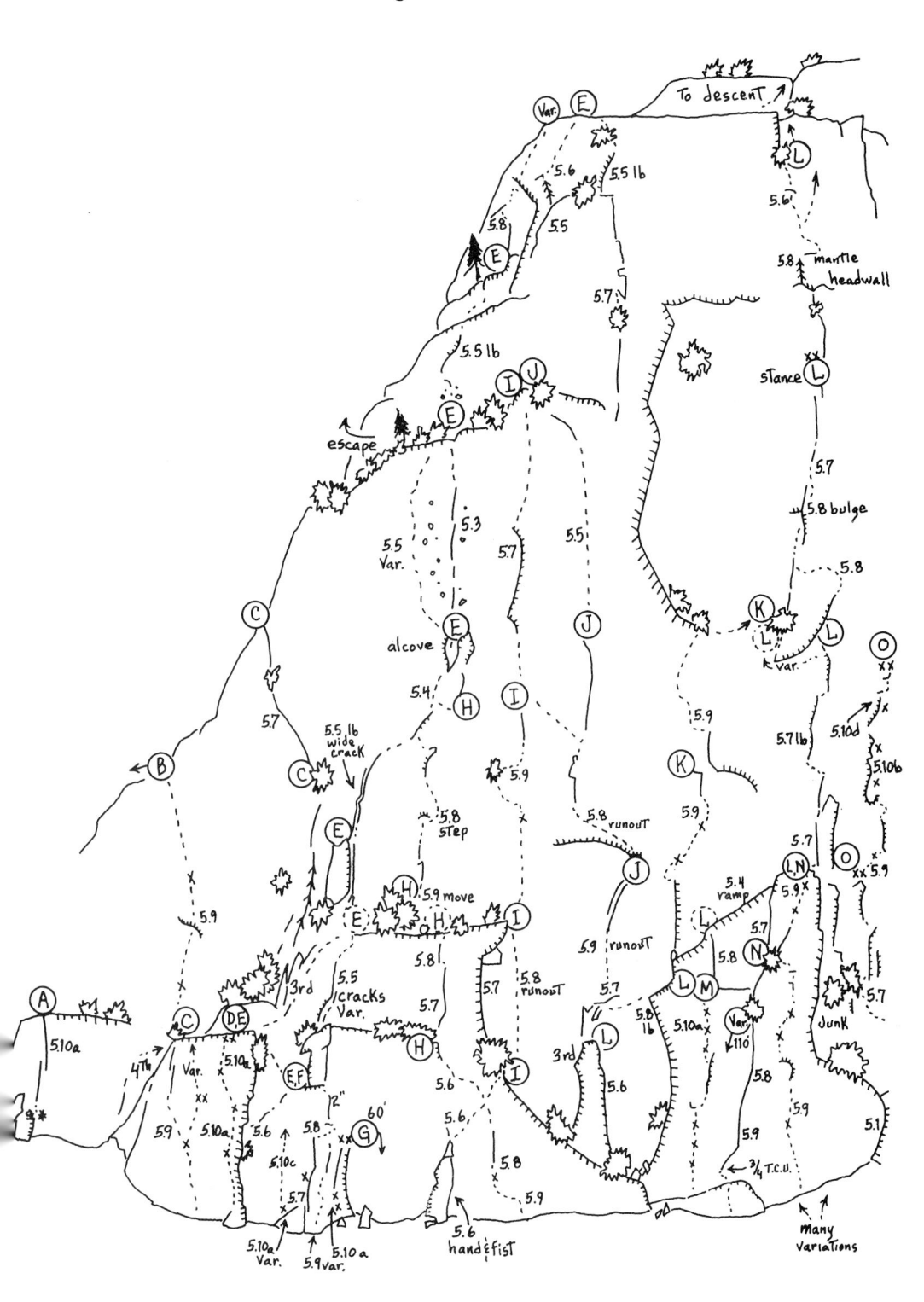

Eagle Creek Area

THREE BROTHERS

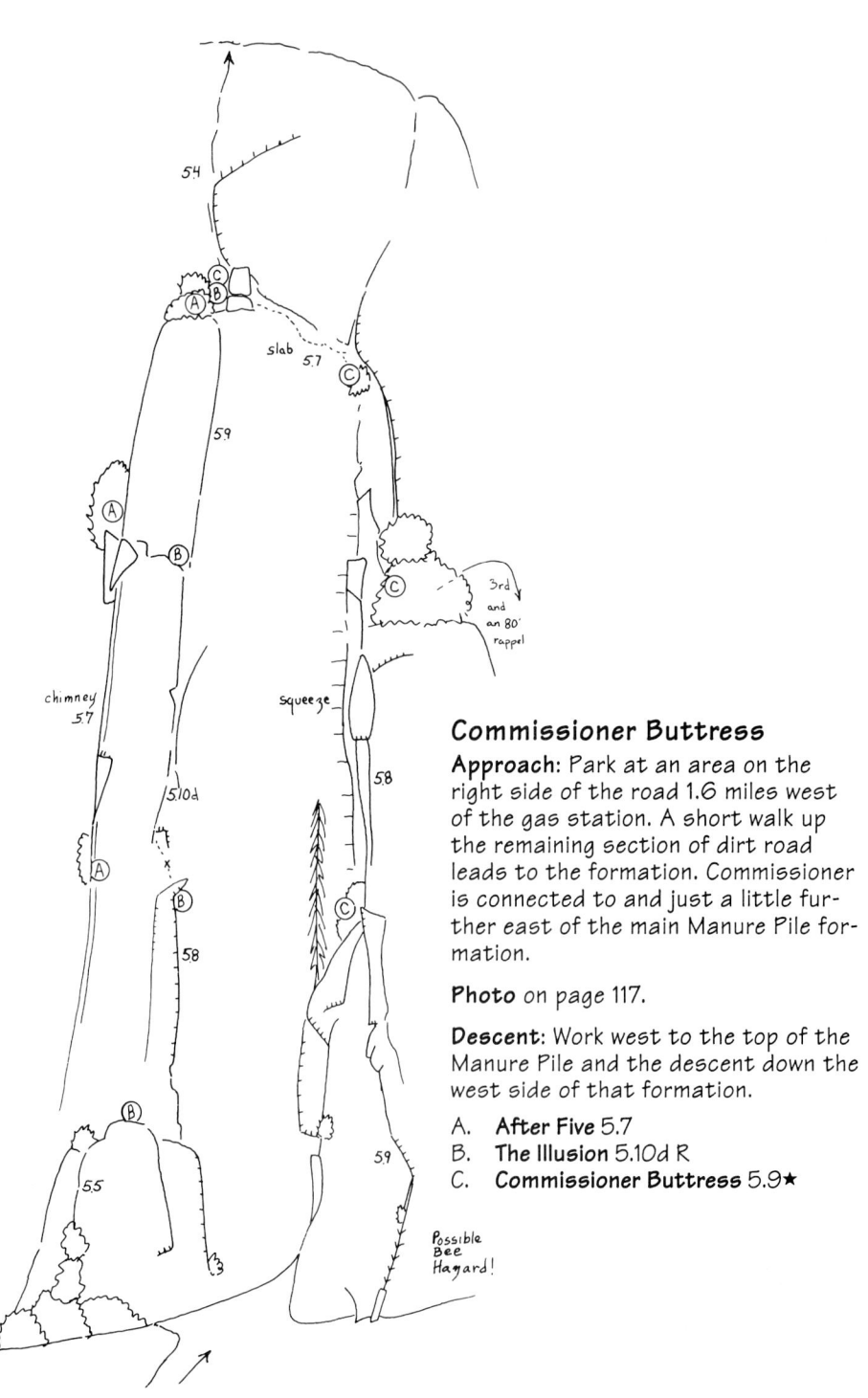

Eagle Creek Area

Commissioner Buttress

Approach: Park at an area on the right side of the road 1.6 miles west of the gas station. A short walk up the remaining section of dirt road leads to the formation. Commissioner is connected to and just a little further east of the main Manure Pile formation.

Photo on page 117.

Descent: Work west to the top of the Manure Pile and the descent down the west side of that formation.

A. **After Five** 5.7
B. **The Illusion** 5.10d R
C. **Commissioner Buttress** 5.9 ★

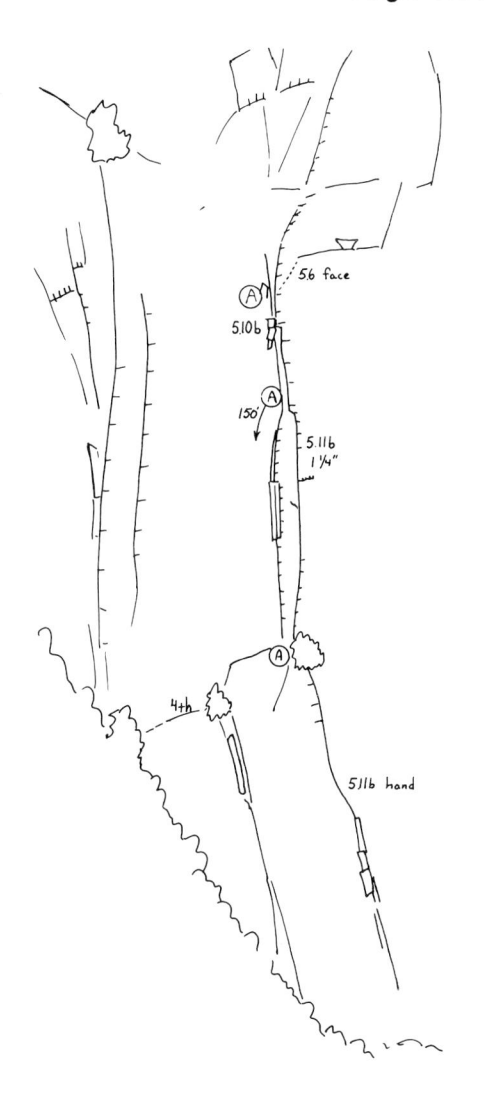

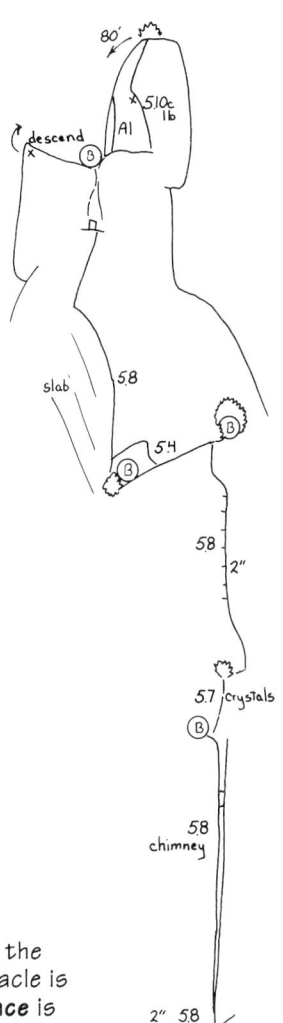

Eagle Creek Area, Upper

Approach: Park in a broad dirt pullout 1.0 mile west of the gas station, at the crossing of Eagle Creek. Split Pinnacle is the yellow spire on the west slopes of the creek. **Essence** is reached by continuing the hike up the gully immediately to the right of Split Pinnacle, trending back to the west, up and to the wall.

A. **Essence** 5.11b★★
B. **Split Pinnacle, East Arête** 5.10c or 5.8 A1+★★

Lower Brother, 4th Street Area

Approach: Park in a dirt turnout on the river side of the road, just past the "S" curves 0.8 mile west of the gas station. The routes are located closest to the road.

Photo on page 130.

- A. **Maple Jam** 5.10a★ Pro: To 3".
- B. **Absolutely Sweet Marie** 5.11d★
- C. **Positively 4th Street** 5.9★★
- D. **Nutty Buddy** 5.8 Pro: To 2½".
- E. **Fuddy Duddy** 5.10a
- F. **Plant Your Fingers** 5.11a Pro: Wires and TCUs.
- G. **My Left Foot** 5.10b R

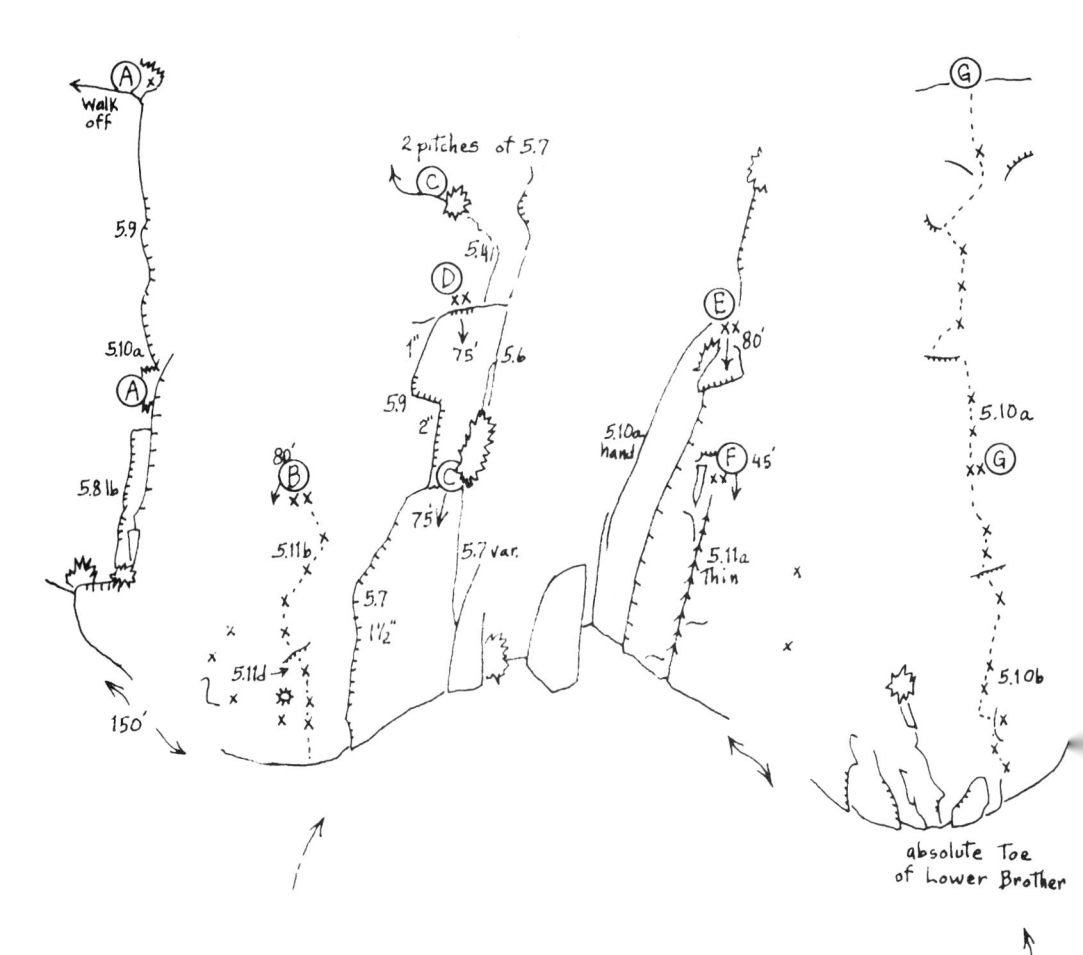

Lower Brother: Base

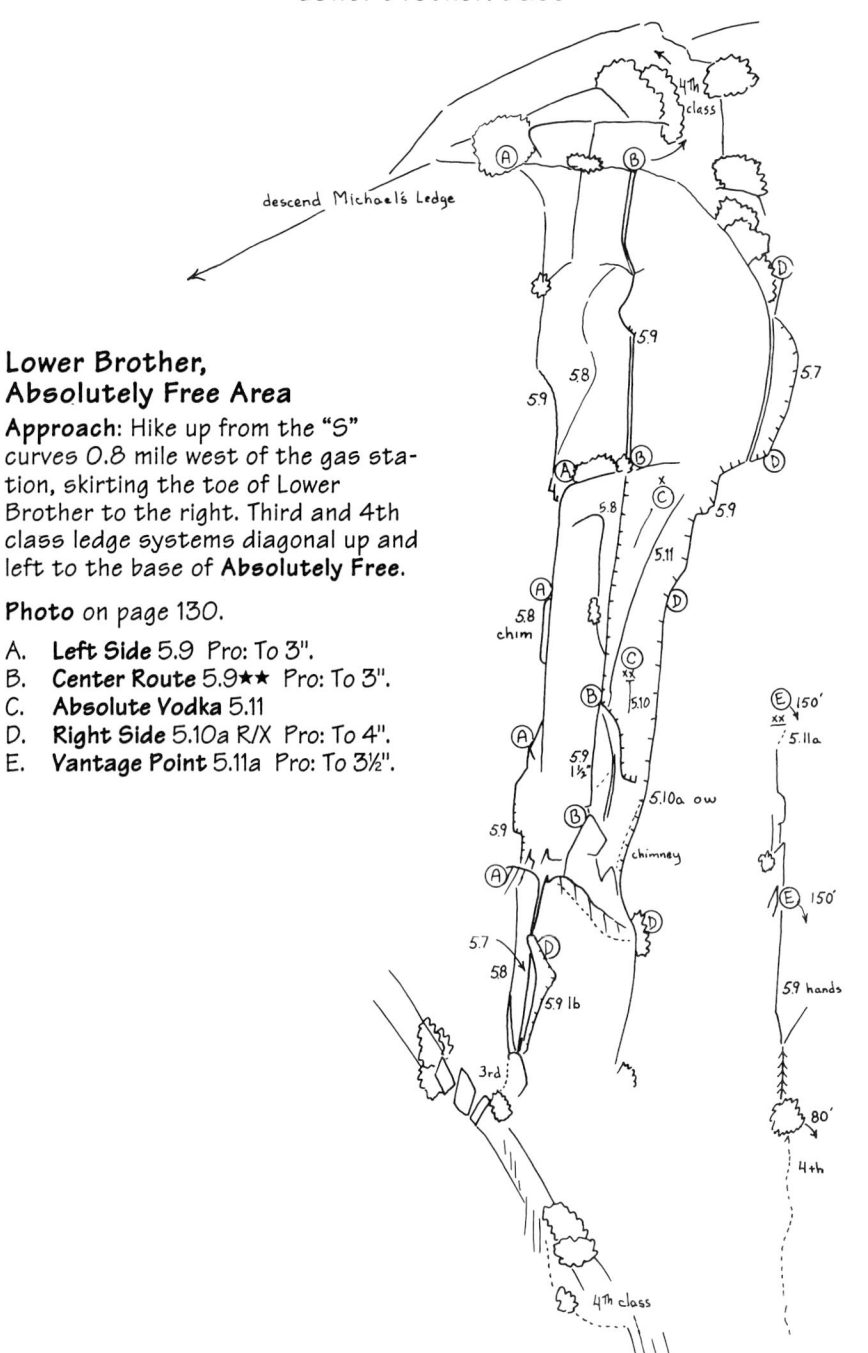

Lower Brother, Absolutely Free Area

Approach: Hike up from the "S" curves 0.8 mile west of the gas station, skirting the toe of Lower Brother to the right. Third and 4th class ledge systems diagonal up and left to the base of **Absolutely Free**.

Photo on page 130.

A. **Left Side** 5.9 Pro: To 3".
B. **Center Route** 5.9★★ Pro: To 3".
C. **Absolute Vodka** 5.11
D. **Right Side** 5.10a R/X Pro: To 4".
E. **Vantage Point** 5.11a Pro: To 3½".

THREE BROTHERS

Lower Brother

1. MANURE PILE BUTTRESS
2. Positively 4th Street 5.9
3. ABSOLUTELY FREE
4. Hawkman's Escape 5.9
5. RIXON'S PINNACLE
6. THE FOLLY
7. Cost of Living 5.10c

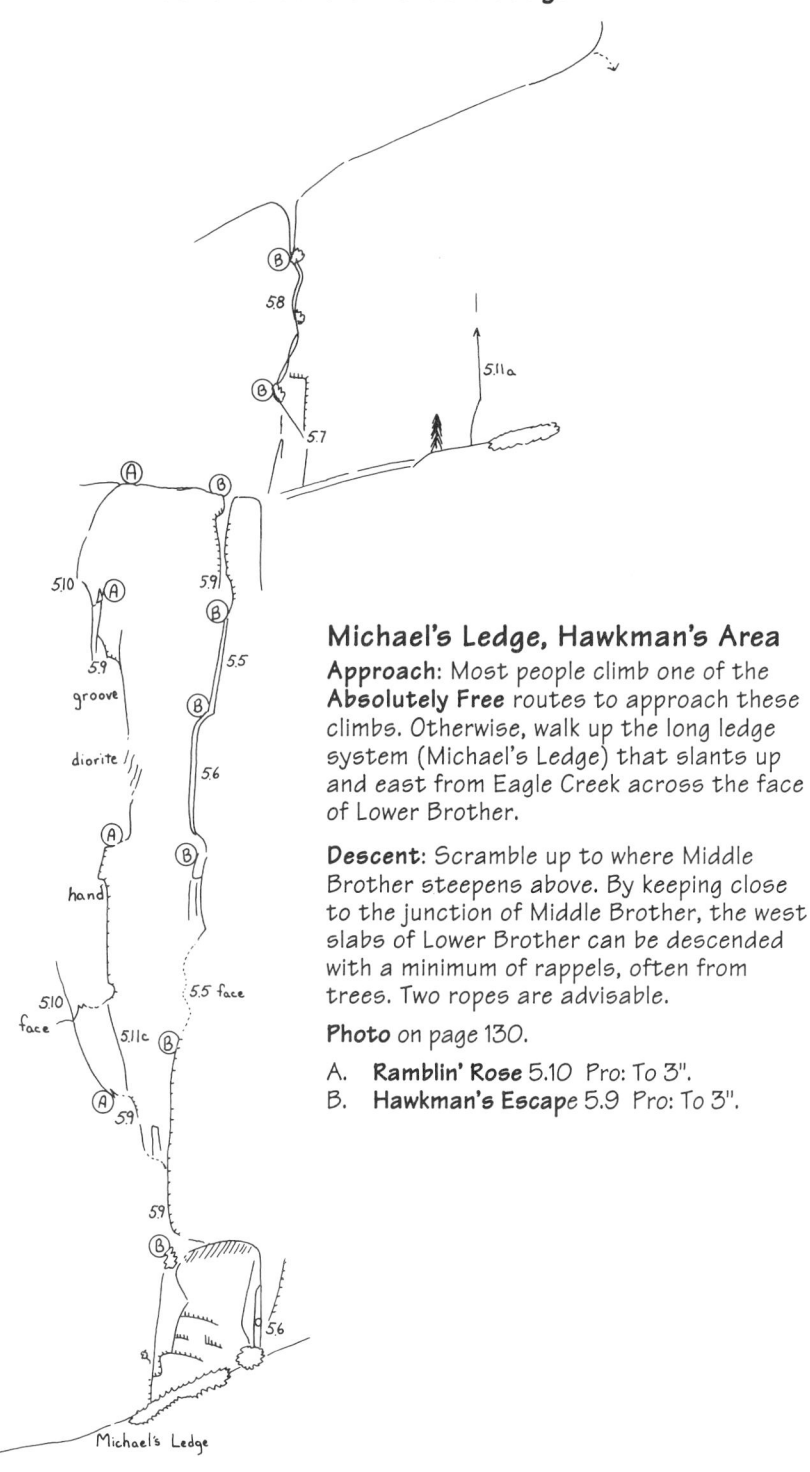

Lower Brother: Michael's Ledge

Michael's Ledge, Hawkman's Area

Approach: Most people climb one of the **Absolutely Free** routes to approach these climbs. Otherwise, walk up the long ledge system (Michael's Ledge) that slants up and east from Eagle Creek across the face of Lower Brother.

Descent: Scramble up to where Middle Brother steepens above. By keeping close to the junction of Middle Brother, the west slabs of Lower Brother can be descended with a minimum of rappels, often from trees. Two ropes are advisable.

Photo on page 130.

A. **Ramblin' Rose** 5.10 Pro: To 3".
B. **Hawkman's Escape** 5.9 Pro: To 3".

THREE BROTHERS

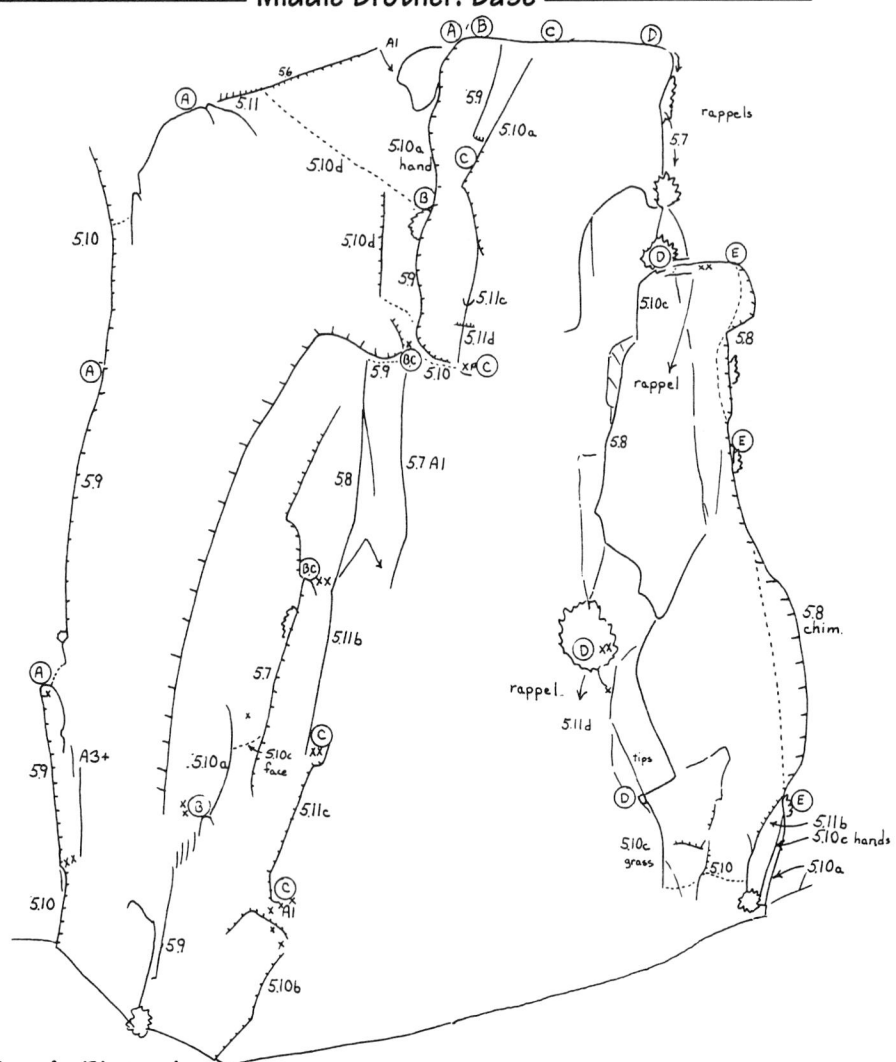

Rixon's Pinnacle

Approach: From a point 0.4 mile west of the gas station, leave the road and hike directly up to meet the cliff. **Photo** on page 130.

Descent: There are rappel anchors off the east side of the pinnacle. While two ropes are needed for most of the rappels, the first rappel is notorious for jamming and thus it is best to make it a short one.

Note: Massive rockfall has occurred in the Koko Ledge area, between Vantage Point and Rixon's Pinnacle, making this area extremely hazardous. The climbing routes in the area if they still exist have been omitted from this guide. Rixon's Pinnacle has experienced major, albeit less frequent, rockfall as well, so discretion and caution are advised here, too.

A. **Far West** 5.11 A1 Pro: To 3".
B. **West Face** 5.10c★★ Pro: To 3".
C. **Direct South Face** 5.11d A1★ Pro: To 3".
D. **South Face** 5.11d
E. **East Chimney** 5.10a★
   Klemens Variation 5.10c
   Final Decision 5.11b

The Folly

Approach: From a point 0.4 mile west of the gas station, leave the road and hike directly up to meet the cliff. Continue hiking up and right along the wall to the following routes.

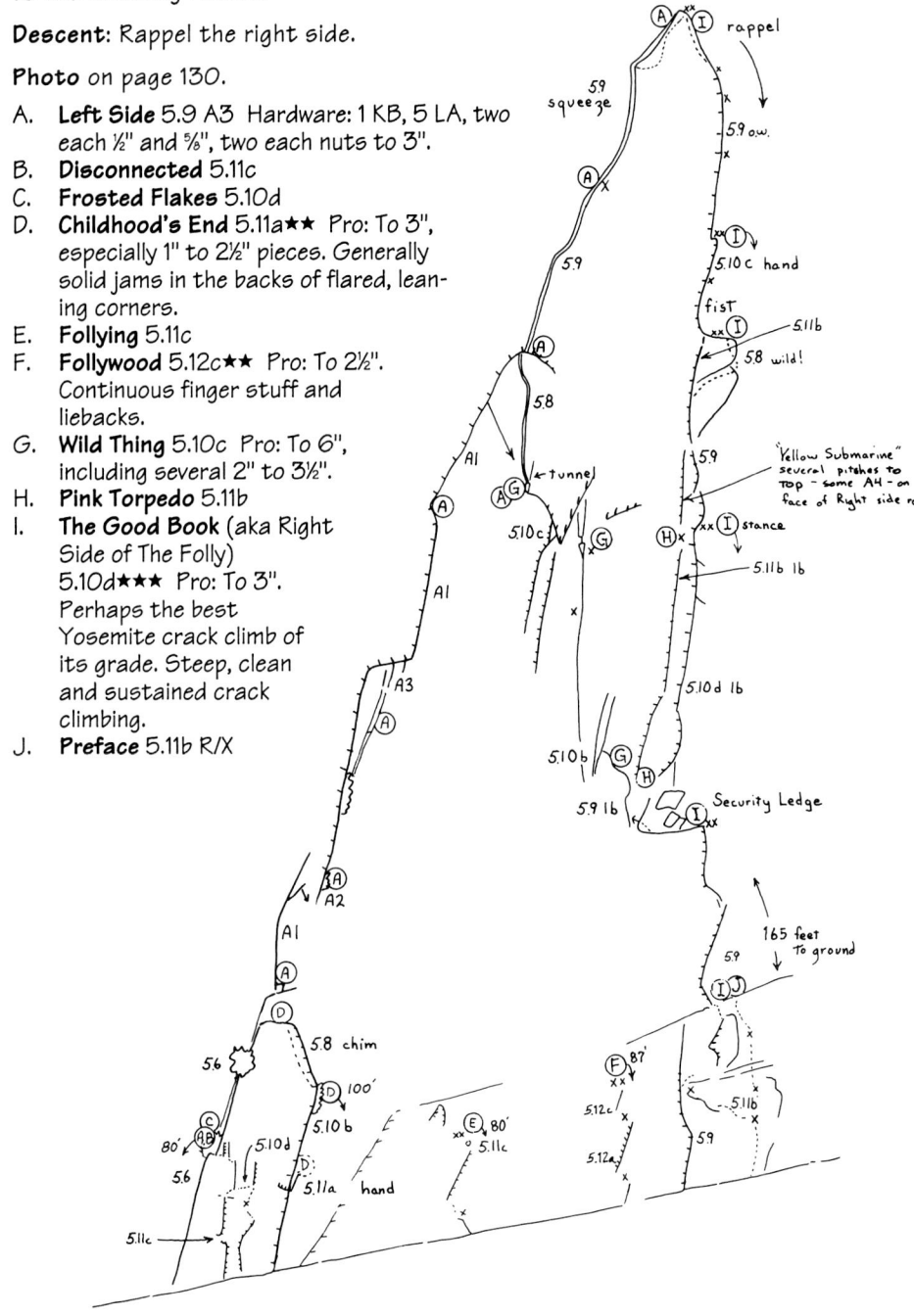

Descent: Rappel the right side.

Photo on page 130.

- A. **Left Side** 5.9 A3 Hardware: 1 KB, 5 LA, two each ½" and ⅝", two each nuts to 3".
- B. **Disconnected** 5.11c
- C. **Frosted Flakes** 5.10d
- D. **Childhood's End** 5.11a★★ Pro: To 3", especially 1" to 2½" pieces. Generally solid jams in the backs of flared, leaning corners.
- E. **Follying** 5.11c
- F. **Follywood** 5.12c★★ Pro: To 2½". Continuous finger stuff and liebacks.
- G. **Wild Thing** 5.10c Pro: To 6", including several 2" to 3½".
- H. **Pink Torpedo** 5.11b
- I. **The Good Book** (aka Right Side of The Folly) 5.10d★★★ Pro: To 3". Perhaps the best Yosemite crack climb of its grade. Steep, clean and sustained crack climbing.
- J. **Preface** 5.11b R/X

Camp 4 Wall, Far Left

Approach: These routes lie along the wall to the right of The Folly. For **Space Doubt** and routes to the right, it is easiest to hike up the streambed that meets the west end of Camp 4.

- A. **Chicken's Choice** 5.10b
- B. **Young and the Restless** 5.10c
- C. **Cost of Living** 5.10c
- D. **Space Doubt** 5.10c

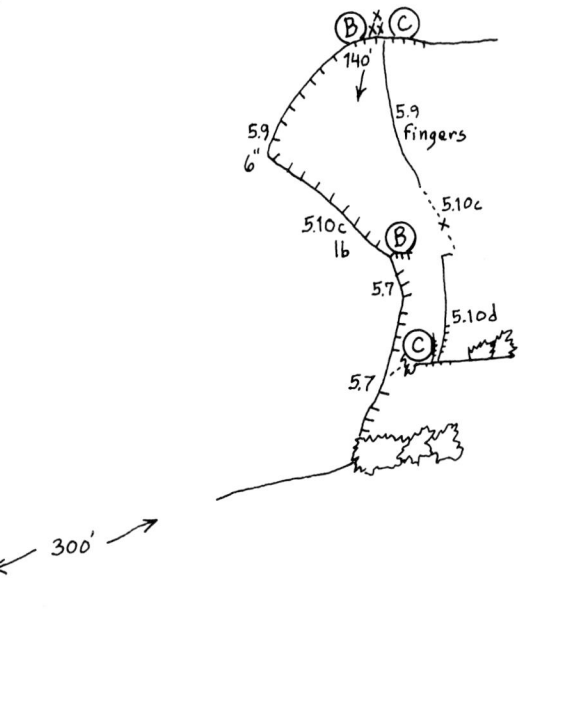

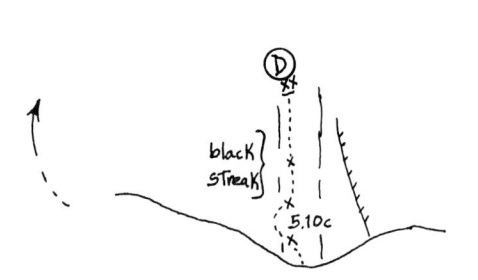

Middle Brother: Base

- E. **Santa Barbara** 5.10d Pro: To 1½".
- F. **General Hospital** 5.11c R Pro: Tiny to 3".
- G. **Chopper** 5.10c ★ Pro: To 5".
- H. **No Love-Chump Sucker** 5.11c
- I. **Days of our Lives** 5.11a Formerly One Life to Live.
- J. **Sample the Dog** 5.12a
- K. **Edge of Night** 5.10c ★ Pro: To 4".
- L. **Secret Storm** 5.10a ★ Pro: To 3".
- M. **Out on a Limb** 5.11b
- N. **Tweedle Dee** 5.8

Camp 4 Wall

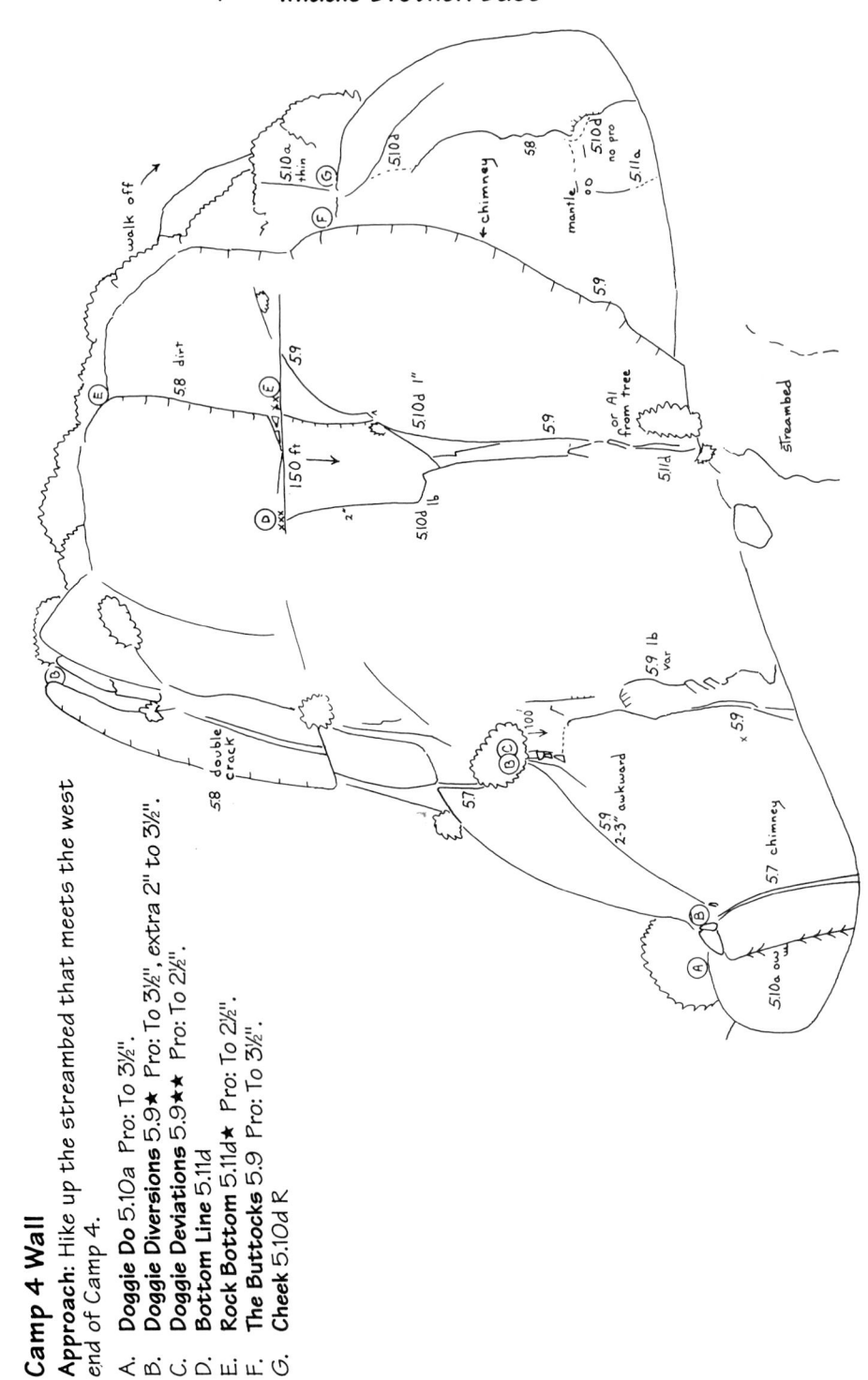

Approach: Hike up the streambed that meets the west end of Camp 4.

A. **Doggie Do** 5.10a Pro: To 3½".
B. **Doggie Diversions** 5.9★ Pro: To 3½", extra 2" to 3½".
C. **Doggie Deviations** 5.9★★ Pro: To 2½".
D. **Bottom Line** 5.11d
E. **Rock Bottom** 5.11d★ Pro: To 2½".
F. **The Buttocks** 5.9 Pro: To 3½".
G. **Cheek** 5.10d R

Camp 4 Wall

Approach: Hike up the streambed that meets the west end of Camp 4.

A. **Cristina** 5.11b Pro: To 3½".
B. **Henley Quits** 5.10a★★ Pro: To 3½".
C. **Cid's Embrace** 5.8★ (Star rating for first 60ft. only.)
D. **Lancelot** 5.9★ Pro: To 3½" including extra 3".
E. **Dynamo Hum** 5.11d★ Pro: Many small to 1¾".

Middle Brother: Base

Camp 4 Wall

Approach: Hike the streambed that meets the west end of Camp 4. **Gillette** is passed enroute. At the top of the talus a 3rd class ledge system leads up and left, past **Apple Seeds**, up to the wooded terrace of Camp Four Tree and the base of **Fallout**.

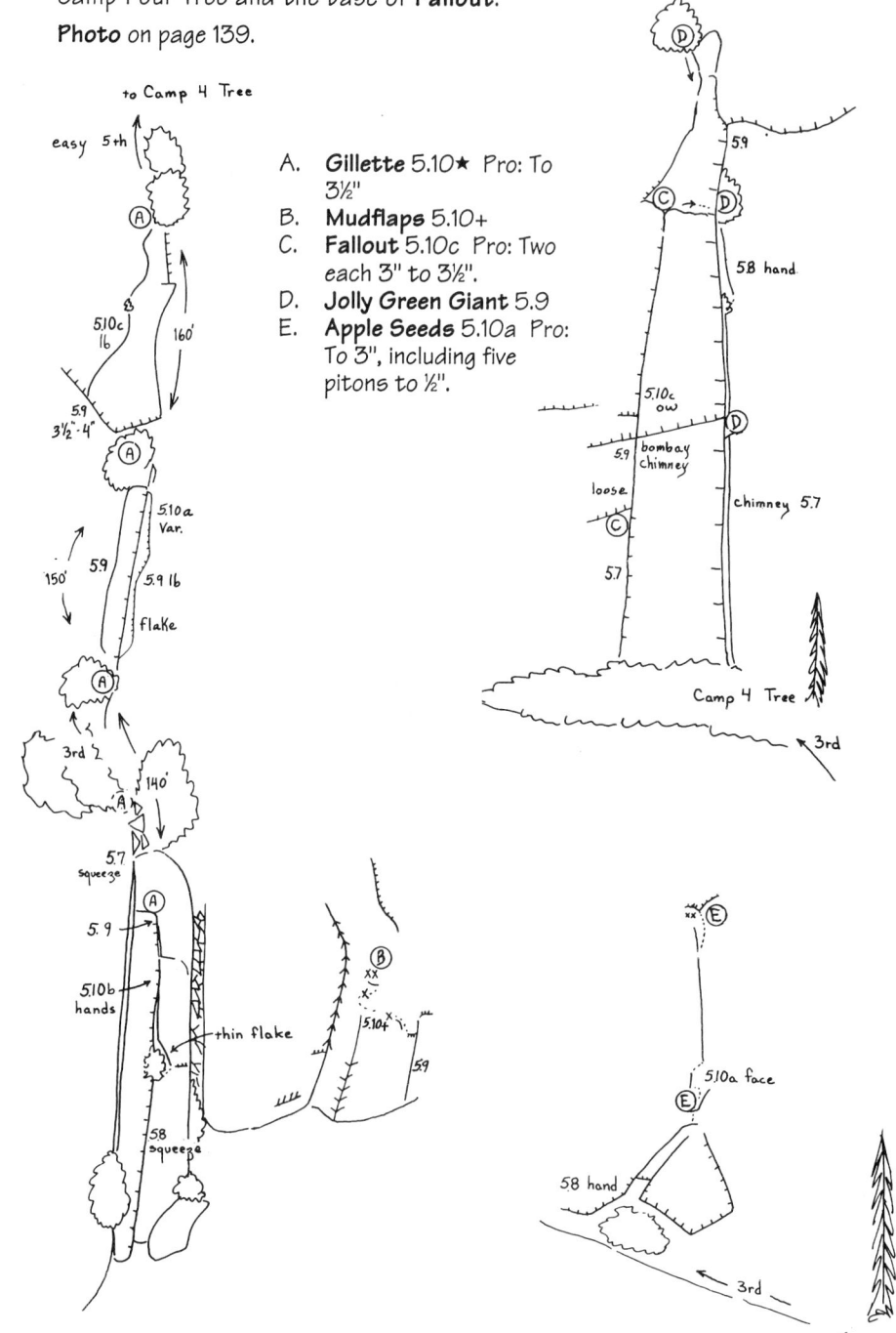

Photo on page 139.

A. **Gillette** 5.10★ Pro: To 3½"
B. **Mudflaps** 5.10+
C. **Fallout** 5.10c Pro: Two each 3" to 3½".
D. **Jolly Green Giant** 5.9
E. **Apple Seeds** 5.10a Pro: To 3", including five pitons to ½".

Camp 4 Wall and Columbia Point Area

1. Apple Seeds 5.10a
2. Sunday Tree 5.6
3. Stay Free 5.11b
4. THE GIRL NEXT DOOR
5. Joe Palmer 5.11b
6. Montgomery Cliff
7. The Right Profiile
8. Psychopath 5.9

Upper Yosemite Falls Trail: West

Montgomery Cliff and Yosemite Falls Trail West

Approach: These climbs all depart from the Upper Yosemite Falls Trail in the vicinity of Columbia Point, the first overlook encountered. For **Stay Free**, leave the trail just after the shady area and diagonal up and left via sandy slopes. No 3rd class is encountered until the end. For **The Girl Next Door**, hike to the second sandy switchback above Columbia Point, go up a dirt slope about 100 feet, then contour around left to the base of the cliff. **Joe Palmer** is approached from a switchback below the Point. The route is about 150 feet to the left. **Montgomery Cliff** is a short yellow wall approached several switchbacks before Columbia Point.

Photo on page 139.

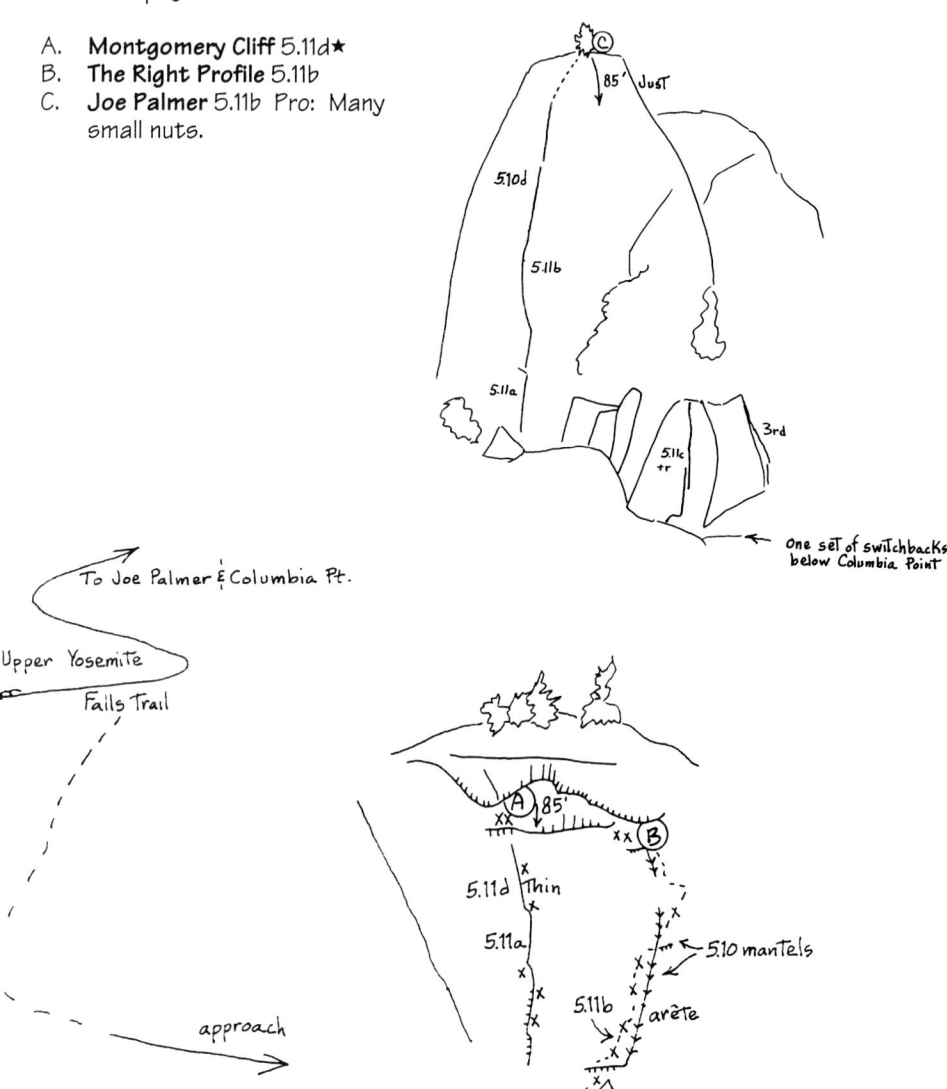

- A. **Montgomery Cliff** 5.11d ★
- B. **The Right Profile** 5.11b
- C. **Joe Palmer** 5.11b Pro: Many small nuts.

Upper Yosemite Falls Trail: West

D. **Stay Free** 5.11b★ Pro: Wires, two each Friends to #3, one each #3.5 to #5.

The Girl Next Door

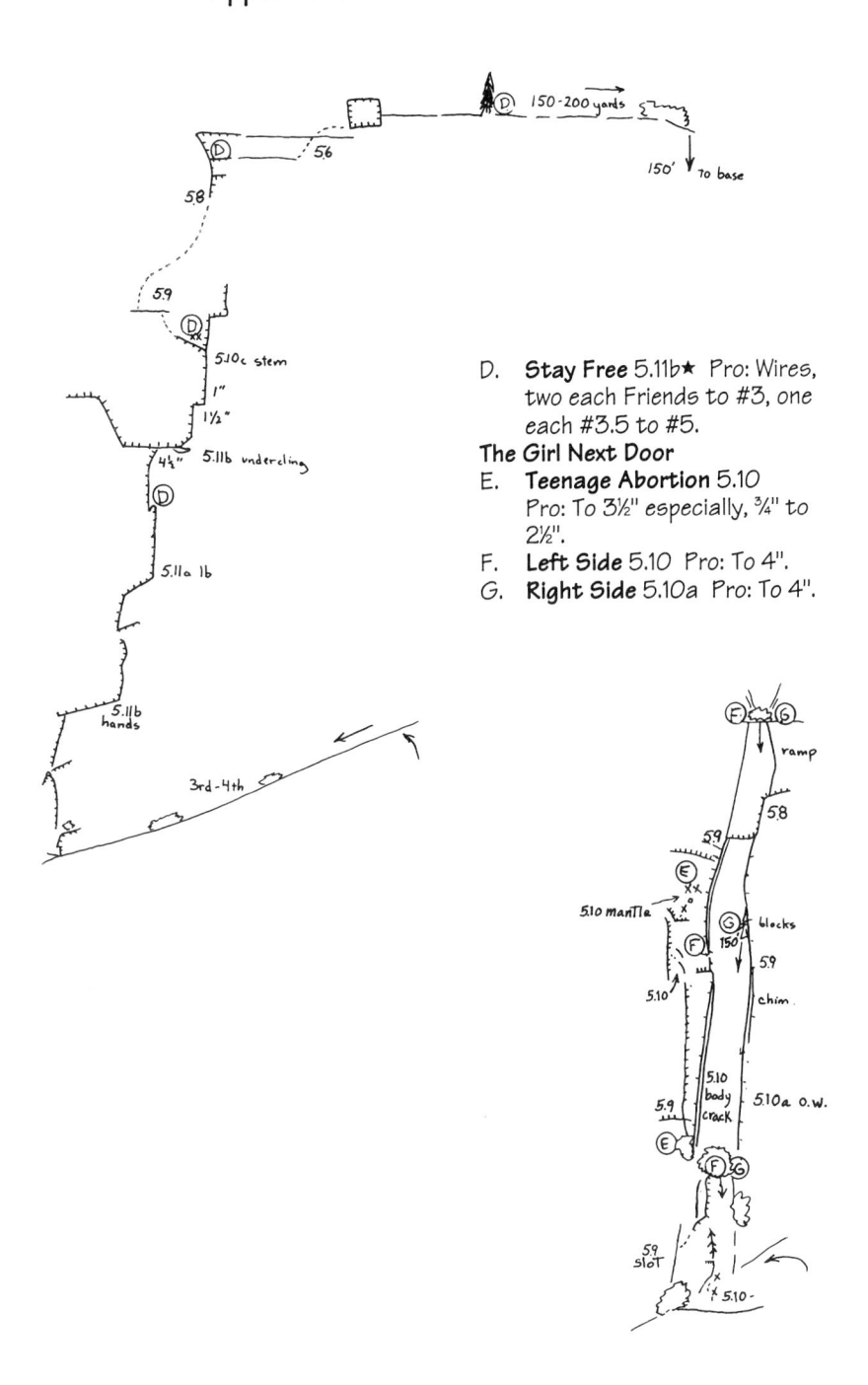

E. **Teenage Abortion** 5.10 Pro: To 3½" especially, ¾" to 2½".
F. **Left Side** 5.10 Pro: To 4".
G. **Right Side** 5.10a Pro: To 4".

Note: In an effort to abide with Park Service concerns over environmental impacts and hikers' safety, numerous climbs adjacent to Upper Yosemite Falls and its trail system have been omitted from this guide.

YOSEMITE FALLS

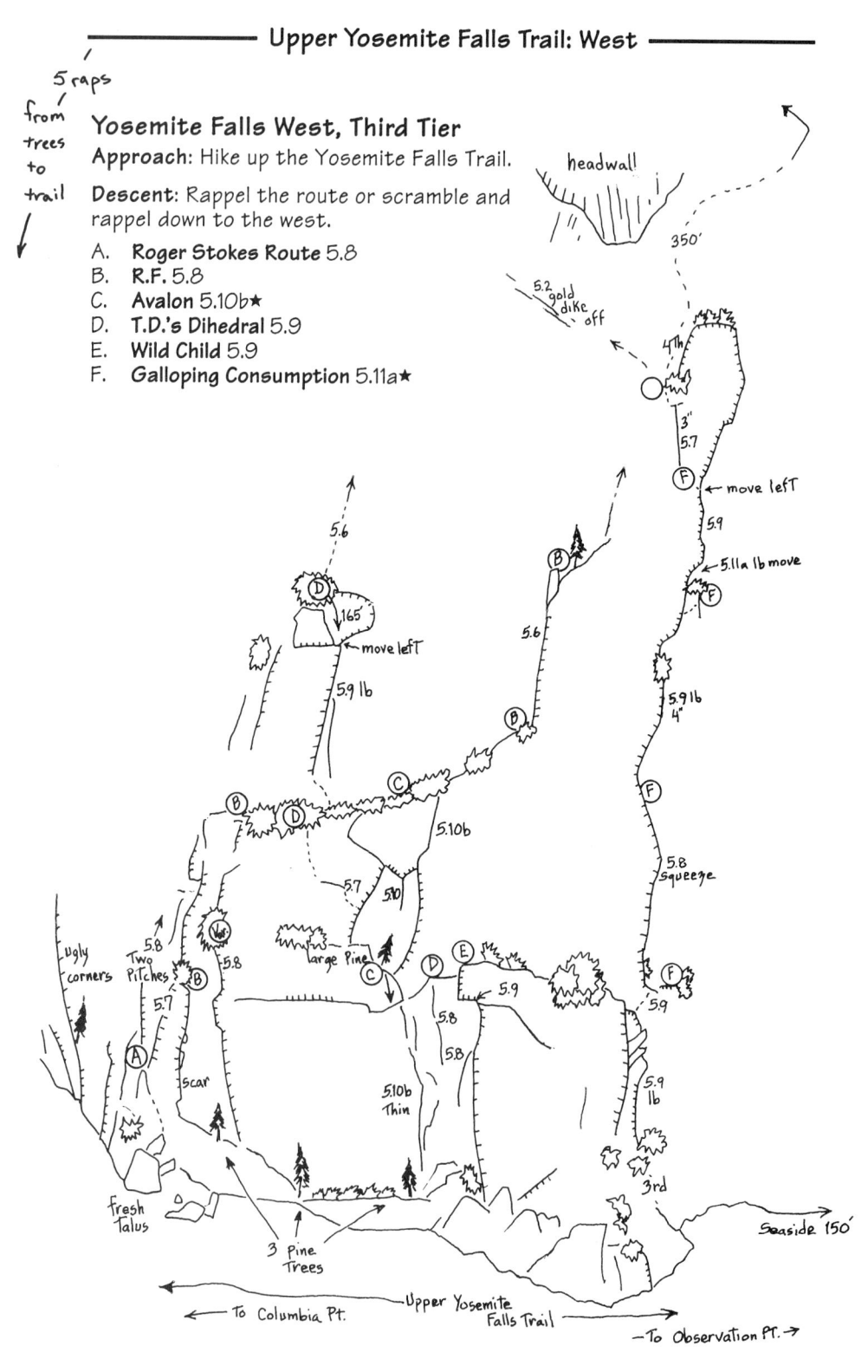

Upper Yosemite Falls Trail: West

Yosemite Falls West, Third Tier

Approach: Hike up the Yosemite Falls Trail.

Descent: Rappel the route or scramble and rappel down to the west.

- A. **Roger Stokes Route** 5.8
- B. **R.F.** 5.8
- C. **Avalon** 5.10b ★
- D. **T.D.'s Dihedral** 5.9
- E. **Wild Child** 5.9
- F. **Galloping Consumption** 5.11a ★

Upper Yosemite Falls Trail: West

Upper Yosemite Falls Trail
G. **Seaside** 5.10c★ Pro: Including two each ⅛" to ¾".
H. **Mindahoonee Wall** 5.11a★★ Pro: Including two each #1-#2 Friends, one each #2.5-#4 Friends and #4 Camalot.

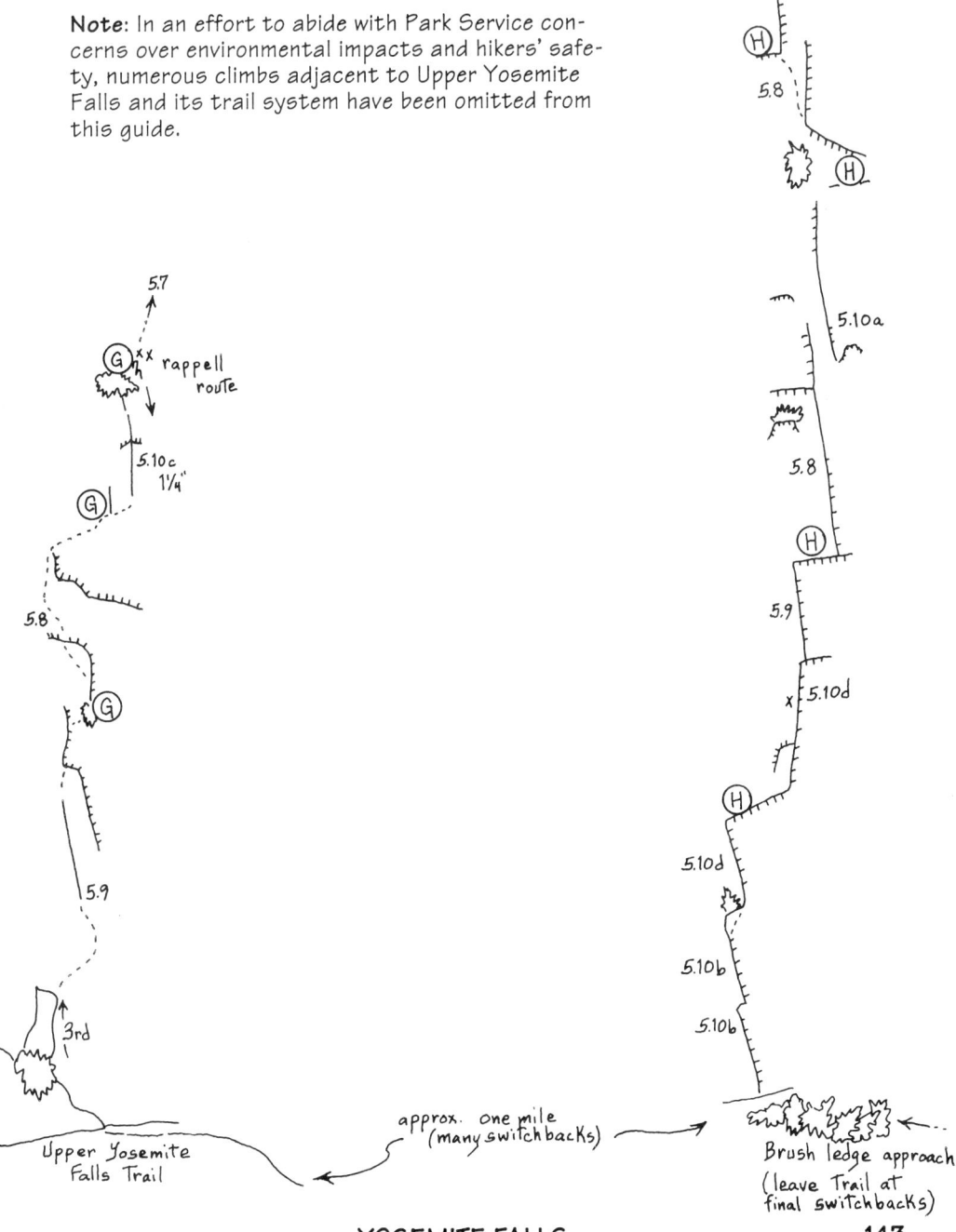

Note: In an effort to abide with Park Service concerns over environmental impacts and hikers' safety, numerous climbs adjacent to Upper Yosemite Falls and its trail system have been omitted from this guide.

back to Trail →

fingers 5.11a

5.8

5.10a

5.8

5.9

5.10d

5.10d

5.10b

5.10b

Brush ledge approach (leave Trail at final switchbacks)

5.7
rappell route
5.10c 1¼"
5.8
5.9
3rd
Upper Yosemite Falls Trail
approx. one mile (many switchbacks) →

YOSEMITE FALLS — 143

Yosemite Falls Area

1. Munginella 5.6
2. Selaginella 5.8
3. Observation Point 5.9
4. Galloping Consumption 5.11a
5. Seaside 5.10c

Yosemite Falls Area

National Park Service photo

1. Mindahoonee Wall 5.11a
2. Sunnyside Bench Regular Route 5.0
3. Sunnyside Bench Lieback Route
4. Yosemite Point Buttress 5.9
5. Slingshot 5.12a
6. Pygmy Pillar 5.7
7. Arrowhead Arete 5.8
8. East Arrowhead Chimney 5.10d

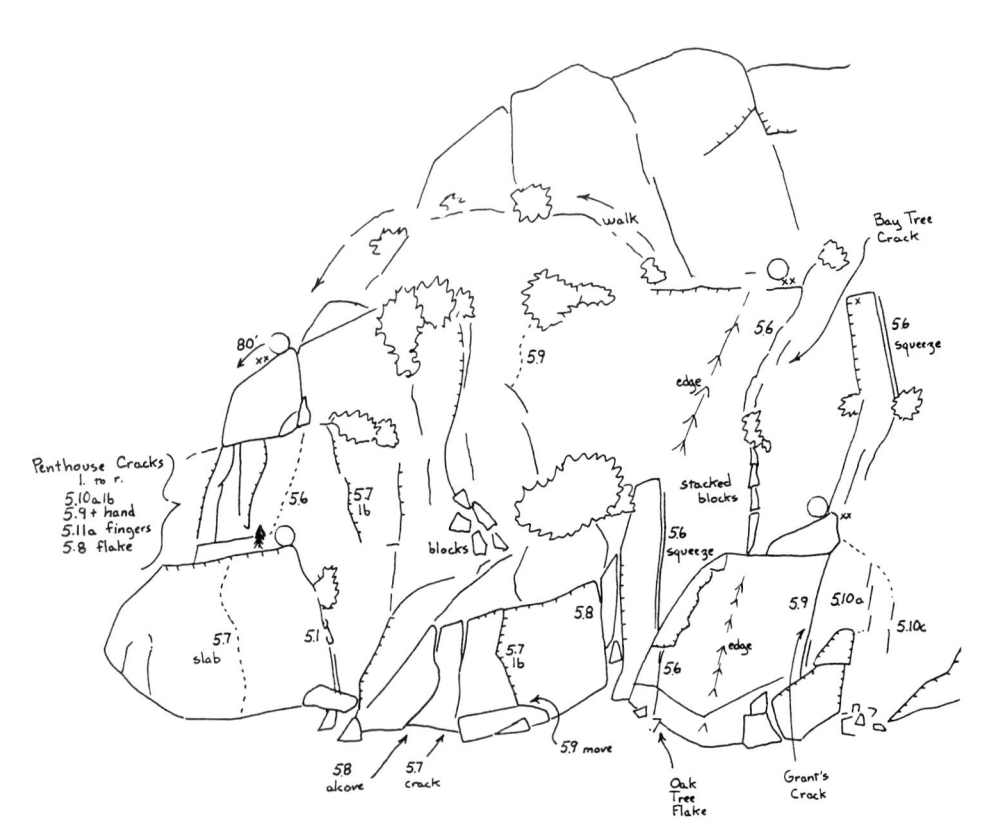

Swan Slab

Approach: This cliff is located directly across the main road from Yosemite Lodge and offers bouldering and moderate free climbs on the complicated left side, with clean and more difficult routes on the main slab itself.

Descent: Routes that lead to the top of the cliff can be walked off in either direction.

Photo on page 144.

- A. **Kokl Duck** 5.11a
- B. **Aid Route** 5.11b★
- C. **Ugly Duckling** 5.10c★ R
- D. **Lena's Lieback** 5.9★
- E. **Goat For It** 5.10a
- F. **Claude's Delight** 5.7★

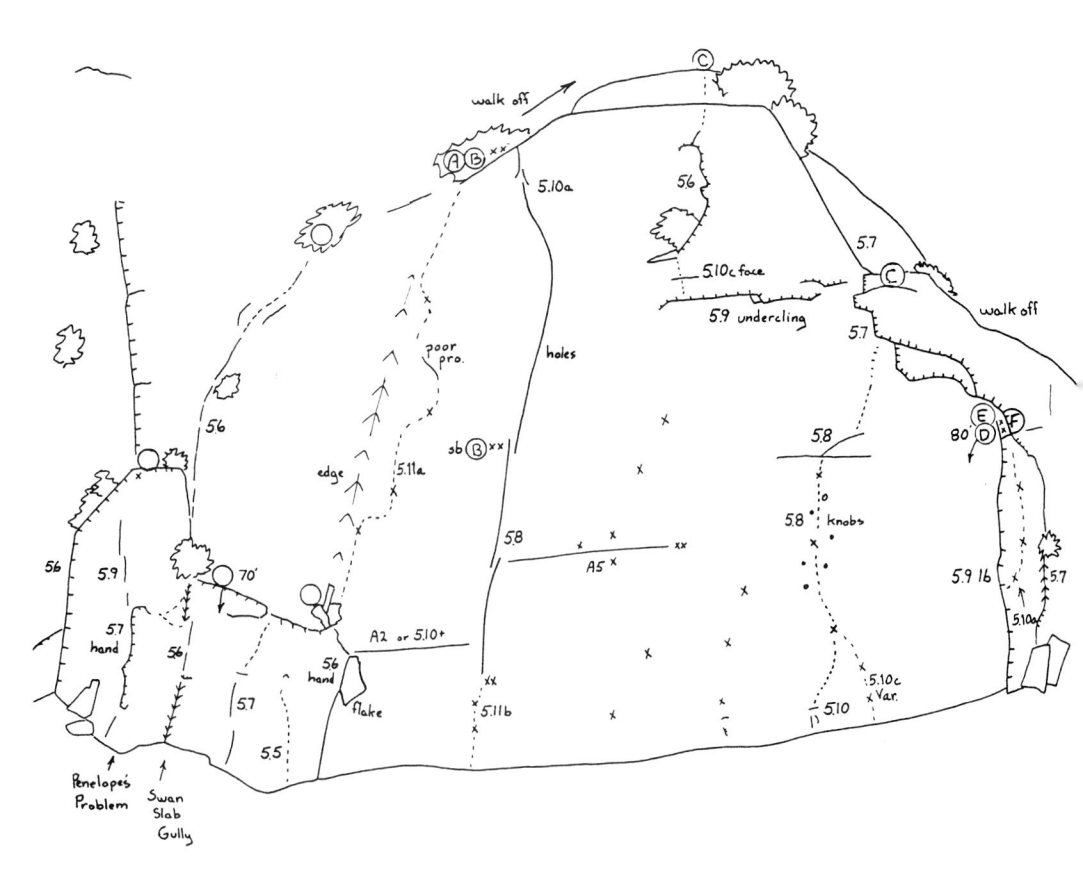

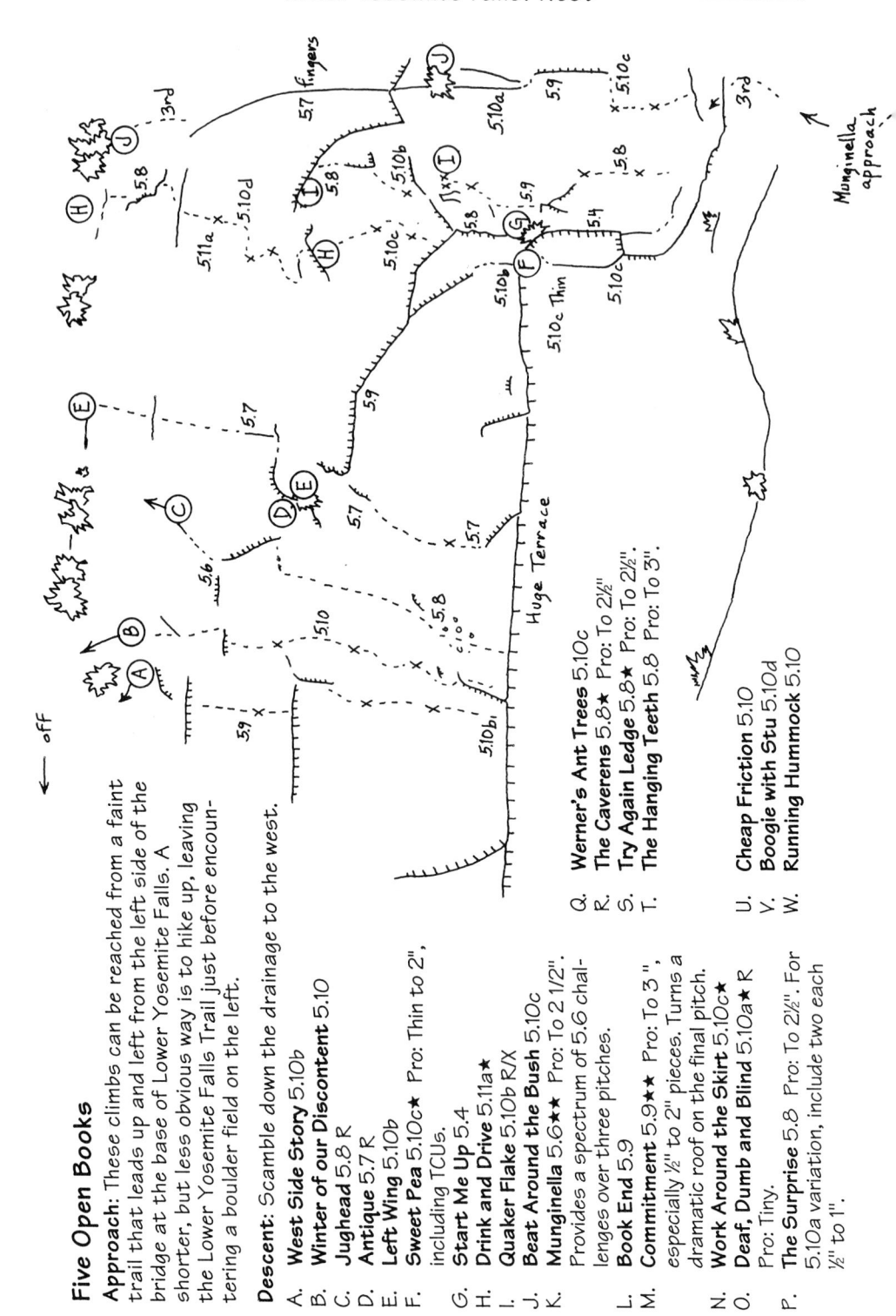

Five Open Books

Approach: These climbs can be reached from a faint trail that leads up and left from the left side of the bridge at the base of Lower Yosemite Falls. A shorter, but less obvious way is to hike up, leaving the Lower Yosemite Falls Trail just before encountering a boulder field on the left.

Descent: Scamble down the drainage to the west.

A. **West Side Story** 5.10b
B. **Winter of our Discontent** 5.10
C. **Jughead** 5.8 R
D. **Antique** 5.7 R
E. **Left Wing** 5.10b
F. **Sweet Pea** 5.10c★ Pro: Thin to 2", including TCUs.
G. **Start Me Up** 5.4
H. **Drink and Drive** 5.11a★
I. **Quaker Flake** 5.10b R/X
J. **Beat Around the Bush** 5.10c
K. **Munginella** 5.6★★ Pro: To 2 1/2". Provides a spectrum of 5.6 challenges over three pitches.
L. **Book End** 5.9
M. **Commitment** 5.9★★ Pro: To 3 ", especially 1/2" to 2" pieces. Turns a dramatic roof on the final pitch.
N. **Work Around the Skirt** 5.10c★
O. **Deaf, Dumb and Blind** 5.10a★ R Pro: Tiny.
P. **The Surprise** 5.8 Pro: To 2½". For 5.10a variation, include two each ½" to 1".
Q. **Werner's Ant Trees** 5.10c
R. **The Caverens** 5.8★ Pro: To 2½"
S. **Try Again Ledge** 5.8★ Pro: To 2½".
T. **The Hanging Teeth** 5.8 Pro: To 3".
U. **Cheap Friction** 5.10
V. **Boogie with Stu** 5.10d
W. **Running Hummock** 5.10

Lower Yosemite Falls: West

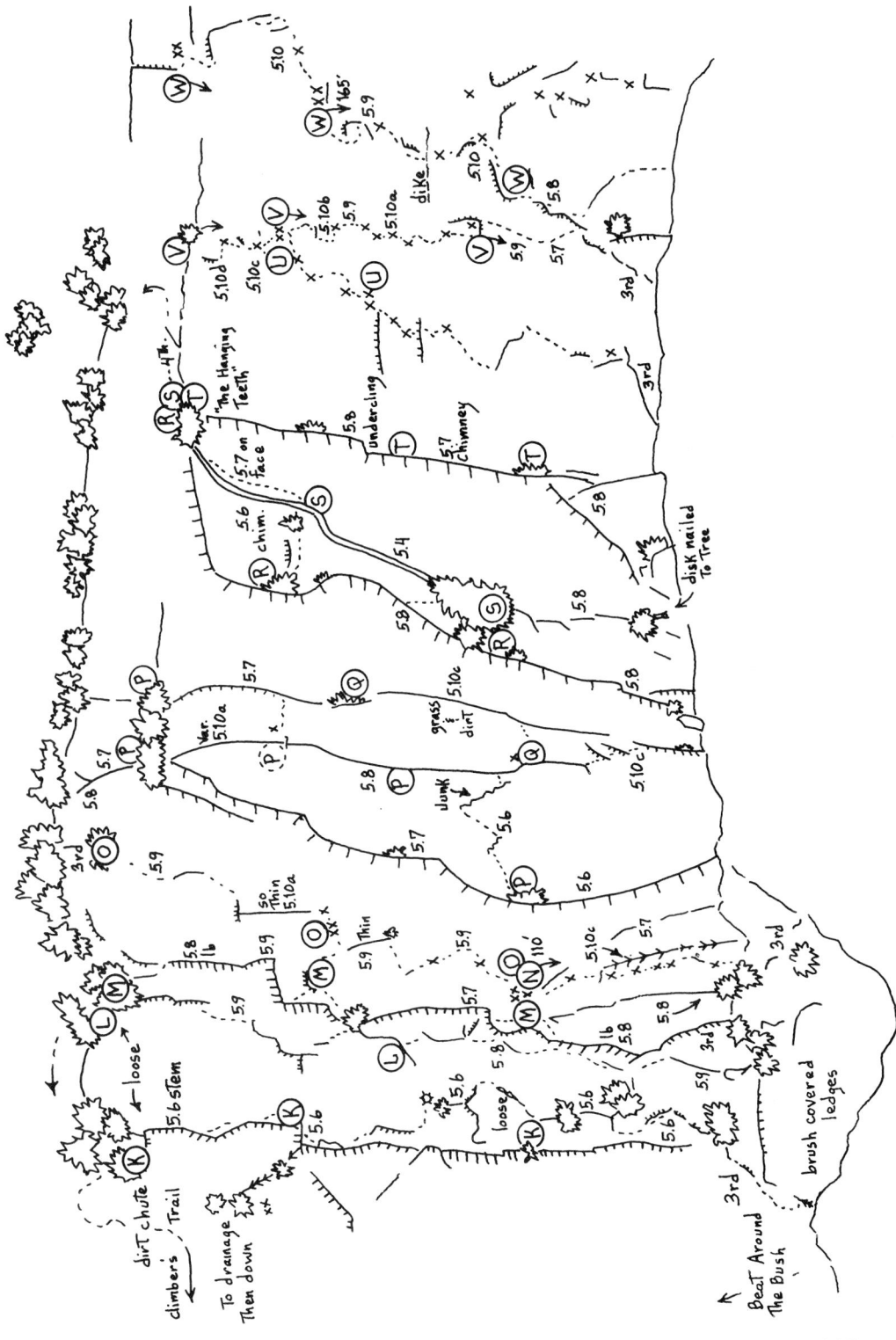

YOSEMITE FALLS — 149

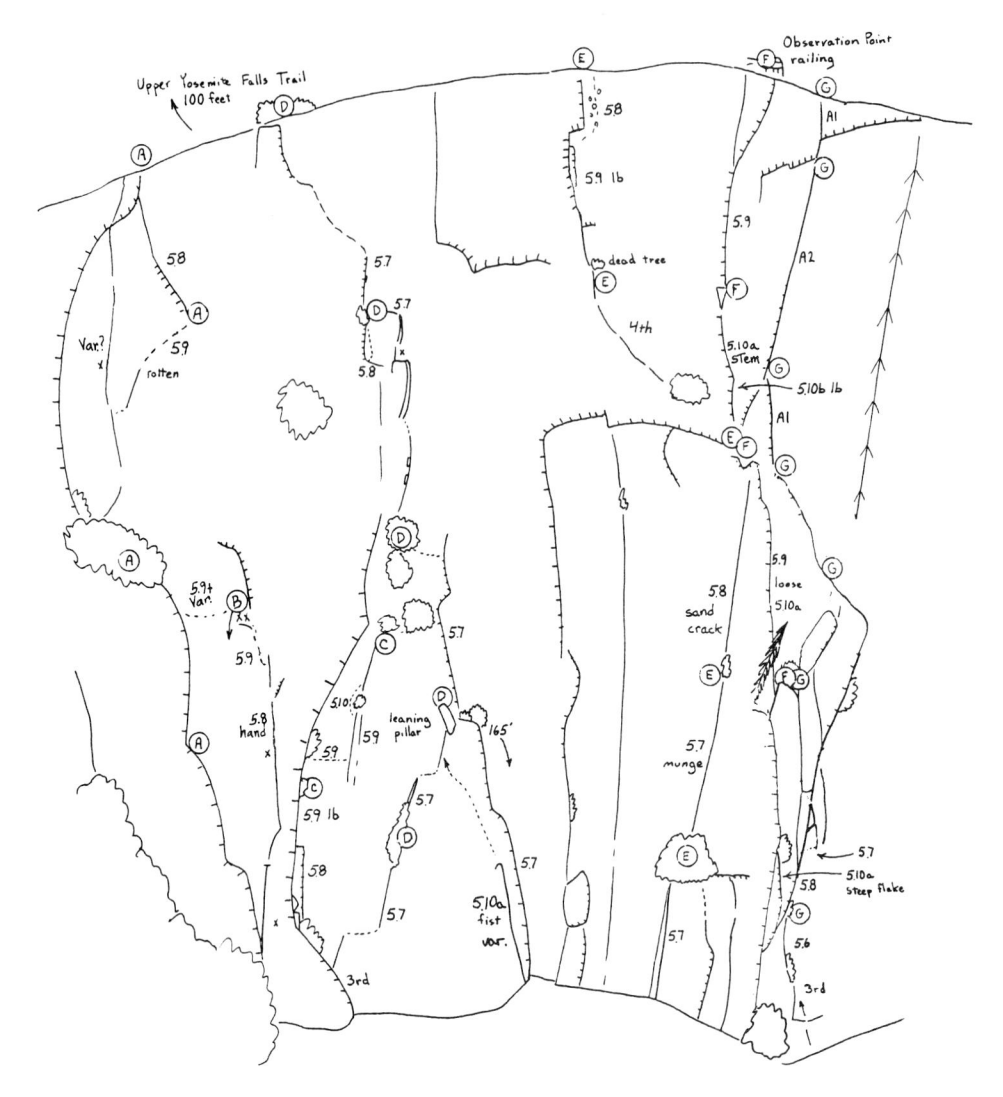

Yosemite Falls, Second Tier

Approach: Climb one of the Five Open Books or ascend the drainage gully just to the west.

Descent: Walk down the Yosemite Falls Trail.

A. **Bacchigaloupe Wall** 5.9
B. **Handshake** 5.9
C. **Marvin Gardens** 5.10
D. **Selaginella** 5.8
E. **Observation Point** 5.9
F. **Indica Point** 5.10b
G. **Mischief** 5.8 A2

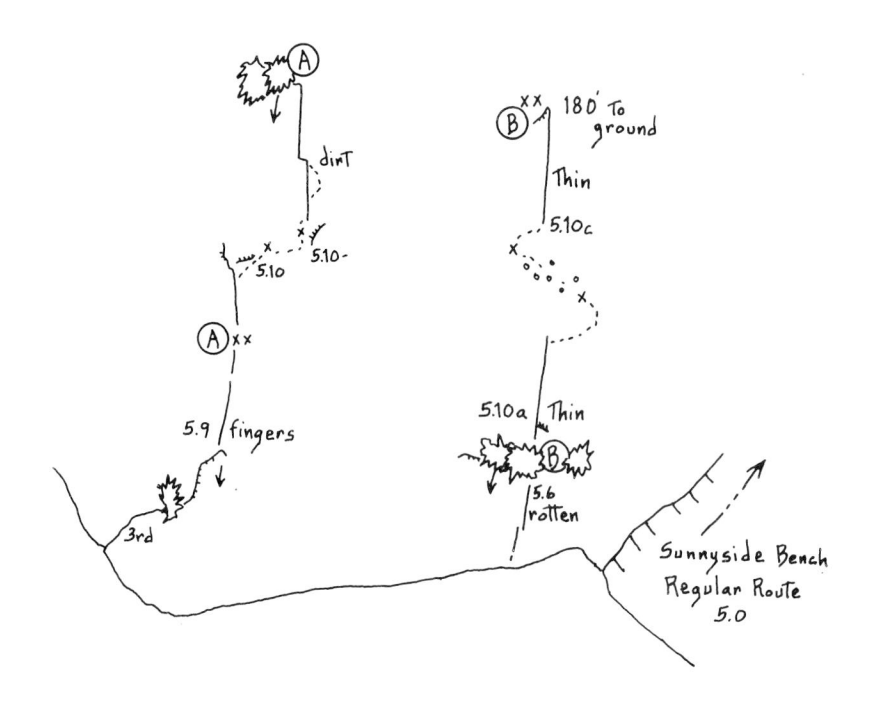

Sunnyside Bench, Far Left
Note: In an effort to abide with Park Service concerns over environmental impacts, routes within the aesthetically scenic Lower Yosemite Falls Amphitheater have been omitted from this guide.
A. **Armed & Dangerous** 5.10-
B. **Moe, Larry, The Cheese** 5.10c Pro: Brass nuts to #2.5 Friend, including TCUs.

Lower Yosemite Falls: East

Sunnyside Bench

A. **Butthole Climbers** 5.10c
B. **Sultans of Sling** 5.10c
C. **Stretch Mark** 5.11b Pro: Brass nuts to #2 Friend.
D. **Raisin** 5.9★ R
E. **Clan of the Big Hair** 5.11c
F. **Mud Flats** 5.11d R
G. **Prune** 5.10a★ R
H. **Fully B.S. or a Tree** 5.11
I. **Lingering Lie** 5.10d R
J. **Lemon** 5.9+
K. **Bench Warmer** 5.10d
L. **Bummer** 5.10c★ Pro: To 2", especially tiny to 1" pieces. A frustrating move gains a small crystal hole. A little spooky to clip the bolt on the second pitch and somewhat vegged.
M. **Lazy Bum** 5.10d★★ Pro: To 2", especially tiny to 1" pieces. Most parties do only the first pitch, which thins and forces moves out left to a distant edge.
N. **Jamcrack Route** 5.9★★ Pro: To 2". Both pitches yield excellent straight-in finger and hand jamming.
O. **To Beer or Not to Be** 5.10
P. **Sunnyside Pinnacle** 5.10
Q. **Lieback Route** 5.8
R. **Blackballed** 5.10b★
S. **Dwindling Stances** 5.10c
T. **Combustible Knowledge** 5.10d★

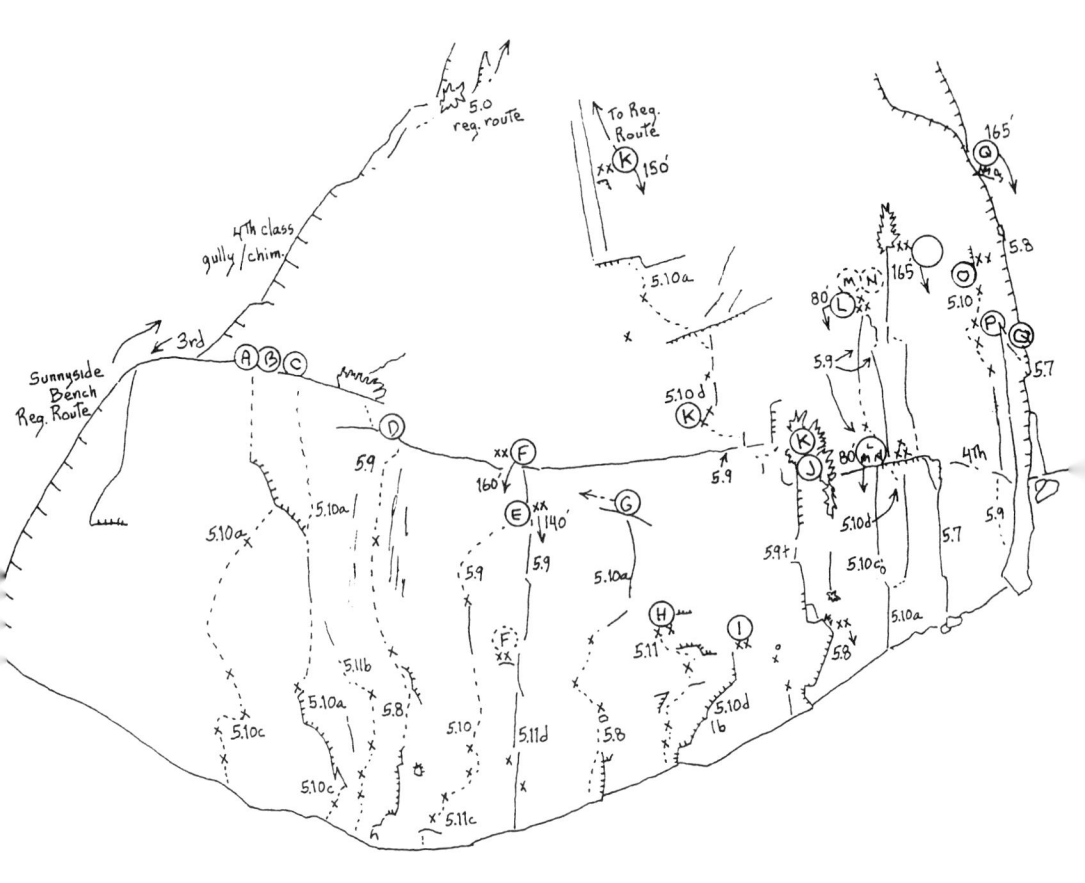

Lower Yosemite Falls: East

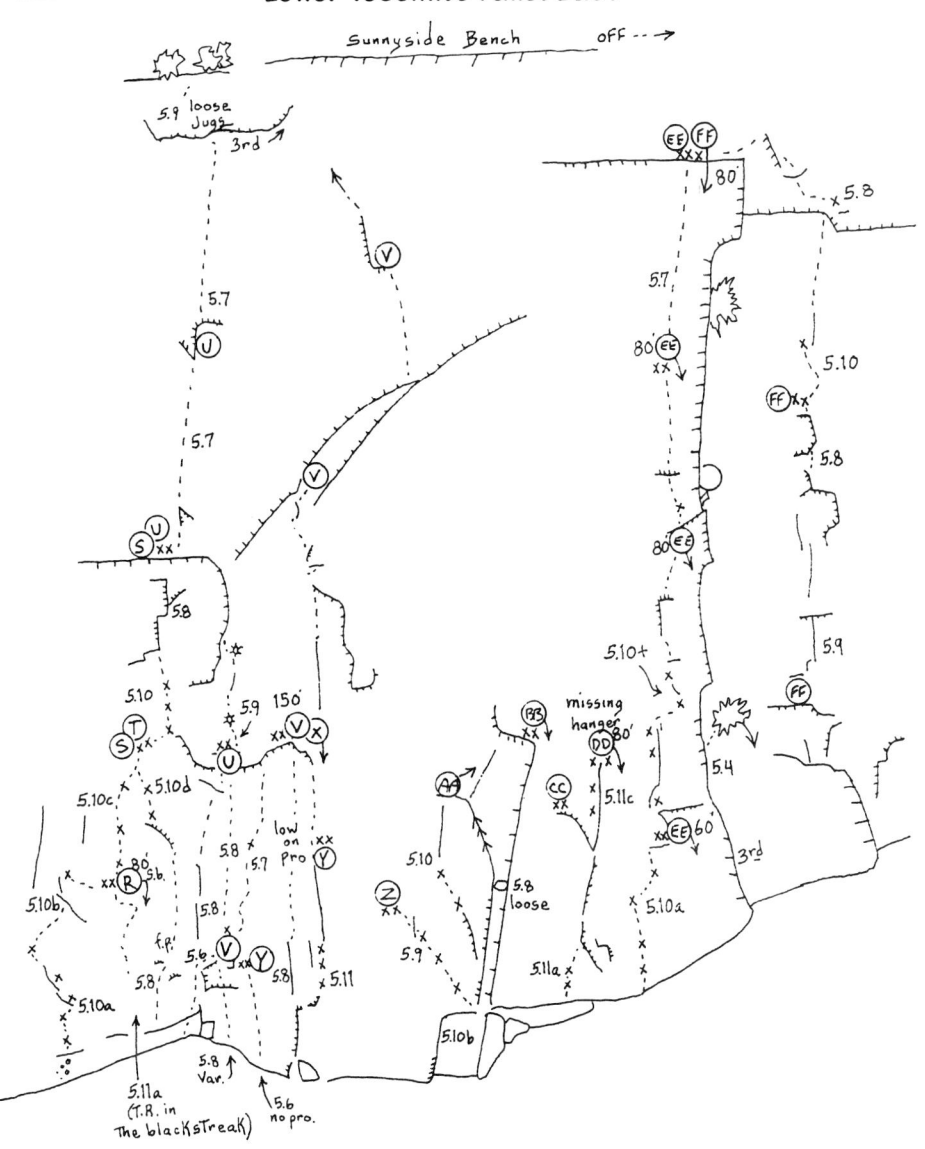

- U. **Ribald** 5.9
- V. **Tiny Tim** 5.7★ X
- W. **Guides Route** 5.6 R/X
- X. **Groove Route** 5.8 R/X
- Y. **Mothballed** 5.11
- Z. **Blueballed** 5.10b★ Pro: Small wires to #1½ Friend.
- AA. **Defoliation** 5.10
- BB. **Scrooged** 5.8
- CC. **Redtide** 5.10+
- DD. **Tidal Wave** 5.11c Pro: To 2½", including TCUs.
- EE. **Fertile Attraction** 5.10+
- FF. **Vegetal Extraction** 5.10

Lower Yosemite Falls: East

Approach: From the government stables at the western end of Yosemite Village, walk uphill to meet the horse/foot path. A nearby open talus slope with yellow "Dangerous to Scramble" signs indicates the start of the approach to Sunnyside Bench and the base of The Lost Arrow. The initial section of this approach is useful in reaching the following routes.

Photo on page 145.

- B. **Pygmy Pillar** 5.7
  Pro: To #3.5 Friend.
- C. **Stack o' Fun** 5.12b ★★
- D. **Crack a Brewski** 5.11d Pro: To 3".
- E. **Police and Thieves** 5.12b ★★
  Pro: #1 TCU for the bottom.

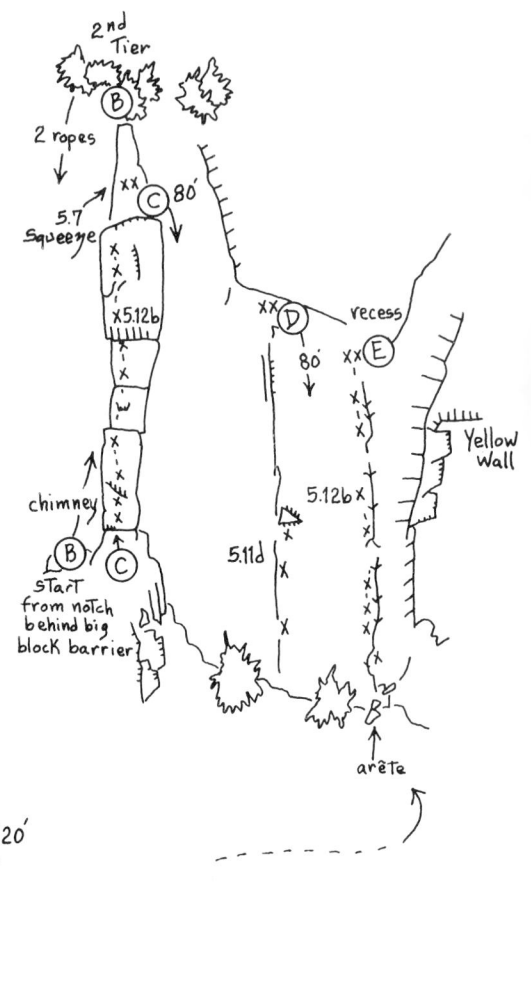

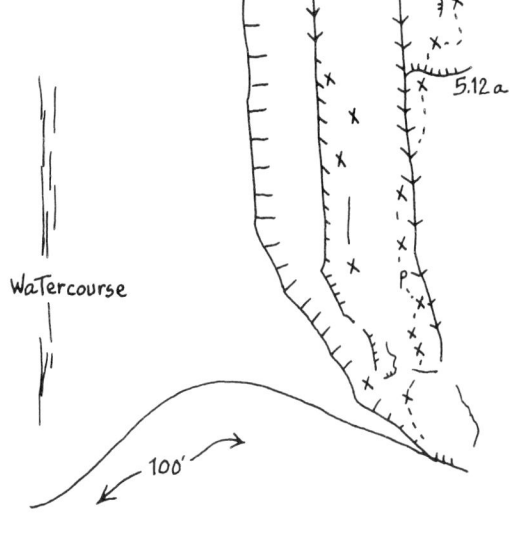

Sunnyside Bench, Far Right

Approach: From the government stables (western end of Yosemite Village) walk uphill to meet the horse/foot path. Continue uphill at sign marked "Government Stock Only."

- A. **Slingshot** 5.12a ★ Pro: Including #1 and #2 Friends.

Upper Yosemite Falls Area

1. Misty Wall V 5.11d A0
2. Lost Arrow Chimney 5.10a
3. Start of Yosemite Point Buttress Direct 5.9
4. Arrowhead Arête 5.8

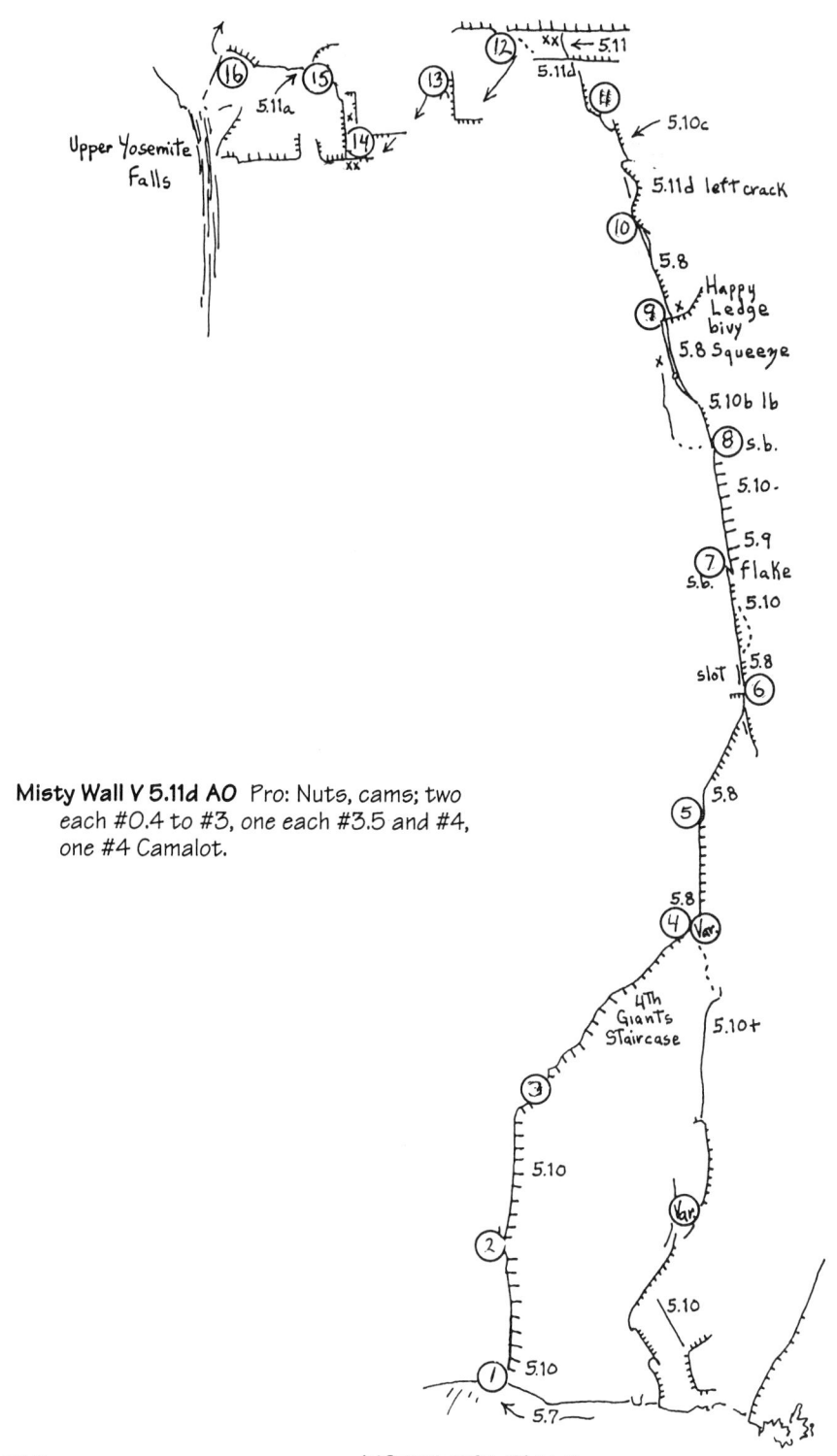

Upper Yosemite Falls: East

Upper Yosemite Falls

- 16
- 15 — 5.11a
- 14 (xx)
- 13
- 12 xx ← 5.11 / 5.11d
- 11 ← 5.10c
- 5.11d left crack
- 10
- 5.8
- 9 — Happy Ledge bivy
- 5.8 Squeeze
- 5.10b 1b
- 8 s.b.
- 5.10-
- 5.9
- 7 flake
- s.b.
- 5.10
- slot — 5.8
- 6
- 5.8
- 5
- 5.8
- 4 Var.
- 4Th Giants Staircase — 5.10+
- 3
- 5.10
- 2
- Var.
- 5.10
- 1 — 5.10
- ← 5.7 —

Misty Wall V 5.11d A0 Pro: Nuts, cams; two each #0.4 to #3, one each #3.5 and #4, one #4 Camalot.

156 — YOSEMITE FALLS

Upper Yosemite Falls: East

Geek Towers

Approach: To get to the base of Geek Towers, it is necessary to gain the top of Sunnyside Bench, the lowest and most prominent wooded tier right of Yosemite Falls. Either climb the Sunnyside Bench 5.0 route or a talus field directly behind the Park Service maintenance yard and fire station. At a point overlooking the lip of Lower Yosemite Falls, a tiny section of 3rd class begins a right-diagonalling wooded ramp. Class 3 friction off the ramp leads to the second tier. The final section involves a march through oak and manzanita, before sandy slopes lead to the base of the Lost Arrow and Geek Towers.

A. **Freestone** 5.11c★★★ Pro: To 5", including extra ⅛" to ¾", two each 2" to 4" pieces. Although shorter, some say this route is harder than Astroman. Stimulating location. Blowing water could be a factor on this route.

B. **Center Route** 5.10a Pro: To 3½".

C. **Right Side** 5.10a A2 Pro: To 3½", including dowel hangers.

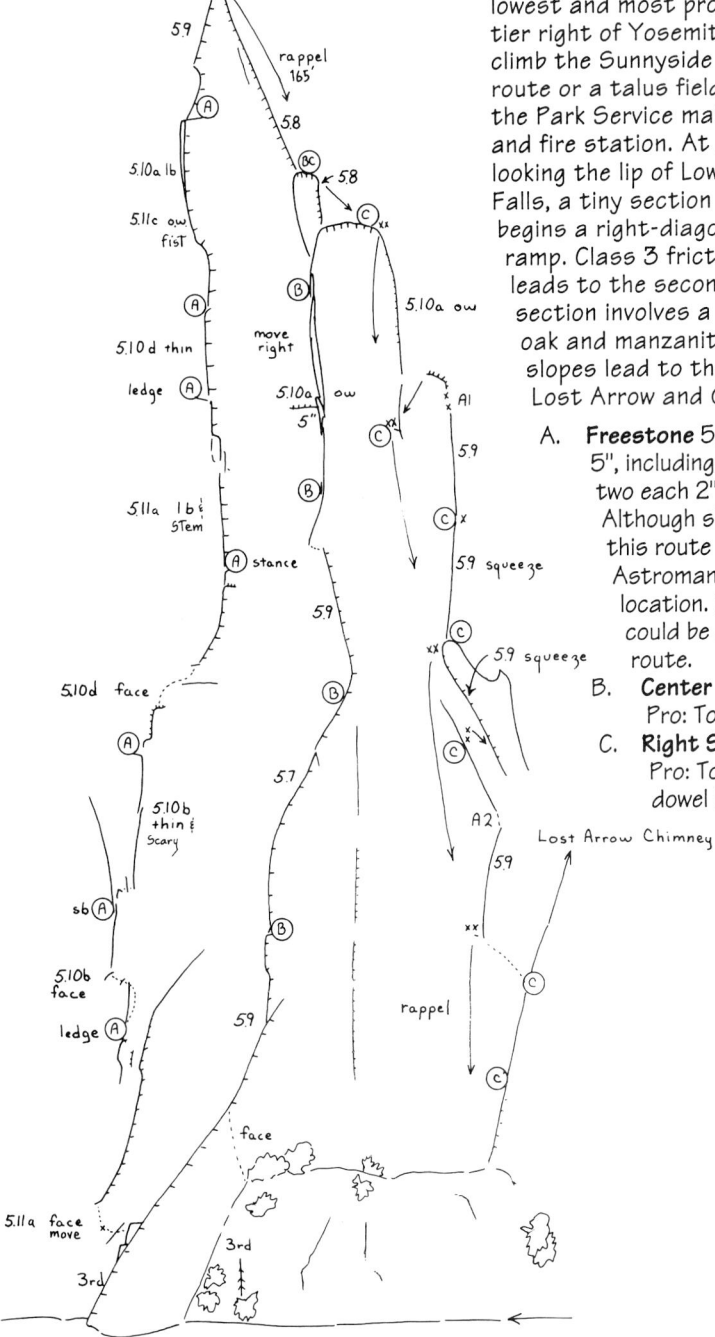

YOSEMITE FALLS

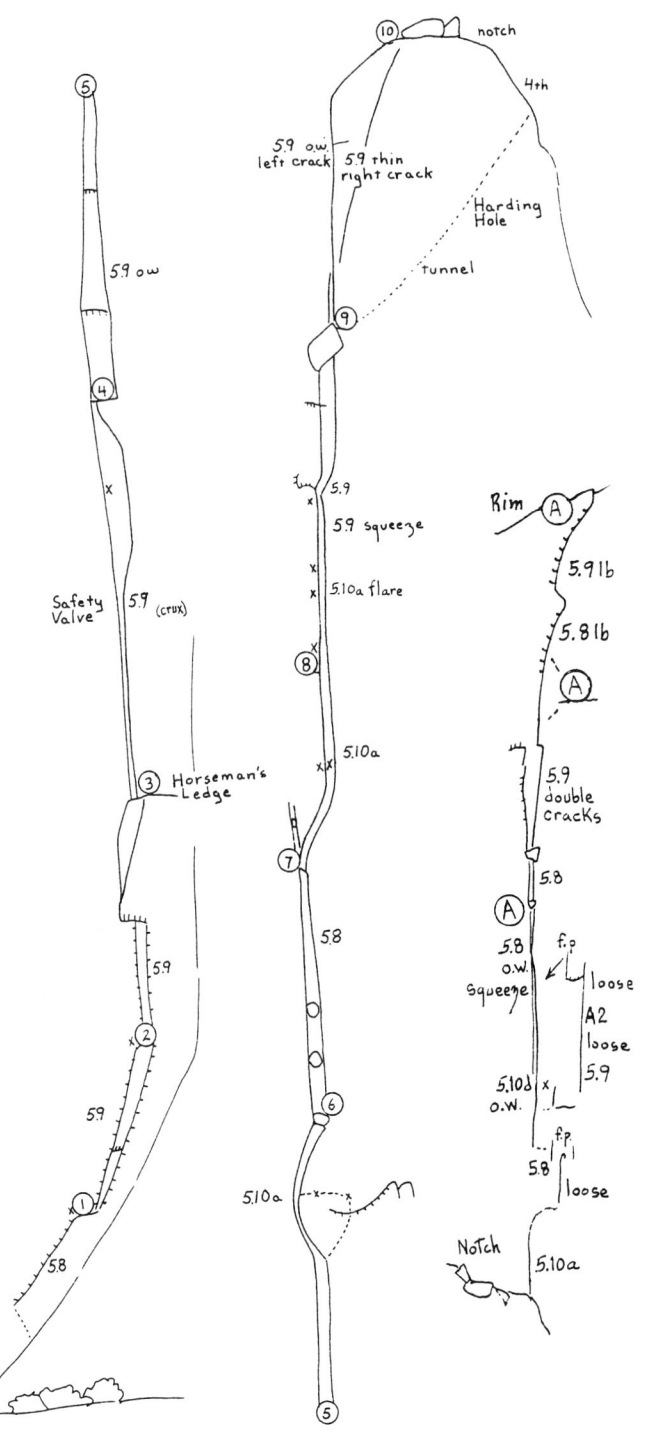

Upper Yosemite Falls: East

Lost Arrow Chimney

Approach: To get to the base of the upper wall it is necessary to gain the top of Sunnyside Bench, the lowest and most prominent wooded tier right of Yosemite Falls. Either climb the Sunnyside Bench 5.0 route or a talus field directly behind the Park Service maintenance yard and Fire Station. At a point overlooking the lip of Lower Yosemite Fall, a tiny section of 3rd class begins a right-diagonalling wooded ramp. Class 3 friction off the ramp leads to the second tier. The final section involves a march through oaks and manzanita before sandy slopes lead to the base of the Lost Arrow.

Descent: It is necessary to have previously fixed ropes from the rim to the Lost Arrow notch or be prepared for a two-pitch free or mixed climb out of the notch.

    Lost Arrow Chimney 5.10a Pro: To 3".
A. **Exit from the Notch** 5.10d or 5.10 A2

Allen Steck collection photo

Allen Steck on Yosemite Point Buttress, 1952

Upper Yosemite Falls: East

Lost Arrow Spire

Approach: This route starts by rappelling from the rim of the valley, near Yosemite Point, into the notch behind the spire. Two ropes need to be fixed for the return to the rim.

One method is to rappel the climbing route, then ascend the fixed ropes back to the rim. A two-bolt station will be found at the 150-foot interval.

The other method is a Tyrolean Traverse. Two "fix" ropes are joined, and one end is then anchored to the rim. This requires that the knot joining the ropes be safely passed during the rappel into the notch. The free end of the fixed ropes is then towed along while climbing.

This is a very spectacular setting. Except for the section leading to Salathé Ledge, the route is almost entirely fixed.

Lost Arrow Tip 5.12b or 5.8/5.10a A2★★ Pro: A few pieces, especially 2½" to 3½" for the upper part of the first pitch. A few rivet hangers/tie-off loops and many carabiners are also needed.

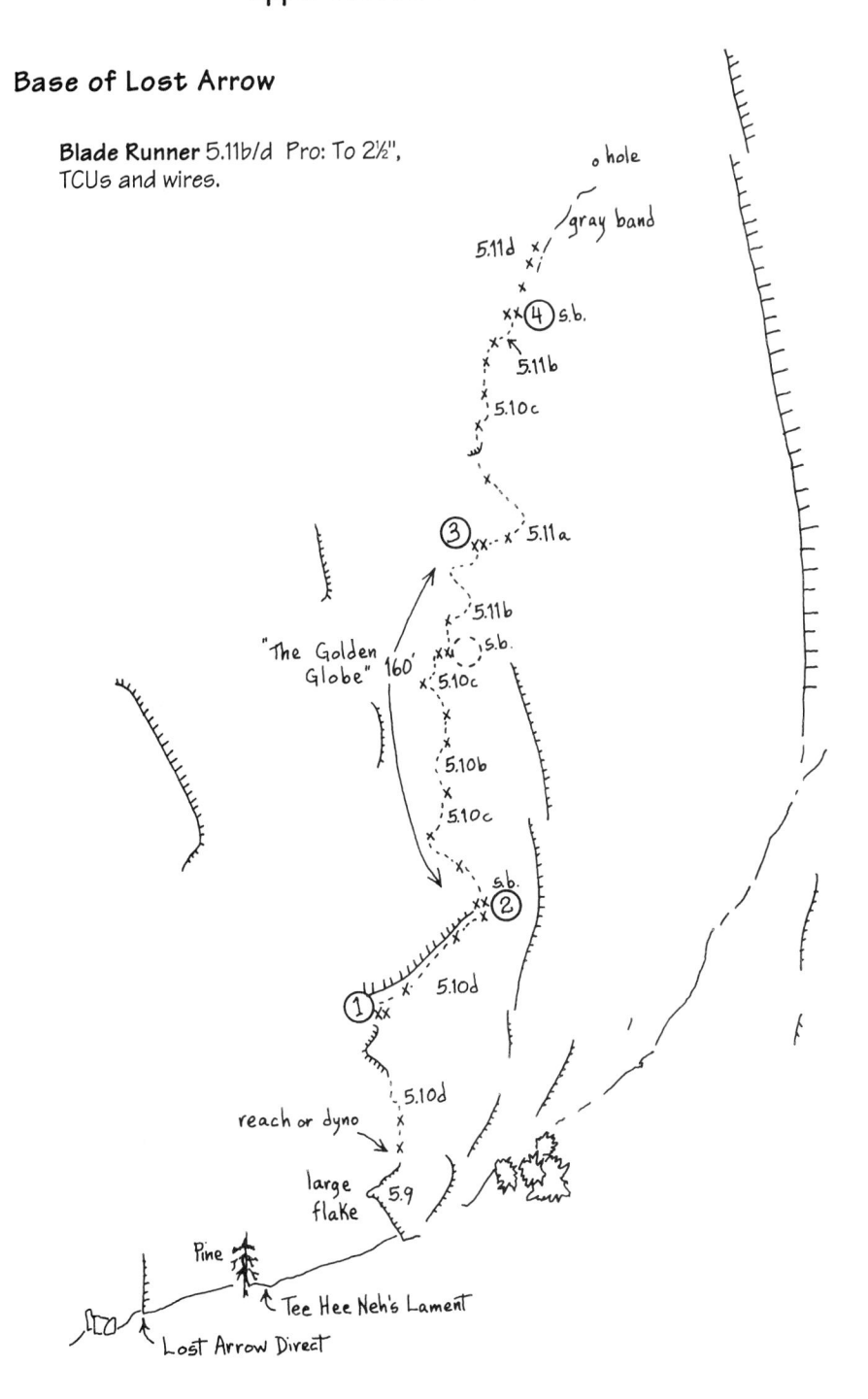

Upper Yosemite Falls: East

Base of Lost Arrow

Blade Runner 5.11b/d Pro: To 2½", TCUs and wires.

Route topo annotations:
- o hole
- gray band
- 5.11d
- ④ s.b.
- 5.11b
- 5.10c
- ③ 5.11a
- 5.11b
- s.b.
- "The Golden Globe" 160'
- 5.10c
- 5.10b
- 5.10c
- s.b.
- ②
- 5.10d
- ①
- 5.10d
- reach or dyno
- large flake 5.9
- Pine
- Tee Hee Neh's Lament
- Lost Arrow Direct

YOSEMITE FALLS — 161

Upper Yosemite Falls: East

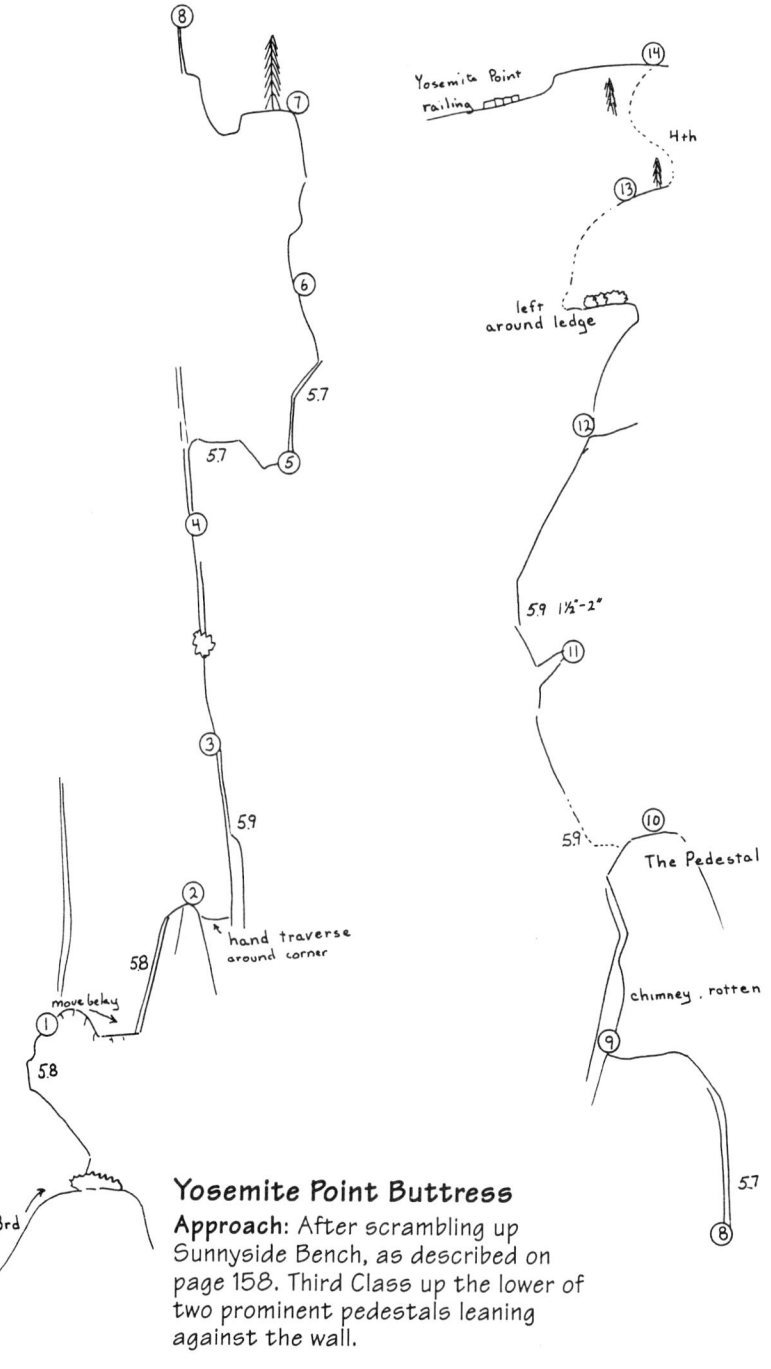

Yosemite Point Buttress

Approach: After scrambling up Sunnyside Bench, as described on page 158. Third Class up the lower of two prominent pedestals leaning against the wall.

Photo on page 155.

Direct Route 5.9

YOSEMITE FALLS

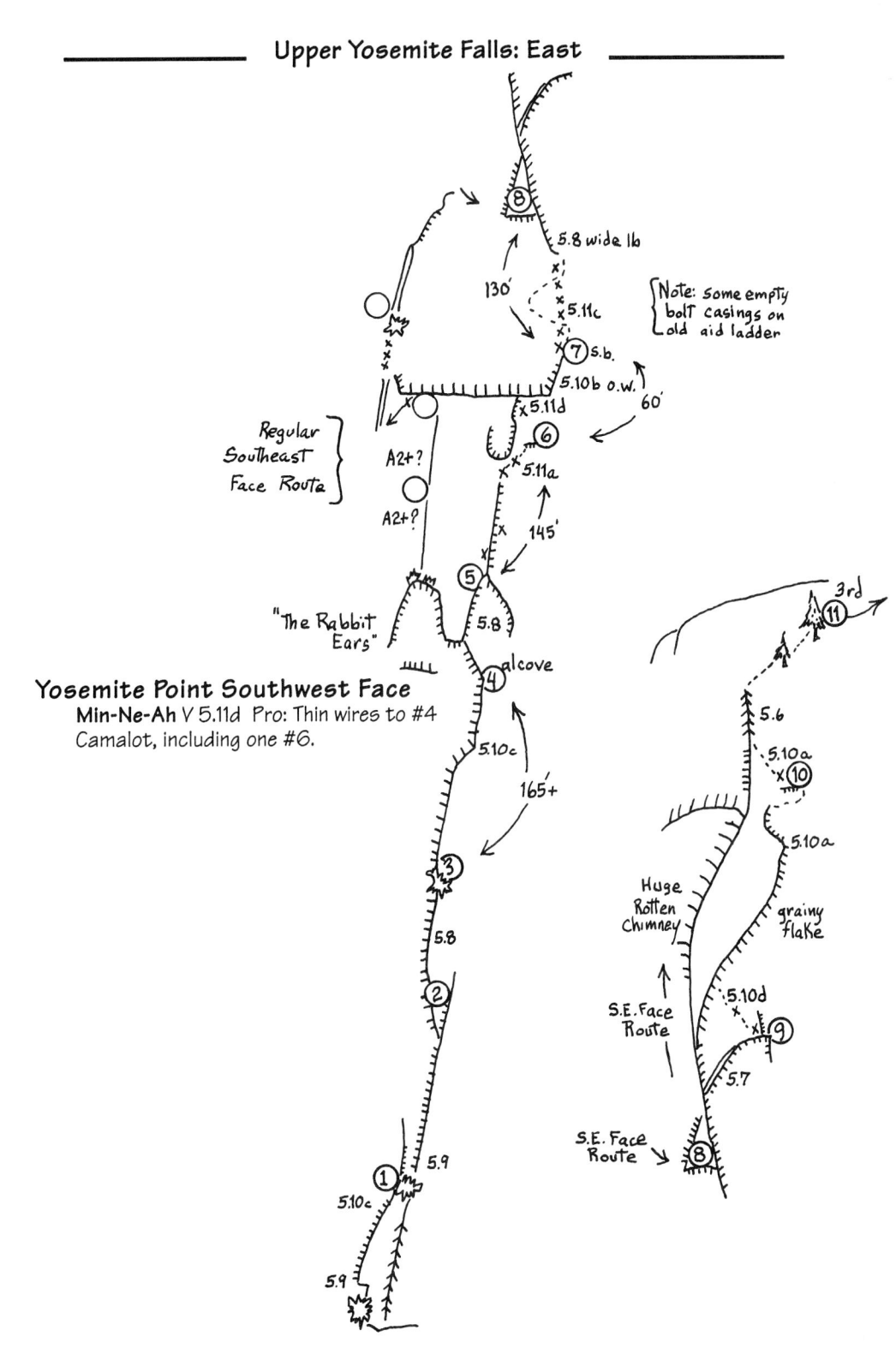

Upper Yosemite Falls: East

5.8 wide lb

130'

5.11c

Note: Some empty bolt casings on old aid ladder

⑧

⑦ s.b.

5.10b o.w.

60'

x 5.11d

Regular Southeast Face Route

A2+?

⑥

x 5.11a

A2+?

145'

⑤

"The Rabbit Ears"

5.8

alcove ④

Yosemite Point Southwest Face
Min-Ne-Ah V 5.11d Pro: Thin wires to #4 Camalot, including one #6.

5.10c

165'+

③

5.8

②

5.9

①

5.10c

5.9

3rd ⑪

5.6

5.10a ⑩

5.10a

Huge Rotten Chimney

grainy flake

5.10d

S.E. Face Route

⑨

5.7

S.E. Face Route ⑧

YOSEMITE FALLS — 163

Yosemite Falls: East

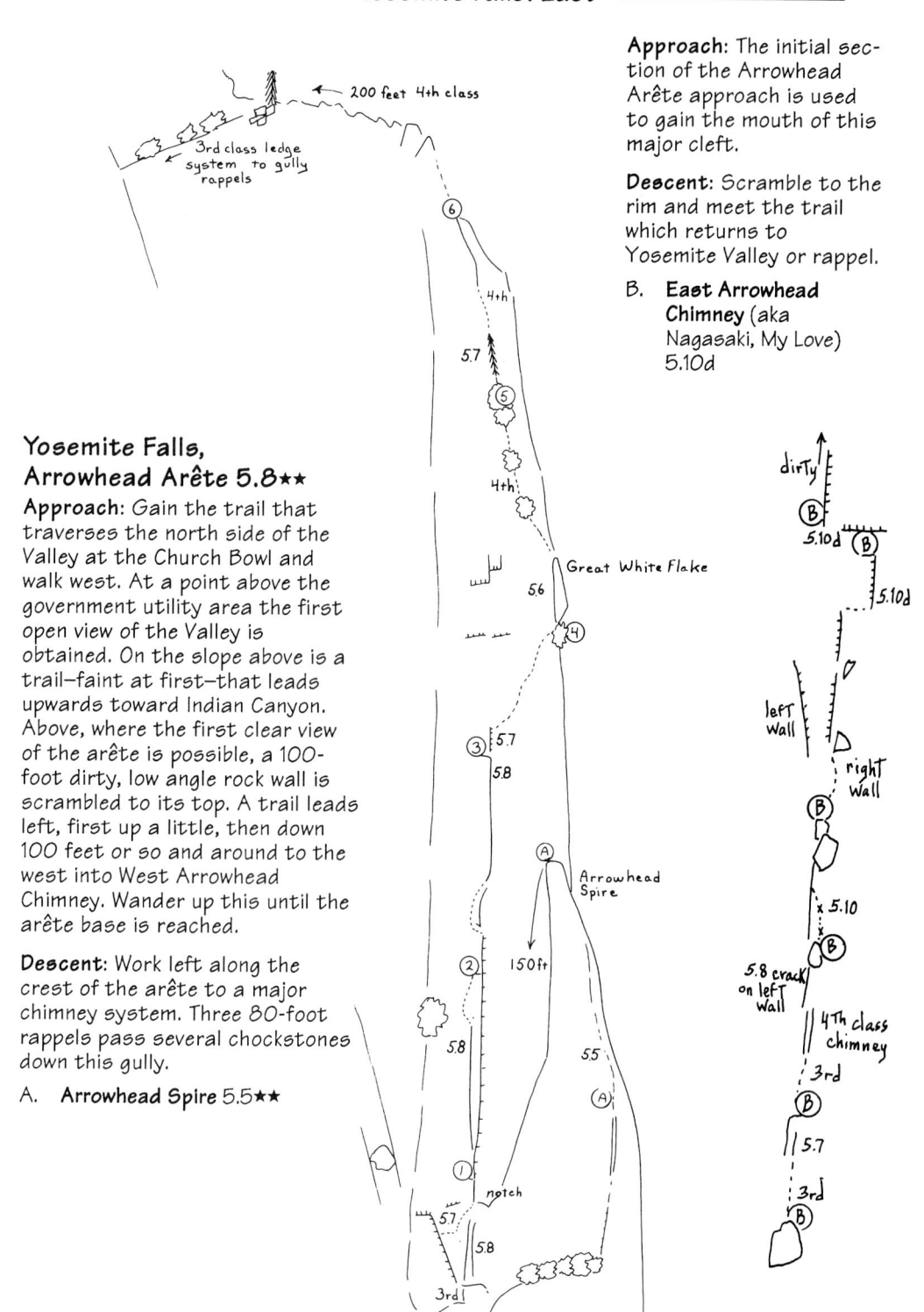

Approach: The initial section of the Arrowhead Arête approach is used to gain the mouth of this major cleft.

Descent: Scramble to the rim and meet the trail which returns to Yosemite Valley or rappel.

B. East Arrowhead Chimney (aka Nagasaki, My Love) 5.10d

Yosemite Falls, Arrowhead Arête 5.8★★

Approach: Gain the trail that traverses the north side of the Valley at the Church Bowl and walk west. At a point above the government utility area the first open view of the Valley is obtained. On the slope above is a trail—faint at first—that leads upwards toward Indian Canyon. Above, where the first clear view of the arête is possible, a 100-foot dirty, low angle rock wall is scrambled to its top. A trail leads left, first up a little, then down 100 feet or so and around to the west into West Arrowhead Chimney. Wander up this until the arête base is reached.

Descent: Work left along the crest of the arête to a major chimney system. Three 80-foot rappels pass several chockstones down this gully.

A. Arrowhead Spire 5.5★★

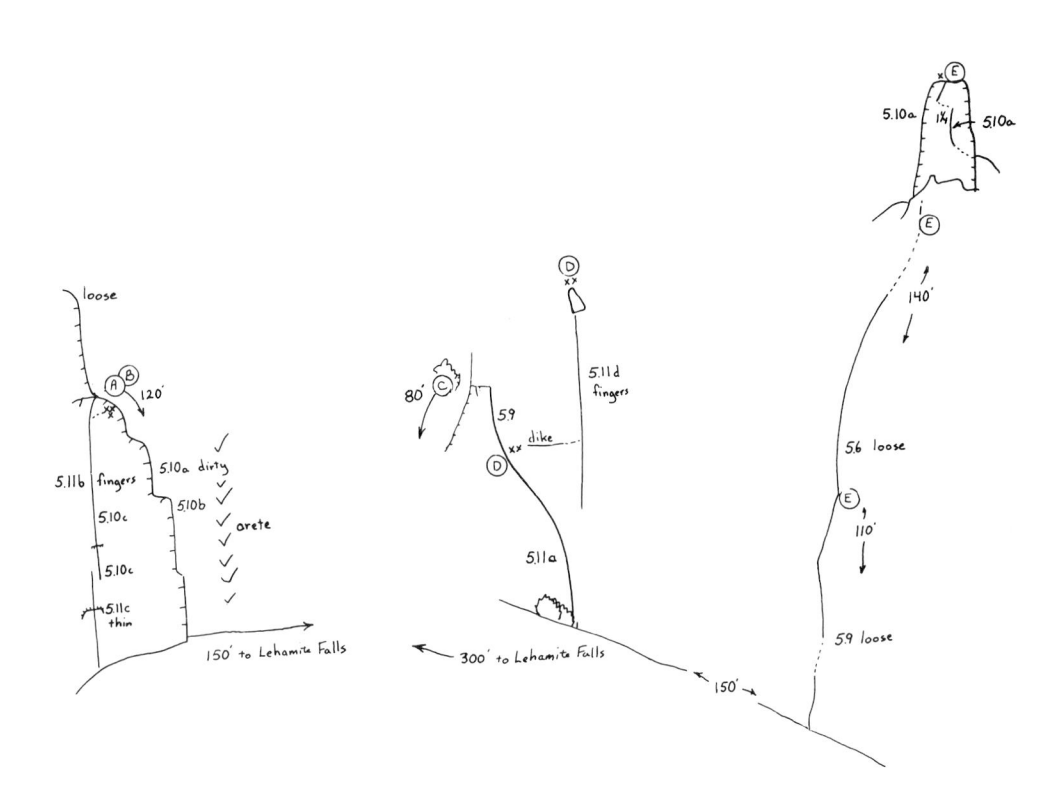

Indian Canyon

Approach: Start up the canyon as described on page 164. Ascend to the east (right) of Indian Creek. Lehamite Creek (the subsidiary waterfall on the right side of the canyon) may be difficult to cross in high water. The climbs are located on either side of Lehamite Falls.

- A. **Maps and Legends** 5.11c★★ Pro: To 2", especially ½" to ¾".
- B. **Police State** 5.10b Pro: To 4".
- C. **Knuckle Buster** 5.11a★★
- D. **The Wand** 5.11d★ R
- E. **A-5 Pinnacle** 5.10a Unstable formation.

Church Bowl

A. **Black is Brown** 5.8★
B. **As It Is** 5.8
C. **Deja Thorus** 5.10a★
D. **Uncle Fanny** 5.7★ Pro: To 2". A prelude to a valley of demanding cracks.
E. **Church Bowl Lieback** 5.8★ Pro: To 2", especially ¼" to 1" pieces. An overlooked, semi-precious stone.
F. **Pole Position** 5.10a★ Pro: QDs. A bit of a squeeze job, but pleasant climbing.
G. **Revival** 5.10a★ Pro: Small to 2".
H. **Gardening At Night** 5.10c
I. **Tammy Fae** 5.10c R
J. **Aunt Fanny's Pantry** 5.4★ Pro: To 2". Ungraceful moves down low, yet a good beginner climb. Rappel the route from bolts on a perch straight down, or tunnel behind the pillar and down a bit. A short rappel from trees leads to Church Bowl Terrace. Another short rappel from bolts on the edge of the ledge ends at the ground.
K. **Jacob's Ladder** 5.10c
L. **Skid Row Messiah** 5.11a R
M. **800 Club** 5.11a★
N. **Book of Revelations** 5.11a★★ Pro: Many small to 2". Tough moves interspersed with awkward rests on the first pitch. On the second pitch, change cracks by moving right to meet a thin finger crack crank crux. The climb continues, but most parties do just two pitches.
O. **Church Bowl Tree** 5.10b★★ Pro: Mainly small to ½". One of the greasiest climbs in the Valley. Balance stand-up moves on fair holds, passing a pair of bolts.
P. **More Balls Than Brains** A3-★ Hardware: Rurps to 1½" angles, rivet hangers.
Q. **Church Bowl Chimney** 5.6★ Pro: To 2½". Physical and potentially humbling.
R. **Energizer** 5.11b★★ Pro: Nine QDs. Starts on the right side of an arête. Hard not to stand on the tree midway.
S. **Atheist** 5.13a★★ Pro: TCUs and nine QDs. A long reach and cranking skills are necessary.
T. **Church Bowl Terrace** 5.8

Church Bowl

- U. **Bitches' Terror** 5.11a★★ Pro: Many QDs. Keen climbing on a blunt arête.
- V. **Bishop's Terrace** 5.8★★★ Pro: To 3½". This classic test piece of 5.8 jamming leads to a novel location.
- W. **Stephanie's Corner** 5.8
- X. **Sacrilege** 5.11a
- Y. **Blasphemy** 5.11a
- Z. **Heretic** 5.10c
- AA. **Catholic Discipline** 5.12 R
- BB. **Bishop's Balcony** 5.5 A3★
- CC. **No Rest for the Wicked** 5.11b★ Pro: A few wireds, #1.5 and #2 Friends and QDs. This is an off-balance lieback.
- DD. **Oral Roberts** 5.12a★★ Pro: QDs and a few pieces to 2½".
- EE. **700 Club** 5.11c★★ Pro: Seven QDs, wired or small TCU optional.

THE ROYAL ARCHES

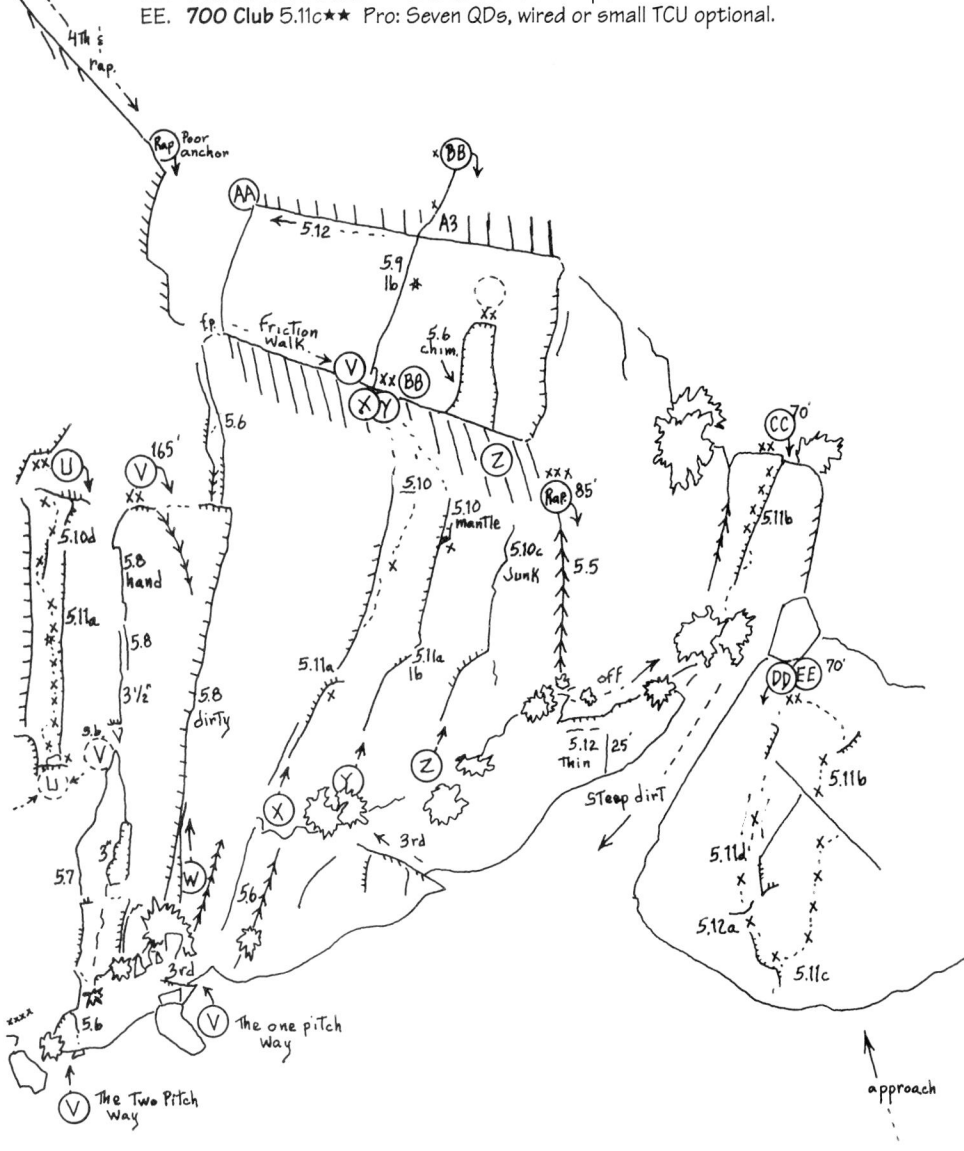

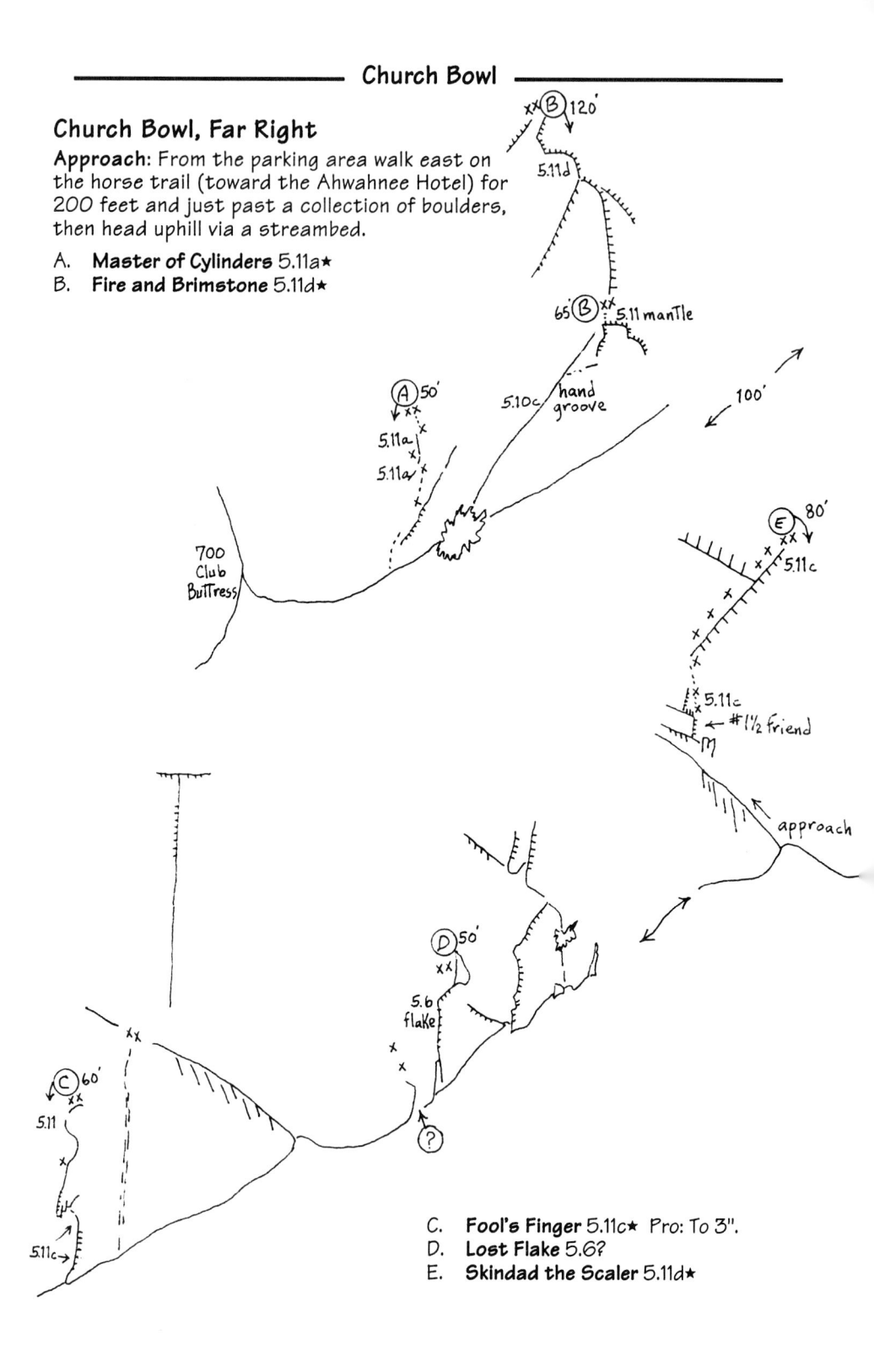

Church Bowl

Church Bowl, Far Right

Approach: From the parking area walk east on the horse trail (toward the Ahwahnee Hotel) for 200 feet and just past a collection of boulders, then head uphill via a streambed.

A. **Master of Cylinders** 5.11a★
B. **Fire and Brimstone** 5.11d★

C. **Fool's Finger** 5.11c★ Pro: To 3".
D. **Lost Flake** 5.6?
E. **Skindad the Scaler** 5.11d★

168 — THE ROYAL ARCHES

My Rhombus/Q.E.D. (aka East of Eden)

Approach: Continue up and left past the Serenity Crack approach, see page 172.

- A. **My Rhombus** 5.10a Pro: To 3½".
- B. **Q.E.D.** (aka East of Eden) 5.11a

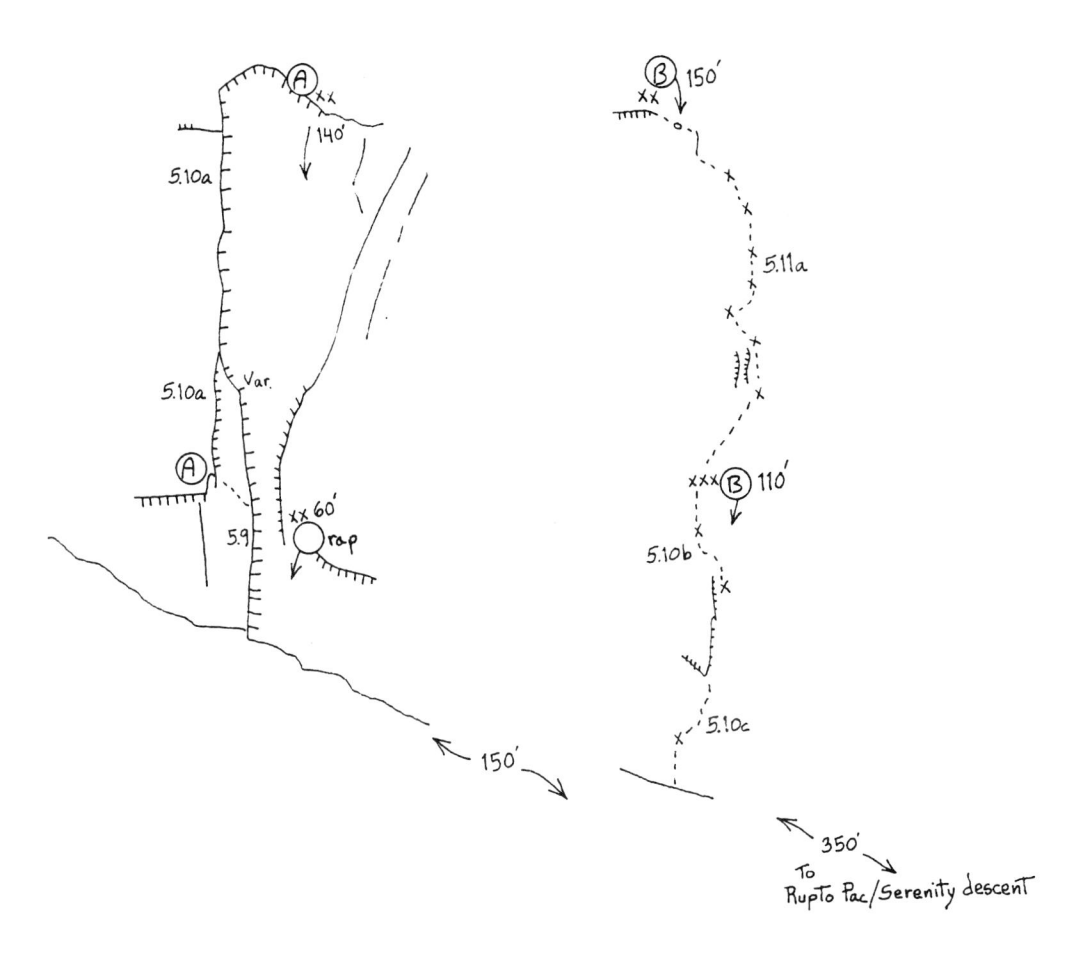

THE ROYAL ARCHES

The Royal Arches

1. Serenity Crack 5.10d
2. Moan Fest 5.10a R
3. DEVIL'S BATHTUB

The Royal Arches

4. Royal Arches Route 5.7 A1 or 5.9
5. King Snake 5.12
6. The Cobra 5.11a
7. Shakey Flakes 5.11a
8. Greasy but Groovy 5.10d
9. Arches Terrace 5.8

Serenity Crack Area

A. **Rupto Pac** 5.11c
B. **Super Slab** 5.9 ★ Some loose blocks and munge.
C. **Peter's Out** 5.12
D. **Trial by Fire** 5.8
E. **Demimonde** 5.11c
F. **Lethal Weapon** 5.11d Very thin crack.
G. **Endorphine** 5.11d A two-pitch bolted face route exiting **Adrenaline**.
H. **Adrenaline** 5.11b ★ Pro: Small wires.
I. **Serenity Crack** 5.10d ★★★ Pro: From ¼" to 2", especially ⅜" to ½" pieces. This climb offers beautifully continuous finger jamming over three pitches. Elegant and civilized. Badly pin-scarred.
J. **New Generation** 5.12a Top-rope.
K. **Maxine's Wall** 5.10c ★ Pro: To 2", only QDs needed for the first pitch. Most parties do only one pitch. Mostly friction and edging.
L. **Firefingers** 5.11b ★★ R Pro: Include #3.5 Friend.
M. **Pigs in Space** 5.12
N. **Mother of the Future** 5.11a
O. **Permanent Waves** 5.10b R Pro: Including #0.5 Friend.
P. **Deviltry** 5.11a R
Q. **Holy Diver** 5.11
R. **Hell's Hollow** 5.10a ★

THE ROYAL ARCHES

Serenity Crack Area

Photo on page 170.

S. **Sons of Yesterday** 5.10a ★★★
Pro: To 3½", especially ¾" to 2" pieces. Offers an enjoyable altitude gain. Stance belays.
T. **Ahwahnee Buttress** 5.10d (First pitch bolt ladder freed?)
U. **Moan Fest** 5.10c R
Pro: Including KBs.

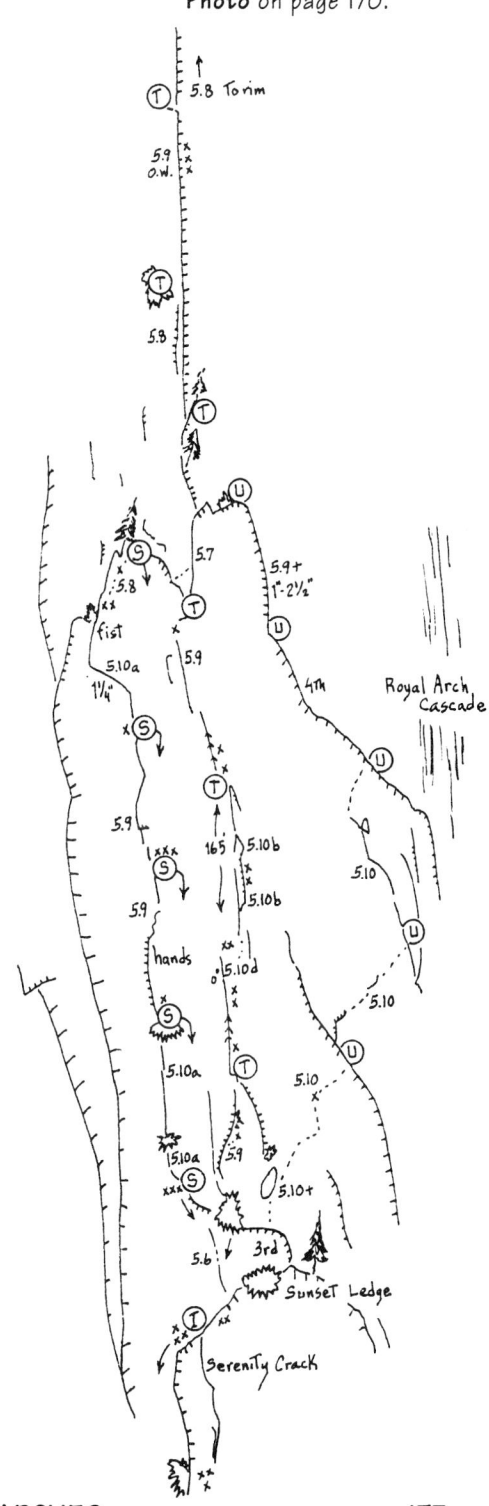

THE ROYAL ARCHES — 173

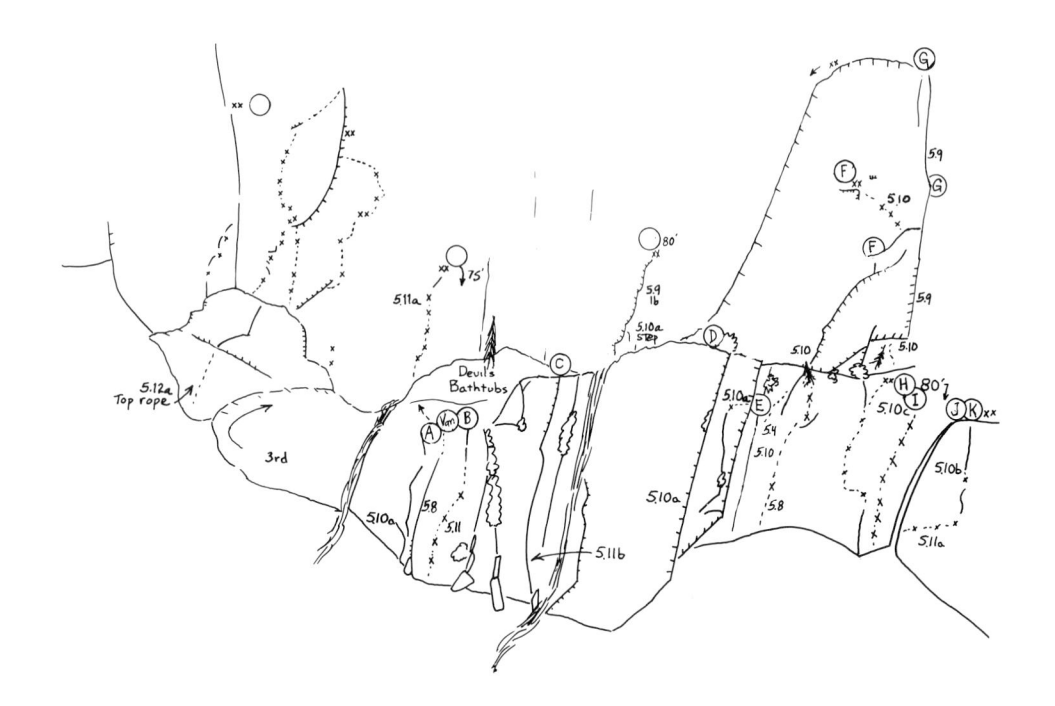

Devil's Bathtub Area

Approach: This area is located a short distance east of the Ahwahnee Hotel along the horse trail. Follow the first creekbed up to the base of the wall.

- A. **Peruvian Flake** 5.10a★
- B. **Astro Turf** 5.11
- C. **Draw the Line** 5.11b★ Pro: Thin.
- D. **Fine Line** 5.10a
- E. **Peeping Tom** 5.10a
- F. **Sea Hag** 5.10
- G. **Sea Cow** 5.10
- H. **Surplus Cheaper Hands** 5.10c R
- I. **Age of Industry** 5.11
- J. **Royal Arches Route** 5.6 (Only first pitch shown.)
- K. **Astro Spam** 5.11a

Devil's Bathtub Area

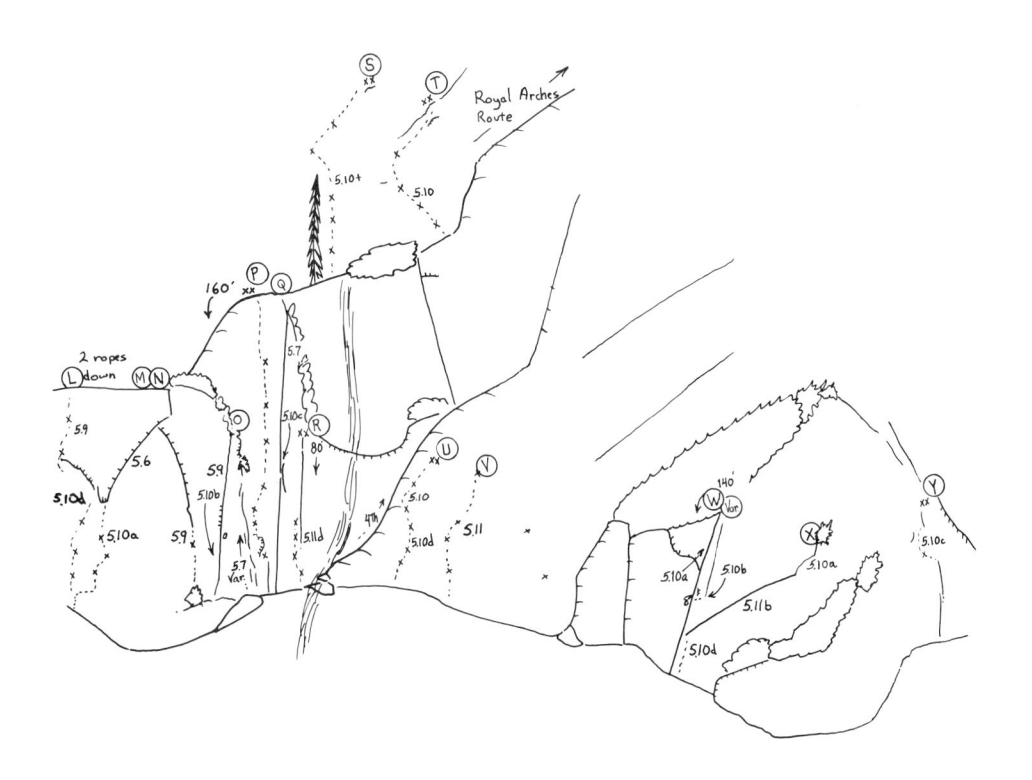

- L. **Distant Driver** 5.10d
- M. **Arête Butler** 5.10a
- N. **Royal Prerogative** 5.9
- O. **Krovy Rookers** 5.10b
- P. **Rum Sodomy in the Lash** 5.10d
- Q. **Ilsa She Wolf of the SS** 5.10c
- R. **The Premature Ejaculation** 5.11d
- S. **Metal Error** 5.10+ R
- T. **Level Two** 5.10
- U. **Feminine Protection** 5.10d
- V. **Facade** 5.11
- W. **Y Crack** 5.10a★
- X. **Fish Fingers** 5.11b R Pro: Many nuts to 1".
- Y. **Way-Homo Sperm Burpers From Fresno** 5.10c Pro: Brass nuts to #2.5 Friend.

The Royal Arches Base, Center

Approach: Hike approximately 0.25 mile east on the horse trail from the Ahwahnee Hotel. Beyond a streambed the trail decends slightly and abuts the wall. Scramble up to the climbs from here.

- A. **Hookie** 5.12a★ Pro: Include brass nuts and TCUs.
- B. **Wise Crack** 5.10a★
- C. **Cornball** 5.7 (Looks loose.)
- D. **Texas Chain Saw Massacre** 5.11a★ (Star rating for second pitch only.) Pro: Include TCUs.
- E. **King Snake** 5.12★ (Good route, but currently grass-filled.) Pro: Many small nuts to 1".
- F. **Poker Face** 5.10b★★
- G. **Aces and Eights** 5.11b★
- H. **Face Card** 5.10c
- I. **King of Hearts** 5.10d R
- J. **Sleight of Hand** 5.10b
- K. **Dire Straits** 5.10
- L. **Stacked Deck** 5.11-
- M. **Public Enema Number One** 5.11c Pro: Many brass nuts.
- N. **Barney Rubble** 5.10d
- O. **The Violent Bear It Away** 5.10c
- P. **Double Trouble** 5.10b

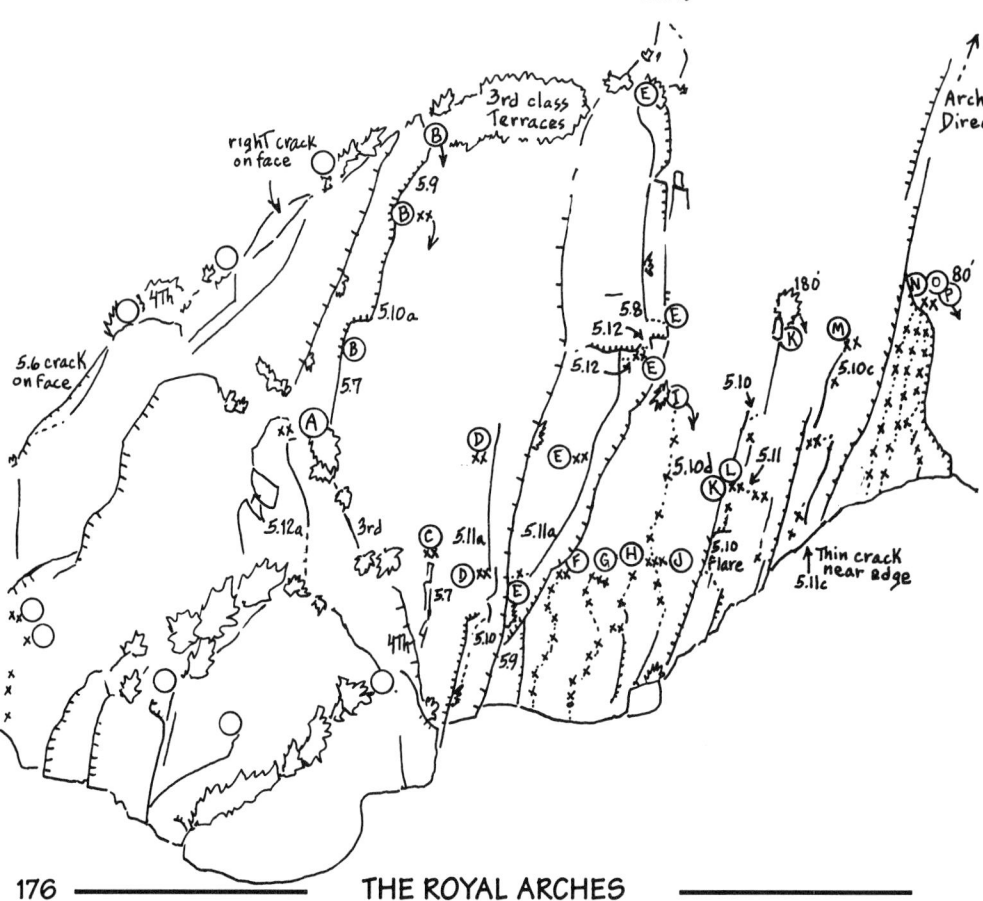

The Royal Arches

The Royal Arches Route

Approach: Hike east from the Ahwahnee Hotel on the horse trail. One hundred feet after crossing a small creek, head up the hill to the first-pitch chimney.

Descent: Scramble down North Dome Gully, see page 184.

Photo on page 170.

The Royal Arches Route
5.7 A1 or 5.9
The Cobra 5.11a ★ R

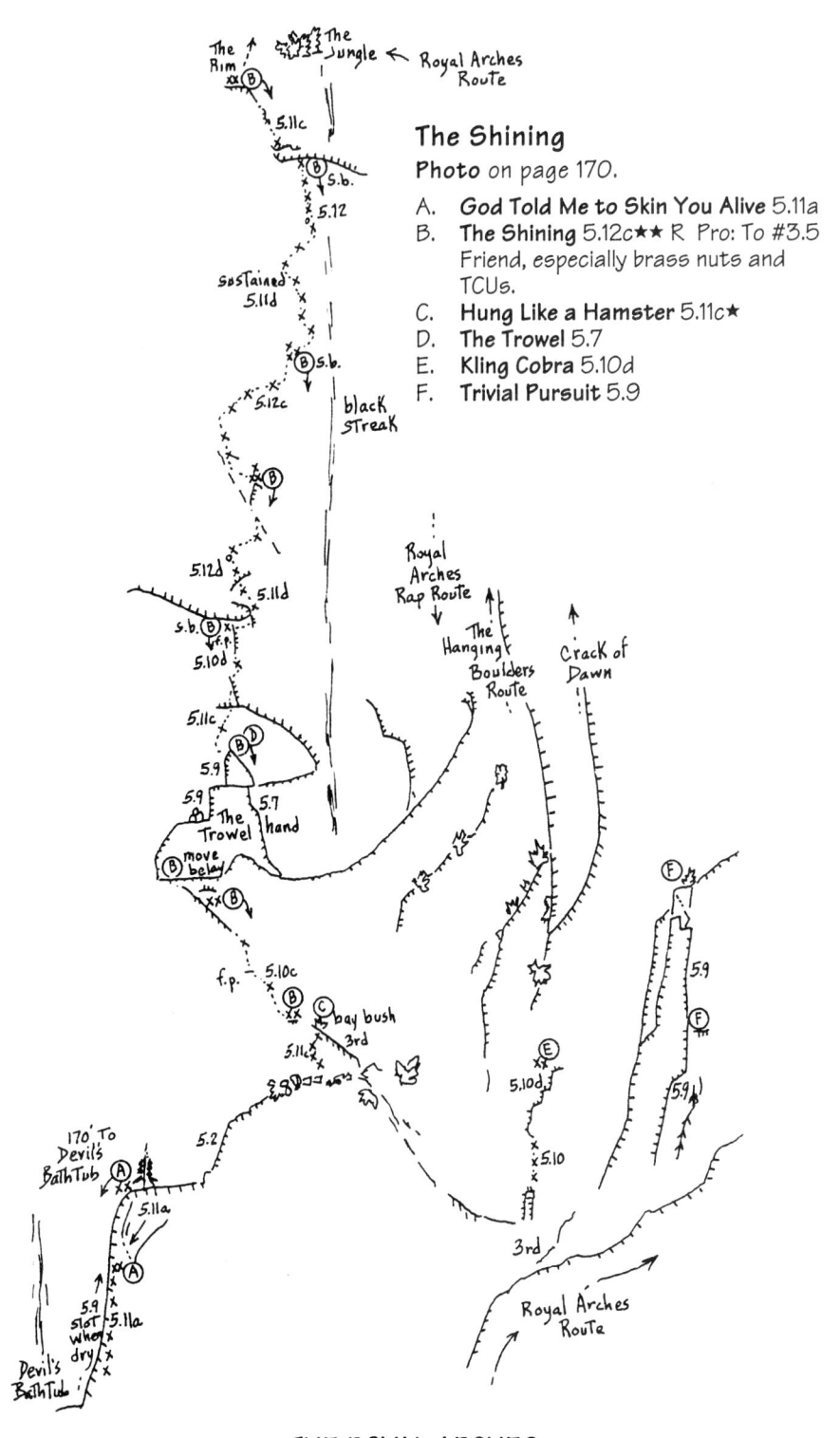

The Royal Arches

The Shining
Photo on page 170.

A. God Told Me to Skin You Alive 5.11a
B. The Shining 5.12c★★ R Pro: To #3.5 Friend, especially brass nuts and TCUs.
C. Hung Like a Hamster 5.11c★
D. The Trowel 5.7
E. Kling Cobra 5.10d
F. Trivial Pursuit 5.9

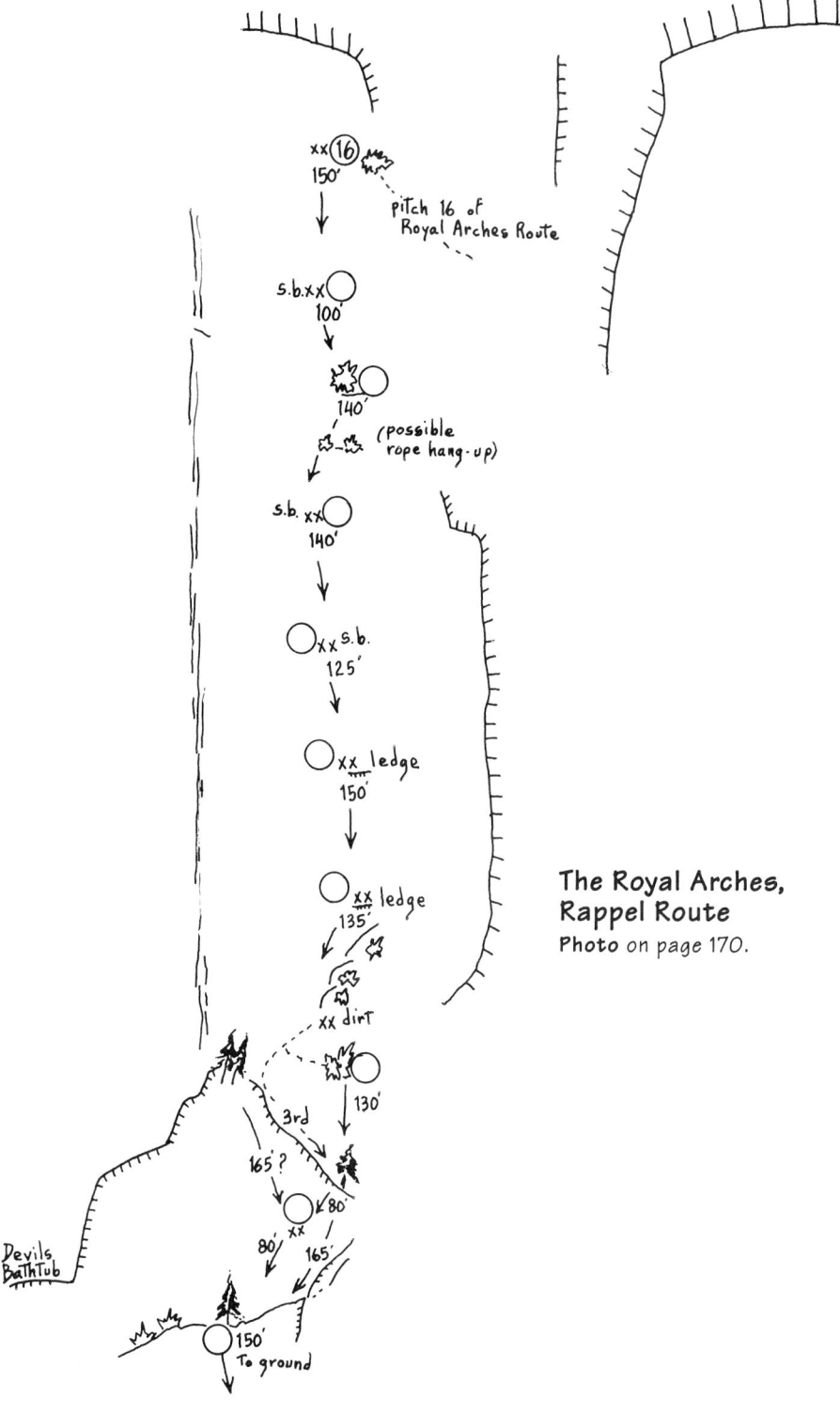

The Royal Arches

The Royal Arches, Rappel Route
Photo on page 170.

- xx (16) 150' — pitch 16 of Royal Arches Route
- s.b. xx 100'
- 140' (possible rope hang-up)
- s.b. xx 140'
- xx s.b. 125'
- xx ledge 150'
- xx ledge 135'
- xx dirt
- 130'
- 3rd 165?
- 80' xx
- 80' / 165'
- Devils BathTub
- 150' To ground

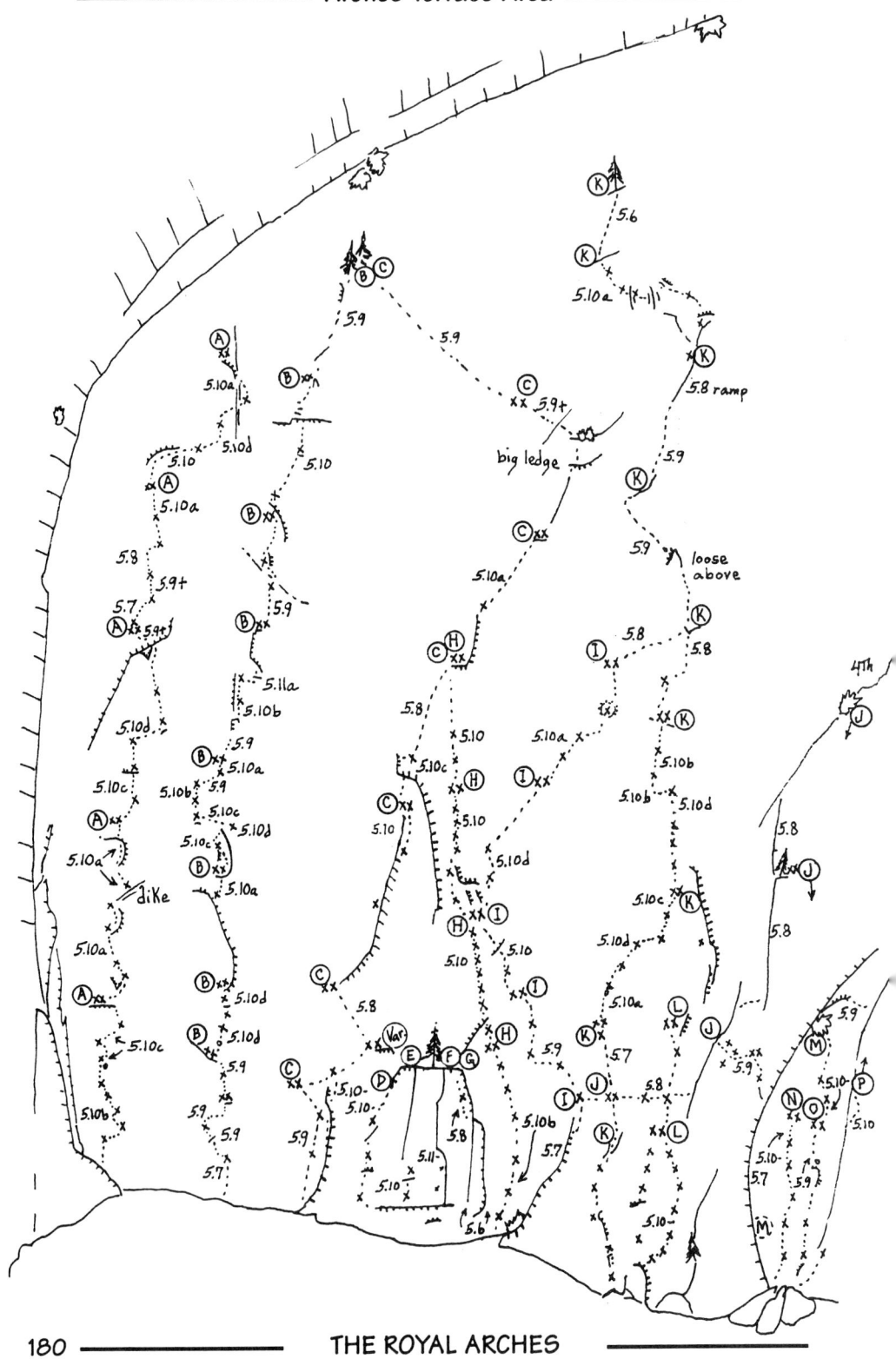

Arches Terrace Area

180 — THE ROYAL ARCHES

Arches Terrace Area

The Royal Arches, Terrace Area

Approach: Walk several hundred yards east along the horse trail from the Ahwahnee Hotel before striking steeply up the hill.

A. **The Rambler** 5.10d★★ (R)
   Pro: Small to ¾", plus a #2.5 Friend.
B. **Shaky Flakes** 5.11a★ (R)
C. **Friday the 13th** 5.10b(R)
   Pro: Small, plus #1 to #3.5 Friends.
D. **Slander Session** 5.10-(R)
E. **Flakes Away** 5.10 (Flattened bolt hangers, still clip-able).
F. **Samurai Crack** 5.11- (chopped bolts).
G. **Hershey Highway** 5.8
H. **Mid-Life Crisis** 5.10★★
I. **Reefer Madness** 5.10d★(R/X)
J. **Arches Terrace** 5.8 ★(R)
   Pro: To 3".
K. **Greasy but Groovy** 5.10d★(R/X)
L. **Surf Nazi** 5.10-
M. **Fallen Arches** 5.9(R)
N. **Wharf Rat** 5.10-
O. **The Mouse That Soared** 5.10-(R)
P. **Lingering Lines** 5.10-(R)
Q. **Crying for Mama** 5.10a(R/X)
R. **Arches Terrace Direct** 5.11a★★
S. **Hang Dog Flyer** 5.12c★★
   pro. small to 2", esp. ¾" to 1½".
T. **10.96** 5.10d★★ pro. ¾" to 3½", esp. 2½" to 3".

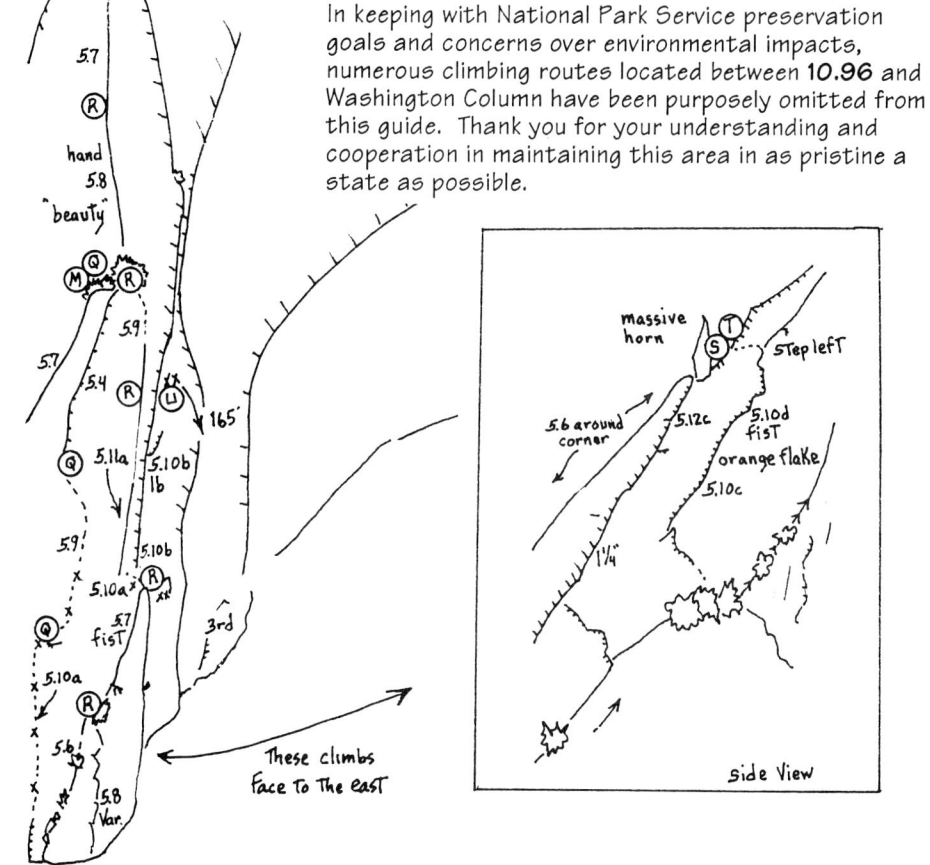

In keeping with National Park Service preservation goals and concerns over environmental impacts, numerous climbing routes located between **10.96** and Washington Column have been purposely omitted from this guide. Thank you for your understanding and cooperation in maintaining this area in as pristine a state as possible.

THE ROYAL ARCHES

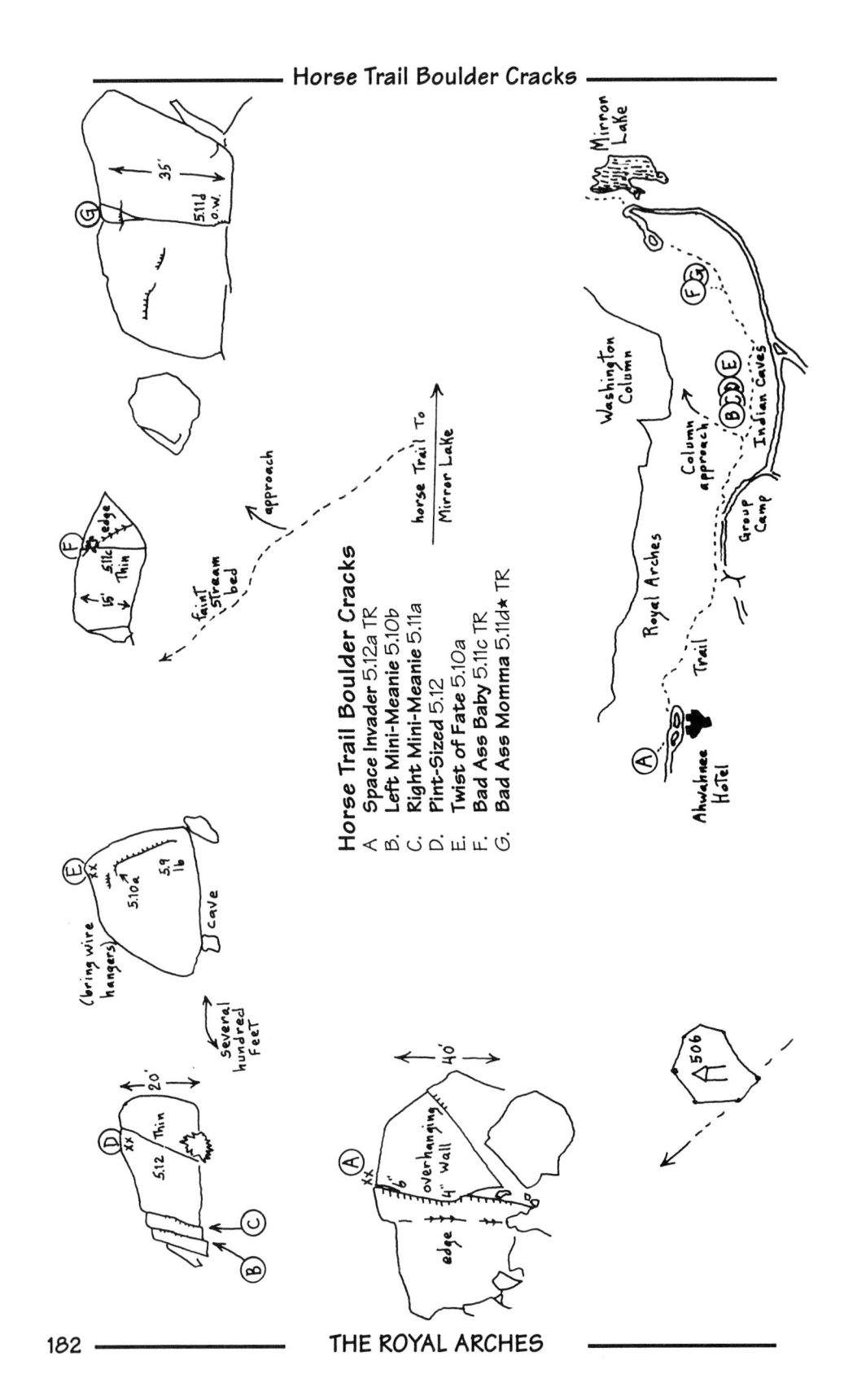

Horse Trail Boulder Cracks

Horse Trail Boulder Cracks
A. Space Invader 5.12a TR
B. Left Mini-Meanie 5.10b
C. Right Mini-Meanie 5.11a
D. Pint-Sized 5.12
E. Twist of Fate 5.10a
F. Bad Ass Baby 5.11c TR
G. Bad Ass Momma 5.11d★ TR

182 — THE ROYAL ARCHES

Washington Column: South Face

1. Space Case 5.10c
2. Direct Route 5.7
3. The Odyssey 5.11

Washington Column, Base

Approach: From the Ahwahnee Hotel or North Pines Campground take the trail toward Indian Caves. Before the caves are reached, however, head up north (near a point where the bike path and the horse trail almost touch), and follow the drainage that comes down from the left side of the Column. A climber's trail skirts the base of the cliff all the way east to the bottom of North Dome Gully.

Descent: Routes that end atop Washington Column necessitate a familiarity with North Dome Gully, the easiest access to and from the rim in the vicinity. The descent down North Dome Gully is the scene of frequent accidents. The trail from the top of the Column traverses east all the way to the forested gully and completely above the death slabs. Don't descend too early; if in doubt and contemplating rappels, keep traversing. If unfamiliar with the descent, don't attempt it at night.

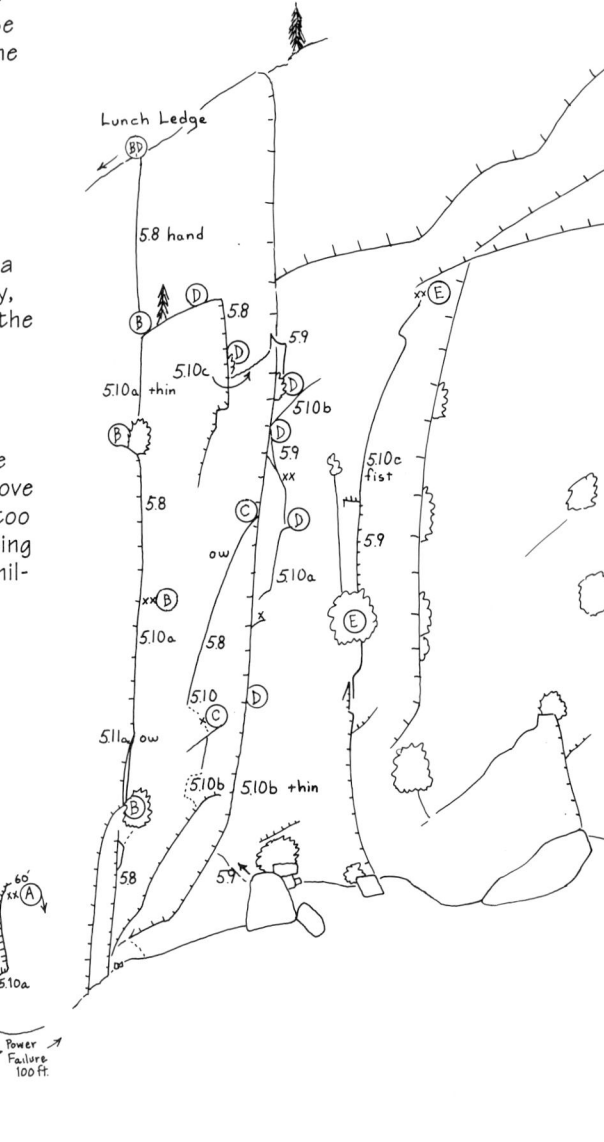

A. **Trial by Jury** 5.10a
B. **Power Failure** 5.11a★★ Pro: To 3½".
C. **The Fang** 5.10b
D. **Space Case** 5.10c★ (Star rating for first pitch only.)
E. **Jesu Joy** 5.10c★ Pro: To 3½".

Washington Column

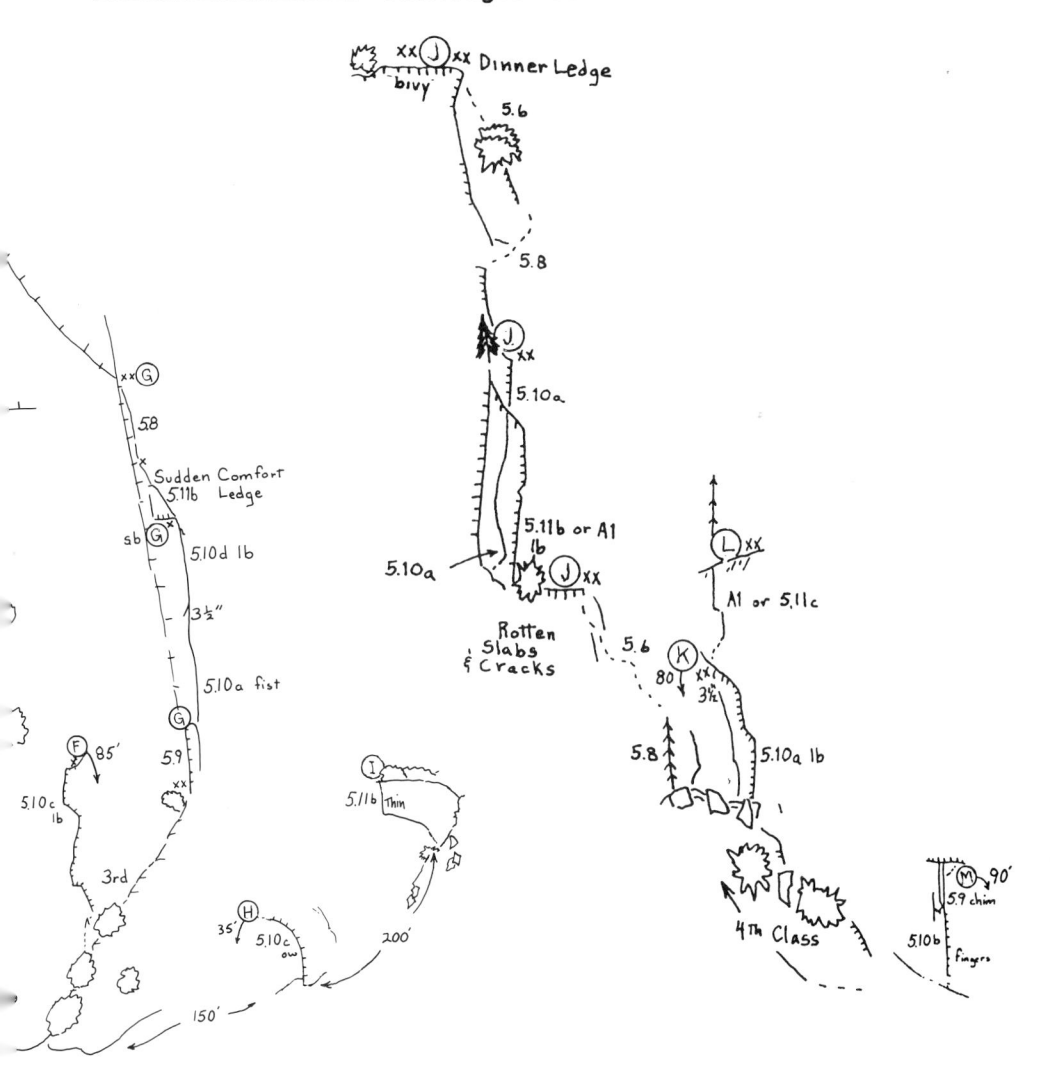

F. **Wing of Bat** 5.10c★ Pro: ¾" to 3½".
G. **Dwindling Energy** 5.11b★★ Pro: Extra large nuts to 3½".
H. **Nowhere Man** 5.10c
I. **Turkey Vulture** 5.11b
J. **Dinner Ledge** 5.10a or 5.11b★
K. **Jojo** 5.10b★★ Pro: To 3½".
L. **The Prow** 5.10a/5.11c★ Only the first pitch is shown.
M. **Tom Cat** 5.10b
   The Panther 5.11d★★ (Not shown.) A short distance to the right of Tom Cat is a striking, straight-in thin crack which leads to a ledge. A bolt protects difficult moves that access the crack.

Washington Column

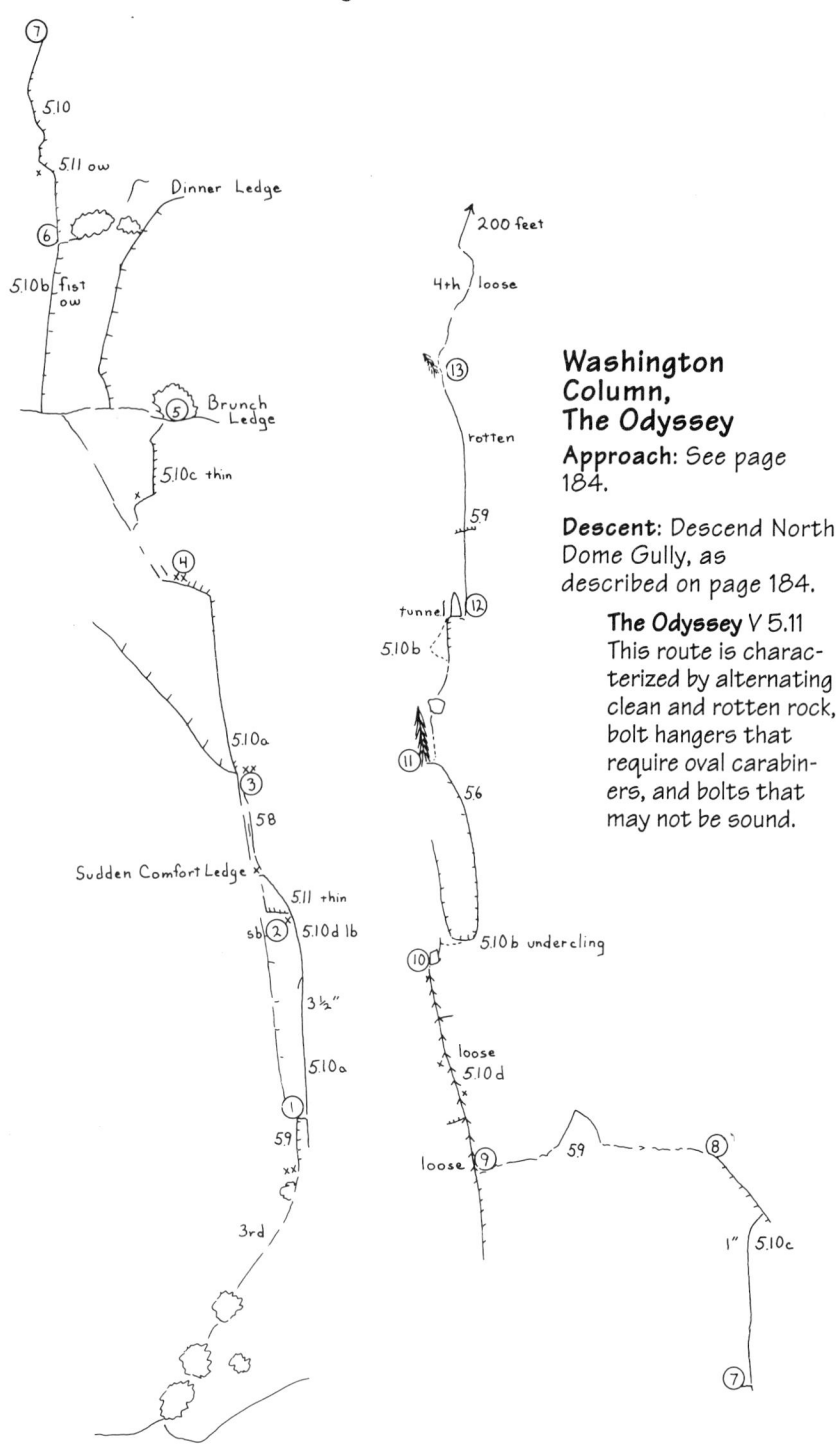

Washington Column, The Odyssey

Approach: See page 184.

Descent: Descend North Dome Gully, as described on page 184.

The Odyssey V 5.11
This route is characterized by alternating clean and rotten rock, bolt hangers that require oval carabiners, and bolts that may not be sound.

Washington Column, Astroman-to-be, 1960   Tom Frost photo

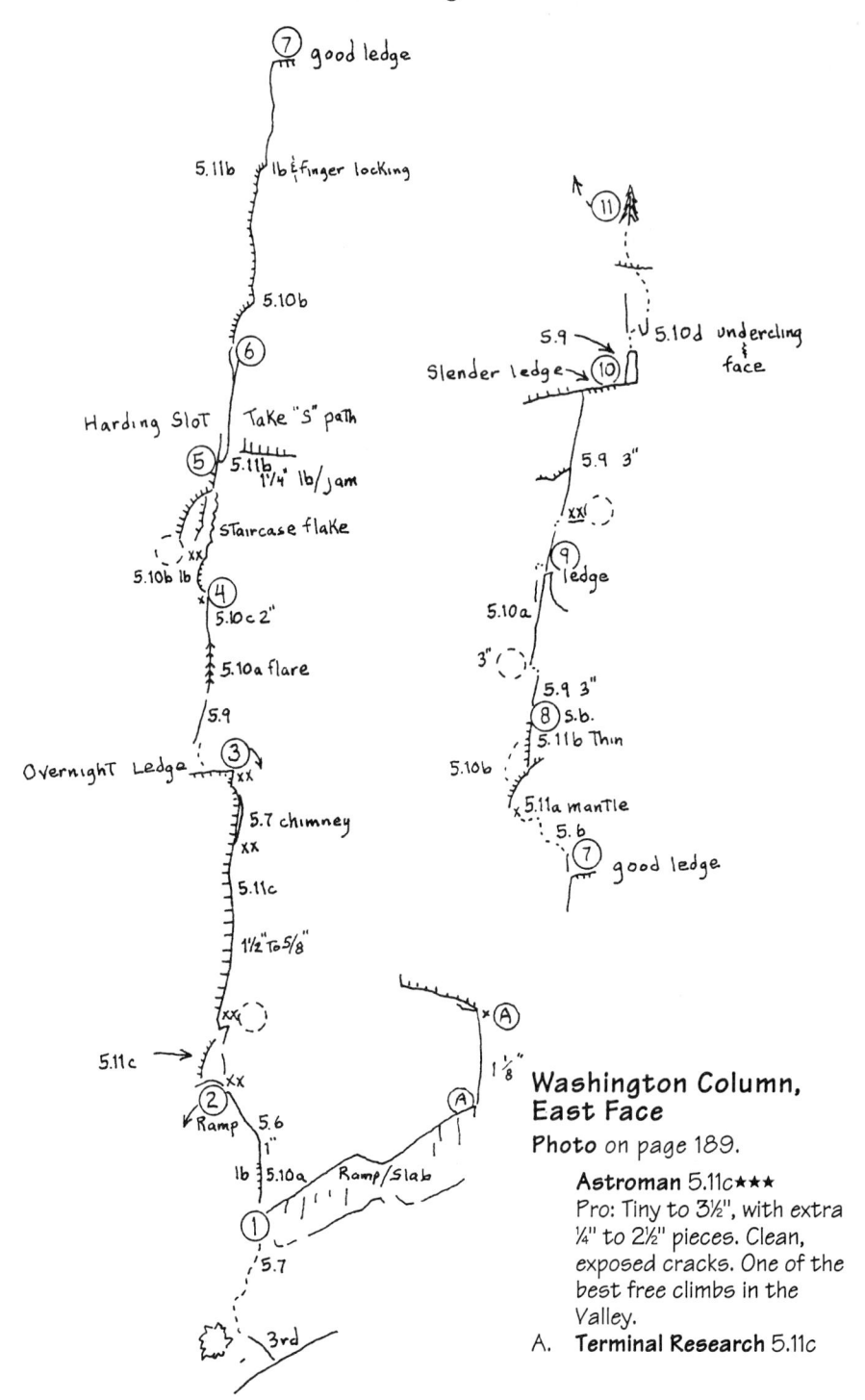

Washington Column

Washington Column, East Face
Photo on page 189.

Astroman 5.11c★★★
Pro: Tiny to 3½", with extra ¼" to 2½" pieces. Clean, exposed cracks. One of the best free climbs in the Valley.

A. **Terminal Research 5.11c**

National Park Service photo

Washington Column: East Face

Astroman

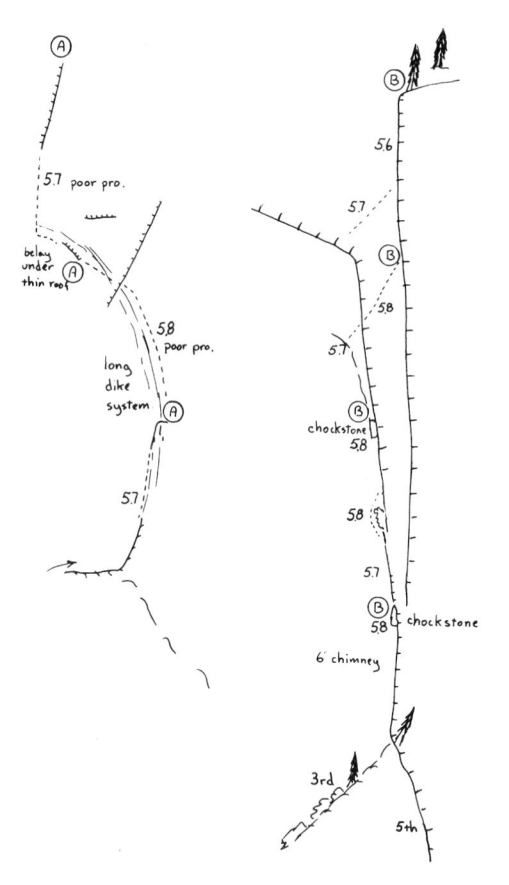

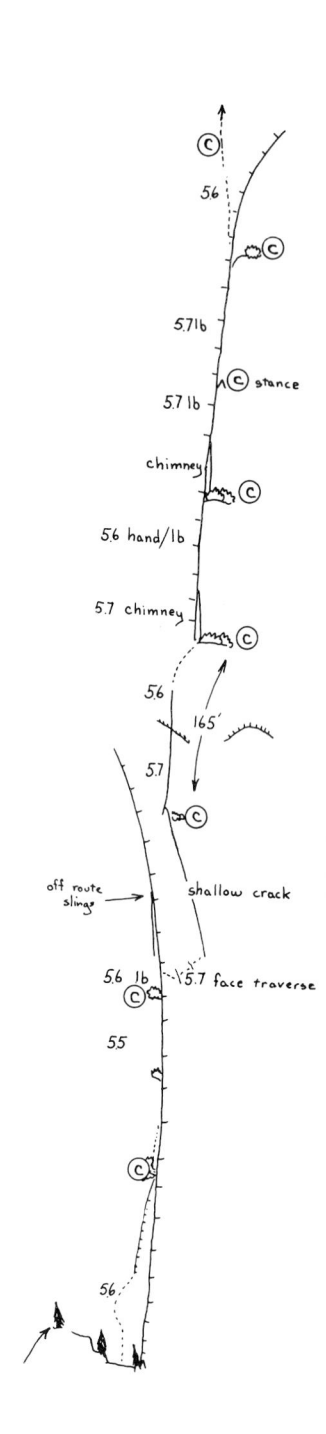

North Dome

Approach: The routes on North Dome are often approached by doing the Royal Arches Route, see page 177. Otherwise, walk in from the Tioga Road on the North Dome Trail, or slog up North Dome Gully, described on page 184.

Descent: Walk off the west side of the dome and hike down North Dome Gully, as described on page 184.

A. **Skid Row** 5.8 Pro: To 2½".
B. **West Face Route** 5.8 Pro: To 3".
C. **South Face Route** 5.7★
   Mass Assault 5.9 From a point near the highest trees, up and right of the huge overhangs on the southeast face, this five-pitch route meanders up the slabs above.

North Dome

1. West Face Route 5.8
2. SOUTHWEST FACE
3. South Face Route 5.7
4. Crest Jewell 5.10a
5. Dakshina 5.11
6. Mass Assault 5.9

North Dome

Approach: The cleanest approach to this route is to hike the trail to the top of North Dome then descend slabs through scattered boulders and brush, heading south/southwest. Large talus and a steep slab below indicate the end of the route and the first of five rappels to the base.

Freaks of Nature 5.11c A0★ Pro: A few small stoppers, one each ¼" to 4" cams.

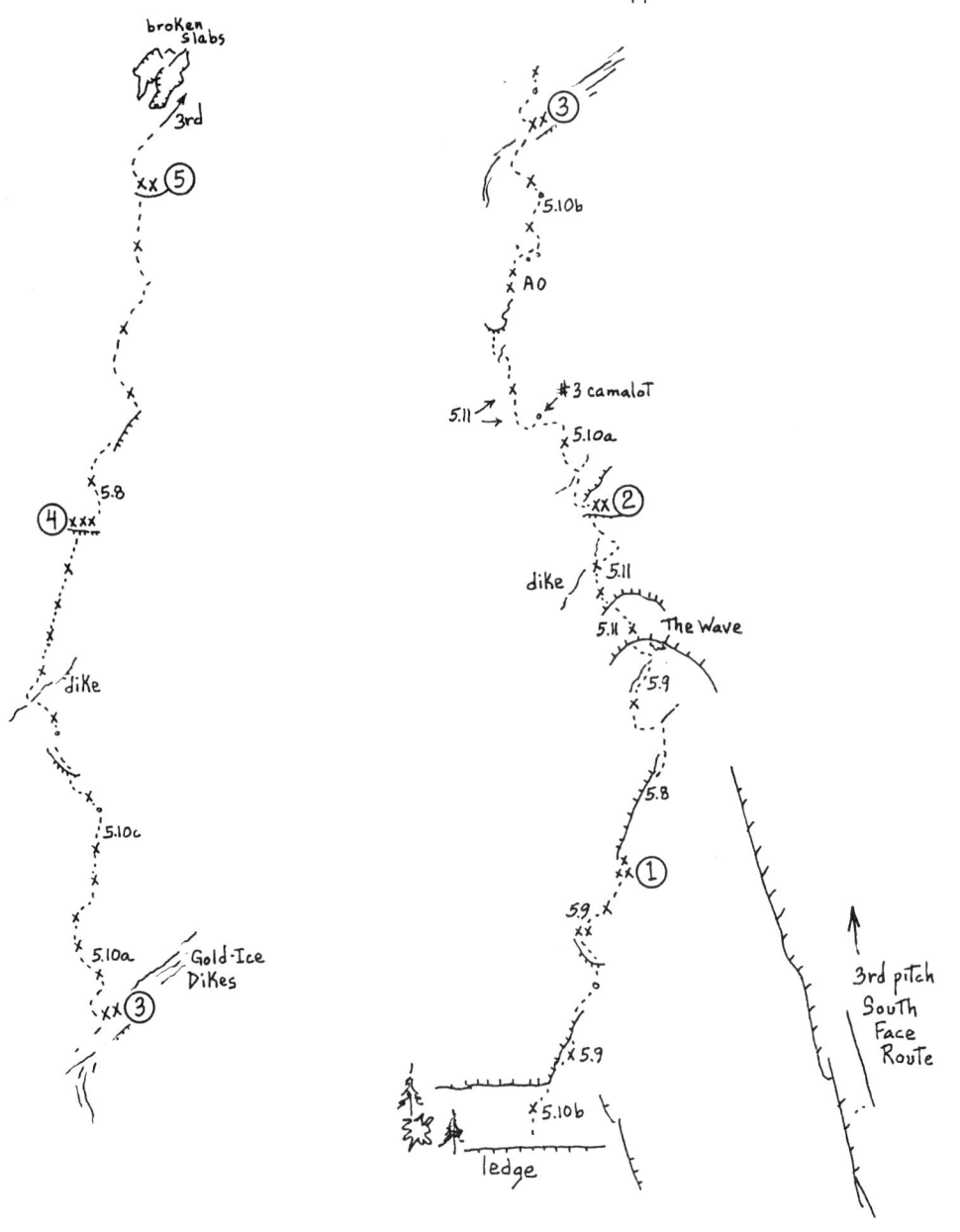

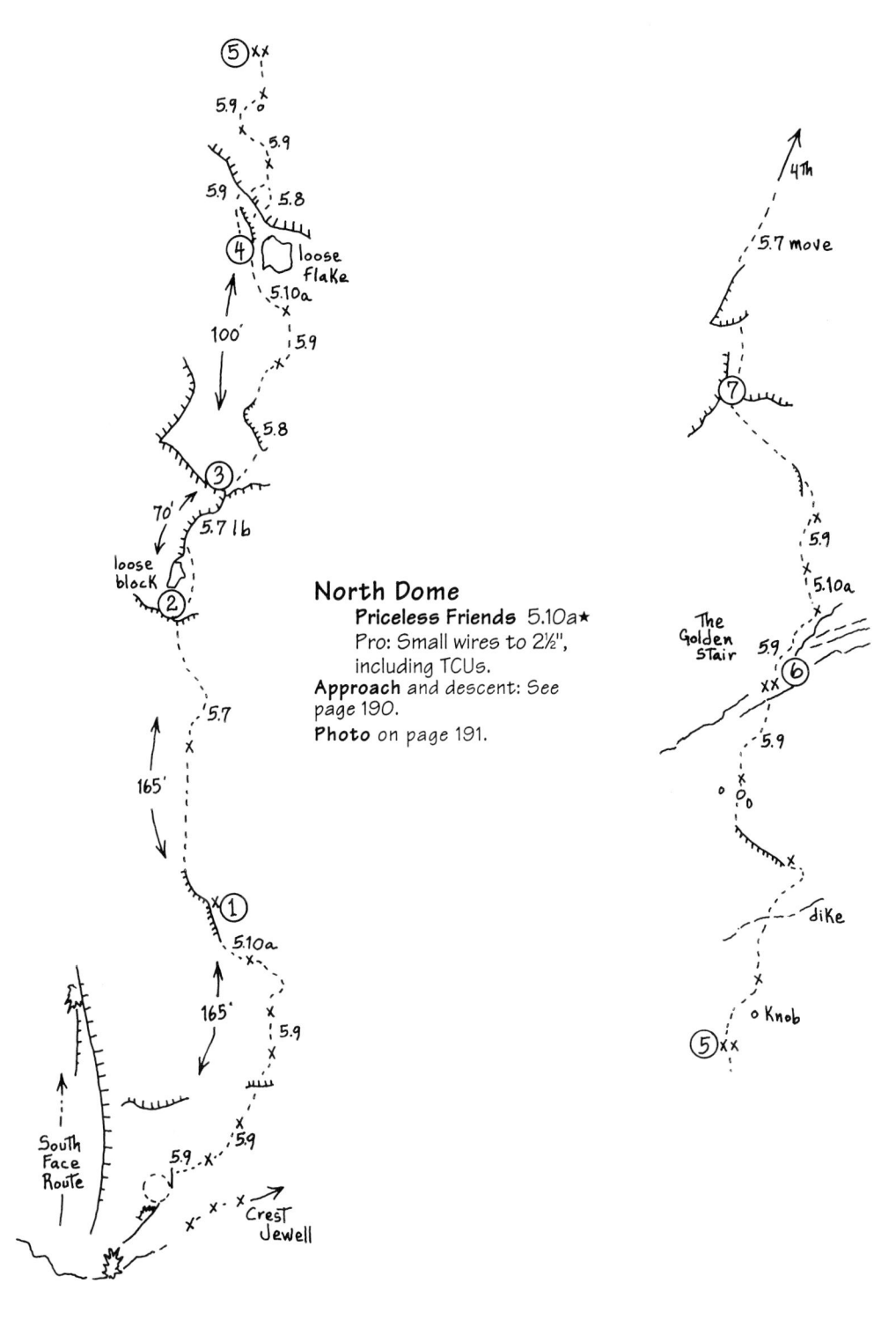

North Dome

Priceless Friends 5.10a★
Pro: Small wires to 2½", including TCUs.
Approach and descent: See page 190.
Photo on page 191.

WASHINGTON COLUMN

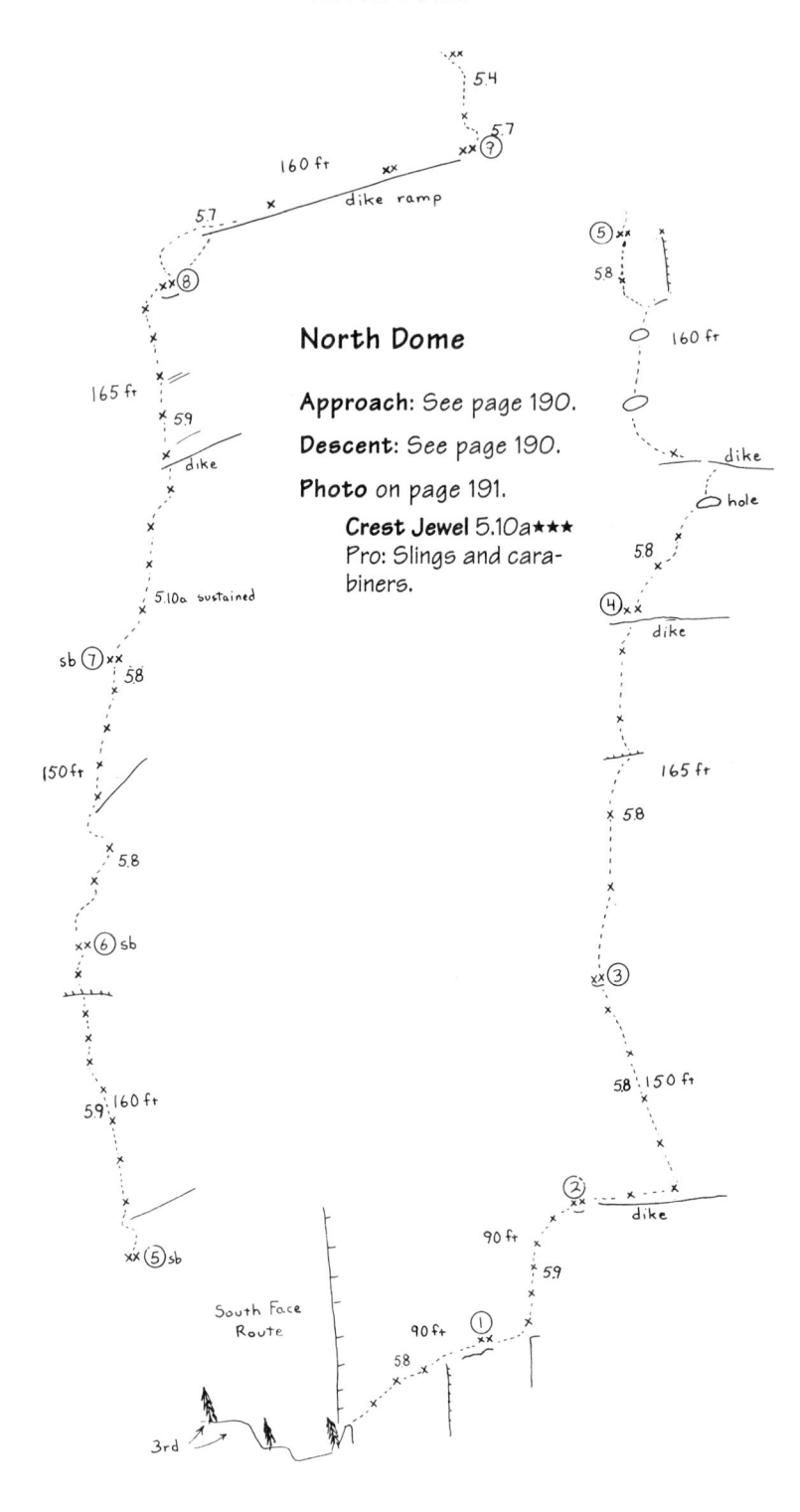

North Dome

Approach: See page 190.

Descent: See page 190.

Photo on page 191.

Crest Jewel 5.10a★★★
Pro: Slings and carabiners.

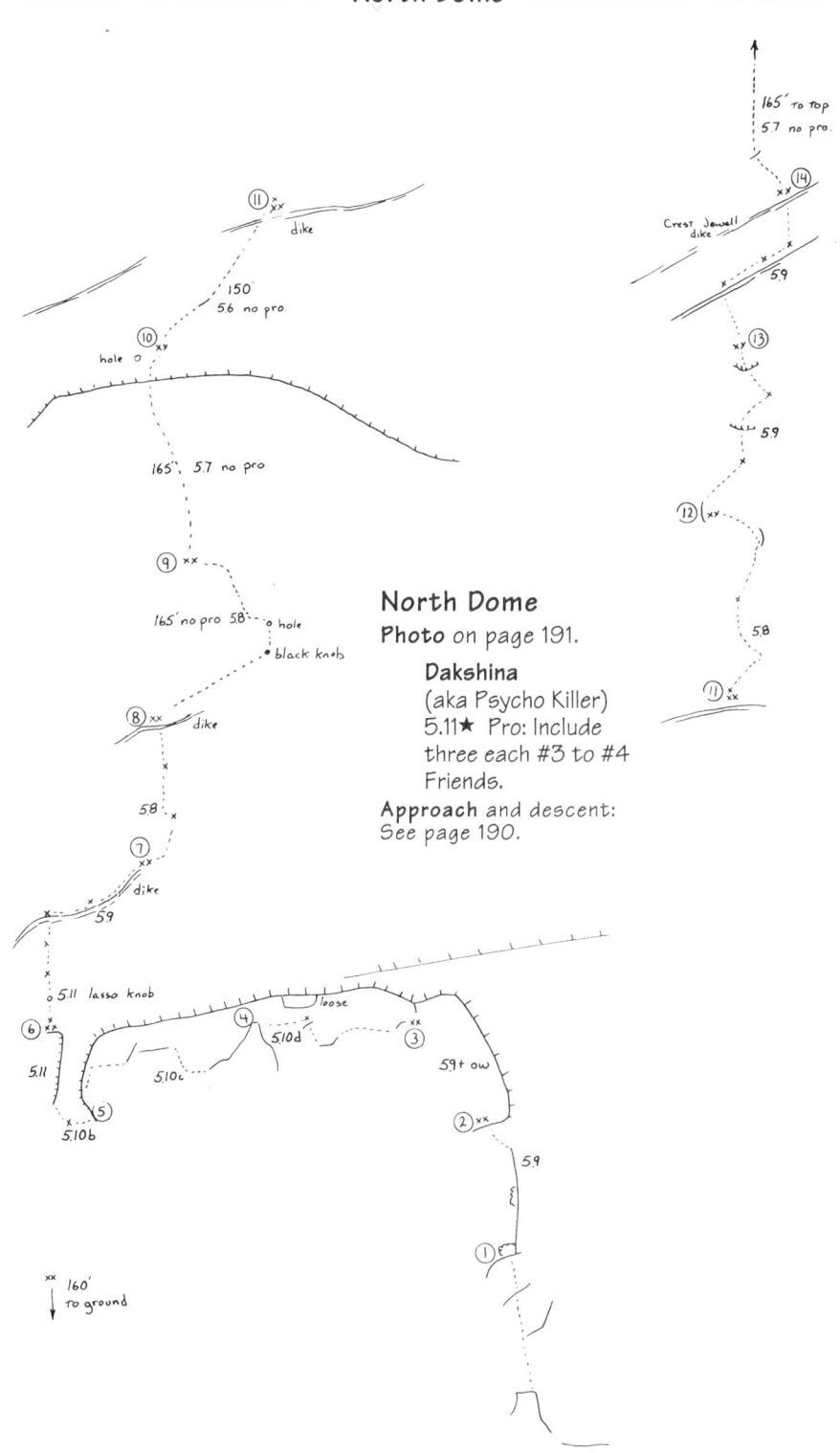

North Dome

Photo on page 191.

Dakshina
(aka Psycho Killer)
5.11★ Pro: Include three each #3 to #4 Friends.

Approach and descent: See page 190.

North Dome

North Dome

Approach: The climb is on the east face of the formation. Hike down and around this side of the Dome, avoiding brush by skirting along the base and staying on the slab when possible. A large tree and right-facing corner mark the start of the climb. **Mass Assault Route** starts near here as well.

Doctor Gravity 5.11b Pro: Wired nuts, all cams to 3½", especially small.

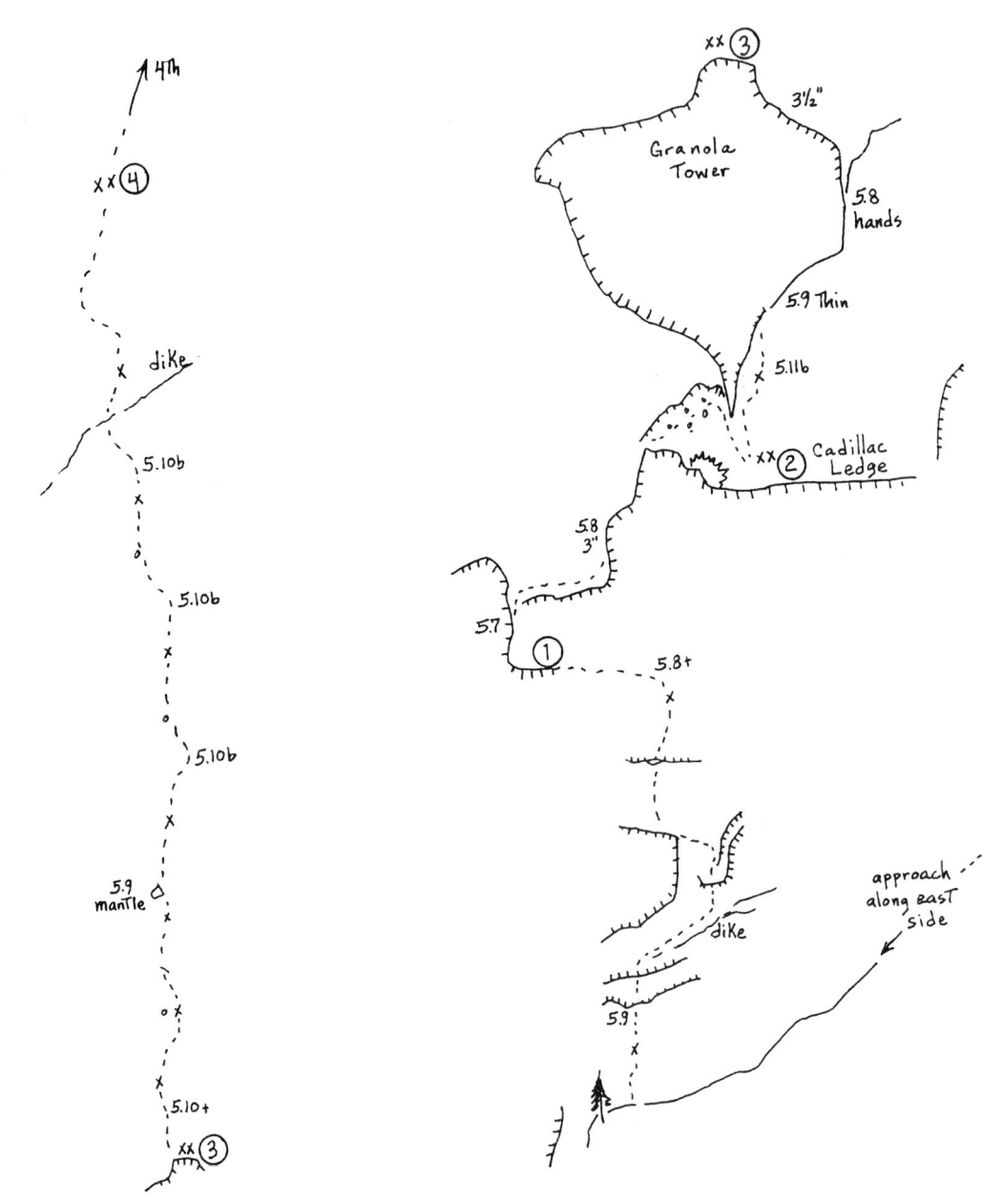

Basket Dome

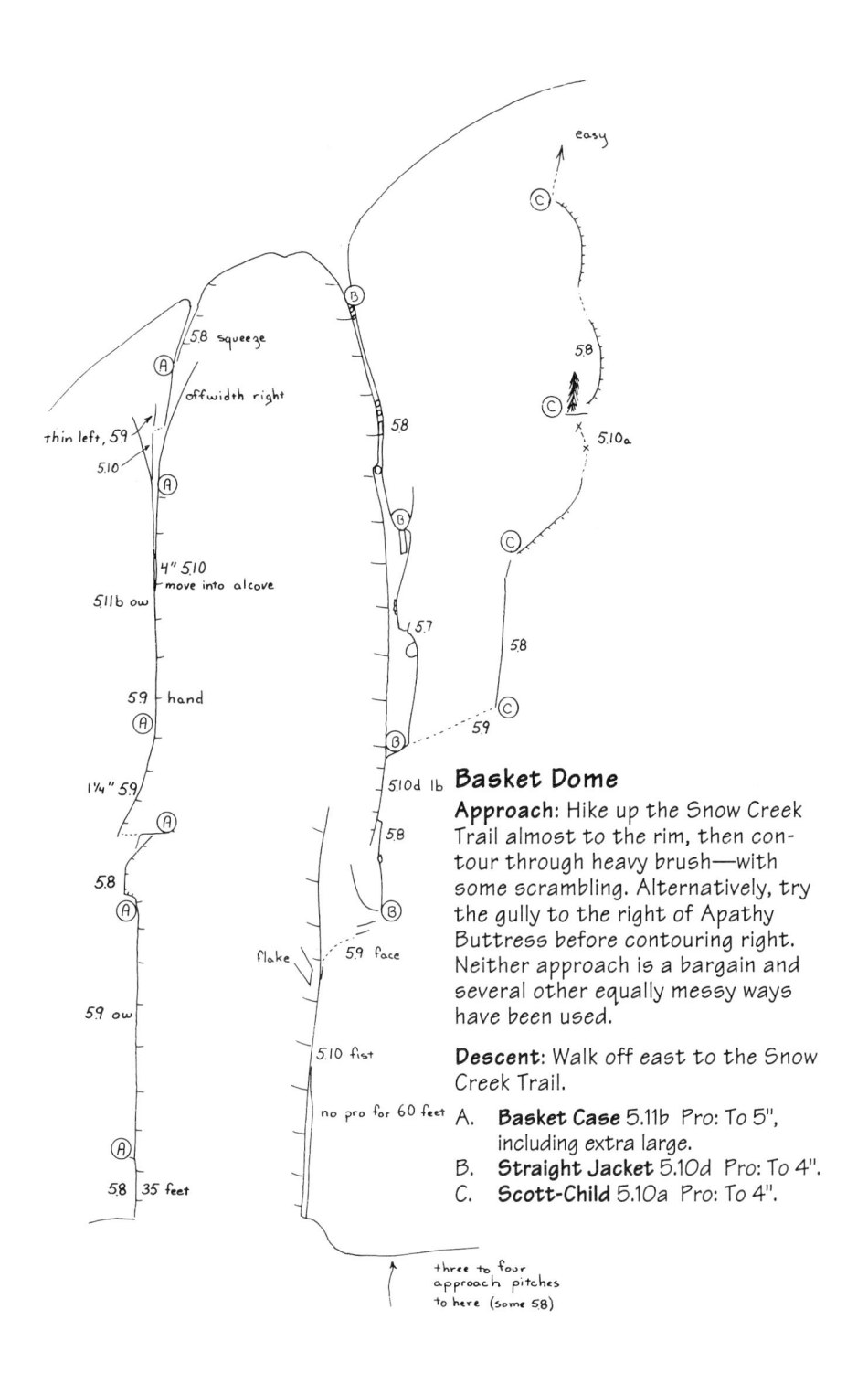

Approach: Hike up the Snow Creek Trail almost to the rim, then contour through heavy brush—with some scrambling. Alternatively, try the gully to the right of Apathy Buttress before contouring right. Neither approach is a bargain and several other equally messy ways have been used.

Descent: Walk off east to the Snow Creek Trail.

A. **Basket Case** 5.11b Pro: To 5", including extra large.
B. **Straight Jacket** 5.10d Pro: To 4".
C. **Scott-Child** 5.10a Pro: To 4".

TENAYA CANYON

Mirror Lake Area

Approach: From the Mirror Lake trailhead, walk east along the north side of the lake for about 1,000 feet until within easy reach of south-facing slabs to the north.

Mirror, Mirror

A. **Left** 5.10b R?
B. **Right** 5.9 R?
C. **Far Right** 5.10d R/X?
D. **Eric's Book** 5.9
E. **Thin Man** 5.10c R? Pro: To 1".
F. **Groundhog** 5.11b X?
G. **Breathalizer** 5.10b R?
H. **Precious Powder** 5.11a ★
I. **Diminishing Returns** 5.10c
J. **Werner's Crack** This former 5.8 route has been reduced to mere talus due to rockfall. Starts to neighboring climbs may be affected. Use caution!
K. **The Prude** 5.9 ★★ Pro: To 3½".
L. **Rurp Rape** 5.10c R

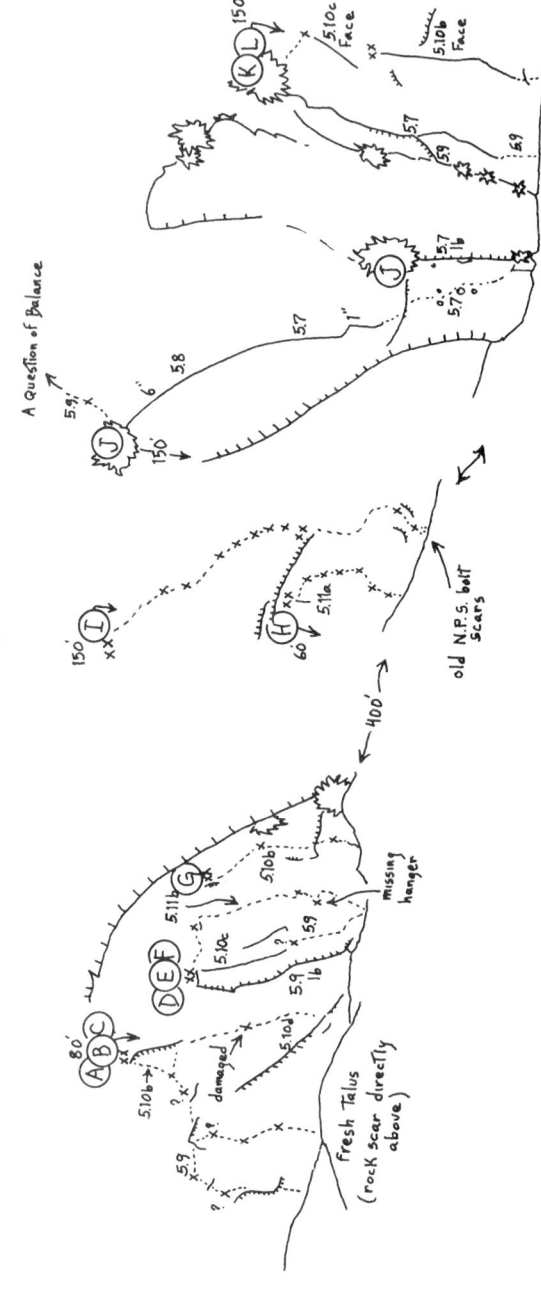

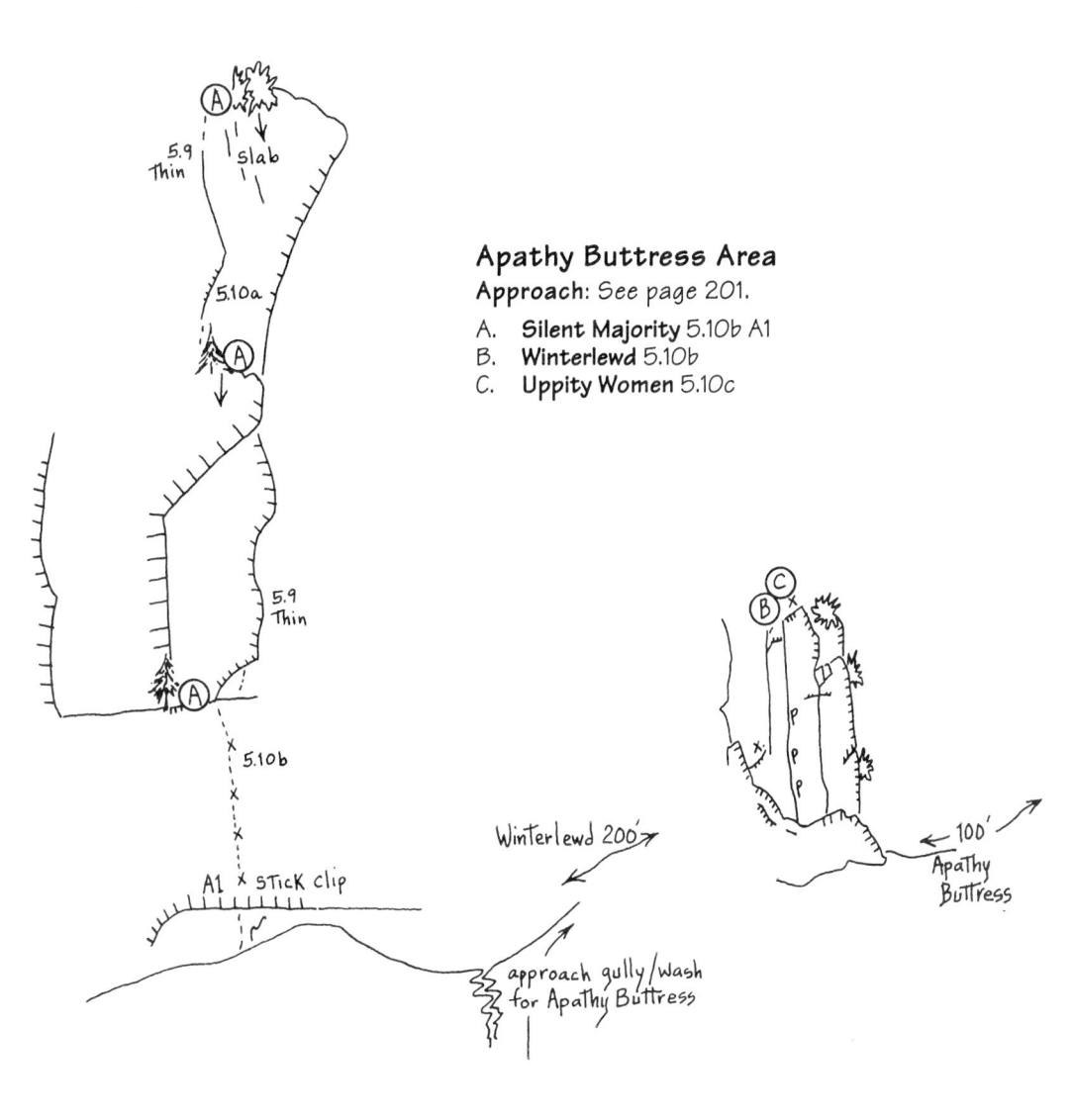

Apathy Buttress Area

Approach: See page 201.

A. **Silent Majority** 5.10b A1
B. **Winterlewd** 5.10b
C. **Uppity Women** 5.10c

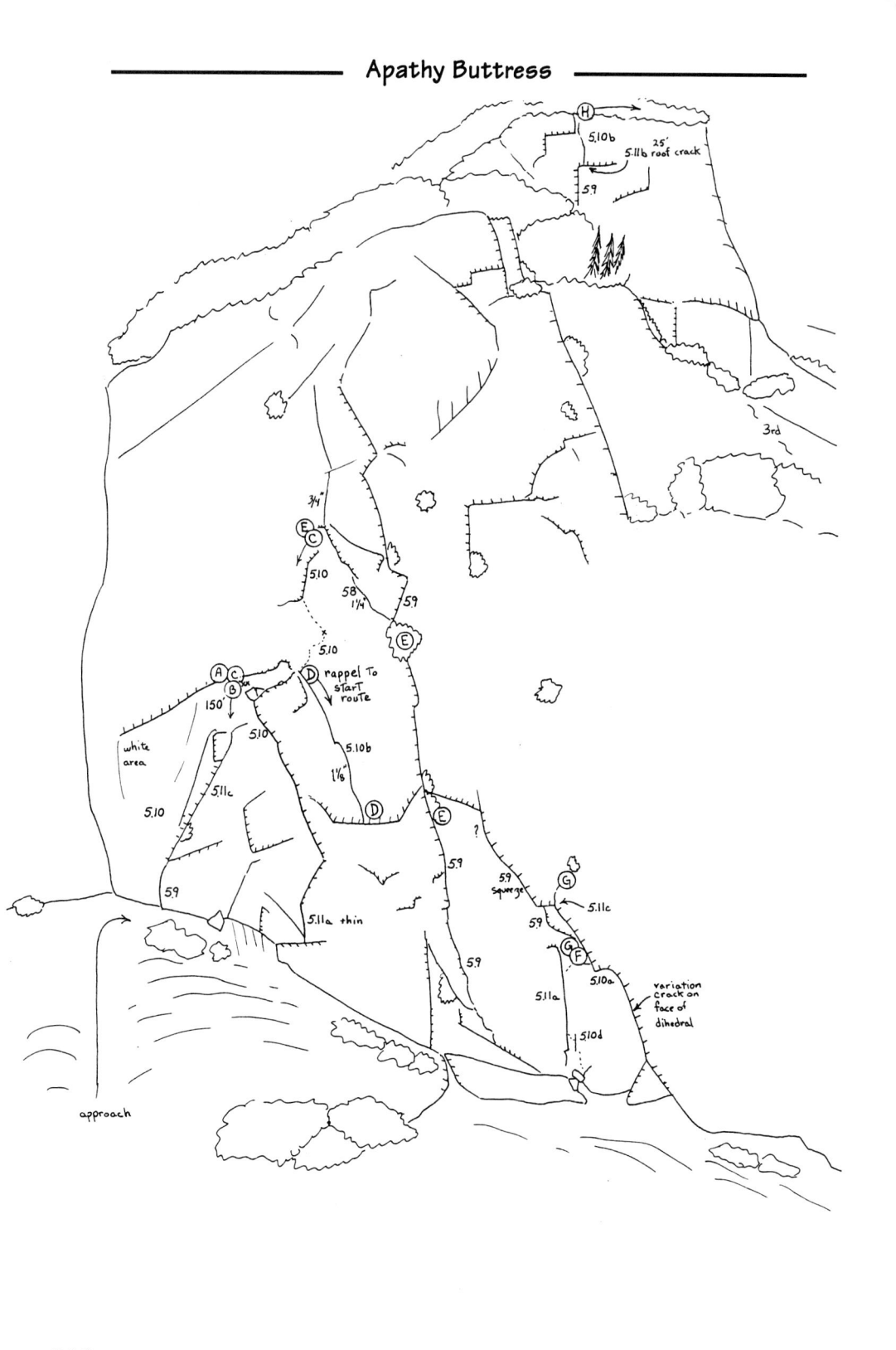

Apathy Buttress

200 — TENAYA CANYON

Apathy Buttress

Approach: Hike east from the Mirror Lake trailhead for about 0.5 mile, and cross the first series of creek beds. These are followed straight up the hill until a traverse right leads to the base of the left side of the wall. **Ken's Dream** is best approached from directly beneath. **Free Clinic** is approached from a gully on the right side of the wall.

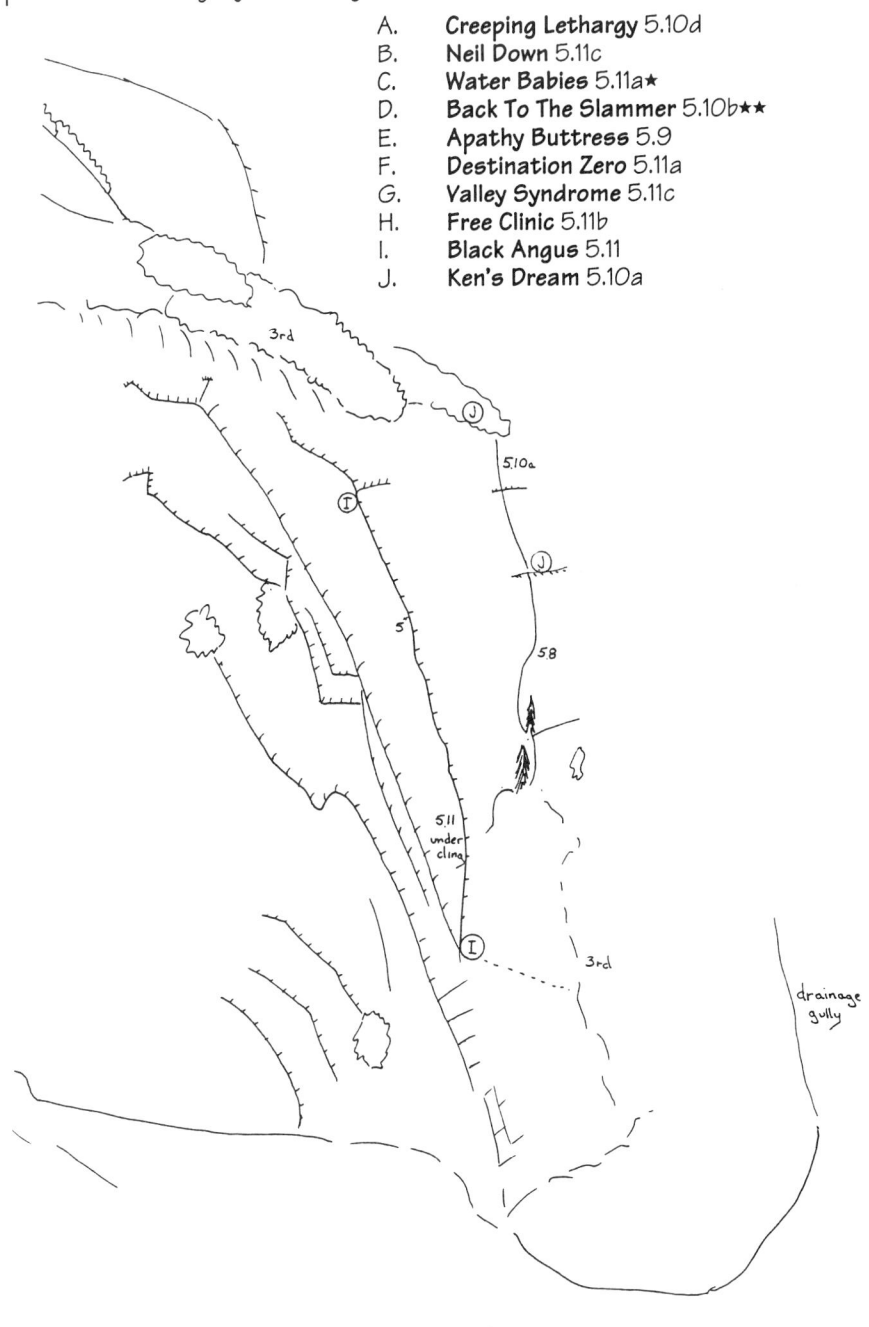

A. Creeping Lethargy 5.10d
B. Neil Down 5.11c
C. Water Babies 5.11a★
D. Back To The Slammer 5.10b★★
E. Apathy Buttress 5.9
F. Destination Zero 5.11a
G. Valley Syndrome 5.11c
H. Free Clinic 5.11b
I. Black Angus 5.11
J. Ken's Dream 5.10a

Mt. Watkins and YaSoo Dome

National Park Service phot

1. Escape From Freedom 5.11c A1
2. Golden Dawn 5.10d
3. YaSoo Dome, South Face Route 5.9
4. The Chief 5.11b A1

Approach: Park at a turnout approximately two miles west of Olmsted Point, at the junction of the May Lake and Snow Creek trails, and indicated at the road by a "Horse Crossing" sign. A blocked-off road to the south can be followed a short distance to an old stone quarry. Skirt this on its left side and gain a ridge which leads toward Mt. Watkins. After following this for a mile, the barren summit of YaSoo Dome will be seen to the left. To get to the YaSoo routes, drop down the brush-choked gully between the summit of YaSoo and the ridge of Mt. Watkins. The east flank of Watkins is rappelled, just to the west of the YaSoo gully, to get to **Golden Dawn**.

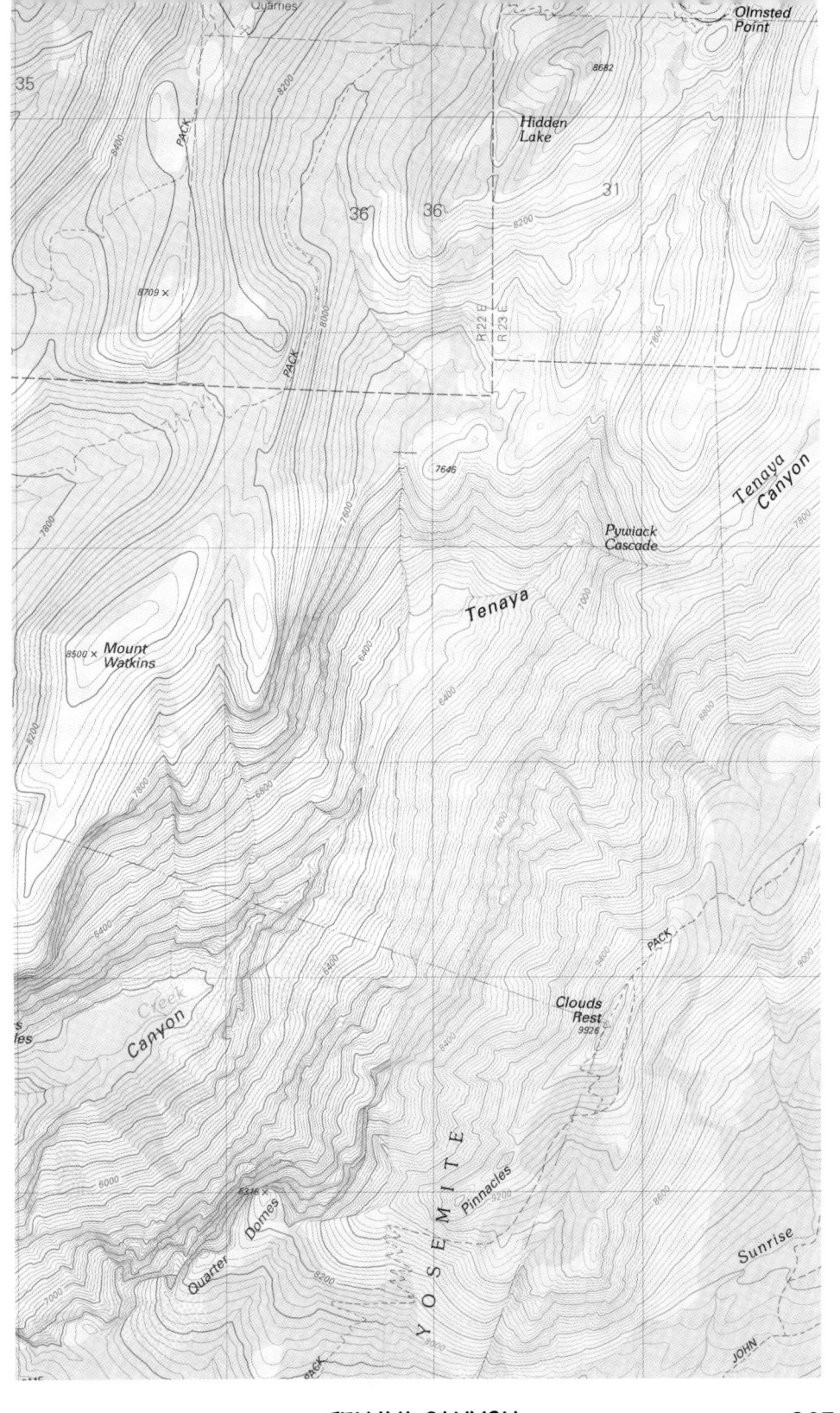

TENAYA CANYON

Mt. Watkins

Descent: See page 202.

Photo on page 202.

Escape From Freedom V/VI 5.11c A1

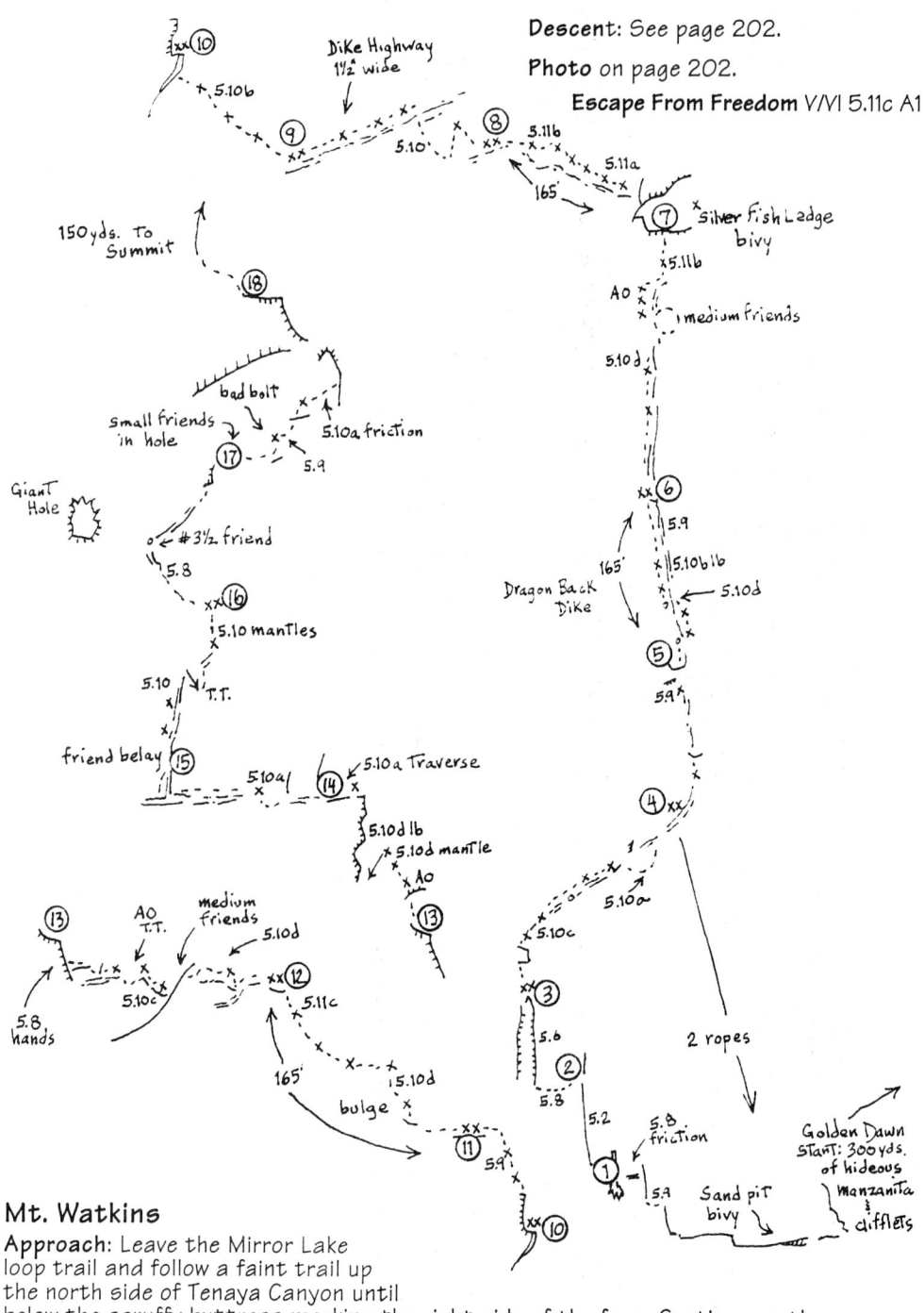

Mt. Watkins

Approach: Leave the Mirror Lake loop trail and follow a faint trail up the north side of Tenaya Canyon until below the scruffy buttress marking the right side of the face. Continue up the canyon a short distance and ascend intricate 5th class slabs for several hundred feet. Approaching from Tioga Road as per **Golden Dawn** is probably more efficient. **Note:** One pendulum, two tension traverses, two points of aid.

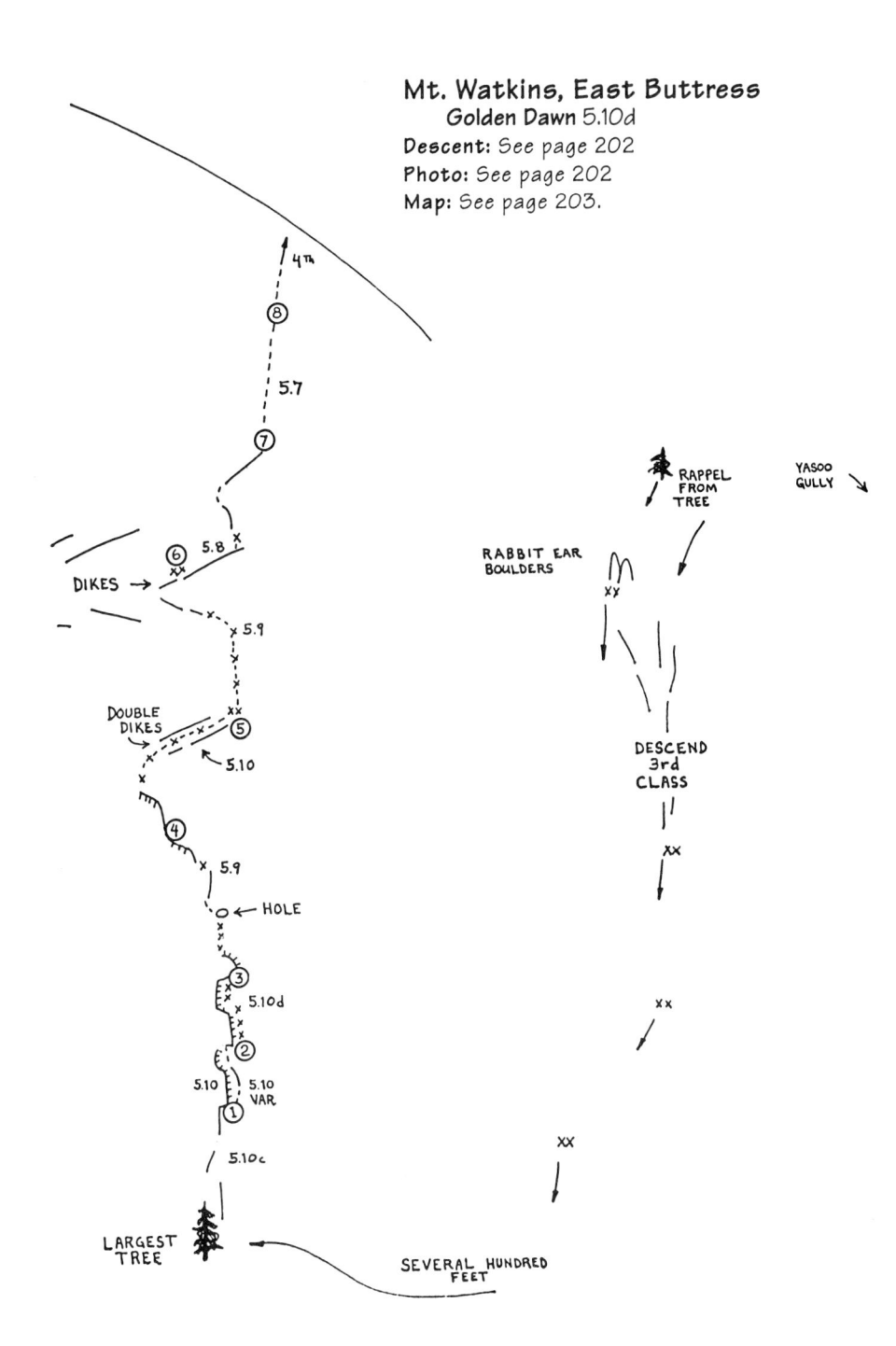

Mt. Watkins

Mt. Watkins, East Buttress
Golden Dawn 5.10d
Descent: See page 202
Photo: See page 202
Map: See page 203.

TENAYA CANYON — 205

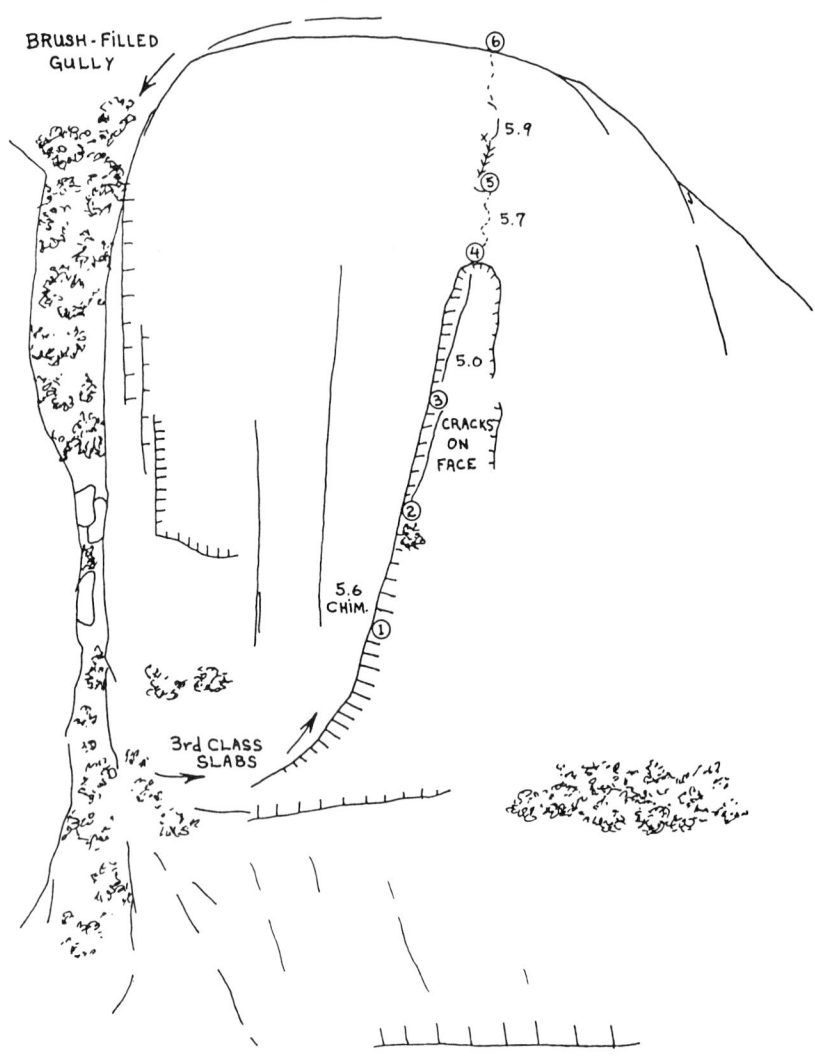

YaSoo Dome

YaSoo Dome
South Face 5.9 This wall is in beautiful Tenaya Canyon, about 0.75 mile east of Mt. Watkins.

Approach: From the afore mentioned parking area (p. 202), descend to the south, crossing a trail, then follow the drainage which flows into Tenaya Canyon and lies just east of YaSoo Dome. Just past a short, steep, brushy section in the drainage, follow talus adjacent to YaSoo to the base of The Chief.

Descent: See page 202
Photo: See page 202
Map: See page 203.

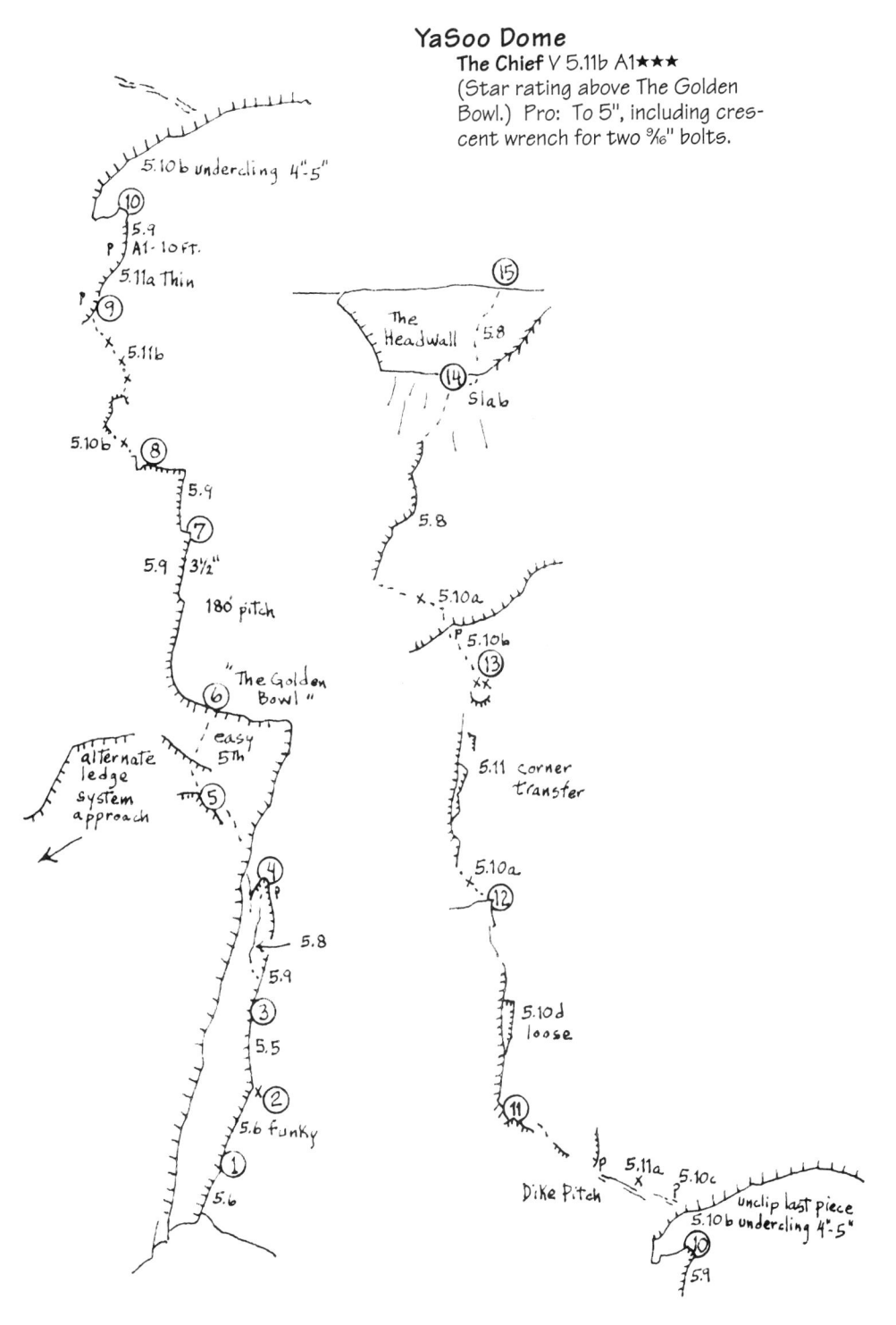

YaSoo Dome

The Chief V 5.11b A1 ★★★
(Star rating above The Golden Bowl.) Pro: To 5", including crescent wrench for two ⅜" bolts.

- 5.10b undercling 4"-5"
- ⑩
- 5.9 P A1 - 10 FT.
- 5.11a Thin
- ⑨
- 5.11b
- 5.10b ⑧
- 5.9
- ⑦
- 5.9 3½"
- 180' pitch
- "The Golden Bowl"
- ⑥
- alternate ledge system approach
- easy 5th
- ⑤
- ④
- 5.8
- 5.9
- ③
- 5.5
- ②
- 5.6 funky
- ①
- 5.6

- ⑮
- The Headwall 5.8
- ⑭ Slab
- 5.8
- 5.10a
- P 5.10b
- ⑬
- 5.11 corner transfer
- 5.10a
- ⑫
- 5.10d loose
- ⑪
- Dike Pitch 5.11a 5.10c
- unclip last piece
- 5.10b undercling 4"-5"
- ⑩
- 5.9

East Quarter Dome, North Face

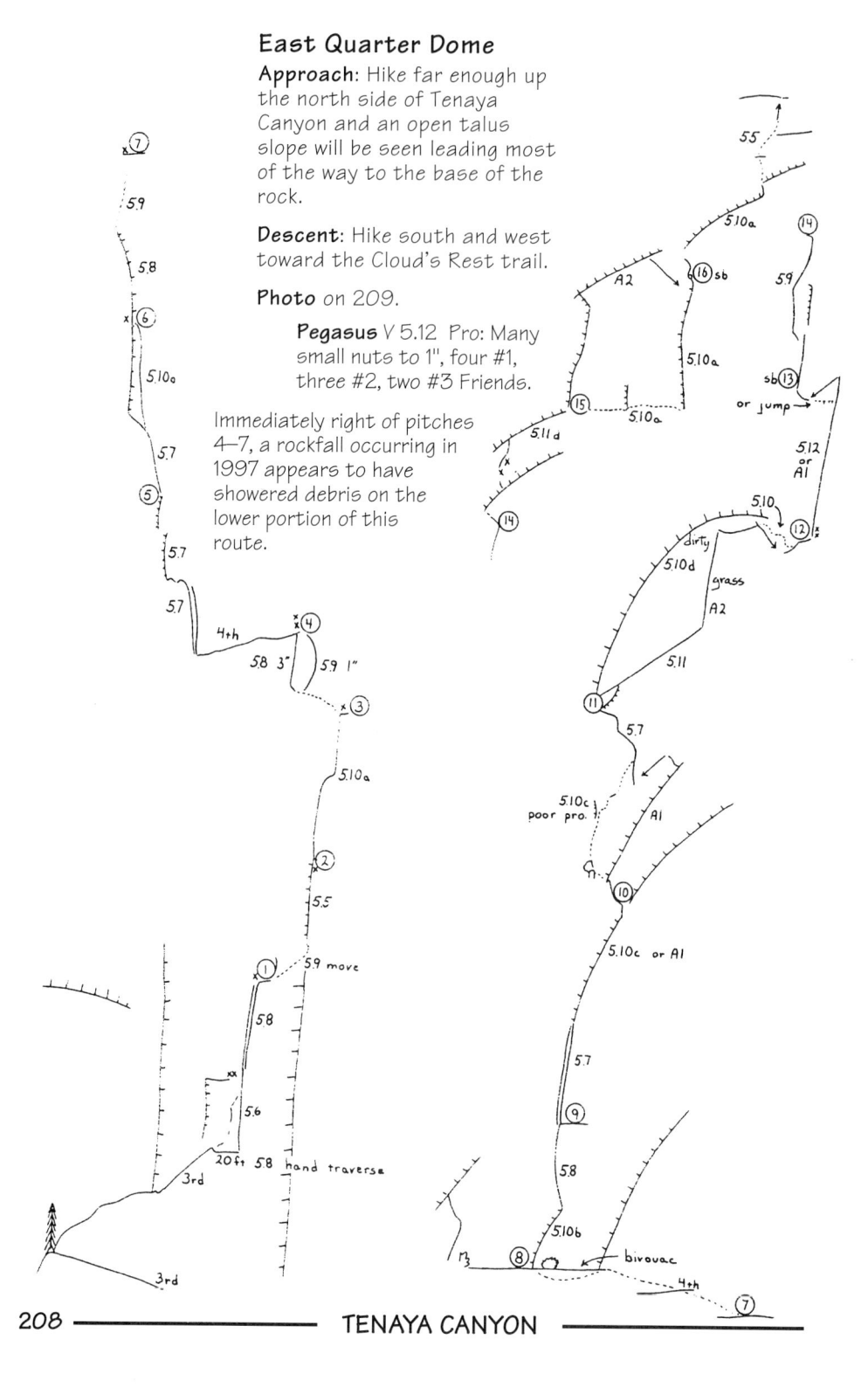

East Quarter Dome

Approach: Hike far enough up the north side of Tenaya Canyon and an open talus slope will be seen leading most of the way to the base of the rock.

Descent: Hike south and west toward the Cloud's Rest trail.

Photo on 209.

Pegasus V 5.12 Pro: Many small nuts to 1", four #1, three #2, two #3 Friends.

Immediately right of pitches 4–7, a rockfall occurring in 1997 appears to have showered debris on the lower portion of this route.

TENAYA CANYON

rockfall area

National Park Service photo

Quarter Dome
Pegasus 5.12

TENAYA CANYON — 209

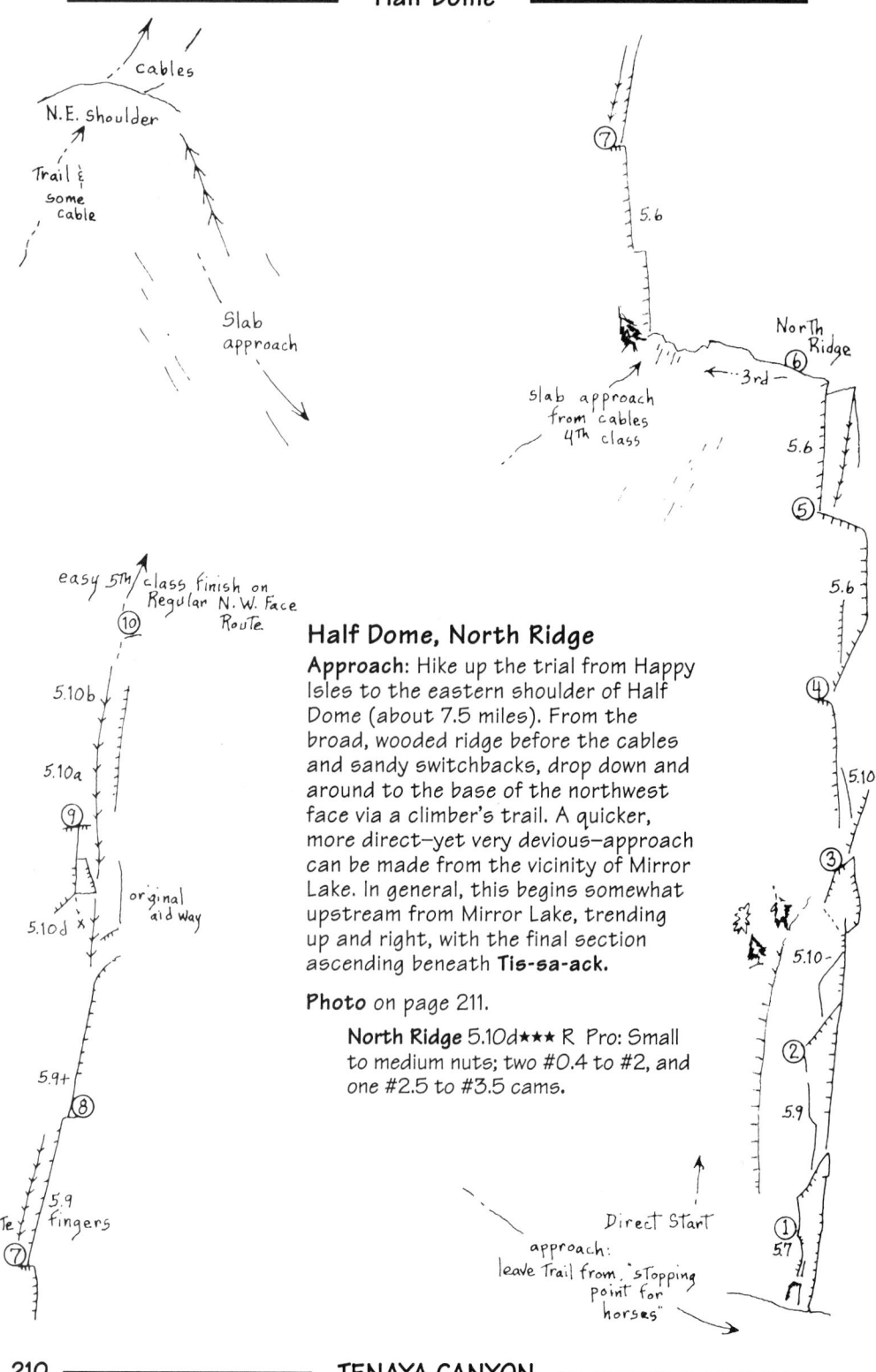

Half Dome

Half Dome, North Ridge

Approach: Hike up the trial from Happy Isles to the eastern shoulder of Half Dome (about 7.5 miles). From the broad, wooded ridge before the cables and sandy switchbacks, drop down and around to the base of the northwest face via a climber's trail. A quicker, more direct—yet very devious—approach can be made from the vicinity of Mirror Lake. In general, this begins somewhat upstream from Mirror Lake, trending up and right, with the final section ascending beneath **Tis-sa-ack**.

Photo on page 211.

    North Ridge 5.10d★★★ R Pro: Small to medium nuts; two #0.4 to #2, and one #2.5 to #3.5 cams.

Half Dome, Northwest Face

1. Final Exam 5.10d
2. North Ridge 5.10d
3. Regular Northwest Face Route 5.9 A2 or 5.12
4. Direct Northwest Face Route 5.13c/d

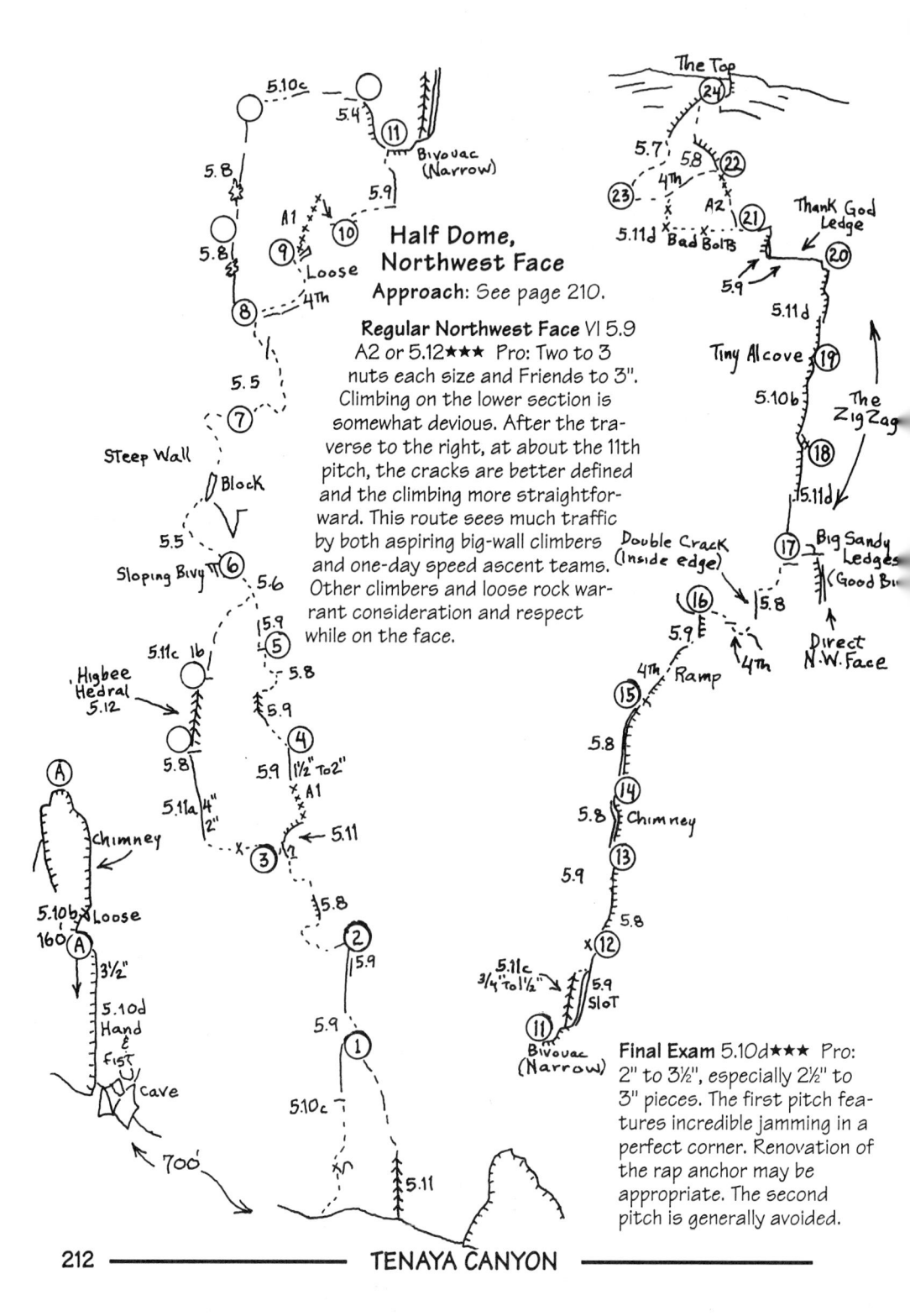

Half Dome

Half Dome, Northwest Face
Approach: See page 210.

Regular Northwest Face VI 5.9 A2 or 5.12★★★ Pro: Two to 3 nuts each size and Friends to 3". Climbing on the lower section is somewhat devious. After the traverse to the right, at about the 11th pitch, the cracks are better defined and the climbing more straightforward. This route sees much traffic by both aspiring big-wall climbers and one-day speed ascent teams. Other climbers and loose rock warrant consideration and respect while on the face.

Final Exam 5.10d★★★ Pro: 2" to 3½", especially 2½" to 3" pieces. The first pitch features incredible jamming in a perfect corner. Renovation of the rap anchor may be appropriate. The second pitch is generally avoided.

Half Dome

Half Dome, Northwest Face
Direct Northwest Face VI 5.13c/d

The Zigzags

Big Sandy Ledges — 5.7 chimney

Northwest Face Route

The Visor

Thank God Ledge

Grand Terrace bivouac

"Bongo Talker"

First Terrace

Bivoac

5.12a
5.7
5.11d
5.11b
5.13a
5.13b
5.13c/d
5.10a
5.10+ flake ow
5.11d
5.10b
5.11d
5.9
5.12b
5.9
5.12b stay left
5.11d
5.11+
5.11+
aid
5.13b
5.9
5.9

Hardware:
Friends:
4	#1
4	#1.5
4	#2
3	#2.5
2	#3
2	#3.5
2	#4

Many TCUs
Many RPs and small wireds

TENAYA CANYON

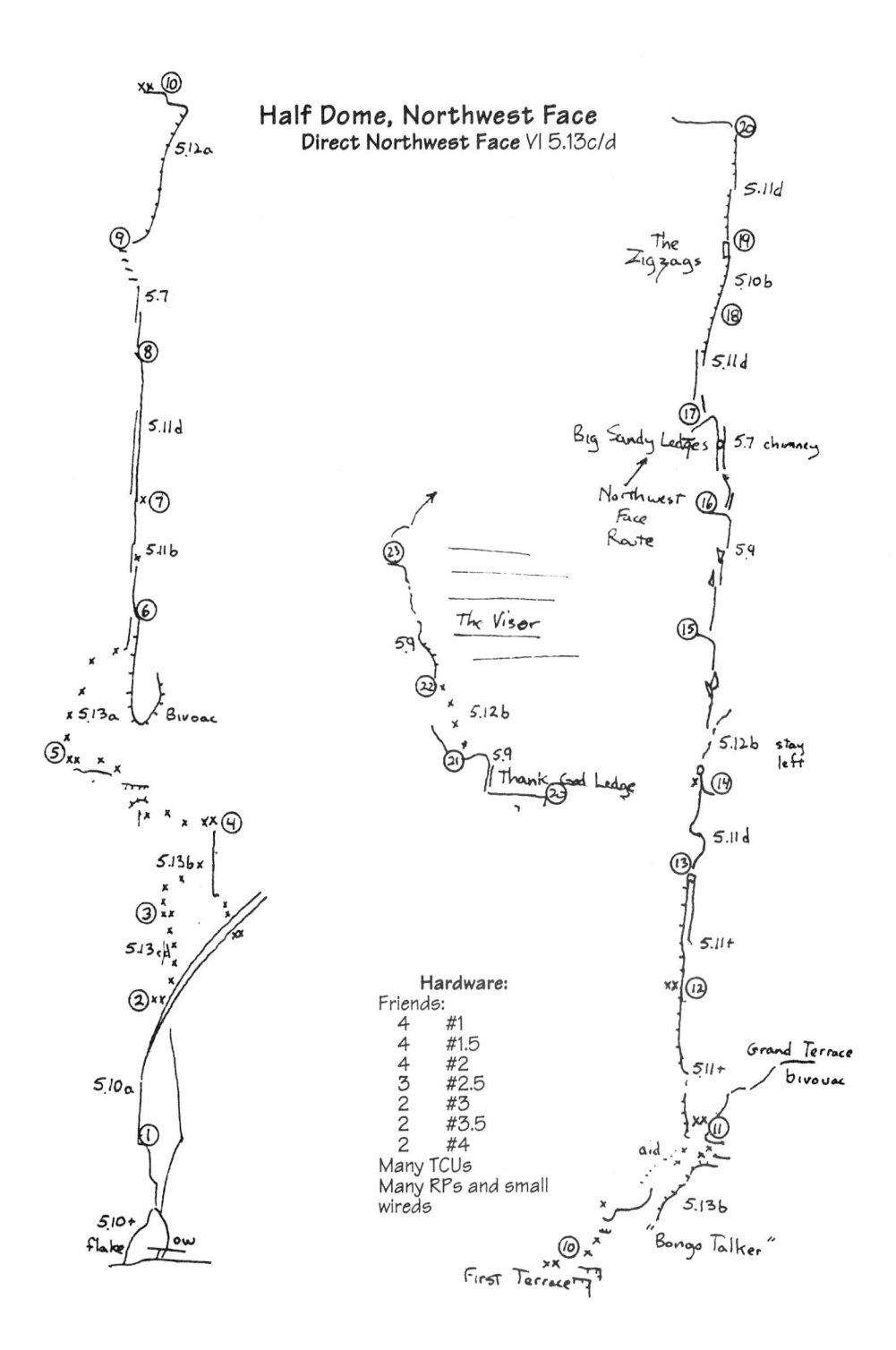

Half Dome

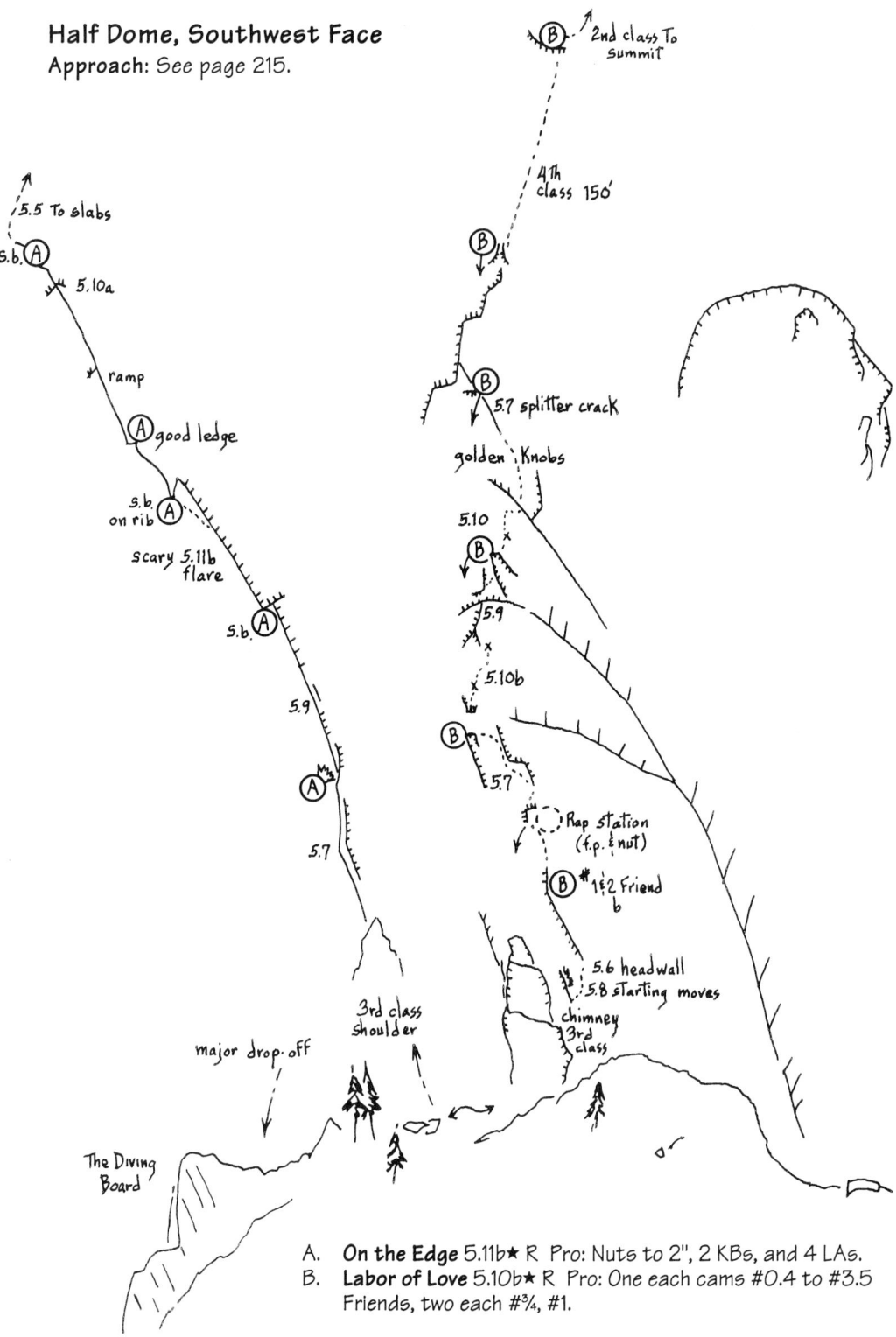

Half Dome, Southwest Face
Approach: See page 215.

Topo annotations:
- 5.5 To slabs
- s.b. (A)
- 5.10a
- ramp
- (A) good ledge
- s.b. on rib (A)
- scary 5.11b flare
- 5.b. (A)
- 5.9
- (A)
- 5.7
- 3rd class shoulder
- major drop-off
- The Diving Board
- 2nd class to summit (B)
- 4th class 150′
- (B)
- (B) 5.7 splitter crack
- golden knobs
- 5.10 (B)
- 5.9
- 5.10b
- (B) 5.7
- Rap station (f.p. & nut)
- (B) #1 & 2 Friend
- 5.6 headwall
- 5.8 starting moves
- chimney 3rd class

A. **On the Edge** 5.11b★ R Pro: Nuts to 2″, 2 KBs, and 4 LAs.
B. **Labor of Love** 5.10b★ R Pro: One each cams #0.4 to #3.5 Friends, two each #¾, #1.

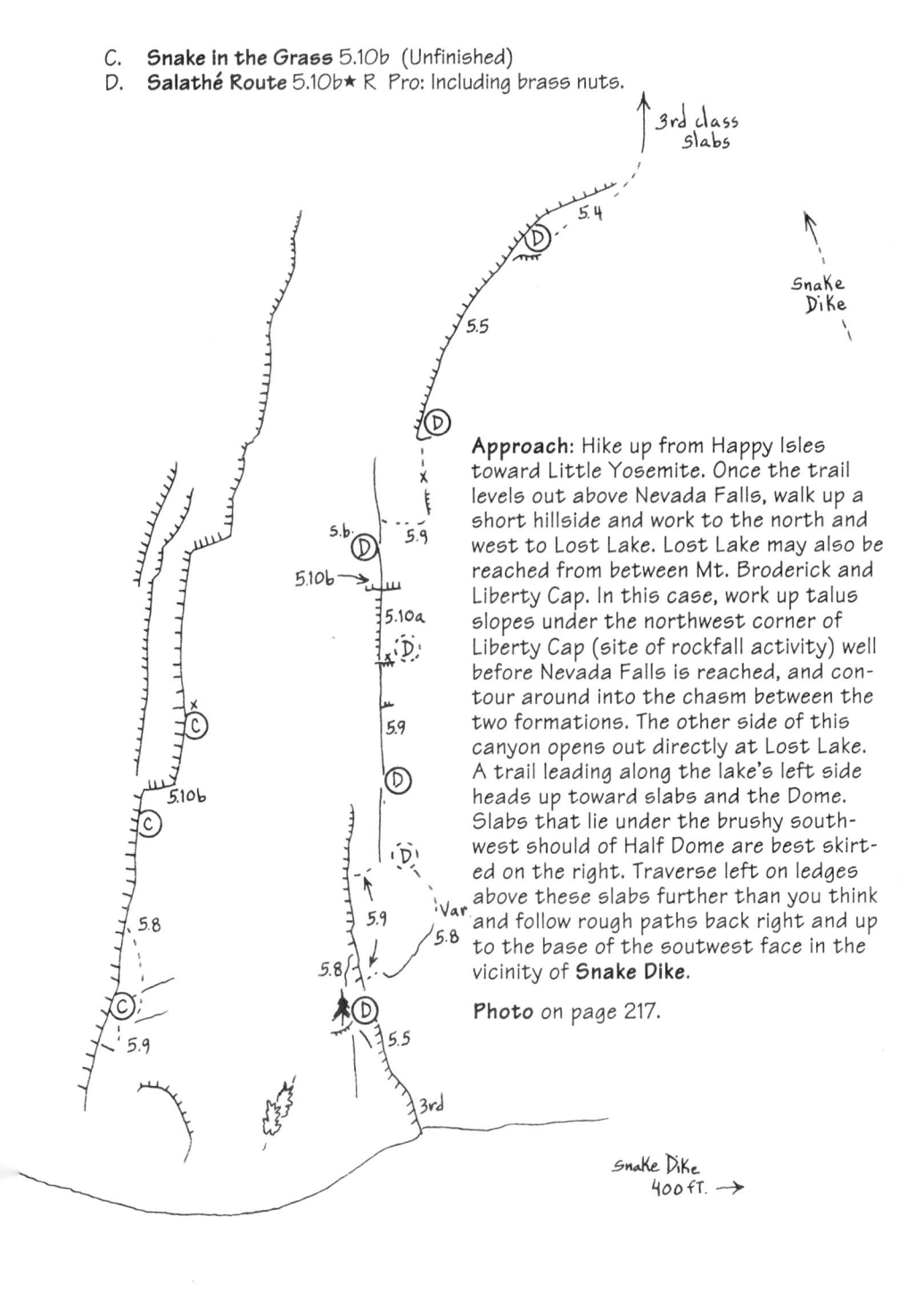

Half Dome

C. **Snake in the Grass** 5.10b (Unfinished)
D. **Salathé Route** 5.10b★ R Pro: Including brass nuts.

Approach: Hike up from Happy Isles toward Little Yosemite. Once the trail levels out above Nevada Falls, walk up a short hillside and work to the north and west to Lost Lake. Lost Lake may also be reached from between Mt. Broderick and Liberty Cap. In this case, work up talus slopes under the northwest corner of Liberty Cap (site of rockfall activity) well before Nevada Falls is reached, and contour around into the chasm between the two formations. The other side of this canyon opens out directly at Lost Lake. A trail leading along the lake's left side heads up toward slabs and the Dome. Slabs that lie under the brushy southwest should of Half Dome are best skirted on the right. Traverse left on ledges above these slabs further than you think and follow rough paths back right and up to the base of the soutwest face in the vicinity of **Snake Dike**.

Photo on page 217.

Snake Dike 400 ft. →

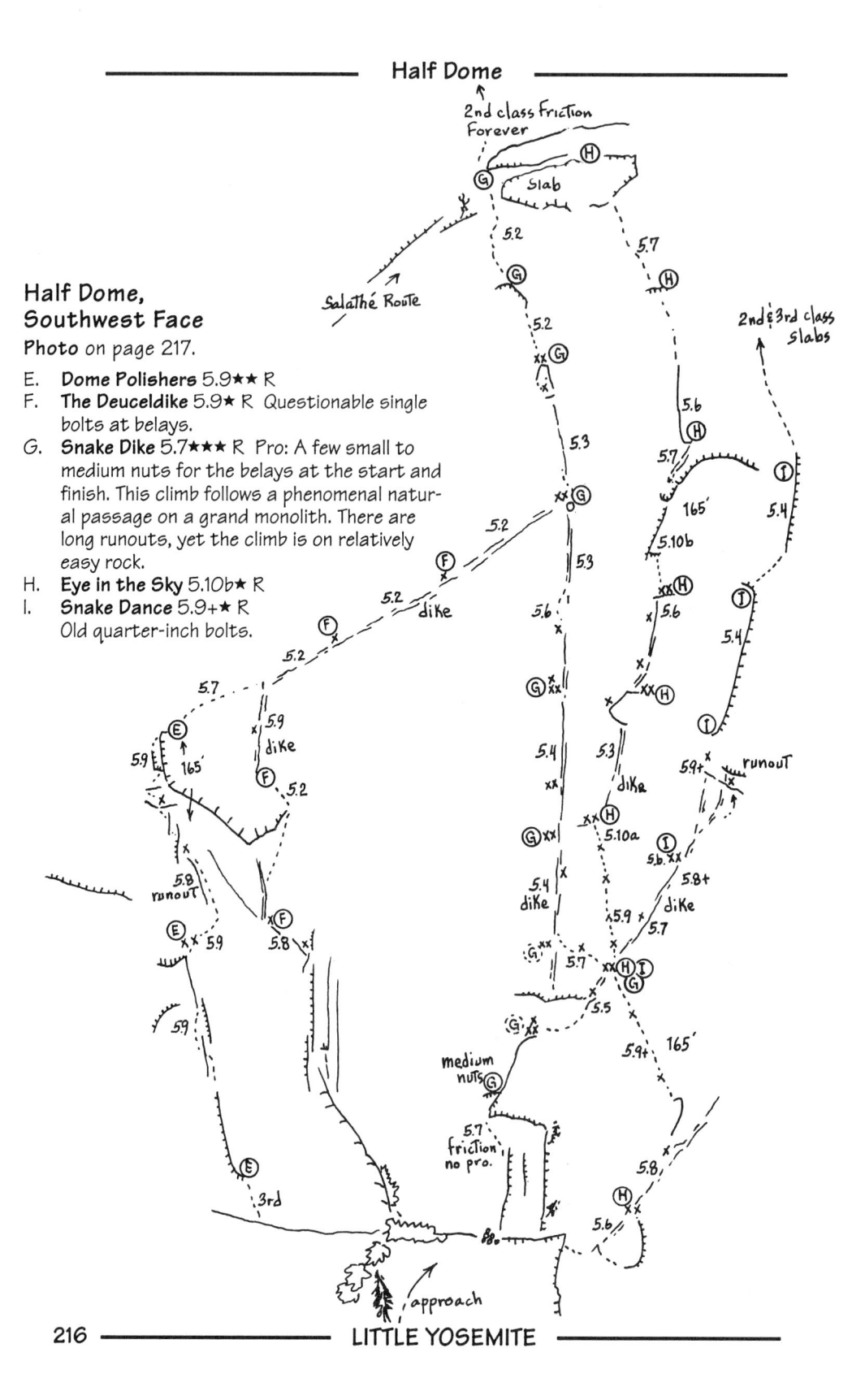

Half Dome, Southwest Face

Photo on page 217.

- E. **Dome Polishers** 5.9★★ R
- F. **The Deuceldike** 5.9★ R Questionable single bolts at belays.
- G. **Snake Dike** 5.7★★★ R Pro: A few small to medium nuts for the belays at the start and finish. This climb follows a phenomenal natural passage on a grand monolith. There are long runouts, yet the climb is on relatively easy rock.
- H. **Eye in the Sky** 5.10b★ R
- I. **Snake Dance** 5.9+★ R
Old quarter-inch bolts.

Half Dome, Southwest Face

1. Salathé Route 5.10b★ R
2. Snake Dike 5.7
3. Autobahn 5.11+

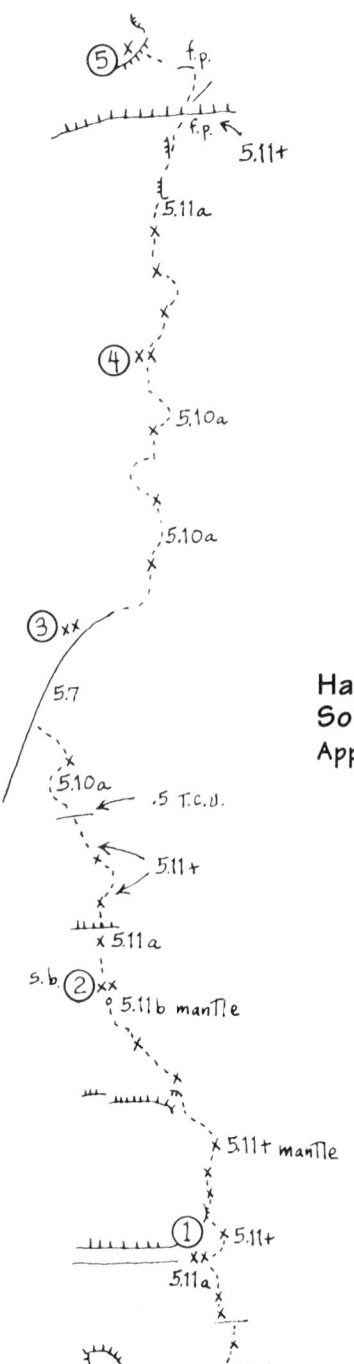

Half Dome

Half Dome, Southwest Face
Approach: See page 215.

Dreamscape IV 5.11+ ★★
Pro: Two each #0.4 and #0.5 TCUs, one each #1 to #3.5 Friends, one each #4 and #5 Rocks.

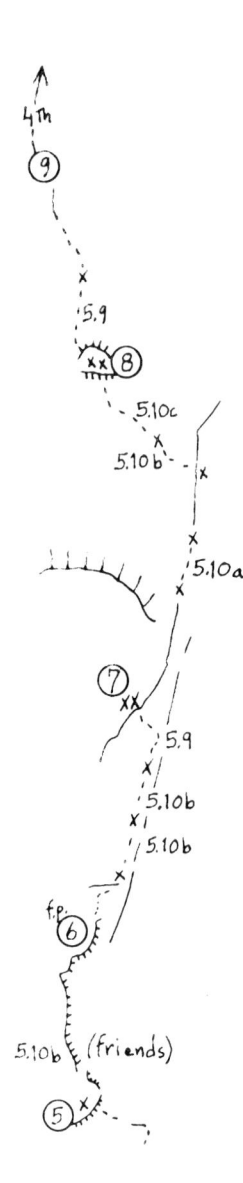

LITTLE YOSEMITE

Half Dome

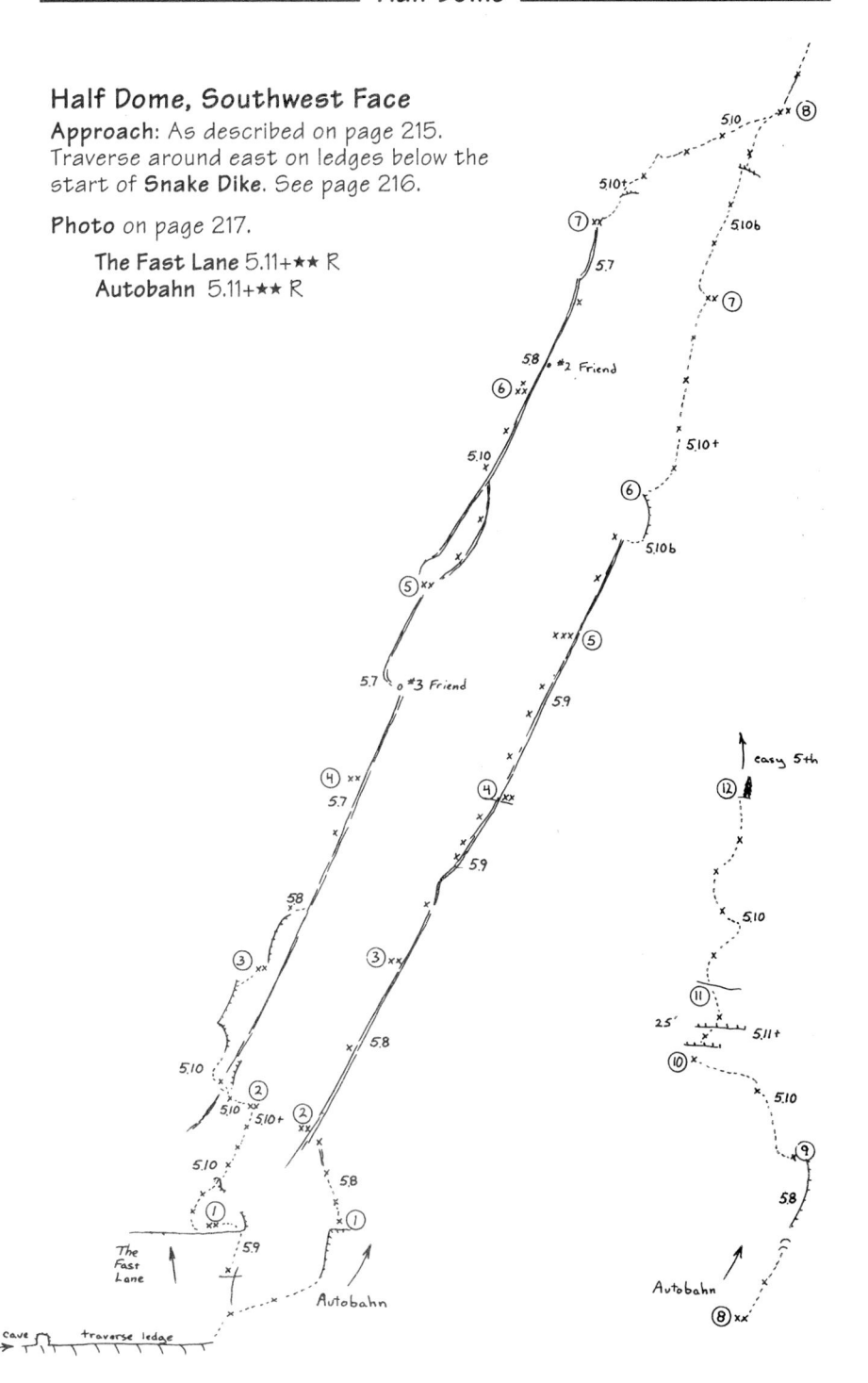

Half Dome, Southwest Face

Approach: As described on page 215. Traverse around east on ledges below the start of **Snake Dike**. See page 216.

Photo on page 217.

The Fast Lane 5.11+ ★★ R
Autobahn 5.11+ ★★ R

Half Dome

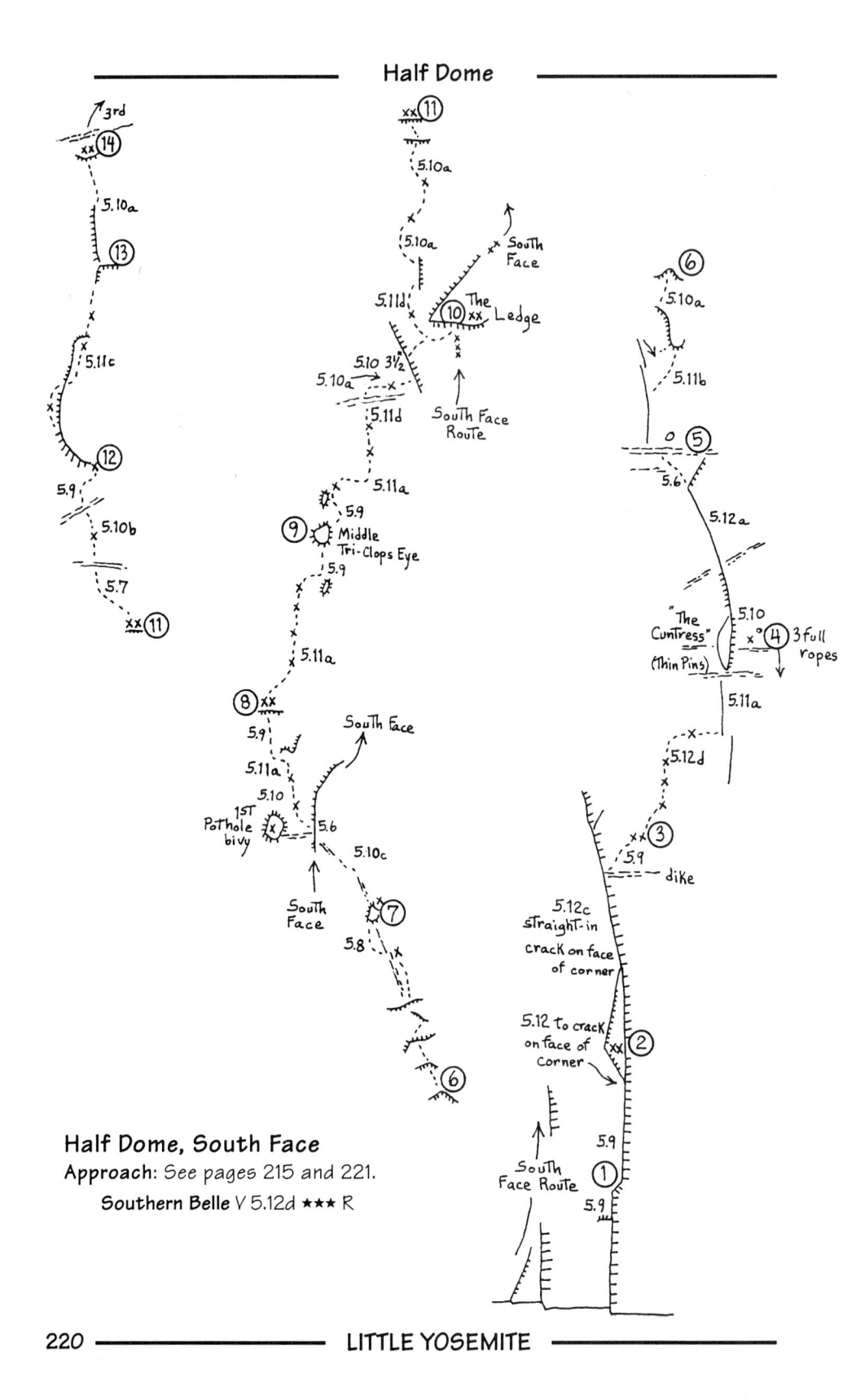

Half Dome, South Face
Approach: See pages 215 and 221.
   Southern Belle V 5.12d ★★★ R

LITTLE YOSEMITE

Half Dome

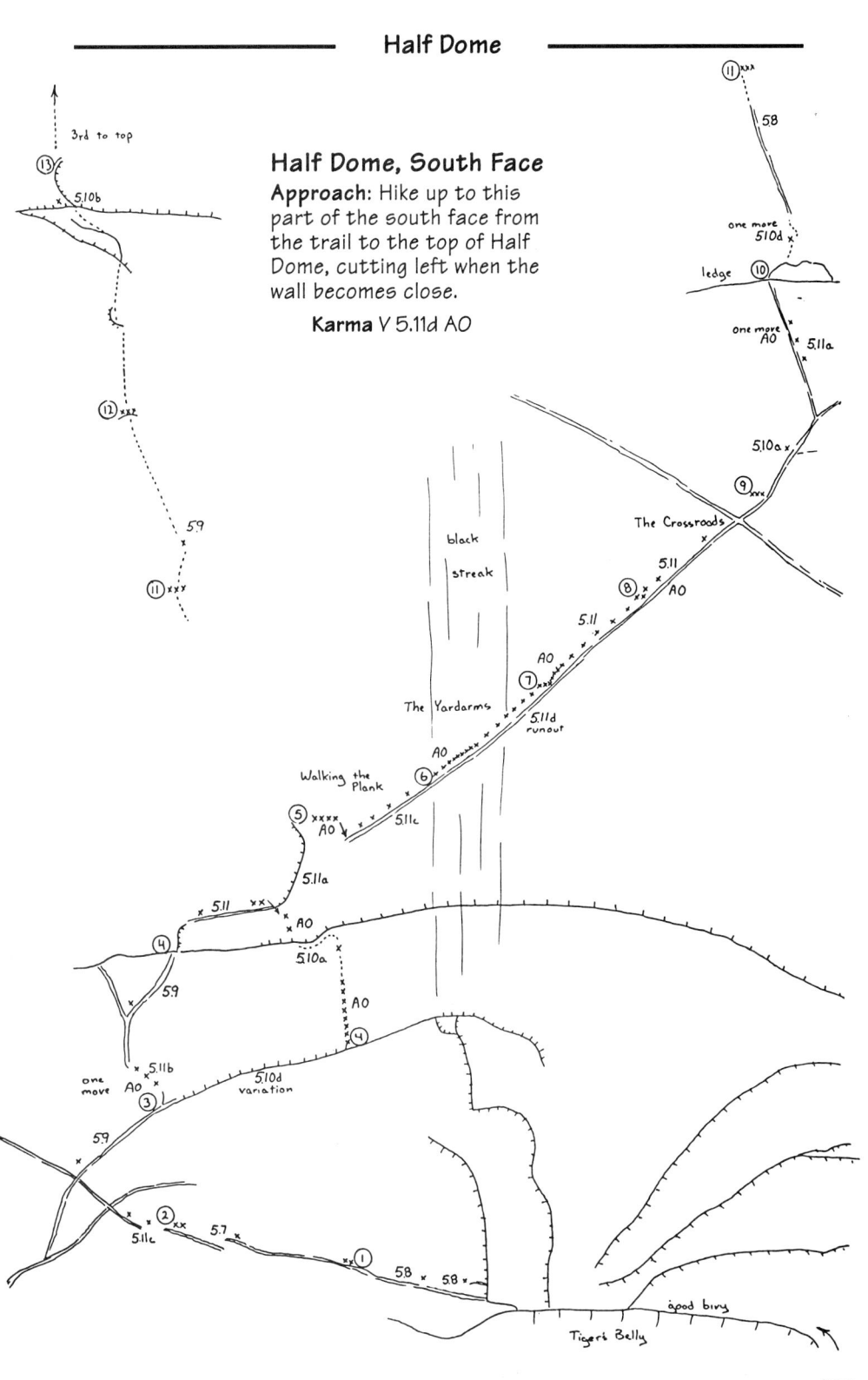

Half Dome, South Face

Approach: Hike up to this part of the south face from the trail to the top of Half Dome, cutting left when the wall becomes close.

Karma V 5.11d A0

Half Dome

Half Dome, South Face

Approach: Hike up the trail from Happy Isles to the northeast flank of Half Dome (about 7.5 miles).

Photo on page 223.

- A. **Call of the Wild** 5.10d   Pro: Double Friends to #4, including two #4 Camalots.
- B. **Happy Gully** 5.8   Pro: To 3".

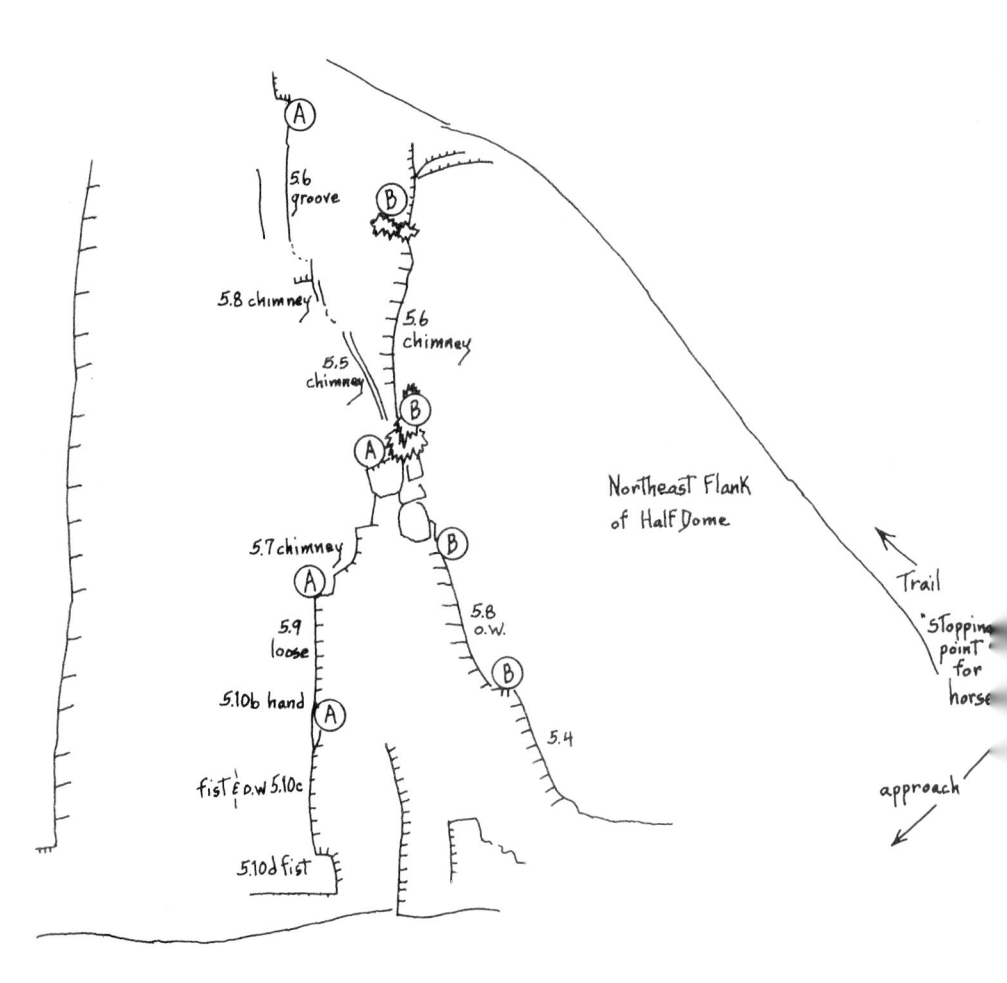

Half Dome, South Face

1. Autobahn 5.11+
2. Karma 5.11d A0
3. Call of the Wild 5.10d

Above Mirror Lake

This climb is located on a rib of rock below Half Dome and the Porcelain Wall/Diving Board. A clean, silver-gray slab is to the southwest; the approach slabs and gullies leading to the Northwest Face of Half Dome are to the left.

Approach: Begin somewhat upstream from Mirror Lake, as for the start of the Half Dome approach, and trend up and right with some Class 4. Then traverse right approximately 300 feet, where the "J" crack of the first pitch should become obvious.

   Porcelain Pup III 5.10b★ Pro: Wired nuts, especially ⅜" to ⅝", two each #0.5 TCU to #2 Friend, one each #2.5 to #3.5 Friend.

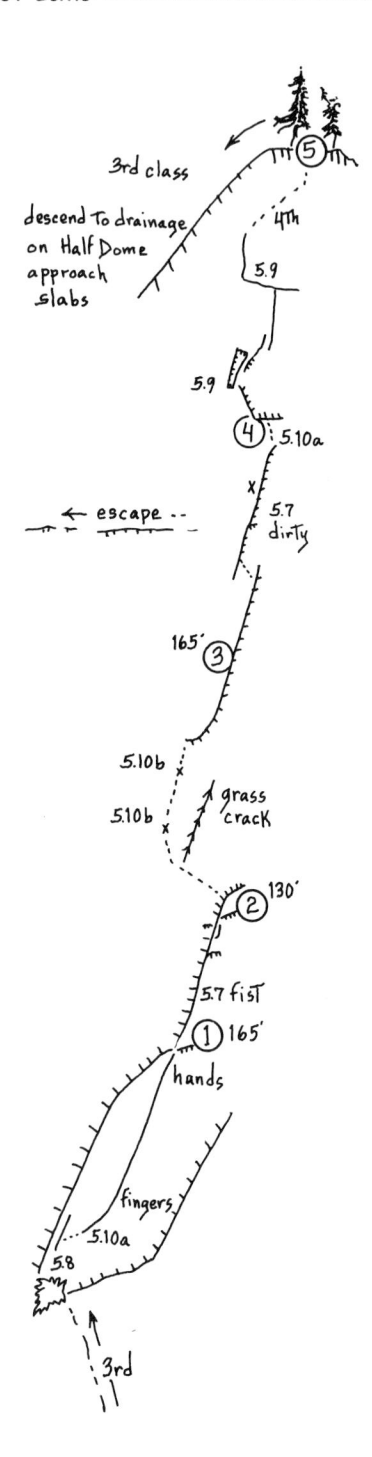

Silver Platter

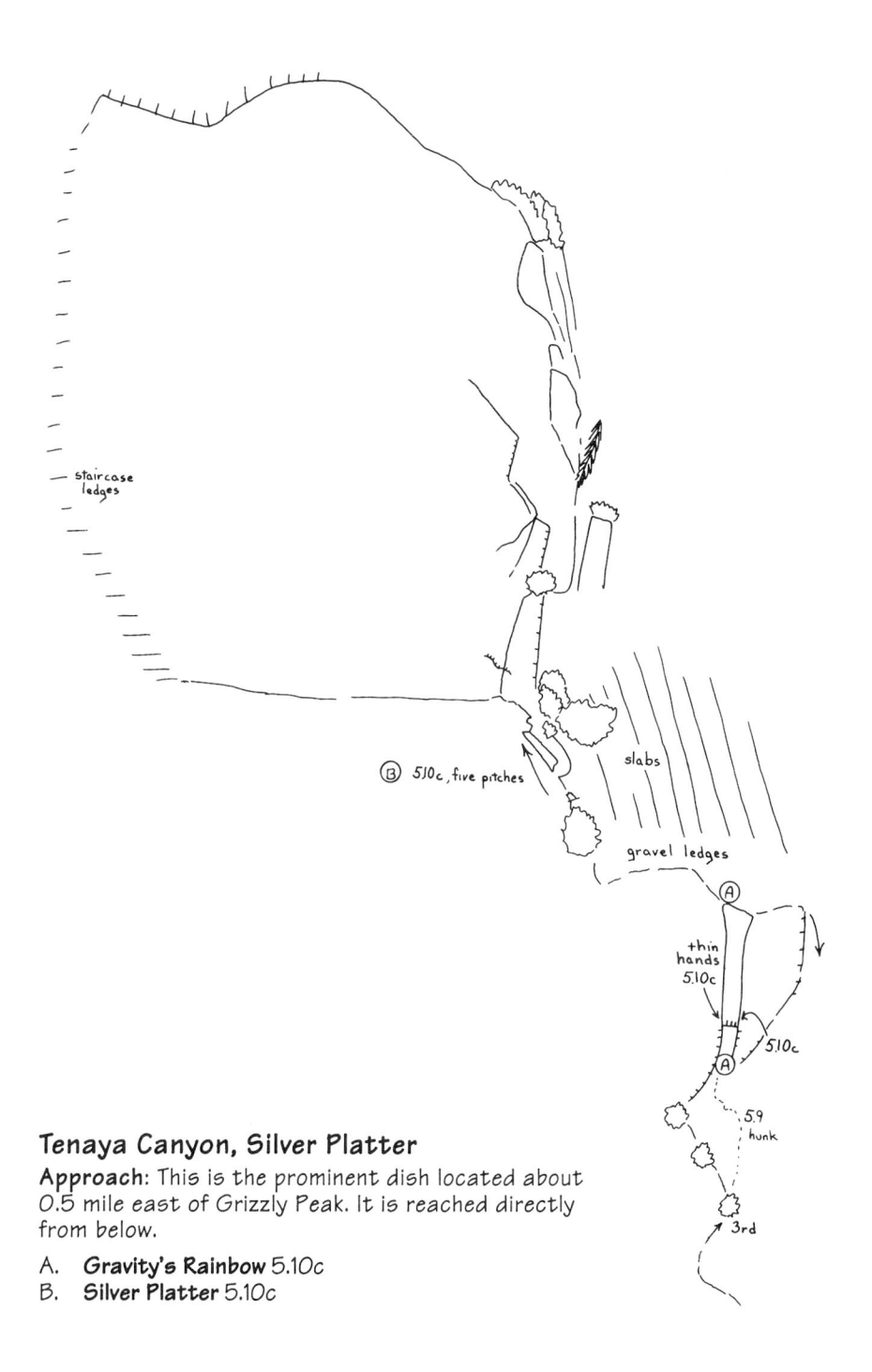

Tenaya Canyon, Silver Platter

Approach: This is the prominent dish located about 0.5 mile east of Grizzly Peak. It is reached directly from below.

A. **Gravity's Rainbow** 5.10c
B. **Silver Platter** 5.10c

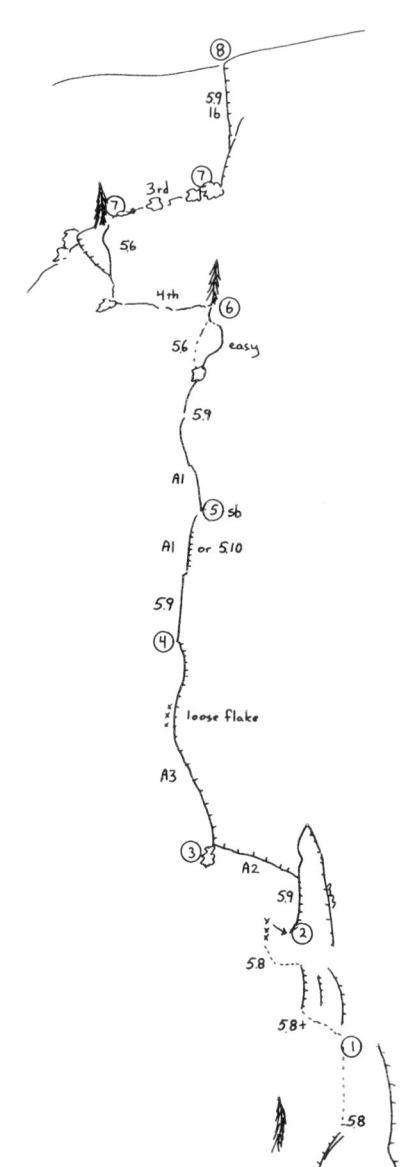

Mt. Broderick

Approach: Hike up the trail from Happy Isles toward Little Yosemite. Mt. Broderick is the major rock to the west of Liberty Cap. This route climbs the center of the west face.

Note: This route has **not** gone free, but is included because of its exclusion in *Yosemite Climbs: Big Walls*.

> **Unemployment Line** 5.9 A3
> Hardware: 2 KBs, 5 LAs, nuts to 3½", Friends.

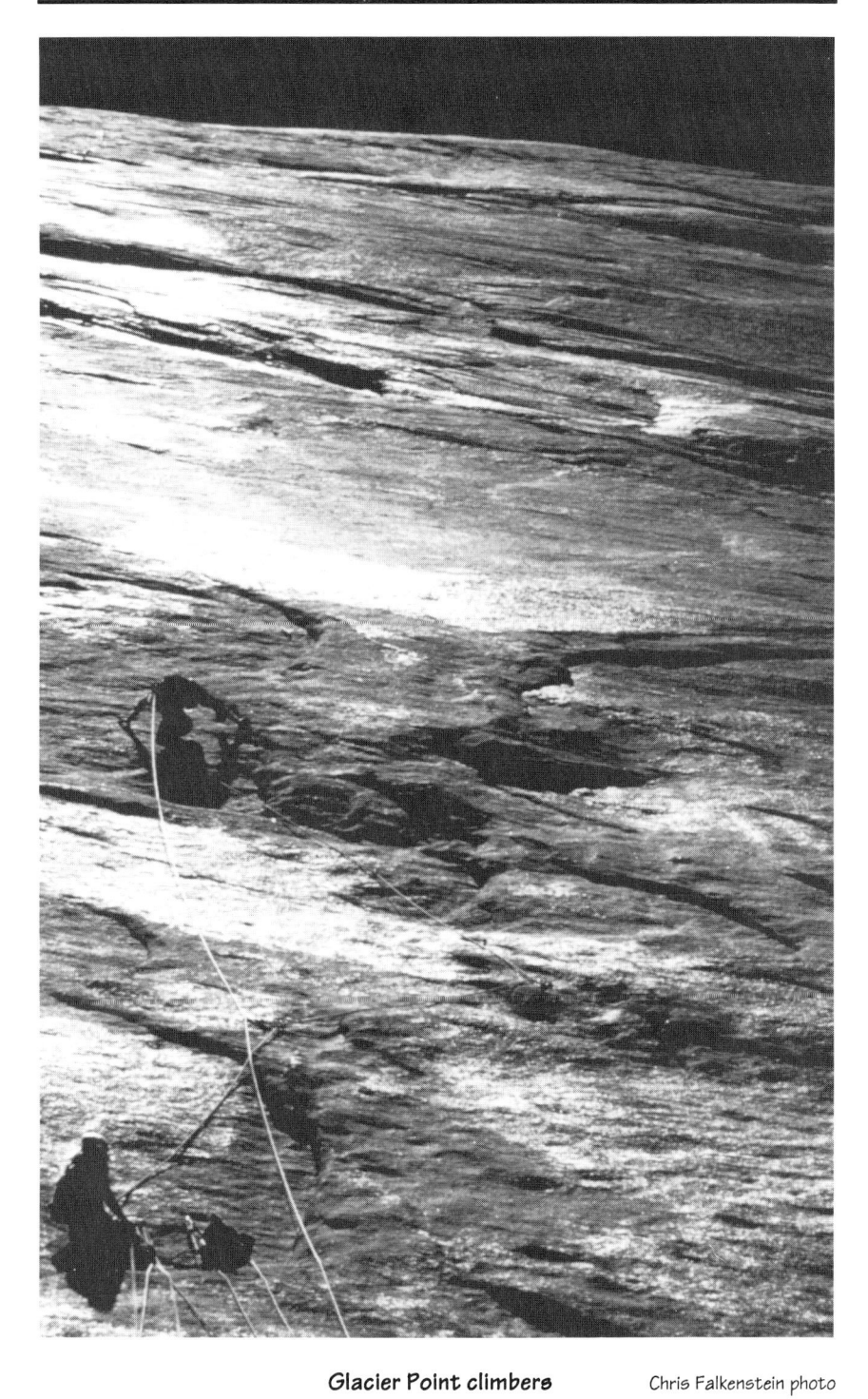

Glacier Point climbers Chris Falkenstein photo

Illiouette Canyon

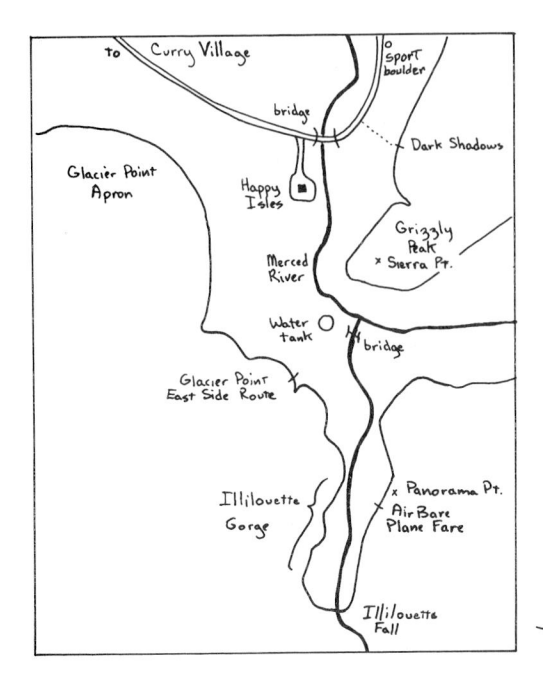

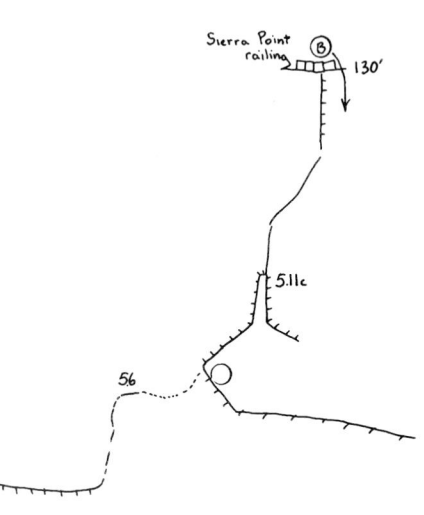

Illiouette Canyon

Approach: Approach all these routes from the parking lot at Curry Village. For **Dark Shadows** cross the first bridge over the Merced and diagonal up and right about 200 yards to a small cliff band. The route is set against a low-angle slab. **Fistibule** lies just below the railing at the top of Sierra Point. **Ape Index** is reached by using the utility road that leads from the Happy Isles Nature Center to the water tank. At the Illiouette bridge follow a vague trail along the west side of the creek for about 0.1 mile. Head straight up to the cliff. The climbs of the **Ape Index** area lie left of conspicuous yellow headwalls. **Plane Fare** lies next to the rockfall below Panorama Point.

A. **Dark Shadows** 5.10a
B. **Fistibule** 5.11c

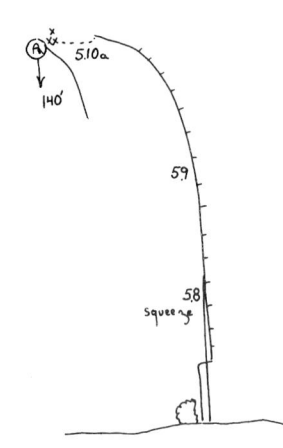

Illiouette Canyon

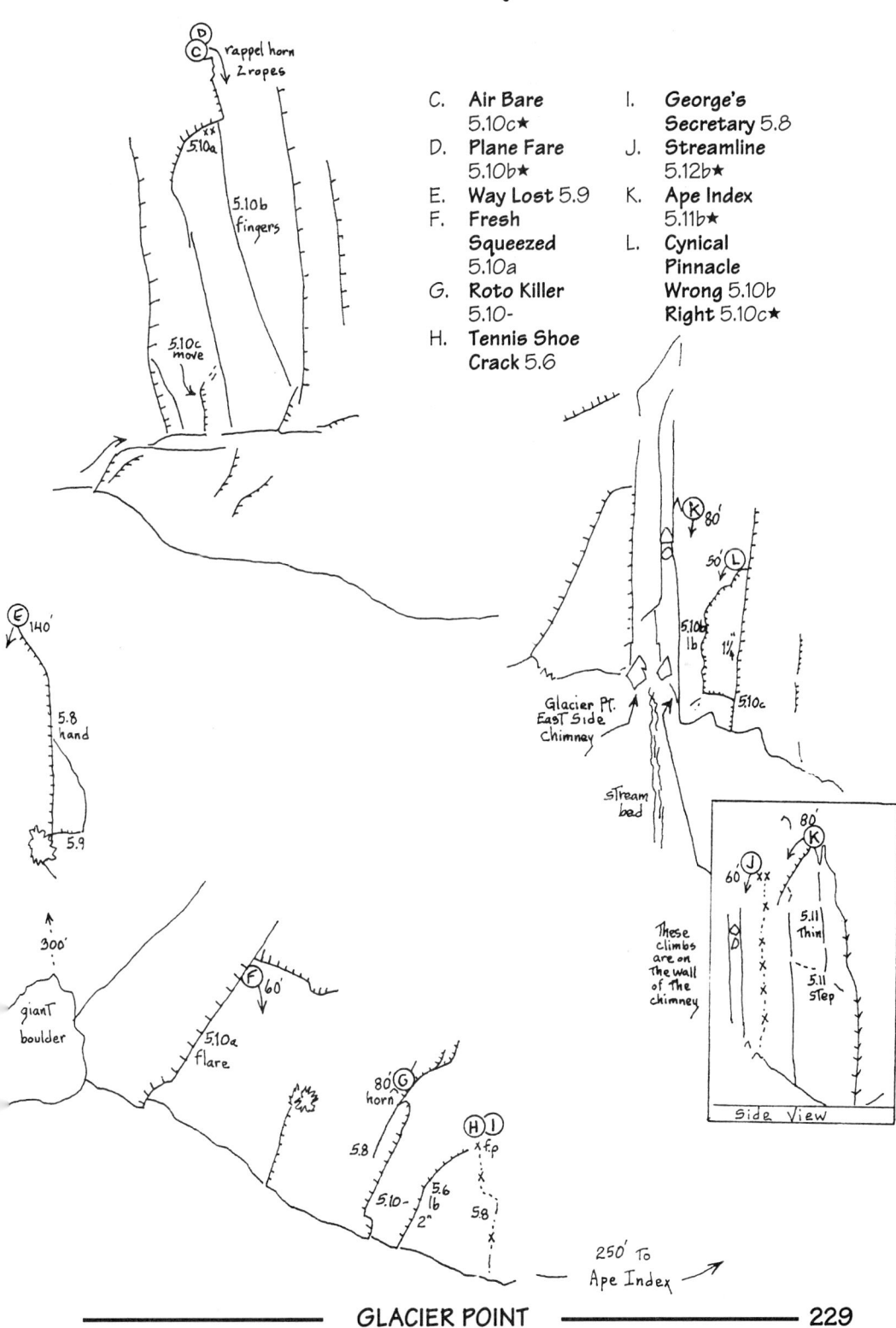

C. Air Bare 5.10c★
D. Plane Fare 5.10b★
E. Way Lost 5.9
F. Fresh Squeezed 5.10a
G. Roto Killer 5.10-
H. Tennis Shoe Crack 5.6
I. George's Secretary 5.8
J. Streamline 5.12b★
K. Ape Index 5.11b★
L. Cynical Pinnacle Wrong 5.10b Right 5.10c★

GLACIER POINT — 229

Glacier Point Apron: East Side

1. Milk Dud 5.10
2. The Calf 5.11c
3. THE GRACK
4. Perhaps 5.10d
5. THE MOUTH
6. Goodrich Pinnacle

Note: The eastern portion of the Glacier Point Apron was decimated by a huge, spontaneous rockfall in the summer of 1996. Although the real impact area was east, or left, of the Cow and The Grack, these climbs lie on the fringe of a bona fide death zone. Future catastrophic events of this nature can not be predicted, therefore the utmost discretion must be used when considering these climbs. Happy Isles and the old approach are wiped out so the only thinkable approach would be from the west, closer to Curry Village.

Glacier Point Apron: Northeast Side

1. Perhaps 5.10d
2. THE MOUTH
3. GOODRICH PINNACLE
4. PATIO PINNACLE
5. Coonyard Pinnacle 5.9 R
6. MONDAY MORNING SLAB
7. Point Beyond 5.8
8. Lucifer's Ledge 5.9
9. The Punch Bowl 5.10a

Glacier Point Apron, East

Approach: The eastern portion of the Glacier Point Apron was decimated by a huge, spontaneous rockfall in the summer of 1996. Use the utmost discretion when considering these climbs!! Happy Isles and the old approach are wiped out, so the only thinkable approach is from the west, closer to Curry Village (as described on p. 234).

- A. **Strange Energy** 5.11b Pro: To 4".
- B. **Synapse Collapse** 5.10b★ Pro: To 2½".
- C. **Shuttle Madness** 5.9★
- D. **Vulture Culture** 5.12a
- E. **Collision Course** 5.12b
- F. **Milk Dud** 5.10a Pro: To 3½".
- G. **Jack the Zipper** 5.12a★
- H. **The Bear** 5.10b
- I. **Psychic Energy** 5.11b
- J. **Transistor Sister** 5.10c★
- K. **Wild At Heart** 5.12b★★
- L. **The Calf** 5.11c★
- M. **Dead Baby** 5.11b★★
- N. **Calf Continuation** 5.10b R
- O. **A Mother's Lament** 5.10c R/X
- P. **Tightrope** 5.11b★ R
- Q. **The Cow**
  Left 5.8★ R Pro: A few pieces for the second pitch. Low-angle, but smooth and runout.
  Center 5.5★ Pro: To 2½".
  Right 5.7
- R. **An Udder Way** 5.10a★ R
- S. **Hoppy's Favorite** 5.10b★ R
- T. **Hoppy's Creed** 5.11

The Grack
- U. Left Side 5.7
- V. Center Route 5.6★★★
- W. Marginal 5.9★★★ R Pro: A few pieces, tiny to 1¼". A sea of friction.
- X. Right Side 5.8 R/X
- Y. Perhaps 5.10d A4 Pro: KBs, RPs to tubes.
- Z. Roller Coaster 5.8 R/X
- AA. Hot Tin Roof 5.9★
- BB. Ochre Fields 5.11a★ R Pro: To 3".

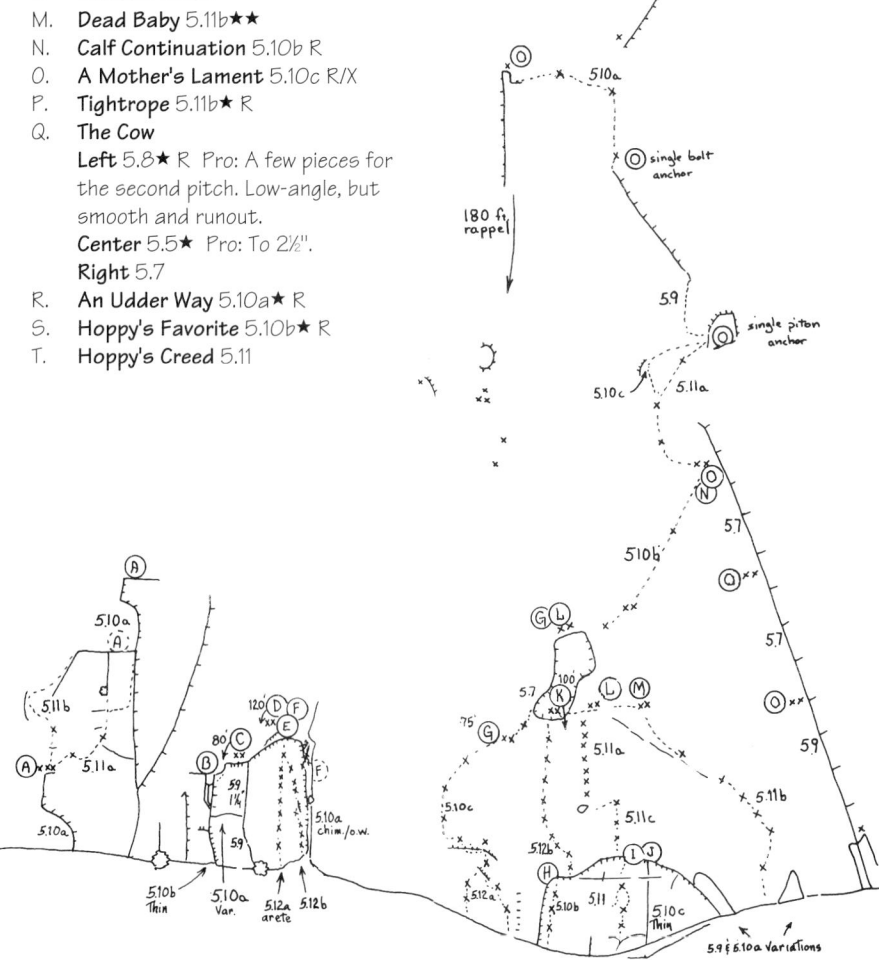

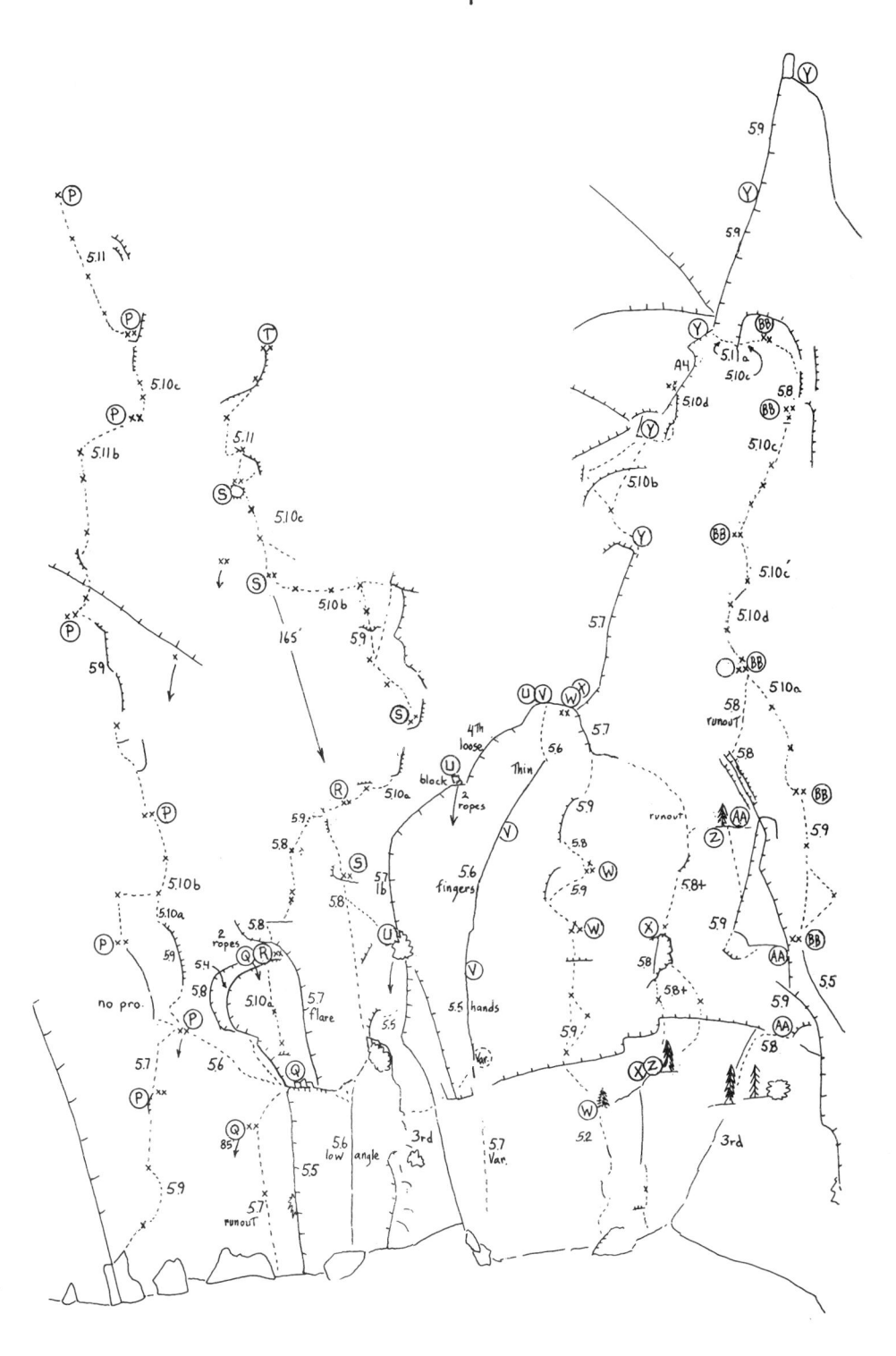

Glacier Point Apron: East

GLACIER POINT — 233

Glacier Point Apron: Center

Glacier Point, Center

Approach: Hike up to meet the formation from a point several hundred feet east of the abandoned dump site at the eastern end of Curry Village. **Descent:** For routes ending at The Oasis, see page 240.

- A. Ochre Fields 5.11a★ R Pro: To 3".
- B. Deep Throat 5.10a★ R

The Mouth
- C. Boche-Hennek Variation 5.9
- D. Regular Mouth 5.9★ R
- E. Mouth to Perhaps 5.11b
- F. Flakey Foont 5.9★ R/X
- G. Misty Beethoven 5.10d★★★ R
- H. Hall of Mirrors 5.12c★★★ R
  Also see page 238.

Goodrich Pinnacle
- I. Left Side 5.9
- J. Right Side 5.9★★★ R Pro: To 2½", especially small pieces. Apron friction with a taste of crack climbing.
- K. Hoosier's Highway 5.10c★ R
- L. McPherson Struts 5.9★ Pro: Thin to ¾".

Patio Pinnacle
- M. Left Side 5.9 R
- N. Regular Route 5.8 R
- O. The Goblet
  - Left 5.4
  - Center 5.6
  - Right 5.4
- P. Angelica 5.9★ R
- Q. Coonyard Pinnacle 5.9 R
- R. Patio to Coonyard 5.10a or 5.8
- S. Coonyard to The Oasis 5.9

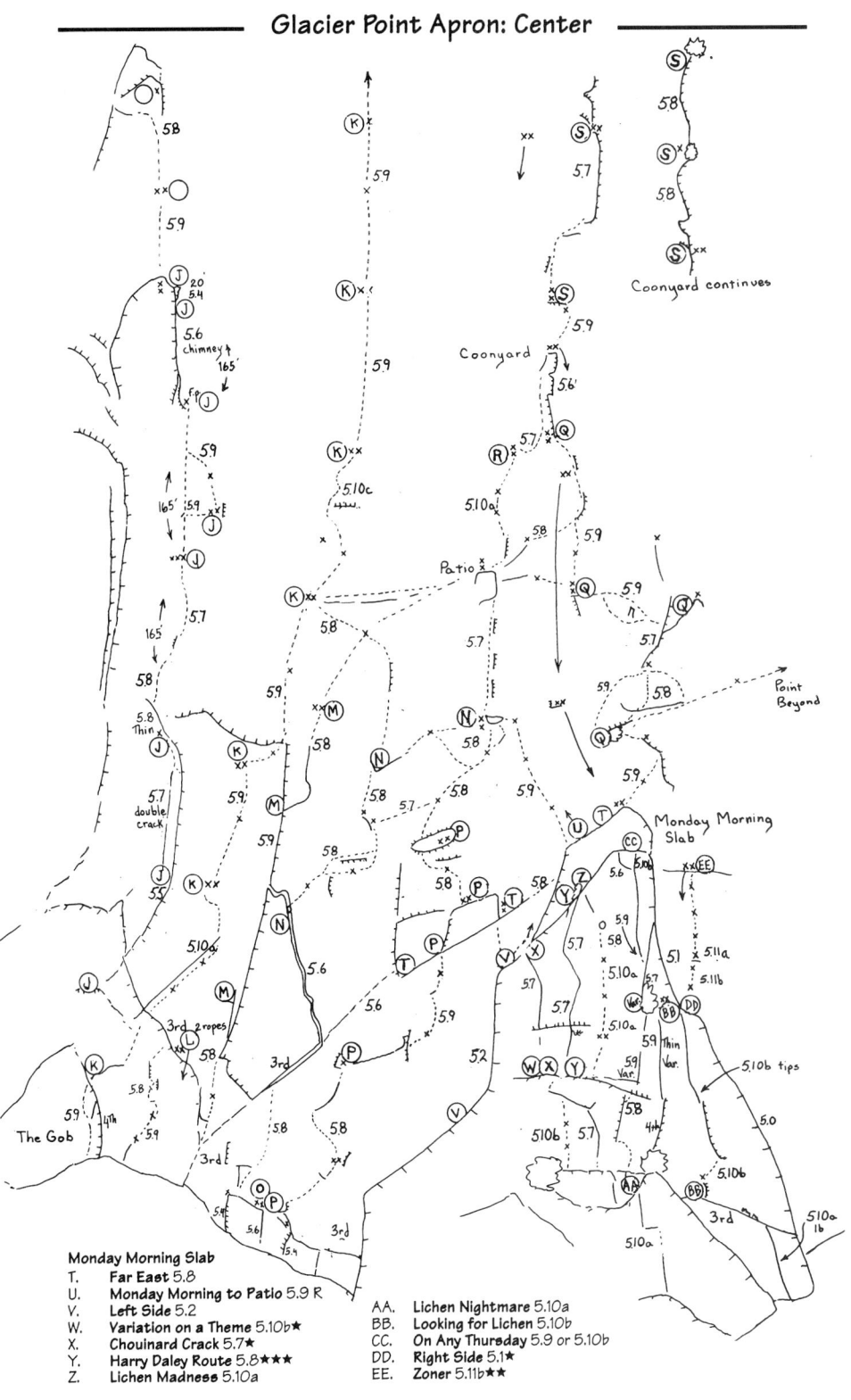

Glacier Point Apron: Center

Monday Morning Slab
- T. **Far East** 5.8
- U. **Monday Morning to Patio** 5.9 R
- V. **Left Side** 5.2
- W. **Variation on a Theme** 5.10b ★
- X. **Chouinard Crack** 5.7 ★
- Y. **Harry Daley Route** 5.8 ★★★
- Z. **Lichen Madness** 5.10a
- AA. **Lichen Nightmare** 5.10a
- BB. **Looking for Lichen** 5.10b
- CC. **On Any Thursday** 5.9 or 5.10b
- DD. **Right Side** 5.1 ★
- EE. **Zoner** 5.11b ★★

GLACIER POINT

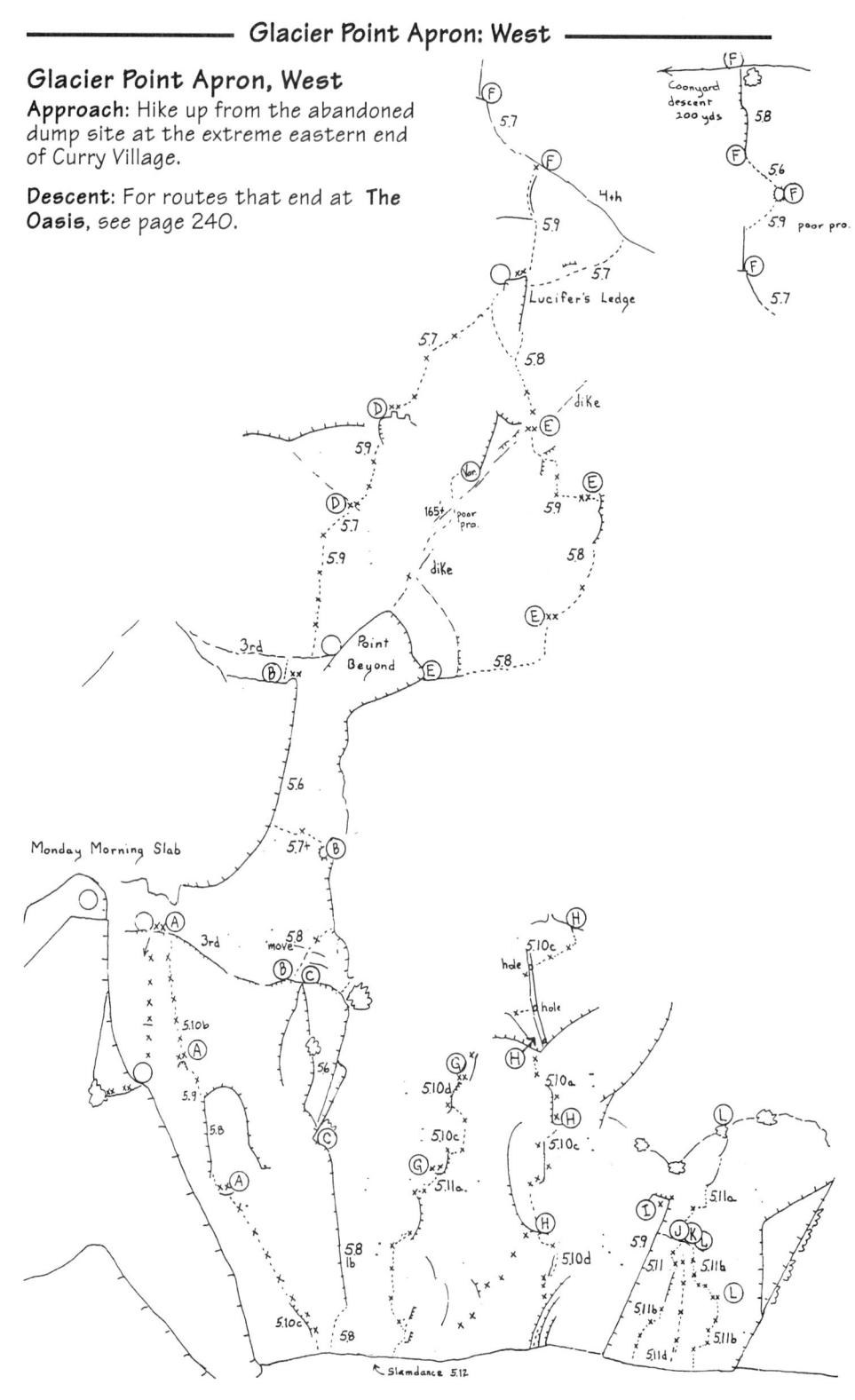

Glacier Point Apron: West

Glacier Point Apron, West

Approach: Hike up from the abandoned dump site at the extreme eastern end of Curry Village.

Descent: For routes that end at **The Oasis**, see page 240.

Glacier Point Apron: West

A. Cold Fusion 5.10c ★★
B. Point Beyond 5.8 ★★
C. Point Beyond, Direct 5.8 ★
D. Angel's Approach 5.9 ★★★
E. Lucifer's Ledge 5.9
F. Lucifer's to The Oasis 5.9 R/X
G. Anchors Away 5.11a ★★★
H. Sailin' Shoes 5.10d ★★
I. 5.9 Grunt
J. Chiropodist Shop 5.11b ★
K. The Token 5.11d ★★ R/X
L. Ephemeral Clogdance 5.11b ★ R
M. The Letdown 5.9
N. Bark at the Moon 5.11b
O. Synchronicity 5.11
P. Nothing on The Apron 5.11c
Q. Lean Years 5.11a ★
R. Blue Funk 5.11a
S. Perfect Master 5.11d ★ Pro: To 1½".
T. Famous Potatoes 5.11b
U. Lonely Dancer 5.10c Pro: To ½".
V. Son of Sam 5.9 Pro: To ⅝".
W. Cosmic Comedy 5.7
X. Dr. Feel Good 5.11a ★ Pro: Tiny to ½".
Y. Afterglow 5.10d
Z. Apron Jam 5.9 ★ Pro: To #4 Camalot.
AA. Green Dragon 5.11b ★★★ R/X
BB. Mr. Natural 5.10c ★★★ Pro: Many ⅜" and ½".
CC. Bad Acid 5.9
DD. Scimitar 5.7, 5.12 ★
EE. Thunderhead 5.11d
FF. This Ain't England 5.11b
GG. The White Dike 5.10d
HH. Lunar Lunacy 5.11d ★ Pro: A few thin pieces.

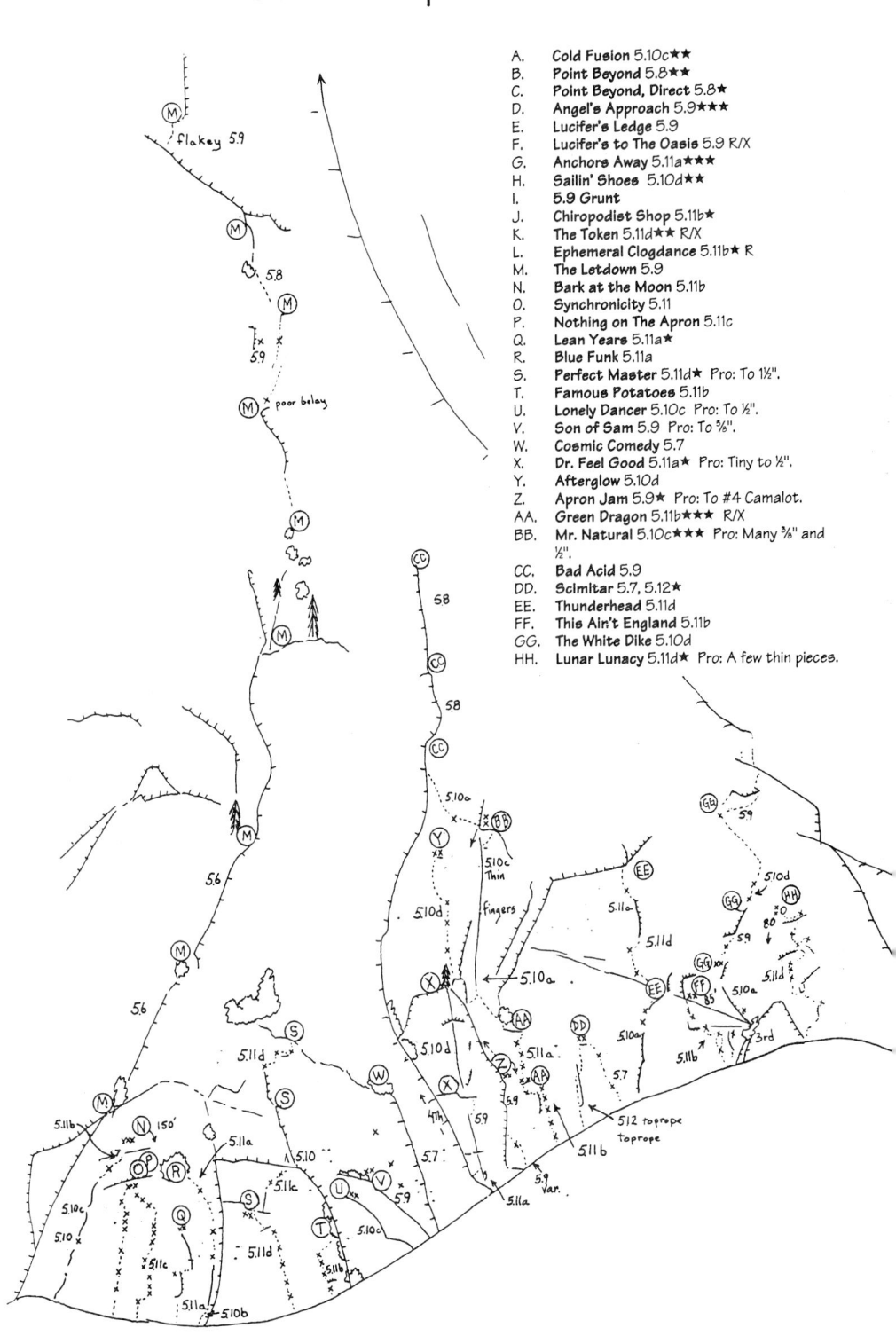

Hall of Mirrors

Approach: This route starts above **Misty Beethoven** on page 234.

Hall of Mirrors 5.12c ★★★ R Pro: #1 to #2 Friends.

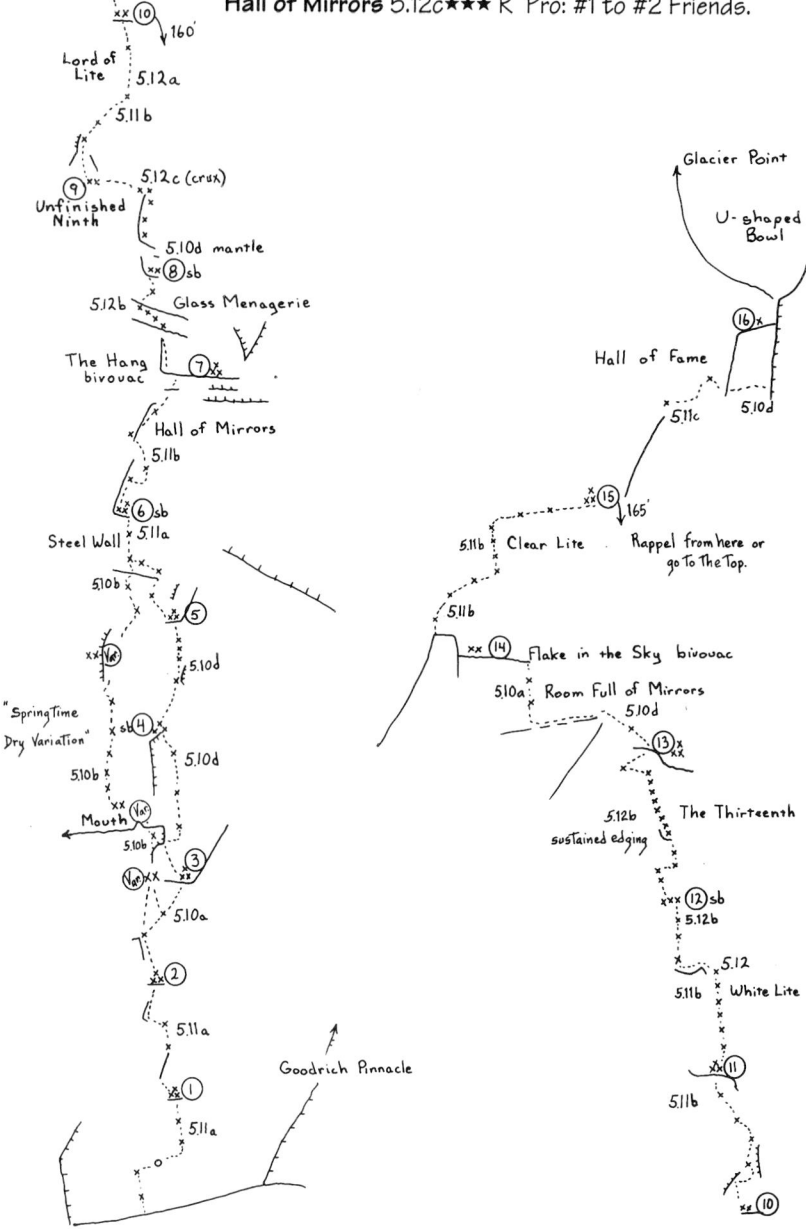

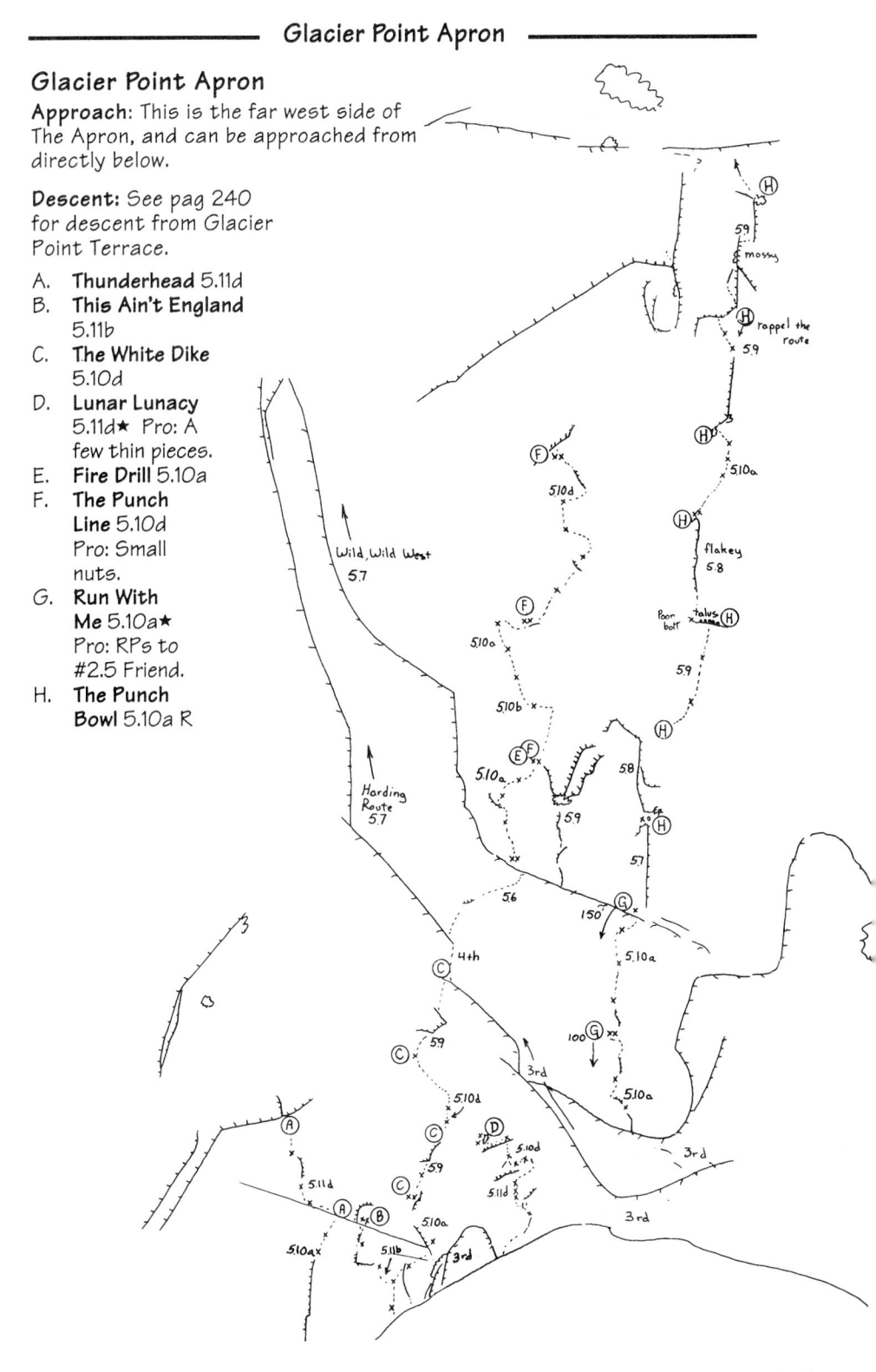

Glacier Point Apron

Approach: This is the far west side of The Apron, and can be approached from directly below.

Descent: See pag 240 for descent from Glacier Point Terrace.

A. **Thunderhead** 5.11d
B. **This Ain't England** 5.11b
C. **The White Dike** 5.10d
D. **Lunar Lunacy** 5.11d★ Pro: A few thin pieces.
E. **Fire Drill** 5.10a
F. **The Punch Line** 5.10d Pro: Small nuts.
G. **Run With Me** 5.10a★ Pro: RPs to #2.5 Friend.
H. **The Punch Bowl** 5.10a R

Glacier Point Apron: Terrace Descent

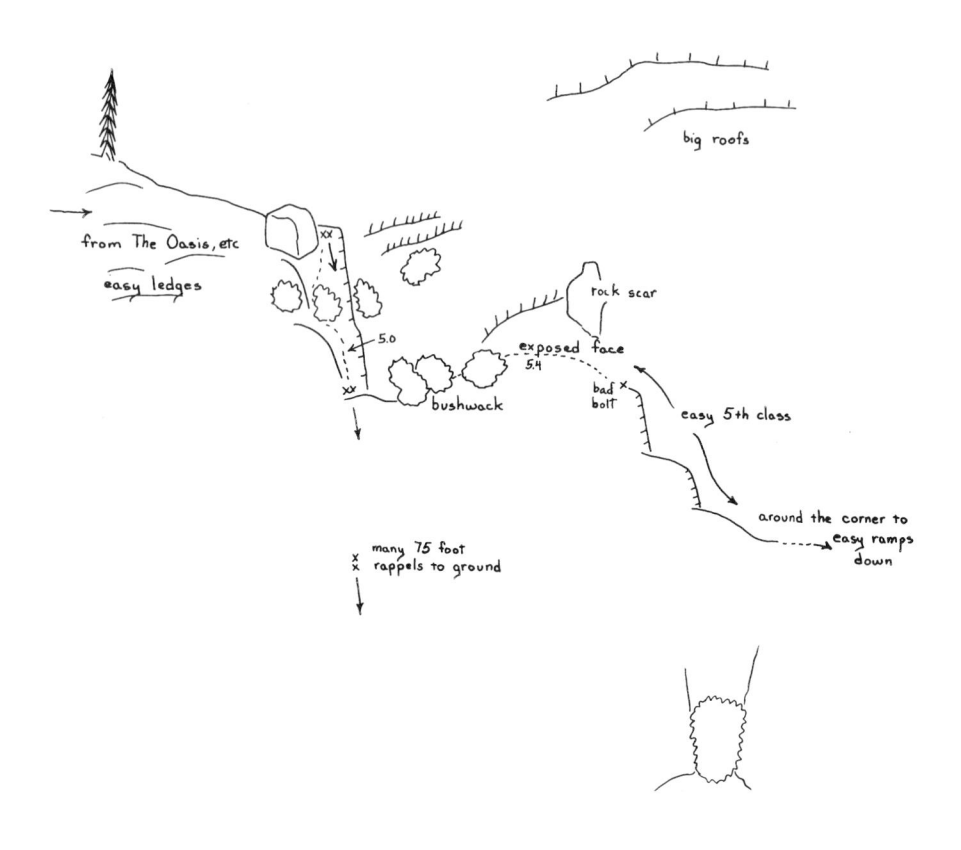

Glacier Point Apron: Terrace Descent

This is the descent for all routes that lead to **The Oasis** and **Glacier Point Terrace**. Walk as far west on the Terrace as you can without having to rope up. From bolt anchors next to a block, make one 70-foot rappel down a low-angle corner. This leads to another ledge with bolts. To follow the Terrace descent, do not rappel again here, but climb up and right through bushes. Traverse across a steep, exposed but easy slab for almost a rope-length to anchors on another ledge. Now rappel down and west for a pitch, following corners and easy ledges. You should see the final, elusive ramps just west of you.

Photo by Chris Falkenstein

Ron Kauk and Daniela Massetti on the Chapel Wall

Glacier Point, Staircase Falls Area

Approach: This is the gray cliff to the right of the Glacier Point Apron and the Ledge Trail. Hike up from the cabins at Curry Village, gaining vague trails adjacent to the watercourse.

A. **Old A5** A3 Hardware: 6 KBs, 14 LAs, some larger angles, nuts, one hook.
B. **Old A3** A3+
C. **Old A2** A2 Hardware: 2 KBs, 5 LAs, one set TCUs, #2 Camalot, rivet hangers, pointed Leeper hook.

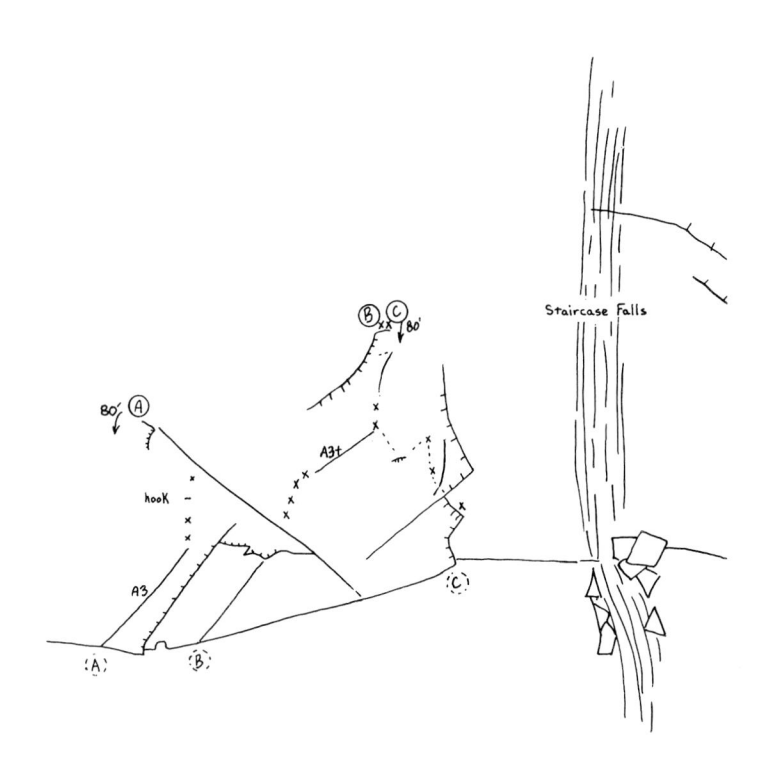

Staircase Falls Area

- D. **The Cafeteria Lieback** 5.11a ★
- E. **Good For Your Soul** 5.11a ★
- F. **Blockbuster** 5.11c A1 Pro: Hooks to a #3 Friend.
- G. **Derelict's Diagonal** A4
- H. **Broken Circuit** 5.12 TR or solo
- I. **Circuit Breaker** 5.11b ★★ TR or solo
- J. **Derelict's Delight** 5.11c Pro: Small.
- K. **Doggie Submission** 5.10b ★ Pro: Extra small.
- L. **Speed Racer** 5.11c R/X Pro: Including tiny RPs.

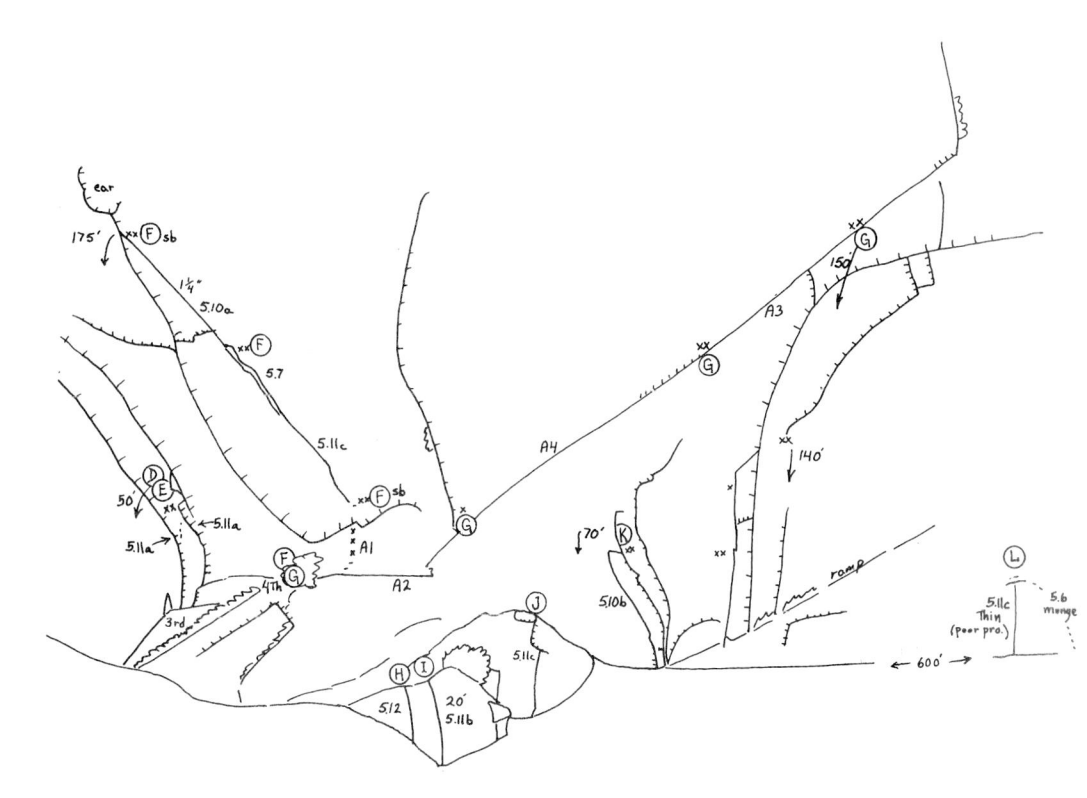

GLACIER POINT

Public Sanitation

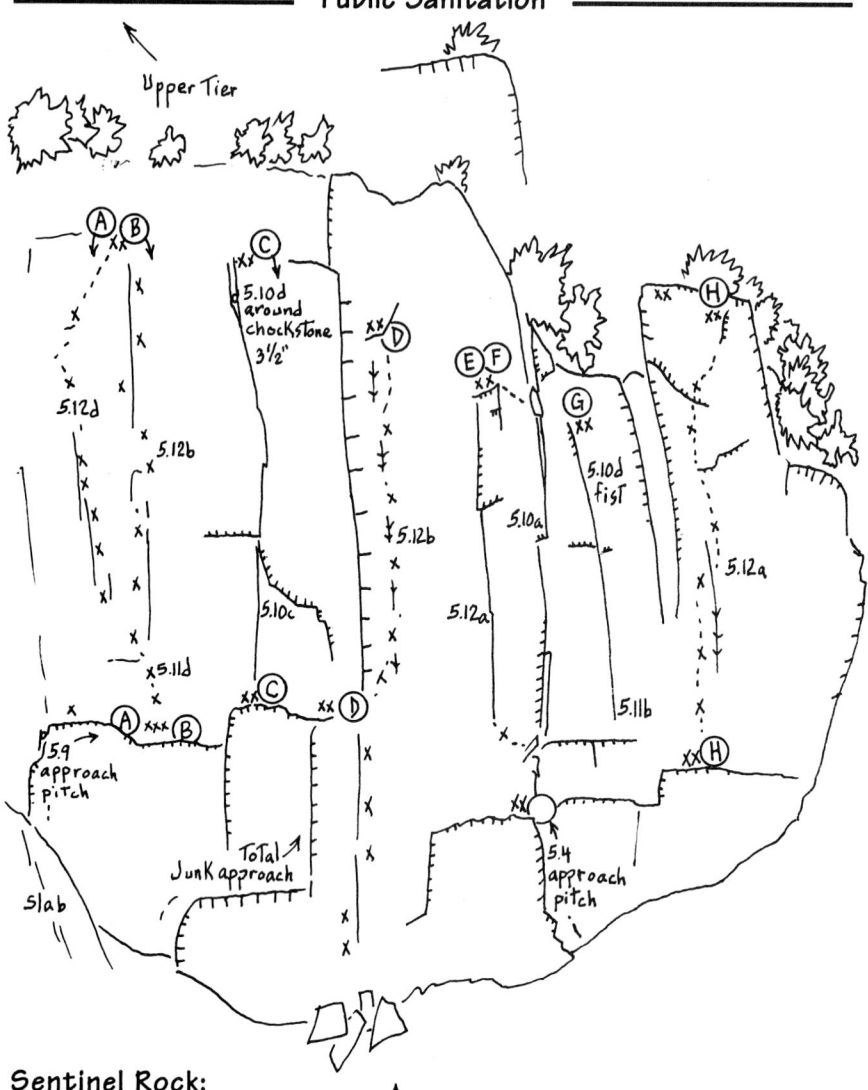

Sentinel Rock: Public Sanitation, Lower Tier

Approach: From Sentinel Bridge continue 0.1 mile toward Curry Village. Leave the road here (dirt shoulder parking next to a small boulder barricade) then hike upward toward the cliff, passing through an obvious talus slope.

A. **Black Fly** 5.13b★★ Pro: Optional to 1".
B. **Final Cut** 5.12b★★★ Pro: Optional to 2".
C. **Wide Thing** 5.10d★ Pro: To 3¾", especially 3" to 3½".
D. **Best Bet Arête** 5.12b★ When in doubt, stay right.
E. **Spike** 5.12a★
F. **Public Sanitation** 5.10
G. **Carpet Bagger** 5.11b★
H. **Wish You Were Here** 5.12a★

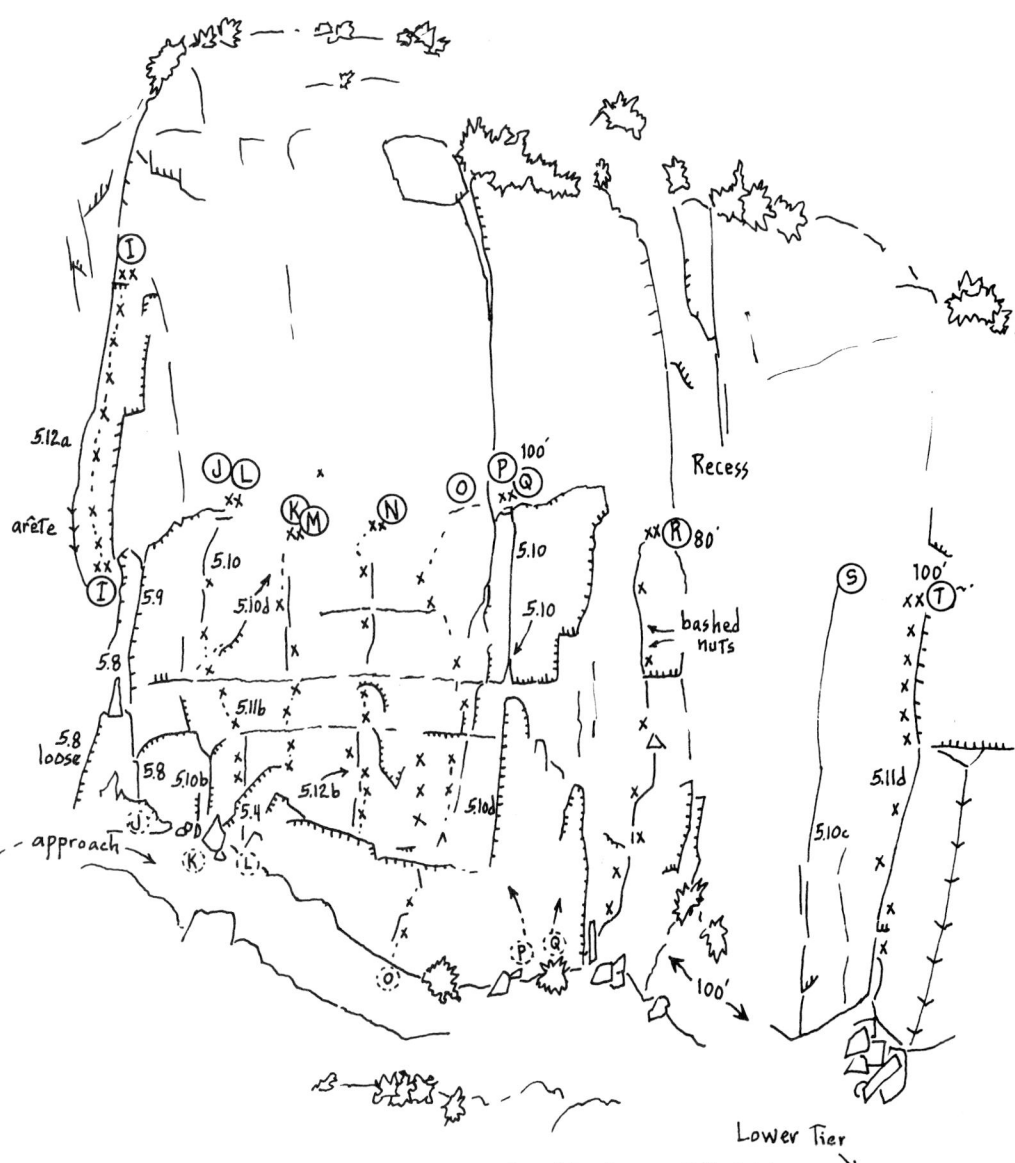

Public Sanitation

Upper Tier
I. **Substance Abuse** 5.12a★★
J. **Sand Jam** 5.9
K. **Solid Waste** 5.10d★ Crosses the line of bolts.
L. **Total Way-ist** 5.11b★★
M. **Waste Not, Whip Not** 5.11★
N. **Tucker's Proud Rock Climb** 5.12b★★★
O. **Afterburner** 5.11c★★★
P. **Sanitary Engineer** 5.10d
Q. **Indisposed** 5.10d
R. **Temple of Doom** 5.12b★★
S. **Bourbon Street** 5.10c
T. **Big Easy** 5.11d ★★★

SENTINEL ROCK — 245

Chapel Wall

Chapel Wall

In keeping with National Park Service preservation goals and concerns over environmental impacts, numerous climbing routes located between Public Sanitation Wall and Chapel Wall have purposely been omitted from this guide. Thank you for your understanding and cooperation in maintaining this area in as pristine a state as possible.

Approach: A horse trail runs along the base of this cliff. For climbs on the left side of the cliff begin from the chapel and walk southwest or down-valley along the trail for several hundred feet. At a level spot leading to the cliff, **Heathenistic Pursuit** can be seen as a huge, left-facing corner 100 feet away. A surge of recent development has taken place on this cliff. Many of the newer routes are bolt-protected vertical faces that exhibit edging cranks and side pulls.

- A. **Colors** 5.12b★★ Pro: QDs.
- B. **New Wave** 5.11d★★ Pro: QDs.
- C. **Heathenistic Pursuit** 5.10b★★ Pro: To 2½".
- D. **Gold Dust** 5.10d★★ Pro: To 2½", plus extra small pieces.
- E. **Berlin Wall** 5.12b★ Pro: QDs.
- F. **Drive By Shooting** 5.12a★★★ Pro: QDs, #2 Friend.
- G. **Cripps** 5.13b★ Pro: QDs, a few pieces.
- H. **Double Dragon** 5.12b★★ Pro: QDs, #1 Friend.
- I. **House of Pain** 5.12a★★ Pro: QDs, a few pieces.

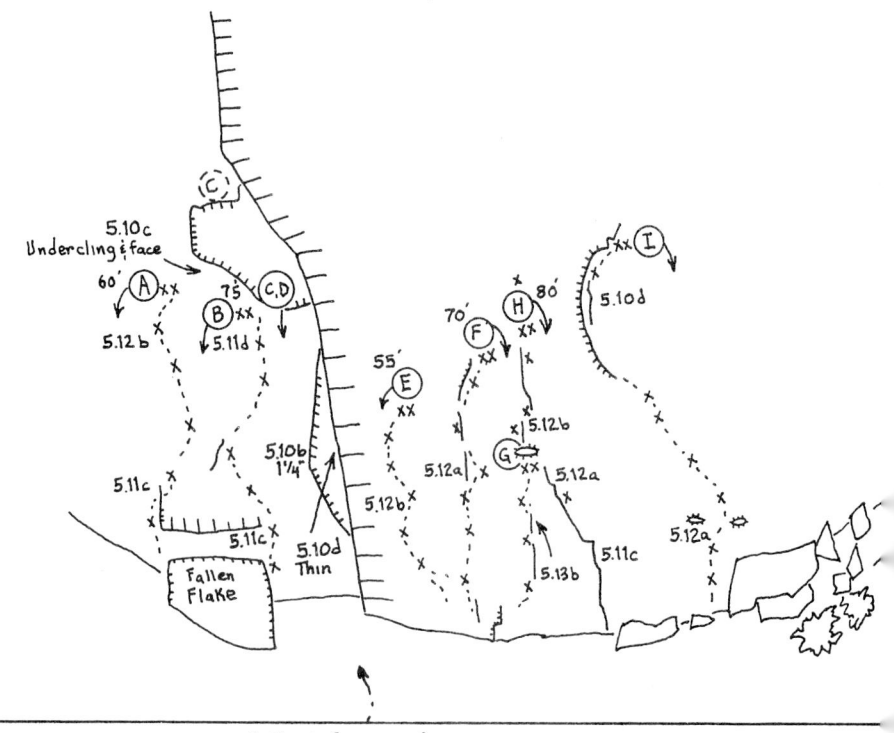

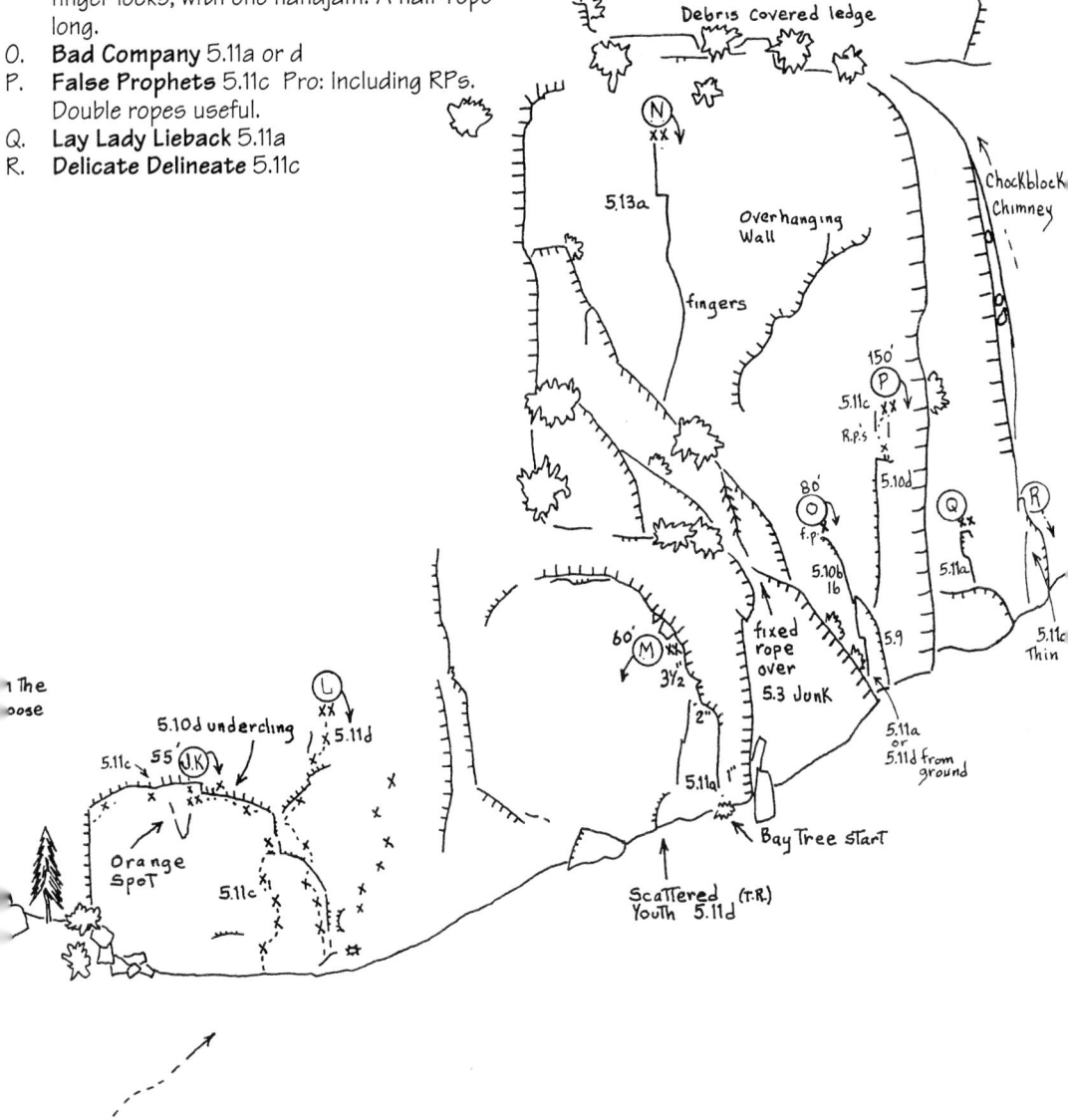

Chapel Wall

For **On The Loose**, etc., see page 248.

J. **Cling Free** 5.11c ★
K. **Mongoloid** 5.11c★★ Pro: QDs.
L. **Max Deviator** 5.11d★ Pro: QDs.
M. **Controlled Burn** 5.11a★★ Pro: ¼" to 3½". A deteriorating bay tree accesses this short, but pumping, crack.
N. **Cosmic Debris** 5.13b★★★ Pro: ⅜" to 1½", especially ¾" pieces. Sustained overhanging finger locks, with one handjam. A half-rope long.
O. **Bad Company** 5.11a or d
P. **False Prophets** 5.11c Pro: Including RPs. Double ropes useful.
Q. **Lay Lady Lieback** 5.11a
R. **Delicate Delineate** 5.11c

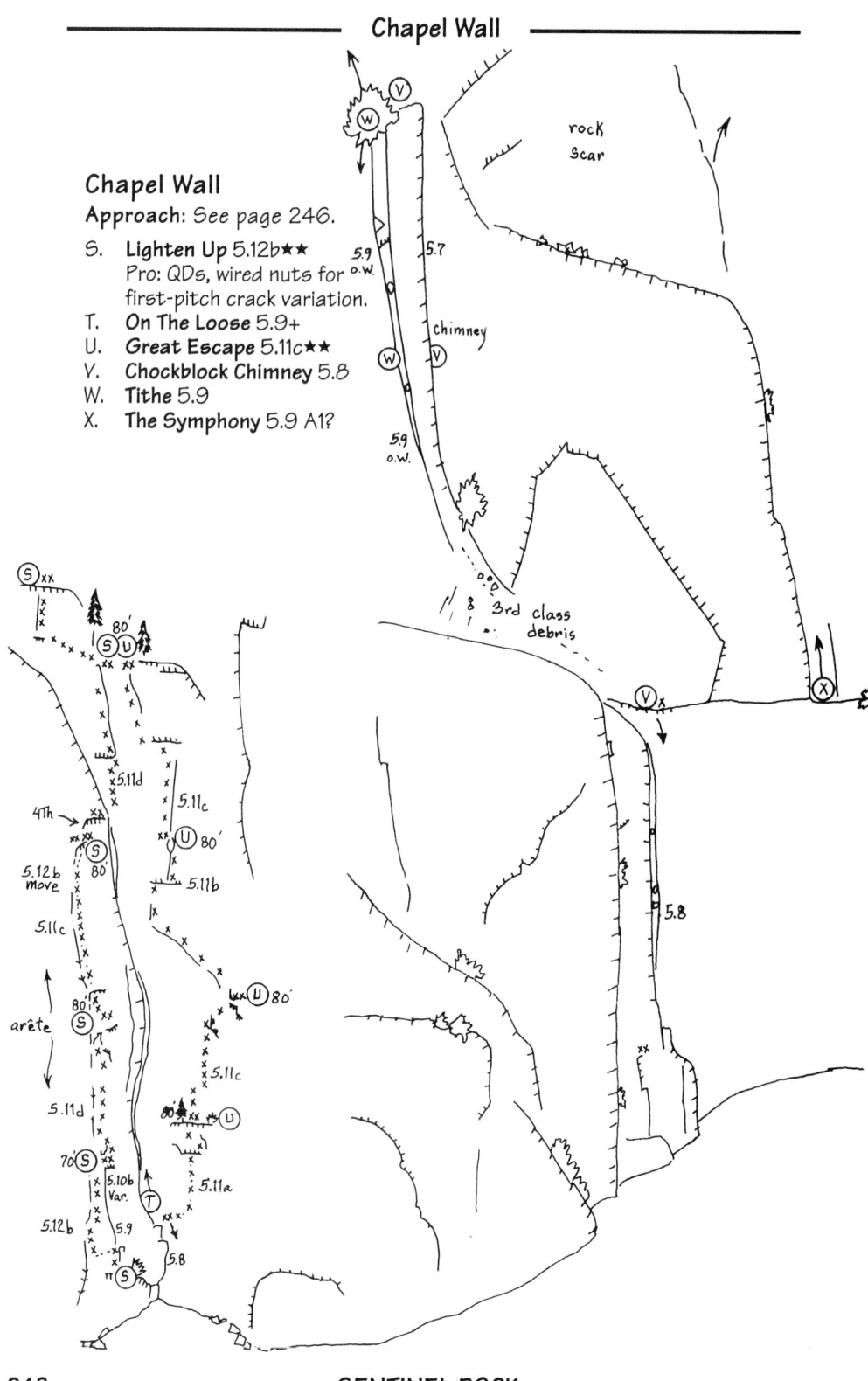

Chapel Wall

Approach: See page 246.

- S. **Lighten Up** 5.12b★★
  Pro: QDs, wired nuts for first-pitch crack variation.
- T. **On The Loose** 5.9+
- U. **Great Escape** 5.11c★★
- V. **Chockblock Chimney** 5.8
- W. **Tithe** 5.9
- X. **The Symphony** 5.9 A1?

Chapel Wall

1. On the Loose 5.9+
2. Cosmic Debris
3. Chockblock Chimney 5.8
4. Shockwave 5.13b
5. Dorn's Crack 5.10c A0
6. Under Siege 5.11b
7. Resurrection 5.10a

Chapel Wall

Approach: See page 246.

Photo on page 249.

- A. **Season of the Bitch** 5.11d Pro: Including wireds and TCUs.
- B. **Freaky Styley** 5.11d★
- C. **The Hidden** 5.12a★
- D. **Little Girl's Route** 5.10d
- E. **Dope Smoking Moron** 5.11
- F. **The Den** 5.8
- G. **Shockwave** 5.13b★★★ Pro: Including #0.4 and #0.5 TCUs.

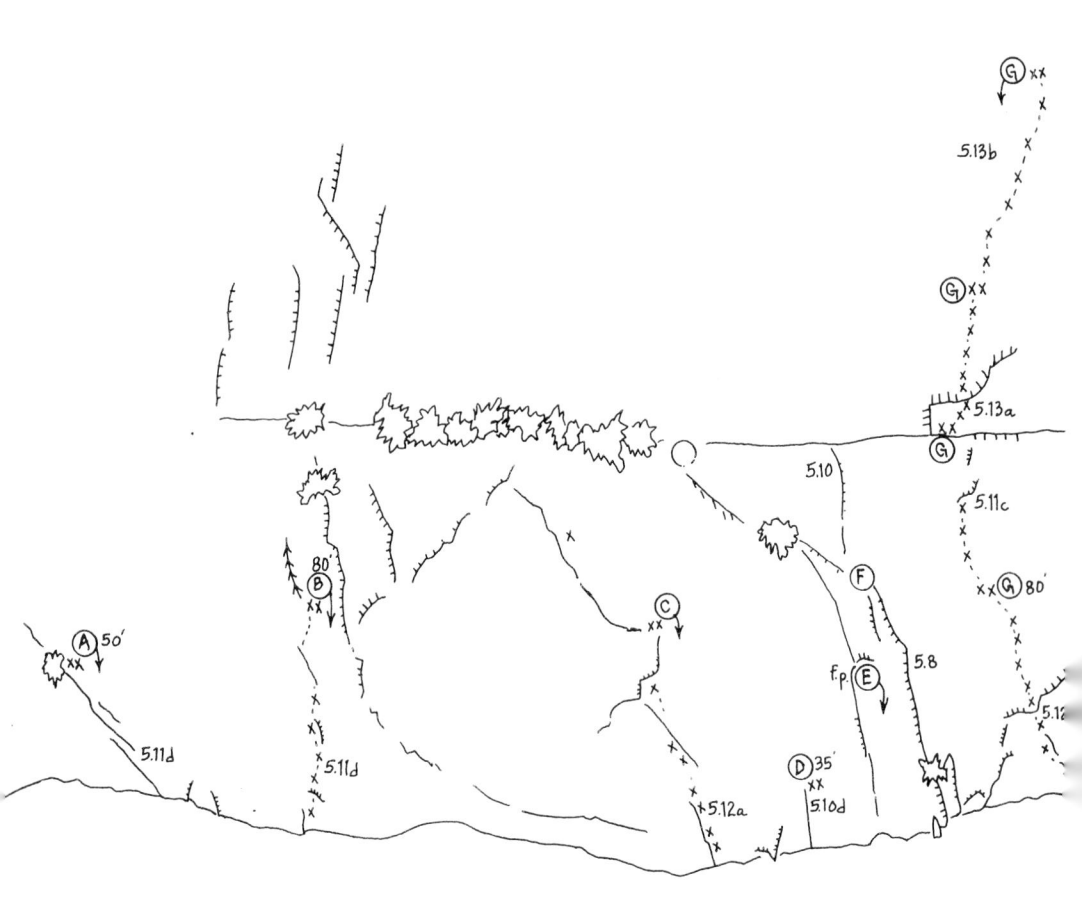

Chapel Wall

Photo on page 249.

H. **Diminishing Standard** 5.12 Pro: Including #0.5 TCU.
I. **Hangover Heights** 5.10d
J. **Morality Check** 5.10 A0
K. **Icons of Filth** 5.7
L. **Earth First** 5.10
M. **Dorn's Crack** 5.10c A0 Pro: To 3", plus 5" to 6".
N. **Dirty Dancing** 5.11

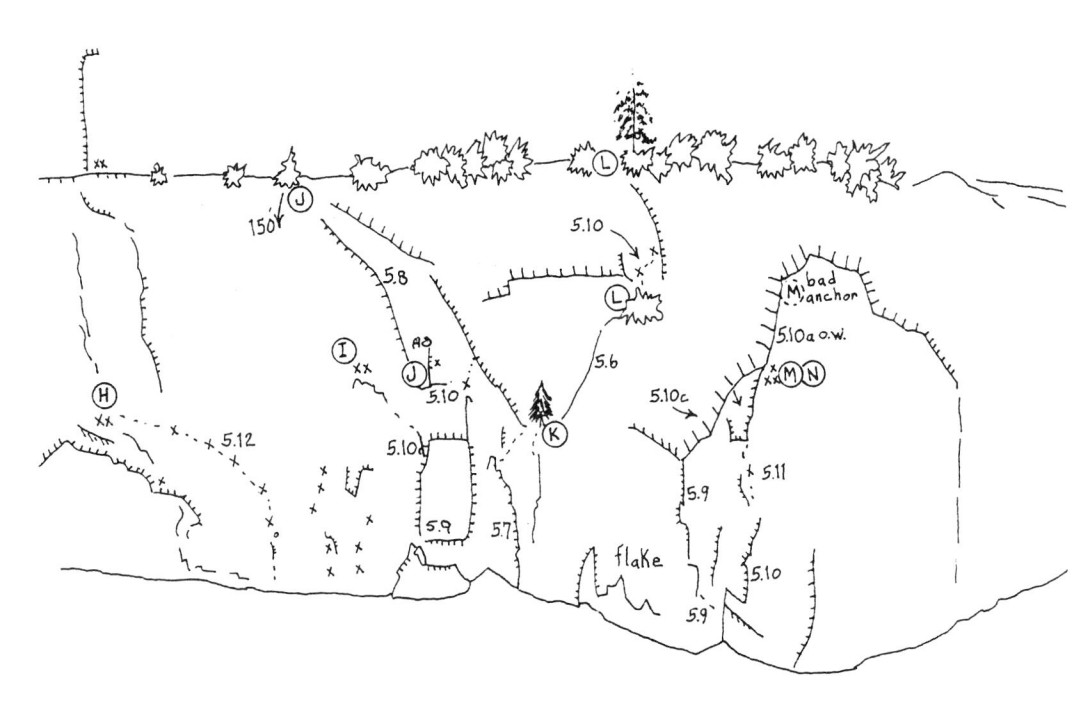

Chapel Wall, Far Right

Approach: See page 246.

- O. **Love Missile F1-11** 5.10b
- P. **Under Siege** 5.11b★
- Q. **Resurrection** 5.10a★
- R. **New Testament** 5.10d★
- S. **Betrayal** 5.9
- T. **Bryan's Crack** 5.8
- U. **By Way of the Flake** 5.10c R Pro: To 3½", including wireds and TCUs.
- V. **Sixth Heaven** 5.10b★

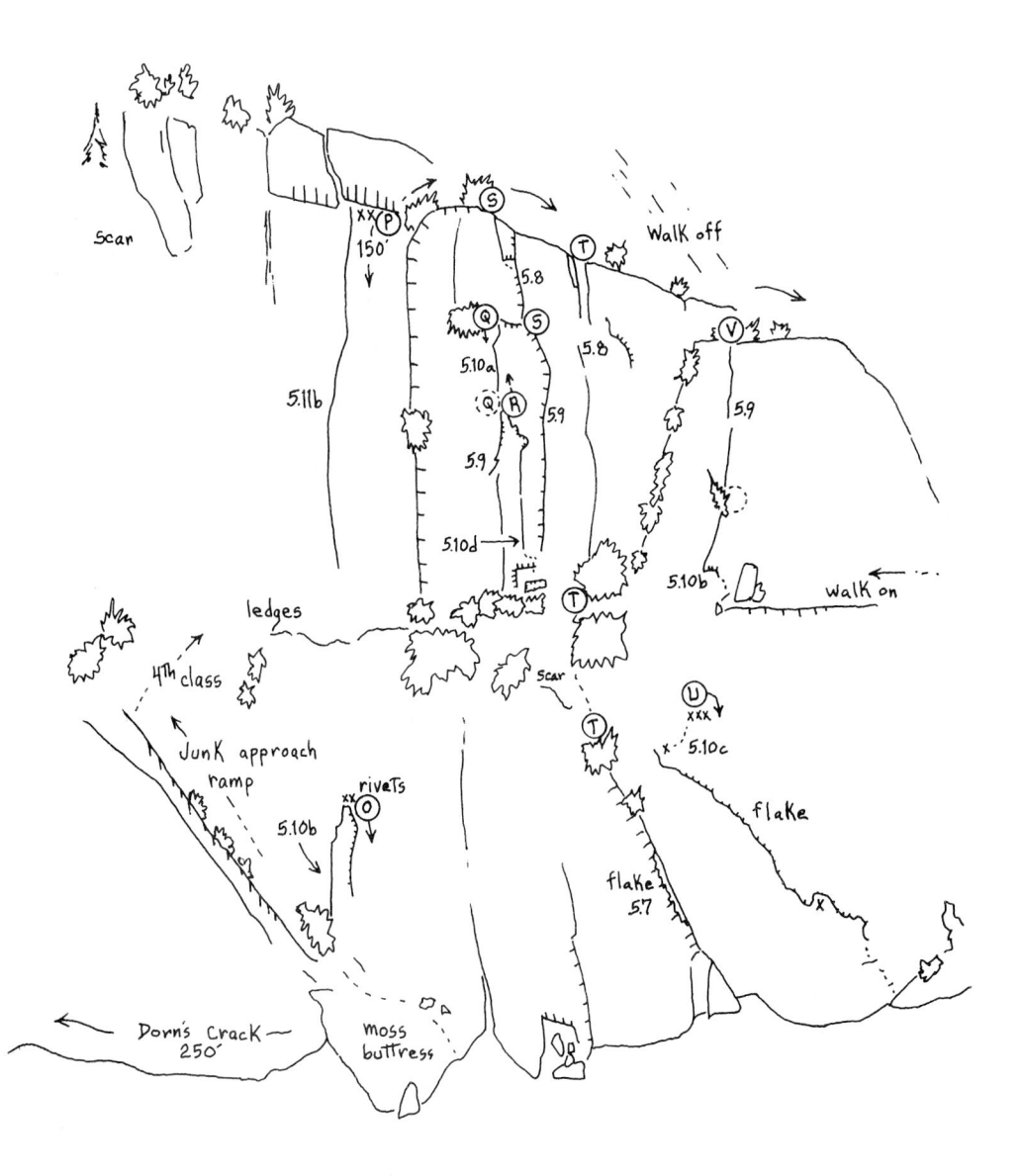

Sentinel Rock: North Face

National Park Service photo

SENTINEL ROCK

Sentinel Rock

Approach: The routes on the north and west faces of Sentinel Rock are approached by 3rd class ledges that traverse up and right across the lower, broken area of the formation. First, hike up the Four-Mile Trail for about a mile to the stream that comes down from the east side of the rock. Leave the trail and hike up the streambed several hundred feet, then move over to the prominent ramp that starts the long scramble up and right. This leads to the base of the Flying Buttress, an 800-foot pillar that sits at the right side of the flat north face and is the start of the **Flying Buttress Direct** and **Steck-Salathé**. The routes on the west face are around the corner. The routes on the north face require further scrambling up and left on ledges. Allow two hours' approach time from Camp 4.

Descent: From the summit, work south to the notch behind Sentinel Rock via manzanita tunnels that skirt small outcrops. From the notch, scramble down the loose, Class 2 gully that leads east to a stream. Further down, descend improbable terrain in the middle of a scruffy buttress that separates two chasms. Eventually, Four-Mile Trail is reached.

Sentinel Rock

Chouinard-Herbert 5.11c or 5.9 A2 ★★ Pro: Nuts to 2½", including extra ¼" to 1½". The beginning and conclusion of this route are somewhat undignified, yet the core of the climb is rewarding and airy.

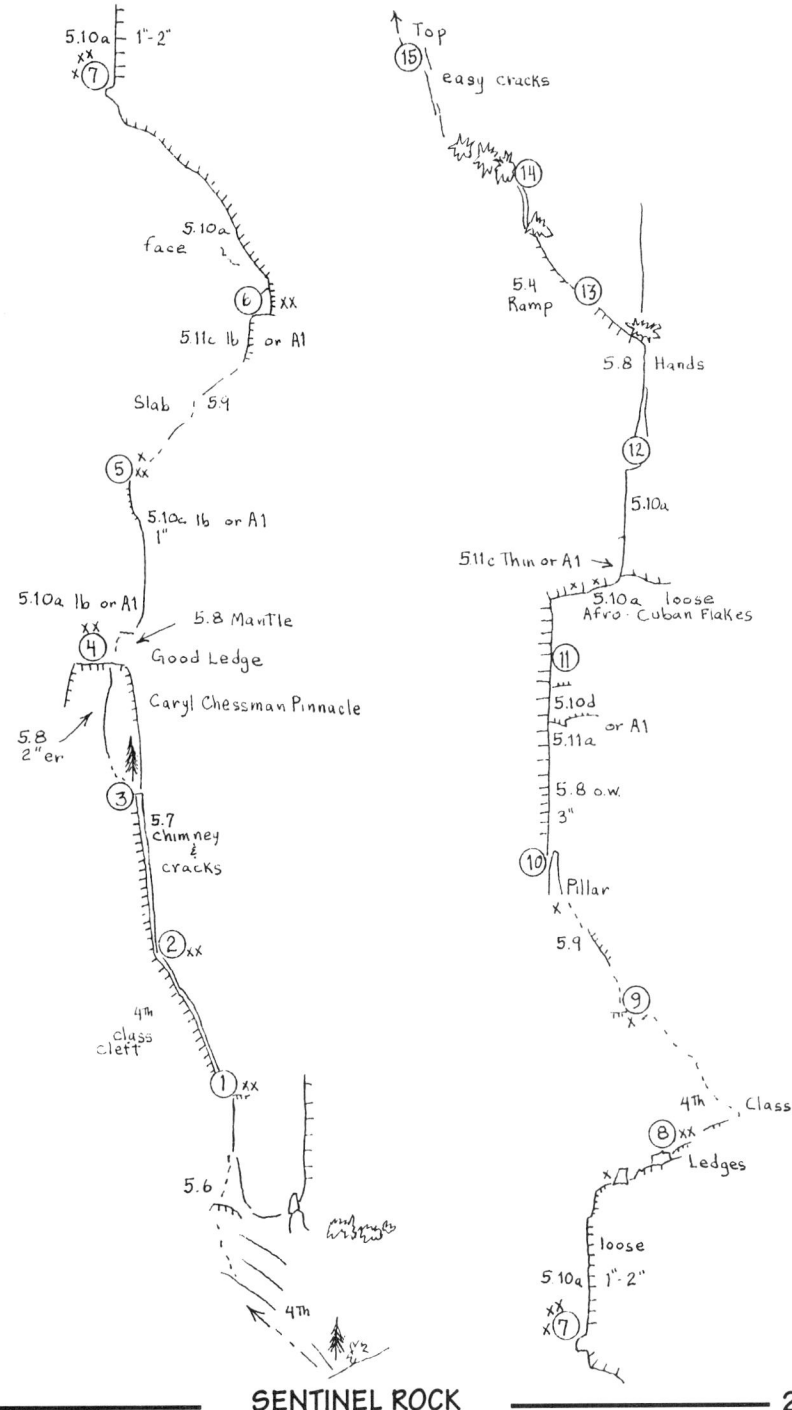

```
                    ↑ Top
5.10a  1"-2"         (15)
 xx                      easy cracks
x(7)
                         (14)
     5.10a
     face
          (6) xx         5.4
          5.11c 1b or A1  Ramp (13)
                              5.8  Hands
    Slab  5.9
  (5) x
      xx                      (12)
      5.10a 1b or A1          5.10a
      1"
                         5.11c Thin or A1 →
5.10a 1b or A1           5.10a  loose
  xx    5.8 Mantle       Afro-Cuban Flakes
 (4)
      Good Ledge         (11)
                         5.10d
      Caryl Chessman Pinnacle  or A1
5.8                      5.11a
2"er
  (3)                    5.8 o.w.
      5.7                3"
      chimney
       &                 (10) Pillar
      cracks             x
                         5.9
  (2) xx                    (9)

   4th                        4th  Class
   class                    (8)xx
   cleft                        Ledges
      (1) xx
                            loose
     5.6                 5.10a  1"-2"
                          xx
                         x(7)
   ← 4th
```

SENTINEL ROCK 255

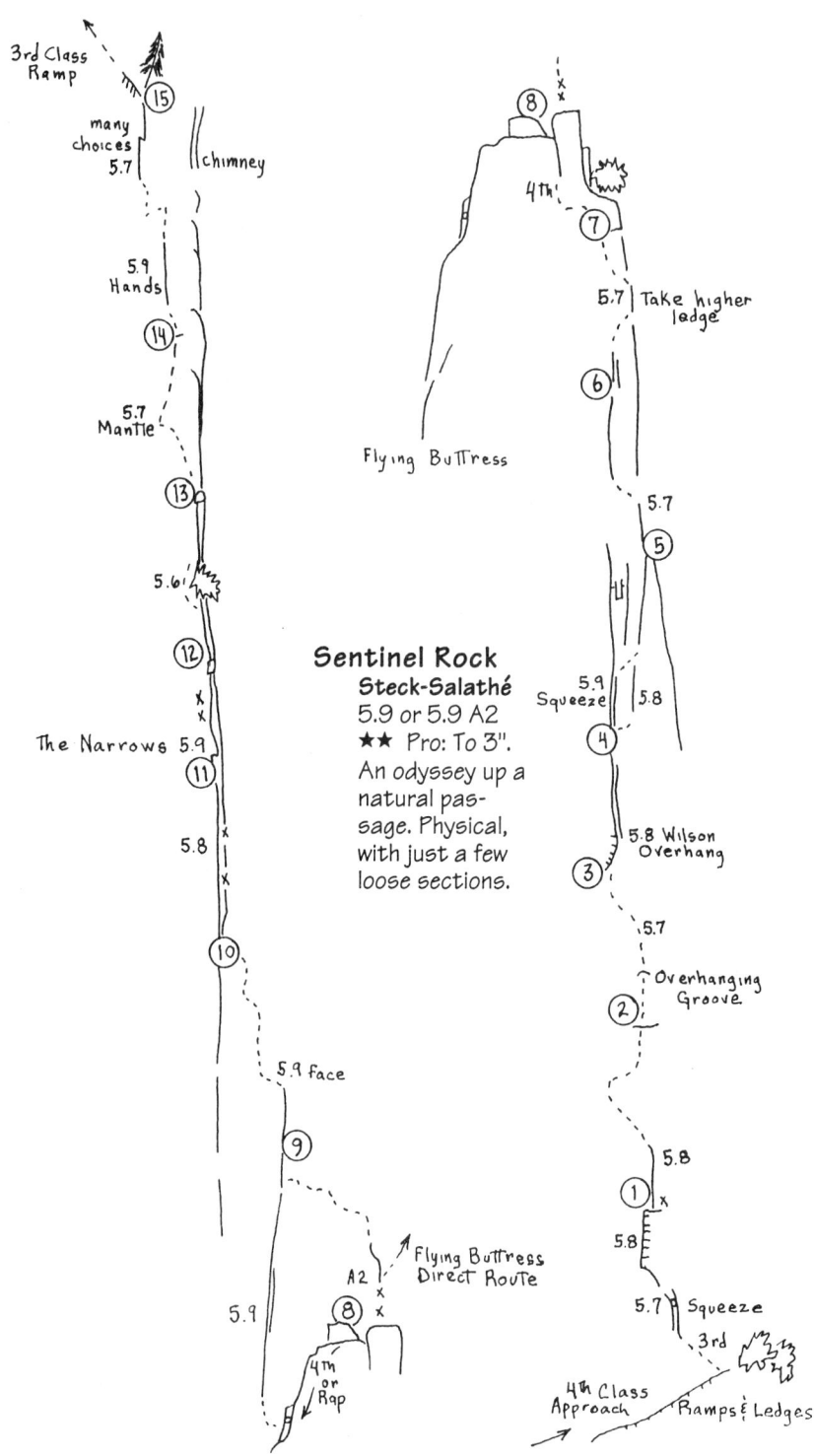

Sentinel Rock

Sentinel Rock
Steck-Salathé
5.9 or 5.9 A2
★★ Pro: To 3".
An odyssey up a natural passage. Physical, with just a few loose sections.

Pitch annotations:
- 15 — 3rd Class Ramp, many choices 5.7, chimney
- 14 — 5.9 Hands
- 13 — 5.7 Mantle
- 12 — 5.6
- 11 — The Narrows 5.9
- 10 — 5.8
- 9 — 5.9 Face
- 8 — A2, 4th or Rap (Flying Buttress Direct Route), 5.9
- 8 (upper) — Flying Buttress, 4th
- 7 — 5.7 Take higher ledge
- 6 — 5.7
- 5 —
- 4 — 5.9 Squeeze, 5.8
- 3 — 5.8 Wilson Overhang
- 2 — 5.7 Overhanging Groove
- 1 — 5.8, 5.8, 5.7 Squeeze, 3rd
- 4th Class Approach — Ramps & Ledges

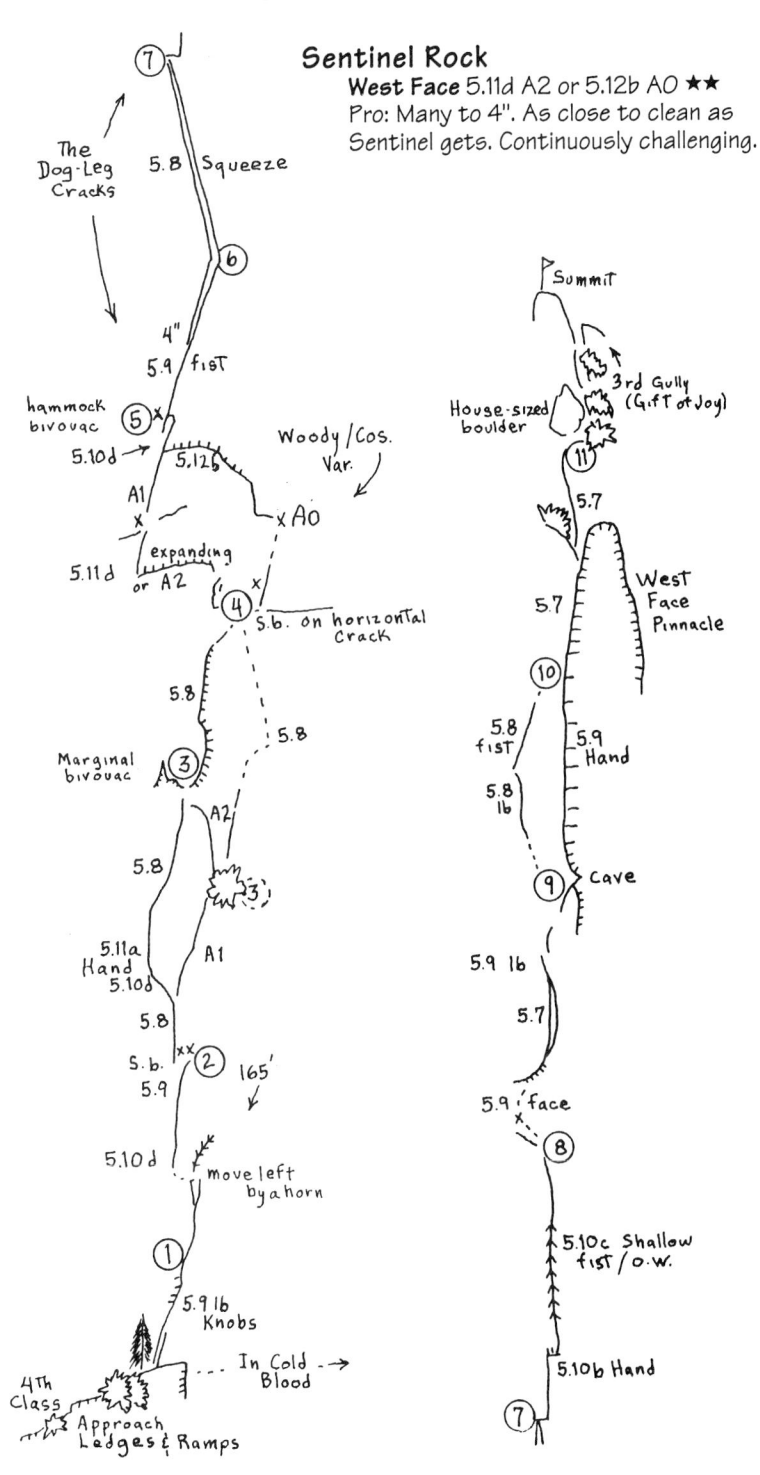

Sentinel Rock

Sentinel Rock
West Face 5.11d A2 or 5.12b A0 ★★
Pro: Many to 4". As close to clean as Sentinel gets. Continuously challenging.

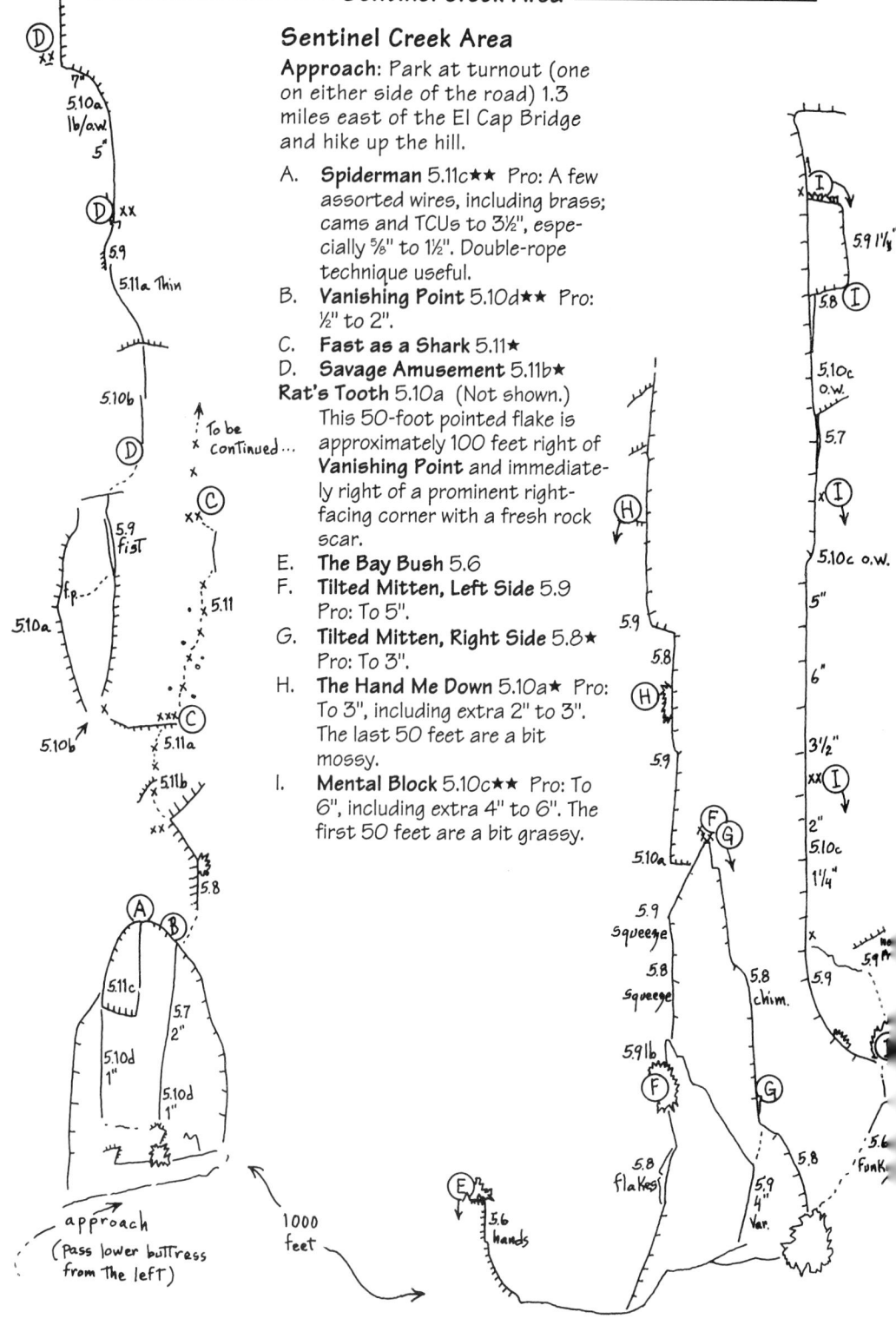

Sentinel Creek Area

Sentinel Creek Area

Approach: Park at turnout (one on either side of the road) 1.3 miles east of the El Cap Bridge and hike up the hill.

A. **Spiderman** 5.11c★★ Pro: A few assorted wires, including brass; cams and TCUs to 3½", especially ⅝" to 1½". Double-rope technique useful.
B. **Vanishing Point** 5.10d★★ Pro: ½" to 2".
C. **Fast as a Shark** 5.11★
D. **Savage Amusement** 5.11b★

Rat's Tooth 5.10a (Not shown.) This 50-foot pointed flake is approximately 100 feet right of **Vanishing Point** and immediately right of a prominent right-facing corner with a fresh rock scar.

E. **The Bay Bush** 5.6
F. **Tilted Mitten, Left Side** 5.9 Pro: To 5".
G. **Tilted Mitten, Right Side** 5.8★ Pro: To 3".
H. **The Hand Me Down** 5.10a★ Pro: To 3", including extra 2" to 3". The last 50 feet are a bit mossy.
I. **Mental Block** 5.10c★★ Pro: To 6", including extra 4" to 6". The first 50 feet are a bit grassy.

SENTINEL ROCK

Sentinel Creek Area

J. **The Sphinxter** 5.9 Pro: Including one 5½" piece.
K. **Unagi** 5.10c
L. **Hari-kiri** 5.10a★
M. **Ying-Yang** 5.10d★★
N. **Mañana** 5.10d★★
O. **Wings of Maybe** 5.12a Pro: Including RPs, TCUs, and #2-#3 Friends.
P. **King Tut's Tomb** 5.10b Pro: To 6".

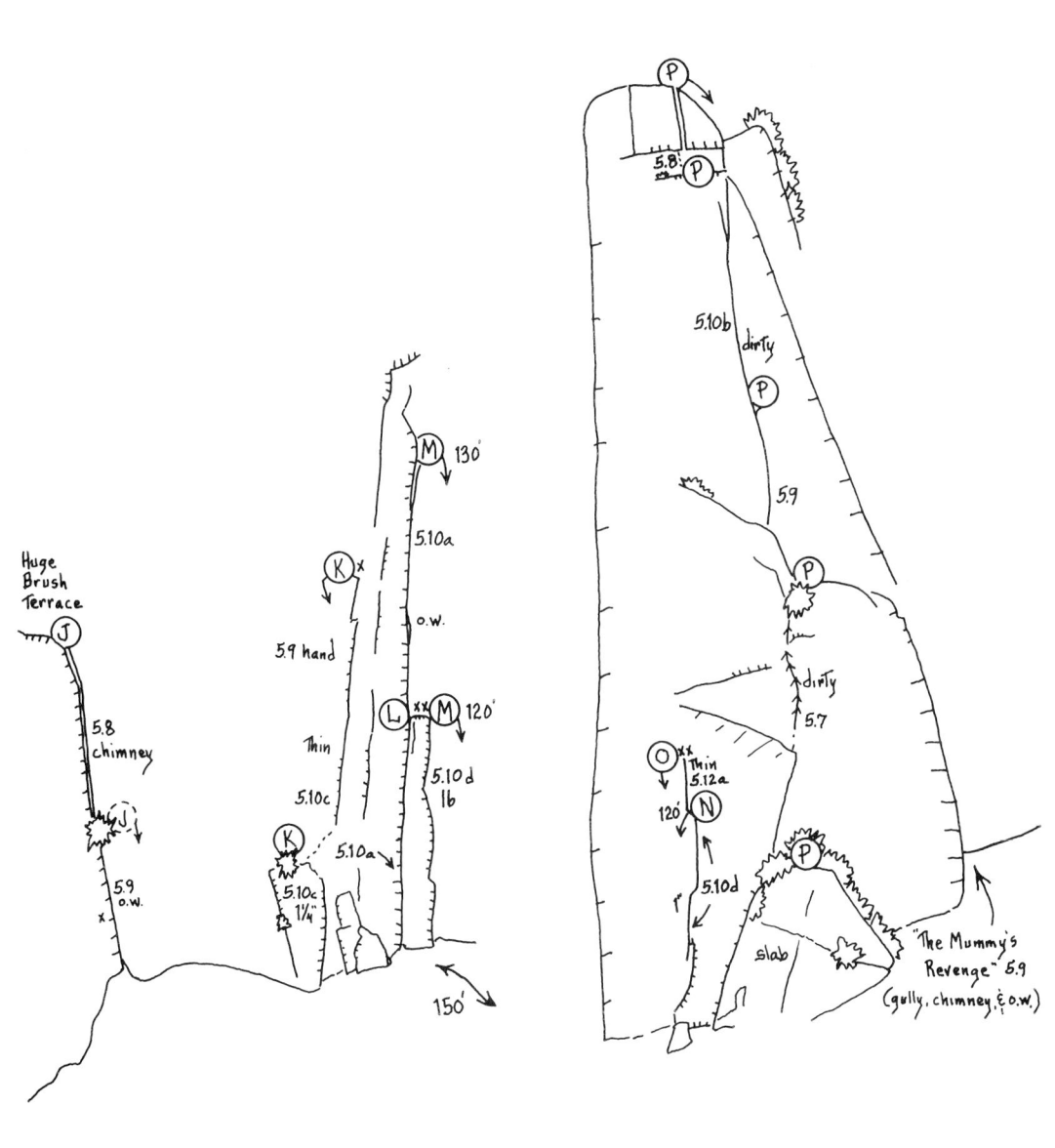

SENTINEL ROCK

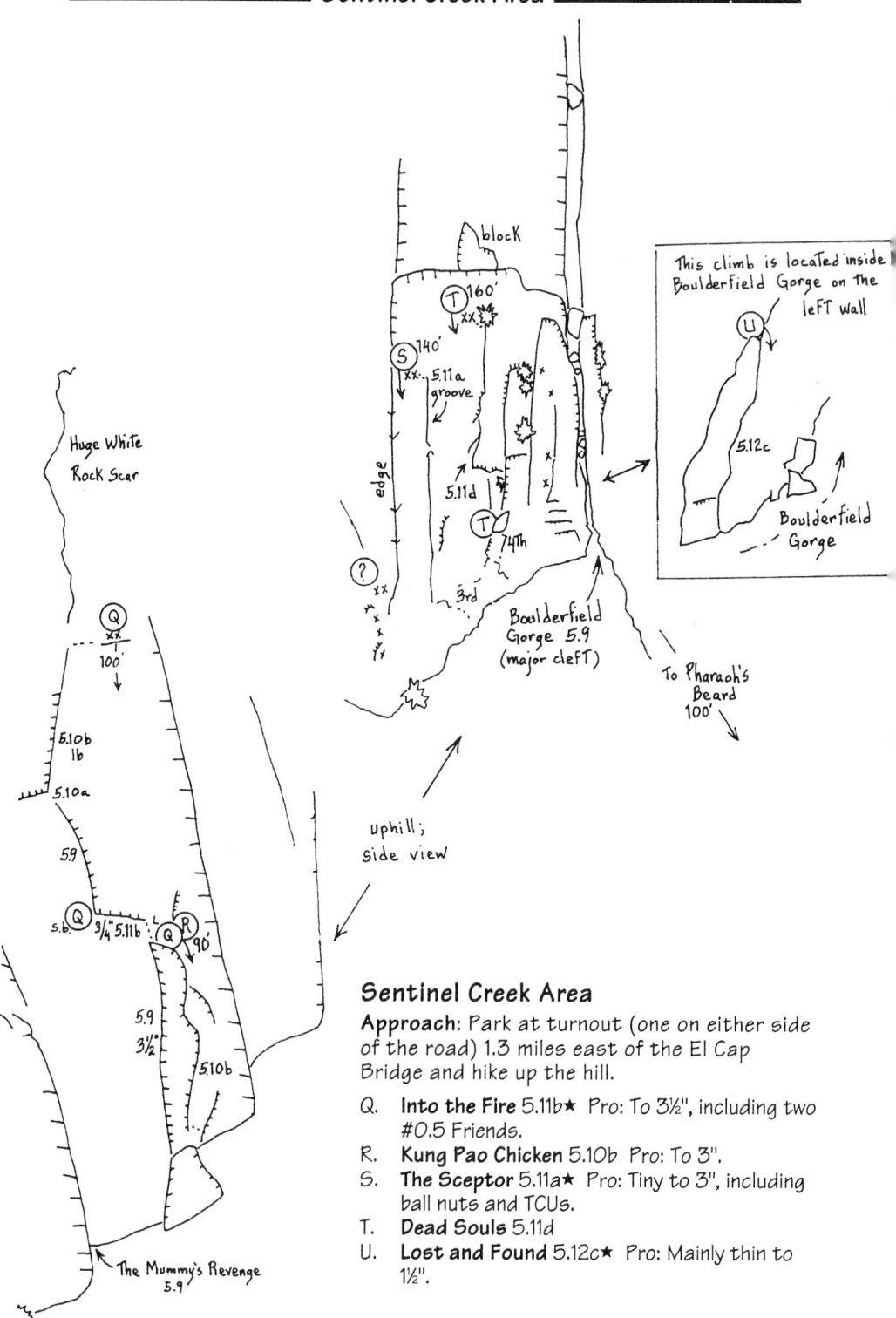

Sentinel Creek Area

Sentinel Creek Area

Approach: Park at turnout (one on either side of the road) 1.3 miles east of the El Cap Bridge and hike up the hill.

- Q. **Into the Fire** 5.11b★ Pro: To 3½", including two #0.5 Friends.
- R. **Kung Pao Chicken** 5.10b Pro: To 3".
- S. **The Sceptor** 5.11a★ Pro: Tiny to 3", including ball nuts and TCUs.
- T. **Dead Souls** 5.11d
- U. **Lost and Found** 5.12c★ Pro: Mainly thin to 1½".

Sentinel Creek Area

1. Vanishing Point 5.10d
2. Tilted Mitten Right 5.8, Left 5.9
3. King Tut's Tomb 5.10b
4. PHARAOH'S BEARD

Pharaoh's Beard Area

Approach: Park at turnout (on either side of the road) 1.3 miles east of the El Cap Bridge and hike up the hill.

Pharaoh's Beard
- A. **Regular Route** 5.8★ Pro: 5"-6" optional.
- B. **Whisker** 5.11d★★ Pro: Many to 1".
- C. **Right Side** 5.10d★ Pro: To 3½".

- D. **Look Before You Leap** 5.11a R/X
- E. **Buried Treasure** 5.11a A0★ Pro: Including three each #4 Friends.
- F. **Sheba** A4+★ Thin hardware.

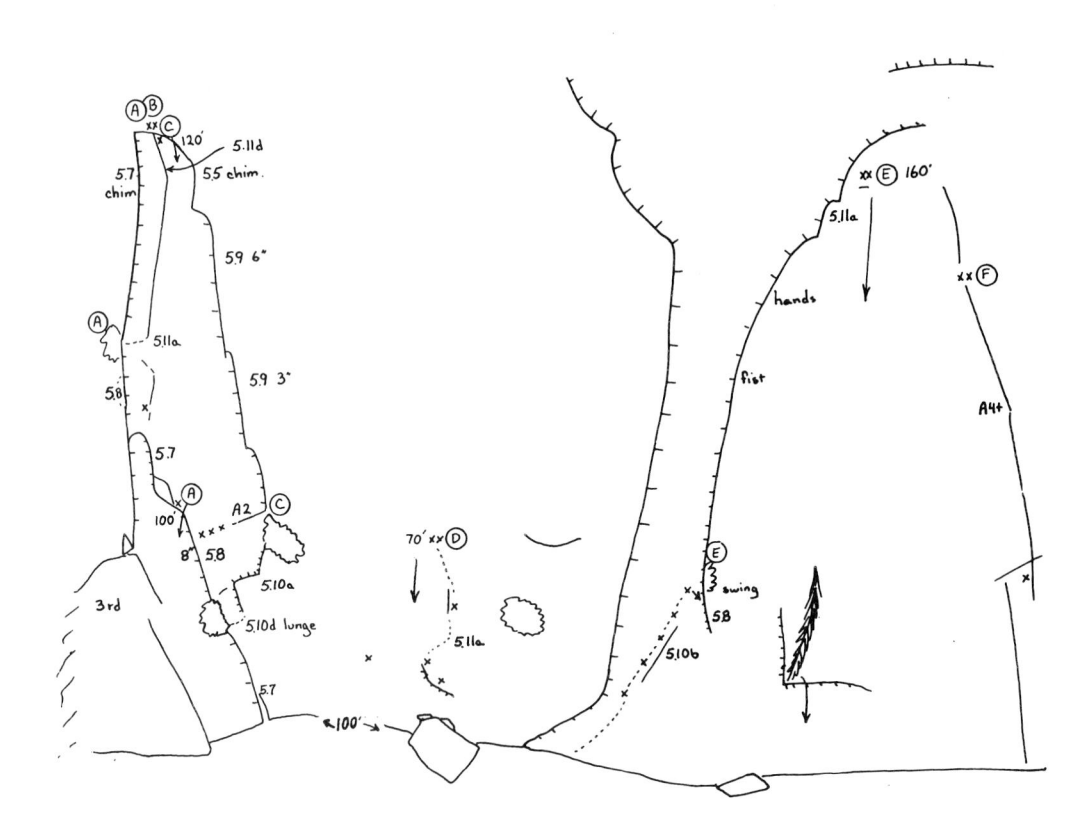

Lost Brother

Approach: Lost Brother is the large square-cut formation located directly across the Valley from Lower Brother. Park at a dirt turnout 1.1 miles east of El Cap Bridge and hike up. The **Northwest Face Route** follows, for the most part, the large corner system on that face. Brushy scrambling leads left across the lower-angle north face. (The route starts just before this sloping traverse leads to a huge drop-off.) **Realm of the Lizard King** lies just up from the toe of the Lower Brother buttress.

A. **Realm of the Lizard King** 5.11c
B. **Northwest Face Route** 5.10c
C. **The Last Resort Pinnacle**
   Left Side 5.9 Pro: To 2½".
   Center 5.10a Pro: To 3".

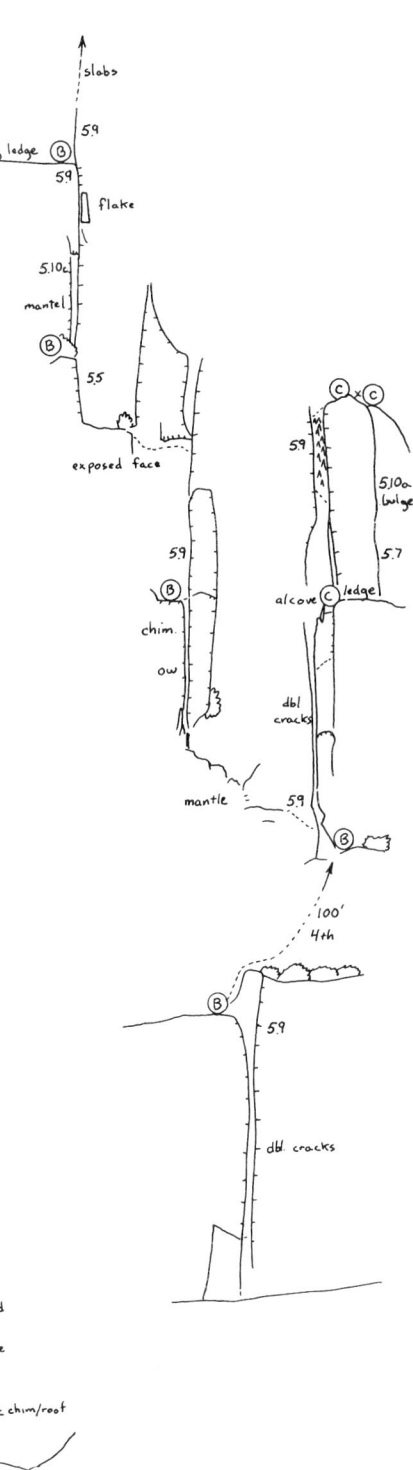

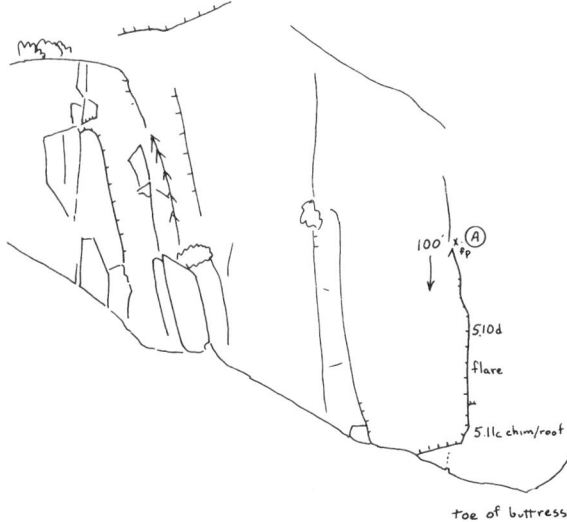

Taft Point Area

Taft Point, From Above

Approach: Park at the Sentinel Dome Trailhead along the Glacier Point Road, then hike the 1.1 miles to Taft Point and The Fissures. (Bring an extra rope for the rappel approach; jumars for an emergency escape are optional.)

A. **Journey to the East** 5.12b★★ Pro: One each to 3".
B. **Dread and Freedom** 5.12d/13a★★
C. **Kundalini Express** 5.13a★★★ (5.12b from the midway anchor)
D. **Notes from the Underground** 5.12★★ (5.11b from the midway anchor)
E. **The Pointy Part** 5.12a/b★★
F. **Jordi-Sattva** 5.10b★ Pro: To 2".

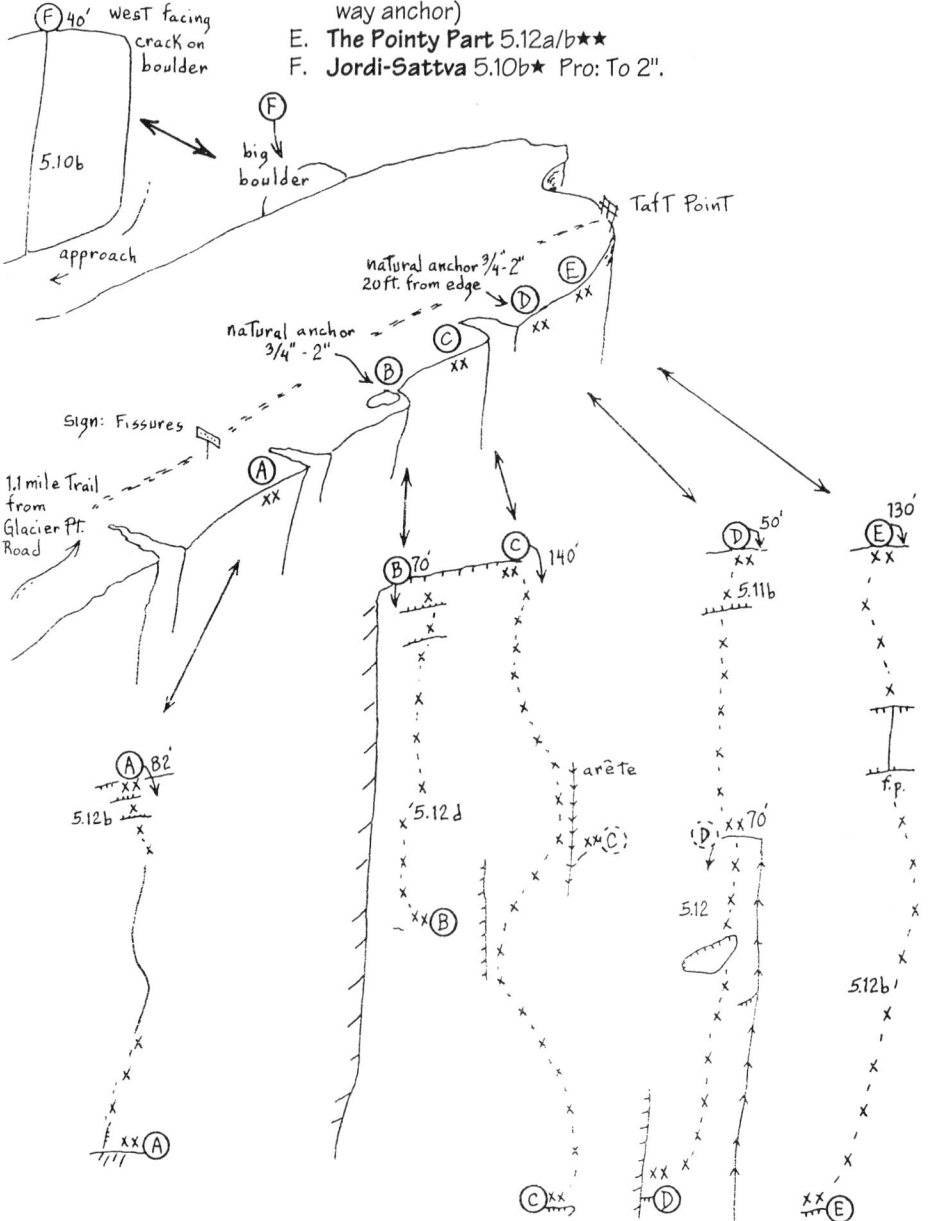

264 — SENTINEL ROCK

Phantom Pinnacle

Approach: Phantom Pinnacle lies on the right side of the very broad gully east of Cathedral Spires and is seen in profile as a needle, slightly separated from the wall behind. Begin hiking at a paved double turnout 1.4 miles east of the Hwy 41/Hwy 140 junction. The rough Spires Gully trail heads directly back into the woods and up. It serves as the approach for all the routes on Higher Spire and Higher Cathedral Rock. Phantom Pinnacle is approached from an inobvious trail that branches off directly uphill from a point where the Spires Gully trail begins a definite diagonal up and right. This ultimately leads to the routes on Lower Spire, but for Phantom, a traverse left off the trail and up around the intervening buttress should be put off until the last opportunity.

    Left Side 5.9★
    Outside Face 5.10d
    Pro: To 3".

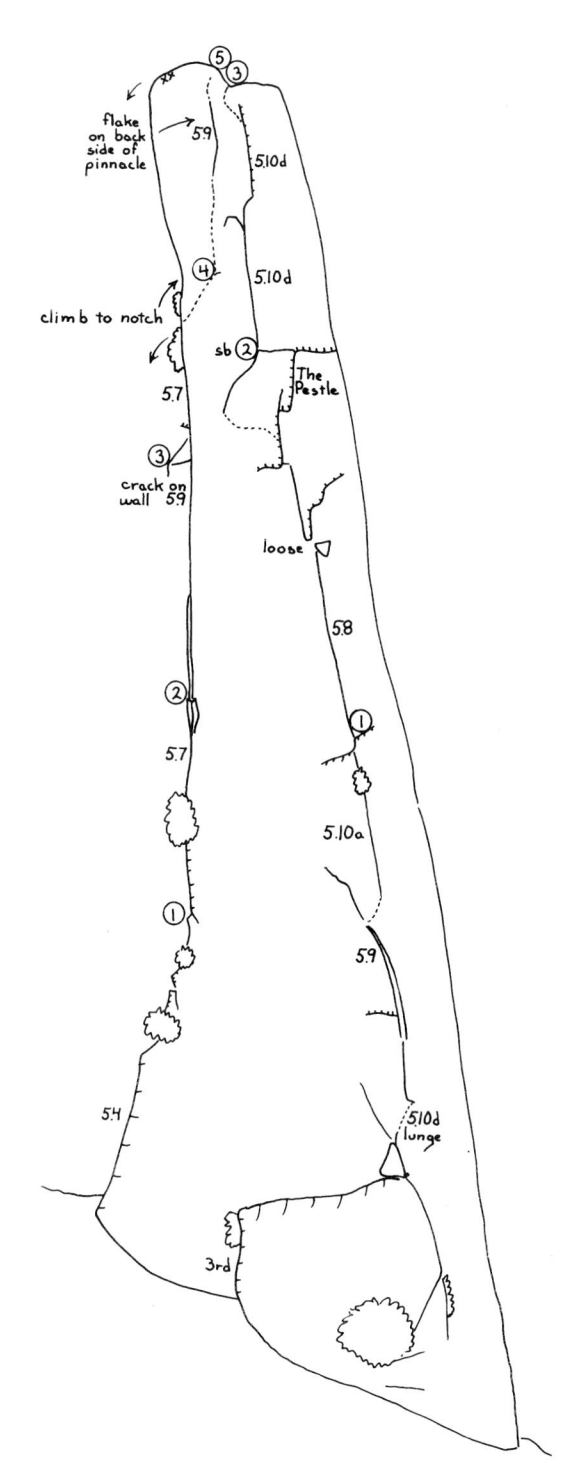

Cathedral Rocks

The approach to the routes of the Higher Cathedral Spire and Higher Cathedral Rock is made from the climber's trail up the Spires Gully. This ultimately leads to the notch between Higher Cathedral Rock and the wall that is up and behind. Start hiking at a road turnout 1.4 miles east of the Hwy 41/Hwy 140 junction at Bridalveil Falls. The trail heads directly back into the woods and up. Lower Cathedral Spire is reached from an inobvious trail that branches off directly uphill from a point where the Spires Gully trail begins a definite diagonal up and right.

The East Buttress of Middle Cathedral Rock is hiked to from a turnout 1.3 miles east of Hwy 41/Hwy 140 junction. For all the routes that ascend the northeast face of Middle Cathedral Rock, park in the same vicinity and hike west to the rock along the horse trail that parallels the road in the woods to the south. The north face apron of Middle can be reached either by hiking up along the wall from the **Direct North Buttress**, or from under Lower Cathedral Rock, below The Gunsight. Park for the latter alternative 0.8 mile east of the Hwy 41/Hwy 140 junction.

Descent: To descend from either Cathedral Spire it is necessary to rappel the regular routes of those rocks. From the summit of Higher Cathedral Rock walk south and around to the upper part of the Spires Gully.

The descent off Middle Cathedral Rock is a bit more complicated. While most of the routes on the northeast face do not lead to the summit, all that do eventually cross the Kat Walk, a narrow ledge system that traverses the rock from the top of the Direct North Buttress east to the East Buttress and on into the Cathedral Chimney, the great chasm between Middle and Higher Cathedral Rocks. The goal of climbers ascending the East Buttress and routes in that vicinity is to scramble up from the top of the technical climbing to the Kat Walk, in this area characterized by open scree slopes and heavy brush. Work left toward the Cathedral Chimney, where some minor downclimbing leads to talus and the Valley floor. A descent of the upper part of the Cathedral Chimney requires rappels, and the goal of the descending climber is to work left toward the chimney below this point.

Other routes on the northeast face of Middle (like **Stoner's Highway**) are best rappelled from their high point, but if the choice is to continue, they most often lead to the Powell-Reed Ledges, a sweeping and broad system that leads up and left into the U-Shaped Bowl. With some careful routefinding, a moderate 5th class scramble can be made up and out the left side of this feature to the Kat Walk. The **Direct North Buttress** and **North Buttress** lead to a spot behind Thirsty Spire, a lone pinnacle at the west end of the Kat Walk. Either work left along the ledge system to the Cathedral Chimney or continue on easy 5th class for 300 feet to brushy slopes that lead to the summit.

From the summit of Middle Cathedral there are several choices. One can walk down to the notch between Middle and Higher, scramble up to the top of Higher, then walk south to the top of the Spires Gully and the trail that leads down from there. Alternatively, steep slabs on the northeast side of the rock can be descended (with possible rappels) to the Kat Walk, where a scramble south leads to the Cathedral Chimney—below the difficulties. Finally, it is possible to bushwhack down the west side of Middle for a descent down The Gunsight, the notch between Middle and Lower Rocks. From the notch between Middle and Higher Rocks, walk down brush-covered slabs that lead west for about 400 feet or until very steep slabs are encountered. Traverse left into a thick brush field, then head straight down toward Bridalveil Creek. About 200 feet above the water, contour north and head uphill for the top of The Gunsight. Scrambling and short rappels lead to talus and the Valley floor.

For the descent from all the routes that lead to the basin above Bridalveil Falls, including all Lower Rock routes, The Gunsight is about the only alternative.

Sue McDevitt on the DNB

Chris Falkenstein photo

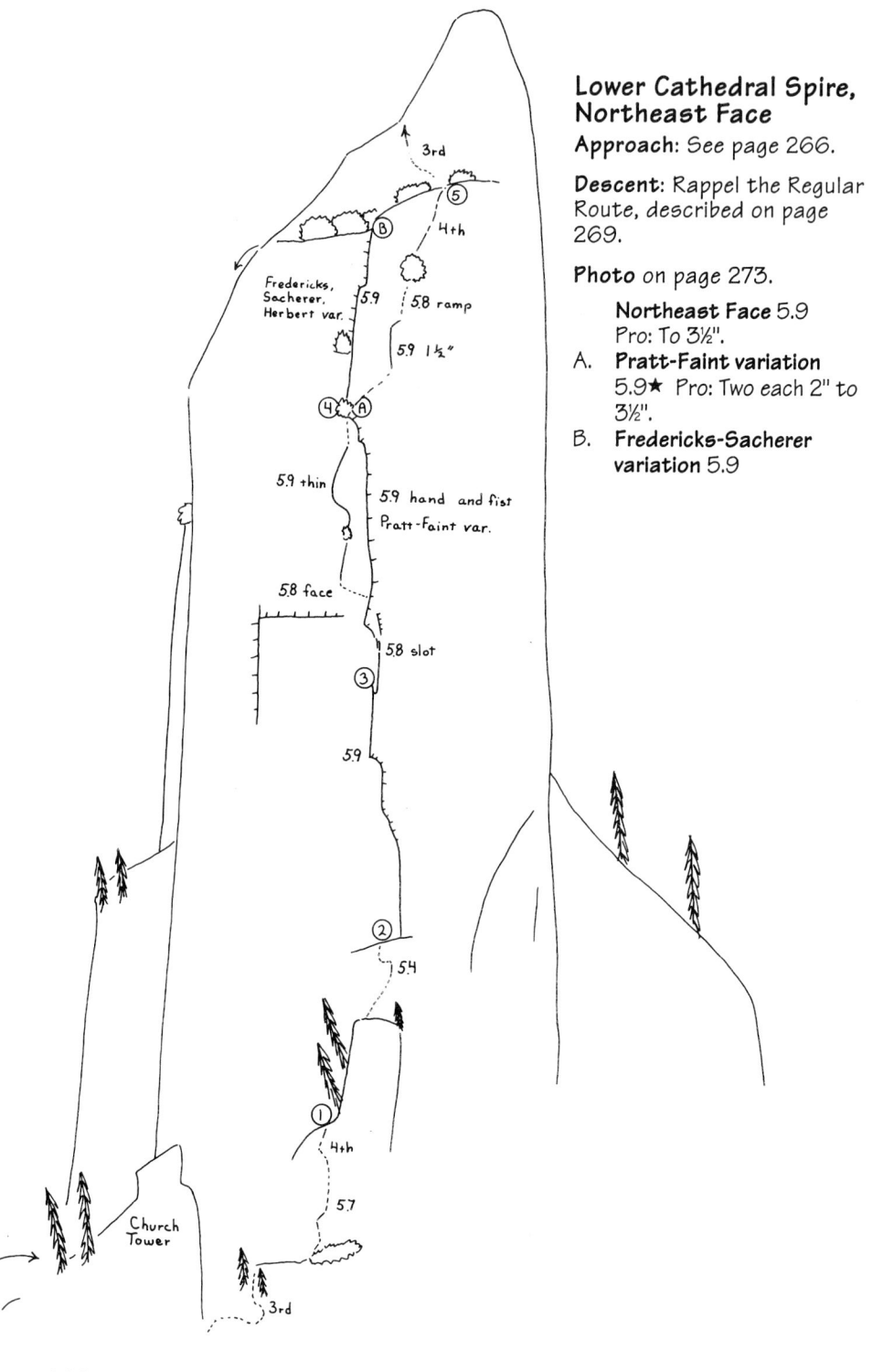

Lower Cathedral Spire: Northeast Face

Lower Cathedral Spire, Northeast Face

Approach: See page 266.

Descent: Rappel the Regular Route, described on page 269.

Photo on page 273.

Northeast Face 5.9 Pro: To 3½".

A. **Pratt-Faint variation** 5.9★ Pro: Two each 2" to 3½".

B. **Fredericks-Sacherer variation** 5.9

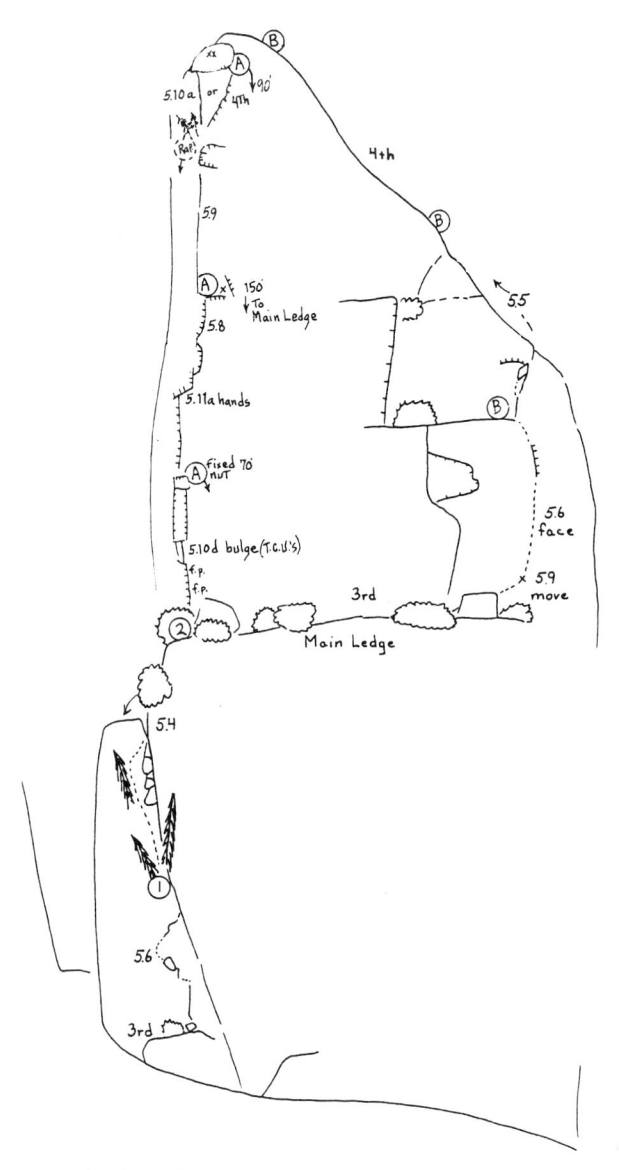

Lower Cathedral Spire
A. **South by Southwest** 5.11a★★★ Pro: Wires, #0.5 TCU to #3½ Friend. Include double #2 to #3 Friends.
B. **Regular Route** 5.9★ Pro: To 2½".

Higher Cathedral Spire

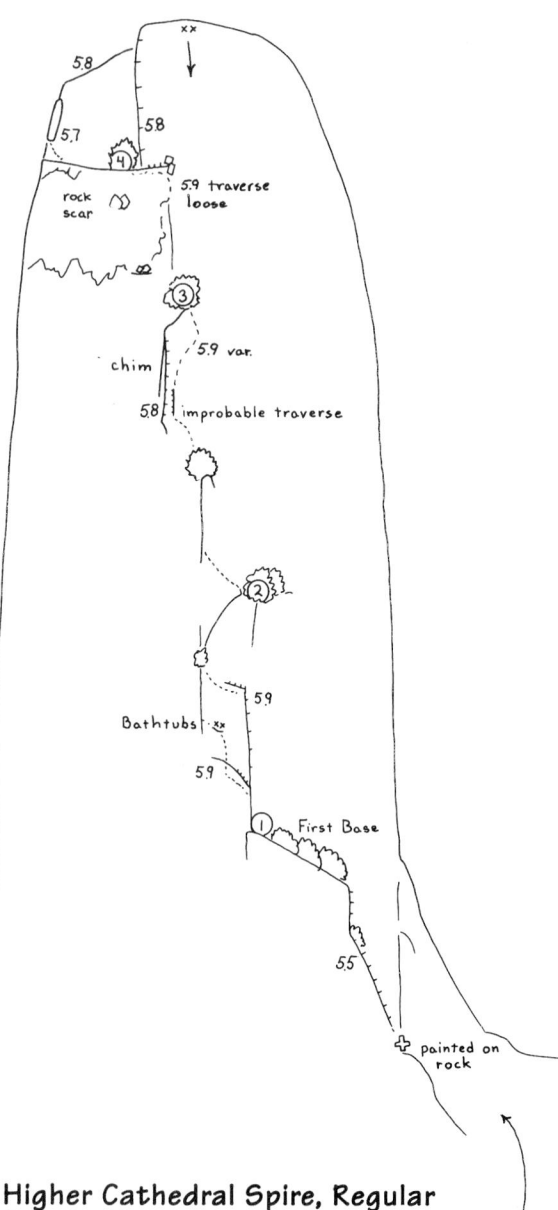

Topo annotations:
- 5.8
- xx
- 5.7
- 5.8
- (4)
- 5.9 traverse loose
- rock scar
- (3)
- 5.9 var.
- chim
- 5.8 improbable traverse
- (2)
- 5.9
- Bathtubs xx
- 5.9
- (1) First Base
- 5.5
- ✚ painted on rock

Higher Cathedral Spire, Regular (Southwest Face) Route

Approach: Described on page 266.

Descent: Rappel the route.

Photo on page 273.

Regular (Southwest Face) Route 5.9★★

Higher Cathedral Spire

Higher Cathedral Spire, Southeast Side

Approach: Described on page 266.

Descent: Rappel the Regular Route, on page 270.

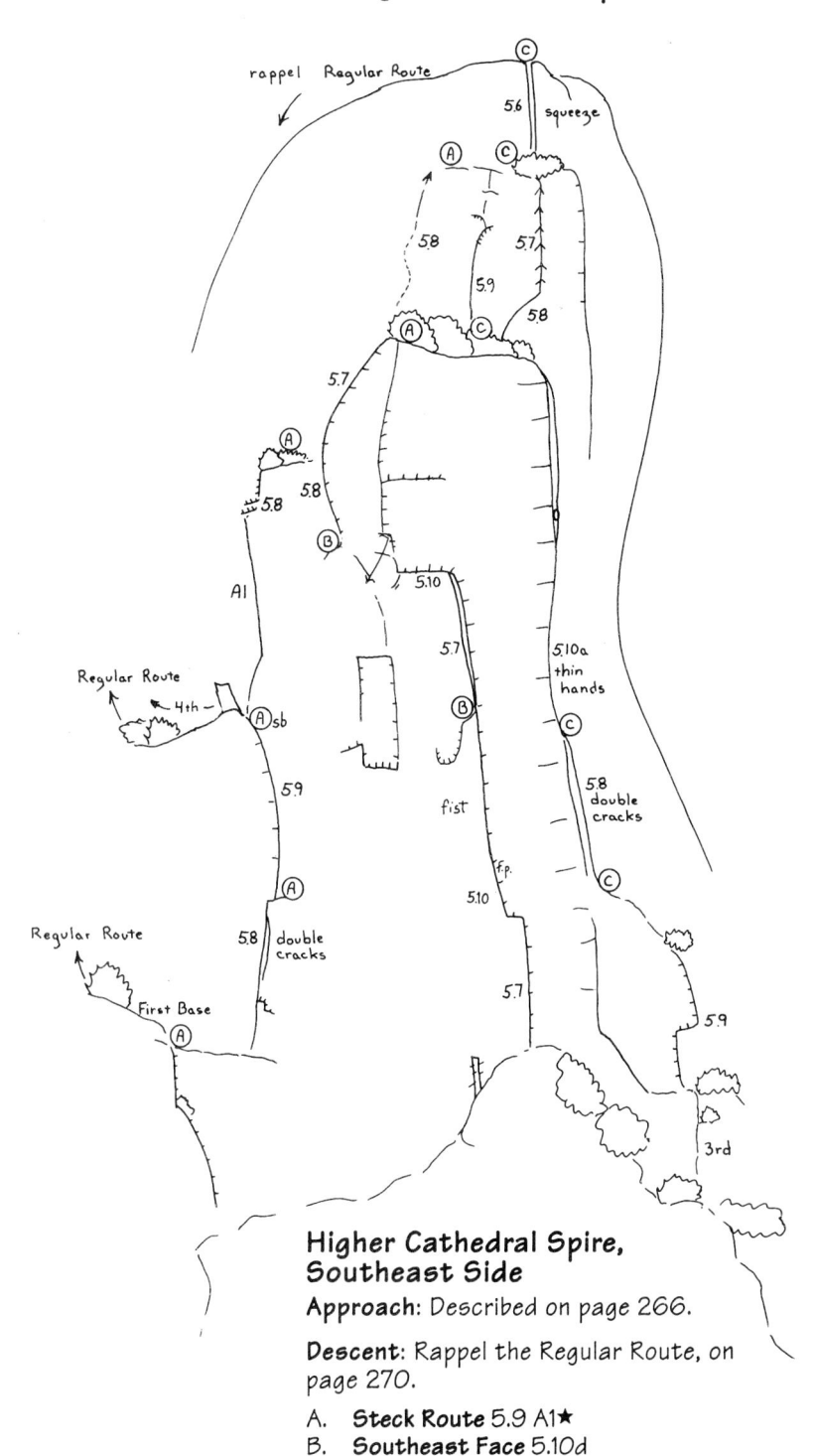

- A. **Steck Route** 5.9 A1★
- B. **Southeast Face** 5.10d
- C. **East Corner** 5.10a★

CATHEDRAL ROCKS

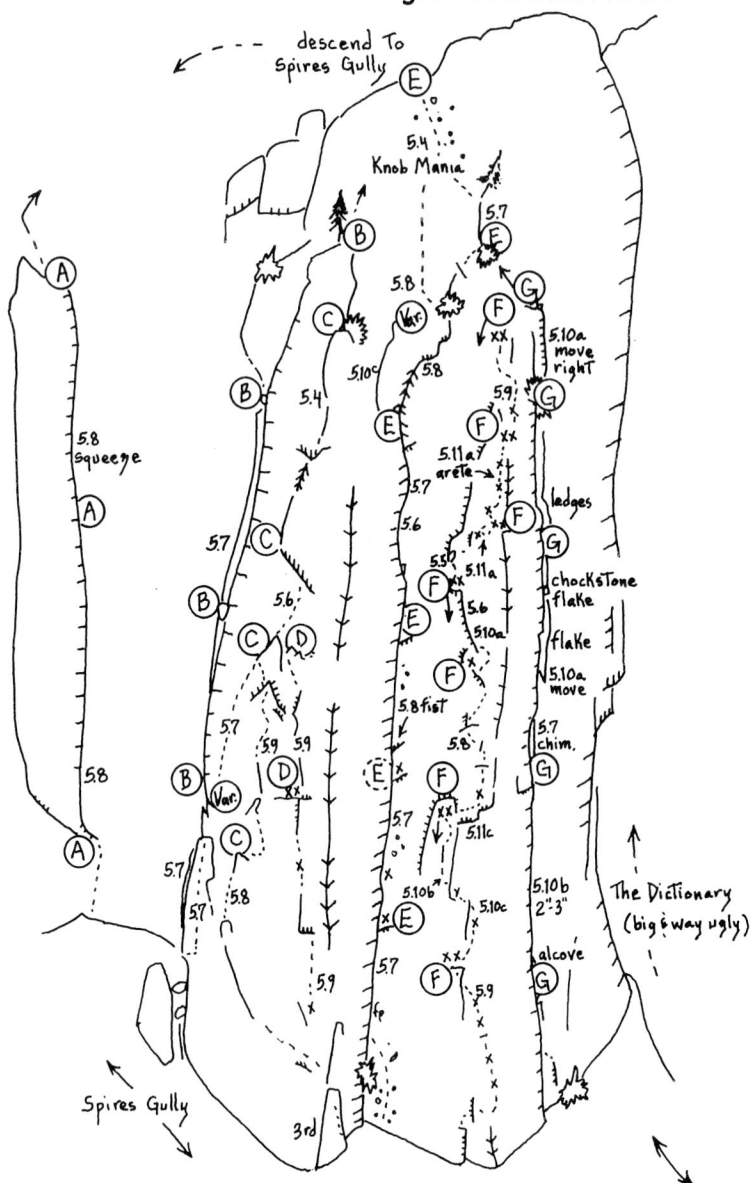

Higher Cathedral Rock, East Face, Left

Approach and Descent: See page 266.

A. **The Syllable** 5.8
B. **The Sequel** 5.8★
C. **Blind Man's Bluff** 5.9★
D. **Blind Alley** 5.9★
E. **The Braille Book** 5.8★★★ Pro: To 3".
F. **Perfect Vision** 5.11c★★★ Pro: Wires, including RPs, cams to 3¾", including TCUs.
G. **Book of Job** 5.10b★ Pro: To 4".
H. **Malice Aforethought** 5.11a★ Pro: One each TCU to #2.5 Friend, including one #4 Friend.

Higher Cathedral Rock: East Face

1. LOWER CATHEDRAL SPIRE
2. HIGHER CATHEDRAL SPIRE
3. Braille Book 5.8
4. Mary's Tears 5.11b
5. Northeast Buttress 5.9
6. The Crucifix 5.12b R
7. Power Point 5.11c R

CATHEDRAL ROCKS

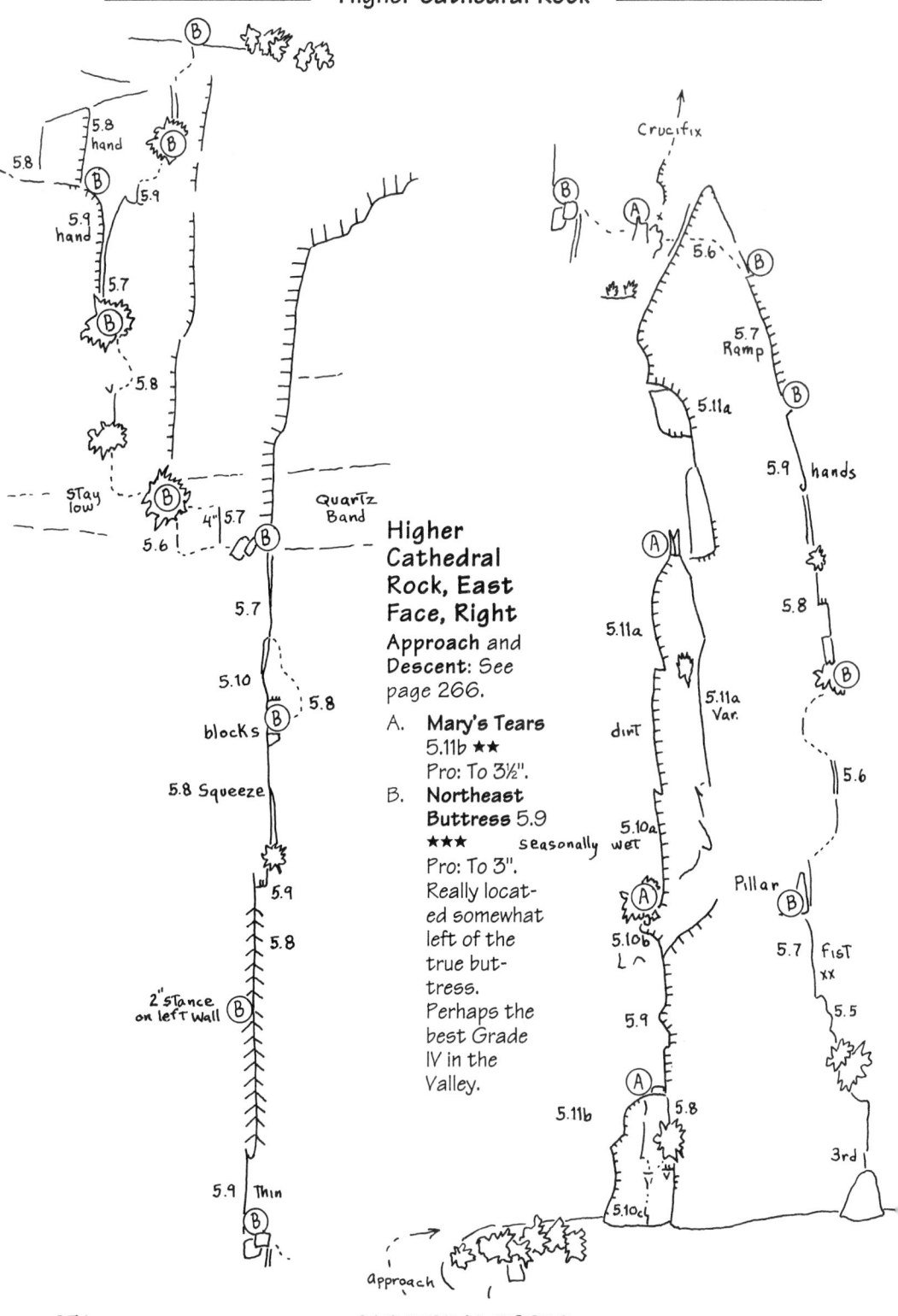

Higher Cathedral Rock, East Face, Right

Approach and Descent: See page 266.

A. **Mary's Tears** 5.11b ★★
Pro: To 3½".

B. **Northeast Buttress** 5.9 ★★★
Pro: To 3". Really located somewhat left of the true buttress. Perhaps the best Grade IV in the Valley.

Higher Cathedral Rock

Higher Cathedral Rock, Northeast Buttress
A. **Power Point** 5.11c★★ R
B. **The Crucifix** 5.12b★★★ R
Pro: Wireds to 4", extra 3" to 4" pieces. This wild climb is played out on a beautiful mosaic wall.

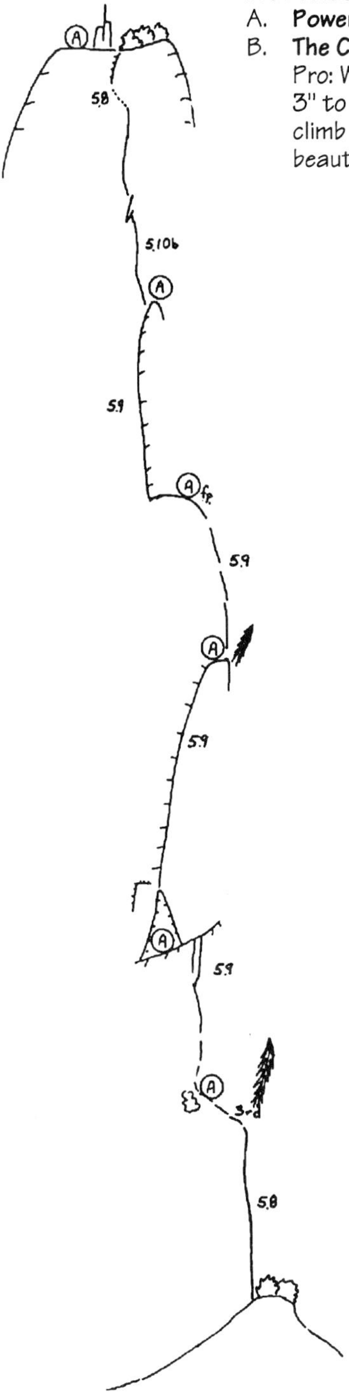

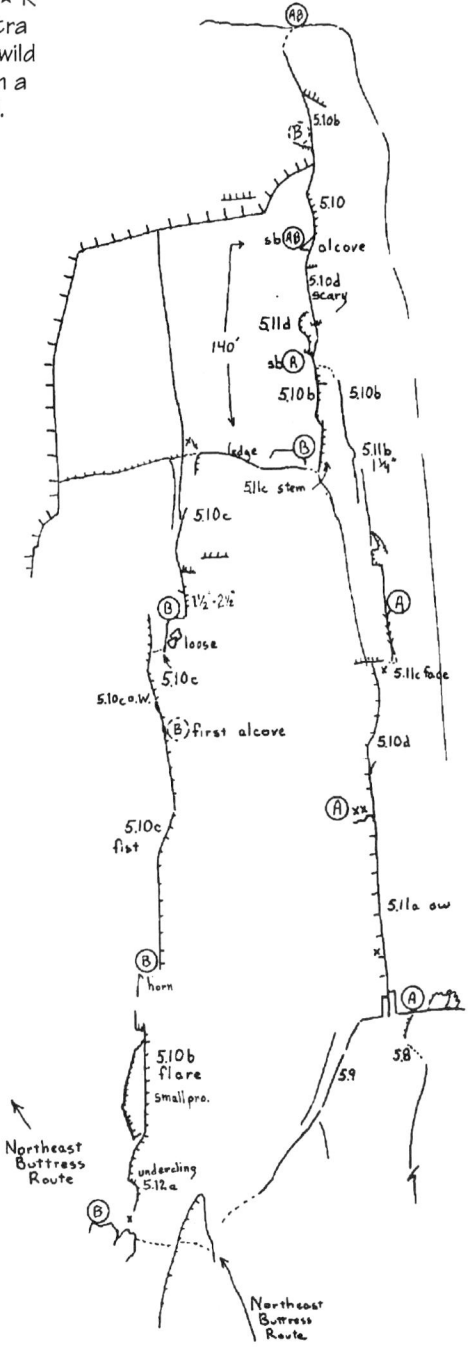

CATHEDRAL ROCKS

Higher Cathedral Rock, North Face
The Affliction 5.11d AO

Higher Cathedral Rock

Higher Cathedral Rock, North Face, Left

The Affliction V 5.11d A0 ★★ R Pro: #3 RP, set of Rocks, two each #0.4 to #4 cams, two each 5".

CATHEDRAL ROCKS — 277

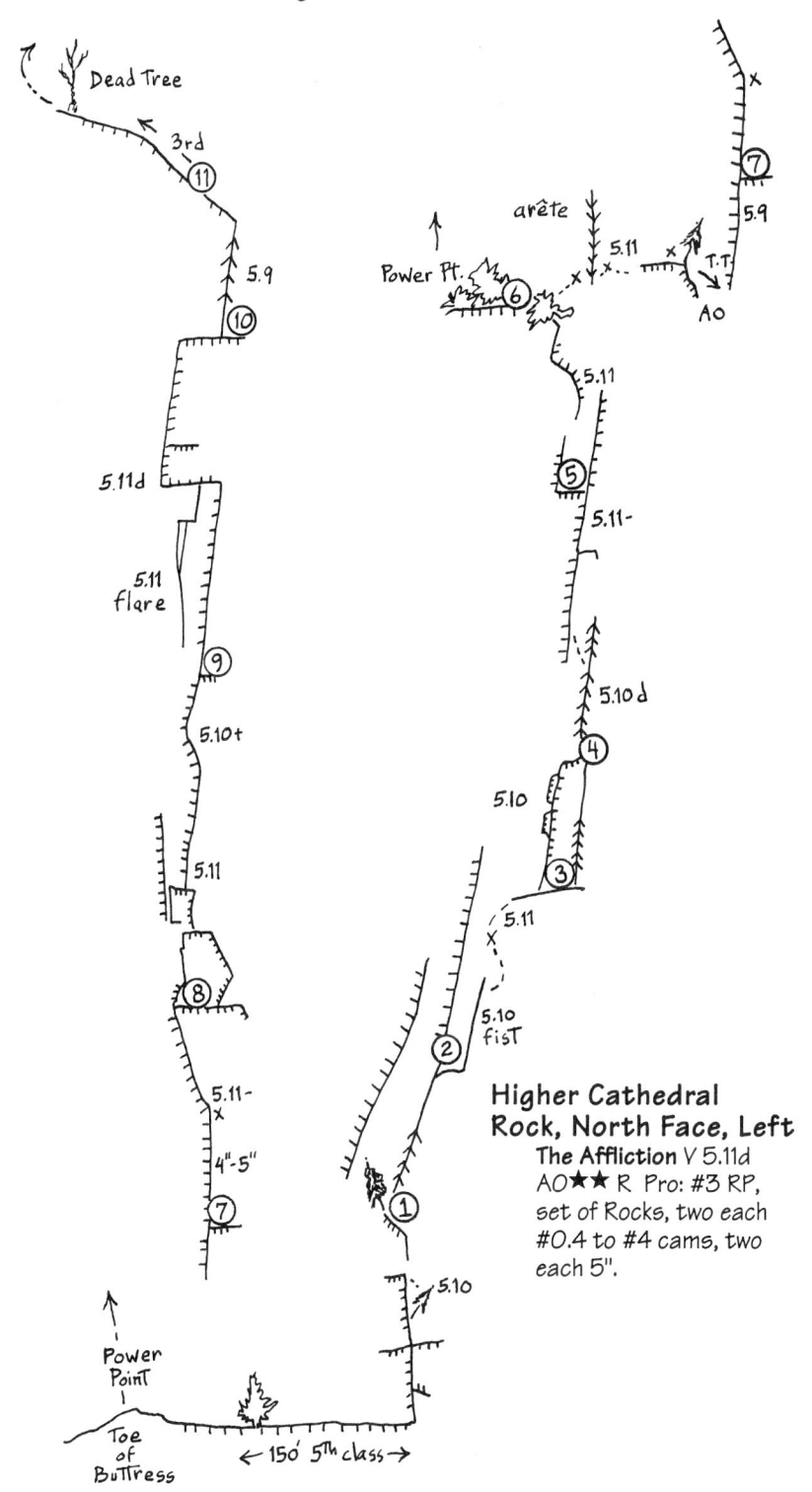

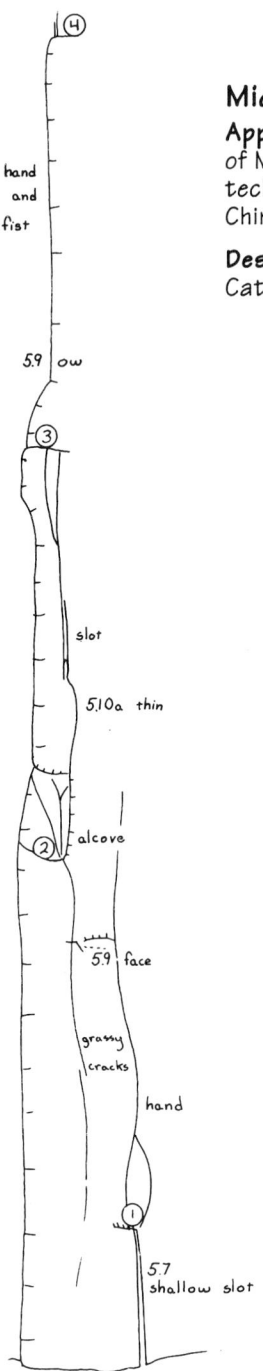

Middle Cathedral Rock

Approach: This route is on the east face of Middle Cathedral Rock, just below the technical climbing in the Cathedral Chimney.

Descent: Rappel and downclimb the Cathedral Chimney.

Alley Cat 5.10a Pro: To 6", including extra 2½" to 3".

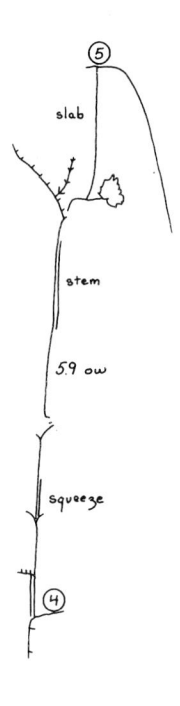

The Cathedral Rocks

1. Braille Book 5.8
2. Power Point 5.11c R
3. East Buttress of Middle 5.9 A1 or 5.10c
4. Sacherer-Fredericks 5.10c
5. Kor-Beck 5.9
6. Space Bubble 5.11a R
7. Central Pillar of Frenzy V 5.10d
8. Stoner's Highway 5.10c
9. Powell-Reed
10. Paradise Lost 5.10c
11. Direct North Buttress ("DNB") 5.10b
12. North Buttress V 5.10a
13. Mother Earth VI 5.11c A4
14. East Buttress of Lower 5.10c
15. Beggar's Buttress 5.11c

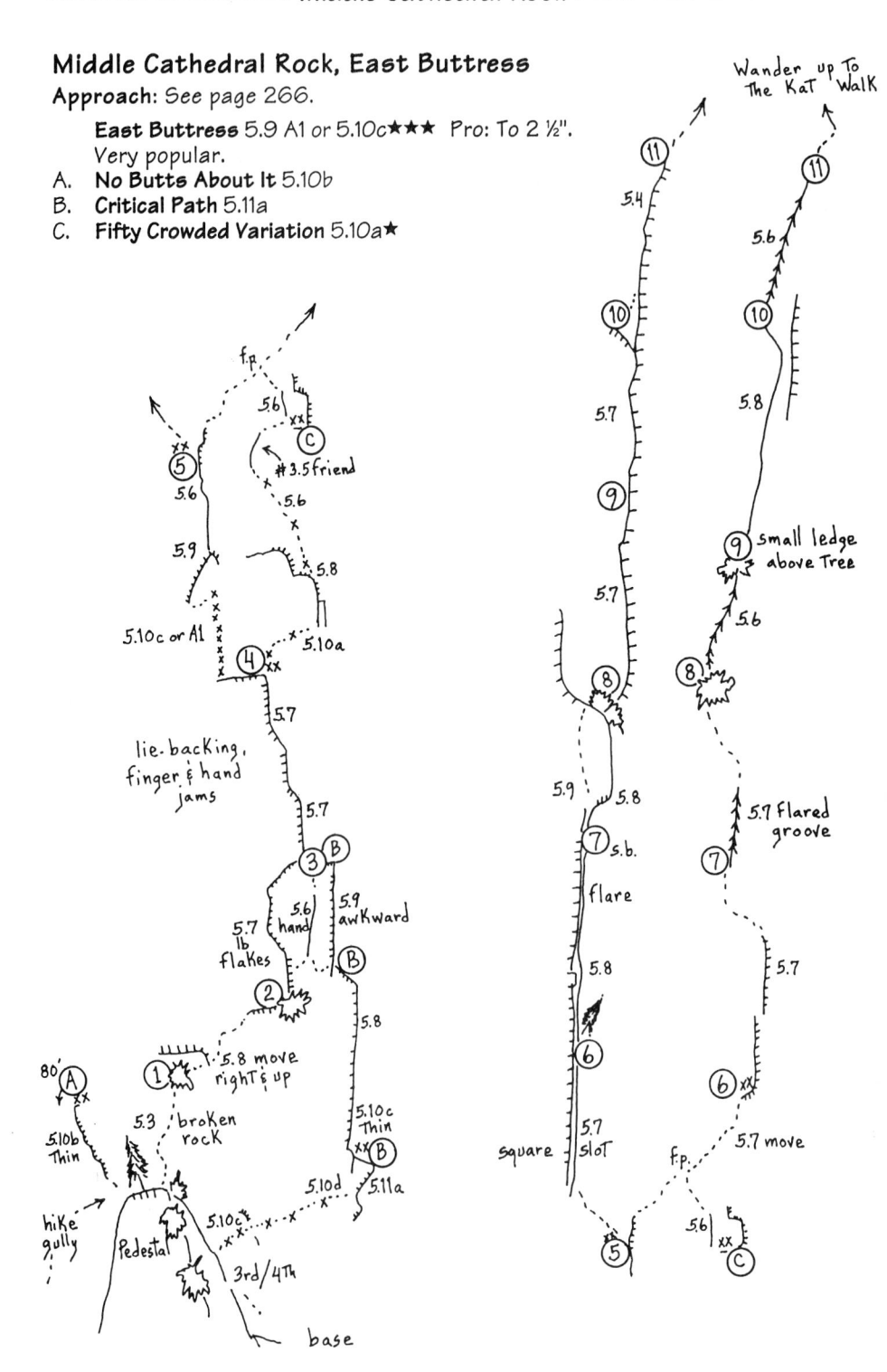

Middle Cathedral Rock, East Buttress
Approach: See page 266.

East Buttress 5.9 A1 or 5.10c★★★ Pro: To 2½".
Very popular.
A. **No Butts About It** 5.10b
B. **Critical Path** 5.11a
C. **Fifty Crowded Variation** 5.10a★

Middle Cathedral Rock

Middle Cathedral Rock: Northeast Face

Approach: See page 266.

Descent: Use the **Kat Walk** descent, page 266.

Sacherer-Fredericks (with direct finish) 5.10c Pro: To 3".

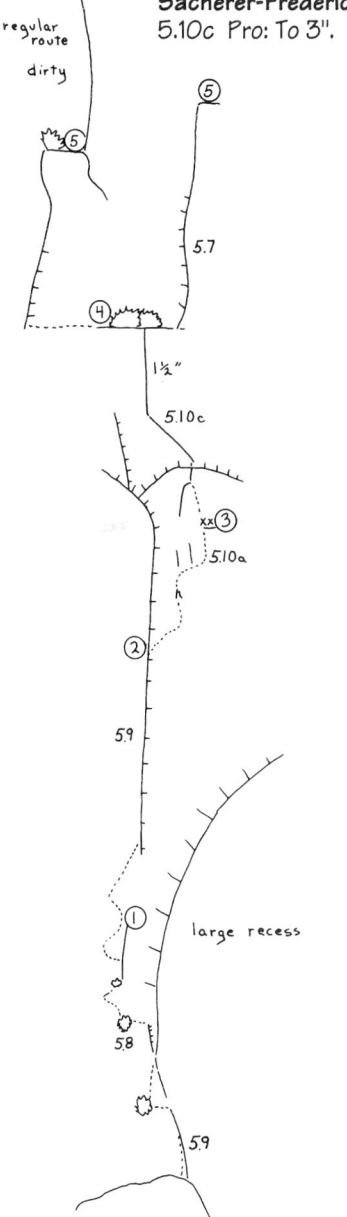

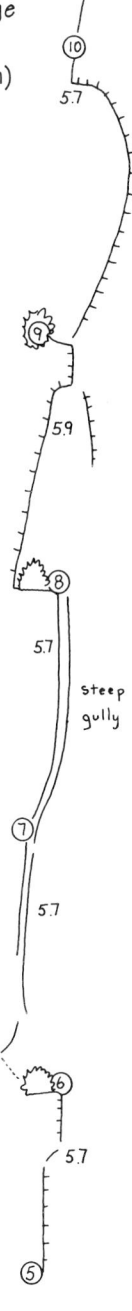

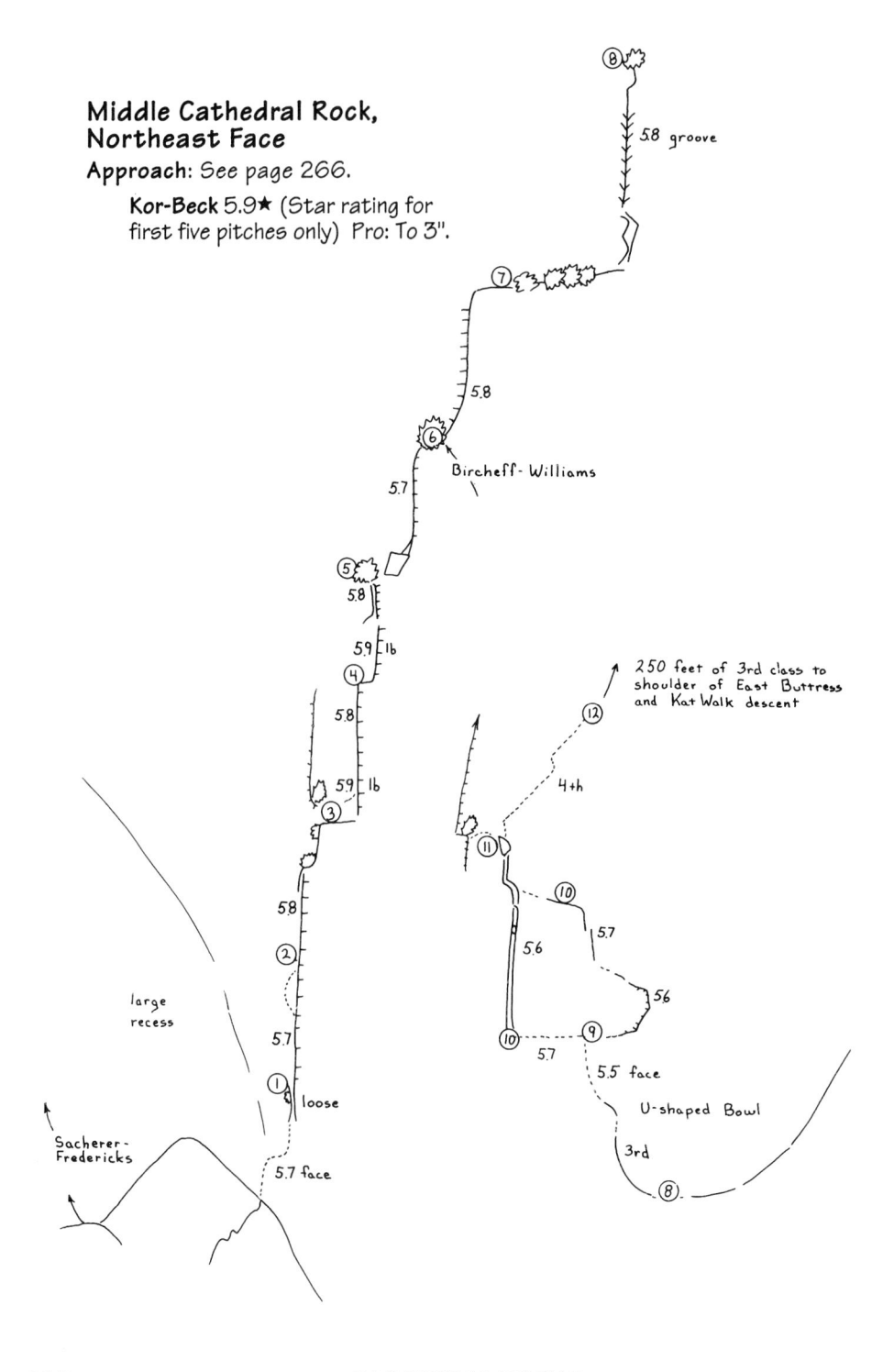

Middle Cathedral Rock, Northeast Face

Approach: See page 266.

Kor-Beck 5.9★ (Star rating for first five pitches only) Pro: To 3".

- 5.8 groove
- 5.8
- Bircheff-Williams
- 5.7
- 5.8
- 5.9 lb
- 5.8
- 5.9 lb
- 5.8
- 5.7
- loose
- 5.7 face
- Sacherer-Fredericks
- large recess
- 250 feet of 3rd class to shoulder of East Buttress and Kat Walk descent
- 4th
- 5.6
- 5.7
- 5.6
- 5.7
- 5.5 face
- U-shaped Bowl
- 3rd

Middle Cathderal Rock

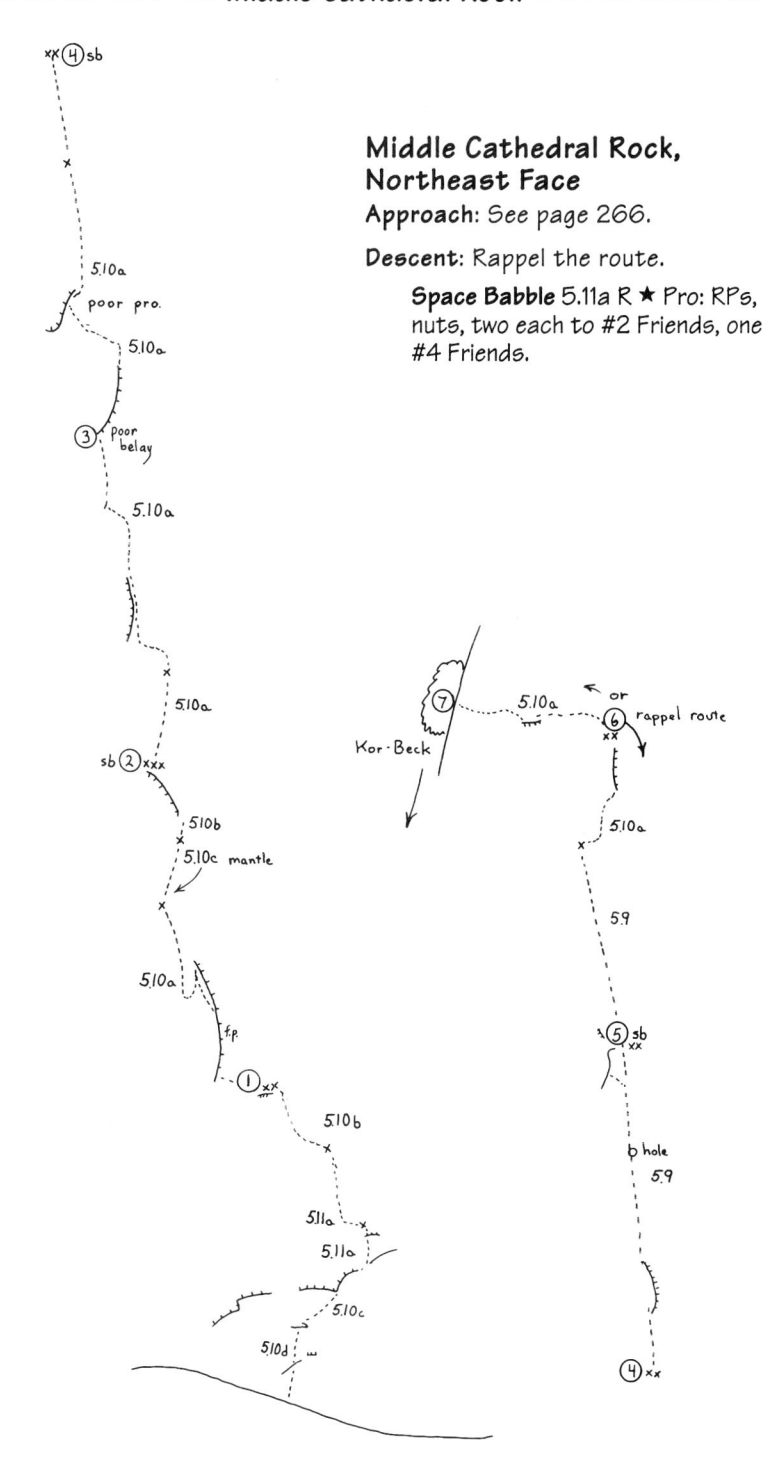

Middle Cathedral Rock, Northeast Face

Approach: See page 266.

Descent: Rappel the route.

Space Babble 5.11a R ★ Pro: RPs, nuts, two each to #2 Friends, one #4 Friends.

Middle Cathedral Rock

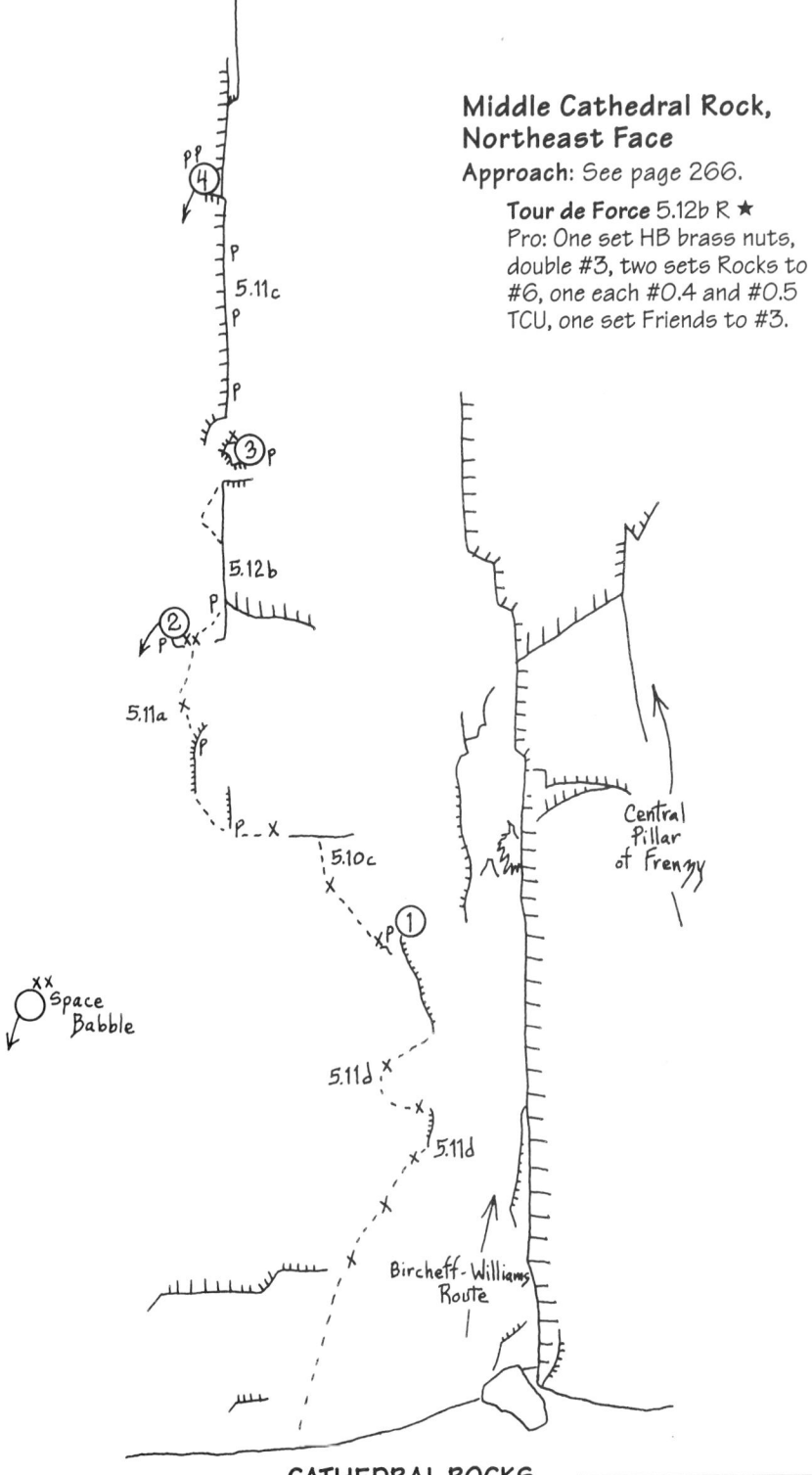

Middle Cathedral Rock, Northeast Face
Approach: See page 266.

Tour de Force 5.12b R ★
Pro: One set HB brass nuts, double #3, two sets Rocks to #6, one each #0.4 and #0.5 TCU, one set Friends to #3.

5.11c
5.12b
5.11a
5.10c
Space Babble
5.11d
5.11d
Bircheff-Williams Route
Central Pillar of Frenzy

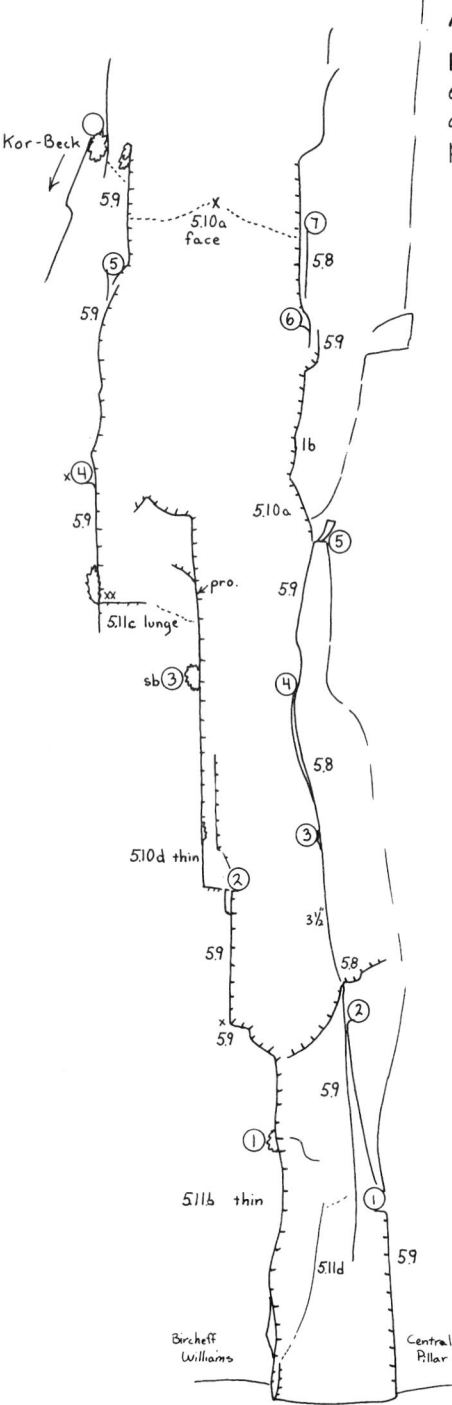

Middle Cathedral Rock

Middle Cathedral Rock, Northeast Face

Approach: See page 266.

Descent: The **Bircheff-Williams** and the escape off the **Central Pillar** can be descended by rappelling **Space Babble**, page 283, or the **Kor-Beck**, page 282.

Bircheff-Williams 5.11b★★ Pro: To 3", including 2 each ½" to ¾".

Central Pillar of Frenzy V 5.10d★★★ Pro: To 3½". This route is usually done in one of three ways: by climbing the first five pitches and rappelling the route; by doing two more pitches and traversing to the **Kor-Beck** to rappel that route; or by continuing to the Powell-Reed Ledges and moving off via the U-Shaped Bowl. Extra thin protection is needed for the upper section of the route.

Chouinard-Pratt V 5.11 Not Shown. This route follows the right side of **The Pillar**.

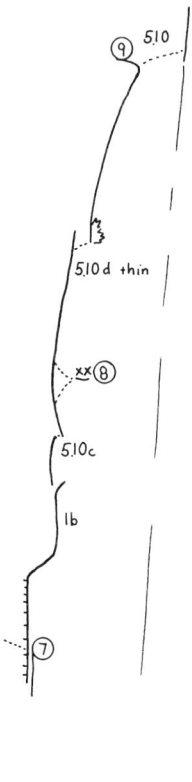

CATHEDRAL ROCKS

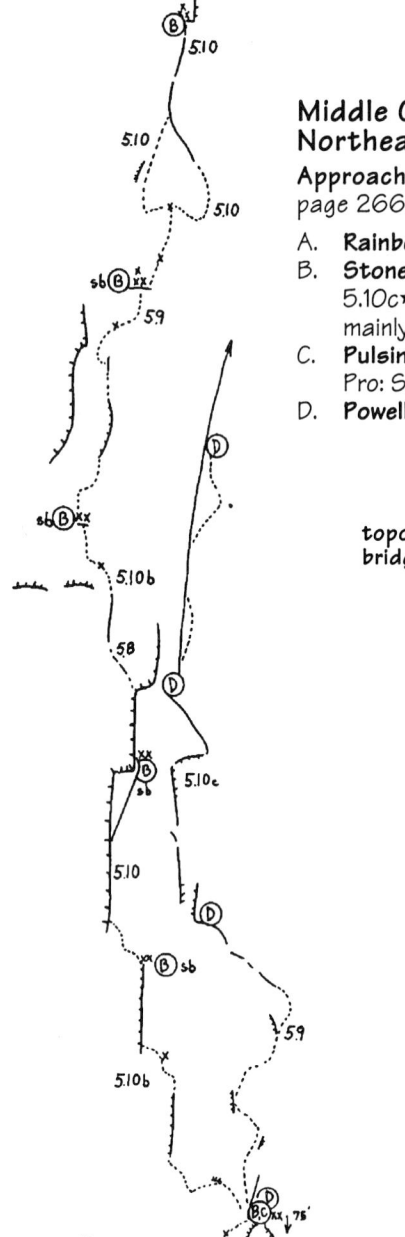

Middle Cathedral Rock, Northeast Face

Approach and Descent: See page 266.

- A. **Rainbow Bridge** 5.11d ★
- B. **Stoner's Highway** 5.10c ★★★ Pro: To 2½", mainly small.
- C. **Pulsing Pustules** 5.11c ★ Pro: Small nuts and TCUs.
- D. **Powell-Reed** 5.10c

topo 182, rainbow bridge

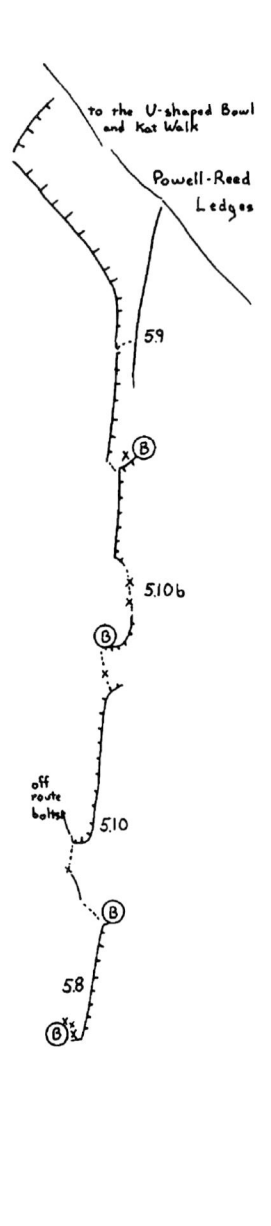

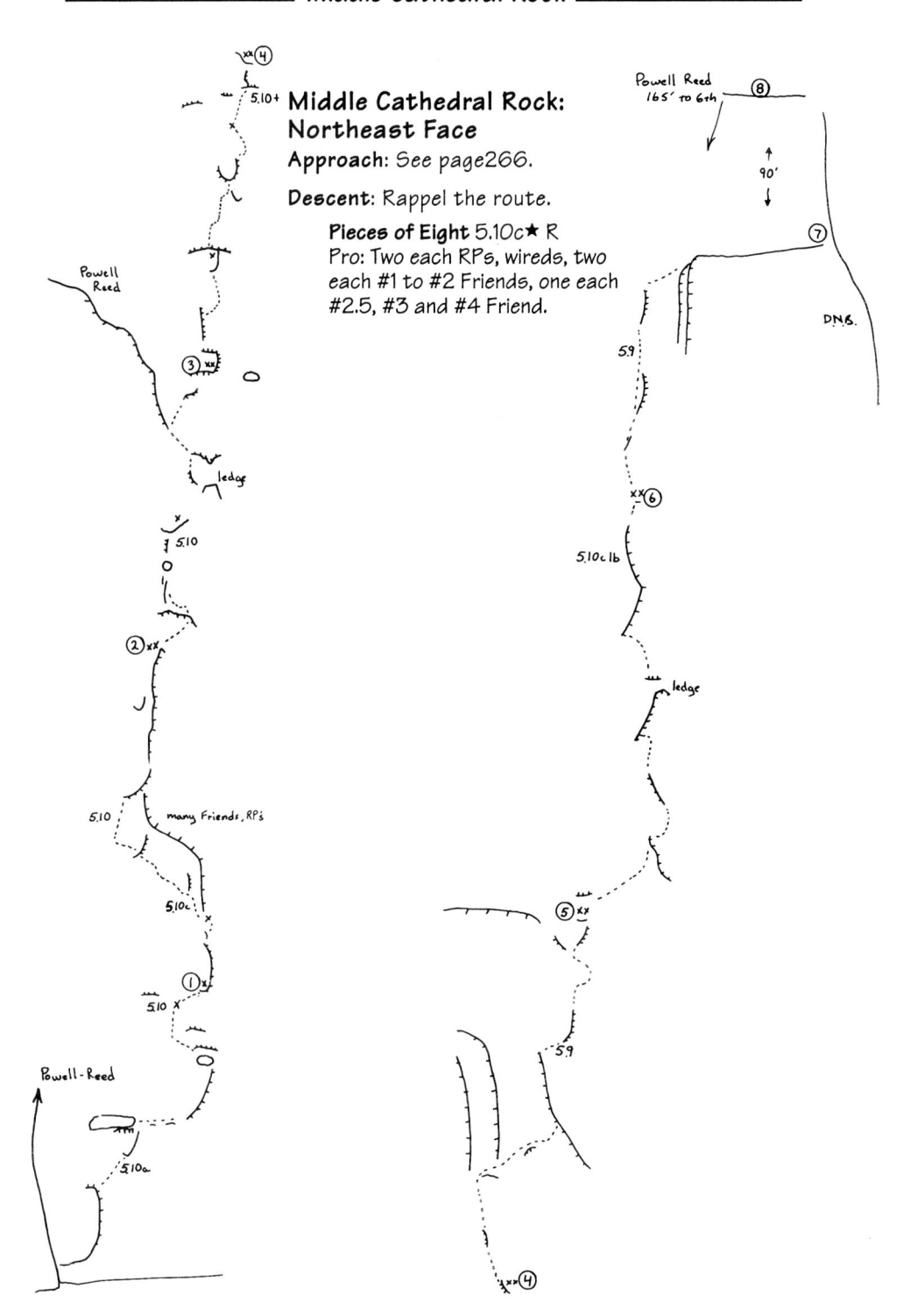

Middle Cathedral Rock: Northeast Face

Approach: See page 266.

Descent: Rappel the route.

Pieces of Eight 5.10c ★ R
Pro: Two each RPs, wireds, two each #1 to #2 Friends, one each #2.5, #3 and #4 Friend.

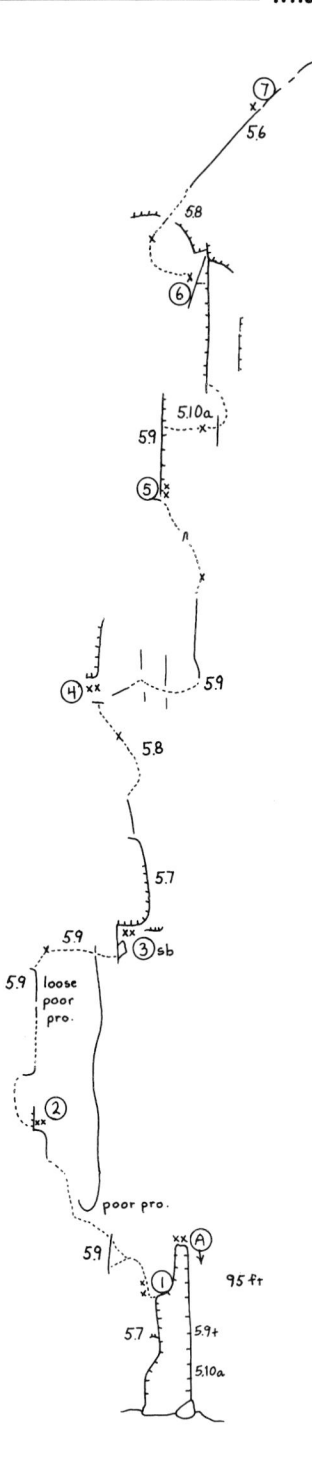

Middle Cathedral Rock: Northeast Face

Approach: See page 266.

Descent: Rappel the route.

Paradise Lost 5.10a ★ R Pro: Small.
A. **Pee Pee Pillar** 5.10a ★★ Pro: To 2".

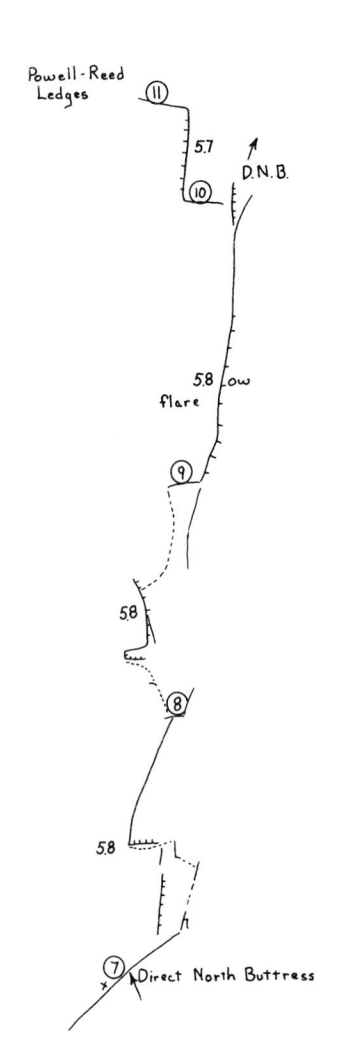

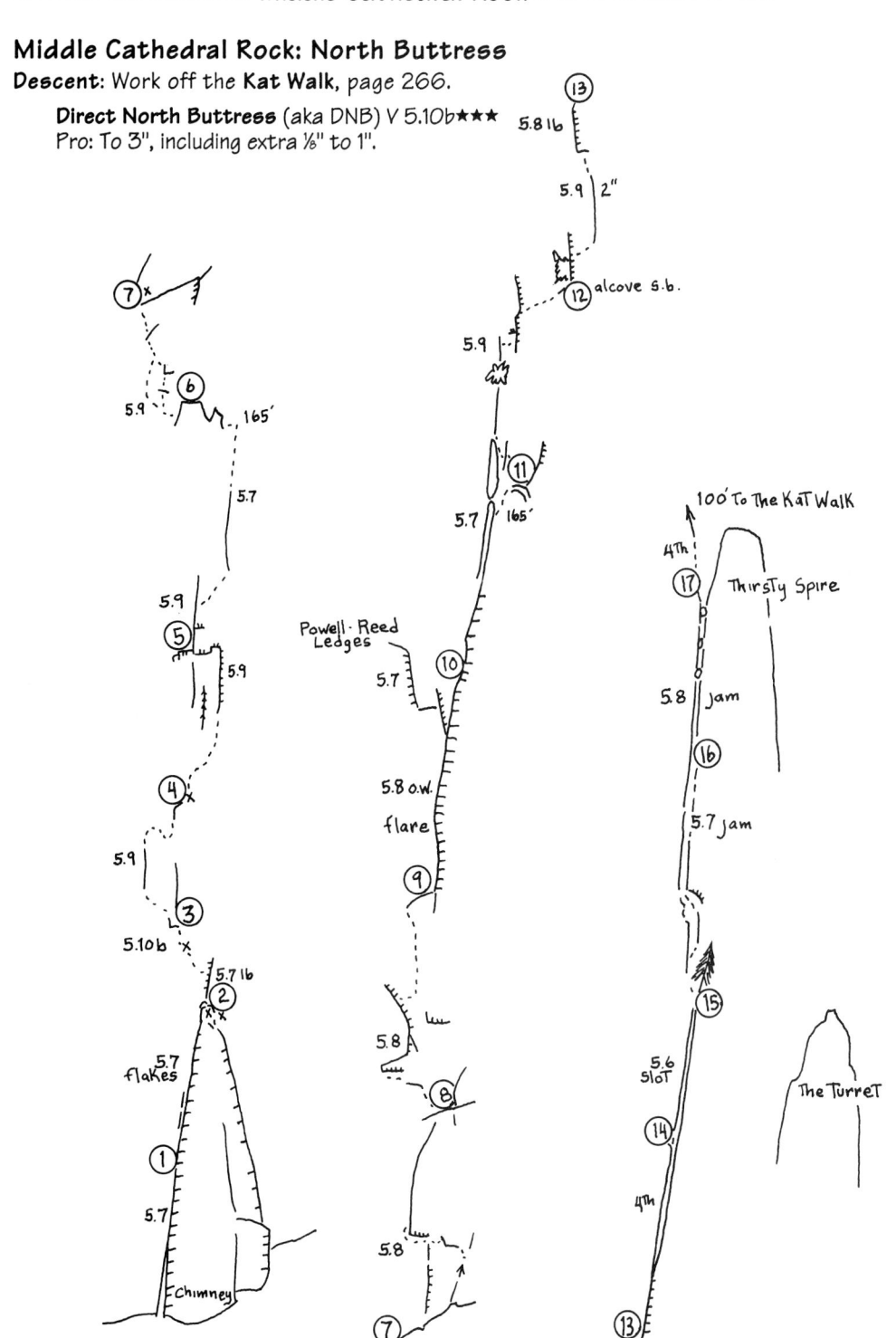

Middle Cathedral Rock: North Buttress

Descent: Work off the **Kat Walk**, page 266.

Direct North Buttress (aka DNB) V 5.10b ★★★
Pro: To 3", including extra ⅛" to 1".

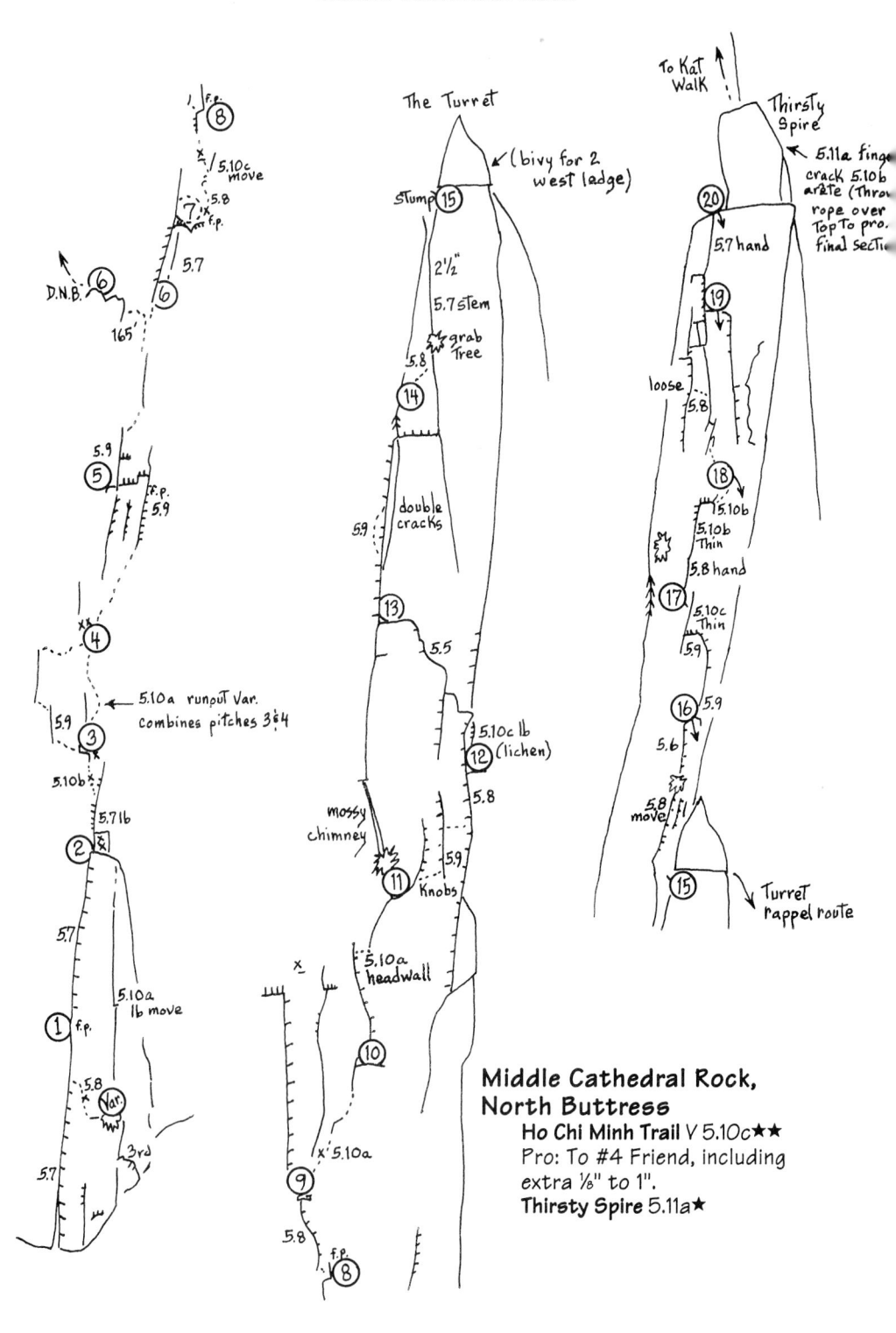

Middle Cathderal Rock

Middle Cathedral Rock, North Buttress
Ho Chi Minh Trail V 5.10c ★★
Pro: To #4 Friend, including extra ⅛" to 1".
Thirsty Spire 5.11a ★

CATHEDRAL ROCKS

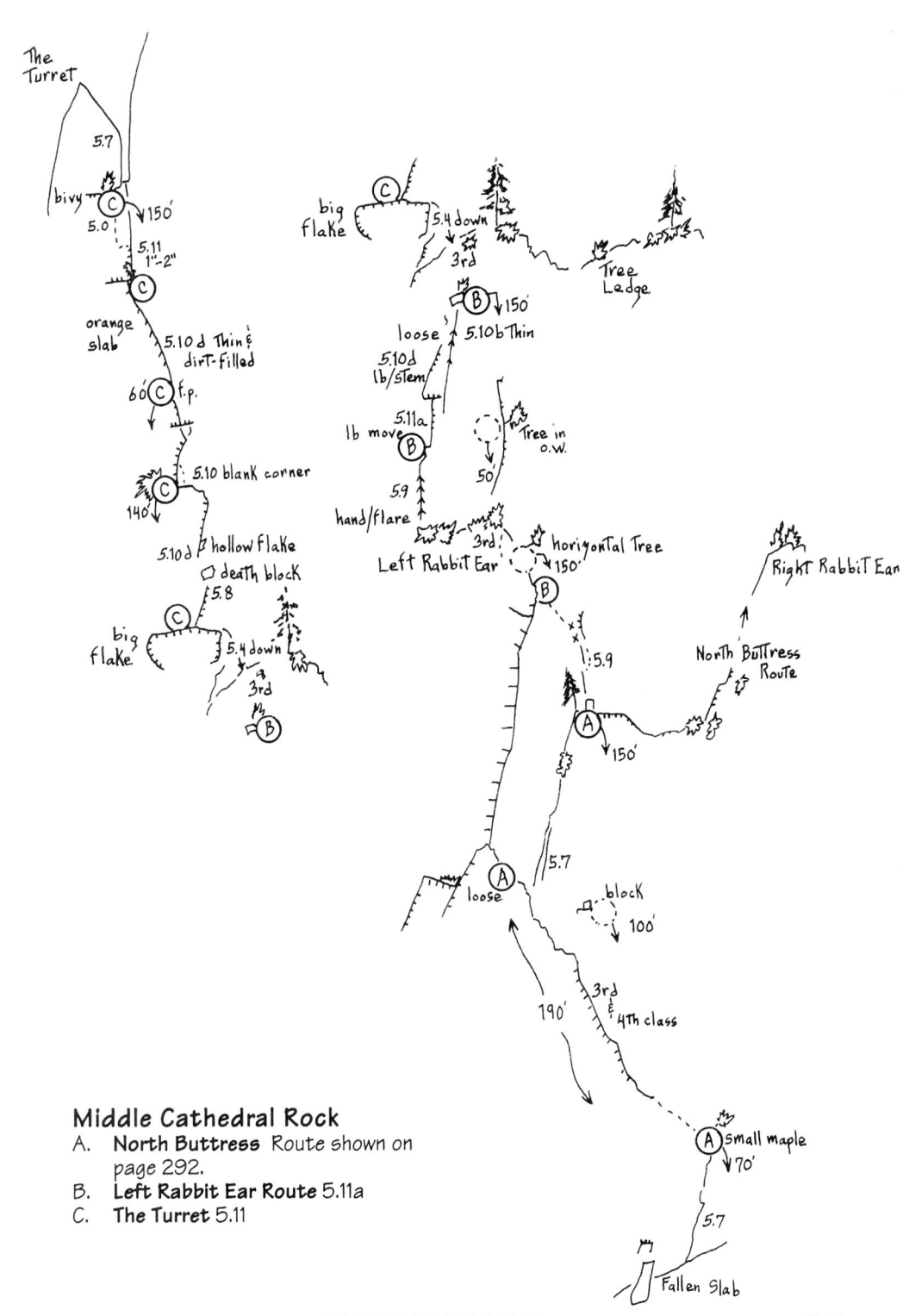

Middle Cathedral Rock

Middle Cathedral Rock
A. **North Buttress** Route shown on page 292.
B. **Left Rabbit Ear Route** 5.11a
C. **The Turret** 5.11

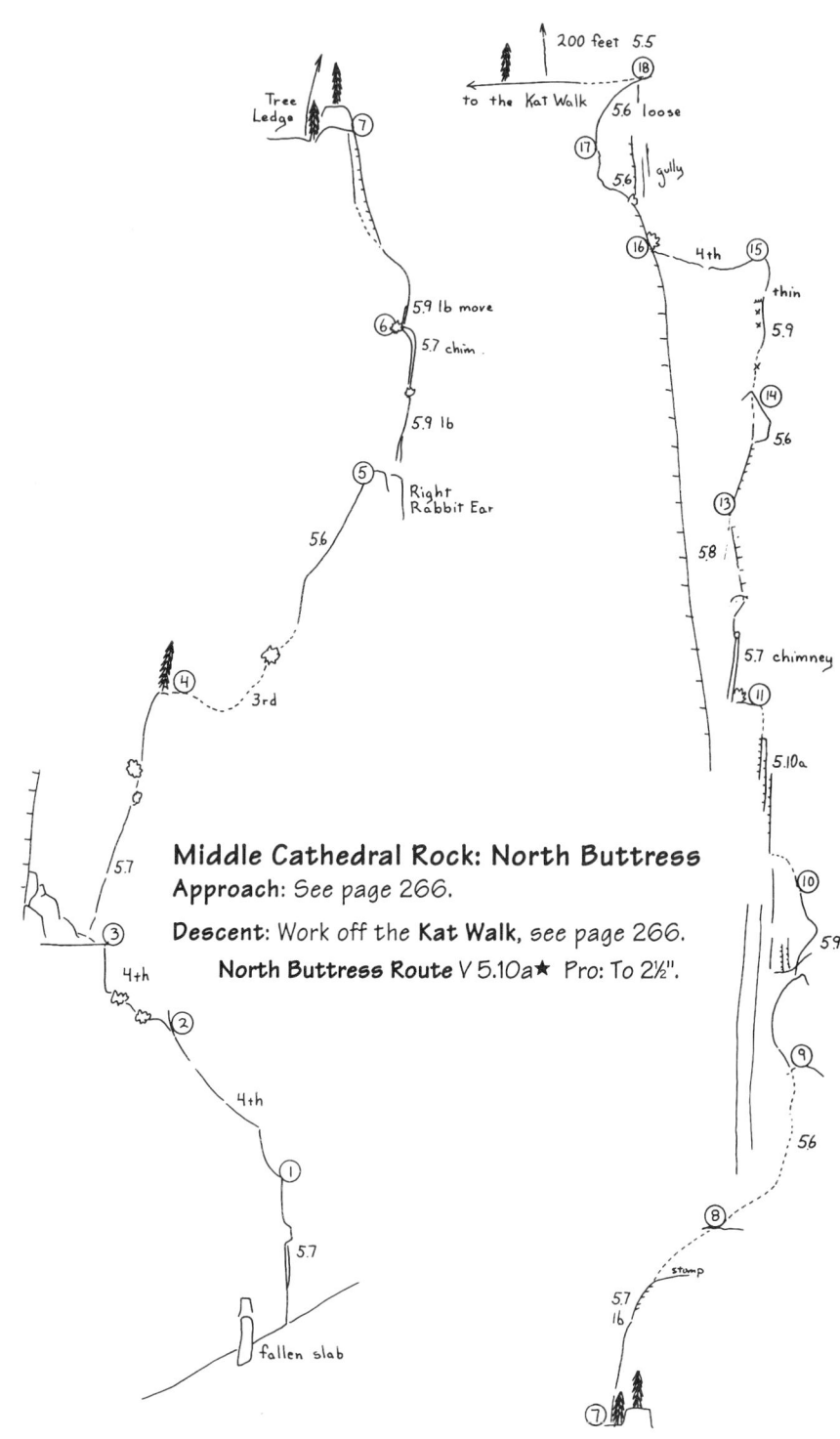

Middle Cathedral Rock

Middle Cathedral Rock: North Buttress
Approach: See page 266.
Descent: Work off the **Kat Walk**, see page 266.
North Buttress Route V 5.10a ★ Pro: To 2½".

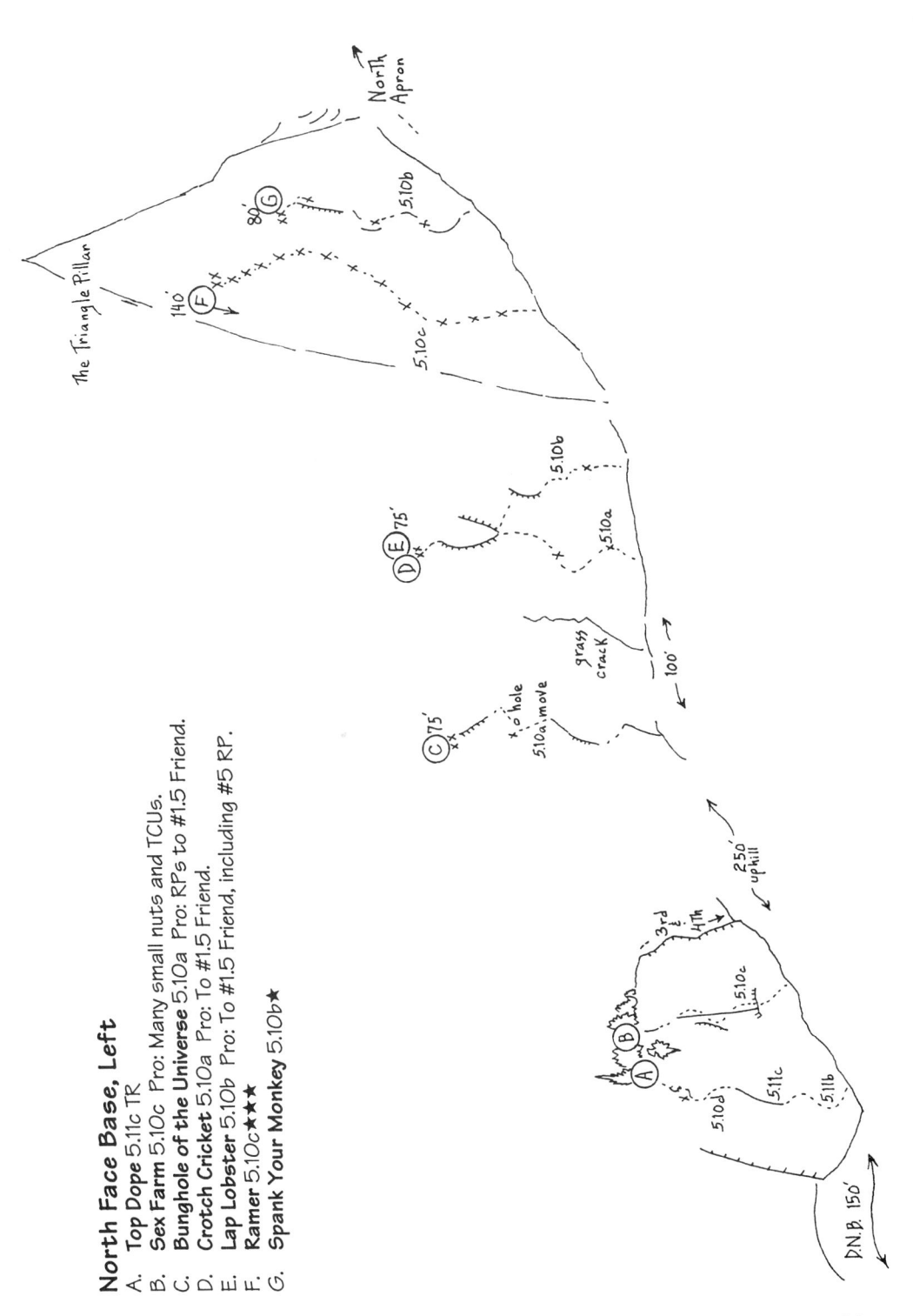

Middle Cathedral Rock

North Face Base, Left
A. Top Dope 5.11c TR
B. Sex Farm 5.10c Pro: Many small nuts and TCUs.
C. Bunghole of the Universe 5.10a Pro: RPs to #1.5 Friend.
D. Crotch Cricket 5.10a Pro: To #1.5 Friend.
E. Lap Lobster 5.10b Pro: To #1.5 Friend, including #5 RP.
F. Ramer 5.10c ★★
G. Spank Your Monkey 5.10b ★

CATHEDRAL ROCKS — 293

Middle Cathedral Rock

North Face Apron

Approach: Walk up along the wall past the North Buttress or, more directly, from below The Gunsight, the notch between Middle and Lower Cathedral Rocks.

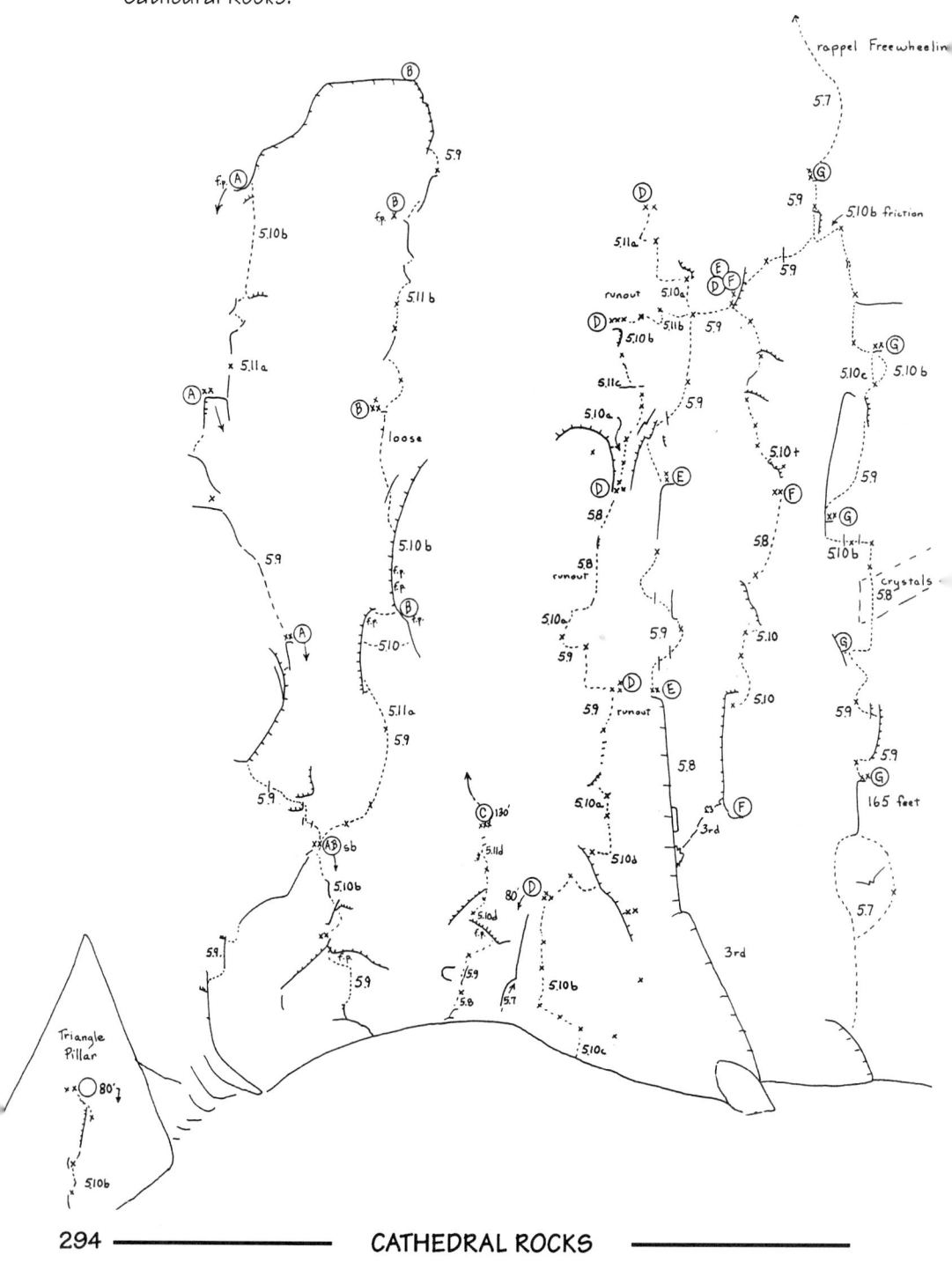

Middle Cathedral Rock

North Face Apron

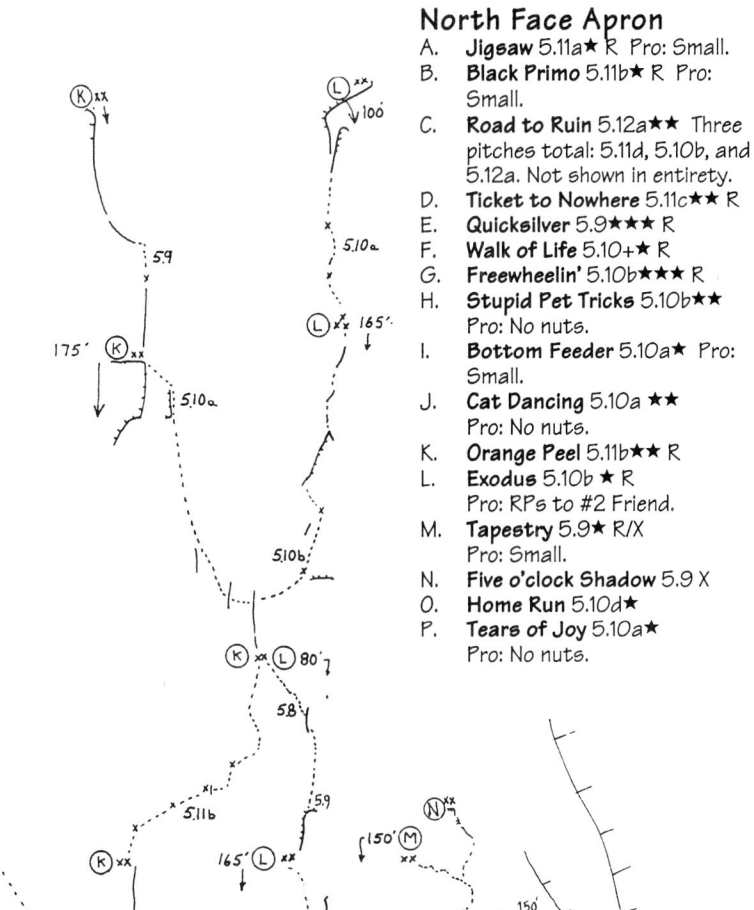

A. **Jigsaw** 5.11a★ R Pro: Small.
B. **Black Primo** 5.11b★ R Pro: Small.
C. **Road to Ruin** 5.12a★★ Three pitches total: 5.11d, 5.10b, and 5.12a. Not shown in entirety.
D. **Ticket to Nowhere** 5.11c★★ R
E. **Quicksilver** 5.9★★★ R
F. **Walk of Life** 5.10+★ R
G. **Freewheelin'** 5.10b★★★ R
H. **Stupid Pet Tricks** 5.10b★★ Pro: No nuts.
I. **Bottom Feeder** 5.10a★ Pro: Small.
J. **Cat Dancing** 5.10a ★★ Pro: No nuts.
K. **Orange Peel** 5.11b★★ R
L. **Exodus** 5.10b ★ R Pro: RPs to #2 Friend.
M. **Tapestry** 5.9★ R/X Pro: Small.
N. **Five o'clock Shadow** 5.9 X
O. **Home Run** 5.10d★
P. **Tears of Joy** 5.10a★ Pro: No nuts.

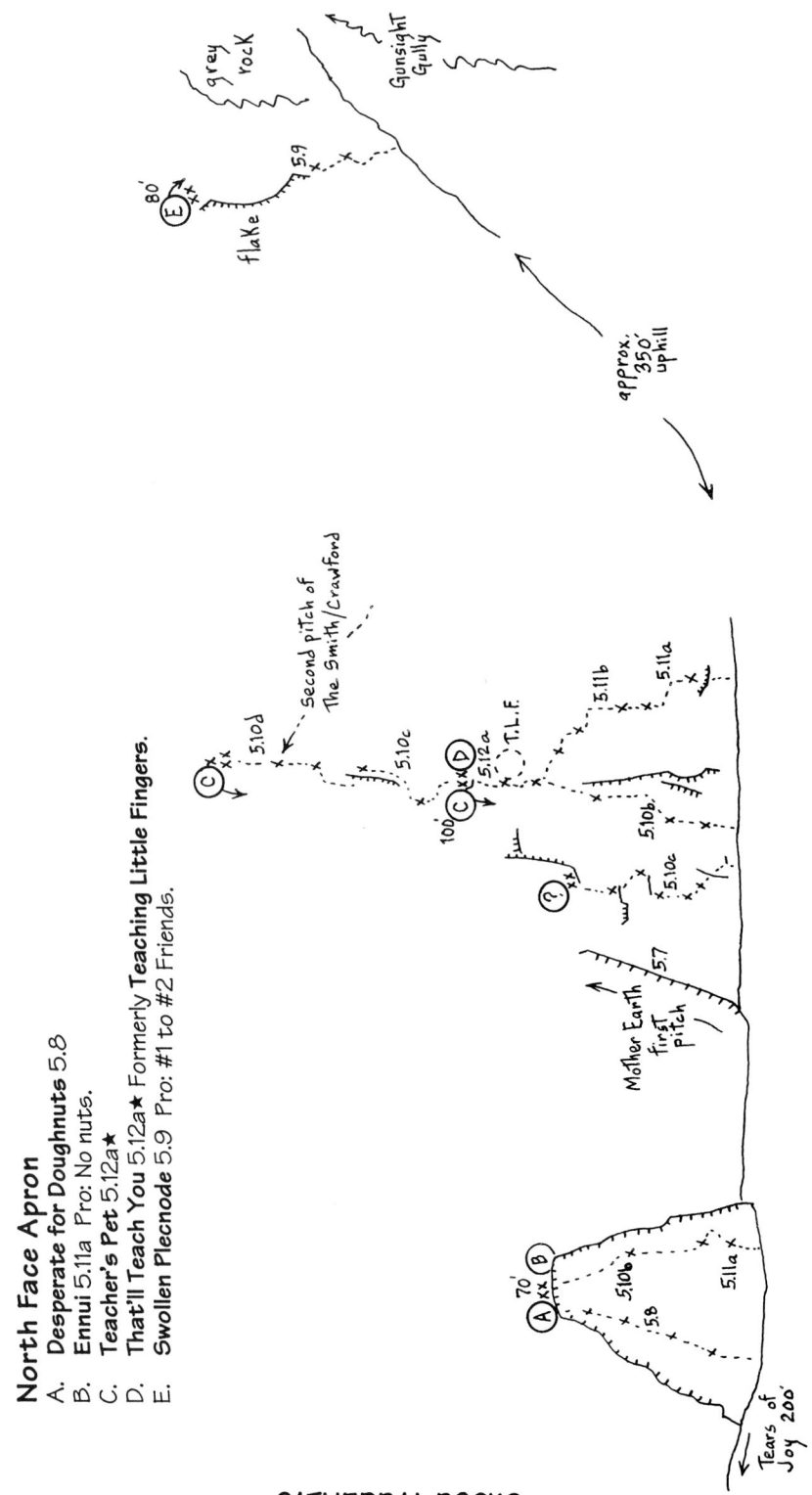

North Face Apron

A. **Desperate for Doughnuts** 5.8
B. **Ennui** 5.11a Pro: No nuts.
C. **Teacher's Pet** 5.12a ★
D. **That'll Teach You** 5.12a ★ Formerly Teaching Little Fingers.
E. **Swollen Plecnode** 5.9 Pro: #1 to #2 Friends.

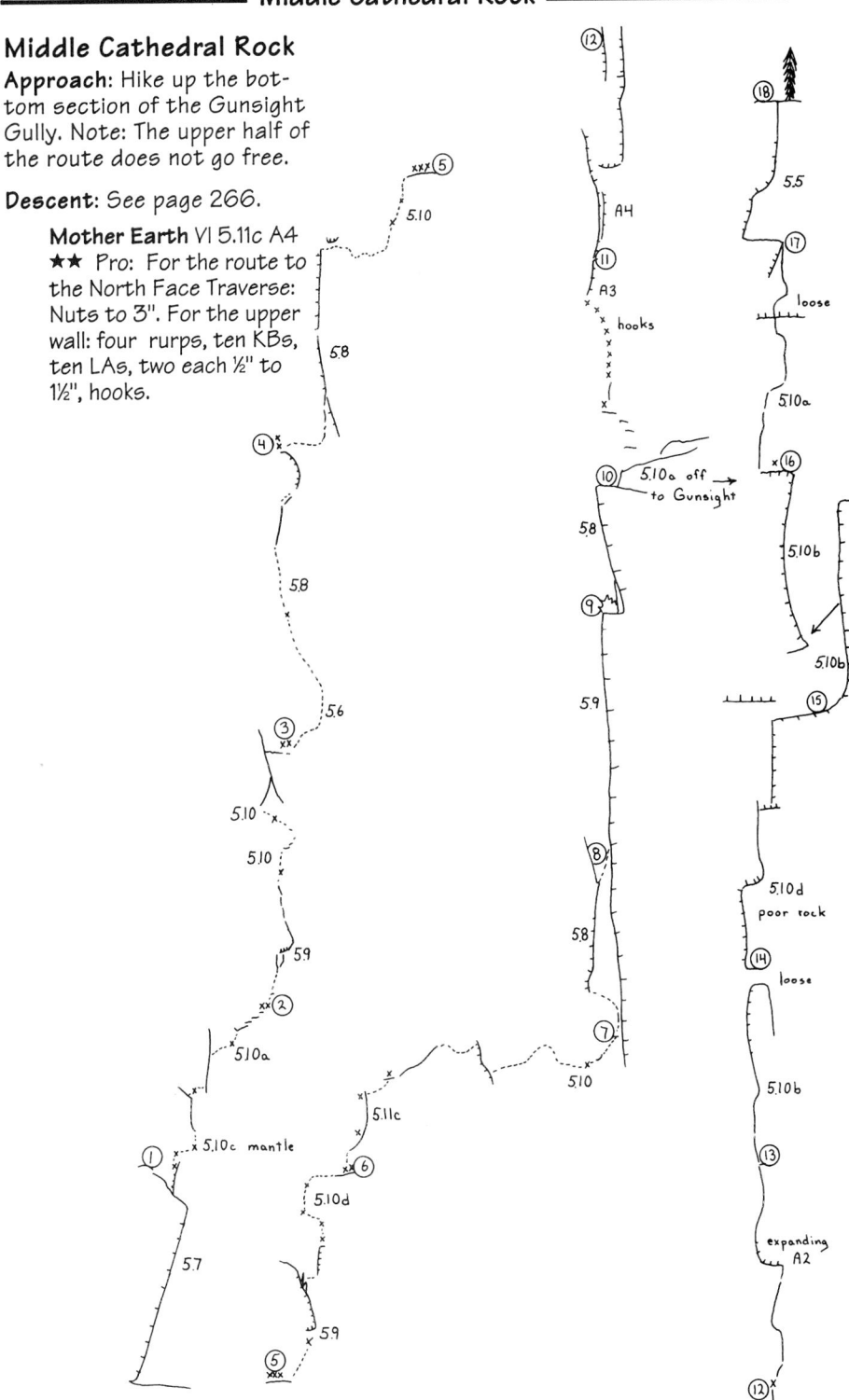

Middle Cathedral Rock

Approach: Hike up the bottom section of the Gunsight Gully. Note: The upper half of the route does not go free.

Descent: See page 266.

Mother Earth VI 5.11c A4 ★★ Pro: For the route to the North Face Traverse: Nuts to 3". For the upper wall: four rurps, ten KBs, ten LAs, two each ½" to 1½", hooks.

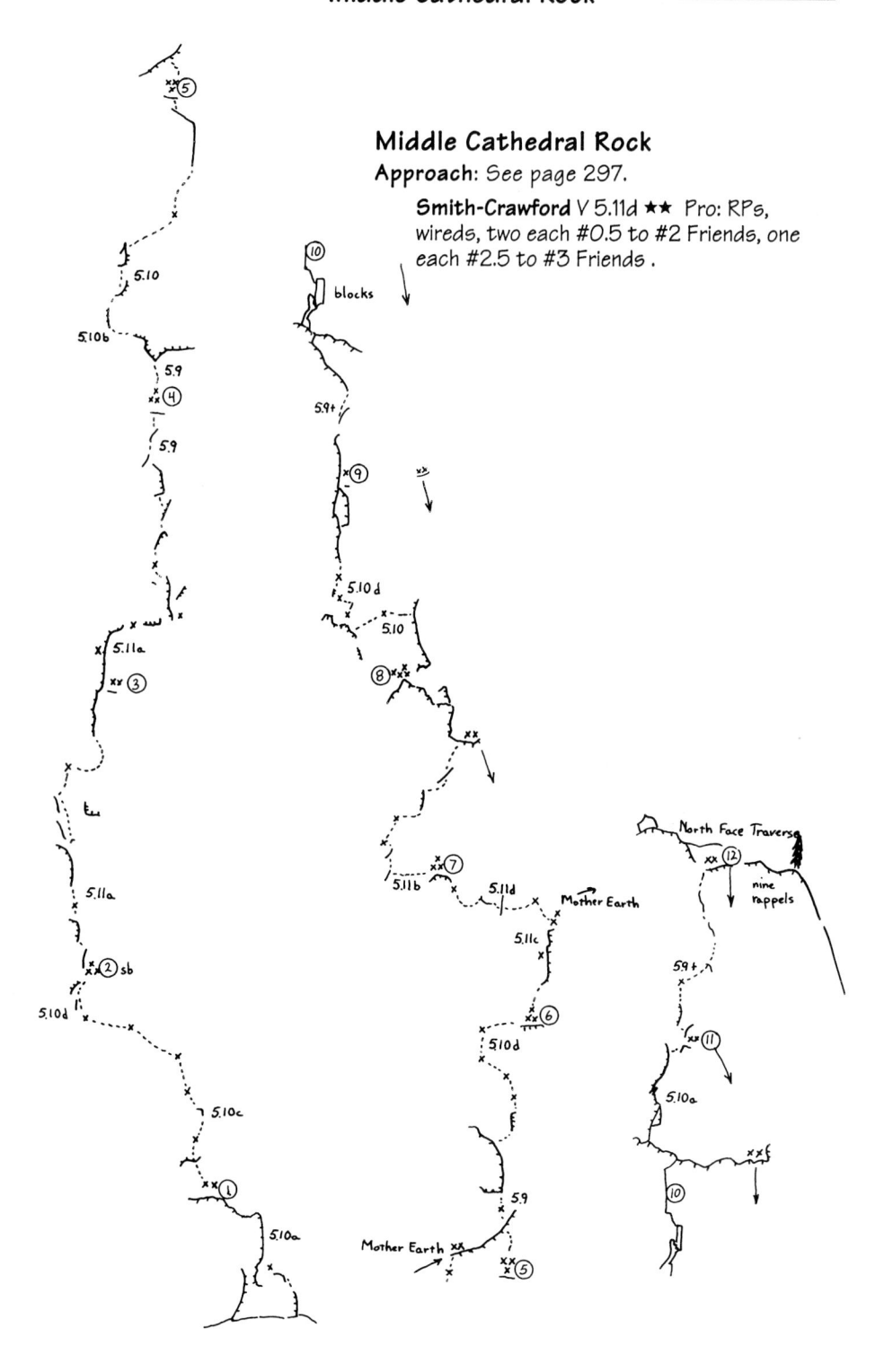

Middle Cathedral Rock

Approach: See page 297.

Smith-Crawford V 5.11d ★★ Pro: RPs, wireds, two each #0.5 to #2 Friends, one each #2.5 to #3 Friends.

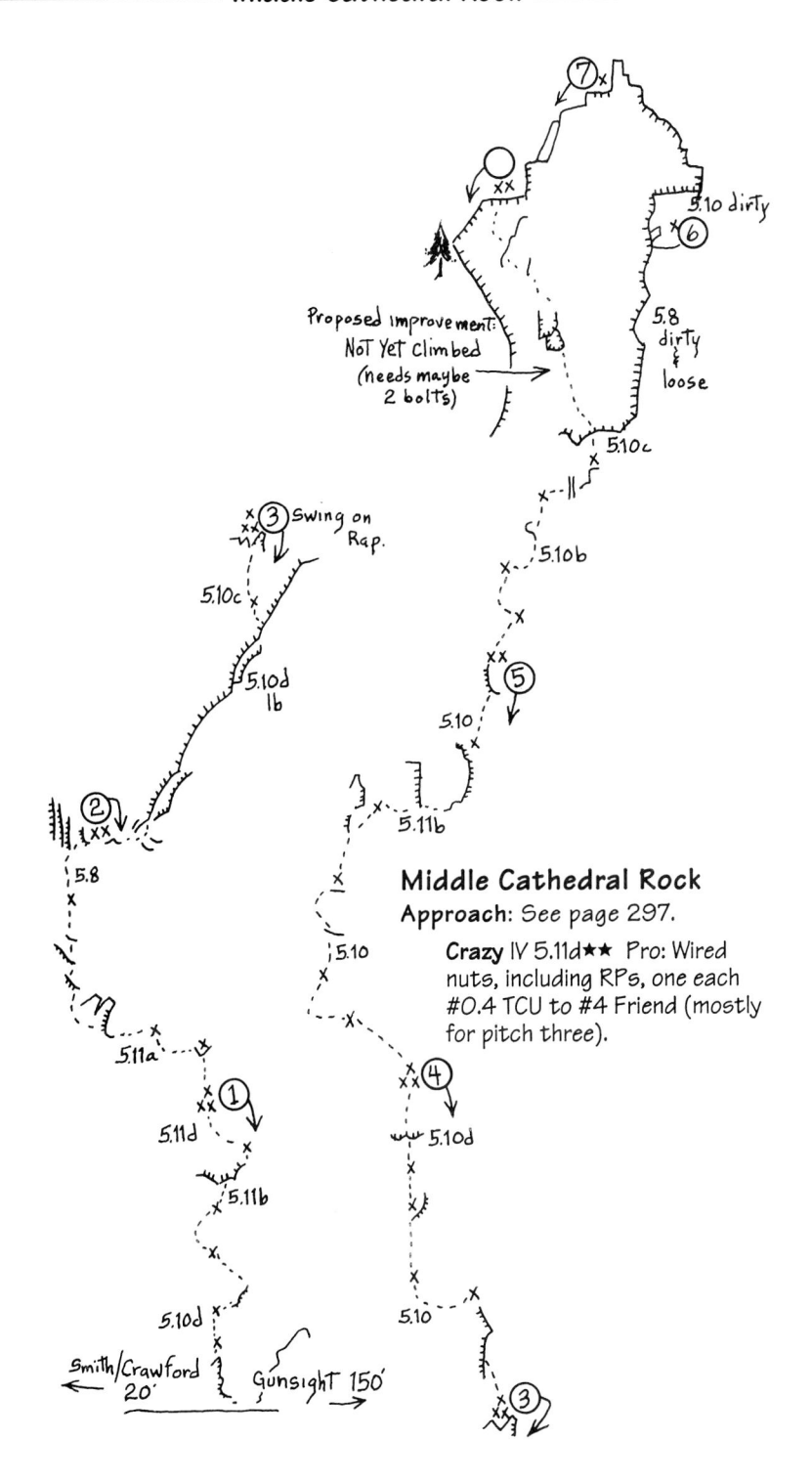

Middle Cathedral Rock

(Topo annotations:)

- ⑦ x
- xx (circle)
- 5.10 dirty
- x ⑥
- 5.8 dirty & loose
- Proposed improvement: Not yet climbed (needs maybe 2 bolts)
- 5.10c
- 5.10b
- xx ⑤
- 5.10
- x ③ Swing on Rap.
- 5.10c
- 5.10d 1b
- ② xx
- 5.8
- 5.11b
- 5.10
- 5.11a
- xx ④
- 5.10d
- xx ①
- 5.11d
- 5.11b
- 5.10d
- 5.10
- Smith/Crawford 20' ←
- Gunsight 150' →
- ③

Middle Cathedral Rock

Approach: See page 297.

Crazy IV 5.11d★★ Pro: Wired nuts, including RPs, one each #0.4 TCU to #4 Friend (mostly for pitch three).

Middle Cathderal Rock

three 4th class pitches to right, bearing upward

poor anchors

piton

5.7

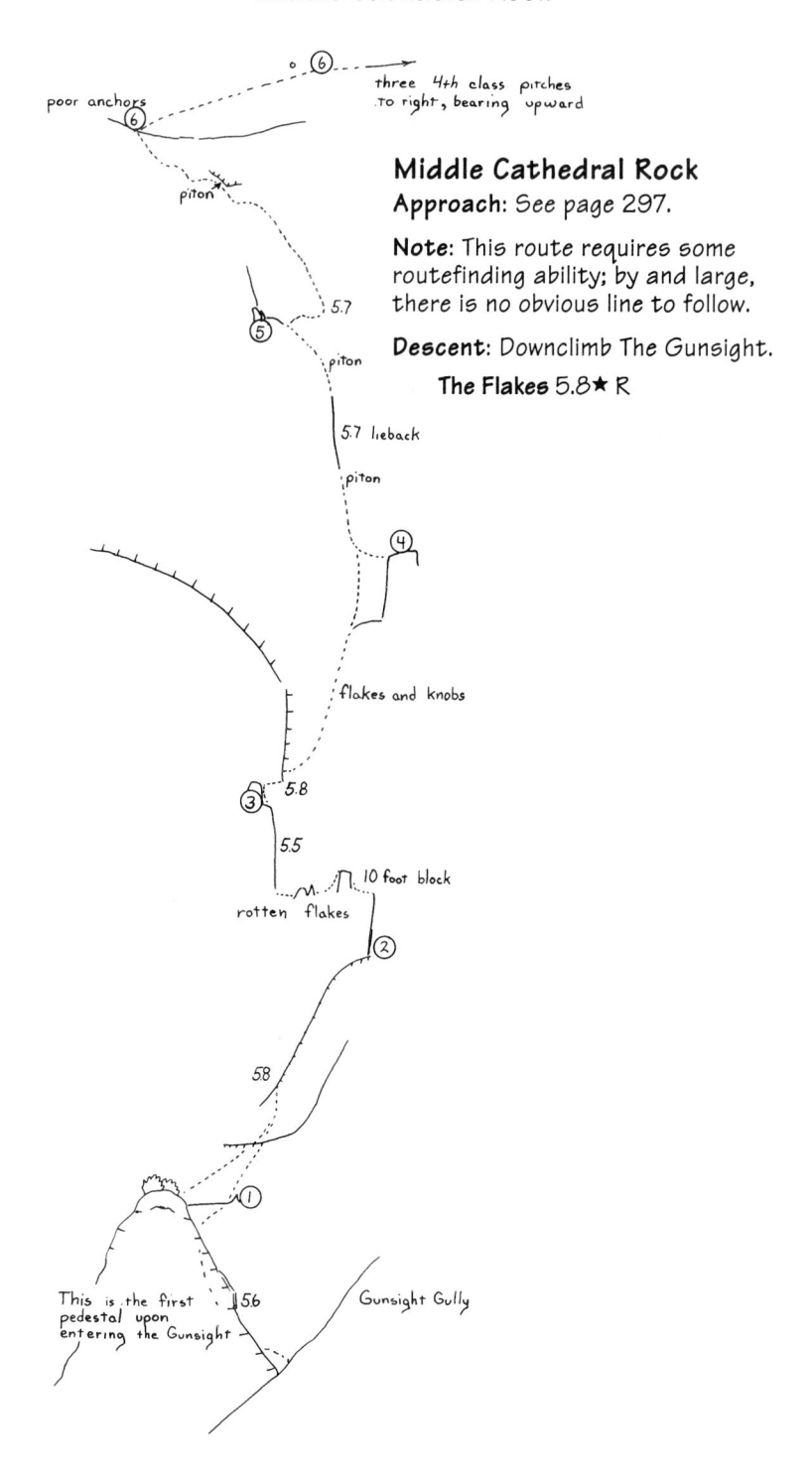

piton

Middle Cathedral Rock
Approach: See page 297.

Note: This route requires some routefinding ability; by and large, there is no obvious line to follow.

Descent: Downclimb The Gunsight.

The Flakes 5.8 ★ R

5.7 lieback

piton

flakes and knobs

5.8

5.5

10 foot block

rotten flakes

5.8

This is the first pedestal upon entering the Gunsight

5.6

Gunsight Gully

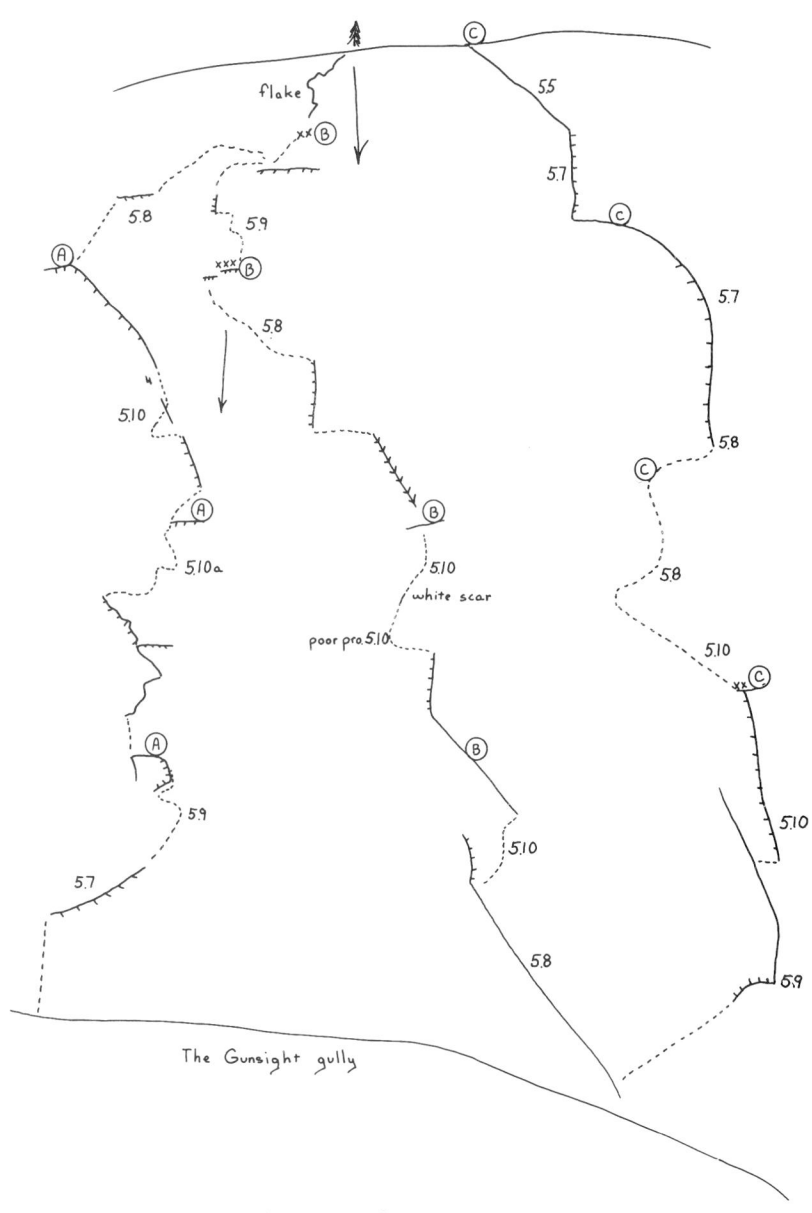

Lower Cathedral Rock, East Face

Approach: Hike up the bottom section of The Gunsight.

- A. **Spooky Tooth** 5.10a★ X Pro: Nuts and pitons ¾" to 1".
- B. **Shake and Bake** 5.10★ X Pro: Nuts and pitons, four KBs, four LAs, two each ½" and ⅝".
- C. **Starfire** 5.10★ X

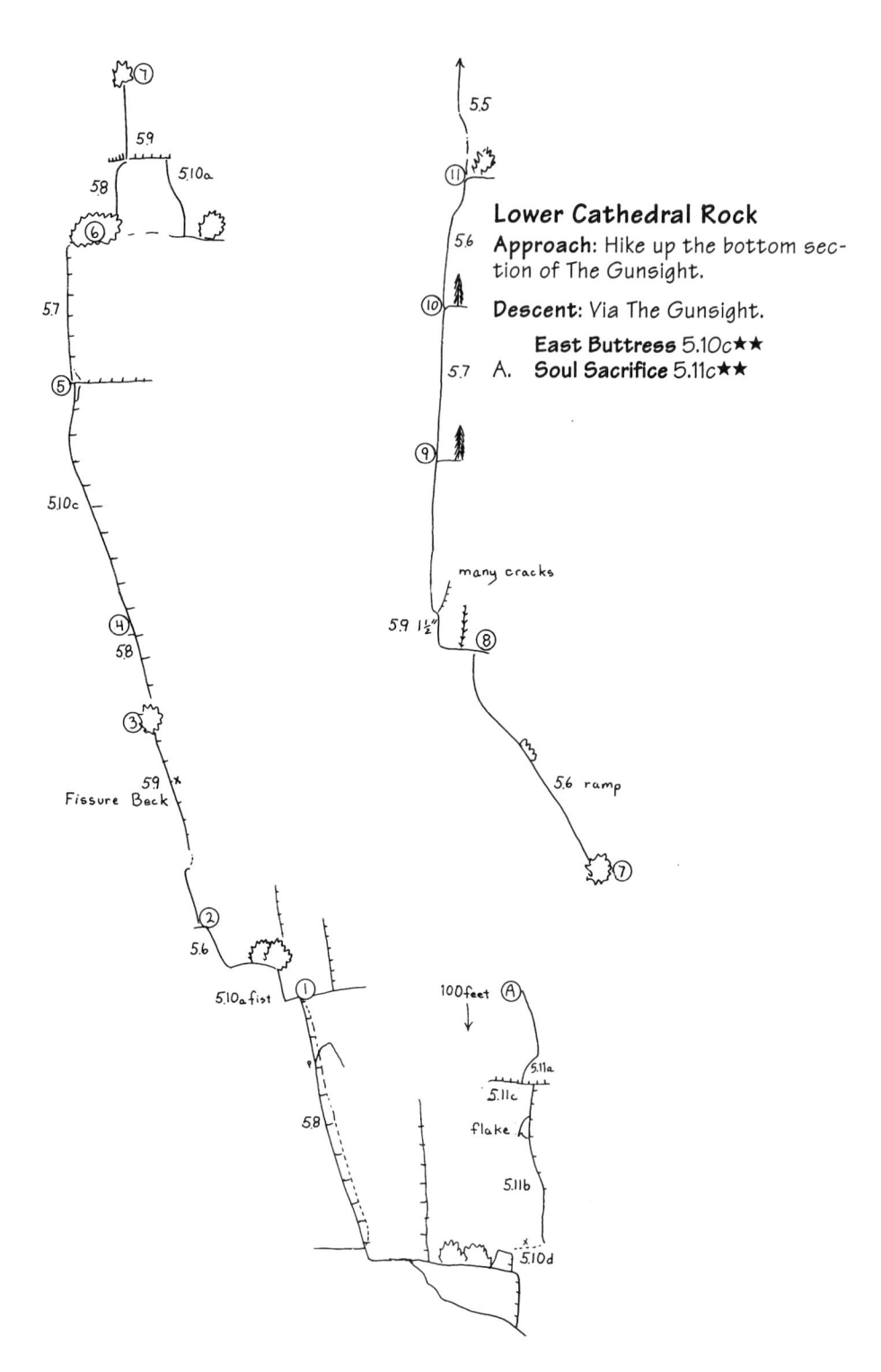

Lower Cathedral Rock

Approach: Hike up the bottom section of The Gunsight.

Descent: Via The Gunsight.

- East Buttress 5.10c ★★
- A. Soul Sacrifice 5.11c ★★

Lower Cathedral Rock

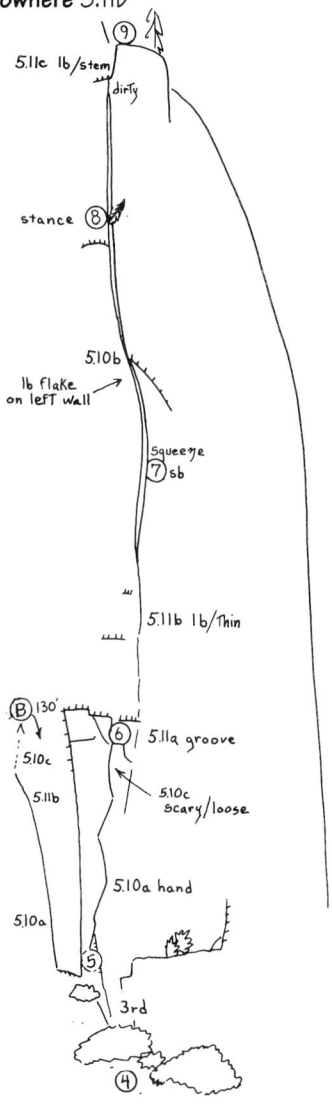

Lower Cathedral Rock: North Buttress

Approach: Walk up and east from the toe of the north buttress to the first major crack system. See page 304.

Descent: Scramble straight back 150 feet to a prominent tree. From here rappel 165 feet to 3rd class terrain near the beginning of **Overhang Bypass**. Descend the wooded buttress (3rd class) used to approach that route.

    Beggar's Buttress 5.11c ★★ Pro: To 3½", including ½" to 2".
A. **Tidbit** 5.11a★ Pro: Including TCUs and one #4 Friend.
B. **Going Nowhere** 5.11b

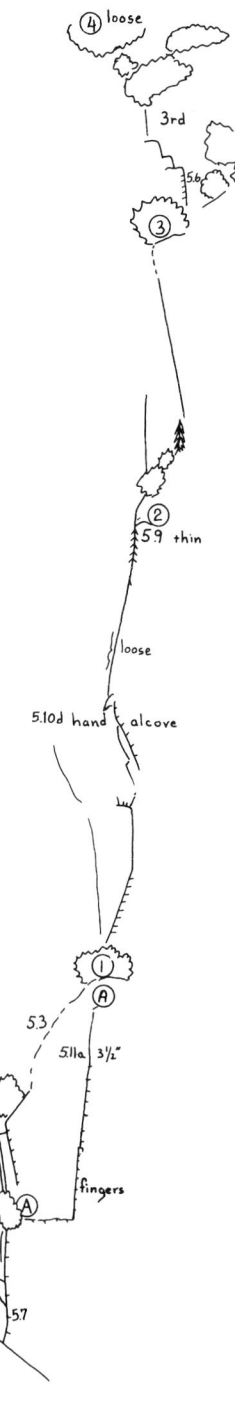

CATHEDRAL ROCKS — 303

Lower Cathedral Rock

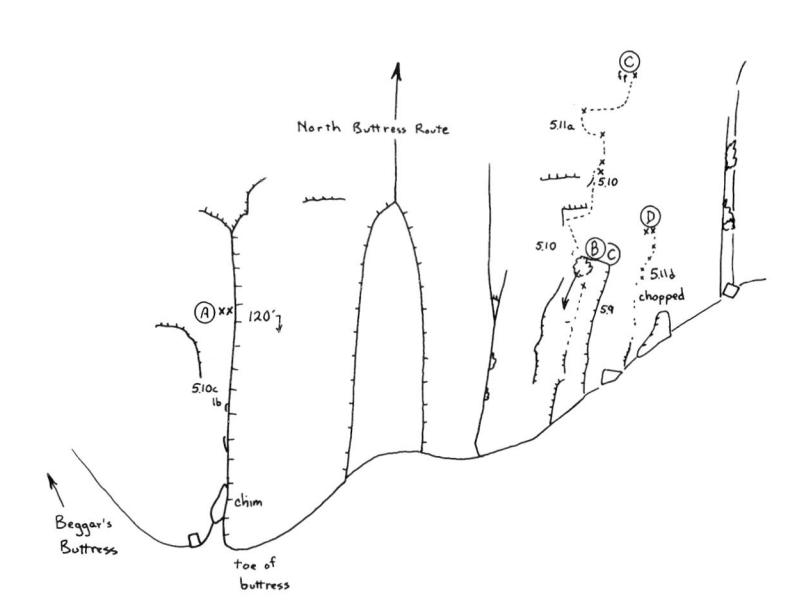

Lower Cathedral Rock, North Buttress

Approach: After driving east into Yosemite Valley, park at the long turnout below Bridalveil Falls, walk toward the rocks and gain the horse trail. Hike to the east and head up the hill from below the toe of the buttress.

- A. **Sub-Mission** 5.10c★ Pro: Small to 3½".
- B. **Compass Rose** 5.10-
- C. **North by Northwest** 5.11a R
- D. **Brass Knuckles** 5.11d Chopped.

Lower Cathedral Rock

Approach: Park at the long turnout adjacent to a straightaway just past Bridalveil Falls. These climbs are below **Overhang Bypass**.

A. **Exfoliator** 5.11b Pro: To 4".
B. **Spectacle** 5.11d★★
C. **Gash** 5.10b★ Pro: To 3".
D. **NWR (Not Worth Repeating)** 5.10b Pro: To 4".

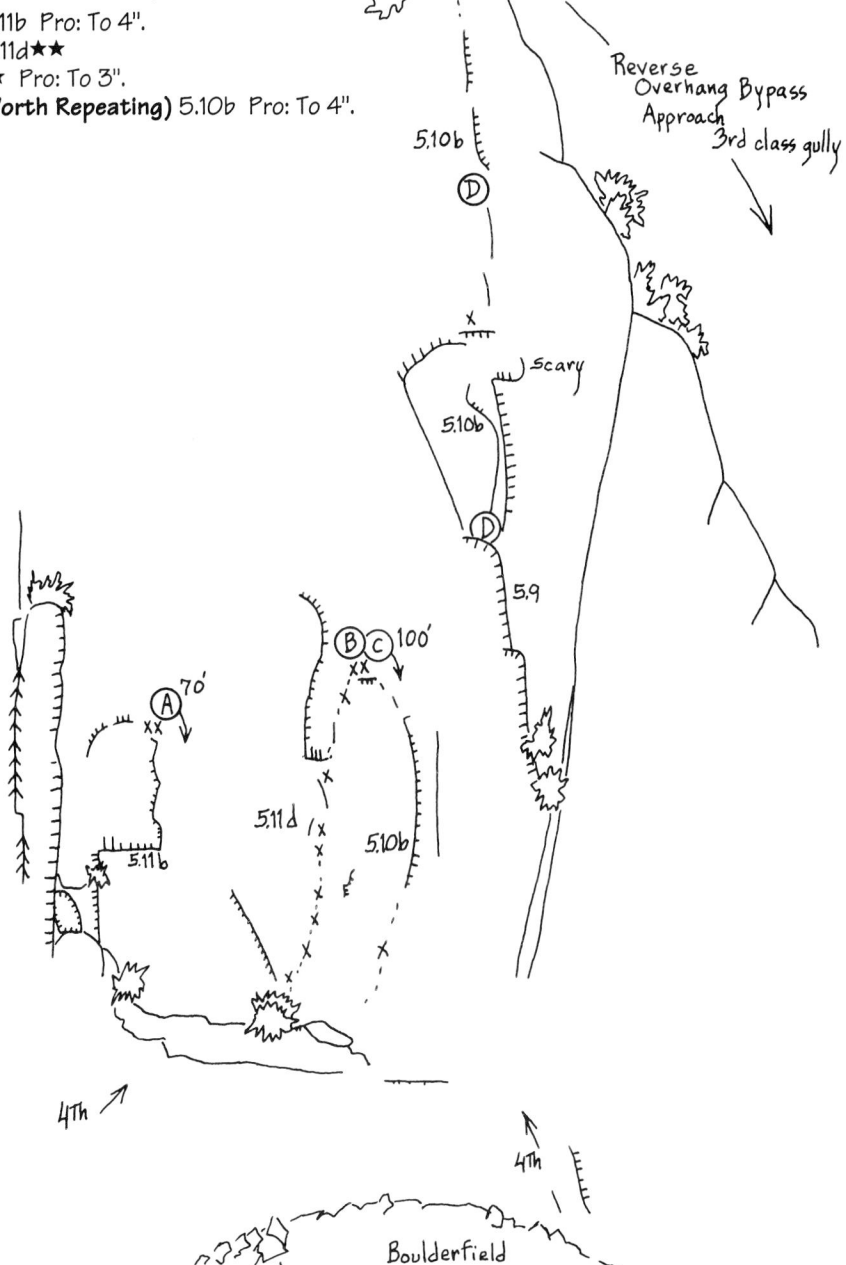

Lower Cathedral Rock

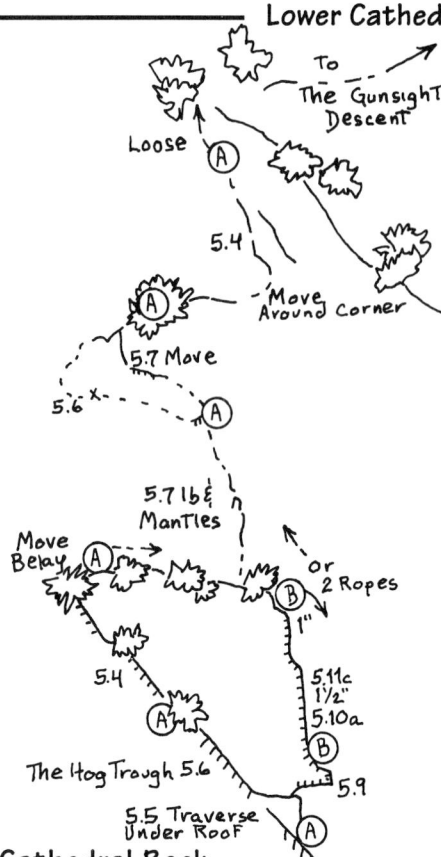

Lower Cathedral Rock, North Buttress Area

Approach: These routes are approached from the long parking turnout below and up-valley from Bridalveil Falls. Scramble up talus and 3rd class rock to the routes marked by the clean, gray corner that is **Overhang Overpass**.

Descent: These routes end on the west slopes of Lower Cathedral Rock. From here, contour along to meet The Gunsight. A short rappel or two may be necessary in this section.

A. **Overhang Bypass** 5.7 ★★ Pro: To 2½". The route is taxed by a fairly involved approach and descent. The rock is compact and cleanly fractured, with the "hog trough" being particularly clean and exposed. However, some loose rock is also found on this route.

B. **Overhang Overpass** 5.11c ★★★ Pro: To 2½", including extra ½" to 1¾" pieces. A burdensome approach and descent are rewarded by this striking corner.

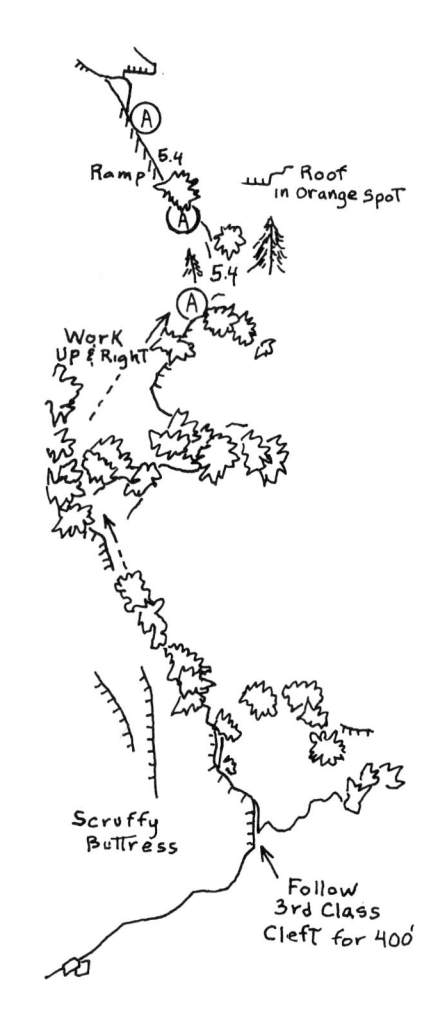

Lower Cathedral Rock

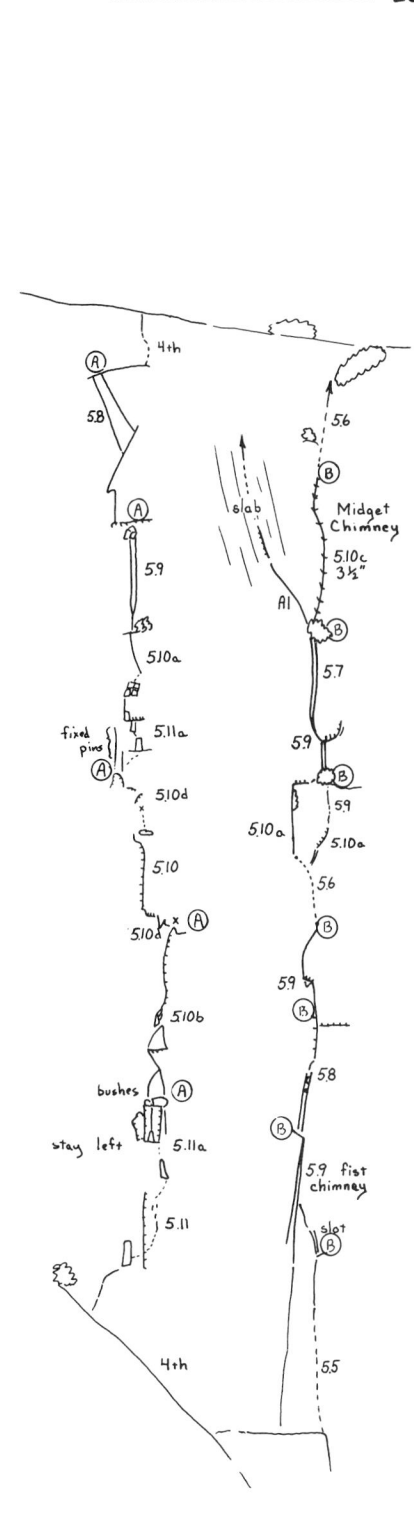

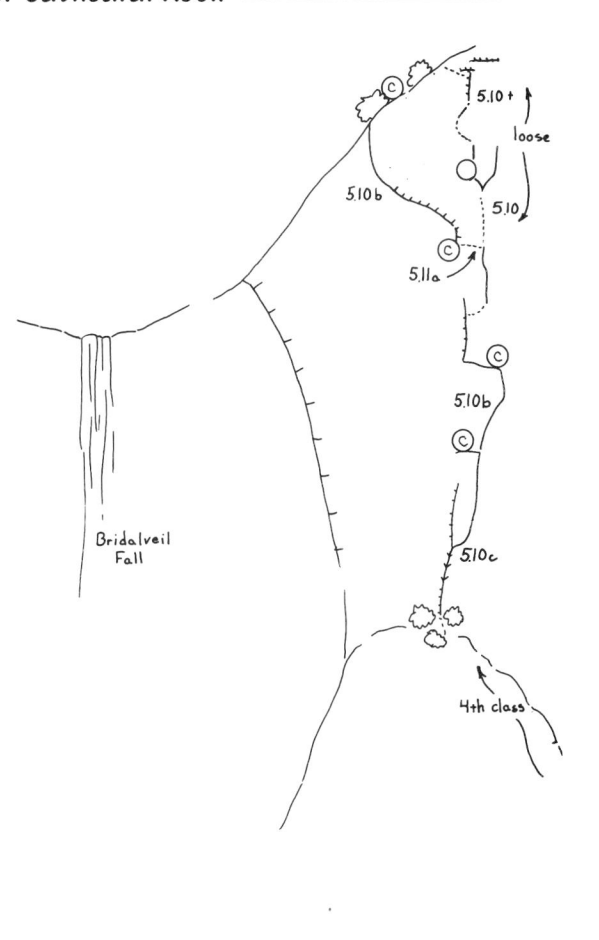

Lower Cathedral Rock, Bridalveil Falls Area

Approach: The footpath to the base of Bridalveil Falls forms a useful portion of the approach. These climbs are best done during times of low water.

Descent: Hike up to and then down The Gunsight. Rattlesnake Buttress necessitates a crossing of Bridalveil Creek, which is only possible during low water.

A. **Return to the Stone Age** 5.11a★ R Pro: Two each RPs, two each Friends to #2, one each #2.5 to #3 Friends.
B. **Bridalveil East** 5.10c★★ Pro: To 3½".
C. **Rattlesnake Buttress** 5.11a Pro: RPs to #4 Friend.

CATHEDRAL ROCKS

Lower Cathedral Rock

1. NORTH BUTTRESS AREA
2. Overhang Bypass 5.7
3. Return to the Stone Age 5.11a R
4. Bridalveil East 5.10c
5. Middle Cathedral Rock, Northwest Face 5.7
6. Middle Cathedral Rock, Northwest Buttress, 5.6

Leaning Tower

7. Rattlesnake Buttress 5.11a
8. The Yellow Corner 5.12a R
9. THE WATCHTOWER
10. THE CRACKER

Leaning Tower: Left

descend Gunsight
(low water only)
or rappel the route

3rd

⑥ 165'

5.9 loose flake

⑤ 70' ···x···5.12a
         ···x···

160' ④ xx
       5.8

blind bolt over → x
roof   5.11a

← 5.11b

xx ③ 165'

5.12a lb

5.10d o.w.
f.p.
5.11b
5.10b

165' plus (Var) ② xx

5.10b

5.11d

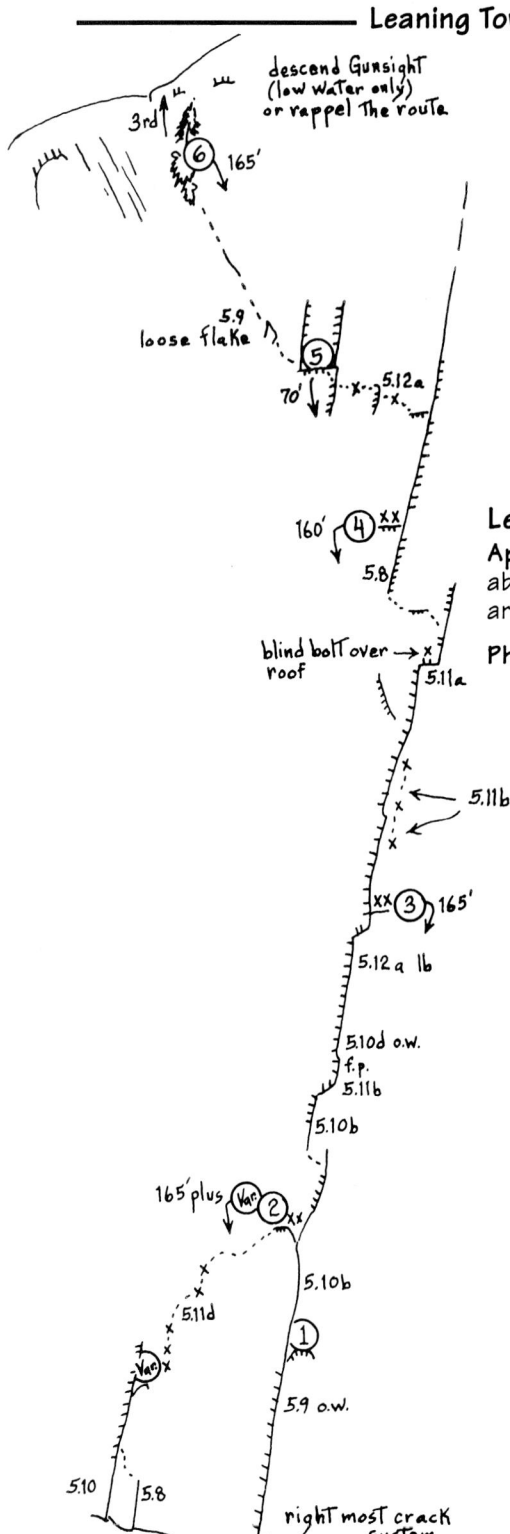

①

5.9 o.w.

(Var)

5.10 5.8

rightmost crack system

Leaning Tower, Yellow Corner

Approach: Hike up talus directly above the Bridalveil Falls parking area.

Photo on pge 309.

Yellow Corner (aka Turning Yeller) IV 5.12a★★ R Pro: One set wireds, two each ¾" to 2½" cams, including one to 3½".

310 — LEANING TOWER

Leaning Tower, Base

Approach: Hike up talus directly above the Bridalveil Falls parking area.

A. The Princess 5.9

The Watchtower
B. The Joker 5.10b R Pro: To 3".
C. The Thief 5.10d ★★ Pro: To 2½", including extra ½" to 2".
D. Megaforce 5.11a ★
E. Barefoot Servants 5.10c Pro: To 5".

The Amoeba
F. Left Side 5.8 Pro: To 2½".
G. Right Side 5.11c

The Cracker
H. Rycrisp 5.7 Pro: To 3½".
I. Beat the Clock 5.10c
J. The Triscuit 5.9 Pro: To 3½".
K. Drop-out 5.10a ★
L. The Chosen Few 5.9 Pro: Optional to 6".
M. Machine Head 5.11c Pro: Wireds, cams to 2", especially 1½"
N. Right Side 5.7

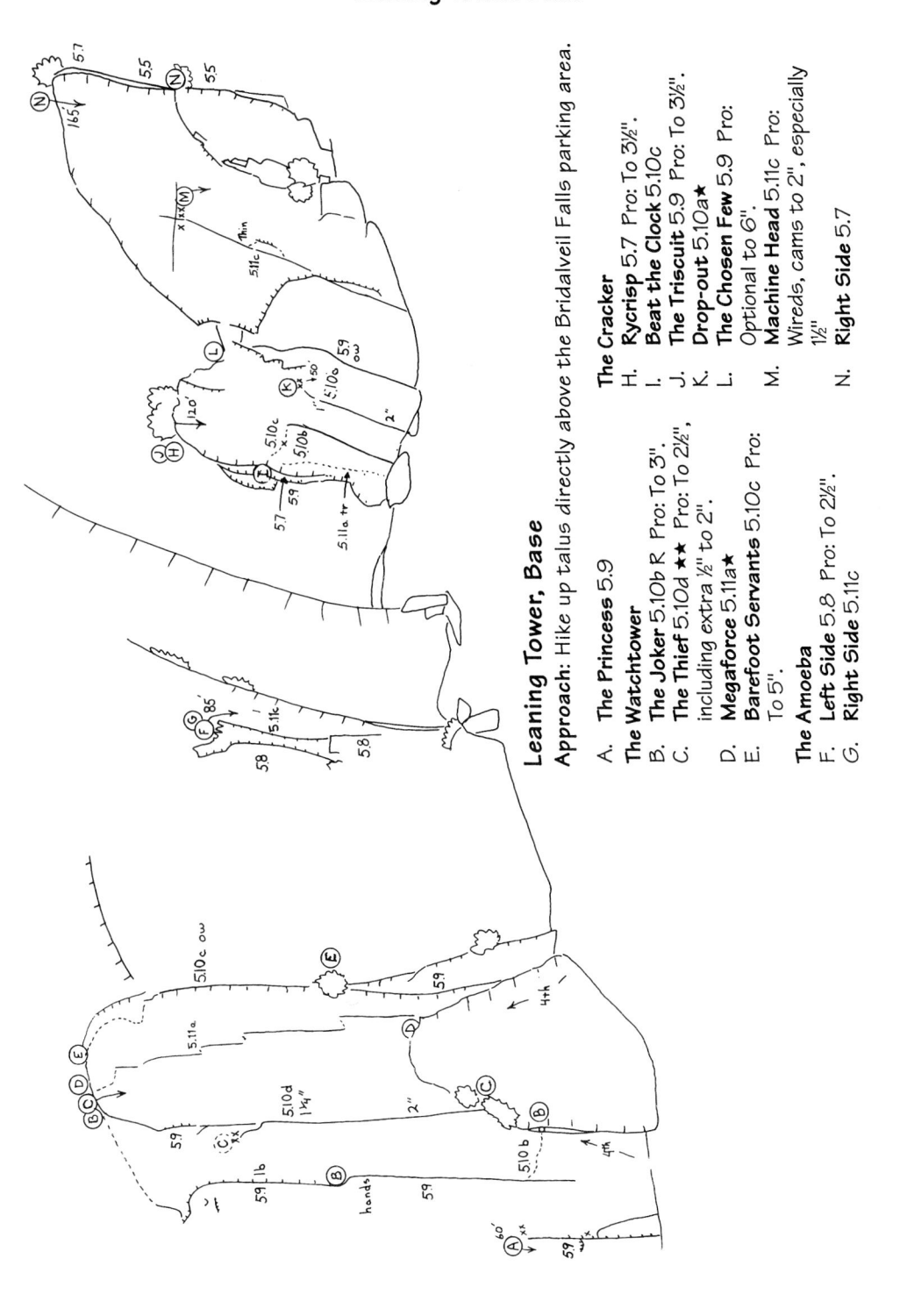

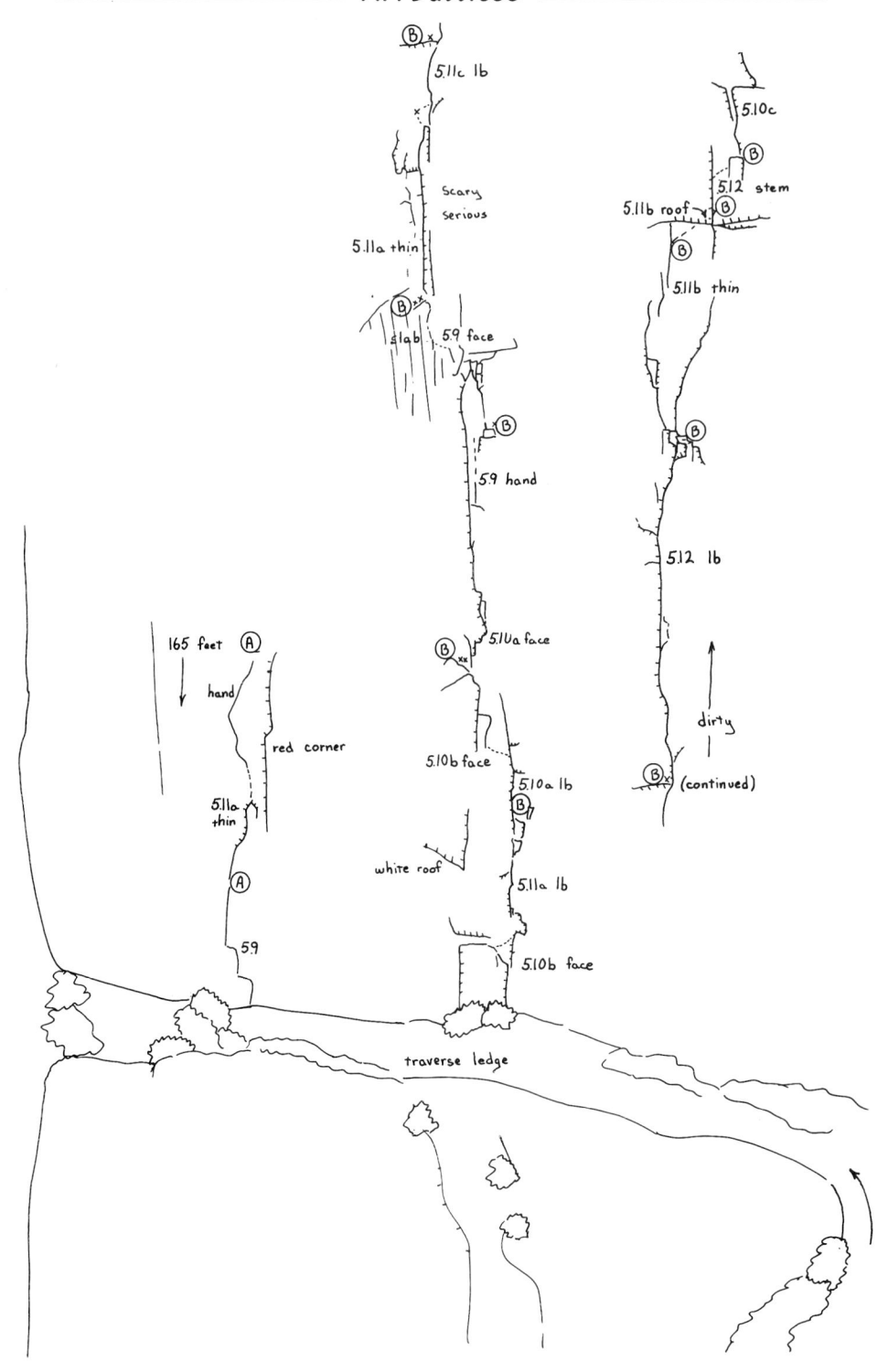

FiFi Buttress

FiFi Buttress

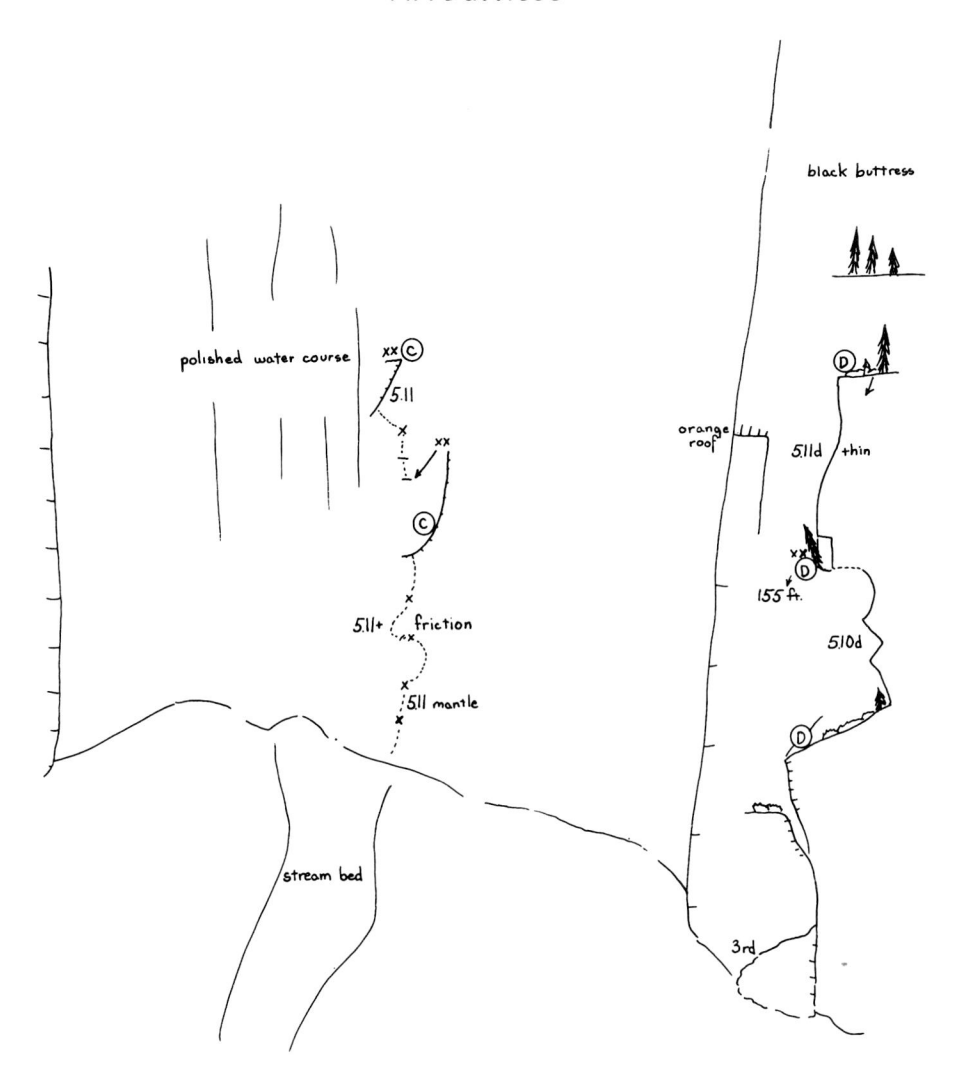

FiFi Buttress, West Face

Approach: This is the first buttress to the west of the Leaning Tower. From the Bridalveil parking lot walk southwest, avoiding the talus field, then follow a streambed that flows down immediately right of the buttress.

Descent: Scramble down to the west via a long diagonal bushwhack ledge.

A. **Sunset Strip** 5.11a
B. **Vortex** 5.12 Pro: Three to four each Friends to #2, two each #3, plus a #4 Friend and a thin rack.
C. **Colony of Slippermen** 5.11+ A1
D. **The Warbler** 5.11d★★

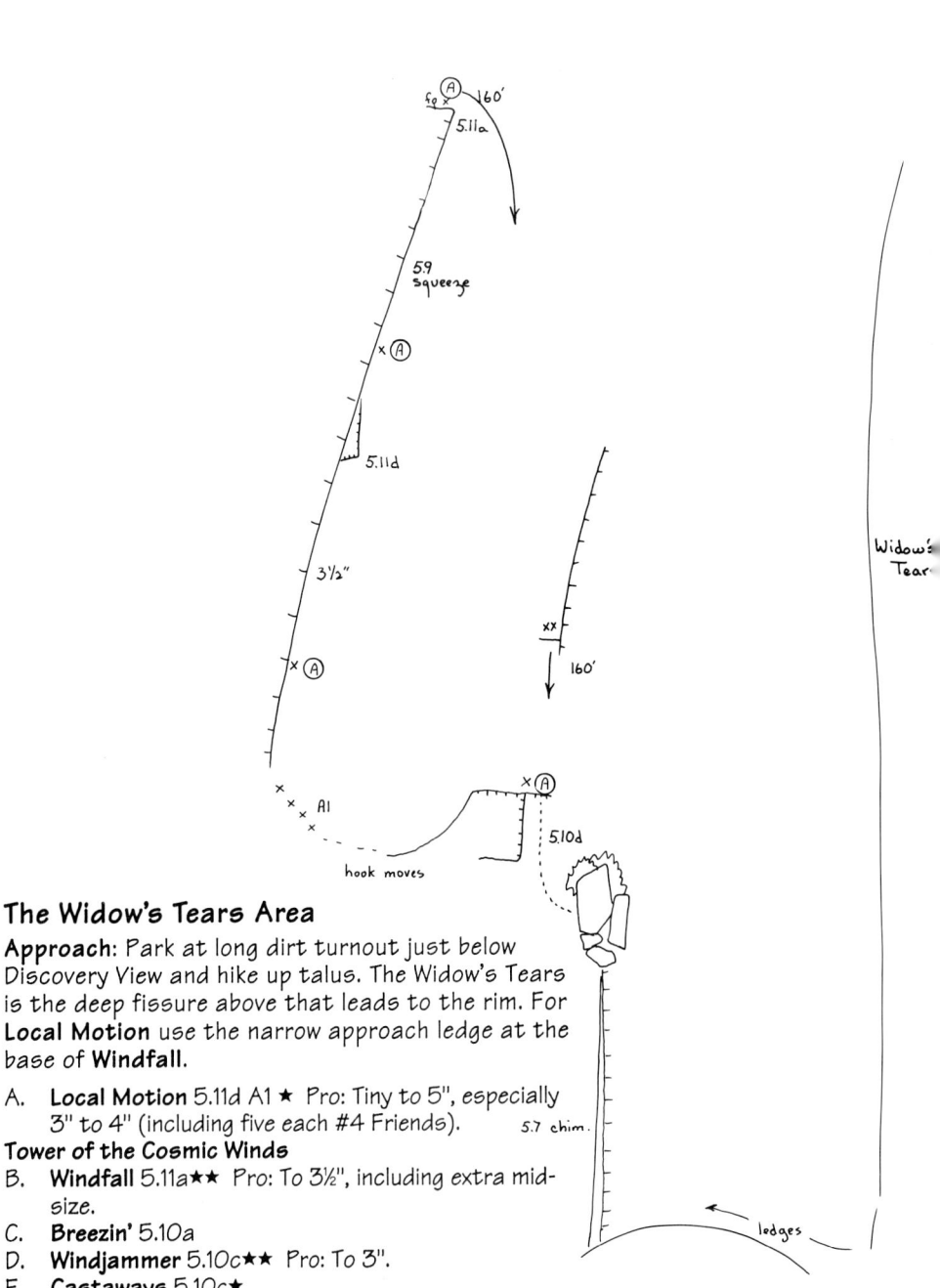

The Widow's Tears Area

Approach: Park at long dirt turnout just below Discovery View and hike up talus. The Widow's Tears is the deep fissure above that leads to the rim. For **Local Motion** use the narrow approach ledge at the base of **Windfall**.

A. **Local Motion** 5.11d A1 ★   Pro: Tiny to 5", especially 3" to 4" (including five each #4 Friends).

Tower of the Cosmic Winds

B. **Windfall** 5.11a★★   Pro: To 3½", including extra mid-size.
C. **Breezin'** 5.10a
D. **Windjammer** 5.10c★★   Pro: To 3".
E. **Castaways** 5.10c★

314 — LEANING TOWER

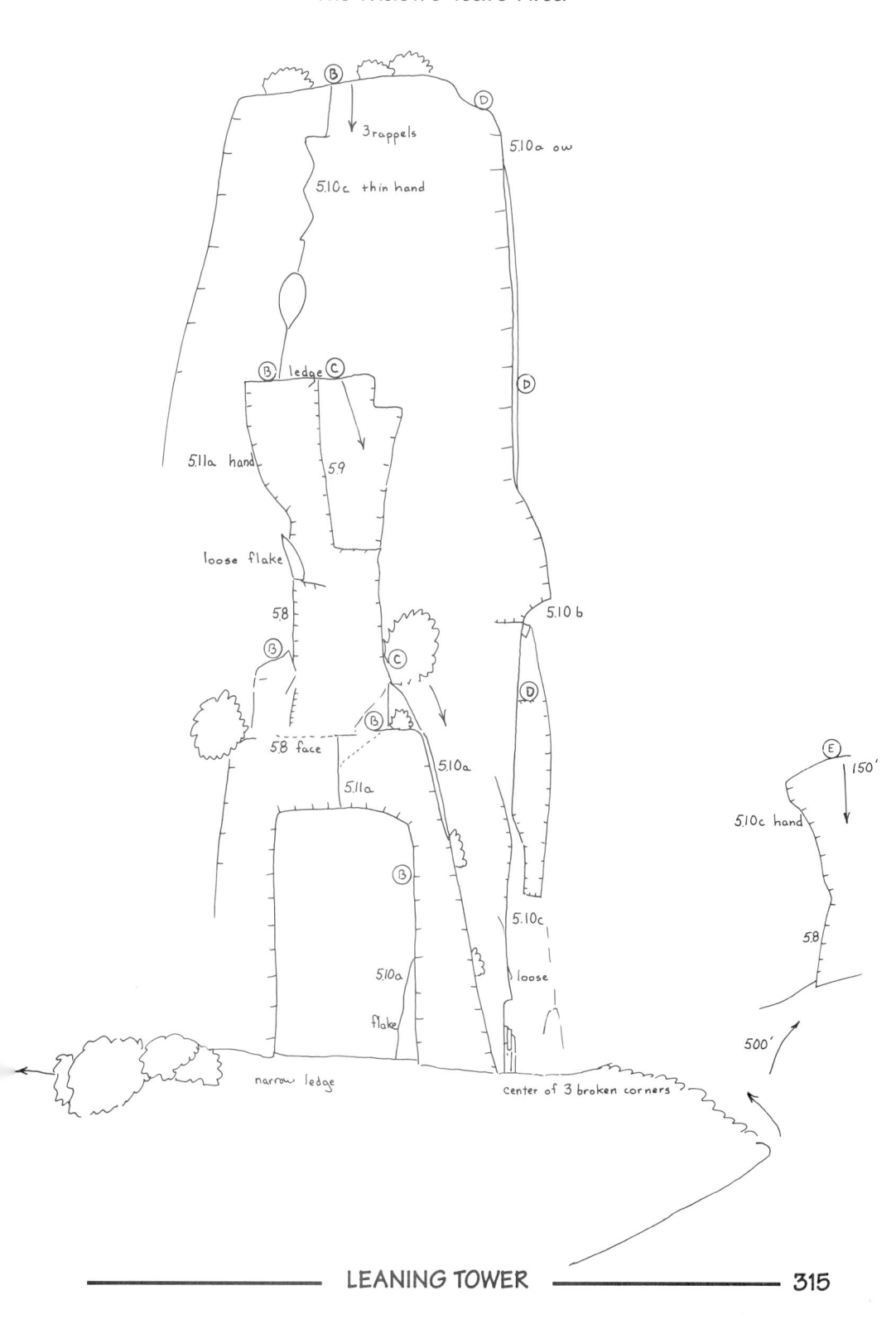

The Widow's Tears Area

LEANING TOWER

Stanford Point

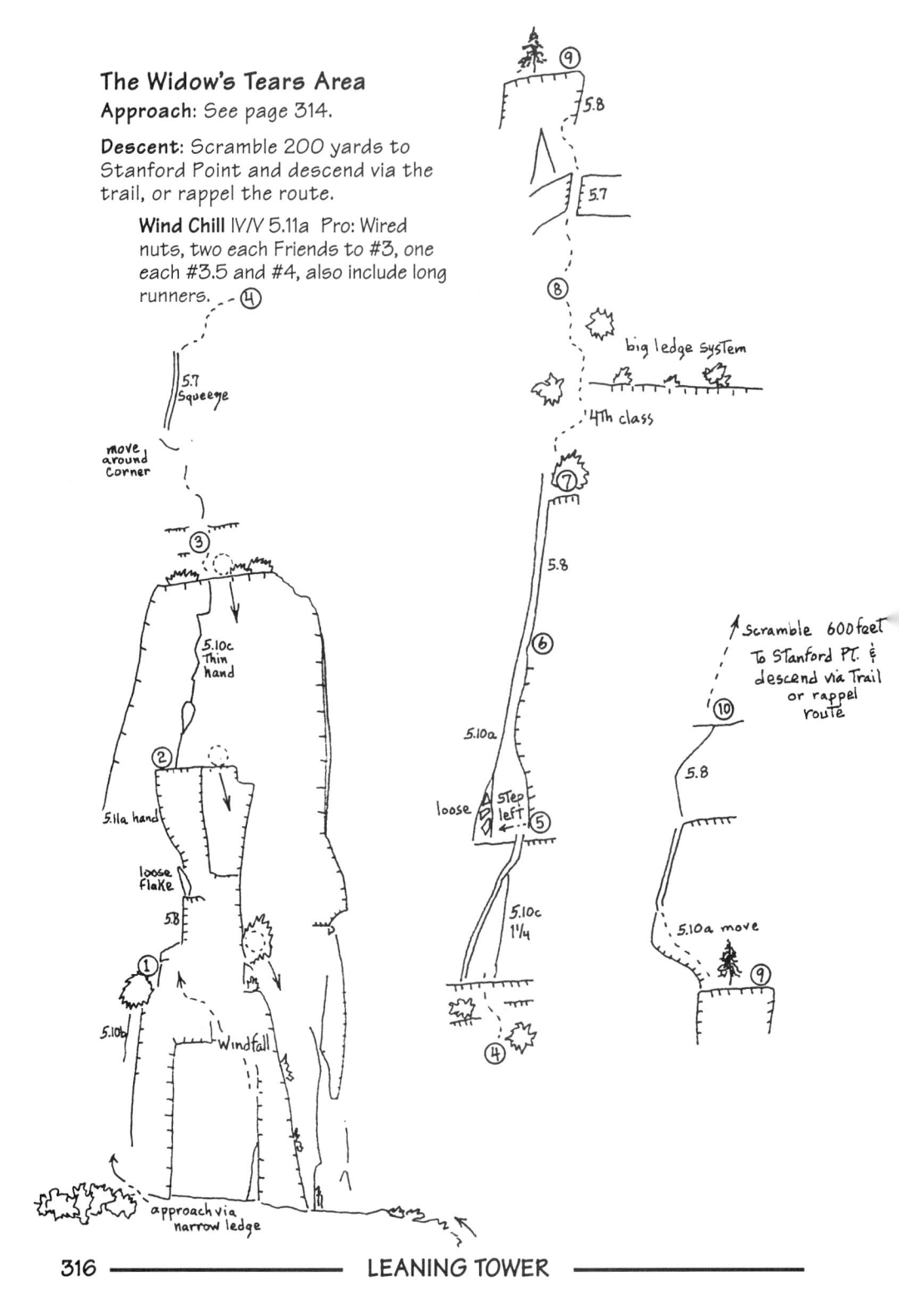

The Widow's Tears Area

Approach: See page 314.

Descent: Scramble 200 yards to Stanford Point and descend via the trail, or rappel the route.

Wind Chill IV/V 5.11a Pro: Wired nuts, two each Friends to #3, one each #3.5 and #4, also include long runners.

5.7 Squeeze

move around corner

5.10c Thin hand

5.11a hand

loose flake

5.8

5.10b

Windfall

approach via narrow ledge

5.8

5.7

big ledge system

4th class

5.8

5.10a

loose / step left

5.10c 1¼

Scramble 600 feet to Stanford Pt. & descend via Trail or rappel route

5.8

5.10a move

LEANING TOWER

Photo by Mark Chapman

Kevin Worrall on The Widow's Tears, 1975

LEANING TOWER

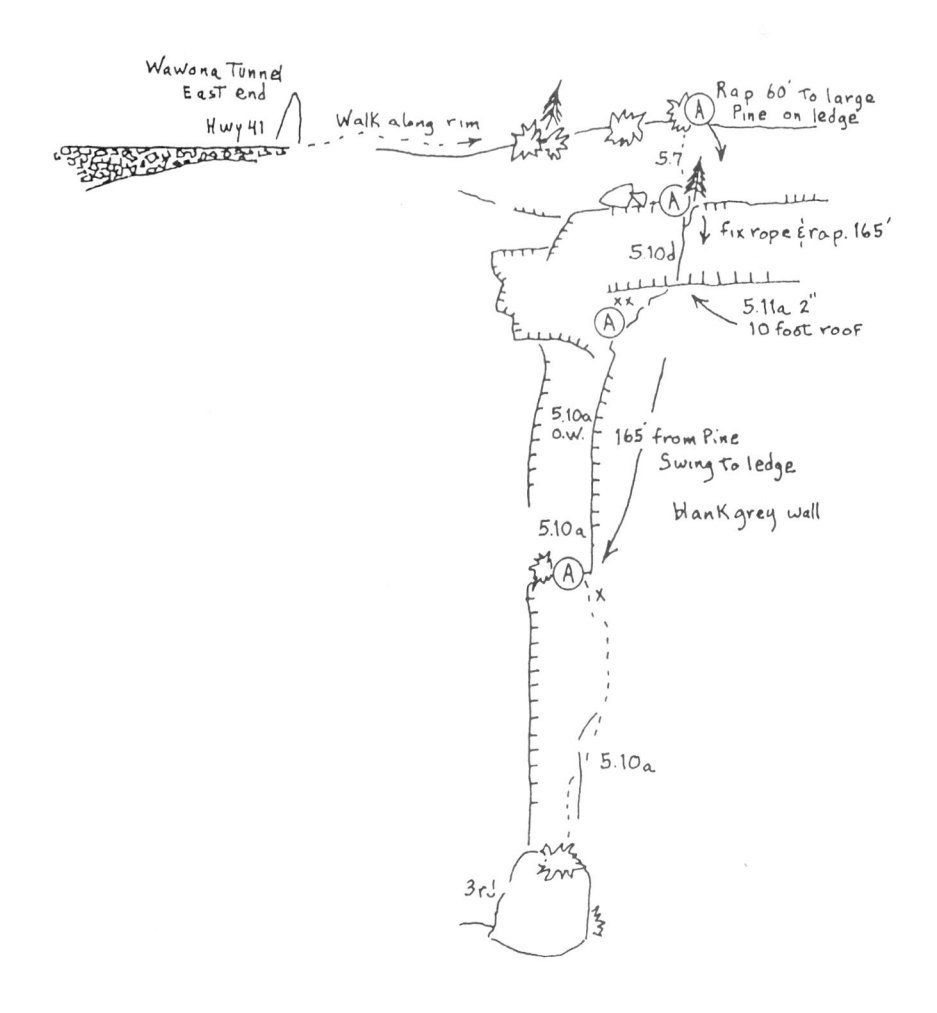

Discovery View

Approach: **Overdrive** is located on the cliff below the Wawona Tunnel near Discovery View, commonly, but not accurately, referred to as Inspiration Point. Although it is possible to approach from below, it is much more convenient to forego the first pitch and come in from above. Do this via a short walk and a couple of rappels.

- A. **Overdrive** 5.11a★ Pro: To 3½", also a "fixed" rappel rope. Semi-obscure, yet close to the road. Features an exhilarating roof experience.

Wawona Tunnel Area

Wawona Tunnel Area

Approach: Park in the lot at Discovery View (eastern end of Wawona Tunnel). Walk into the tunnel and pass through the eastern vent shaft. After exiting the shaft, traverse several hundred yards west to a point directly above and across from the Hwy 120/Hwy 140 junction then downclimb to the base of this overhanging white corner.

D. **Pump Dummy** 5.11c/d★ Pro: To 3½", including extra 1½" to 2".

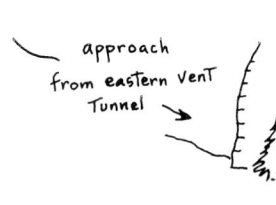

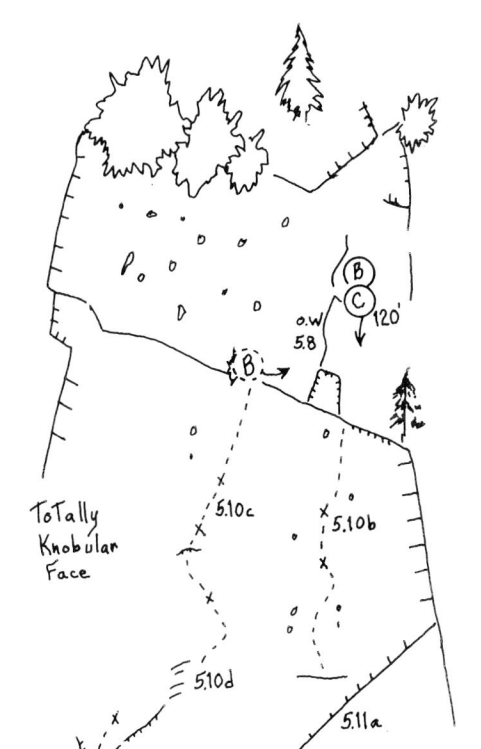

Below Wawona Tunnel

Approach: Scrub Scouts and **Flagman** are located on Flagman Buttress. This knobby 150-foot-high tablet of stone is directly across the river from the Mojo Tooth. Park in the small lot at the Hwy 120/Hwy 140 junction. Crossing the river is possible during periods of low water only!

B. **Scrub Scouts** 5.10c
C. **Flagman** 5.11a

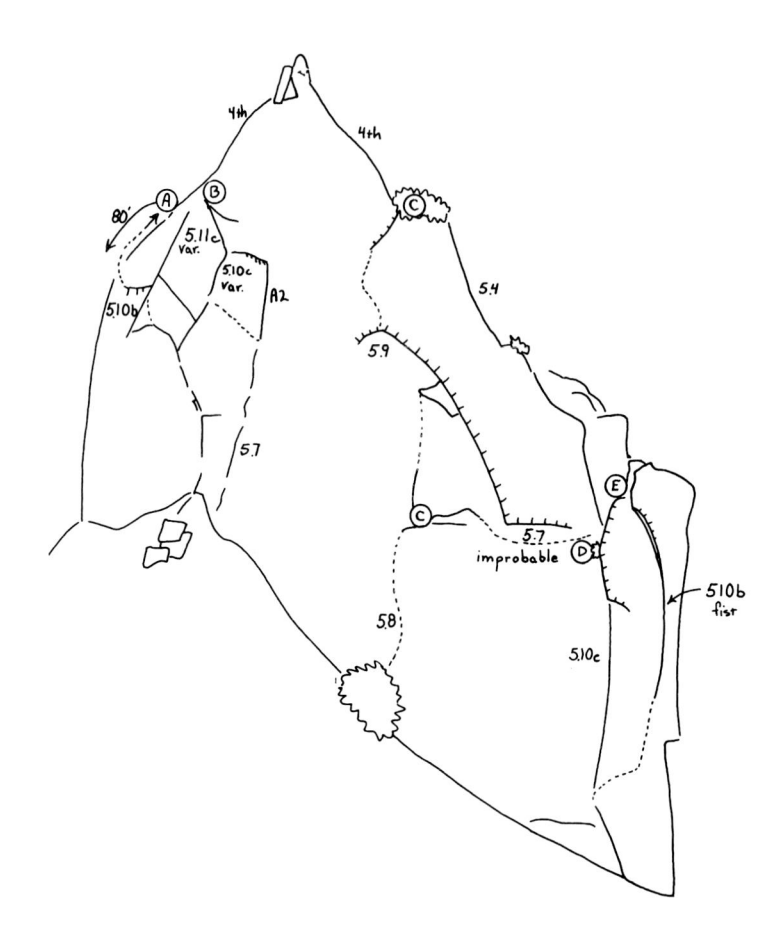

Pulpit Rock

Approach: Park in the lot at the Hwy 140/Hwy 120 junction. The river crossing is possible during periods of low water only.

Southeast Face
A. **Notch Route** 5.10b R
B. **East Face** 5.7 A2 or 5.10c
C. **Tree Route** 5.9 ★
   Improbable Traverse 5.7
D. **Original Sin** 5.10c
E. **Pulpit Pooper** 5.10b ★ Pro: To 3½".

Northwest Face
F. **Sky Pilot** 5.10c
G. **The Sermon** 5.10b★★ Pro: To 3½".
H. **Waste of Time** 5.10c
I. **Magilla Gorilla** 5.11b★★
J. **Gorilla Cookies** 5.10d

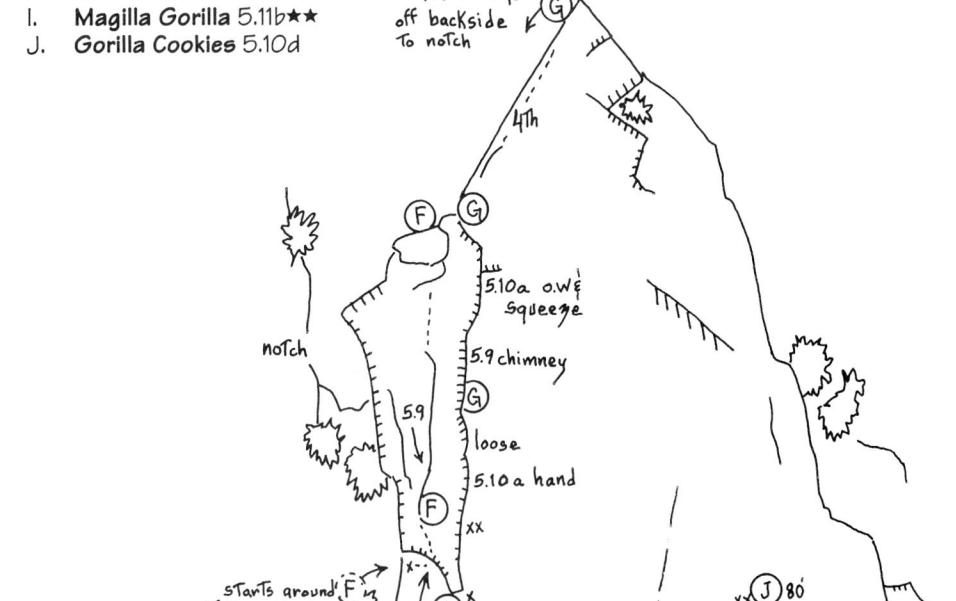

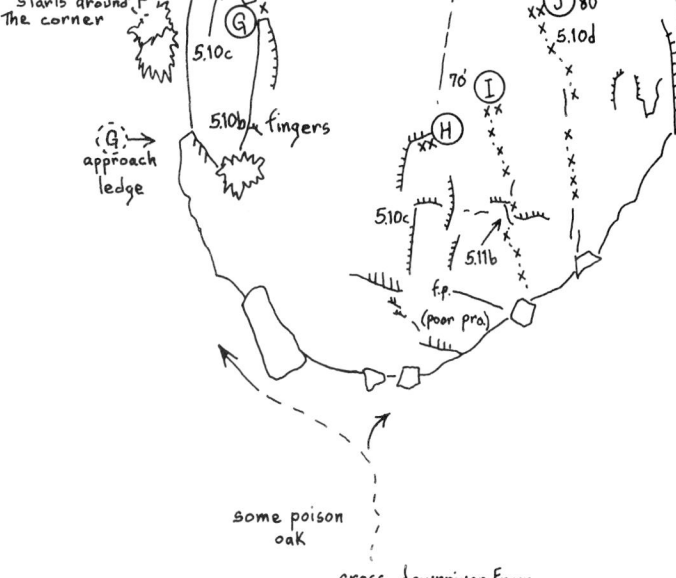

Pulpit Rock: West

High Pressure Cliff

Approach: **High Pressure** is located downstream about 0.25 mile from Pulpit Rock and may be reached from above or below. Beware poison oak that grows in abundance in this area.

A. **High Pressure** 5.11b★ Pro: To 3½", including extra ⅛" to ½".
   Open Trench 5.10a This is the next crack system to the right of High Pressure. Extremely ugly approach climbing leads to redeeming double hand cracks which ultimately break through a small roof near the top of the cliff.
   Lost on Venus 5.7 This is the flake system to the right of **Open Trench**.

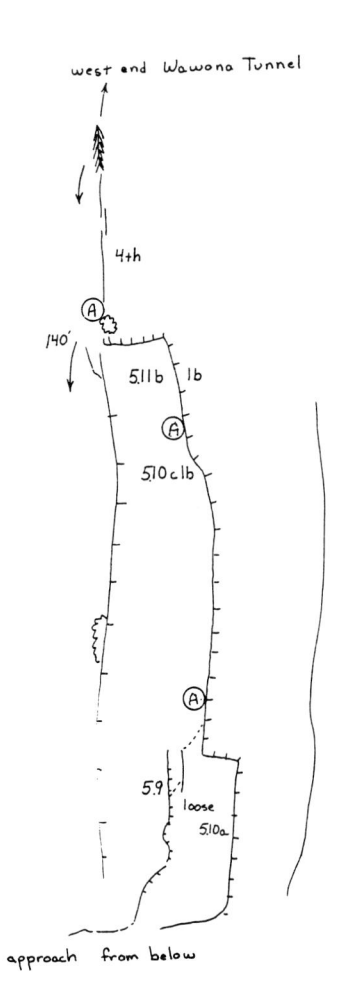

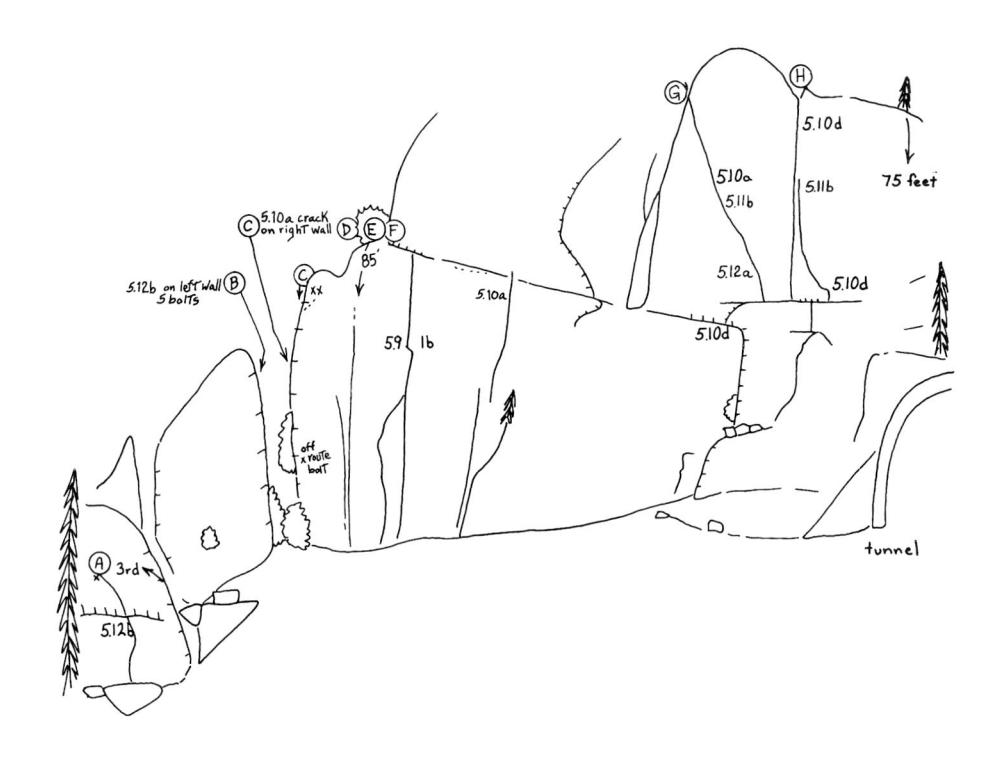

Wawona Tunnel, West End
A. **A Dog's Roof** 5.12b★ Pro: Especially ½" to 1".
B. **A Bit of OK** 5.12b★
C. **Walk On By** 5.10a
D. **Your Pizza Is Ready** 5.8/9
E. **Eat at Degnan's** 5.9+★
F. **Pohono The Barbarian** 5.10a
G. **Landshark** 5.12a
H. **Dancin' Days** 5.11c

Wawona Tunnel, West

Approach: Park in a dirt turnout a couple of hundred feet beyond the western end of Wawona Tunnel. This low cliff is within a stone's throw of the road.

A. **I Don't Know** 5.10a Pro: Thin to 2½", including TCUs.
B. **I Don't Remember** 5.9 Pro: Medium and large stoppers, #1.5 to #2.5 Friends.

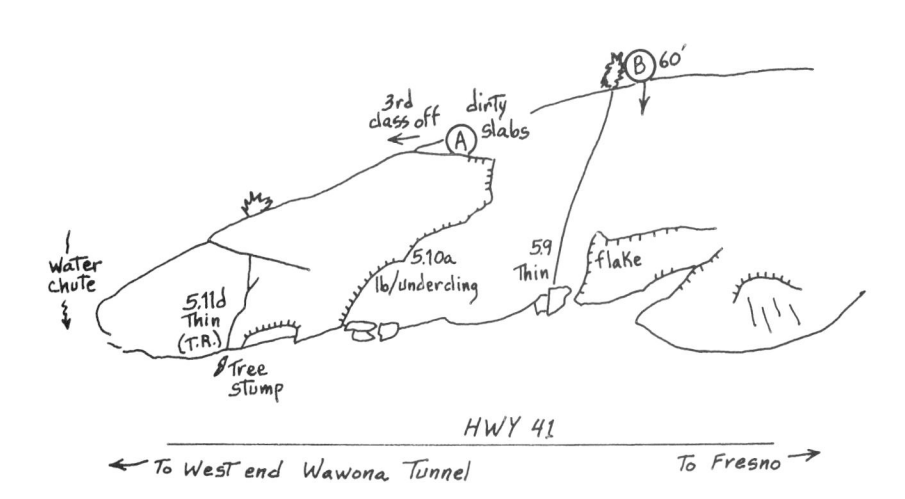

Cream Area

Approach: These climbs are located on a faceted buttress below Highway 41. Park a half mile past the west end of the Wawona Tunnel, just before the long stone wall.

A. **Cream** 5.11a★★ Pro: 2" to 6", including extra 4" to 6" pieces. A bizarre approach, yet a remarkable crack. A must for the offwidth aficionado. The crux is a slightly overhanging section perhaps 60 feet up, where the knee has to come out for a move. Physical, but fairly secure, above.
B. **Jam Session** 5.10b★ Pro: 2" to 5". The junior version of **Cream**.
C. **Cartwheel** 5.10a
D. **Monkey Do** 5.10c Pro: To 3".
E. **Energy Crisis** 5.11d★★ Pro: To 2", including extra #1.5 and especially #2 Friends. Basically, this climb is 85 feet of off-hand jamming. The technical crux is a slightly thinner, bulging section at the halfway point, but endurance over the distance is the name of the game.
F. **Shiver-Me-Timbers** 5.8

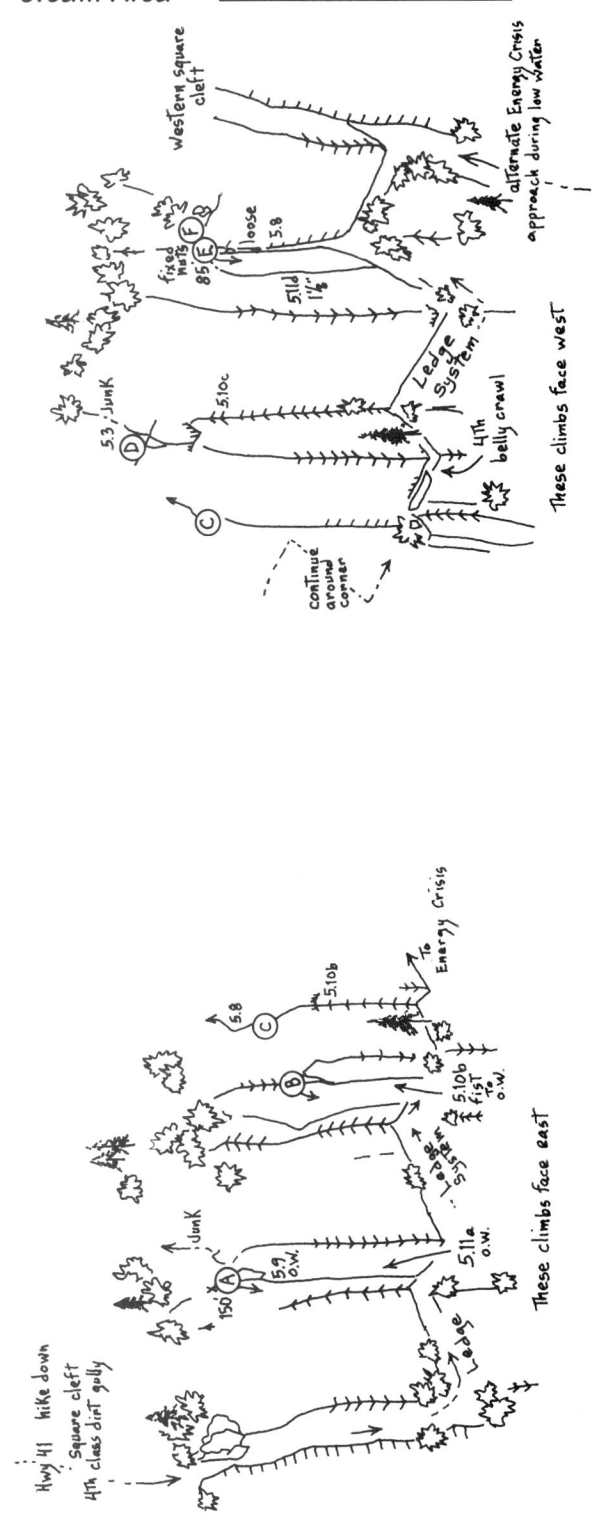

Turtleback Dome: Overview

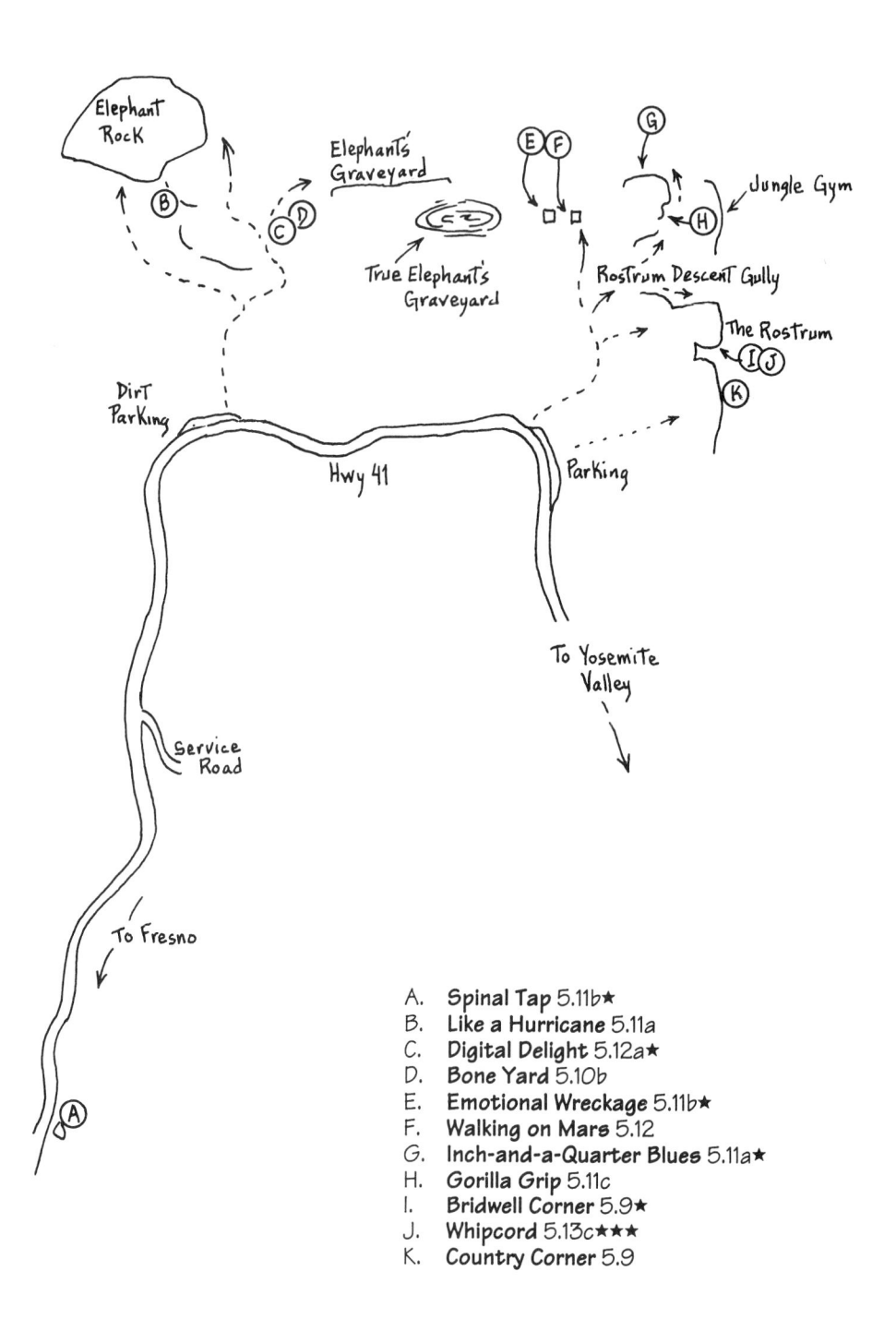

A. Spinal Tap 5.11b★
B. Like a Hurricane 5.11a
C. Digital Delight 5.12a★
D. Bone Yard 5.10b
E. Emotional Wreckage 5.11b★
F. Walking on Mars 5.12
G. Inch-and-a-Quarter Blues 5.11a★
H. Gorilla Grip 5.11c
I. Bridwell Corner 5.9★
J. Whipcord 5.13c★★★
K. Country Corner 5.9

Turtleback Dome: Overview

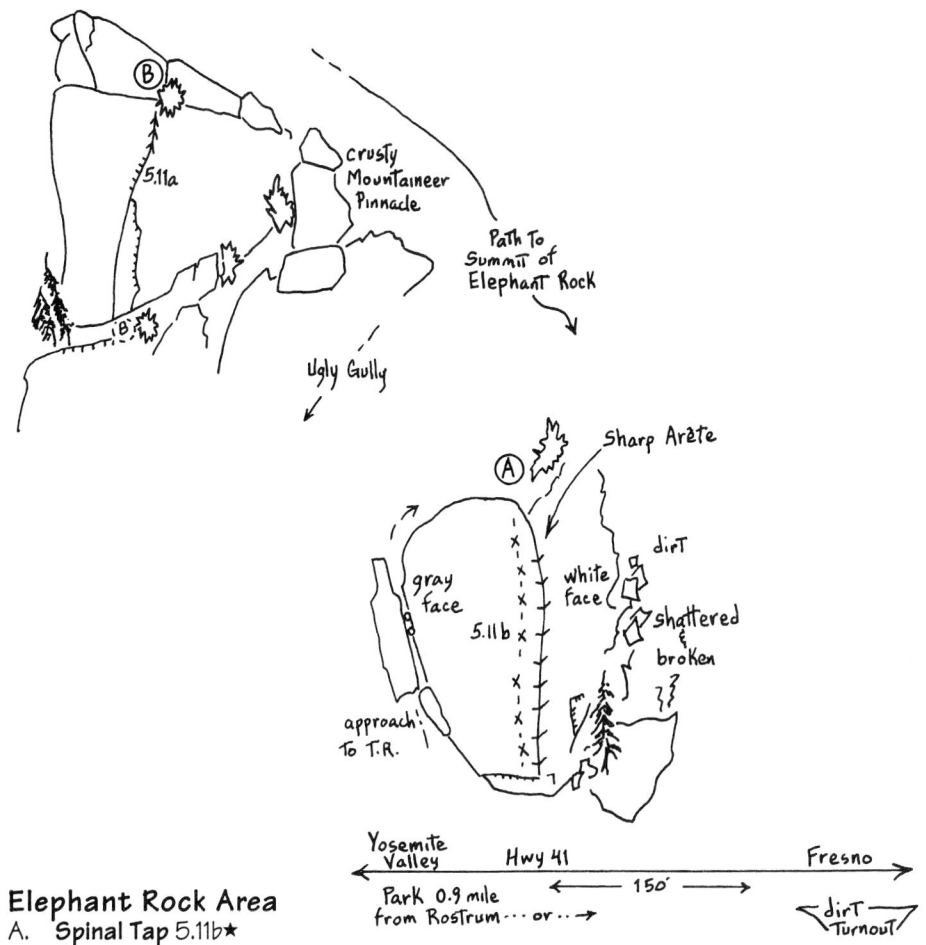

Elephant Rock Area
A. **Spinal Tap** 5.11b★
B. **Like a Hurricane** 5.11a
C. **Digital Delight** 5.12a★ Pro: To 3", especially ¾" to 1½". This is a southwest facing, straight-in thin crack encountered after passing through the rock barrier of the Elephant's Graveyard Cliff approach.
D. **Bone Yard** 5.10b Ascend a finger to hand crack on the left margin of a 70-foot band of rock located east and above **Digital Delight**.

Turtleback Dome: Overview

The Rostrum Area

E. **Emotional Wreckage** 5.11b★
F. **Walking on Mars** 5.12 This short yet severely overhanging hands to thin crack faces toward Elephant Rock and is located within an area of giant talus boulders.
G. **Inch-and-a-Quarter Blues** 5.11a★ Pro: Include several #1.5 to #2 Friends. This climb is located several hundred feet further and around the corner from **Gorilla Grip**.
H. **Gorilla Grip** 5.11c About midway down The Rostrum descent gully, contour left (down-river) along steep dirt. This route climbs a thin crack starting from a debris-strewn platform.
I. **Bridwell Corner** 5.9★
J. **Whipcord** 5.13c★★★ Pro: Small gear needed only for bottom belay. Two approaches are possible. However, coming in from above by rappelling from the summit of The Rostrum will probably prove the more popular approach. To approach from below, climb across to the eastern side of The Rostrum by exiting the **North Face Route** at a point two pitches above the big midway ledge on that route.
K. **Country Corner** 5.9 Pro: TCUs to #3 Friend. Approach by descending slabs several hundred feet east of The Rostrum.

Elephant Rock Area

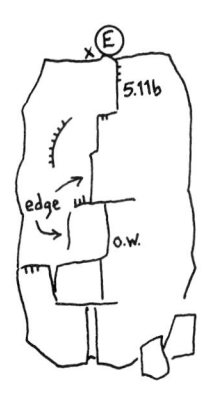

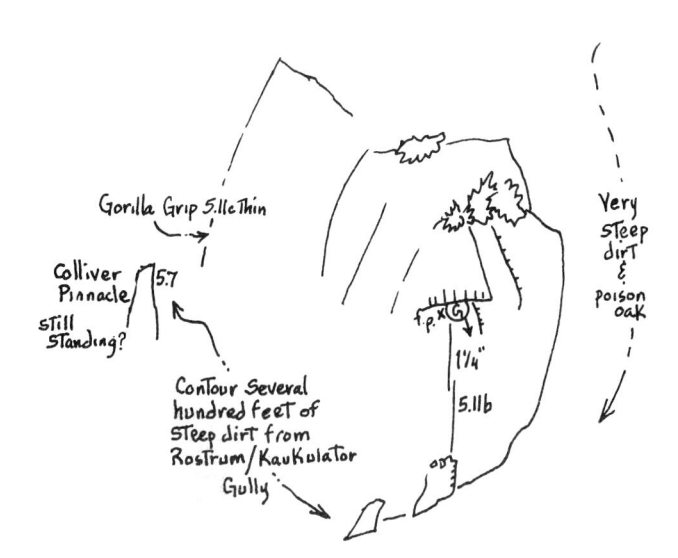

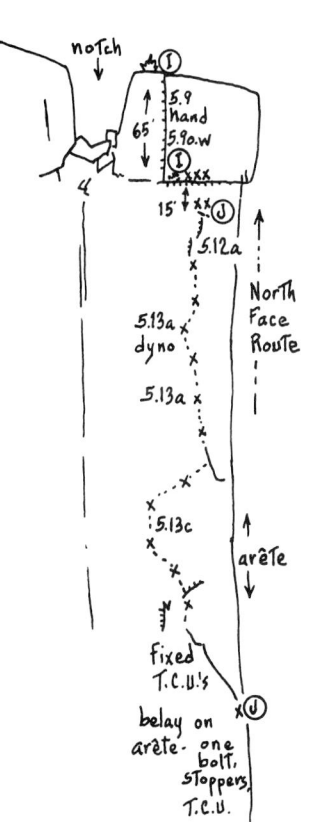

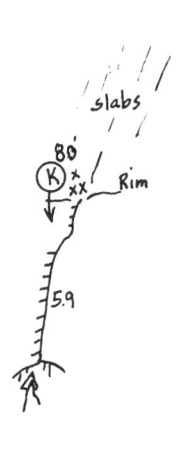

LOWER MERCED CANYON: SOUTH — 329

The Rostrum: East

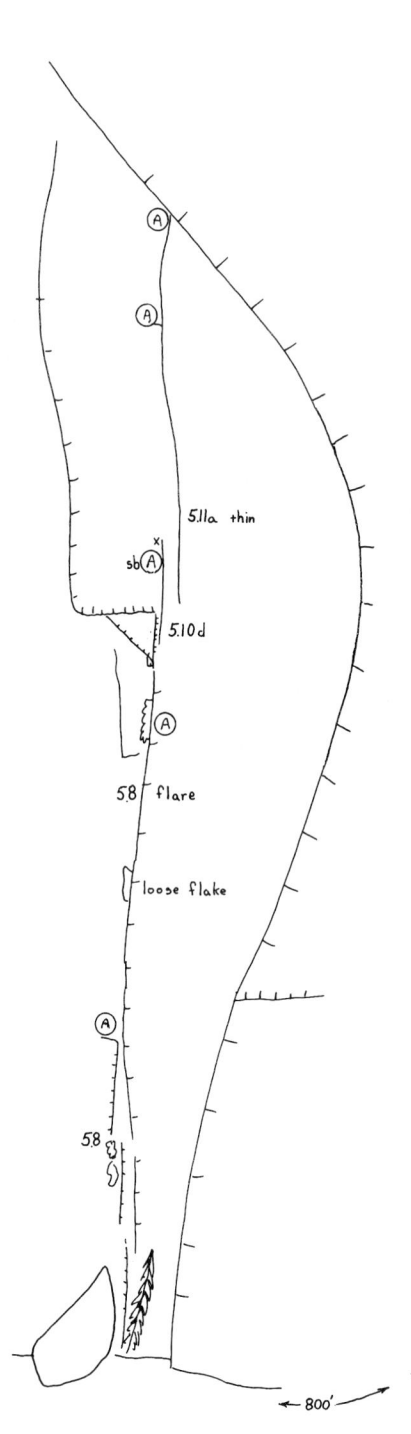

Super Nova Area

Approach: This is the sliver/gray wall left (east) of the Rostrum. Wade across the river (low water only), then hike up talus.

Photo on page 331.

A. **Super Nova** 5.11a★ Pro: To 4", including extra #0.5 to #2 Friends. Although this has an one-star rating, the initial sections are somewhat dubious.
B. **Dime Bag** 5.10c★
C. **Crack the Whip** 5.11b★★

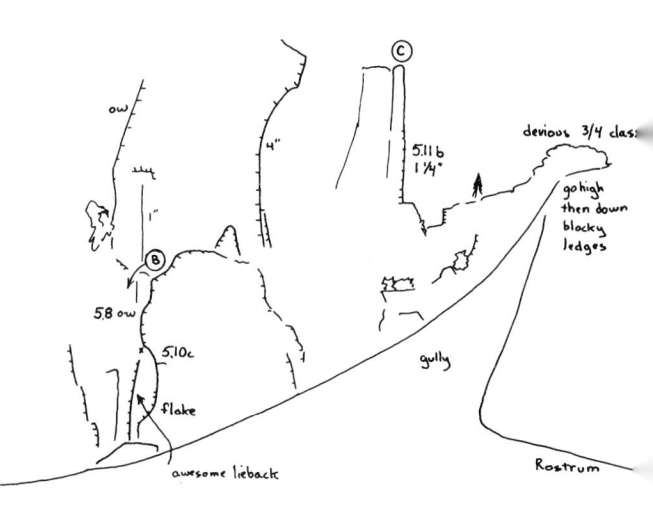

The Rostrum Area

1. Super Nova 5.11a
2. Country Corner 5.9
3. Dime Bag 5.10c
4. Crack the Whip 5.11b
5. Rostrum North Face Route 5.11c
6. Gorilla Grip 5.11c
7. Inch and a Quarter Blues 5.11a

The Rostrum

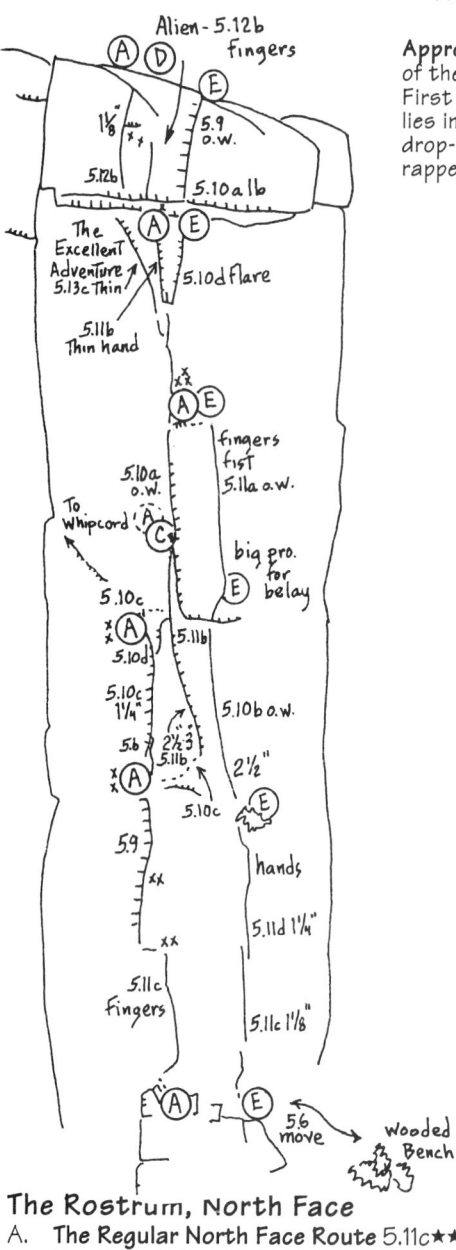

Approach: Park above on Hwy. 41 at the west end of the long stone wall west of the Wawona Tunnel. First hike down slabs, then a steep dirt gully that lies immediately west of the Rostrum. There is a drop-off beyond here which requires four 70-foot rappels to reach the base of the north face.

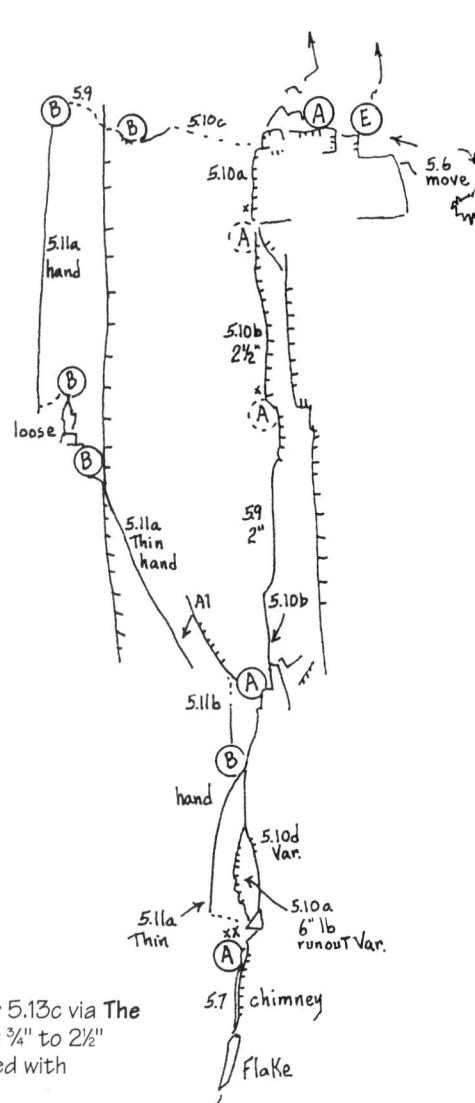

The Rostrum, North Face
A. **The Regular North Face Route** 5.11c★★★ or 5.13c via **The Excellent Adventure** Pro: To 3½", especially ¾" to 2½" pieces. A narrow column of granite splintered with astounding cracks.
B. **Mad Pilot** 5.11b A1★
C. **Uprising** 5.11b★★★ Pro: ¾" to 3½" pieces, with extra 2½" to 3". Overhanging off-hand/fist combat.
D. **Alien** 5.12b★★★ Pro: To 2".
E. **Blind Faith** 5.11d Pro: To 6". Physical climbing up sharp fractures. The first pitch by itself is popular.

The Rostrum

LOWER MERCED CANYON: SOUTH

The Rostrum

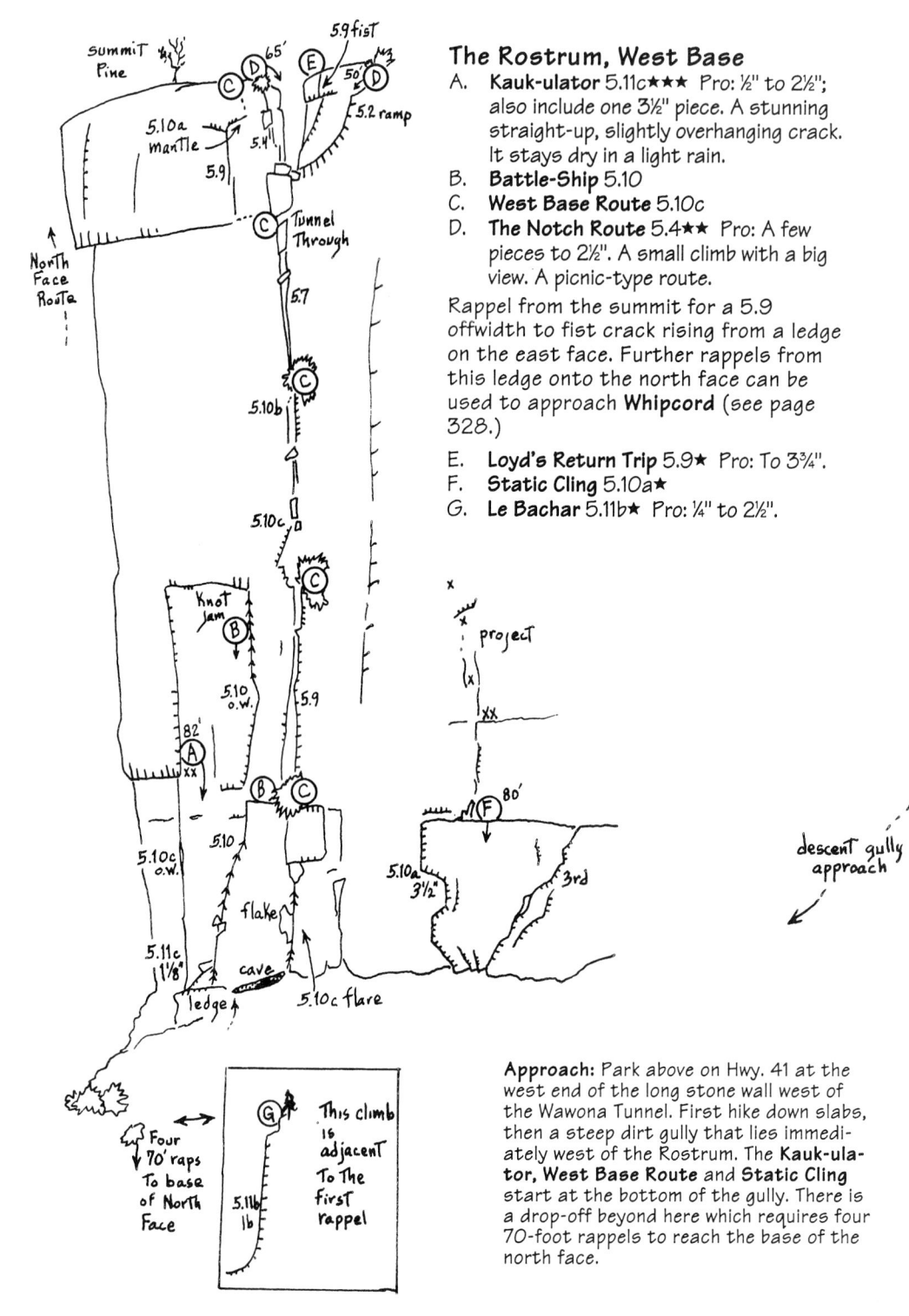

The Rostrum, West Base

A. **Kauk-ulator** 5.11c★★★ Pro: ½" to 2½"; also include one 3½" piece. A stunning straight-up, slightly overhanging crack. It stays dry in a light rain.
B. **Battle-Ship** 5.10
C. **West Base Route** 5.10c
D. **The Notch Route** 5.4★★ Pro: A few pieces to 2½". A small climb with a big view. A picnic-type route.

Rappel from the summit for a 5.9 offwidth to fist crack rising from a ledge on the east face. Further rappels from this ledge onto the north face can be used to approach **Whipcord** (see page 328.)

E. **Loyd's Return Trip** 5.9★ Pro: To 3¾".
F. **Static Cling** 5.10a★
G. **Le Bachar** 5.11b★ Pro: ¼" to 2½".

Approach: Park above on Hwy. 41 at the west end of the long stone wall west of the Wawona Tunnel. First hike down slabs, then a steep dirt gully that lies immediately west of the Rostrum. The **Kauk-ulator, West Base Route** and **Static Cling** start at the bottom of the gully. There is a drop-off beyond here which requires four 70-foot rappels to reach the base of the north face.

LOWER MERCED CANYON: SOUTH

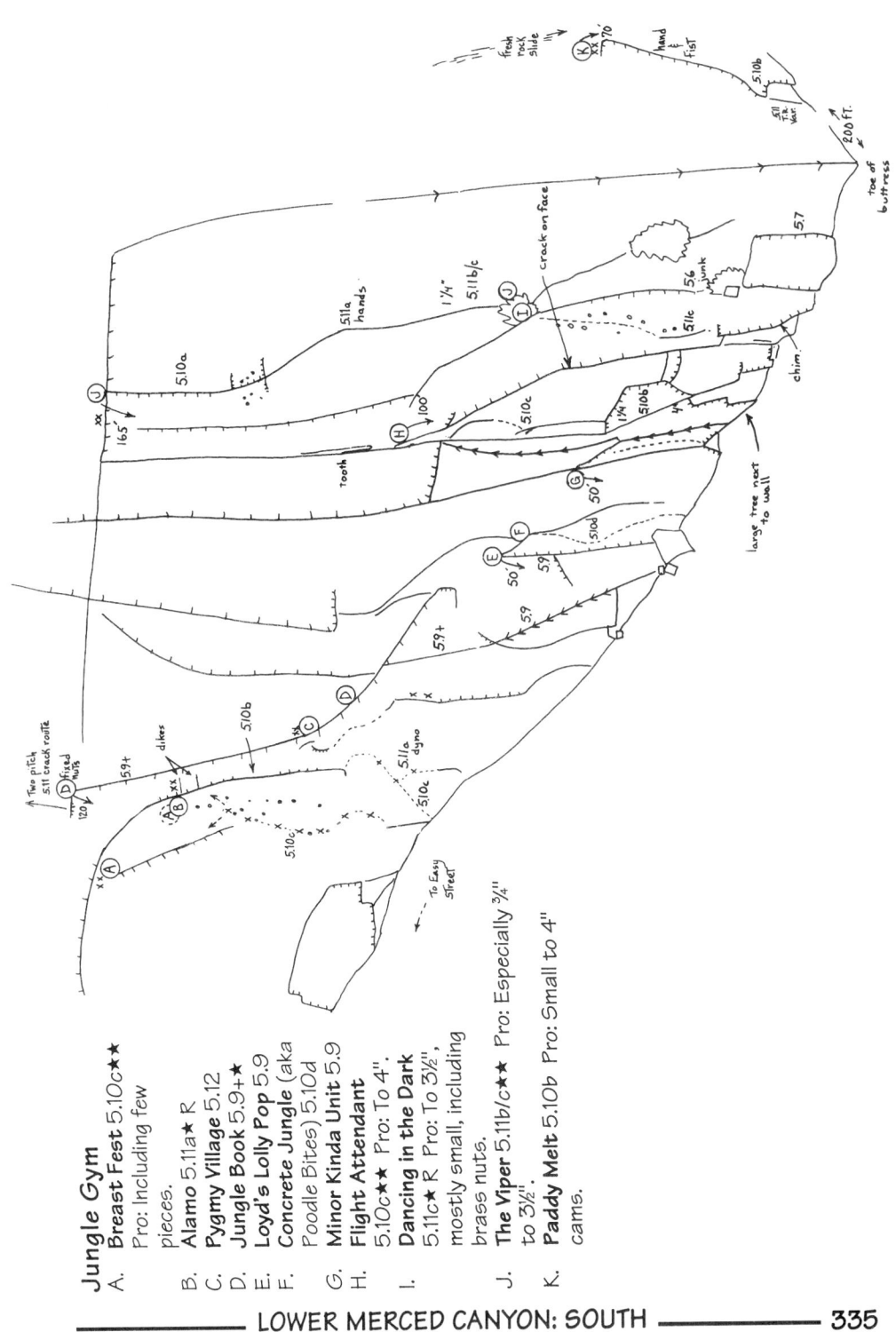

The Rostrum: West

Jungle Gym
A. **Breast Fest** 5.10c ★★ Pro: Including few pieces.
B. **Alamo** 5.11a ★ R
C. **Pygmy Village** 5.12
D. **Jungle Book** 5.9+ ★
E. **Loyd's Lolly Pop** 5.9
F. **Concrete Jungle** (aka Poodle Bites) 5.10d
G. **Minor Kinda Unit** 5.9
H. **Flight Attendant** 5.10c ★★ Pro: To 4".
I. **Dancing in the Dark** 5.11c ★ R Pro: To 3½", mostly small, including brass nuts.
J. **The Viper** 5.11b/c ★★ Pro: Especially ¾ to 3½".
K. **Paddy Melt** 5.10b Pro: Small to 4" cams.

LOWER MERCED CANYON: SOUTH — 335

Elephant's Graveyard

1. Razor's Edge 5.12
2. Slit Your Tires 5.11d
3. Pet Semetary 5.11b
4. Eagle 5.10a

Elephant's Graveyard

Approach: This small cliff is located just to the east of Elephant Rock. See page 338.

A. **Razor's Edge** 5.12★★
B. **Battlescar** 5.11d A1
C. **Slit Your Tires** 5.11d★
D. **Pet Semetary** 5.11b★
E. **Eagle** 5.10a
F. **The Elephant Guy** 5.10

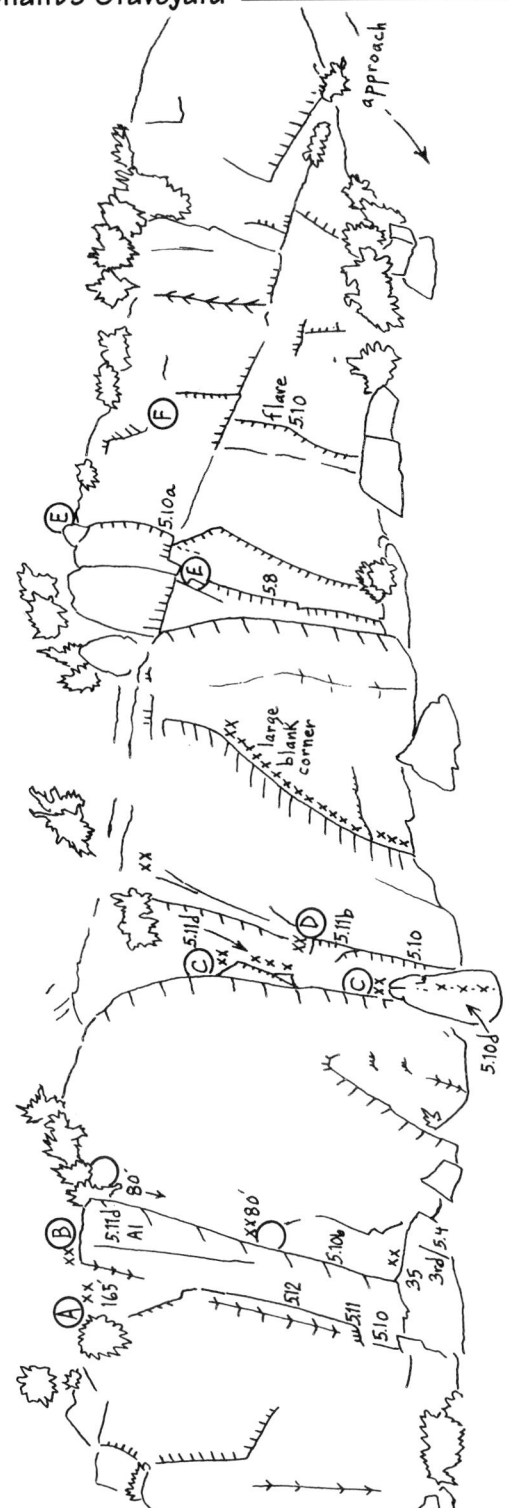

LOWER MERCED CANYON: SOUTH

Elephant Rock

Approach: This cliff can be approached from below from Hwy 140 or from above off Hwy 41. From below, park at The Cookie and walk down the road until even with the huge Monster Boulder that lies on the opposite side of the river. This is the best crossing, but can only be made during periods of low water. Once across hike up the talus.

To approach Elephant Rock (as well as Elephant's Graveyard) from Hwy 41, park in the banked, graveled turnout west of the stone wall that is The Rostrum parking. The rim is reached within minutes, though careful scouting is needed to find a Class 2 descent that intrudes the short crown of cliffs between Elephant Rock and Elephant's Graveyard. This leads down the east side of Elephant Rock. Some of the short routes at the top of Elephant Rock an be reached from above by careful scouting and judicious rappelling.

Descent: Descend most of the routes by rappel. The descent from the top of **Crack of Doom** and the like can be made by scrambling east on ledges to an improbable traverse that leads to rappel anchors down **Real Error** (see page 343). Descend routes that lead to the top of **Worst Error** by rappelling the **Right Side** route.

Elephant Rock

1. Hotline 5.12a
2. Fatal Mistake 5.11a A1
3. Cracks of Doom and Despair 5.10a
4. Hairline 5.11b
5. Elephantiasis 5.10d R

Elephant Rock

Elephant Rock, East Face

Approach: Walk to the top of Elephant Rock and rappel to the start of these climbs.

- A. **Take Da Plunge** 5.12c★ TR Pro: To 2".
- B. **Candy-O** 5.11d★ R Poor finish.
- C. **Left Guru Crack** 5.10c★ Poor finish.
- D. **Right Guru Crack** 5.10a★ Poor finish.
- E. **Elephant Talk** 5.11b★★
- F. **Killing Yourself to Live** 5.12a★ R Pro: To 2½", including many thin.
- G. **Keeper of the Flame** 5.13a★★★

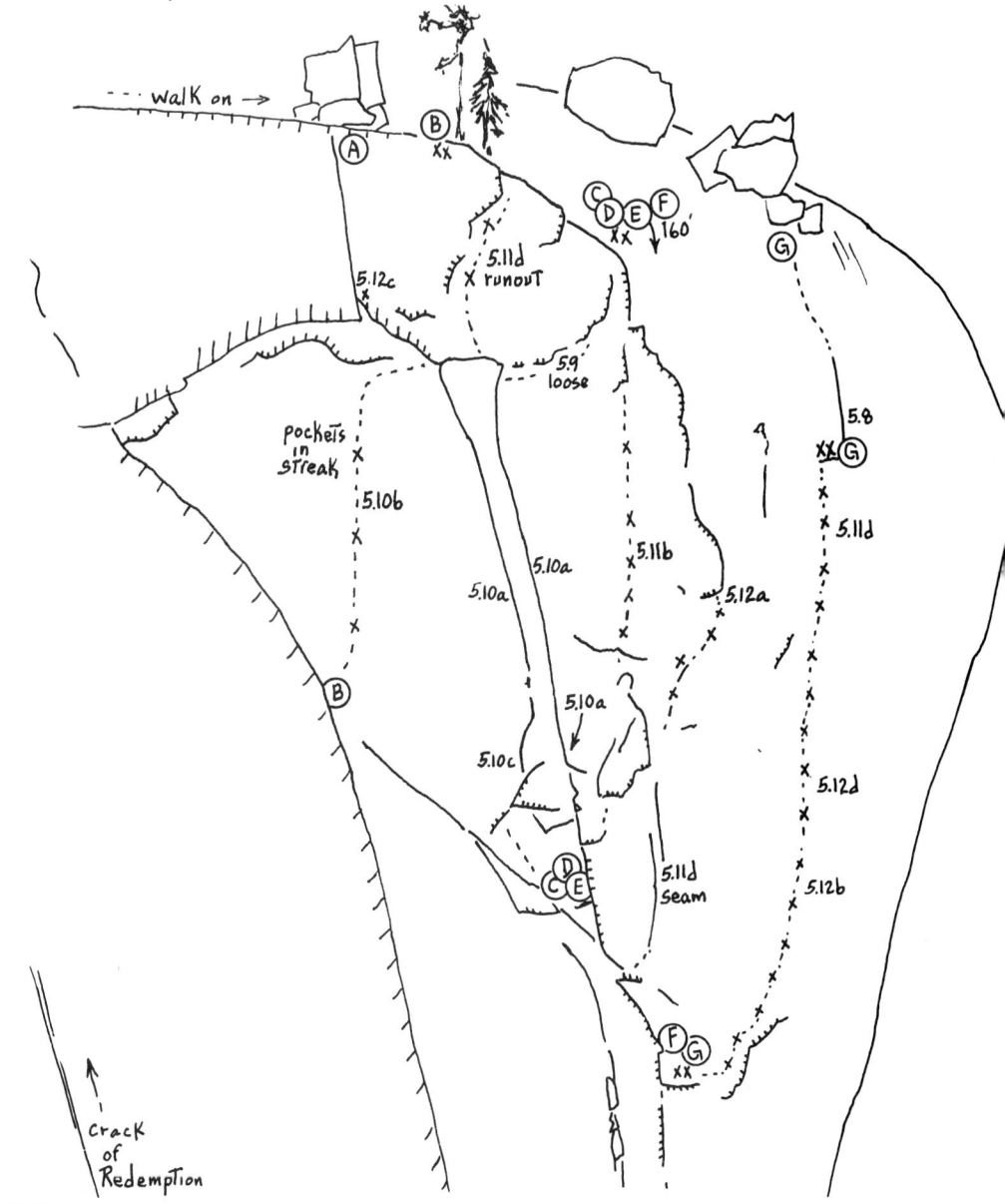

Elephant Rock

Elephant Rock, Top
Approach: Described on page 338.

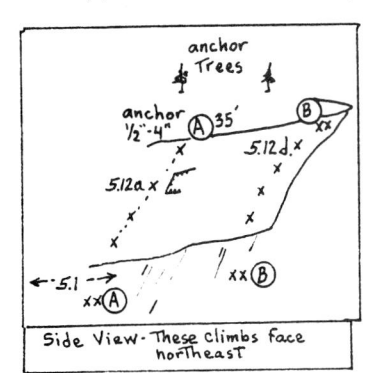

A. **Fly Swatter** 5.12a★ Pro: ½" to 4" for anchor.
B. **Isaiah 2:21** 5.12d★
C. **Sky** 5.11c★★ Pro: To 5".
D. **Hocus Pocus** 5.11d★★
E. **Elephantiasis** 5.10d★ R Pro: Tiny wireds to 2½", including 2 medium-thick LAs.
F. **Pink Elephant** 5.9★
G. **Crack of Destiny** 5.8/9
H. **The Hundredth Monkey** 5.11b★★ Pro: QDs.
I. **Fun Terminal** 5.12a★★★ Pro: QDs.
J. **Wicked Gravity** 5.12c★★★ Pro: QDs.
K. **Bucket Brigade** 5.11d★★★ Pro: QDs.
L. **Elephant Malt** 5.9 R

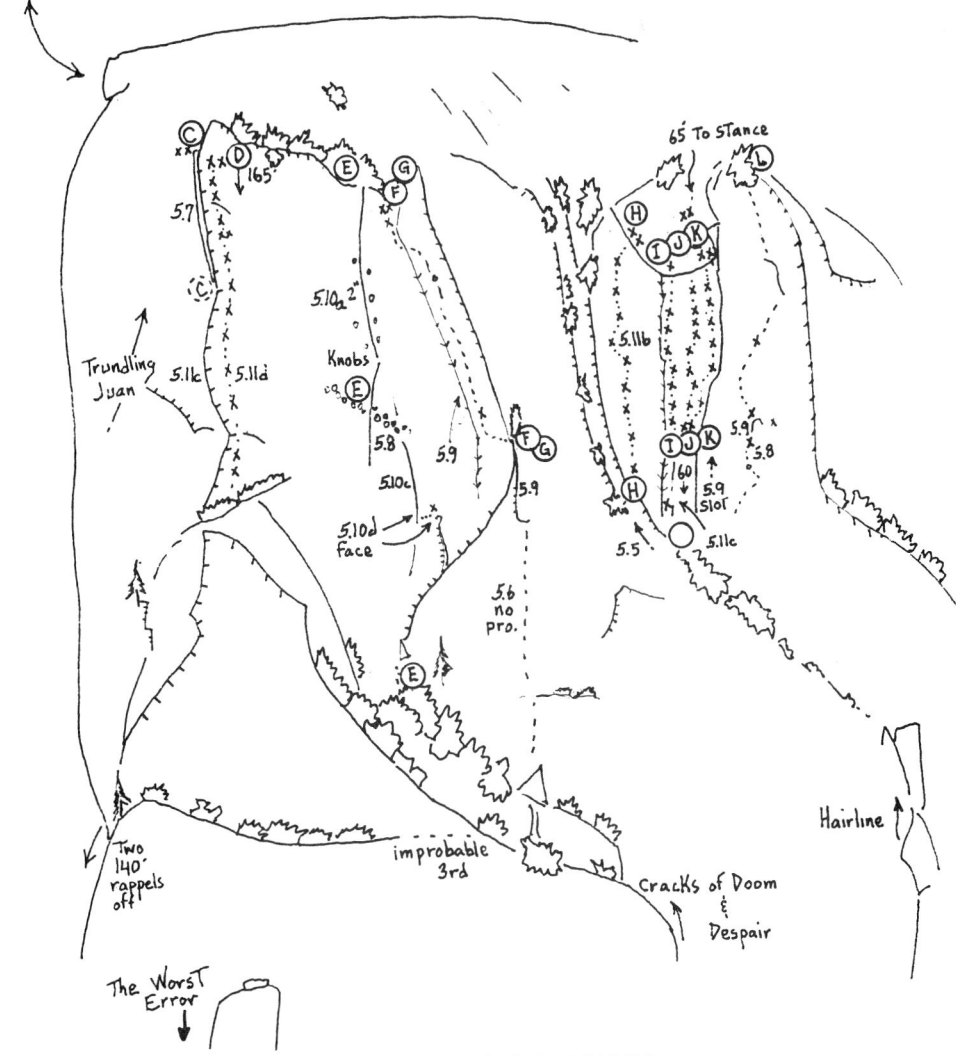

Boulder Cracks

Elephant Rock Boulders

Approach: Park at The Cookie. Only in times of low water can the river crossing can be made at a point even with the huge Monster Boulder.

Monster Boulder 5.11a TR
Jaws 5.12a TR

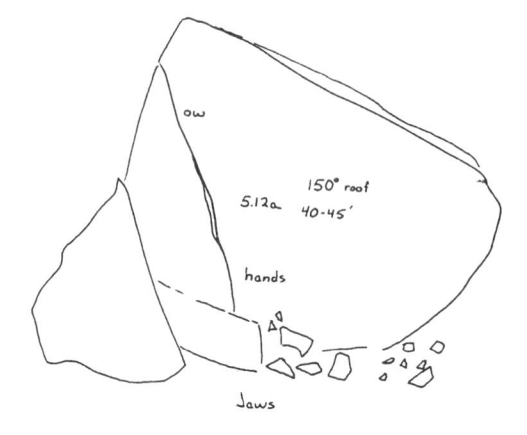

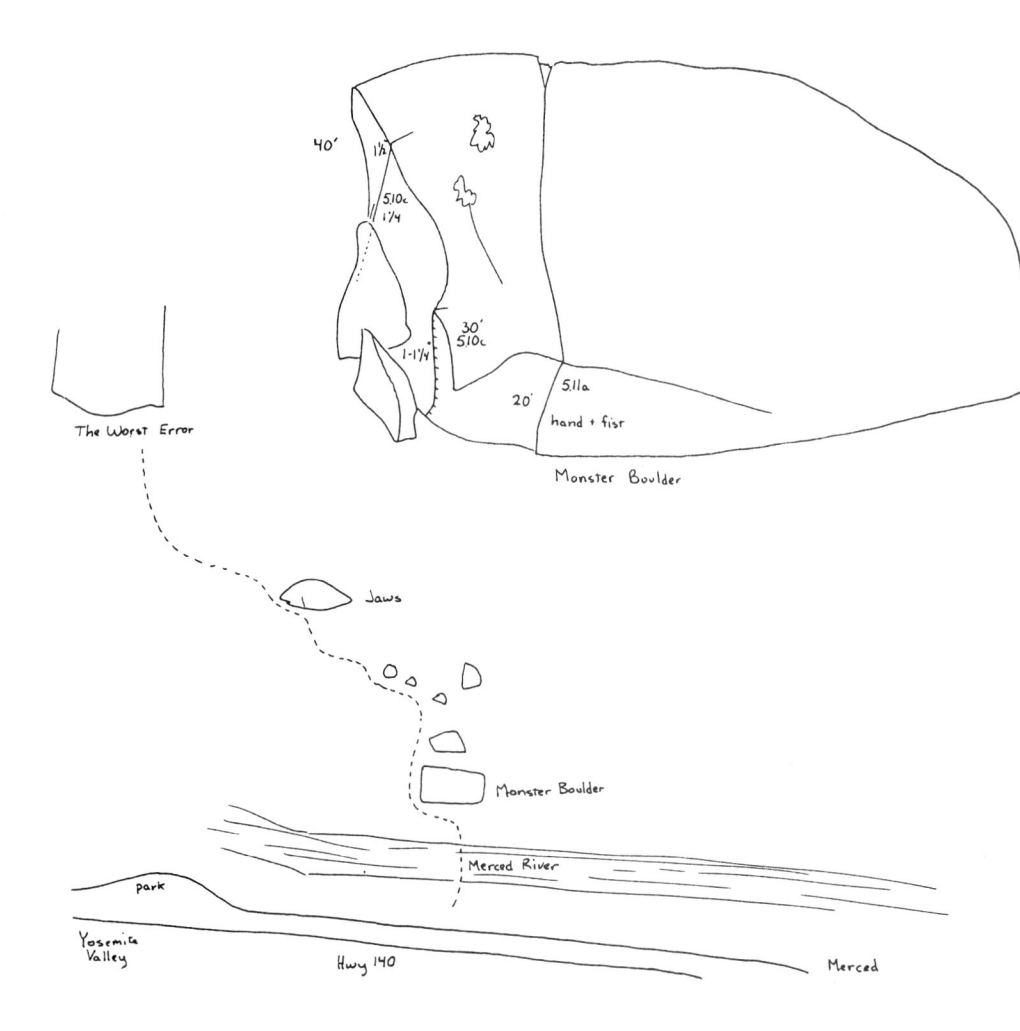

LOWER MERCED CANYON: SOUTH

Elephant Rock

Elephant Rock, East Side

Approach: As described on page 338.

- A. **Reality Check** 5.10c★ Pro: To 4", including extra ½" to 1½".
- B. **Plumb Line** 5.10d★ Pro: To 6", including extra 2½" to 3".
- C. **Trundling Juan** 5.10b★ Pro: To 5".
- D. **Straight Error** 5.10c★★ Pro: To 3", including extra 2" to 3".
- E. **Real Error** 5.7
- F. **Foaming at the Crotch** 5.10a Pro: To 3½".

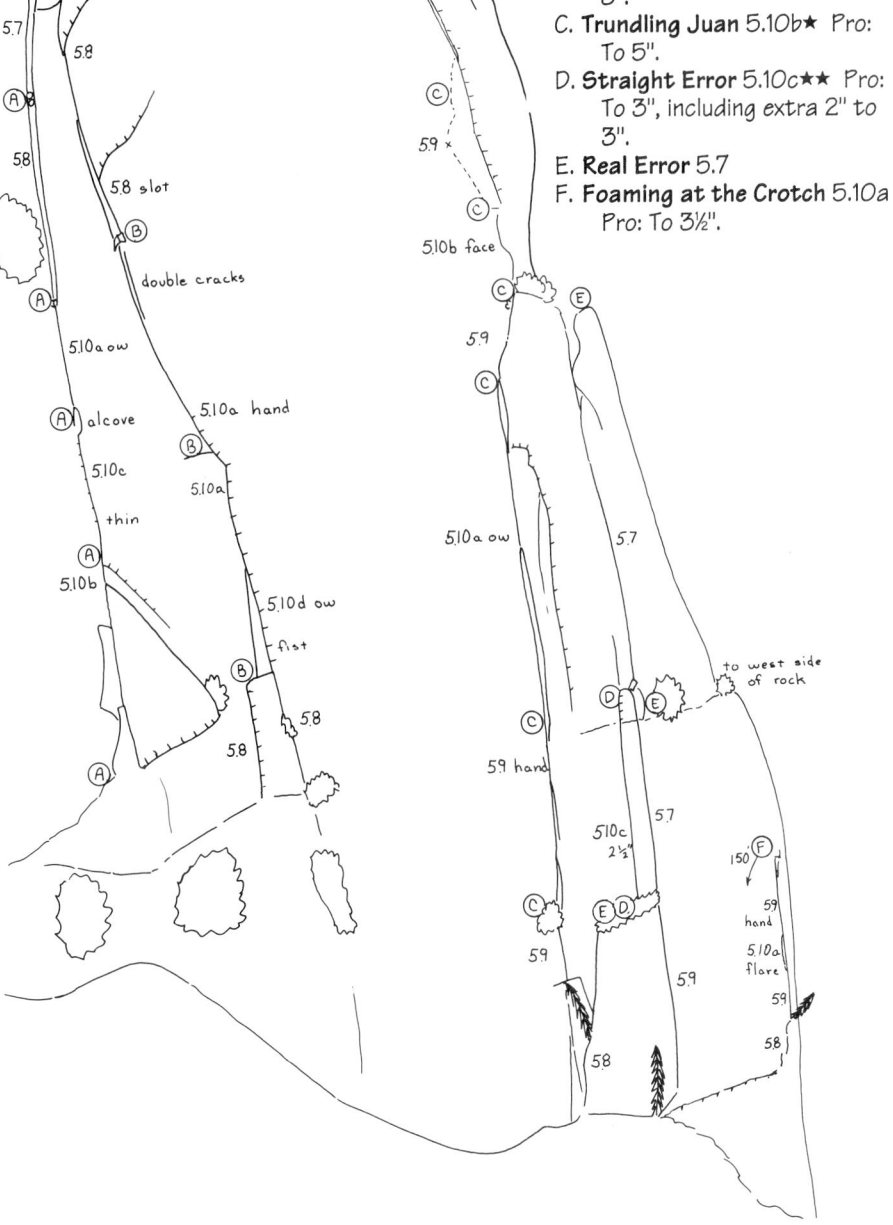

LOWER MERCED CANYON: SOUTH

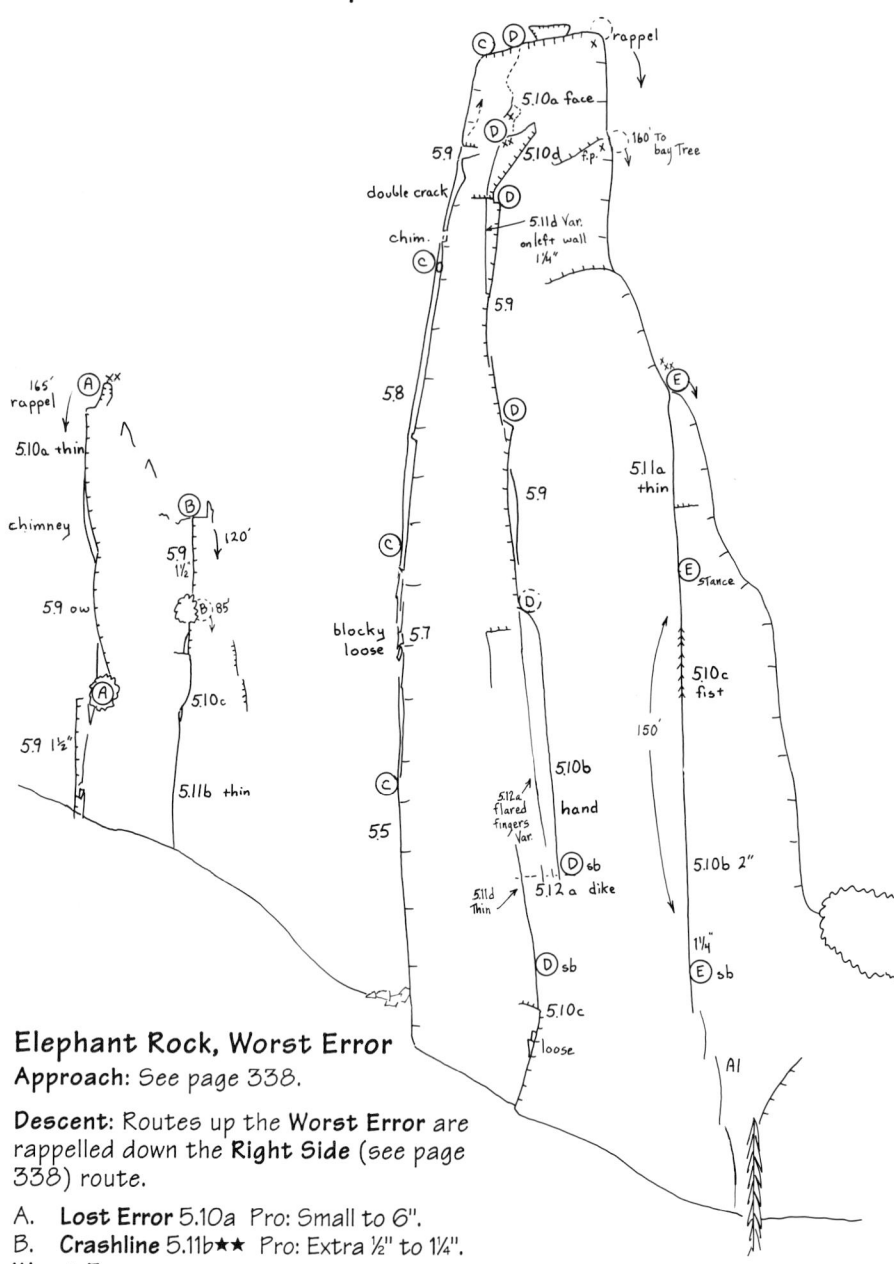

Elephant Rock Area

Elephant Rock, Worst Error
Approach: See page 338.

Descent: Routes up the **Worst Error** are rappelled down the **Right Side** (see page 338) route.

- A. **Lost Error** 5.10a Pro: Small to 6".
- B. **Crashline** 5.11b★★ Pro: Extra ½" to 1¼".

Worst Error
- C. **Left Side** 5.9★ R
- D. **Hotline** 5.12a★★★ Pro: To 3", including extra 1½" to 2½".
- E. **Fatal Mistake** 5.11a A1★★★ Thus far, free attempts on the first pitch have been unsuccessful. A standard ploy has been to climb **Pink Dream**, then arrange two rappels to reach the top of the first pitch. This is an indistinct point, and extra gear should be considered for these rappel/belay stations. Usually the first rappel is short, and the rope pulled; the second long and the rope fixed.

Killer Pillar Chris Falkenstein photo

Elephant Rock, West Side
Approach and **Descent**: See page 338.

A. **Pink Dream** 5.10a★★★ Pro: To 3½", including extra 2" to 3". A #11 hex is useful.
B. **Nightmare Continuation** 5.11d★ R
C. **Right Side Route** 5.10a★ Pro: To 3". Very physical.
D. **Crack of Doom** 5.10a★ Pro: To 3".
E. **Crack of Despair** 5.10a★ Pro: To 5".
F. **Hairline** 5.11b★★ Pro: To 3", including extra 1" to 2½". Approach from above via **The Killer Pillar** rappels or by downclimbing the adjacent gully. This is followed by more downclimbing and further rappelling. Alternately, an approach from below can be made that concludes by traversing out on a skinny tree limb to gain the crack.
G. **Moongerms** 5.12a★★
H. **Crack of Deliverance** 5.9
I. **Elephant's Eliminate** 5.12d

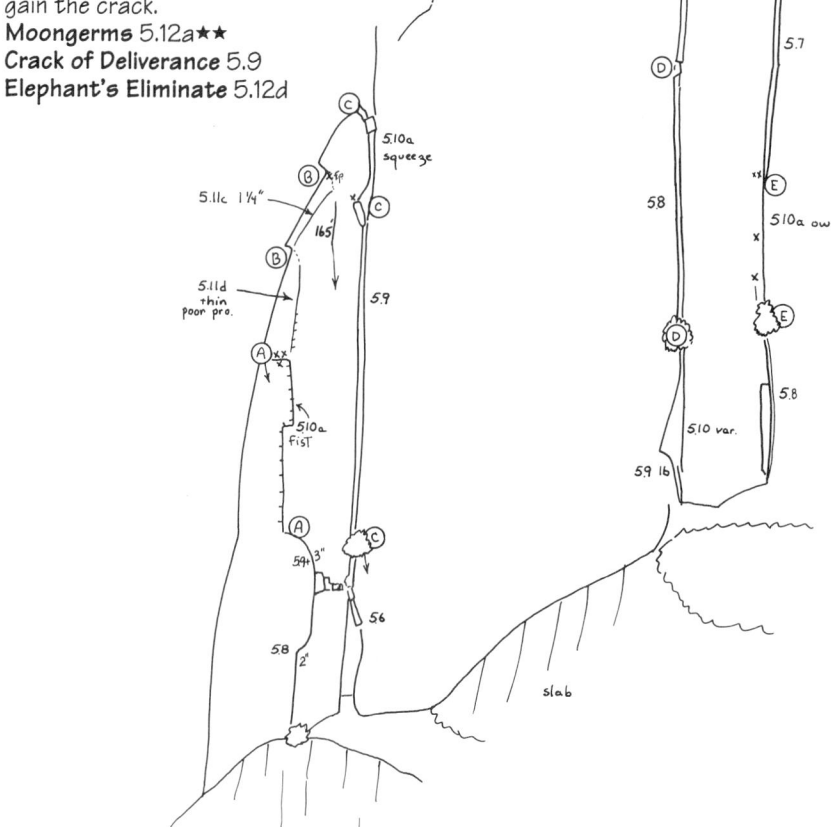

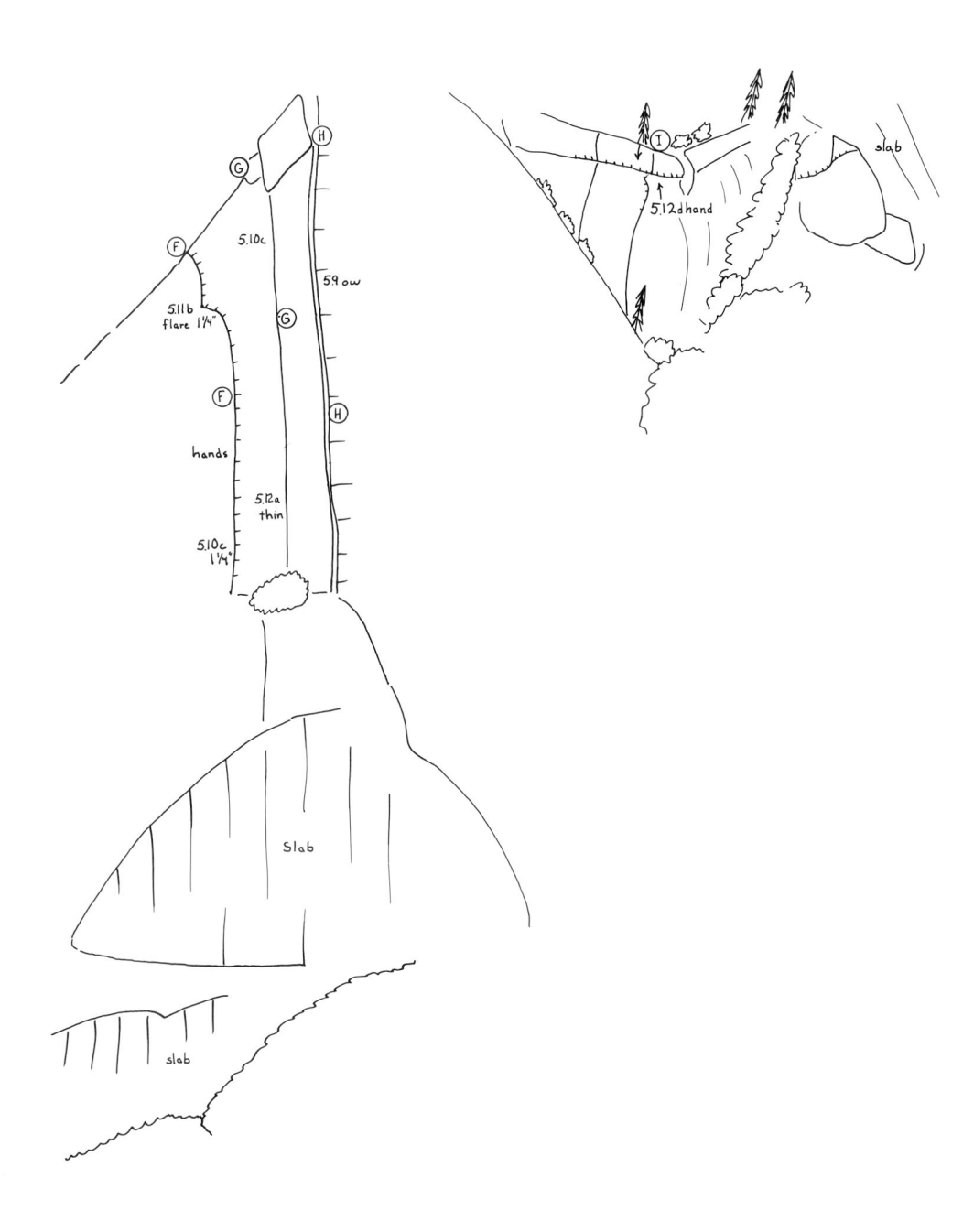

Elephant Rock Area

LOWER MERCED CANYON: SOUTH

First Ascent List

Parkline Slab and Narrow Escape
Haley Anna Ken Yager, Pat Ranstrom and Grant Hiskes,1990
Dressed To Kill Walt Shipley and Ken Yager,1990
Woody Woodpecker Don Reid and Ron Skelton, 1/85
Sawyer Crack Bruce Price and Jerry Anderson, 4/72
Eagle's Eyrie Ron Skelton and Greg Magruder, 4/25/88
Crossover Unknown
Color Me Gone Don Reid and Ron Skelton, 2/85
The Hawaiian Don Reid and Ron Skelton, 1/85
Fly By Dave Caunt and Eric Mayo, late 1980s
Too High Unknown, late 1980s
Farm Alarm Unknown, late 1980s

Parkline Pinnacle
Cool Cliff 170 Jerry Anderson, Bruce Price and John Yates, 3/70   FFA John Dill and Phil Gleason, 1973
Stonequest Ron Skelton and Mark Tuttle, late 1980s
Center Route Bill Price, John Yates and Jerry Anderson, 3/70   FFA Claude Fiddler, 1972
Aids Curve Unknown
The Chase Dave Caunt and Eric Mayo, late 1980s
Right Side Dave Huson and Clyde Deal, 3/63
The Soloist Ron Skelton, 1989
The Perpetrator Unknown
Costa Rica Tucker Tech, Steve Routhbun and John Dossi, late 1980s
Teeter Tower Jack Delk and Bill Sorenson, 2/70
A Desperate Kneed John Yablonski, Don Reid and Rick Cashner, 1981
Narrow Escape Peter Haan, Jim Bridwell and Mark Klemens, 4/71
Remember Ribbon Falls Rick Cashner and Dale Bard, 1980

U.S.G.S. Wall
Spud Launcher Dan McDevitt and Kevin Fosburg 1991
Bush League Ed Barry 1992
Polish Finger Massage Dan and Sue McDevitt 1992
Coup d'état Ken Ariza, 1988

Arch Rock Island
666 Dave Schultz and John Bachar, late 1980s
Short Circuit Stone Masters, mid-1970s

Arch Rock
Dirty Litttle Secret Greg Murphy and Bruce Morris, 3/88
Constipation Bill Price and Kurt Rieder, 1979
Anticipation Mark Chapman and Jim Donini, 1974
Supplication Barry Bates and Bev Johnson, 1971
Application Barry Bates and Peter Haan, 10/71
TKO Unknown
Punchline Unknown
Entrance Exam Chuck Pratt, Chris Fredericks, Larry Marshik and Jim Bridwell, 8/65
Blotto Henry Barber and Ajax Greene, 5/75
English Breakfast Crack Chris Fredericks and Kim Schmitz, 7/66
Midterm Chuck Pratt and Tom Frost, 8/64
Sidetrack Jim Bridwell and Dale Bard, 1974
Leanie Meanie Jim Donini, Rab Carrington and Mark Chapman, 1972
Gripper Jim Bridwell, Bruce Kumph and Mark Klemens, 8/70

─────────── First Ascent Index ───────────

Gripped Bill Price et al, 1978
Two "D" Don Reid and Tucher Tech, '87
Bachar's Ring Job John Bachar and Ron Kauk, late 191980s
New Dimensions Mark Klemens and Jim Bridwell, 5/70; **FFA** Barry Bates and Steve Wunsch, 1972
The Voyage Vern Clevenger and Ray Jardine, 5/75
Klemens Escape Mark Klemens and Jim Bridwell, 1970
Inchworm John Bachar and Rick Cashner, 1984
Grokin' Ed Barry and Chris Falkenstein, 9/86
Now Werner Braun Rick Cashner and Don Reid, 2/83
Omakara John Bachar et al, 6/83
Later Werner Braun and Doug McDonald, 2/83
GRE Elliott Robinson and Steve Annecone, 11/88
SAT Elliott Robinson and Peter Carrick, 3/88
Ultimate Emotion Elliott Robinson and Peter Carrick, 3/88
Skateaway Greg Murphy, (solo) 3/88
The Bin Greg Murphy and Bruce Morris, 3/88
Arch Rock Pinnacle Warren Harding and George Whitmore, 4/55
Per-Spire-ation Kevin Worrall, Mark Chapman, Matt Pollock and Bruce Pollock, 1974
Pass or Fail Rick Sylvester and Gib Lewis, 11/71
Cross Country Crack Chuck Pratt and Tim Kimbrough, 10/65
Kindergarten Crack John Evans and Chuck Pratt, 8/65
Quickie Quizzes Mark Klemens and Dave N. Gerughty, 1970
Nerf Test Phil Gleason and Rick Sylvester, 11/71
Extra Credit Walt Shipley and Werner Braun, 1986
Julliette's Flake, Left Chuck Pratt and Jim Bridwell, 8/65
Julliette's Flake, Right Warren Harding and Rich Calderwood, 1960
Cosmic Messenger Bob Williams et al, 1980
Goldfingers Chick Holtkamp and Eric Zschiesche, 5/80
Torque Converter Dave Anderson and Chick Holtkamp, 5/80
Stealth Technology Don Reid 2/85

Dog Dik and Finger Lickin'

Short but Thick Kevin Worrall, John Bachar and Ed Barry, 1975
Opposition John Bachar and Werner Braun, 1985
Happy Days Werner Braun, Rick Cashner and Chris Belizzi, 4/82
Pink Pussycat Don Reid and Greg Sonagere, 11/82
Fist Puppet Walt Shipley and Bill Russell, 1986
Finger Lickin' Mark Chapman and Kevin Worrall, 1973
Fun Flake Mark Chapman and Kevin Worrall, 1973
Pandora's Box Mark Chapman and Kevin Worrall, 1973
Petty Larceny Unknown
Snatch Power Bob Ashworth, Bruce Pollock and Matt Pollock, 1973
Jawbone Mark Chapman and Kevin Worrall, 1973
Pinky Paralysis John Bachar and Jim Bridwell, 1975
Health Insurance Alan Roberts and Joe Rousek, 10/88
High Profile Joe Rousek and Alan Roberts, 10/88
R and R Alan Roberts and Joe Rousek, 10/88
No Exit Joe Rousek and Alan Roberts, 10/88

Roadside Attraction

Outta Hand Dale Bard and Rick Cashner, 1982
Hand Out Rick Cashner and Don Reid, 1982
Roadside Attraction Unknown
Roadside Infraction Scott Cosgrove (TR)
Dale's Pin Job John Bachar, 12/86
Roadside Destruction Tucker Tech and Ray Olson, 1989
Van Belle O Drome Hidetaka Suzuki 1990; Peter Croft, second ascent without bolts
Van Belle Syndrome Peter Croft 1991
Back to the Future Ron Kauk, 5/86

First Ascent Index

Kat Pinnacle Area
Kat Pinnacle via Tyrolean Traverse Dewitt Allen, Torcom Bedayan and Robin Hansen, 11/40
Northwest Corner Mark Powell and Don Wilson, 12/56; 5.10 last pitch variation Chuck Pratt and Tom Gerughty, 7/65
Katchup John Long and Tony Zeek, 1972
Southwest Corner Yvon Chouinard and Tom Frost, 4/60
Compass Rick Cashner, 1981
A la Moana John Yablonski and Werner Braun, 1981

Bobcat Buttress
Cat Fight Ken Yager, Grant Hiskes and Mike Barker, 1/91
Tiger By The Tail Ken Yager, 1991
Don't Give Up the Ship Walt Shipley TR 1991
Scratching Post Ken Yager, Grant Hiskes, Jerry Anderson and Mike Barker, 1/91
Pussy Licked Jerry and Sigrid Anderson, Ken Yager, Grant Hiskes and Mike Barker, 1/91
Pussy Whipped Ken Yager, Grant Hiskes, Mike Barker and Jerry Anderson, 1/91

The Cookie Area
Mystic Mint Dan and Sue McDevitt 1992
Twinkie Ray Jardine and Chris Nelson, 1973
Nutter Butter Dan and Sue McDevitt 1992
Tennessee Strings Rob Robinson, Cade Lloyd, 12/86
Coffin Nail Charlie Porter, 1972
Hardd Henry Barber and Ron Kauk, and Steve Wunch, 5/75
Banana Dreams Vern Clevenger et al, 5/74
Crack-A-Go-Go Harvey Carter and Pete Pederson, 5/67 **FFA** Pete Livesey and Ron Fawcett, 1974
Orangutan Arch Steve Wunsch and John Bragg, 1974
Outer Limits Jim Bridwell and Jim Orey, 1971
Satanic Mechanic Dimitri Barton and Pete Takeda 1989
Elevator Shaft Jim Bridwell and Phil Bircheff, 6/65
Cookie Monster Bill Price, et al, 1979; **FFA** First pitch, Kurt Smith and Scott Cosgrove, 1987
Cookie Cutter Bill Price, et al, 1979; **FFA** Second pitch, Dave Schultz and Ed Barry 1990
Twilight Zone Chuck Pratt and Chris Fredericks, 9/65
Chips Ahoy Dan and Sue McDevitt 1991
Ginger Snaps Dan and Sue McDevitt 1992
America's Cup Kim Carrigan and Geoff Weigand, 1985
Red Zinger Ray Jardine and Dave Altman, 9/79
Meat Grinder Royal Robbins and TM Herbert, 3/68
Meat Grinder Arête Dave Schultz 1990
Beverly's Tower Gerry Czamanske and Warren Harding, 1959; **FFA** Roger Breedlove and Alan Bard, 5/73
Aftershock Tony Yaniro and Max Jones, 1981
Waverly Wafer Jim Bridwell, Barry Bates and Beverly Johnson, 10/70
Butterballs Henry Barber et al, 5/73
Wheat Thin Peter Haan and Jim Bridwell, 8/71
Butterfingers Jim Bridwell and Charley Jones, 8/71
Ladyfingers John Long and Mike Graham, 5/74
The Cookie Chuck Pratt and Dick Sykes, 8/58
The Cookie, Left Royal Robbins and Loyd Price, 2/68
The Cookie, Center Tom Kimbrough, Tom Hargis and Roman Laba, 1965
The Cookie, Right Royal Robbins and Loyd Price, 2/68
Cookie Continuation Unknown
The Big Fig Charlie Row and Bob Ramee 1979; **FFA** Dave Schultz? 1990?
Vendetta Loyd Price and Roger Gordon, 6/67; **FFA** Royal Robbins and Galen Rowell, 1968; Last pitch variation Jim Donini and Mark Chapman, 1973; Second pitch variation Urmas Franosch mid-1980s
Infraction Bob Finn and Don Reid, 1977

First Ascent Index

Anathema Barry Bates et al, 1972
The Last In Line Chris Synder and Ken Ariza, 5/88
Jardine's Hand Ray Jardine et al, 1979
The Cleft Chuck Pratt and Wally Reed, 1958; **FFA** Chuck Pratt and Chris Fredericks, 1965
Catchy Jim Pettigrew, Jim Bridwell and Mark Klemens, 10/71
Catchy Corner Jim Bridwell and Dale Bard, 1974
Pringles Dan and Sue McDevitt, 1991
Zipperhead Doug McDonald and Pete Takeda, 1989
Void Continuation Dimitri Barton and Steve Gerberding, 1984
The Void Tom Higgins et al, 1971
The Stigma Dennis Miller and Brian Birmingham, 1970; **FFA** (first pitch) Alan Watts, 1986
The Enigma
 via 5.8 finish Barry Miller and Ray Barlow, 9/64
 via 5.9 finish TM Herbert et al
Ramp of Deception Jim Bridwell et al, 1971
Abstract Corner Jim Bridwell et al, 1971
Shortcake Jim Bridwell and Dale Bard, 1971
Enema Jim Donini and John Bragg, 1974
Ray's Pin Job Kurt Smith and Dave Hatchettt, 5/85
Something for Nothing Kurt Smith and Dave Hatchettt, 5/85
Gunning For Buddha Ed Barry, Tucker Tech, 1990
Terminator, Left Don Reid, 2/85
Terminator, Right Bruce Brossman and Mike Breidenbach, early 1970s

Oreo Cliff
Animal Crackers Kurt Smith and Dave Hatchett, 1987
Original Chips Ahoy Dave Caunt and Troy Johnson, 1987
Ninja Crack Kurt Smith and Dave Hatchett, 1987
Fig Neutron Charlie Fowler, Ed Collins, Dave Hattchett, and Kurt Smith, 1987
Spuds McKenzie Dave Hatchett and Kurt Smith, 1987
What's Your Fantasy Kurt Smith, Stu Richie, and Dave Hatchett, 1987
Snap, Crackle, and Pop Dave Hatchett and Ed Collins, 1987
Capital Punishment Chuck Pratt, Bruce Price and Jerry Anderson, 1972
Corn Corner Bob Ashworth et al, 1970s
Hobknob George Meyers and Merrill Wilson, 10/86

Wildcat Falls Area
Joe's Garage Rick Cashner and Ed Barry, 1979
Gait of Power Ron Kauk and John Bachar, 1976
Tunnel Vision John Bachar et al, 6/82
Romantic Tension Jonny Woodward and Dimitri Barton, 5/85
Klingon Jonny Woodward and Dimitri Barton, 5/85
Miramonte Steve Schneider and Dimitri Barton, 10/85
Uncertain Ending Ray Jardine and John Lakey, 10/78
Obscure Destiny Ray Jardine and John Lakey, 5/77
Skunk Crack Ray Jardine and John Lakey, 5/77
Tales of Power Ron Kauk et al, 9/77
Separate Reality Ron Kauk et al, 1978
Guilloutine Ken Ariza, Frank Lucido, Peter Kern, 1988
Through Bein' Cool Rick Cashner, Dimitri Barton and Dave Neilson, 4/86
Prime Time Rick Cashner, Dimitri Barton, Dave Neilson and Grant Hiskes, 4/86

Cascade Area
Pat Pinnacle Wayne Merry and Mike Borghoff, 1958
Jack Pinnacle, Left Tom Gerughty and Dave Calfee, 6/64
Jack Pinnacle, Right Wayne Merry and Warren Harding, 1957
Domehead Bill Russell and Pat Ranstrum, 1983
Scorpion Man Bill Russell and Pat Ranstrum, 1983

First Ascent Index

Stinger Walt Shipley et al 1991
Hat Pin Walt Shipley et al 1991
Stand and Quiver Walt Shipley et al 1991
The Knife Don Reid, 2/84
Flailing Dog Cliff Howard and Larry Zulim, 1979
Gilligan's Chicken Drone Stephens and Bob Ashworth, 1973
Chicken Fever Unknown
Sherrie's Crack Kevin Worrall and George Meyers, 1976
Nurdle Bob Ashworth and George Meyers, 1973
Knob Job Kevin Worrall and George Meyers, 1973
"G" Man Steve Grossman mid-1980s
Book 'em, Dano Dimitri Barton and Dave Neilson
Knuckleheads Dan and Sue McDevitt 1991
Trough of Justice Chris Cantwell et al, 1980
People's Court Paul Crawford, Paul Teare and Scott Woolums, 4/84
Desperado Ron Skelton, Dan McDevitt and Mark Tuttle 1989
Desperate Straights Rick Sylvester and Mike Farrell, 1973
Cat's Squirrel Bill Price and Augie Klein, 1980
Cat's Squirrel Continuation Unknown
Nine Lives Bruce Morris and Dave Sessions, 10/82
Nine Lives Continuation Ron Skelton and Greg Magruder 6/88
Blackheads Jim Beyer and Bob Sullivan, 9/78
Skinheads Dan and Sue McDevitt 1991
Underclingon Ron Skelton and Dan McDevitt 3/88
The Tube Jim Bridwell, Kevin Worrall, Dale Bard and George Meyers, 1974
Guardian Angel Larry Zulim and Cliff Howard, 1979
Gay Bob's Mike Borris and Larry Zulim, 1979
Tricky Fingers Jim Beyer, 4/78
Brainbucket Dave Schultz, Kurt Smith, Mike Hatchettt and Joe Hedge, 4/86
Babble On Jim Beyer, Mike Sawyer and Bob Sullivan, 1978
Porker Party Dave Schultz, John Middendorff and Joe Hedge, 1984
Showtime Ron Skelton and Mark Tuttle, 5/89
Rocky Horror Show Ron Skelton and Mark Tuttle, 5/89
Wart Hog Grant Hiskes et al, 1984
My-Toe-Sis Ray Jardine and Chris Ball, 5/78
Eraser Flake Walt Shipley and Tucker Tech, 1/86
Sunblast Don Reid and Grant Hiskes, 12/81; **FFA** 5.13 section Dave Schultz
The Wedge Ray Jardine and John Lakey, 5/75
Psychological Warfare Walt Shipley 1991
Bolt Adventures Tucker Tech et al, 1989
Toxic Avenger Tucker Tech et al, 1989
Flary Tales Tucker Tech and Mike Laden, 1989
Maltese Falcon Mike Laden and Tucker Tech, 11/88
Eraser Head Tucker Tech, Mike Laden and Ed Barry, 12/88
White Cloud Jim Beyer and Misa Giesey, 1979
A Boy And His Knob Mike Laden and Tucker Tech, 1988
Filthy Rich Alan Bartlett and Don Reid, 6/83
Wicked Aretation Tucker Tech and Mike Laden, 1989
Golden Needles Jim Beyer and Janice Linhares, 1979
Scurv Jim Beyer and Bob Sullivan, 1979
Jug Monkey Mike Laden and Tucker Tech, 1989
Mud Shark Billy Sernick, Charleen Sernick and Jack Dodalou, 1980
Fish Crack Henry Barber et al, 1975
Free Press Galen Rowell and Sibylle Hechtel, 11/71
Crimson Cringe Ray Jardine and John Lakey, 4/76
Polished Flake Dave Bengston and Alan Roberts, late-1980s
Phoenix Ray Jardine and John Lakey, 5/77
On the Spot Ken Yager and Rick Cashner, 1990
Cascade Crack Unknown, early 1970s
Verde Bruce Pollock, Jim Bridwell and Jim Pettigrew, 1975
Flake Off Bruce Pollock, Jim Bridwell, Jim Pettigrew and Mark Klemens, 1975

False Verde Bob Finn and Don Reid, 1974
The Gerbil Launcher Tucker Tech et al, 1989
Notably Knobular Dave Harden and Dave Clay, 1/88
Just Scraping By Tucker Tech et al, 1989
On the Wedge Tucker Tech et al, 1989
Solo Crack Don Reid, 1974

This and That Cliff
Meat Puppet Dimitri Barton, mid-1980s
Weird Scenes in the Gold Mine Ken Ariza and Dave Hatchett, 1986
King Cobra Grant Hiskes and Dave Schultz, 1984
Psuedo Desperation Don Reid and Jim Howard, 5/88
Agent Orange Don Reid and Grant Hiskes, 10/84
Blame it on 800 Bill Russell, late 1980s
Gotham City Bill Price and John Long, 1980
Robin Bill Price and Tony Yaniro, 1981
Stubs Werner Braun, Dale Bard and Ed Barry, 1980
Title Fight Hidetaka Suzuki, 1988
Master Lock Ron Kauk, 1987
Tips John Bachar and Ron Kauk, 1975; **FFA** Jonny Woodward and Ron Kauk, 1985
Back in the Saddle Dimitri Barton et al, 1984
Whim Matt Donohoe and Pat Stewart, 1970
Said and Done Bob Finn, John Yablonsky, Richard Harrison and Don Reid, 1977
Grateful Pinheads Joe Hedge and Dave Hatchett, late 1980s
Slamming Left Ray Olson and Tucker Tech, 5/89
Slamming Right Ray Olson and Tucker Tech, 5/89
Stumped Ray Olson, Tucker Tech, 5/89
This and That Jim Donini and Jim Bridwell, 1972
Slap that Bitch Tucker Tech, late 1980s
Summary Judgment Ron Skelton, Brad Young and Mark Tuttle, 5/90
Humdinger John Long, Ron Fawcett and Eric Ericksson, 1979; second pitch Jonny Woodward et al; first pitch traverse variation Ron Skelton, Brad Young and Mark Tuttle, 5/90
Pink Banana Chris Cantwell, Bruce Morris, Mike Hernandez and Donald Cantwell, 1981; FFA Greg Murphy, Nathan, and Elliott Robinson, 4/87
Cramming Steve Wunsch, Matt Donohoe, George Meyers, Jim Donini and Rab Carrington, 1972
Scram Ken Yaeger, 12/90
Secret Agent Unknown early 1990s
Cleaver Unknown early 1990s

New Diversions Cliff
Falcon Chris Cantwell, Larry Zulim, Becky Plourd and Sue Moore, 1981
Rocket Man Chris Cantwell et al, 1981; **FFA** Paul Crawford and Jay Smith, 9/82
Highlander Dave Schultz, 1988
Chicken Pox Steve Wunsch and Diana Hunter, 1972
New Deviations Jack Johnson and Mike Whawski, 1992
New Diversions Rick Sylvester, Claude Wreford-Brown and Jerry Coe, 6/71
Burst of Brilliance Eric Kohl, 1990
Wasp Steve Wunsch and Rab Carrington, 1972
Strangers in the Night Jim Donini, Rab Carrington, Bev Johnson and Steve Wunsch, 1972
Electric Gully Jerry Coe and Rick Sylvester, 4/71
Radical Chic Dimitri Barton and Joe Hedge, 5/85
Chicken Pie Jerry Coe and Rick Sylvester, 4/71
Catch a Wave Scott Cosgrove et al, 1986
Jugs Henry Barber et al, 1974
Spring Chicken Murray Judge and Roger Whitehead, 8/83
Shake, Rattle and Drop Rick Sylvester, Chris Hassig and Alex Behr, 11/74
Chimney for Two Steve Shea and Jerry Coe, 4/71
Holidays Scott Cosgrove and Jenny Naquin, 1/86
Tail End George Meyers, 1975

First Ascent Index

Knob Hill and The Owl
Pot Belly Bill Griffin and Bruce Price, 4/73
Movin' To Montana The Anderson Family, 1992
Sloth Wall Steve Miller, Jerry Anderson and Elsie Anderson, 10/72
Anti-Ego Crack Steve Miller and Jerry Anderson, 10/72
Sloppy Seconds Jerry and Elsie Anderson, 9/72
Chicken Pie Jerry Anderson, 3/73
Knob Hill Rapist Chuck Pratt, Tim Auger and Jerry Anderson, 4/73
Deception Gully Chuck Pratt, Tim Auger and Jerry Anderson, 4/73
Wrong Address Tucker Tech, late 1980s
Arlington Heights Charlie Porter et al, 1972
Hampton Estates Alan Bartlett, Alan Roberts and Bill Critchlow, 9/82
Trix Ray Jardine and Chris Ballinger, 5/78
Pimper's Paradise Scott Cosgrove and Dave Griffith, 10/86
White Owl Dimitri Barton et al, 1984
Loose Tooth City Tucker Tech and Don Reid, 3/87
Block Horror Picture Show Tucker Tech and Don Reid, 3/87
Teenage Warning Don Reid and Tucker Tech, 3/87
Dromedary, The Hump Barry Bates and Bev Johnson, 1971
Dromedary Direct Barry Bates, Matt Donohoe and Herb Swedlund, 1971
Dromedary Frank Sacherer and Gordon Webster, 11/65
The Shaft Matt Donohoe and George Meyers, 1971
The Owl Bypass unknown
Stroke (My Erect Ear Tufts) Dave Altman and Rob Oraveitz, 10/86
The Owl Roof John Lakey and Ray Jardine, 5/77
Floating Lama Doug McDonald, 1987
Mirage Dale Bard and Rick Cashner, 1980
Color Purple Ken Arize and Pete Takeda, 6/88
Pygmy Sex Circus Brian Knight and Norman Boles, 5/89
Wicked Jones Crusher Dimitri Barton and Roy McClanahan, 4/86
Walrus Don Reid and Rick Cashner, 1/77
Traffic Jam Paul Cowan, early 1970s

Goldrush Area
5.8 Chimney Matt Donohoe, 1970
William's Climb The Anderson Family and Rob Kroeckel, 12/89
Mongolian Clusterfuck Jim Donini et al, 1972
Siberian Swarm Screw Jim Donini, Steve Wunsch, John Bragg, Kevin Bein and Bev Johnson, 1972
Siberian Swarm Screw Direct Start Walt Shipley and Bill Russell, 1980s
Gang Bang Paul Cowan and Ray Jardine, 1974
Handjob Jim Donini, Steve Wunsch et al, 1972
Fun 5.9 unknown
Polymorphous Perverse Bruce Morris and Dave Altman, 11/77
Shit on a Shingle Ken Ariza, Dave Hatchett and Kurt Smith
Mainliner Bruce Morris and Dave Altman, 11/77
Rest for the Wicked Bruce Morris, Stu Richie and Dimitri Barton, 10/87
Goldrush Jim Bridwell, Steve Wunsch and Jim Donini, 1972
Andy's Inferno Sheridan Anderson et al, '64

Reed's Pinnacle Area
Danger Will Robinson Brian Bennett and Bob Ost, 9/86
Anal Tongue Darts Brian Bennett and Bob Ost, 9/86
Olga's Trick Rik Rieder, Mike Breidenbach and Drone Stephens, 1972
Crazy Train Mike Hatchettt and Ken Ariza, 5/86
Isotope John Bachar, Dimitri Barton, Ron Kauk and Werner Braun, 1983
Chingango Chuck Pratt et al, 6/65
The Iota Wally Reed and Bill Henderson, 1956
The Tooth Tom Higgins and Pat Ament
Crossroads Ron Kauk, 1990

Phantom John Bachar, 10/86
Micron Eric Zschiesche
The Remnant, Left Pat Ament and Larry Dalke, 10/67; **FFA** Royal Robbins and Loyd Price, 1968
The Remnant, Center John Bachar et al, 1986
The Remnant, Right Wally Reed and Herb Swedlund, 1960
Reed's Pinnacle, Left Frank Sacherer, Wally Reed and Gary Colliver, 11/62; **FFA** Frank Sacherer, Dick Erb and Larry Marshik, 1964
Goosebumps Mark Tuttle and Ron Skelton, 4/89
Reed's Pinnacle, Direct (last pitch) Frank Sacherer, Mark Powell, Wally Reed, Gary Colliver and Andy Lichtman, 5/64; (2nd pitch) Frank Sacherer, Wally Reed and Chris Fredericks, 6/64; (all pitches) Royal Robbins, Gordon Webster and Terry Burnell, 10/66
Reed's Pinnacle, Blazing Buckets John Middendorf, 1986
Reed's Pinnacle, Regular Route Wally Reed and Herb Swedlund, 1957
Survival Sampler Alfred Randall and Bryan Burdo, mid-1980s
Bong's Away, Left Jim Bridwell, 1970
Bong's Away, Center Barry Bates and Mark Klemens, 1970
Bong's Away, Right unknown
Magical Mystery Tour Charlie Porter and Dave Altman, 1975
Duck and Cover Dave Schultz and Jim Cambell, 1987
Old Five Ten Pat Ament and Tom Higgins, 1975
Midnight Rampest John Middendorf and Tucker Tech mid-1980s
Lunatic Fringe Barry Bates and Bev Johnson, 1971
Beyond the Fringe Dan Nguyen and Clint Cummins, 11/87
Flatus Chuck Pratt and Tom Bauman, 5/68
The Rorp Wally Reed and Frank Sacherer, 7/63
Tooth or Consequences Charles Cole and Lidija Painkiher, 5/86
Stone Groove Jim Bridwell and Galen Rowell, 5/71
Independence Pinnacle, Independent Route Jim Bridwell and Mark Klemens, 8/70
Independence Pinnacle, Center Dave Hampton, Barry Bates and Matt Donohoe, 7/70
Independence Pinnacle, Steppin' Out Mark Klemens and Jim Bridwell, 1971
The Gray Bullet Don Reid and Dennis Oakeshott, 10/82
Rocket in My Pocket Jim Elias, Bruce Morris and Kevin Lollard, 10/83
Center Direct Mark Chapman, Kevin Worrall, Ron Kauk and Ed Barry, 1987
Cosmic Ray Ray Jardine and Rick Cashner, 5/79
Ejesta Charlie Porter, Bob Ashworth and Jeff Stubbs, 1/74
Porter's Pout Charlie Porter and Bruce Pollock, 1974
Sylvester's Meow Rick Sylvester and Sue Odom, 12/86
Fasten Your Seat Belts John Bachar and Rick Cashner, mid-1980s
Free Ride John Bachar and Rick Cashner, mid-1980s
Magic Carpet Ron Skelton and Rick Cashner, 5/88
Cro Magnon Capers Kevin Worrall, Werner Braun and Rick Cashner, 1979
Nothing Good Ever Lasts Joe Hedge, 1986
Spring Fever Don Reid and Rick Cashner, 4/83
Headhunter John Bachar and Rick Cashner, mid-1980s
Fireside Chat Walt Shipley and John Middendorf, 12/85

Five and Dime Cliff

Bijou Heather Baer and Jeff Schoen, 1992
Chump Change Doug McDonald, 1985
Keystone Corner Don Reid and Jay Fiske, 10/75
Copper Penny Charlie Porter et al, 1973
Five and Dime Barry Bates et al, 1971
Whack and Dangle Ajax Greene and Don Peterson, 4/76
Penny Ante unknown
Ride the Lightning John Collins, Ed Collins and Craig Delbrook, 8/88
The Anti-Christ Ed Collins and Craig Delbrook, 1990
The Reception Mike Breidenbach and Mike Farrell, 1974
Inner Reaches Chuck Pratt, Tim Auger and Jerry Anderson, 4/73
Crack n' Face Ed Barry et al, mid-1980s

First Ascent Index

Fantasy Island
Jupiter unknown
Fantasy Island Dave Shultz, 1990

Mojo Tooth
Sub Atomic unknown, early 1990s
Fluke unknown
Tongue and Groove Andreas Maurer, 1975
Scratch and Sniff Jonny Woodward (on-sight solo), 5/88
Mojo Tooth Peter Haan and Darwin Alonso, 10/70
New Traditionalist Peter Chesko, Rick Cashner and Werner Braun, 4/82
Yankee Clipper Ken Yager, 5/90
Cereal Killer Tucker Tech and Don Reid, 3/89
Figment Mike Breidenbach and Bruce Hawkins, 1975
Grape Nuts Mike Breidenbach and Bruce Hawkins, 1975
Euellogy Bruce Hawkins, Mike Breidenbach and Bruce Brossman, 1975
Mighty Crunchy Andreas Maurer, 1975
Bad News Bombers Steve Annecone and Tom Hayes, 4/85
Deception Pete Takeda, Kevin Fosberg and Tucker Tech, 1989
Jomo Pete Takeda, Kevin Fosberg and Tucker Tech, 1989
Natural End Will Gilmer and Jay Anderson, 10/83
Golden Shower Pete Takeda, Kevin Fosberg and Tucker Tech, 1989
Yellow Peril Pete Takeda, Kevin Fosberg and Tucker Tech, 1989
Motor Drive Kevin Fosberg, Pete Takeda and Tucker Tech, 1989
Vibrator Pete Takeda and Tucker Tech, 1989
Yuk Tucker Tech et. al., 1989
Rehab Doll Tucker Tech et. al., 1989
Skid Roper Tucker Tech et. al., 1989
Tooth Fairy Tucker Tech et. al., 1989
Old 5.11 Kevin Fosberg, 1989
Hey Walt Walt Shipley, 1985
Highway Star Chris Falkenstein, Don Reid and Edd Kuropat, 1/75

Last Resort Cliff
Turning Point Rick Cashner and Don Reid, 9/77
Side Kick Chris Falkenstein, Don Reid and TM Herbert, 11/75
Tiger's Paw Don Reid and Rick Cashner, 1978
Plumkin Rik Reider and Doug Scott, 1972
Moon Age Daydream Don Reid and Rick Cashner, 1978
The Steal Rick Cashner and Angie Morales, 1978
Sex, Drugs and Violence Don Reid and Rick Cashner, 11/77
P.M.S. Tucker Tech and Mike Sciacca, 1985
B and B Rick Cashner, Ray Jardine and Frank Brown, 10/78
No Falls Wall Chris Cantwell and Mike Borelli, 1980
Black Sunday Chris Cantwell and Bruce Morris, 1980
Shattered Rick Cashner, Ray Jardine and Frank Brown, 1979
Ready or Not Rick Cashner and Ray Jardine, 5/79
Slumgullion Jim Bridwell, Kevin Worrall and Marco Milano, 1978
Neutron Escape Ray Jardine and Rick Cashner, 1979
Radioactive Rick Cashner and Ray Jardine, 1979
Atomic Finger Crack Ray Jardine and Rick Cashner, 5/79

Audubon Buttress to Little Wing
Wild Turkey Dale Bard and Ron Kauk, 1974
The Dove Kevin Worrall and Jane Witucki, 1975
Birds of a Feather Kevin Worrall and Jane Witucki, 1975
Eagle Feather John Long, Jim Bridwell and Kevin Worrall, 1974
Duncan Imperial Kevin Worrall, Werner Braun and Ed Barry, 1977
Catch-U Steve Wunsch and John Bragg, 1974
W'allnuts Steve Wunsch and Jim Donini, 1973

First Ascent Index

Scuz Ball Don Reid, 2/85
Squeeze-n' Tease Rick Cashner and Angie Morales, 9/77
L.D. Getaway Rick Cashner and Angie Morales, 9/77
Andy DeVine Rick Cashner and Angie Morales, 9/77
Machine Gun Scott Cosgrove, 1988
He Can't Shout, Don't Hear You Bob Ashworth and Jeff Stubbs, 4/74
Kryptonite Dave Schultz, 1990
Gunks Revisited Ron Kauk and Kim Carrigan, 1980
Honor Thy Father Ajax Greene and Matt Cox, 4/76
Leisure Time George Meyers, Bob Ashworth and Mike Breidenbach, 4/76
The Riddler Bruce Pollock, Matt Pollock, Mark Chapman and Charlie Porter, 1/74
Little Wing Mark Chapman, Charlie Porter and Bruce Pollock, 1/74
Dolly Dagger Alan Bartlett, 1984
Building Blocks Alan Bartlett and Bill Frey, 1984
Crash Landing Dave Schultz et al, mid-1980s
Angelina Rick Cashner and Angie Morales, 9/77
Little Thing Tony Yaniro and Alan Nelson, 1981
Red House unknown
Too Much Paranoias Rick Cashner and Don Reid, 3/82

Ribbon Falls Area

The Slabs Wolfgang Heinritz, Andrzej Ehrenfaucht and Les Wilson, 5/63
West Buttress Frank Sacherer and Bob Kamps, 6/62
Golden Bough Roger Breedlove and Ed Drummond, 6/79
Gold Wall Layton Kor and Tom Fender, 5/65
Silent Line Rick Cashner and Werner Braun, 4/82
Fool's Gold Don Reid and Rick Cashner, 8/83
Thin Line Werner Braun and Scott Cosgrove, 10/86
West Portal Chris Fredericks and Steve Roper, 9/63
Straight In Werner Braun and Rick Cashner, 9/81
Ribbon Candy FFA Jonny Woodward and Scott Cosgrove, 5/88
Chockstone Chimney Les Wilson, Wolfgang Heinritz, Andrzej Ehrenfeucht and Leif Patterson, 12/62 **FFA** Ray Jardine and Mark Moore, 5/76
The Lionheart Ray Jardine and Mark Moore, 5/76
Gold Leaf Tucker Tech and John Harpole, 4/87
Nottingham Ray Jardine and Mark Moore, 5/76
The Hourglass, Left Bob Kamps and Joe McKeown, 7/62 **FFA** Peter Haan, Rick Linkert and Mike Farrell, 9/71
The Hourglass, Right Bob Kamps and Frank Sacherer, 7/62 **FFA** Sacherer and Tom Gerughty, 8/64
The Rappel Chimney Wolfgang Heinritz, Les Wilson, Leif Patterson and Andrzej Ehrenfeucht, 4/63
Hidden Chimney Les Wilson, Wolfgang Heinritz and Andrzej Ehrenfeucht, 7/63

El Capitan

El Capitan Gully J.L. Staats, 6/05 Staats' climbing partner, Charles Bailey, was killed in a fall near the top.
K-P Pinnacle Ted Knoll and Jack Piontaki, 5/41 **FFA** Mark Powell, Larry Hawley, Bryan Milton and Merle Alley, 1955
Salami Ledge Route Les Wilson and Wolfgang Heinritz, 1965 **FFA** Tucker Tech et al, late-1980s
El Capitan, West Chimney Ethel Mae Hill, Owen Williams and Gordon Patten, 10/37 **FFA** Galen Rowell and Tom Fender, 1966
West Face TM Herbert and Royal Robbins, 6/67 **FFA** Ray Jardine and Bill Price, 5/79
J.M. Barrie Dick Dorworth and Rick Sylvester, 5/68
Phyllis(Variation) Michael Forkash and Peter Lehrach, 6/81
Peter Pan Bob Kamps and Jim Sims, 7/62
Cuthulu Eric Weinstein and Dave Anderson, 10/75
Indubious Battle Ray Jardine and Kris Walker, 5/75
Peter Left Mead Hargis and Kim Schmitz, 1971
Tinkerbell, Left Bruce Kumph and Joe Cote, 10/69

First Ascent Index

Tinkerbell, Right Jim Bridwell and Kim Schmitz, 1971
Lost Boys Dave Bircheff and Roger Breedlove, 1975
Wendy Frank Sacherer and Bob Kamps, 7/62 **FFA** Kim Schmitz and Marty Martin, 6/70
Smee's Come-on Dave Bircheff and Roger Breedlove, 1976
Captain Hook, Left unknown
Captain Hook, Right Glen Denny, Eric Beck and Dave Cook, 3/63 **FFA** Tom Gerughty and Chris Fredericks, 1965
Captain Crunch Tony Yaniro and Paul Vance, 1977
Delectable Pinnacle, Left Jim Baldwin, 5/62
Delectable Pinnacle, Center Art Gran and Eric Beck, 5/62 **FFA** Dale Bard mid-1970s?
Cosmic Charley Brian Knight, Graig Delbrook, and Ken Ariza late-1980s
Meteorite, Ken Ariza et al, late-1980s
Delectable Pinnacle, Right Warren Harding and Brian Small, 5/62
La Escuela Yvon Chouinard and TM Herbert, 5/62 **FFA** Steve Wunsch and Mark Chapman, 1973
La Escuela, Direct Eric Beck and Steve Williams, 10/69
The Slack, Left Chuck Pratt and Royal Robbins, 5/65
The Slack, Center Charlie Raymond and Wally Reed, 8/58 **FFA** Pat Ament and Larry Dalke, 1967
Sacherer Cracker Frank Sacherer and Mike Sherrick, 1964
The Mark of Art Mark Chapman and Art Higbee, 1974
Short but Thin Tobin Sorenson and John Bachar, 5/74
Fifteen Seconds of Fame, FA Unknown-**FFA** Clint Cummins, 5/88
La Cosita, Left Bob Kamps, Galen Rowell, Dan Doody and Wally Upton, 6/62
Sparkling Give-away Pete Takeda and Eric Kohl, 12/91
LaArista Chris Craig and Mike Creel, 2/88
La Cosita, Right TM Herbert and Steve Roper, 5/63
Little John, Left Dan Doody, Bob Kamps, Galen Rowell and Wally Upton, 8/62
Hardly Pinnacle Dale Bard et al, 1972 (Section above pinnacle Michael Forkash and John Tuttle, 9/85)
Little John, Center Tom Frost and Harry Daley, 1961
Moonchild Dave and Mike Hattchet, 1987
Little John, Right Jack Turner and Royal Robbins, 4/62
Sunday Driver Ken Ariza, Mark Carpenter and Dimiti Barton, mid-1980s
Moby Dick, Left Bob Kamps and Frank Sacherer, 10/63
Moby Dick, Center Herb Swedlund and Penny Carr, 5/63 **FFA** Frank Sacherer and Steve Roper, 5/63
Masquerade Charles Cole and Rusty Reno, 10/88
Moby Dick, Ahab Frank Sacherer and Jim Bridwell, 9/64
Reed's Leads Wally Reed and Mike Borghoff, 1963
Seedy Leads FA-Mark Chapman and Rick Sylvester, 8/71. FFA-Clint Cummins and Dan Nguyen, 3/88 . Variation, Clint Cummins and Dan Nguyen, 10/88
Thread of Life Clint Cummins and Dan Nguyen, 10/88
Dust in the Wind Joel Ager and Clint Cummins, 11/89
Salathe Wall Royal Robbins, Chuck Pratt and Tom Frost, 9/61 Free Blast (free to Mammoth Ledges) Jim Bridwell, John Long, Kevin Worrall, Mike Graham, John Bachar and Ron Kauk, 5/75. **FFA**, Todd Skinner and Paul Piana, 1988
Pterodactyl Terrace, Left Jim Sims and Steve Roper, 4/63
Pterodactyl Terrace, Right Glen Denny and Eric Beck, 4/63 **FFA** Vern Clevenger et al, 1975
Pine Line Jeff and Greg Schaffer, 7/66
Nose Route Warren Harding, Wayne Merry and George Whitmore, 11/58 (free variations to Camp IV) Ray Jardine et al, 1980. **FFA**, Lynn Hill 9/93
Duty Now For the Future Kurt Smith, 1987
General Dynamics Kurt Smith and Dave Hattchet, 1987
Base Hits Kurt Smith, Charlie Fowler, Stu Richie, and Ken Ariza, 1987
Negative Pinnacle, Left Gary Colliver, 1964
Negative Pinnacle, Center Jim Beyer, 1978
Party Mix Dave Caunt, Charlie Fowler, Troy Johnson, and Kurt Smith, 1987
Negative Pinnacle, The High Arc Tom Cochrane, 1964 **FFA** Peter Mayfield and Augie Klein, 1981

First Ascent Index

Rock Neurotic Dave Caunt, Rob Settlemeyer, and John Barbella, 3/86
Armageddon Dave Yerian, Greg Sonagere, Craig Connel, Dave Rubine and Ray Olson, 1978. **FFA** Dimitri Barton, 1978
Lunar Landscape Ron Skelton and Greg Magruder, 1990
Say Mama, Say Daddy John Middendorf and Scott Cosgrove, 5/84
Simulkrime John Middendorf and Tucker Tech, mid-1980s
Blazo John Middendorf, mid-1980s
Gollum, Left Peter Haan, Rick Linkert and David Moss, 3/72
Gollum, Right Joe Kelsey, Roman Laba and John Hudson, 9/67
Dock of the Bay Bill Price and Larry Zulim, 1981
The Footstool, Left Clyde Deal and Steve Roper, 1/63
The Promise John Bachar and Dimitri Barton, 1983
The Believer John Bachar et al, 1984
The Bluffer Eric Kohl and Cade Loyd, 1992
The Footstool, Right Mark Powell, Beverly Powell and Bill Feuerer, 1959
Life Worth Living Scott Cosgrove and Ken Ariza, 1985
El Cap Tree Direct Glen Denny and Frank Sacherer, 12/61
El Cap Tree, Regular Route Al Steck, Will Siri, Bill Dunmire and Bob Swift, 3/52
Blank Out Eric Zschiesche and Peter Croft, 1984
Champagne on Ice Steve Schneider, Dave Caunt, 1982. (second pitch) Steve Schneider and Rob Oraveitz, 10/85
Submen Steve Schneider, Rob Oraveitz and John Middendorf, 10/85
El Matador Dimitri Bevc and Steve Schneider, 10/85
Snake Knez Fran;abcek and Walace, 5/83
East Buttress Allen Steck, Will Siri, Willi Unsoeld and Bill Long, 6/53 **FFA** Frank Sacherer and Wally Reed, 8/64
End of the World Werner Braun and Don Reid, 1/83
Eura Mura Knez Fran;abcek, Lidija Painkiher and Igor Skamprle, 5/83
El Capitan, East Ledge Traverse Allen Steck, Bill Dunmire and Jim Wilson, 9/54
El Capitan, East Ledges, West Side Henry Kendall and Bill Pope, 3/61
El Capitan, East Ledges, East Side Henry Kendall and Gerry Czamanske, 12/58
Schultz's Ridge John Shonle and Steve Roper, 10/59
The White Zone Chris Cantwell and Mark Grant, 1980
Annette Funicello Chris Cantwell and Mark Grant, 1980
Gidget Goes to Yosemite Ron White and Bert Levy, 10/88
Bikini Beach Party Chris Cantwell and Mark Grant, 1980
Demon's Delight Ed Barry and Dave Hitchcock, 9/78
Supertoe Chris Cantwell and Larry Zulim, 5/82
Superstem Unknown, 1992
Rectum Ranch Brian Bennett et al, 6/90
Brown Sugar John Bragg and Peter Barton, 10/72
Free Bong Larry Zulim and Chris Cantwell, 5/82
Deucey's Elbow Walt Shipley and Tucker Tech, 10/89
Deucey's Nose Walt Shipley and Tucker Tech, 10/89
Ain't That a Bitch Dale Bard and Ed Barry, 1976
Abazaba Charlie Porter and Walter Rosenthal, 1972 (**FFA** first pitches) Scott Cosgrove and Walt Shipley, 4/86
End Game Walt Shipley, Tucker Tech and Scott Cosgrove
Creamatorium Mark Blanchard, Simon King, and ConradVan Bruggen 3/76
Moratorium Bruce Price, Bill Griffin and Bob Edwards, 11/69 **FFA** Pete Livesey and Trevor Jones, 8/75
Burden of Dreams Dave Rubine and Tom Davis, 1990

Loggerhead Buttress

Orange Juice Avenue Chris Falkenstein and Don Reid, 12/75
Chester the Molester Tucker Tech et al, 1989
Yeast Infection Tucker Tech et al, 1989
Sink Like a Stone Jeff Schoen, 1993
Lycra Virgin Ron Kauk, 5/86
Material Girl Jeff Schoen, 1993
Goodhead Jeff Schoen, 1993

First Ascent Index

Hammerhead Tucker Tech and Ray Olsen, 1989
Lagerhead Tucker Tech and Ray Olsen, 1989
Head Banger Tucker Tech and Ray Olsen, 1989
Loggerhead Ledge Route 5.7 Unknown
Log Jam Tucker Tech et al, 1989
Simian Sex Tucker Tech and ray Olson, 4/90
Dick Wrenching Classic Tucker Tech et al, 1989
Monkey Hang Tucker Tech et al, 1989
Conquest of the Stud Monkey Don Reid and Jim Howard, 5/89
Edge-u-cator Tucker Tech and Ray Olsen, 1989
Sorry Poopsie Don and Susan Reid 6/89
Teenage Mutant Blowjobs Ray Olson and Tucker Tech, 5/90
Agricultural Manuvers in the Dark Tucker Tech et al, 1989
Cherry Picker Tucker Tech et al, 1989
Deflowered Tucker Tech et al, 1989
Le Nocturne Brian Bennett and Michael Forkash, 1985
D.U.I. Tucker Tech et al, 1989
Drunk Tank Tucker Tech et al, 1989
Swillar Pillar Tucker Tech et al, 1989
Sober Up Tucker Tech et al, 1989
Mr. Happy Unknown
Happy's Favorite Tucker Tech et al, 1989
Sow Sow Sow Tucker Tech et al, 1989
Brown Eyed Girl Tucker Tech et al, 1989
Stay Lady Stay Back Tucker Tech et al, 1989
Here on the Inside Urmas Franosch and Bruce Morris, 1983
Chow Chow Chow Dave Yerian and Bruce Morris, 1982

El Capitan: East Ledges Area

The Silent Freeway Brian Knight and Linus Platt, 10/88
Slab Happy Pinnacle, Left Royal Robbins and Jack Turner, 5/62 **FFA** Mark Chapman and Art Higbee, 2/74
Slab Happy Pinnacle, Center Royal Robbins, Tom Frost and Harry Daley, 5/61 **FFA** Vern Clevenger, George Meyers and Tom Carter, 1974
The Happy Ending Kevin Fosburg and Jordy Morgan, 10/88
Slab Happy Pinnacle, The Dihardral Tom Frost and Royal Robbins, 5/61 **FFA** Frank Sacherer and Tom Gerughty, 8/64
Never Say Dog, Jonny Woodward and John Sherman, 5/88
The Big Juan, Jonny Woodward and Derrell Hensel, 9/88
Golden Years Tom Davis, Kelly Rich, Dave Rubine, and Jeff Gorris, 5/92

Manure Pile Area

Chairman Ted Scraps the Time Machine Greg Murphy and Melanie Findling, 3/87
God's Creation Chris Cantwell and Eric Zichi, 4/81
Jump for Joy Yvon Chouinard and Joy Herron, 1967
Beer Pressure Walt Shipley, 1987
After Six Yvon Chouinard and Ruth Schnieder, 6/65
After Seven unknown
Just Do-Do It Unknown
C.S. Concerto Yvon Chouinard, Chuck Pratt and Mort Hempel, 1967
Fecophilia Yvon Chouinard et al, 1972
Easy Wind Kevin Worrall and Bill Westbay, 1975
The Mouse King George Meyers et al, 1976
Nutcracker Royal and Liz Robbins, 5/67
Renus Wrinkle Eric Mayo, Brian Bennett, and Bob Ost, 9/88
The Gardener Did It Chris Cantwell and Mike Borelli, 4/81
Dynamic Doubles Dan and Sue McDevitt, 1991
Flexible Flyer Tucker Tech, 11/89
After Five TM Herbert et al, 1968
The Illusion Tom Higgins, Galen Rowell, Loyd Price and John Kanepej, 11/71
Commissioner Buttress Galen Rowell and Joe Faint, 3/69

First Ascent Index

True Grit Dave Altman and Will Crljenko, 5/74
Essence Werner Braun and Don Reid, 1/83
Split Pinnacle, Regular Jack Reigelhuth, Raffi Bedayan, Dick Leonard and Muir Dawson, 5/38
Split Pinnacle, East Arete Chuck Pratt and Krehe Ritter, 9/58

Lower Brother

Lower Brother, West Face, North Corner H.B. Blanks, Boynton Kaiser and Elliot Sawyer, 10/34
Lower Brother, West Face, Middle Don Goodrich and Gary Lundberg, 4/52
Lower Brother, Southwest Arete David Brower and Morgan Harris, 6/37
Maple Jam Chris Falkenstein and Dennis Miller, 1973
Absolutely Sweet Marie, Dave Caunt and Rob Settlemeyer, 1991
Nutty Buddy Brian Birmingham and Dave Bircheff, 3/72
Positively 4th Street Dennis Miller, Jeff Mathis and Chris Falkenstein, 3/73
Fuddy Duddy Bruce Brossman and Gene Foley, 5/75
Plant Your Fingers Unknown
My Left Foot Ron Skelton and Brad Young, 3/91
Absolutely Free, Left Jim Bridwell, Bev Johnson and Mark Klemens, 9/70
Absolutely Free, Center Sheldon Smith, Mark Klemens and Rick Sylvester, 8/70
Absolute Vodka Tucker Tech et al, late-1980s
Absolutely Free, Right Mark Klemens and Jim Bridwell, 5/70
Vantage Point Don Reid and Werner Braun, 1/84
Lower Brother, Michael's Ledge Charles Michael, in the 1920's
Ramblin' Rose Kevin Worrall and Mark Chapman, 1975
Hawkman's Escape John Dill and Phil Gleason, 1972 (last pitch variation) Peter Haan and Ed Drummond

Middle Brother

Middle Brother, Southwest Arete, Left Nick Clinch, Dave Harrah, Sherman Lehman and John Mowat, 5/50
Middle Brother, Southwest Arete, Right David Brower and Morgan Harris, 5/41
Middle Brother, from Michael's Ledge John Salathe, Anton Nelson, Dave Hammack and Rob Hahn, 6/51
Betsy Pinnacle Betsy Nelson and Rick Sylvester, 8/70
Lower Brother, Southeast Face Wally Reed and Charlie Raymond, 8/58
Koko Ledge, Left Bill Amborn and Bob Klose, 1961 **FFA** Kevin Bein, 1968
Koko Ledge, Center unknown **FFA** Pete Livesey et al, 1975
Koko Ledge, Right Glen Denny and Jim Posten, 7/61 **FFA** unknown
Koko Ledge, Far Right Barry Bates and Sergio Roch, 1970
Koko Continuation Glen Denny and Frank Sacherer, 8/62
Limbo Ledge Jim Baldwin and Steve Roper, 10/62 **FFA** Pete Livesey et al, 1975
Watermelon Rind John Svenson, Sharon Young, Kent Stokes and Bob Schneider, 9/71
Merry Old Ledge Warren Harding and Gerry Czamanske, 4/59
Midwall Tom Fender and Kim Schmitz, 4/66
Licenced to Fly Jim Elias and Bruce Morris, 11/84
Skunk Weed Scott Burke and Dave Caunt, 1981
Roachweed Bruce Morris and Jim Elias, 10/83
Rixon's Pinnacle, Far West Royal Robbins and Dick McCracken, 6/63
Rixon's Pinnacle, West Face Tom Frost Bill Feuerer, 1959 **FFA** Pat Ament et al, 1971
Rixon's Pinnacle, Direct South Face Glen Denny and Gary Colliver, 3/63
Rixon's Pinnacle, South Face Chuck and Ellen Wilts, 1948 **FFA** Tobin Sorenson and John Bachar, 1974
Rixon's Pinnacle, East Chimney Don Goodrich and Dick McCracken, 1956 **FFA** Royal Robbins and Dave Rearick, 1960 **Final Decision** Anders Lundahl and Eva Selim, 1981 **Klemens Variation** Mark Klemens, 1970
The Plume Don Reid and Chuck Goldmann, 1/79
The Folly, Left Layton Kor and Jim Bridwell, 9/64
Disconnected Chris Cantwell and Eric Zichi, 5/81
Frosted Flakes Eric Kohl, 1986
Childhood's End Ray Jardine and John Lakey, 4/76

First Ascent Index

Follying Walt Shipley, 5/86
Follywood Dave Bengston and Alan Roberts, 1988
The Folly, Wild Thing Ray Jardine and Ian Wade, 4/73 **FFA** Lou Dawson and Don Peterson, 1973
Pink Torpedo John Sherman and Todd Skinner, 1985
Yellow Submarine unknown
The Folly, Right Side Warren Harding and Tom Fender, 1965 **FFA** Dale Bard, Jim Bridwell, Kevin Worrall and Ron Kauk, 1973
Preface John Bachar and Tobin Sorenson, 1975

Camp 4 Wall Area
Chicken's Choice Sigrid and Jerry Anderson, 1/86
Young and the Restless Werner Braun, Rick Cashner, Grant Hiskes, Scott Cole and Dimitri Barton, 4/82
Cost of Living Rick Cashner and Don Reid, 4/79
Space Doubt Alan Nelson and Y. Matsumoto, 1980
Santa Barbara Brian Knight and Rondo Powell, 10/92
General Hospital Rik Rieder, Phil Gleason and Chris Wegener, 1972
Chopper Mead Hargis and Rick Sylvester, 1971
No Love-Chump Sucker Cade Loyd, Jordy Morgana and Ray Munoz, 1/89
Days of Our Lives Walt Shipley et al, mid-1980s
Sample the Dod Cade Loyd, Ray Munoz, and Pete Takeda, 1/89
Edge of Night Chris Fredericks, Rich Doleman and Jim Bridwell, 10/67
Secret Storm Peter Haan and Roger Breedlove, 1971
Out on a Limb Eric Kohl et al, 191980s
Tweedle Dee Frank Sacherer and Jim Baldwin, 6/63
Doggie Do Chris Fredericks
Doggie Diversions Joe Faint and Yvon Chouinard, 6/67
Doggie Deviations Kim Schmitz and Jim Bridwell, 1968
Bottom Line Bill Price and Dimitri Barton, 1983
Rock Bottom Kevin Worrall and George Meyers, 5/74 **FFA** John Long et al, 1980
The Buttocks Kim Schmitz and Don Peterson, 1969
Cheek Jim Bridwell et al, 1972
Christina Mead Hargis and Dave Davis, 1971 **FFA** John Long et al
Henley Quits Mark Klemens and Rick Sylvester, 7/70
Cid's Embrace Rick Sylvester and Mark Klemens, 7/70
Lancelot Rick Sylvester and Mark Klemens, 1970
Camp 4 Tree Mort Hempel and Bob Kamps, 1960 **FFA** (Dynamo Hum) Tobin Sorenson and John Long, 8/75
Eagle Peak, Southeast Face Jon Linberg and Ron Hayes, 6/52
Gillette Pete Livesey and Ron Fawcett, 8/74
Mudflaps Tucker Tech and Troy Johnson, late-1980s
Fallout Jim Donini and Steve Wunsch, 10/72
Jolly Green Giant John Bragg and Rab Carrington, 10/72
Apple Seeds Bob Sullivan and Jim Beyer, 10/78
Sunday Tree Leigh Ortenburger and Bill Briggs, 10/58
Montgomery Cliff Eric Kohl and Cade Loyd, 1992

Upper Yosemite Falls Area
The Right Profile Eric Kohl and Kevin Fosburg, 1991
Stay Free Dave Schultz and Walt Shipley, 6/86
Teenage Abortion Tucker Tech et al, late 1980s
The Girl Next Door, Left John Bragg and Bev Johnson, 6/72
The Girl Next Door, Right John Bragg, Bob Harding and Al Rubin, 6/72
Joe Palmer Michael Forkash and Andy Burnham, 10/86
Trailside Slasher Tucker Tech et al, late-1980s
Israeli Bomber Walt Shipley and Phil Chapman, 1986
Trailside Bandit Tucker Tech et al, late-1980s
Happy Trails Tucker Tech et al, 9/89
Pit Stop Phil Chapman and Walt Shipley, 1986
Psychopath Charlie Porter, 1972

Roger Stokes Route Marshall Ravenscroft and Tim Kemple, 8/82
RF Greg Schaffer and Rob Foster, 8/66
Avalon John Tuttle, Brian Bennet and Michael Forkash, 1986
T.D.'s Dihedral Tim Kemple and Marshall Ravenscroft, 2/82
Wild Thing Tim Kemple and Marshall Ravenscroft, 8/82
Galloping Consumption Chuck Pratt anf Steve Roper, 10/70. **FFA**-Don Reid and Alan Roberts, 4/87
Seaside Kevin Worrall and Mike Breidenbach, 1973
Diversions Marshall Ravenscroft and Tim Kemple, 4/82
Smoky Pillar Jim Bridwell, George Meyers, Vern Clevenger and Larry Bruce, 1973
Colonel unknown
Dumbo Go Home John Middendorf and Tucker Tech, 1985
Chain Reaction Rik Rieder, Mark Chapman, Ed Barry and Rab Carrington, 9/72
The Peanut Tom Higgins and Gary Colliver, 6/67
No Teats Susan Lilly and Tucker Tech, 10/86
Taboo Treat Don Reid and Bob Bartlett, 7/76
Forbidden Pinnacle Mark Klemens and Bruce Pollock, 5/72
Forbidden Pinnacle Continuation Kevin Fosgurg et al, late-1980s
Mindahoonee Wall Warren Harding, Mike Corbett,and Bill Surnick, late-1970s. **FFA**-Walt Shipley and Kevin Fosburg, early-1990s

Upper Yosemite Falls, West

Aquamist Nathan King, 1965
Via Aqua Dave Rearick, Herb Swedlund and Glen Denny, 4/60 **FFA** Dick McCracken and Steve Roper, 1960
Puke Ledge Ron Cagle and Jerry Anderson, 1970
Spray Fest Walt Shipley Eric Kohl, early-1990s
Slut Wagon Eric Kohl, 11/89
Brush Off Ed Barry and Mark Chapman, 1972
Razor Train Eric Kohl and Walt Shipley, 11/89
Hole Train Eric Kohl and Walt Shipley, 11/89
Taste Buds Eric Kohl and Walt Shipley,1189
Shift City Eric Kohl, 1990
White Rain Eric Kohl, 1990
Peril Drops Eric Kohl, 1990

Swan Slab

Penelope's Problem John Long and Tony Zeek, 1972
Swan Slab Aid Route Joe Oliger and Steve Roper, 4/61 **FFA** Loyd Price et al, 1967
Kohl Duck Eric Kohl, late -1980s
Swan Song Ron Skelton et al, late-1980s
Re-sole Fusion Dave Tucker et al late-1980s
Ugly Duckling Kevin Worrall and George Meyers, 1974
Lena's Lieback Kim Schmitz and Jim Madsen
Goat For It Mark Carpenter et al, late-1980s
Claude's Delight Claude Fiddler and Peter Olander, 8/72
Werner's Oversight Mark Moore and Dave Hitchcock, 1972

Yosemite Falls

West Side Story Tucker Tech and Sue Harrington,11/89
Winter of Our Discontent TuckerTech and Sue Harrington,11/89
Jughead TuckerTech et al, late-1980s
Antique Unknown
Left Wing Tucker Tech et al, late-1980s
Sweet Pea Walt Shipley and Werner Braun, 4/87
Start Me Up Unknown
Drink and Drive Tucker Tech and Walt Shipley, 12/87
Quaker Flake Tucker Tech and Kevin Fosburg, 12/87
Munginella Tom Fender and Vic Tishous, 1966
Book End Tucker Tech et al, 12/87

First Ascent Index

Commitment Jim Bridwell, Dave Bircheff and Phil Bircheff, 6/66
Work Around the Skirt Tucker Tech et al, late-1980s
Deaf, Dumb and Blind Jeff Hornerbrook and Mark Carpenter, 1986
The Surprise Pete Spoecker and Steve Herrero, 4/65
Werner's Ant Trees Werner Braun, Jerry Coe and Jerry Anderson, 8/70
The Caverns Jim Pettigrew and Jerry Anderson, 1/70
Try Again Ledge Ed Leeper, Dave Trantor and Steve Herrero, 6/64
The Hanging Teeth Jim Bridwell and Vic Tishous, 1968
Cheap Friction Tucker Tech, Pete Takeda, and Kevin Fosburg, late-1980s
Boogie With Stu Tracy Dortin, Walt Shipley, Steve Gerberding and Stu Richie, 1986
Running Hummock Tucker Tech et al, 11/89
Auntie Gravity Steve Monks and L. Broomhead, 9/80
The Fin Les Wilson and Glen Denny, 10/61 **FFA** John Long and Jay Wilson, 6/74
The Green Strip Al Macdonald and Les Wilson, 2/62 **FFA** Tom Higgins and Mike Dent, 1965
The Eggplant Kent Stokes and John Svenson, 10/71 **FFA** Walt Shipley and Xavier Bongard, late-1980s
Eclipse Alan Bartlatt, Don Reid and Rick Cashner, 1978
Blackout Don Reid and Rick Cashner, 1978
Pass-out Eric Kohl, et al, 1992
Azimuth Coordinator Keith Reynolds and Eric Kohl,1992
Black Wall Glen Denny and Al Macdonald, 10/61
Fawlty Towers Alec Sharp and Arni Strapcans, 8/77
Dagger Walt Shipley and Russ Walling, 10/85
Black Wall Glen Denny and Roger Derryberry, 9/63 **FFA** (Shadow Wall) Pete Livesey, Ron Fawcett and Geoff Birtles, 10/77
Guiding Light Rick Cashner and Don Reid, 1978; 2nd pitch-Don Reid and George Meyers 1986; 3rd pitch to top-Walt Shipley and Keith Renyolds, 1993
Center Route Jonny Woodward(T.R.), 9/88
Lightweight Guides Grant Hiskes et al,1985
Full Stem Ahead Rob Robinson and Chris Synder, 12/86
The Podium Grant Hiskes and Ken Yager, 10/86
Tunderbird Eric Kohl et al, 1991
Public Opinion Grant Hiskes and Ken Yager, 10/86
Not What it Seams Mark Carpenter et al, late-1980s
Firewater Keith Reynolds et al, 1990
An Historic Adventure Brian Knight, Tom Borges, and Joel Hawk, 9/89
Exciter Kevin Fosgurg and Walt Shipley, 1990
Dangerbird Walt Shipley and Eric Kohl, 1989
Edge of Darkness Tucker Tech et al, 1990
Edge of Feckness Tucker Tech et al, 1990
Cisco Eric Kohl et al, 1991
Pocket Pussy Eric Kohl, 1991
Dark Star Andy Burnham and Michael Forkash, 10/86
Nanbeeb Michael Forkash and Andy Burnham, 10/86
Isosceles Revisited Urmas Franosch, Steve Plunkett and Michael Forkash, 11/86
I Saw a Sleaze Revisit Ed Walt Shipley and Eric Kohl, late-1980s
Lower Yosemite Fall, West Corner Alan M. Hedden and L. Bruce Meyer, 9/42
Lower Yosemite Fall, West Side Herb Swedlund and Errol Bohannon, 1959
Beat the Rap(Bolted arete climbs) Ron Skelton/ Ed Barry, 1990
Ten Years After Ken Ariza and Kurt Smith, 8/85
Mistfitz Kurt Smith, Dave Griffith, and Chris Beigh, 8/85
Play Misty for Me Kurt Smith, Dave Hatchettt, Ken Ariza and Dave Griffith, 9/85
Powerslave Kurt Smith, Dave Hatchettt and Ken Ariza, 9/85
Lower Yosemite Fall, Right Side John Svenson and Kent Stokes, 10/71 **FFA**(Fight or Flight), Kevin Fosburg and Walt Shipley, 11/89
Mean Streak Kevin Fosburg and Cade Loyd, 11/89
Sunnyside Bench, 5.2 Route David Brower and William Van Voorhis, 7/35
Sunnyside Bench, MW Route Art Gran and Jack Hansen, 9/60
Just Say Moe Brian Bennett, Norman Boles, and Eric Mayo, 6/91
Armed and Dangerous Mark Carpenter et al,1988

— First Ascent Index —

Larry, Moe-The Cheese Brian Bennett and John Tuttle 10/86
Sunnyside Bench, Regular Route unknown
Butthole Climbers Brian Bennett and John Tuttle, 1986
Sultans of Sling Brian Bennett, George Watson and Norman Boles, 1985
Stretch Mark Mike Forkash, Brian Bennett, and Vince DePasque 6/90
Raisin unknown
Mud Flats Kim Schmitz and Don Peterson, 10/69 **FFA** Roger Greatrick and Carl Jonasson, 4/84
Clan of the Big Hair Tucker Tech and Pete Takeda 4/87
Prune Mike Caldwell and Eric Craig, 1974
Fully B.S. or a Tree Tucker Tech et al, late-1980s
Lingering Lie unknown
Lemon Dave Sessions and Scott Burke, 8/79
Bench Warmer Tucker Tech et al, late-1980s
Bummer Bruce Morris, Scott Cole and Peter Thurston, 10/77
Lazy Bum Eric Beck and Steve Williams, 1971 **FFA** Chris Falkenstein et al, 1972
Jamcrack Route Loyd Price and Kim Schmitz, 1967 **FFA** Kim Schmitz and Jim Madsen
To Beer or Not to Be Tucker Tech and Steve Ortner, 3/88
Sunnyside Pinnacle unknown
Lieback Route unknown
Black Balled Dan McDevitt and Sue Bonovich. (Direct Var. T.R.- Bill LeFever, 6/87)
Dwindling Stances Tucker Tech et al, 10/87
Combustable Knowledge Mark Carpenter and Dave Bengston, 11/86
Ribald Tucker Tech et al, 10/89
Tiny Tim Tim Fitzgerald and Bob Korte, 6/66
Guide's Route Roy McClanahan, 1986
Groove Route Tucker Tech and John Harpole, 12/87
Mothballed Tucker Tech et al, late-1980s
Blueballled Elliot Robinson, Bruce Morris, and Mike Hernandez, 9/87
Defoliation Tucker Tech and John Harpole, 2/88
Scrooged Tucker Tech et al, late-1980s
Redtide unknown
Tidal Wave Al Swanson et al, 8/91
Safe to Surf Bob Ost and Matt Hilden, 10/85
Fertile Attraction Tucker Tech and Pete Takeda, 2/88
Vegetal Extraction Tucker Tech and Pete Takeda, 2/88
The Easter Egg Rob Foster and Greg Schaffer, 3/67
Slingshot Dan and Sue McDevitt, 1990
Pygmy Pillar Mike White and Ron Cagle, 1970
Stack O' Fun Kevin Fosburg, 1991
Crack a Brewski Eric Kohl and Kevin Fosburg, 1991
Police and Thieves Kevin Fosburg and Cade Loyd, 1991

Yosemite Falls: Upper Tiers

Bacchiagaloupe Wall Pete Spoecker and Steve Herrero, 4/65. **FFA**-Don Reid, Greg Sonagere, and Alan Bartlett, 12/81
Handshake Mark Ingdal et al, early-1980s
Marvin Gardens Bill Matthies, Tom Tumiano and Brent Reynolds, 9/86
Selaginella Wally Reed and Jim Posten, 9/63
Observation Point Les Wilson, Wolfgang Heinritz and Andrzej Ehrenfeucht, 11/62 **FFA** Frank Sacherer and Wally Reed, 1964
Indica Point Walt Shipley and Dimitri Barton, 1985
Mischief Marshall Ravenscroft and Tim Kemple, 4/82
Gorge Traverse Dave Hammack and George Larrimore, 1950

Upper Yosemite Falls: East

Easy's Playhouse Eric Kohl, 1990
Bitches Galore Eric Kohl, 1991
Dark Cloud Walt Shipley and Eric Kohl, 9/90
Eight Ball Slippin' Eric Kohl, 1990
Easy-Duz-it Eric Kohl, 1990

_____ First Ascent Index _____

Whipping Post Unknown
Misty Wall Dick McCracken and Royal Robbins, 6/63. (Near **FFA**-Walt Shipley and Kevin Fosburg, early-1990s)
Geek Towers, Left (Freestone) Jim Bridwell, Ron Kauk and Dale Bard, 10/74
Geek Towers, Center Jim Bridwell and John Syrett, 6/74
Geek Towers, Right Mark Klemens and Jim Bridwell, 7/71
Lost Arrrow Chimney John Salathe and Anton Nelson, 9/47 **FFA** Chuck Pratt and Frank Sacherer, 1964
Lost Arrow Spire, Direct Warren Harding and Pat Callis, 6/68
ABC Route Ron Kauk and Jerry Moffat, 6/85
Lost Arrow Tip Fritz Lippmann, Jack Arnold, Anton Nelson and Robin Hansen, 9/46 **FFA** Dave Schultz et al, 5/84
Blade Runner Robb Settlemeyer and Dave Caunt, 3/90
Seand Paradise Knez Fran;abcek and Fre;abser Marjan, 4/82
Yosemite Point, Czech Route Jan Porvazik and A. Behia, 10/78
East of Paradise Knez Fran;abcek and Freser Marjan, 4/83
Yosemite Point Buttress Allen Steck and Bob Swift, 1952 (free variations) Yvon Chouinard and Tom Frost, 1960; Frank Sacherer and Don Telshaw, 8/64 (direct outside face) Galen Rowell and Scott Walker, 1963
Yosemite Point, Southeast Face Gordon Webster and TM Herbert, 6/65. **FFA**(Min-Ne-Ah) Scott Cosgrove and Walt Shipley, 6/90
Yosemite Point Couloir Dave Brower, Morgan Harris and Torcom Bedayan, 6/38
Castle Cliffs Dave Brower and Morgan Harris, 5/40
West Arrowhead Chimney Torcom Bedayan and Fritz Lippmann, 12/41
Arrowhead Spire, South Arete Dave Brower and Richard Leonard, 9/37
Arrowhead Spire, East Face Fritz Lippmann and Anton Nelson, 12/46
Arrowhead Spire, Northeast Side John Fiske and Dick Scheible, 8/58
Arrowhead Arete Mark Powell and Bill Feuerer, 10/56
East Arrowhead Chimney Mark Powell and Warren Harding, 12/56. **FFA**-(Nagasaki My Love) Elliot Robinson and Steve Annecone, 3/88
East Arrowhead Buttress, Overhang Route Mark Powell and Wayne Merry, 8/57
East Arrowhead Buttress, Overhang Bypass Mark Powell, Wally Reed and Warren Harding, 3/57

Indian Canyon

Maps and Legends Drew Davol and John Tuttle **FFA** Joe Hedge and Drew Davol, 1986
Police State Urmas Franosch, John Tuttle and Bill Rose
Knuckle Buster Chris Falkenstein and Dennis Oakeshott, 1975
The Wand Dimitri Barton, 1982
A-5 Pinnacle Larry Zulim, Bob Jasperson and Scott Cole, 1981
Yoghurt Rick Sylvester and Barry Bates, 8/70
Chocolate Dihedral Rick Sylvester, Matt Donohoe and Barry Bates, 8/70

Church Bowl

Black is Brown Kim Schmitz and Frank Trummel, 1966
As It Is Walt Shipley(solo), late-1980s
Deja Thorus Jim Beyer and Misa Giesey, 1978
Uncle Fanny Bruce Price and Michael McLean, 1/70
Church Bowl Lieback unknown
Pole Position John Harpole et al, late-1980s
Revival unknown
Gardening At Night Clint Cummins and Joel Ager, 11/89
Tammy Fae Mark Carpenter et al, late-1980s
Jacobs Ladder Mark Carpenter and Jeff Hornibrook, late-1980s
Skid Row Messiah Walt Shipley et al, 1989
800 Club Bill Russell, Walt Shipley, and Eric Kohl, 1990
Aunt Fanny's Pantry Sheridan Anderson and Leo Le Bon, 1965
Book of Revelations Gordon Webster and Chuck Ostin, 10/65 **FFA** Bob Finn and Chris Falkenstein, 1974
Church Bowl Tree Mike Jefferson and Dave Collins, 8/70**FFA** unknown
More Balls Than Brains Dana Brown, 1980

First Ascent Index

Church Bowl Chimney unknown
Energizer Dan and Sue McDevitt, 1990
Atheist Dave Bengston, 1990
Church Bowl Terrace Jim Bridwell and Hamish Mutch, 12/65
Bitches' Terror Walt Shipley and Eric Kohl, 1990
Bishop's Terrace Russ Warne, Dave McFadden and Steve Roper, 12/59 **FFA** Chuck Pratt and Herb Swedlund, 1960
Stephanie's Corner Stephanie McCormack and Walt Shipley, Early-1990s
Sacrilege Walt Shipley and Tucker Tech, 3/87
Blasphemy Walt Shipley and Tucker Tech, 3/87
Heretic Walt Shipley and Tucker Tech, 4/87
Catholic Discipline Dimitri Barton, late-1980s
Bishop's Balcony Frank Sacherer and Gary Colliver, 11/62
No Rest for the Whicked Walt Shipleyand Eric Kohl, 1990
Oral Roberts Mark Carpenter, 1988
700 Club Mark Carpenter and Scott Stow,1988
Master of Cylinders Eric Kohl, 1992
Fire and Brimstone Chick Holtkamp and Chris Ballinger, 9/81
Fool's Finger Bill Price
Lost Flake unknown
Skindad The Scaler Walt Shipley and Kevin Fosburg, 1991

Royal Arches Area

My Rhombus Dan McDevitt and Sue Bonovich, 1986
Q.E.D. (aka East of Eden) Jonny Woodward and Killin Belz, 5/88
East of Eden Bob Gaines and Jay Smith, 9/85
Rupto Pac Eric Mayo and Brian Bennett, 1984
Super Slide Gene Drake and Rex Spaith, 1971
Peter's Out Peter Croft and Tami Knight, 1978
Trial by Fire Chris Falkenstein and Don Reid, 3/74
Demimonde Eric Mayo, Andy Roberts, Dave Caunt , and Rick Harlin, 1991
Lethal Weapon Tom Herbert and Jason Campbell, 1987
Endorphine Charles Cole and Rusty Reno, 1987
Serenity Crack Glen Denny and Les Wilson, 10/61 **FFA** Tom Higgins and Chris Jones, 1967
Adrenaline Mark Hudon et al, 1976
New Generation Tom Herbert and Jason Campbell
Maxine's Wall Les Wilson and Al Macdonald, 3/62 **FFA** Pete Livesey and Andreas Maurer, 1973
Firefingers Charles Cole et al
Pigs in Space Peter Croft, Tami Knight and Larry Zulim, 10/78
Mother of the Future Joel Auger, Clint Cummins, and Nancy Kerrebrock, 11/89
Permanent Waves Chris Hash, Gene Hash and Scott Burke, 11/86
Deviltry John Tuttle and Michael Forkash, mid-1980s
Hell's Hollow Ken Ariza, Doe DeRoss, Nick Arms and Mark Carpenter, mid-1980s
Holy Diver Ed Collins, Ken Ariza, and Tucker Tech, 9/88
God Told Me to Skin You Alive unknown
Sons of Yesterday John Tuttle, Drew Davol and Vince Depasque, 1986
Moan Fest Dimitri Barton and Steve Gerberding, 4/84
Ahwahnee Buttress George Sessions, George Whitmore, Jerry Dixon and Merle Alley, 5/59. **FFA-** Dave Sessions and Tucker Tech, 4/89
Peruvian Flake Bruce Morris, Kevin Leary and Bill Taylor
Astro Turf Tucker Tech, Cade Loyd, and Pete Takeda, 3/88
Draw the Line Mark Carpenter and Nick Arms, 1986
Fine Line Grant Hiskes and Doe DeRoss, 1985
Peeping Tom Grant Hiskes, Neal Newcomb and Tim Noonan, 1985
Sea Hag Tucker Tech and Pete Takeda, late-1980s
Sea Cow Tucker Tech, Stephanie McCormack, and Neil Sugarman, late-1980s
Surplus Cheaper Hands John Tuttle, Norman Boles and George Watson
Age of Industry unknown
Royal Arches Route Ken Adam, Morgan Harris and W. Kenneth Davis, 10/36

First Ascent Index

God Told Me to Skin You Alive unknown
The Shining Scott Burke and Chris Hash, 6/88
The Trowel Eric Beck and Jim Harper, 5/62
Hung Like a Hamster Pete Takeda, Cade Loyd, and Tucker Tech, 3/88
The Hanging Boulders Les Wilson, Wolfgang Heinritz and Andrzej Ehrenfeucht, 10/62
The Crack of Dawn Royal Robbins, Chuck Pratt and Tom Frost, 9/59
Kling Cobra Cade Loyd, Pete Takeda, and Tucker Tech, 2/88
Trivial Pursuit Tucker Tech et al, late-1980s
Astro Spam Norman Boles and Brian Bennett, 1986
Arete Butler Norman Boles, George Watson and Brian Bennett, 1986
Distant Driver Tucker Tech and Neil Sugarman, 2/88
Royal Prerogative Don Reid and Rick Cashner, 2/78
Krovy Rookers Norman Boles and Brian Bennett, 1986
Rumsodomy in the Lash Norman Boles, 9/89
Ilsa She Wolf of the S.S. George Watson, Norman Boles and Brian Bennett,
The Premature Ejaculation Brian Knight, early-1990s
Metal Error Tucker Tech and Neil Sugarman, 2/88
Level Two Tucker Tech and Neil Sugarman, 2/88
Feminine Protection Tucker Tech and Allan Weidner, late-1980s
Facade unknown
Y Crack Gene Drake et al, 1975. Variation- Glen Van Aken and Mark Kirner 6/89
Fish Fingers Jonny Woodward and Maria Cranor, 5/85
Way Homo Sperm Burpers From Fresno Eric Mayo and Brian Bennett, 6/89
The Cobra Mark Powell and Bob Kamps, 6/66 **FFA** Tobin Sorenson and Tim Sorenson, 1975
Royal Cornpad Ray Jardine and Linda McGinnis, 4/76
Hookie Jason Campbell, 1987
Wise Crack Chris Falkenstein, Chuck Cochrane and Dennis Oakeshott, 1979
Cornball unknown
Texas Chain Saw Massacre Chris Cantwell and Augie Klein, 1980
King Snake Chris Cantwell and Mark Grant, 1980
Poker Face Dan McDivett and Sue Bonavich, 3/86
Aces and Eight's Ron Wright and John Gregson, 10/89
Face Card unknown
King of Hearts unknown
Sleight of Hand Bob Ost and Norman Boles, 1/85
Dire Straits Allen Weidnel and Tucker Tech
Stacked Deck Tucker Tech and Neil Sugarman
Public Enema Number One Brian Bennett and Norman Boles, 9/93
Barney Rubble Barney Ng, Keith Kishiyama, and Dave Ryan, 11/89
The Violent Bear it Away John Tuttle and Vince Depasque, 1986
Double Trouble unknown
Arches Direct Royal Robbins and Joe Fitschen, 6/60
The Rambler Steve Gerberding, Scott Burke, Chris Hash, and Gene Hash, 6/86
Shaky Flakes Chris Flakenstein, Ken Bishop, Edd Kuropat, Tom Carter and Mark McPheron, 1973
Friday the 13th Dimitri Barton and Scott Burke, 9/85
Slander Session unknown
Flakes Away Chris Cantwell, 9/78
Samurai Crack Bill Price and Chris Cantwell, 9/78
Hershey Highway Lance Lynch and Malcolm Jolly, 1978
Mid-Life Crisis Bruce Morris, Dave Yerian, et al late-1980s
Reefer Madness Pat Timson and Don Harter, 1976
Arches Terrace Rich Calderwood and Merle Alley, 12/57 **FFA** Merle Alley, Rich Calderwood, John Ohrenschall and George Sessions, 1958
Greasy but Groovy John Long, Rick Accomazzo and Richard Harrison, 5/74
Surf Nazi unknown
Fallen Arches Yvon Chouinard and Dave Bathgate, 10/66 **FFA** Yvon Chouinard and Tom Frost, 10/66
Wharf Rat unknown
The Mouse That Soared Tucker Tech and Pete Takeda, 11/87

First Ascent Index

Lingering Lines Tucker Tech and Cade Loyd, 11/87
Crying for Mama Charles Cole and John Middendorf, 1986
Arches Terrace Direct Bob Grow, Rick Sylvester and Kelly Minnick, 10/70
Hangdog Flyer Ray Jardine and John Lakey, 9/76
10.96 Jim Bridwell, John Long and Mark Klemens, 1972
The Plank Don Reid and Alan Roberts, 10/85
Liberace's Lost Lover Tucker Tech et al, late-1980s
Stranger Than Friction Tucker Tech et al, late-1980s
Movin' Like a Stud Pat Timpson, Julie Brugger, Bob Crawford and Dave Anderson, 1978
Benzoin and Edges Pat Timpson, Jeff Vance, Don Harter, Rick LeDuc and Bruce Hildenbrand, 4/78
Finish Work Tucker Tech et al, late-1980s
The Kids are All Right Jerry, Sigrid, Lynnea, and William Anderson, 5/86
Poodle With a Mohawk Rick Molinar, Bob Ost, and Karl Sonnberger, 7/87
The Bellyshooter Bob Ost and Brian Young, 8/87
Lynnea's Birthday Surprise Jerry, Sigrid and Lynnea Anderson, 5/86
Lower Arch Traverse Krehe Ritter, Mara Unterman and Judy Beyers, 8/57

Washington Column

Lunch Ledge Hervey Voge, Richard Leonard, Jules Eichorn and Bester Robinson, 9/33
Direct Route John Dyer, Robin Hansen and DeWitt Allen, 8/40
Piton Traverse Morgan Harris, Jack Reigelhuth and Richard Leonard, 5/35
Trial by Jury Brad Young and Tom Kastner, 5/89
Power Failure Ray Jardine, Linda McGinnis and Mark Vallance, 10/75
The Fang Ray Jardine et al, 1975
Lunch Ledge Direct Yvon Chouinard and Wally Reed, 7/61 (free variation; Space Case) Ray Jardine and Linda McGinnis, 10/76
Direct Direct Route Bill Bostick, Jack Delk, and Bill Sorenson, 3/71
Jesu Joy Ray Jardine and Rick Sylvester, 10/75
Wing of Bat Don Reid and Mike Corbett, 1/84
Dwindling Energy Ray Jardine and Mark Vallance, 10/75
Nowhere Man Don Reid and Dave Yerian, 1984
Too Munge Fun Tucker Tech and John Harpole, 6/87
Turkey Vulture Jeff Smith and Kevin Lathrop, 1981
The Odyssey Ray Jardine and John Lakey, 5/76
Dinner Ledge Direct Jim Madsen and Kim Schmitz, 1967
Dinner Ledge Don Goodrich and Dave Dows, 4/52 **FFA** John Hudson and Chris Fredericks, 1966
Obscurity Traverse Bill Loughman and Don Goodrich, 10/55
Jojo Bruce Pollock, Matt Pollock and Luke Freeman, 1972
Tom Cat Ken Ariza and Tommy Thompson, mid-1980s
East Face Warren Harding, Glen Denny and Chuck Pratt, 7/59 **FFA (Astroman)** John Bachar, John Long and Ron Kauk, 5/75
The Panther Joe Hedge, Dave Hatchett, Ken Ariza, and Ed Collins, 10/86
Terminal Research Randy Leavitt, Gary Zaccor and Tony Yaniro, 1980

Tenaya Canyon

Skid Row Alan Bartlett and Dimitri Barton, 5/82
North Dome, West Face Art Gran and Steve Roper, 4/62 **FFA** Peter Barton and Mark Chapman, 1972
North Dome, Southwest Face Bev Clark and Chuck Pratt, 4/68
Freaks of Nature Mike McGrale, Cary Hansen, and Jeff Snedden, 9/93
North Dome, South Face Mark Powell and Wally Reed, 8/57 **FFA** Mort Hempel, Irene Ortenburger and Steve Roper, 1960
Priceless Friends Mike McGrale, Urmas Franosch, Marlo Finney, and Marty Lewis, 10/88
Crest Jewell Dan Dingle and Michael Lucero, 9/81
Dakshina Dan Dingle and Ken Black, 8/83. **FFA-** Ken Black and Ian Cummings, 6/84
Mass Assault Ken Boche, Dennis Hennek, Judy Sterner, Russ McLean, Sibylle Hechtel, Tim Auger and Mike Farrell, 3/72
North Dome, Doctor Gravity Mike McGrale et al, 6/90

First Ascent Index

Basket Dome, Basket Case Jim Donini and TM Herbert, 6/72 **FFA** Mark Klemens and Jim Bridwell, 7/72
Basket Dome, Straight Jacket Dale Bard, Jim Bridwell and Ron Kauk, 1977
Scott-Child Doug Scott and Greg Child, 1982
Mirror Mirror, Left Eric Brand and Jonell Geller, 8/85
Mirror Mirror, Right Eric Brand and Tom Shores, 8/86
Mirror Mirror, Far Right unknown
Eric's Book Eric Barrett et al, 1979
Thin Man Eric Barrett et al, 1979
Groundhog Eric Kohl and Eric Brand, 11/86
Breathalizer Eric Kohl and Eric Brand, 11/86
Precious Powder Bruce Morris and Jim Elias, 10/83
Diminishing Returns Hal Thompkins and Lin Murphy 5/90
Werner's Crack Werner Braun and Bruce Steakly, 6/71
The Prude David and Alan Bard, 3/72
Rurp Rape Bruce Steakly, 1971
Silent Majority Clint Cummins, Jim Lutz, and Joel Ager, 6/87
Winterlewd Lin Murphy, Jane Koski, and Mia Ongelma, 1/90
Uppity Women Lin Murphy and Denise Matenson, 5/90
Creeping Lethargy Dimitri Barton et al, 1986
Neil Down Dimitri Barton, Ken Ariza and Tracy Dorton, 5/86
Water Babies Dimitri Barton, Ken Ariza and Tracy Dorton, 2/86
Back To The Slammer Ken Ariza et al, 1988
Apathy Buttress Dimitri Barton , Ken Ariza and Tracy Dorton, 2/86
Destination Zero Bruce Morris and Ken Ariza, 1986
Valley Syndrome Dimitri Barton, Ken Ariza and tracy Dorton, 1986
Free Clinic Dimitri Barton and Ken Ariza, 1986
Black Angus unknown
Ken's Dream Dimitri Barton and Ken Ariza, 1986
Snow Creek Slabs Bob Summers and Ken Boche, 6/69
Sex Drive Tucker Tech, Dan and Sue McDevitt, 1988
BHOS Dome Doug Scott, TM Herbert, Don Lauria and Dennis Hennek, 4/70
Watkins Gully Robin Hansen, Fritz Lippmann and Rolf Pundt, 9/46
Upper Watkins Pinnacle Al Baxter, Ulf Ramm-Ericson and Rupert Gates, 5/47 **FFA** Joe Oliger, Wayne Hildebrand and Steve Roper, 1961
Middle Watkins Pinnacle Al Baxter and Rupert Gates, 12/46
Lower Watkins Pinnacle Mark Powell, Herb Swedlund, Wally Reed, George Sessions and Merle Alley, 7/57
Lower Watkins Pinnacle, Direct Tucker Tech and Walt Shipley, 1991
Watkins Pinnacles (from Tenaya Canyon) Gary Hemming, Dick Long, Jim Wilson and Larry Lackey, 5/58
Mt. Watkins, Escape From Freedom Urmas Franosch and Bruce Morris, 7/88
Mt. Watkins, Golden Dawn Bruce Morris and Urmas Franosch, 7/83
Yasoo Dome, South Face Jim Baldwin and Kit Carr, 7/63
Yasoo Dome, The Chief Al Swanson, Arthur James FoleyIII, and brian Warshow, 8/92
Clouds Rest, Northwest Face Bob Kamps and Bud Couch, 7/63
Clouds Rest, Northwest Ledges Dick Long and Jack Davis, 8/52
Quarter Dome, North Face Yvon Chouinard and Tom Frost, 9/62 **FFA** (Pegasus) Max Jones and Mark Hudon, 1980
Quarter Dome, Route of All Evil Matt Donohoe and Cliff Jennings, 1971
West Quarter Dome, North Face Phil Koch and Dave Goeddel, 9/69
Ahwiyah Point, Northeast Gully Dave Brower and Morgan Harris, 8/37
Ahwiyah Point, Northwest Buttress Wayne Merry and Warren Harding, 1957

Half Dome

North Ridge Chuck Wilts and Royal Robbins, 6/61. **FFA-** Walt Shipley ans John Harpole, 1989
Final Exam Mark Klemens and Jim Bridwell, 1971
Regular Northwest Face Route Royal Robbins, Jerry Gallwas and Mike Sherrick, 7/57 **FFA** Jim Erickson and Art Higbee, 1976

―――――― First Ascent Index ――――――

Direct Northwest Face Royal Robbins and Dick McCracken, 6/63. **FFA**-Todd Skinner and Paul Piana, 1993
West Corner Bob Kamps and Dave Rearick, 6/61
On the Edge Dale Bard and George Meyers, 1975
Labor of Love Walt Shipley and Stephanie McCormack, 7/91
Snake in the Grass Tucker Tech and Steve Ortener, 1989
Dome Polishers Tucker Tech and steve Ortner, 1988
Salathé Route (Southwest Face Route) John Salathé and Anton Nelson, 10/46 **FFA** Frank Sacherer, Bob Kamps and Andy Lichtman, 1964
The Deuceldike Charles Cole, Rusty Reno and John Middendorf, 4/85
Snake Dike Eric Beck, Jim Bridwell and Chris Fredericks, 7/65
Eye in the Sky Mark Spencer, Shirley Spencer, Dan Abbot and David Abbot, 4/85
Snake Dance Claude Fiddler and Bob Jones, 1973
Dreamscape Scott Burke, Tory Elbrader, and Jeff Folett, 5/88
The Fast Lane Dimitri Barton, Scott Burke and Chris Hash, 6/86
Autobahn Charles Cole, Rusty Reno and John Middendorf, 4/85
South Face Route Warren Harding and Galen Rowell, 7/70
Southen Belle Walt Shipley and Dave Schultz, 6/87. **FFA-** Dave Schultz and Scott Cosgrove, 1988
Karma Dave Schultz, Ken Yager and Jim Campbell, 7/86
Call of the Wild Peter Haan and Roger Briggs, 7/75
Happy Gully Joe Faint, Warren Harding and Chris Fredericks, 5/66
Diving Board, from Mirror Lake Charles Michael, prior to 1927
Cold, Rain, and Snow Greg Murphy and Elliott Robinson, 1989
Porcelain Pup Walt Shipley and Rob Orovitz, 5/87
Diving Board, Sunshine Buttress Dick Long, Al Macdonald and Jim Wilson, 8/62
Diving Board, West Side Ken Adam and W. Kenneth Davis, 1938
The Silver Platter Ray Jardine and John Lakey, 4/76
Gravity's Rainbow Ray Jardine and John Lakey, 4/76
Grizzly Peak, West Face Dick Houston and Ralph McColm, 6/42
Bare Necessities Mark Chapman and Rik Rieder, 7/72
Grizzly Peak, South Gully David Brower and Moragan Harris, 6/38
Sierra Point, Southeast Farce Greg Shaffer, Roger Evje and Rob Foster, 6/66

Little Yosemite

Mt. Broderick, Unemployment Line Alan Bartlett, Jim May and Steve Gerberding, 11/82
South Face Bob Kamps, Joe Fitschen and Chuck Pratt, 6/60
Liberty Cap, West Corner Dick McCracken and Steve Roper, 6/60
Liberty Cap, South Face Mark Powell, Royal Robbins and Joe Fitschen, 9/56
Liberty Cap, Southern Buttress Mike Loughman and Dick Armstrong, 6/57
Leverage Joe Faint and Chris Fredericks, 5/66
Base Pinnacle Mark Klemens and Bruce Pollock, 5/72
Sugarloaf Dome, South Face John Salathé and Cliff Hopson, 11/51 **FFA** Yvon Chouinard and Tom Frost, 1960
Nevada Fall, Left Side Royal Robbins and Lin Ephraim, 7/60
Nevada Flake, The Slot Machine unknown **FFA** Bruce Morris and Paul Cowen, 10/77
Nevada Flake, Center Route Bill Amborn, Tom Naylor and Steve Roper, 1/61
Nevada Flake, Right Side Glen Denny and Charles Fisher, 4/61
Vernal Fall, Right Side Allen Steck, Jim Wilson and Dick Long, 10/66
Vernal Fall, Gold's Gym Chris Snyder and Kevin Fosburg, 10/88
Mt. Starr King, Northeast Slopes George Bayley and E.S. Schuyler, 1876
Mt. Starr King, East Face John Roebig, Ron Schroder and Tom Distler, 7/69
Mt. Starr King, West Face Ken Boche and Lee Panza, 5/70
Mt. Starr King, Nuts and Bolts Tim Harrison and Ken Boche, 1971
Mt. Starr King, Northwest Face Ken Boche and Mary Bomba, 9/70
Panorama Cliff Dave Brower and Morgan Harris, 10/36
Dark Shadows Dave Yerian, Bruce Morris and Malcolm Jolley, 10/78
Fistibule Werner Braun and Walt Shipley, 4/86
Air Bare Eric Mayo et al, 1982
Plane Fare Eric Mayo et al, 1982
Way Lost Tucker Tech and Lee Price, 10/86

First Ascent Index

Fresh Squeezed Grant Hiskes and Sean Plunkett, 84
Roto Killer Tucker Tech et al, late-1980s
Tennis Shoe Crack George Watson, Jim and Kyle Edmondson, 7/88
George's Secretary George Watson, Jim and Kyle Edmondson, Mike Forkash, and Nancy Beebe, 7/88
Streamline Kevin Fosburg and John Harpole, 8/89
Ape Index Werner Braun et al, 1981
Cynical Pinnacle Chris Cantwell et al, 1981

Glacier Point Apron
Mud, Sweat and Beers Tony Dailley and Bob Madison, 8/73
Strange Energy Dean Miller, Bruce Morris and Chris Cantwell
Synapse Collapse Bruce Morris and Steve Cerrada, 1979
Shuttle Madness unknown
Vulture Culture Mark Spencer, 3/90
Collision Course Mark Spencer, 5/90
Milk Dud Jack Roberts et al, 9/71
Zap the Gipper Scott Cosgrove, 10/85
Jack the Zipper Tony Yaniro, Nick Turvey and Scott Cole, 1978
The Bear Mark Spencer and Jeff Maurer, 7/90
The Calf Joe McKeown and Jim Harper, 7/63 **FFA** John Long et al, 1974
Wild At Heart Mark Spencer, 10/90
Dead Baby Dave Austin and Dimitri Barton, 11/78
Psychic Energy John Pruett et al, 10/86
Transistor Sister unknown
Mr. Rabbit Ray Sebastian and Tim Felton, late-1980s
Dead Squirrel Ray Sebastian and Tim Felton, late-1980s
Calf Continuation Dennis Oakeshott and Vern Clevenger, 1975
A Mother's Lament Rab Carrington and Rik Rieder, 9/72
Tightrope Vern Clevenger, Tom Carter et al, 1975
The Cow, Left Ken Boche and Mary Bomba, 3/70
The Cow, Center Jeff and Greg Schaffer, 7/66
The Cow, Right Ken Boche, 5/70
An Udder Way Bill Zauman and Dave Jensen, 1977
Hoppy's Favorite Dennis Oakeshott and Vern Clevenger, 1974
Hoppy's Creed Dave Diegleman et al, 1978
The Grack, Left Side Bob Kamps and Andy Lichtman, 8/63
The Grack, Center Route Bill Sorenson and Jack Delk, 1967
The Grack, Marginal Ken Boche, Mary Bomba and Joe McKeown, 5/70
The Grack, Right Side TM Herbert and Ken Boche, 3/70
Perhaps Bob Kamps and Andy Lichtman, 8/63
Roller Coaster Ken Ariza, Mike Hatchett and Mark Carpenter, 1986
Hot Tin Roof Ed Barry, Matt Pollock and Bruce Pollock, 1973
Ochre Fields Carl Austrom and Darryl Jones, 4/78
Deep Throat Dennis Oakeshott and Paul Weir, 1974
The Mouth Variation Ken Boche and Dennis Hennek, 1966
Regular Mouth Bob Kamps and Tom Cochrane, 1964
Mouth to Perhaps Rick Accomazzo and Mike Breidenbach, 1974
Flakey Foont Vince Goetz, Rick Lee and Al Hu, 8/72
Misty Beethoven Mark Wilford et al, 1975
Hall of Mirrors Chris Cantwell, Bruce Morris, Scott Burke, Dave Austin and others, 1978-80. (**Dry Variation-** Jonny Woodward and Derrell Hensel, 5/92
Goodrich Pinnacle, Left Side Don Goodrich and Krehe Ritter, 5/59 **FFA** Bob Kamps and Andy Lichtman, 1962
MacPherson Struts Bob Gaines and Yvonne MacPherson, 6/88
Goodrich Pinnacle, Right Side Royal Robbins, Liz Robbins and TM Herbert, 5/64
Goodrich to the Oasis Eric Beck, Mike Cohen and Tom Gerughty, 1966
Goodrich-Coonyard Traverse Jeff Dozier and Loyd Price, 7/66
Hoosier's Highway Steve Shea, Molly Higgins, Larry Bruce and Lou Dawson, 1974
Patio Pinnacle, Left Side Gordon Webster and Joh Morton, 1965
Patio Pinnacle, Regular Jeff Foott, 8/63

First Ascent Index

Monday Morning to Patio Mark Chapman and Ed Barry, 1973
Angelica Fremont Bainbridge, Conrad Van Bruggen, Simon King, Gordon Rhodes and Jeff Panetta, 1978
Coonyard Pinnacle Bill Amborn, Joe McKeown and Rich Calderwood, 9/60 **FFA** Chuck Ostin and Frank Sacherer, 1961
Patio to Coonyard Russ McLean and Ken Boche, 4/65
Coonyard to the Oasis Layton Kor and Yvon Chouinard, 9/60
The Hinterland (Oaisis to the rim) Bob Kamps and Joe McKeown, 1962
Monday Morning Slab, Far East Dennis Hennek and Ken Boche, 5/65
Monday Morning Slab, Left Side unknown
Monday Morning Slab, Variation on a Theme Paul Cowan et al, 1974
Monday Morning Slab, Chouinard Crack Yvon Chouinard et al
Monday Morning Slab, Harry Daley Route Ken Weeks and Harry Daley, 1960
Monday Morning Slab, Lichen Madness unknown
Monday Morning Slab, Right Side Don Goodrich and Mac Fraser, 1958
Monday Morning Slab, Lichen Nightmare Rik Rieder and John Long, 1972
Monday Morning Slab, Looking for Lichen Brian Knight, Linus Plalt and Michael Harris, 5/86
On Any Thursday Mark Spencer and Kevin Wilcox, 6/88
Zoner Mark Spencer, Shirley Spencer and Floyd Hayes, 7/85
Cold Fusion Mark Spencer, 4/90
Point Beyond Don Goodrich and Bill Loughman, 1955 **FFA** Howard Sturgis and Ron Harrison, 1959
Point Beyond Direct Yvon Chouinard and Ken Weeks, 1965
Angel's Approach Tom Higgins et al
Lucifer's Ledge Ken Boche and Dave Bircheff, 9/65
Lucifer's to the Oasis Ken Boche and Russ McLean, 9/65
Anchors Away Tim Harrison and Mike Breidenbach, 1972
Sailin' Shoes Bruce Morris, Dave Austin, Chuck Neifield, Gary Robbe, Peter Thurston and Val Lecont, 5/78
5.9 Grunt unknown
Chiropodist Shop Rick McGregor, 10/81
The Token Scott Burke et al
Ephemeral Clogdance Rick McGregor and Robert Parker, 1981
The Letdown Bob Kamps and Tom Higgins, 9/67
Bark at the Moon Ken Ariza, Mark Carpenter and Dave Walters, 1986
Synchronousity Drew Bedford and Mike Ortz
Nothing on the Apron Bruce Morris, Ken Ariza, Gary Rabbe and Stu Ritchie, 5/86
Lean Years Chris Cantwell and Bruce Morris, 6/79
Blue Funk Mike Artz and Drew Bedford
Perfect Master Bruce Morris and Chris Cantwell, 12/79
Famous Potatoes Todd Montgomery and Trent Smith, 9/86
Lonely Dancer Dave Yerian, Shary McVoy and Bruce Morris, 1979
Son of Sam Dave Austin and Bruce Morris, 4/78
Cosmic Comedy Leon Borowski, Kevin Minto and Claude Fiddler, 11/72
Dr. Feel Good Bruce Morris, Mike Herandez and Scott Cole, 5/81
Afterglow Chris Cantwell and Scott Burke, 9/81
Apron Jam Galen Rowell and Gordon Webster, 10/65
Green Dragon Chris Cantwell and Dean Young, 9/79
Mr. Natural Chris Cantwell and Bruce Morris, 9/79
Bad Acid Al Swanson and Norman Boles
Scimitar unknown
Thunderhead Jim Beyer and Janice Linhares **FFA** Jonny Woodward and Maria Cranor, 5/85
This Ain't England Greg Anderson and Gordon Jenkins, 6/92. (Direct Variation- Greg Anderson and Gordon Jenkins, 6/92.)
The White Dike Brian Bennett, George Watson and Eric Mayo, 1986
Lunar Lunacy Gene Drake and Bob Bartlett, 6/77. **FFA**- Bob Gaines, 6/87
Fire Drill Brian Bennett and John Tuttle, 1986
The Punch Line Al Swanson, Brian Bennett and Brian Bailey, 1986
Run With Me Brian Bennett and John Tuttle, 1986
The Punch Bowl Bob Kamps and Tom Higgins, 9/66

First Ascent Index

Harding Route Warren Harding and Bea Vogel, 6/57
Wild, Wild, West Greg Shaffer, Jeff Shaffer, Rob Foster and Roger Evje, 6/66
Glacier Point Terrace Dave Brower and Morgan Harris, 6/37
Flake Route Jerry Gray et al, 6/62

Staircase Falls

Old A5 Peter Chesko et al, 1982
Old A3 unknown
Old A2 Dana Brown and Jeff Perrin, 10/88
The Cafeteria Lieback Brian Knight and Jason Cambell, 8/88
Good For Your Soul Jason Cambell and Brian Knight, 8/88
Blockbuster Don Reid, Grant Hiskes and Dimitri Barton, 9/84
Derelict's Diagonal Chuck Goldman and Mathew Moore, 1979
Broken Circuit unknown
Circuit Breaker unknown
Derelict's Delight Mike Corbett, 1976 FFA Dan Phillips and John Ockerman, 10/85
Doggie Submission John Tuttle and Brian Bennett, 1986
Speed Racer Jason Campbell and Tom Herbert, 1987
Once is Enough Bill Price, Larry Zulim and Jim Hevner, 1980

Public Sanitation

Black Fly Scott Cosgrove, 1991
Final Cut Cade Loyd, 1990
Wide Thing Cade Loyd and Jeff Folett, 1989
Best Bet Arete Cade Loyd, 1990
Spike Paul Parker and Jeff Folett, 1990
Public Sanitation Rick Sylvester and Roy Kligfield, 9/71
Carpet Bagger Kevin Fosburg and John Harpole, 1990
Wish You Were Here Cade Loyd, 1990
Substance Abuse Kevin Fosburg, 1991
Sand Jam Brian Knight et al, 1990
Solid Waste unknown
Total Way-ist Tucker Tech, 1990
Waste Not, Whip Not Tucker Tech and Kevin Fosburg, 1990
Tucker's Proud Rock Climb Ed Barry, early-1990s
Afterburner Dan and Sue McDevitt, 1993
Sanitary Engineer unknown
Indisposed unknown
Temple of Doom Kevin Fosburg and Cade Loyd, 1991
Bourbon Street Dan and Sue McDevitt, 1993
Big Easy Dan and Sue McDevitt, 1993

Chapel Wall

Crack Baby Kevin Fosburg and Eric Gomper, 10/90
Betty Comes Alive Dave Gardener and Eric Gomper, 7/89
Betty Does Yosemite Tucker Tech, 1990
Raging Bull Eric Gomper and Dave Gardener, 7/89
Mr. Clean Eric Gomper and Dave Gardener, 7/89
Psycho-Betty Eric Gomper and Linda Gil-Martin, 7/89
Switchblade Dan McDevitt, 1991
Lamb Chop unknown
Pork Chop unknown
Home-Boys Dan and Sue McDevitt
Fly-Girls Dan and Sue McDevitt
Ninety-six Degrees in the Shade Andrew Stevens and Dan McDevitt, early-1990s
Pink Panther Dan and Sue McDevitt, 1991
Mr. Pink-eyes Dan and Sue McDevitt, 1991
Rock-Shock Andrew Stevens and Dan McDevitt, early-1990s
Exploited Pete Takeda and Cade Loyd, 1989
Scavenger Ken Ariza, Pete Takeda, and Cade Loyd, 11/88

— First Ascent Index —

Cathedral Spires Area

Phantom Pinnacle, Left Side Bill Dunmire and Bob Swift, 9/50 **FFA** Rich Calderwood and Mike Borghoff, 1957
Phantom Pinnacle, Outside Face Chris Fredericks and Joe Faint, 6/65 **FFA** Mike Graham, Roger Breedlove and Jim Bridwell, 4/76
Hangover Buttress Rich Calderwood and Jerry Dixon, 6/60
Harris's Hangover Oscar Cook, Bill Dunmire and Bob Swift, 8/49
The Ski Jump Chuck Pratt and Bob Kamps, 7/59
Spireview Point George Sessions and dick Irvin, 4/54
Church Tower, East Arête Ken Adam, Olive Dyer and Morgan Harris, 10/35 variation Dick Houston, Ed Koskinen, Bill Horsfall and Newton McCready, 5/41
Church Tower, Soutwest Notch unknown
Church Tower, North Face John Salathé, Anton Nelson, DeWitt Allen and Fritz Lippmann, 6/46
Lower Cathedral Spire, Regular Route (via Flake) Richard Leonard, Jules Eichorn and Bestor Robinson, 8/34 (current route) Roy Gorin, Paul Estes, Jerry Ganapole and Raffi Bedayn, 5/48
Lower Cathedral Spire, South by Southwest, Walt Shipley and Keith Reynolds, 7/93
Lower Cathedral Spire, Northeast Chimney Chuck Pratt and Steve Roper, 6/58 **FFA** Tom Kimbrough and Roman Laba, 1966
Lower Cathedral Spire, Northeast Face Mark Powell, Frank Sacherer and Bob Kamps, 9/63 variations Chuck Pratt and Joe Faint, 1965; Chris Fredericks, Frank Sacherer and TM Herbert, 1965
Lower Cathedral Spire, Lower North Face Les Wilson and Wolfgang Heinritz, 7/62
Lower Cathedral Spire, Upper North Face Galen Rowell and Al Macdonald, 6/62
Higher Cathedral Spire, Regular Route Jules Eichorn, Bestor Robinson and Dick Leonard, 4/34 **FFA** Chuck Wilts and Spencer Austin, 1944
Higher Cathedral Spire, Steck Route Allen Steck, Fletcher Hoyt and William Hoyt, 8/48
Higher Cathedral Spire, Southeast Route Keith Edwards and Fred Cady, 6/70. **FFA-** Keith Reynolds and Alvino Pon, late-1980s
Higher Cathedral Spire, East Corner Tom Gerughty and Chuck Pratt, 7/65
Higher Cathedral Spire, North Couloir Upper Part Dick Long and Jim Wilson, 4/54 complete route Dick Long, Ray D'Arcy and Wally Reed, 6/61

Higher Cathedral Rock

The Syllable Rick Sylvester and Sibylle Hechtel, 11/71
The Sequel Joe Faint and Chuck Pratt, 10/66
Blind Man's Bluff Roger Breedlove and Bill St. Jean, 1976
Blind Alley Joel Ager and Clint Cummins, 7/90
Braille Book Jim Bridwell, Chris Fredericks and Brian Berry, 6/66
Perfect Vision Clint Cummins and Joel Ager, 6/90
Book of Job Rick Sylvester and Ben Read, 11/71 **FFA** Jim Donini and Rik Rieder, 6/72
The Dictionary Ken Jern, J. McMillan and J. Catland, 1970
Malice Aforethought Brad Young and Ron Skelton, 8/90
Mary's Tears Bill Price and Mike Borris, 5/80
Higher Cathedral Rock, Northeast Buttress Dick Long, Ray D'Arcy and Terry Tarver, 6/59 **FFA** Frank Sacherer and Jeff Dozier, 1964
Higher Cathedral Rock, Northeast Corner Chuck Pratt and Joe Kelsey, 10/70 Free variation (Powerpoint) Werner Braun and Scott Cosgrove, 4/86
Crucifix Jim Bridwell and Kevin Worrall, 1973 **FFA** Peter Croft et al, 1985
The Affliction Walt Shipley and Scott Cosgrove, 7/90
Higher Cathedral Rock, North Face Yvon Chouinard, Chuck Pratt and Bob Kamps, 7/60
Cathedral Chimney Dave Brower and Morgan Harris, 10/36
Cork Screw Peter Markle and Jim Pettigrew, 1974
Backlashing Tucker Tech et al, late-1980s
Penny Pinnacle, South Face Torcom Bedayan and Fritz Lippmann, 4/46
Penny Pinnacle, West Face unknown, 1950's
Penny Pinnacle, North Face unknown
Penny Pinnacle, East Arete Mark Powell and Bill Feuerer, 5/59
Nickel Pinnacle, from the notch Mark Powell and George Whitmore, 11/54 **FFA** Mort Hempel and Steve Roper, 1960

First Ascent Index

Nickel Pinnacle, East Face Chuck Kroger and Kep Stone, 4/68
Penny-Nickel Arete Chuck Pratt, George Sessions and Krehe Ritter, 9/58
John's Other Chimney John Ohrenschall and Mary Ann Corthell, 6/53

Middle Cathedral Rock

Alley Cat Dave Anderson, Mark Moore and K. Eastman, 5/75
Kat Walk Ralph Griswold, 9/29
No Butts About It Phil Bard et al, 1983
East Buttress Warren Harding, Jack Davis and Bob Swift, 1954. **FFA** Frank Sacherer and Ed Leeper, 1965 right variation Yvon Chouinard and Mort Hempel, 1961
Fifty Crowed Variation Clint Cummins and Nancy Kerrebrock, 10/87
Critical Path Clint Cummins and Anne Smith, 6/91
Sacherer-Fredericks Frank Sacherer and Chris Fredericks, 7/64
Kor-Beck Layton Kor and Eric Beck, 4/63 **FFA** Eric Beck and Mark Klemens, 1966
Space Babble Ron Kauk and Kevin Worrall, 1976
Tour de Force Scott Burke and Jeff Folett, 9/87
Bircheff-Williams Phil Bircheff and Steve Williams, 6/69 **FFA** Kevin Worrall and George Meyers, 1973
Central Pillar of Frenzy (first eight) Jim Bridwell, Roger Breedlove and Ed Barry, 5/73 finish Jim Bridwell, John Long and Billy Westbay, 5/75 direct start John Long and Ron Fawcett, 1979
Chouinard-Pratt Chuck Pratt and Yvon Chouinard, 10/60 direct finish Chuck Pratt and Bob Kamps, 6/64
Rainbow Bridge Chris Cantwell, Scott Burke and Bruce Morris, 1980
Stoner's Highway Kevin Worrall, John Long, Ed Barry, Peter Barton and Vern Clevenger, 1973
Pulsing Pustules Brian Bennett and Norman Boles, 7/91
Powell-Reed Mark Powell and Wally Reed, 7/57 **FFA** Bob Kamps and Tom Higgins, 1964
Pieces of Eight Scott Burke and Steve Schneider, mid-1980s
Paradise Lost Ray Jardine and Rik Rieder, 6/72
Pee Pee Pillar Peter Barton, Eric Schoen, George Meyers and Bob Ashworth, 1974
Direct North Buttress Yvon Chouinard and Steve Roper, 6/62 **FFA** Frank Sacherer and Eric Beck, 1965
Picnic Peter Barton, Eric Schoen and George Meyers, 1974
Ho Chi Minh Trail Clint Cummins and Joel Ager et al, 5/89
Thirsty Spire (finger crack) Clint Cummins and Joel Ager, 5/89
Top Dope Eric Mayo and Brian Bennett, 6/90
Sex Farm Brian Bennett and Norman Boles, 7/91
North Buttress Warren Harding, Frank Tarver, Craig Holden and John Whitmer, 5/54 **FFA** Frank Sacherer and Jim Bridwell, 1964
Left Rabbit Ear Route Clint Cummins and Joel Ager, 5/89
The Turret Bob Kamps and Mark Powell, 7/62 **FFA** Jim Donini and John Bragg, 1973
Bunghole of the Universe Brian Bennett and Norman Boles, 7/91
Crotch Cricket Brian Bennett, Eric Mayo, and Andy Roberts, 9/91
Lap Lobster Brian Bennett, Eric Mayo, and Andy Roberts, 9/91
North Face Route Chuck Pratt, Bob Kamps and Steve Roper, 6/59
Ramer Chris Breemer, Jeff Gorris, and Tom Harper, 10/92
Spank Your Monkey Brian Bennett, Stu Ritchie and Norman Boles, 1984
Jigsaw Kevin Worrall, George Meyers and Mark Chapman, 1976
Black Primo Kevin Worrall, John Long and George Meyers, 5/74
Road to Ruin Bob Gaines, Jay Smith, and John Mallory, 6/88
Ticket to Nowhere Bob Gaines, John Mallery, Tom Callahan, Mike Paul and Franciso Blanco, 1983-1986
Quicksilver Kevin Worrall, George Meyers and Vern Clevenger, 1973
Walk of Life Ron Kauk, Kevin Worrall and Mark Chapman, 6/86
Freewheelin' Kevin Worrall, George Meyers and Roger Breedlove, 1973
Stupid Pet Tricks Brian Bennett, Vince Deposque and Jack Wenzel, 1985
Bottom Feeder Norman Boles, Brian Bennett and Stu Ritchie, 1984
Cat Dancing P. Landrum, John Haek and Bruce Casey, 9/79
Orange Peel George Meyers and Bruce Hawkins, 1975
Exodus Jay Smith and Gary Anderson, 8/83

First Ascent Index

Tapestry Heidi Pesterfield and Brian Bennett, 1986
Five O'clock Shadow Jay swmith and Penny Fogel, 7/87
Home Run Jonny Woodward and Derrell Hensel, 5/92
Tears of Joy Gene Drake, Rick Stockwell and Bob Bartlett, 6/77
Desperate for Doughnuts Brad Young and Tom Barney, 10/91
Ennui Eric Mayo and Brian Bennett, 9/91
Mother Earth (to traverse ledges) George Meyers, John Long, Kevin Worrall and Mark Chapman, 1975 complete route John Long, Mark Chapman and Ron Kauk, 1978
Teacher's Pet Derrel Hensel and Jonny Woodward, 10/89
That'll Teach You (formerly-Teaching Little Fingers) Derrel Hensel and Jonny Woodward, 10/89
Teaching Little Fingers Eric Gompper, Dan Parks and Ralph Shaffer, 8/85
Smith-Crawford Jay Smith and Paul Crawford, 9/84
Crazy Jay Smith, Paul Van Betten, and Sal Mamusia, 8/87
Swollen Plecnode Eric Mayo and Brian Bennett, 8/92
The Flakes Frank Sacherer and Mark Powell, 6/64
North Face Traverse Dick Long, George Mandatory, Jack Davis and Bob Skinner, 7/54
Thirsty Spire Dick Long and Bob Skinner, 7/54
Northwest Face Les Overstreet, Jerry Gray and George Ewing, 9/57 **FFA** Margaret Young and Steve Roper, 1959
Northwest Buttress Bill Dunmire, Marj Dunmire, Jack Davis, Dale Webster, Dick Long and Dick Houston, 4/53
Gunsight unknown

Lower Cathedral Rock

Spooky Tooth John Yablonski, Fred East and Richard Harrison, 1976
Shake and Bake Rick Accomazzo and Richard Harrison, 1976
Starfire Rick Accomazzo and Richard Harrison, 1976
East Buttress Mark Powell, Jerry Gallwas and Don Wilson, 6/56 **FFA** Steve Thompson and Chris Fredericks, 1965
Soul Sacrifice Werner Braun et al, 1981
Beggar's Buttress Kevin Worrall and Mark Chapman, 5/76
Tidbit Don Reid and Grant Hiskes, 1978
Going Nowhere Werner Braun and Scott Cosgrove, 9/86
Submission Chuck Cochrane, mid-1970s. FFA-Don Reid and Grant Hiskes, 8/84
Compass Rose Tucker Tech and Lynn Wolfe, 9/89
North by Northwest Dimitri Barton et al, 1986
Brass Knuckles Chris Cantwell and Bruce Morris, 1981
Exfoliator Eric Kohl and Kevin Fosburg, 1992
Spectacle Joe Hedge and Kevin Fosburg, 1992
Gash Joe Hedge and Kevin Fosburg, 1992
N.W.R. Walt Shipley and Kevin Fosburg, 1992
The Roof Tom Frost and Henry Kendall, 4/58
Overhang Route Dick Leonard, Doris Leonard and Bestor Robinson, 9/35 **FFA** Mark Powell and Bill Feuerer, 1956
Overhang Bypass Bill Dunmire, Ed Robbins, Bill Long and Dick Long, 6/52
Overhang Overpass Jim Donini et al, 1974
West Face Frank Sacherer and Wally Reed, 8/63
Return to the Stone Age Ed Barry and Scott Cosgrove, 10/85
Bridalveil Fall, East Buttress Royal Robbins and TM Herbert, 9/63
Bridalveil East Mark Powell and Warren Harding, 8/57 **FFA** via Midget Chimney Frank Sacherer and John Morton, 1964 free var. from pitch 3 Royal Robbins and Rich Calderwood, 1961

Leaning Tower Area

Rattlesnake Buttress Layton Kor and Fred Beckey, 6/65 **FFA** Werner Braun and Rick Cashner, 5/82
The Yellow Corner Layton Kor and Tom Fender, 6/65. FFA(Turning Yeller) Walt Shipley and Tucker Tech, 1992. Clean start variation- Walt Shipley and Jory Morgan, 1992
Direct Assistance Route Layton Kor, John Hudson and Dick Williams, 6/66
The Princess Brian Bennett, Brian Hoffmann and Michael Forkash, 1986

―――――――――――― First Ascent Index ――――――――――――

The Watchtower, The Joker Mark Chapman and Kevin Worrall, 1975
The Watchtower, The Thief Mark Chapman and Kevin Worrall, 1975
The Watchtower, Magnum Force Doug and Maurice Reed, 1983
The Watchtower, Barefoot Servants Don Reid, Alan Bartlett and Alan Roberts, 6/80
The Amoeba, Left Side Rick Sylvester and Larry Young, 8/71
The Amoeba, Right Side Michael Forkash and Andy Burnham, 10/85
Rycrisp Rick Sylvester and Jim Downs, 8/71
Beat the Clock Michael Forkash and Norman Boles, 1986
The Triscuit Alan Bartlett et al, 1982
Drop-out Rick Sylvester and Larry Young, 8/71
The Chosen Few Jim Bridwell and Mark Klemens, 1971
Machine Head Norman Boles and Alex Dropshoff, 4/87
The Cracker, Southwest Corner Bill Sorenson and Ann Rehder, 6/69
Cracker, Right Side Mike Loughman and others of the U.C. Hiking Club, 1959
Leaning Tower, Northeast Slopes Charles Michael, in the 1920's
Leaning Tower, East Face Russ McLean and Ken Boche, 5/70
Leaning Tower Traverse Chuck Wilts, Ellen Wilts and G.B. Harr, 9/57
Leaning Chimney Dave Brower, Ken Adam, Morgan Harris, Richard Leonard and Carl Rosberg, 10/40
Fifi Buttress Dick McCracken and Steve Roper, 5/60
Sunset Strip Chick Holtkamp and Eric Zschiesche, 4/82
The Vortex Chick Holtkamp and Randy Russell, 10/80 FFA Chick Holtkamp and Eric Zschiesche, 5/82
Colony of Slippermen Chris Cantwell and Mark Grant, 1981
The Worbler Werner Braun and Ed Barry FFA Chris Bellizzi et al, 5/82
Stanford Point, North Face Dave Brower, L. Bruce Meyer, Morgan Harris and Alan Hedden, 9/42
Local Motion Doug McDonald and Werner Braun, 5/86
Wind Chill Elliott Robinson and Greg Murphy, 5/90
Tower of the Cosmic Winds, Windfall Mark Chapman and Kevin Worrall, 5/76
Tower of the Cosmic Winds, Breezin' Mark Chapman and Kevin Worrall, 5/76
Tower of the Cosmic Winds, Windjammer Mark Chapman and Kevin Worrall, 1975
Castaways Mark Chapman and Kevin Worrall, 1976
Inspiration Buttress Joe Faint and Mike Borghoff, 6/65

Wawona Tunnel
Overdrive Dale Bard, Ron Kauk, Nic Taylor and George Meyers, 1976
Pump Dummy Keith Reynolds and Walt Shipley, 9/90
A Dog's Roof Ray Jardine, 5/77
A Bit of O.K. Kevin Fosburg et al, 1993
Tips Are For Kids Kevin Fosburg et al, 1993
Walk On By Ken Yager et al, early-1990s
Your Pizza Is Ready unknown
Eat at Degnan's Royal Robbins, 1965
Pohono the Barbarian unknown
Landshark Jonny Woodward and Chris Peisker, 5/85
Dancin' Days Bob Williams et al, 1980
Short but in the Shade Jerry and Sigrid Anderson, 12/90
I Don't Know Jerry, Sigrid, Lynnea, and William Anderson, 12/90
I Don't Remember Jerry, Sigrid, Lynnea, and William Anderson, 12/90
Green Carpet Treatment Rick Sylvester and Jerry Coe, 10/70
Deadline Dihedral Rick Sylvester and Jerry Coe, 10/70
You Asked For It Rick Sylvester and Jerry Coe, 10/70
Autumn Crescent Rick Sylvester and Jerry Coe, 10/70
Jungle Train Rick Sylvester and Matt Donohoe, 8/70

Lower Merced Caynon: South
Scrub Scouts Ken Yager and Walt Shipley, 1990
Flagman Ken Yager and Walt Shipley, 1990
Shadyside Bench Alan Gillespie and Bill Nelson, 11/68
High Pressure Jim Bridwell and John Bragg, 1972

―――――――― First Ascent Index ――――――――

Open Trench Ed Barry et al, 1972
Lost on Venus Ed Barry and Mark Chapman, 1972
Pulpit Rock, from the Notch unknown, 1950's? **FFA** Royal Robbins, 1966
Pulpit Rock, East Face Dave Rearick and Tom Frost, 1960 **FFA** var. Don Reid and Ken Yager, 11/86
Pulpit Rock, Tree Route Raffi Bedayn, Carl Jensen and Randolph May, 5/39 **FFA** Tom Frost, 1960
Pulpit Rock, Improbable Traverse Wally Reed and Mark Powell, 7/57 variation Frank Sacherer and Jim Yensen, 1962 **Original Sin** variation Rick Cashner and Don Reid, 1980
Pulpit Rock, Pulpit Pooper Jim Orey and Jack Roberts, 6/72
Pulpit Rock, Sky Pilot Ken Yager and Jim Cambell, late-1980s
Pulpit Rock, The Serman Ron Kauk and Jim Orey, 1974
Pulpit Rock, Waste of Time Bill Russell et al, 1991
Pulpit Rock, Magilla Gorilla Bill Russell et al, 1991
Pulpit Rock, Gorilla Cookies Bill Russell et al, 1991
Cream Mark Klemens et al, 8/71
Jam Session Mark Klemens and Jim Bridwell, 1971
Cartwheel Mark Klemens and Jim Bridwell, 1971
Monkey Do Don Reid and Rick Cashner, 10/77
Energy Crisis Bill Price and Randy Grandstaff, 1980
Shiver-Me-Timbers Mike Borris, 1979
Waltzing Mathilda Greg Murphy and Elliott Robinson, 1992
The Mosstrum Bob Bauman, Chuck Pratt and Bruce Kumph, 9/68

The Rostrum Area

Country Corner Don Reid and Jim Howard, 5/92
Super Nova Ray Jardine and John Lakey, 9/76
Dime Bag Dale Bard and Werner Braun, 1975
Crack the Whip Don Reid and Grant Hiskes, 9/84
Vegemite Elliott robinson and Greg Murphy, 1989
The Rostrum, Bridwell Corner Jim Briwell and Loyd Price?
The Rostrum, Whipcord Ed Barry, 1993
The Rostrum, Regular North Face Route Glen Denny and Warren Harding, 7/62 **FFA** (to last pitch) Ron Kauk and John Yablonski, 1977 **FFA** (entire route) Kim Carrigan et al, 1985
The Rostrum, Mad Pilot Rob Rohn and Peter Croft, 5/81
The Rostrum, Up Rising Kevin Fosburg and Chris Snyder, 5/88
Alien Tony Yaniro, 1980
The Rostrum, Blind Faith Dale Bard and Ron Kauk, 10/75
Kauk-ulator Ron Kauk and John Yablonsky, 1975
The Rostrum, West Base Route (from the bench) Gerry Czamanske and Larry Wood, 9/59 **FFA** Don Reid and Rick Cashner, 6/82 (route to the bench) Chuck Pratt and John Fiske, 9/60
The Rostrum, from the notch Dave Brower, Ken Adam, Richard Leonard and Rolf Pundt, 10/41
The Rostrum, Loyd's Return Trip Loyd Price
Static Cling Don Reid and Rick Cashner, 1984
Le Bachar John Bachar, Mike Lechlinski and Mari Gingery, 1982
Gorilla Grip Doug McDonald et al, late-1980s
Inch and a Quarter Blues Dale Bard and Kevin Worral, mid-1970s
Easy Street Jim Bridwell and Jim Pettigrew, 1972
Breast Fest Ken Yager et al, 1990
Alamo Al Swanson, Ken Yager, Dave Schultz and Grant Hiskes, 10/86
Jungle Book Ron Kauk and Jim Pettigrew, 1974. (Crack above-Jay Smith et al, late-1980s)
Loyd's Lolly Pop Dave Schultz, Ken Yager and Grant Hiskes, 10/86
Concrete Jungle Ken Yager et al, 1990
Minor Kinda Unit Dave Schultz, Ken Yager and Grant Hiskes, 10/86
Flight Attendant Ken Yager, Dave Schultz and Grant Hiskes, 10/86
Dancing in the Dark Scott Cosgrove and Al Swanson, 11/86
The Viper Werner Braun and John Middendorf, 10/85
Paddy Melt Jerry and Sigrid Anderson, Ken Yager, and Grant Hiskes, 1/91

First Ascent Index

Elephant's Graveyard
Walking on Mars unknown, mid-1970s
Emotional Wreckage Walt Shipley et al, 1987
Razor's Edge Mark Hudon and Max Jones, 1979
Battlescar Ed Barry and Doug MacDonald, 1987
Slit Your Tires Tucker Tech and Ray Olson, 4/90
Pet Semetary Tucker Tech and Ray Olson, 1990
Eagle Ron Kauk and George Meyers, 1973
The Elelphant Guy Dave Altman, Dave Anderson, and Eric Jansen, 1978
Boneyard Troy Johnson and Dimitri Barton, 1987
Digital Delight Dimitri Barton, Ken Ariza, and Joe Hedge, 1987

Elephant Rock
Take Da Plunge undetermined
Candy-O Kurt Smith, Dave Altman, and Tucker Tech, 10/88
Left Guru Crack undetermined
Right Guru Crack Charles Cole and Rusty Reno, 1986
Elephant Talk Kurt Smith and Tucker Tech, 10/88
Killing Yourself to Live Kurt Smith and Tucker Tech, 10/88
Keeper of the Flame Kurt Smith and Ken Ariza, 1988
Flyswatter Kevin Fosburg and Tom Borges, 1992
Isaiah 2:21 Kevin Fosburg and Tom Borges, 1992
Crack of Redemption Chuck Pratt and Chris Fredericks, 7/65
Reality Check Ray Jardine and Linda McGinnis, 10/76
Plumb Line Dale Bard, Jim Bridwell and Kevin Worrall, 5/74
Trundling Juan Ray Jardine and John Lakey, 10/76
Straight Error Mark Chapman and Jim Bridwell, 1973
Real Error Galen Rowell, Joe McKeown and Scott Walker, 6/62
Foaming at the Crotch Lance Rowlands and Tucker Tech, 10/85
Sky Dale Bard and Ron Kauk, 1976
Hocus Pocus Eric Kohl et al, early-1990s
Elephantiaisis John Yablonski and Richard Harrison, 1977
Pink Elephant Tucker Tech and Ray Olson, 4/89
Crack of Destiny Galen Rowell and Joe Faint, 3/70
The Hundredth Monkey Deanne Gray and Rolland Arsons, 1990
Fun Terminal Dimitri Barton and Ron Kauk, late-1980s
Wicked Gravity Dimitri Barton and Ron Kauk, late-1980s
Bucket Brigade Dimitri Barton and Ron Kauk, late-1980s
Elephant Malt Tucker Tech and Ken Ariza, late-1980s
Lost Error Don Reid, Rick Cashner and Ken Yager, 7/77
Crashline John Yablonski, Rick Cashner and Don Reid, 8/77
Worst Error, Left Side Warren Harding and Wayne Merry, 9/57
Worst Error, Hotline Jim Bridwell and Mark Chapman, 1973. **FFA** Ron Kauk and John Bachar, 1975. (3rd pitch variation- Merry and Werner Braun, 1991)(Summit variation- Werner Braun and Scott Cosbrove, 1984)
Worst Error, Fatal Mistake Charlie Porter and Walter Rosenthal, 1972 **FFA** (above 1st pitch) Dale Bard and Werner Braun, 1975
Pink Dream Barry Bates and Steve Wunsch, 1971
Nightmare Continuation John Bachar and Rick Cashner, 1984
Worst Error, Right Side Frank Sacherer and Galen Rowell, 11/62
A Shot in the Dark Rob Ramey and Nick Badyrka, 9/78
Crack of Doom Chuck Pratt and Mort Hempel, 10/61
Crack of Despair Frank Sacherer and Galen Rowell, 10/62 **FFA** Frank Sacherer, Chuck Pratt and Tom Gerughty, 1964
Crack of Deliverance Galen Rowell and Al Macdonald, 9/64
Hairline Jim Bridwell, Kevin Worrall, Dale Bard and George Meyers, 1974
Moongerms John Bachar and Werner Braun, 5/82
Elephant's Eliminate Ray Jardine and John Lakey, 5/78
Token of Our Extreme Ed Barry and Rick Cashner, early-1980s
Blue Ribbon Don Reid and Michael Brocado, early-1980s
Too Big For Her Top Peter Chesko and Bill Russell, mid-1980s

Arch Rock: Across the River
Cross-Train Crack Ken Ariza and Cade Loyd, 11/88
Rolo-Solo Ken Ariza and Cade Loyd, 11/88
Teacher's Pet Dave Yerian, Cade Loyd, Ken Ariza, and Merry McGrath-Braun, 11/88
Revenge of the Nurds Dave Yerian and Bruce Morris, 11/88
October Country Darwin Alonso and Jack Roberts, 9/71

Rated Route Index

5.0–5.5

- [ ] Monday Morning Slab, Right Side 5.1★ (235)
- [ ] Mothballed 5.1 (153)
- [ ] Monday Morning Slab, Left Side 5.2 (235)
- [ ] Delectable Pinnacle, Left Side 5.3★ (101)
- [ ] Aunt Fanny's Pantry 5.4★ (166)
- [ ] The Footstool, Right Side 5.4★ R (110)
- [ ] The Goblet, Left 5.4 (234)
- [ ] The Goblet, Right 5.4 (234)
- [ ] The Iota 5.4 (74)
- [ ] Start Me Up 5.4 (148)
- [ ] Arrowhead Spire 5.5★★ (164)
- [ ] Bishop's Balcony 5.5★ (167)
- [ ] The Cow, Center 5.5★ (232)
- [ ] Original Route, Arch Rock Pinnacle 5.5 (34)
- [ ] Sloppy Seconds 5.5 (66)

5.6

- [ ] After Six ★★ (124)
- [ ] The Bay Bush, The (258)
- [ ] Chimney for Two (65)
- [ ] Church Bowl Chimney ★ (166)
- [ ] The Goblet, Center (234)
- [ ] The Grack, Center Route ★★★ (232)
- [ ] Guides Route R/X (153)
- [ ] Lost Flake (168)
- [ ] Munginella ★★ (148)
- [ ] Royal Arches Route (174)
- [ ] Tennis Shoe Crack (229)
- [ ] Too High (26)

5.7

- [ ] After Five (126)
- [ ] Andy Devine (87)
- [ ] Anti-Ego Crack ★ (66)
- [ ] Antique R (148)
- [ ] Birds of a Feather (85)
- [ ] Captain Hook, Left (100)
- [ ] Chouinard Crack ★ (235)
- [ ] Claude's Delight ★ (146)
- [ ] Cornball (176)
- [ ] Cosmic Comedy (237)
- [ ] The Cow, Right (232)
- [ ] The Cracker, Right Side (311)
- [ ] Delectable Pinnacle, Right Side (101)
- [ ] Electric Gully (65)
- [ ] Farm Alarm (26)
- [ ] Gilligan's Chicken (53)
- [ ] The Grack, Left Side (232)
- [ ] He Can't Shout, Don't Hear You ★ (87)
- [ ] Icons of Filth (251)
- [ ] Improbable Traverse (320)
- [ ] Inner Reaches (78)
- [ ] Jack Pinnacle, Right (53)
- [ ] The Kids are All Right (181)
- [ ] Loggerhead Ledge Route (118)
- [ ] Lost on Venus (322)
- [ ] North Dome, South Face Route ★ (190)
- [ ] Northwest Corner, Kat Pinnacle ★ (40)
- [ ] Overhang Bypass ★★ (306)
- [ ] Pat Pinnacle (53)
- [ ] Pine Line ★★ (106)
- [ ] Pot Belly ★ (66)
- [ ] Psuedo Desperation (63)
- [ ] Pulpit Rock, East Face (320)
- [ ] Pygmy Pillar (154)
- [ ] Real Error (343)
- [ ] The Remnant, Right Side (74)
- [ ] The Rorp ★ (75)
- [ ] Rycrisp (311)
- [ ] Scuz Ball (87)
- [ ] Sloth Wall ★ (66)
- [ ] Snake Dike ★★★ R (216)
- [ ] Southwest Corner, Kat Pinnacle ★ (40)
- [ ] Tinkerbell, Left (100)
- [ ] Tiny Tim ★ X (153)
- [ ] The Trowel (178)
- [ ] Turkey Pie ★ (66)
- [ ] Uncle Fanny ★ (166)
- [ ] Yuk (81)

5.8

- [ ] After Seven ★ (124)
- [ ] Agricultural Manuvers in the Dark (119)
- [ ] The Amoeba, Left Side (311)
- [ ] Angelina (87)
- [ ] Arches Terrace (181)
- [ ] As It Is (166)
- [ ] Bishop's Terrace ★★★ (167)
- [ ] Black is Brown ★ (166)
- [ ] Blazo X (108)

Rated Route Index

5.8 cont.

- ☐ Bongs Away, Left ★ (74)
- ☐ Braille Book, The ★★★ (272)
- ☐ Bryan's Crack (252)
- ☐ Building Blocks (87)
- ☐ C.S. Concerto ★ (124)
- ☐ Caverens, The ★ (148)
- ☐ Chicken Pox (65)
- ☐ Chockblock Chimney (248)
- ☐ Church Bowl Lieback ★ (166)
- ☐ Church Bowl Terrace (166)
- ☐ Cid's Embrace (137)
- ☐ Cool Cliff 170 (26)
- ☐ The Cow, Left ★ (232)
- ☐ The Den (250)
- ☐ Desperate for Doughnuts (296)
- ☐ The Dove (85)
- ☐ Dromedary (70)
- ☐ Ejesta (75)
- ☐ Elevator Shaft ★ R (44)
- ☐ Escape (45)
- ☐ Far East (235)
- ☐ Figment (80)
- ☐ The Flakes ★ R (300)
- ☐ The Footstool, Left Side (110)
- ☐ George's Secretary (229)
- ☐ Golden Needles ★ (57)
- ☐ Gollum, Right Side ★ (108)
- ☐ The Grack, Right Side R/X (232)
- ☐ The Gray Bullet (75)
- ☐ Grove Route (153)
- ☐ The Hanging Teeth (148)
- ☐ Happy Gully (222)
- ☐ Harry Daley Route ★★★ (235)
- ☐ Hayley Anna ★ (26)
- ☐ Hershey Highway (181)
- ☐ Holidays R/X (65)
- ☐ Jughead R (148)
- ☐ Jugs R/X (65)
- ☐ Juliette's Flake, Left Side (35)
- ☐ Just Scraping By (59)
- ☐ Keystone Corner ★ (78)
- ☐ Kindergarten Crack (34)
- ☐ Knob Hill Rapist R/X (66)
- ☐ L.D. Getaway (87)
- ☐ Lieback Route (152)
- ☐ Little John, Left ★ (105)
- ☐ Little John, Right ★★★ (105)
- ☐ Mischief (150)
- ☐ Mojo Tooth (80)
- ☐ Movin' to Montana ★ (66)
- ☐ Mud Shark (57)
- ☐ Nerf Test (35)
- ☐ North Dome, West Face Route (190)
- ☐ Notably Knobular (59)
- ☐ Nurdle ★ (53)
- ☐ Nutcracker ★★★ (124)
- ☐ Nutty Buddy (128)
- ☐ Patio Pinnacle, Right Side R (234)
- ☐ Patio Pinnacle, Regular Route R (234)
- ☐ Pharoah's Beard, Regular Route ★ (262)
- ☐ Point Beyond ★★ (237)
- ☐ Point Beyond, Direct ★ (237)
- ☐ Rectum Ranch (115)
- ☐ RF (142)
- ☐ Roger Stokes Route (142)
- ☐ Scrooged (153)
- ☐ Selaginella (150)
- ☐ The Sequel ★ (272)
- ☐ Shiver-Me-Timbers (325)
- ☐ Skid Row (190)
- ☐ Sorry Poopsie ★ (119)
- ☐ Squeeze-n-Tease (87)
- ☐ Stepahnie's Corner (167)
- ☐ Stonequest ★★ R (26)
- ☐ The Surprise (148)
- ☐ The Syllable (272)
- ☐ Tilted Mitten, Right Side ★ (258)
- ☐ Trial By Fire (172)
- ☐ Try Again Ledge ★ (148)
- ☐ Tweedle Dee (135)
- ☐ Wart Hog (53)
- ☐ Werner's Crack (198)

5.9

- ☐ 5.9 Grunt (237)
- ☐ Absolutely Free, Center Route ★★ (129)
- ☐ Absolutely Free, Left Side (129)
- ☐ Angel's Approach ★★★ (237)
- ☐ Angelica ★ R (234)
- ☐ Apathy Buttress (201)
- ☐ Application (32)
- ☐ Apron Jam ★ (237)
- ☐ Arlington Heights ★ (68)
- ☐ Bacchigaloupe Wall (150)
- ☐ Bad Acid (237)
- ☐ Betrayal (252)
- ☐ Blazing Buckets (74)
- ☐ Blind Alley ★ (272)
- ☐ Blind Man's Bluff ★ (272)
- ☐ Block Horror Picture Show (69)
- ☐ Bongs Away, Right (74)
- ☐ Book End (148)
- ☐ Brown-Eyed Girl (119)
- ☐ The Buttocks (136)
- ☐ Center Route (26)
- ☐ The Chase ★★ R (26)
- ☐ Chicken Pie ★★ (65)
- ☐ Chockstone Chimney (93)
- ☐ The Chosen Few (311)
- ☐ The Cleft ★ R (45)

Rated Route Index

5.9 cont.

- [ ] Color Me Gone ★ (26)
- [ ] Commissioner Buttress ★ (126)
- [ ] Commitment ★★ (148)
- [ ] The Cookie, Center Route ★ (45)
- [ ] The Cookie, Right Side ★★ (45)
- [ ] Coonyard Pinnacle R (234)
- [ ] Coonyard to The Oasis (234)
- [ ] Costa Rica ★ R (26)
- [ ] Country Corner (328)
- [ ] Crack of Deliverance (346)
- [ ] Crack of Destiny (341)
- [ ] Cross-Country Crack (34)
- [ ] Crossover ★ (26)
- [ ] Deception Gully (66)
- [ ] The Deuceldike ★ R (216)
- [ ] Dirty Little Secret (32)
- [ ] Doggie Deviations ★★ (136)
- [ ] Doggie Diversion ★ (136)
- [ ] Dolly Dagger (87)
- [ ] Dome Polishers ★★ R (216)
- [ ] Dynamic Doubles ★ (124)
- [ ] Eagle's Eyrie (26)
- [ ] Easy Wind R (124)
- [ ] Elephant Malt R (341)
- [ ] The Enigma ★★ (45)
- [ ] Entranc★★xam ★ (32)
- [ ] Eric's Book (198)
- [ ] Fallen Arches (181)
- [ ] False Verde (59)
- [ ] Fecophilia ★ R (124)
- [ ] Fifteen Seconds of Fame (104)
- [ ] Filthy Rich (57)
- [ ] Five o'Clock Shadow X (295)
- [ ] Flakey Foot ★ R/X (234)
- [ ] Flatus (75)
- [ ] Fluke (80)
- [ ] The Folly, Left Side (133)
- [ ] Fun (72)
- [ ] Fun Flake (37)
- [ ] Gidget Goes to Yosemite ★ (114)
- [ ] God's Creation (124)
- [ ] Gold Leaf (93)
- [ ] Goodrich Pinnacle, Left Side (234)
- [ ] Goodrich Pinnacle, Right Side ★★★ R (234)
- [ ] Grape Nuts ★ (80)
- [ ] Half Dome, Regular Northwest Face ★★★ (212)
- [ ] Hampton Estates (68)
- [ ] Handshake (150)
- [ ] Hawkman's Escape (131)
- [ ] Higher Cathedral Rock, Northeast Buttress ★★★ (274)
- [ ] Higher Cathedral Spire, Regular (Southwest Face) Route (270)
- [ ] Hot Tin Roof ★ (232)
- [ ] I Don't Remember (324)
- [ ] Infraction (45)
- [ ] Jack Pinnacle, Left (53)
- [ ] Jamcrack Route ★★ (152)
- [ ] Jolly Green Giant (138)
- [ ] Jug Monkey ★ (57)
- [ ] Jump for Joy ★ (124)
- [ ] Klemens' Escape ★ (32)
- [ ] Kor0Beck ★ (282)
- [ ] La Cosita, Left ★ (105)
- [ ] La Cosita, Right ★★★ (105)
- [ ] Lancelot ★ (137)
- [ ] The Last Resort Pinnacle, Left Side (263)
- [ ] Lemon (152)
- [ ] Lena's Lieback ★ (146)
- [ ] The Letdown (237)
- [ ] Lost Boys (100)
- [ ] Lower Cathedral Spire, Fredericks-Sacherer Variation (268)
- [ ] Lower Cathedral Spire, Northeast Face (268)
- [ ] Lower Cathedral Spire, Pratt-Faint Variation ★ (268)
- [ ] Lower Cathedral Spire, Regular Route ★ (269)
- [ ] Loyd's Lolly Pop (335)
- [ ] Loyd's Return Trip ★ (334)
- [ ] Lucifer's Ledge (237)
- [ ] Lucifer's to The Oasis R/X (237)
- [ ] Marginal ★★★ R (232)
- [ ] Mass Assualt (190)
- [ ] McPherson Struts ★ (234)
- [ ] Minor Kinda Unit (335)
- [ ] Mirror, Mirror Right (198)
- [ ] Moby Dick, Left ★ (106)
- [ ] Monday Morning To Patio R (235)
- [ ] The Mouse King R (124)
- [ ] The Mouth, Boche-Hennek Variation (234)
- [ ] The Mouth, Regular ★ R (234)
- [ ] Nautral End (80)
- [ ] New Deviations ★★ (65)
- [ ] Observation Point (150)
- [ ] On The Loose (248)
- [ ] The Owl Bypass ★ (70)
- [ ] Pass or Fail (34)
- [ ] Patio Pinnacle, Left Side R (234)
- [ ] Peter Pan ★ (100)
- [ ] Phantom Pinnacle, Left Side ★ (265)
- [ ] Pink Elephant ★ (341)
- [ ] Positively 4th Street ★★ (128)
- [ ] Prime Time (50)
- [ ] The Princess (311)
- [ ] The Prude ★★ (198)
- [ ] Quicksliver ★★★ R (295)
- [ ] Radical Chic R (65)
- [ ] Raisin ★ R (152)
- [ ] Ramp of Deception ★★ (45)
- [ ] Reed's Pinnacle Regular Route ★★★ (74)
- [ ] Ribald (153)
- [ ] Royal Arches Route (177)

Rated Route Index

5.9 cont.

- [ ] Royal Prerogative (175)
- [ ] Said and Done (63)
- [ ] Sand Jam (245)
- [ ] Sawyer Crack (26)
- [ ] Scruv (57)
- [ ] Shit on a Shingle (72)
- [ ] Shuttle Madness ★ (232)
- [ ] Side Kick (84)
- [ ] Simulkrime R/X (108)
- [ ] Snake Dance ★ R (216)
- [ ] Solo Crack (59)
- [ ] Son of Sam (237)
- [ ] The Sphinxter (259)
- [ ] Steck Route ★ (271)
- [ ] Steck-Salathé (256)
- [ ] Super Slab ★ (172)
- [ ] Swollen Plecnode (296)
- [ ] The Symphony (248)
- [ ] Tapestry ★ R (295)
- [ ] TD's Dihedral (142)
- [ ] Tilted Mitten, Left Side (258)
- [ ] Tinkerbell, Right (100)
- [ ] Tithe (248)
- [ ] Traffic Jam (71)
- [ ] Tree Route ★ (320)
- [ ] The Triscuit (311)
- [ ] Trivial Pursuit (178)
- [ ] Unemployment Line (226)
- [ ] Walrus (71)
- [ ] Way Lost (229)
- [ ] Wendy (100)
- [ ] Whim (63)
- [ ] Wild Child (142)
- [ ] Woody Woodpecker (26)
- [ ] Worst Error, Left Side (344)
- [ ] Wrong Address (68)
- [ ] Yasoo Dome, South Face (206)
- [ ] Yosemite Point Buttress, Direct Route (162)
- [ ] Your Pizza is Ready (323)
- [ ] Wasp 5.9d (65)

5.10a

- [ ] A-5 Pinnacle (165)
- [ ] Absolutely Free, Right Side R/X (129)
- [ ] Alley Cat (278)
- [ ] Apple Seeds (138)
- [ ] Arête Butler (175)
- [ ] Armed and Dangerous (151)
- [ ] B and B (84)
- [ ] Babble On (53)
- [ ] Bad News Bombers (80)
- [ ] Banana Dreams (44)
- [ ] Beer Pressure R (124)
- [ ] Beverly's Tower ★★ (44)
- [ ] Bikini Beach Party (114)
- [ ] Black Sunday (84)
- [ ] Bongs Away, Center (74)
- [ ] Bottom Feeder ★ (295)
- [ ] Bottom Feeder ★ (295)
- [ ] Breezin' (314)
- [ ] Brown Sugar R (115)
- [ ] Bunghole of the Universe (293)
- [ ] Cartwheel (325)
- [ ] Cat Dancing ★★ (295)
- [ ] Cereal Killer (80)
- [ ] Chairman Ted Scraps the Time Machine (122)
- [ ] Chingando ★ (74)
- [ ] Compass Rose (304)
- [ ] Conquest of the Stud Monkey ★ (119)
- [ ] The Cookie, Left Side (45)
- [ ] Copper Penny ★ (78)
- [ ] Crack of Despair (346)
- [ ] Crack of Doom (346)
- [ ] Crest Jewel ★★★ (194)
- [ ] Crotch Cricket (293)
- [ ] Dark Shadows (228)
- [ ] Deaf, Dumb and Blind ★ R (148)
- [ ] Deep Throat ★ R (234)
- [ ] Deja Thorus ★ (166)
- [ ] Desperate Straights ★ (53)
- [ ] Dinner Ledge ★ (185)
- [ ] Doggie Do (136)
- [ ] Drop-out ★ (311)
- [ ] Dust in the Wind (106)
- [ ] Eagle (337)
- [ ] Elephant Rock, Right Side Route (346)
- [ ] Euellogy ★ (80)
- [ ] Fifty Crowded Variation ★ (280)
- [ ] Fine Line (174)
- [ ] Flary Tales (57)
- [ ] Foaming at the Crotch (343)
- [ ] Fool's Gold (90)
- [ ] Free Press ★★ (57)
- [ ] Free Ride ★ R/X (77)
- [ ] Fresh Squeezed (229)
- [ ] Fuddy Duddy (128)
- [ ] Gang Bang (72)
- [ ] Geek Towers, Center Route (157)
- [ ] Geek Towers, Right Side (157)
- [ ] The Girl Next Door, Right Side (141)
- [ ] Goat For It (146)
- [ ] Golden Bough (89)
- [ ] Gollum, Left Side (108)
- [ ] Guru Crack, Right ★ (340)
- [ ] Hand Job (72)
- [ ] The Hand Me Down (258)
- [ ] Hari-kiri ★ (259)
- [ ] The Hawaiian (26)
- [ ] Health Insurance (37)

Rated Route Index

5.10a cont.

- ☐ Hell's Hollow ★ (172)
- ☐ Henley Quits ★★ (137)
- ☐ Higher Cathedral Spire, Southeast Side, East Corner ★ (271)
- ☐ Highway Star ★ (82)
- ☐ The Hourglass, Right Side (93)
- ☐ I Don't Know (324)
- ☐ Jaw Bone ★ (37)
- ☐ Just Do-D- It (124)
- ☐ Katchup (40)
- ☐ Ken's Dream (201)
- ☐ King Cobra (63)
- ☐ The Last Resort Pinnacle, Center (263)
- ☐ LeNocturne (119)
- ☐ Lichen Madness (235)
- ☐ Lichen Nightmare (235)
- ☐ Loose Tooth City (69)
- ☐ Lost Arrow Chimney (158)
- ☐ Lost Error (343)
- ☐ Lynnea's Birthday Surprise (181)
- ☐ Magical Mystery Tour ★ (75)
- ☐ Maple Jam ★ (128)
- ☐ Middle Cathedral Rock, North Buttress ★ (292)
- ☐ Milk Dud (232)
- ☐ Moby Dick, Center ★★★ (106)
- ☐ Mongolian Clusterfuck R (72)
- ☐ Mr. Happy (119)
- ☐ My Rhombus (169)
- ☐ Neutron Escape (84)
- ☐ New Diversions ★★★ (65)
- ☐ Nottingham (93)
- ☐ Now (34)
- ☐ On the Wedge (59)
- ☐ Open Trench (322)
- ☐ Orange Juice Avenue ★ (118)
- ☐ Pandora's Box (37)
- ☐ Paradise Lost ★ R (288)
- ☐ Patio To Coonyard (234)
- ☐ Pee Pee Pillar ★★ (288)
- ☐ Peeping Tom (174)
- ☐ Peruvian Flake ★ (174)
- ☐ Pink Dream (346)
- ☐ Plumkin (84)
- ☐ Pole Position ★ (166)
- ☐ Porter's Pout (75)
- ☐ Priceless Friends ★ (193)
- ☐ The Prow ★ (185)
- ☐ Prune ★ (152)
- ☐ Pterodactyl Terrace, Left R (106)
- ☐ The Punch Bowl R (239)
- ☐ R and R (37)
- ☐ Rat's Tooth (258)
- ☐ The Reception (78)
- ☐ Red House (87)
- ☐ Reed's Pinnacle Direct ★★★ (74)
- ☐ Reed's Pinnacle, Left Side (74)
- ☐ Rehab Doll (81)
- ☐ Renus Wrinkle ★ (124)
- ☐ The Resurrection (252)
- ☐ Revival ★ (166)
- ☐ Riddler ★ (87)
- ☐ Rixon's Pinnacle, East Chimney ★ (132)
- ☐ Roto Killer (229)
- ☐ Run With Me ★ (239)
- ☐ Sacherer Cracker ★★★ (104)
- ☐ Say Mama, Say Daddy R (108)
- ☐ Scott-Child (197)
- ☐ Secret Storm ★ (135)
- ☐ Sex, Drugs and Violence (84)
- ☐ Shake and Bake ★ X (301)
- ☐ Siberian Swarm Screw ★ (72)
- ☐ Skateaway (34)
- ☐ Sober Up (119)
- ☐ Sons of Yesterday ★★★ (173)
- ☐ Sow Sow Sow (119)
- ☐ Spooky Tooth ★ X (301)
- ☐ Static Clinb ★ (334)
- ☐ Stay Lady Stay Back (119)
- ☐ The Steal (84)
- ☐ Straight In (90)
- ☐ Swillar Pillar (119)
- ☐ Tears of Joy ★ (295)
- ☐ This and That (63)
- ☐ Tiger's Paw (84)
- ☐ The Tooth (74)
- ☐ Trial by Jury (184)
- ☐ Twist of Fate (182)
- ☐ Udder Way, An ★ R (232)
- ☐ Walk on By (323)
- ☐ Weird Scenes in the Gold Mine (63)
- ☐ Wise Crack (176)
- ☐ Y Crack ★ (175)

5.10b

- ☐ Anathema ★★ (45)
- ☐ Avalon ★ (142)
- ☐ Back To The Slammer ★★ (201)
- ☐ The Bear (232)
- ☐ Blackballed ★ (152)
- ☐ Bluballed ★ (153)
- ☐ Bone Yard (327)
- ☐ Book of Job ★ (272)
- ☐ Breathalizer (198)
- ☐ Calf Continuation R (232)
- ☐ Cat Fight ★ (41)
- ☐ Chicken Fever (53)
- ☐ Chicken's Choice (134)
- ☐ Church Bowl Tree ★★ (166)

Rated Route Index

5.10b cont.

- [ ] Crack 'n Face (78)
- [ ] Cynical Pinnacle, Wrong (229)
- [ ] Dick Wrenching Classic (118)
- [ ] Doggie Submission * (243)
- [ ] Domehead (53)
- [ ] Double Trouble (176)
- [ ] Dressed to Kill R (26)
- [ ] East Buttress ** (113)
- [ ] Exodus * R (295)
- [ ] Eye in the Sky * R (216)
- [ ] Falcon (65)
- [ ] The Fang (184)
- [ ] Fasten Your Seat Belts * R/X (77)
- [ ] The Flake (50)
- [ ] Freewheelin' *** R (295)
- [ ] Friday the 13th (181)
- [ ] Gash * (305)
- [ ] Gay Bob's (53)
- [ ] Gripper *** (32)
- [ ] Happy's Favorite (119)
- [ ] Heathenistic Pursuit ** (246)
- [ ] Hoppy's Favorite * R (232)
- [ ] Independent Route * (75)
- [ ] Indica Point (150)
- [ ] Jam Session * (325)
- [ ] Jojo ** (185)
- [ ] The Joker R (311)
- [ ] Jordi-Sattva * (264)
- [ ] King Tut's Tomb (259)
- [ ] Knob Job * (53)
- [ ] Knuckleheads ** (53)
- [ ] Krovy Rookers (175)
- [ ] Kung Pao Chicken (260)
- [ ] Labor of Love * R (214)
- [ ] Lap Lobster (293)
- [ ] Left Mini-Meanie (182)
- [ ] Left Wing (148)
- [ ] Leisure Time * (87)
- [ ] The Lionheart (93)
- [ ] Looking for Lichen (235)
- [ ] Love Misslie F1-11 (252)
- [ ] Lunar Landscape R (108)
- [ ] Middle Cathedral Rock, Direct North Buttress *** (289)
- [ ] Midterm *** (32)
- [ ] Mirror, Mirror Left (198)
- [ ] Moby Dick, Ahab * (106)
- [ ] My Left Foot R (128)
- [ ] New Traditionalists * R (80)
- [ ] No Butts About It (280)
- [ ] No Falls Wall (84)
- [ ] Notch Route R (320)
- [ ] NWR (Not Worth Repeating) (305)
- [ ] On Any Thursday (235)
- [ ] Orange Peel ** R (295)
- [ ] Paddy Melt (335)
- [ ] Party Mix * (107)
- [ ] Per-Spire-ation (34)
- [ ] Permanent Waves R (172)
- [ ] Plane Fare * (229)
- [ ] The Plank (181)
- [ ] Poker Face (176)
- [ ] Police State (165)
- [ ] Porcelain Pup * (224)
- [ ] Pulpit Pooper * (320)
- [ ] Pygmy Sex Circus (71)
- [ ] Quaker Flake R/X (148)
- [ ] Quickie Quizzes * (32)
- [ ] Reed's Leads (106)
- [ ] The Remnant, Left Side (74)
- [ ] Salathé Route * R (215)
- [ ] Scratching Post (41)
- [ ] The Sermon ** (321)
- [ ] Shake, Rattle and Drop (65)
- [ ] The Silent Freeway, Center Route * (120)
- [ ] Silent Majority (199)
- [ ] Sixth Heaven * (252)
- [ ] Skid Roper (81)
- [ ] The Slack, Left Side (104)
- [ ] Sleight of Hand (176)
- [ ] Snake in the Grass (215)
- [ ] Spank Your Monkey * (293)
- [ ] Stone Groove ** (75)
- [ ] Strangers in the Night (65)
- [ ] Stupid Pet Tricks ** (295)
- [ ] Sunday Driver (105)
- [ ] Synapse Collapse * (232)
- [ ] Teenage Mutant Blowjobs (119)
- [ ] Tom Cat (185)
- [ ] Too Much Paranoia (87)
- [ ] Tooth Fairy (81)
- [ ] Trough of Juice * (53)
- [ ] Trundling Juan (343)
- [ ] Uncertain Ending * (49)
- [ ] Variation on a Themem * (235)
- [ ] Vendetta * (45)
- [ ] Waterfall Route Start R (111)
- [ ] West Side Story (148)
- [ ] Wicked Jones Crusher * (71)
- [ ] Winterlewd (199)

5.10

- [ ] Aids Curve 5.10 (26)
- [ ] Battle-Ship 5.10 (334)
- [ ] Cheap Friction (148)
- [ ] Defoliation (153)
- [ ] Dire Straights (176)
- [ ] Dynamite Crack (42)
- [ ] Earth First (251)
- [ ] Eat at Degnan's 5.10* (323)

Rated Route Index

5.10 cont.

- [ ] Elephant Guy (337)
- [ ] Gillette 5.10★ (138)
- [ ] The Girl Next Door, Left Side (141)
- [ ] Gold Wall (92)
- [ ] Hangover Heights (251)
- [ ] Jungle Book ★ (335)
- [ ] Level Two (175)
- [ ] Marvin Gardens (150)
- [ ] Meat Puppet (63)
- [ ] Moonchild R (105)
- [ ] Morality Crack (251)
- [ ] Opposite World R/X (57)
- [ ] Public Sanitation (244)
- [ ] Ramblin' Rose (131)
- [ ] Running Hummock (148)
- [ ] Salami Ledge (96)
- [ ] Sea Cow (174)
- [ ] Sea Hag (174)
- [ ] Slumgullion (84)
- [ ] The Soloist 5.10★ R (26)
- [ ] Starfire ★ X (301)
- [ ] Sunnside Pinnacle (152)
- [ ] Teenage Abortion (141)
- [ ] To Beer or Not To Be (152)
- [ ] Vegetal Extraction (153)
- [ ] Winter of Our Discontent (148)

5.10c

- [ ] Air Bare ★ (229)
- [ ] Anal Tongue Darts (74)
- [ ] Barefoot Servants (311)
- [ ] Beat Around the Bush (148)
- [ ] Beat The Clock (311)
- [ ] Benzoin and Edges (181)
- [ ] Beyond the Fringe (75)
- [ ] Bijou ★ (78)
- [ ] Bourbon Street (245)
- [ ] Breast Fest ★★ (335)
- [ ] Bridalveil East ★★ (307)
- [ ] Bummer ★ (152)
- [ ] Butthole Climber (152)
- [ ] By Way of the Flake R (252)
- [ ] Castaways ★ (314)
- [ ] Chopper ★ (135)
- [ ] Chow Chow Chow ★ (119)
- [ ] Cold Fusion ★★ (237)
- [ ] Compass (40)
- [ ] Cost of Living (134)
- [ ] Crazy Train (74)
- [ ] Cynical Pinnacle, Right ★ (229)
- [ ] The Dihardral ★ (120)
- [ ] Dime Bag ★ (330)
- [ ] Diminishing Returns (198)
- [ ] Dorn's Crack (251)
- [ ] Dromedary Direct (70)
- [ ] Dwindling Stances (152)
- [ ] Eagle Feather ★ (85)
- [ ] Edge of Night ★ (135)
- [ ] English Breakfast Crack ★ (32)
- [ ] Face Card (176)
- [ ] Fallout (138)
- [ ] Flight Attendant ★★ (335)
- [ ] Gardening At Night (166)
- [ ] Generator Crack ★ TR (64)
- [ ] Goosebumps (74)
- [ ] Gravity's Rainbow (225)
- [ ] Guru Crack, Left ★ (340)
- [ ] Heretic (167)
- [ ] Ho Chi Minh Trail ★★ (290)
- [ ] Honor Thy Father ★ (87)
- [ ] Hoosier's Highway ★ R (234)
- [ ] Ilsa She Wolf of the SS (175)
- [ ] Jacob's Ladder (166)
- [ ] Jesu Joy ★ (184)
- [ ] La Arista (105)
- [ ] Lonely Dancer (237)
- [ ] Lost Brother, Northwest Face Route (263)
- [ ] Lower Cathedral Rock, East Buttress ★★ (302)
- [ ] Lunatic Fringe ★★★ (75)
- [ ] Mainliner (72)
- [ ] Maxine's Wall ★ (172)
- [ ] Meat Grinder ★★ (44)
- [ ] Mental Block ★★★ (258)
- [ ] Miramonte (49)
- [ ] Moan Fest R (173)
- [ ] Moe, Larry, The Cheese (151)
- [ ] Monkey Do (325)
- [ ] Mother's Lament, A R/X (232)
- [ ] Mr. Natural ★★★ (237)
- [ ] Narrow Escape (28)
- [ ] Nowhere Man (185)
- [ ] Original Chips Ahoy ★ (42)
- [ ] Original Sin (320)
- [ ] Outer Limits ★★★ (44)
- [ ] Pieces of Eight ★ R (287)
- [ ] Polymorphous Perverse (72)
- [ ] Powell-Reed (286)
- [ ] Ramer ★★★ (293)
- [ ] Reality Check (343)
- [ ] Rixon's Pinnacle, East Chimney, Klemens Variation (132)
- [ ] Rixon's Pinnacle, West Face ★★ (132)
- [ ] The Rostrum, West Base Route (334)
- [ ] Rurp Rape R (198)
- [ ] Sacherer-Fredericks (281)
- [ ] Scrub Scouts (319)
- [ ] Seaside ★ (143)
- [ ] Secret Agent (63)
- [ ] Sex Farm (293)
- [ ] Sherrie's Crack ★★ (53)

Rated Route Index

5.10c cont.

- ☐ Silber Platter (225)
- ☐ The Silent Freeway ★ (120)
- ☐ Sky Pilot (321)
- ☐ Snap, Crackle, and Pop (42)
- ☐ Snatch Power ★ (37)
- ☐ Space Case (184)
- ☐ Space Doubt (134)
- ☐ Split Pinnacle, East Arête (127)
- ☐ Stoner's Highway ★★★ (286)
- ☐ Straight Error (343)
- ☐ Stroke (My Erect Ear Tufts) R (70)
- ☐ Sub-Mission ★ (304)
- ☐ Sultans of Sling (152)
- ☐ Supplication ★ (32)
- ☐ Surplus Cheaper Hands R (174)
- ☐ Sweet Pea ★ (148)
- ☐ Tammy Fae R (166)
- ☐ Thin Man (198)
- ☐ Through Bein' Cool (50)
- ☐ Transistor Sister ★ (232)
- ☐ Tricky Fingers (53)
- ☐ Turning Point ★ (84)
- ☐ Twinkie (44)
- ☐ Two "D" (32)
- ☐ Ugly Duckling ★ R (146)
- ☐ Unagi (259)
- ☐ Uppity Women (199)
- ☐ The Violent Bear It Away (178, 181)
- ☐ Voyage ★ (32)
- ☐ Waste of Time (321)
- ☐ Waverly Wafer ★★★ (44)
- ☐ Way-Homo Sperm Burpers from Fresno (175)
- ☐ Werner's Ant Trees (148)
- ☐ Wheat Thin ★★★ (45)
- ☐ Wild Thing (133)
- ☐ Wild Turkey ★ (85)
- ☐ Wing of Bat ★ (185)
- ☐ William's Climb (72)
- ☐ Windjammer ★★ (314)
- ☐ Work Around the Skirt ★ (148)
- ☐ Yeast Infection (118)
- ☐ Young and The Restless (134)

5.10d

- ☐ 10.96 (181)
- ☐ Afterglow (237)
- ☐ Agent Orange ★ (63)
- ☐ Ahwahnee Buttress (173)
- ☐ Armageddon R (108)
- ☐ Barney Rubble (176)
- ☐ Bench Warmer (152)
- ☐ The Bin ★ (34)
- ☐ Blotto ★ (32)
- ☐ Boogie with Stu (148)
- ☐ Book 'em Dano (53)
- ☐ Brainbucket (53)
- ☐ Call of the Wild (222)
- ☐ Catchy ★★★ (45)
- ☐ Central Pillar of Frenzy ★★★ (285)
- ☐ Cheek R (136)
- ☐ Combustable Knowledge ★ (152)
- ☐ Concrete Jungle (335)
- ☐ Conductor Crack TR (64)
- ☐ Cramming ★★★ (63)
- ☐ Creeping Lethargy (201)
- ☐ Cuthulu R (100)
- ☐ Danger Will Robinson (74)
- ☐ Deucey's Elbow (115)
- ☐ Distant Driver (175)
- ☐ Dr. Feel Good ★ (237)
- ☐ Drunk Tank (119)
- ☐ East Arrow Chimney (164)
- ☐ Elephantiasis ★ R (341)
- ☐ End of the World (113)
- ☐ Eraser Head R/X (57)
- ☐ Exit From The Notch (158)
- ☐ Extra Credit (35)
- ☐ Far Right (198)
- ☐ Feminine Protection (175)
- ☐ Fertile Attraction (153)
- ☐ Final Exam ★★★ (212)
- ☐ Finger Lickin' ★★ (37)
- ☐ Fire Drill (239)
- ☐ Five and Dime ★★★ (78)
- ☐ Flexible Flyer (124)
- ☐ Frosted Flakes (133)
- ☐ The Gerbil Launcher (59)
- ☐ Gold Dust ★★ (246)
- ☐ Golden Dawn (205)
- ☐ The Good Book ★★★ (133)
- ☐ Gorilla Cookies (321)
- ☐ Greasy but Groovy (181)
- ☐ Half Dome, North Ridge ★★★ R (210)
- ☐ Harldy Pinnacle ★ (105)
- ☐ Higher Cathedral Spire, Southeast Side, Southeast Face (271)
- ☐ Home Run ★ (295)
- ☐ Humdinger ★ (63)
- ☐ The Illusion R (126)
- ☐ Independence Pinnacle, Center Route ★ (75)
- ☐ Indisposed (245)
- ☐ King of Hearts (176)
- ☐ Kling Cobra (178)
- ☐ Lazy Bum ★★ (152)
- ☐ Lingering Lie R (152)
- ☐ Little Girl's Route (250)
- ☐ Little John, Center (105)
- ☐ Little Wing ★★ (87)
- ☐ Manana ★★ (259)

Rated Route Index

5.10d cont.

- [ ] The Mark of Art ** (104)
- [ ] Meatheads TR (50)
- [ ] Metal Error R (175)
- [ ] Midnight Rampest R (75)
- [ ] Mighty Crunchy * (81)
- [ ] Mindahoonee Wall ** (143)
- [ ] Misty Beethoven *** R (234)
- [ ] Movin' Like a Stud (181)
- [ ] Mudflaps (138)
- [ ] New Testament * (252)
- [ ] No Exit (37)
- [ ] Nothing Good Ever Lasts (77)
- [ ] Old Five Ten * R (75)
- [ ] Olga's Trick * (74)
- [ ] People's Court (53)
- [ ] Perhaps (232)
- [ ] The Perpetrator (26)
- [ ] Phantom Pinnacle, Outside Face (265)
- [ ] Pharaoh's Beard, Right Side * (262)
- [ ] Pink Banana (63)
- [ ] Plumb Line (343)
- [ ] The Punch Line (239)
- [ ] The Rambler (181)
- [ ] Redtide (153)
- [ ] Reefer Madness (181)
- [ ] Romantic Tension * (48)
- [ ] Rum Sodomy in the Lash (175)
- [ ] Salin' Shoes ** (237)
- [ ] Sanitary Engineer (245)
- [ ] Santa Barbara (135)
- [ ] Scorpion Man (53)
- [ ] Serenity Crack *** (172)
- [ ] The Shaft (70)
- [ ] Shattered (84)
- [ ] Simian Sex ** (118)
- [ ] Skinheads *** (53)
- [ ] The Slack, Center Route (104)
- [ ] Slamming Right (63)
- [ ] Slap that Bitch (63)
- [ ] Solid Waste * (245)
- [ ] Spuds McKenzie (42)
- [ ] Steppin' Out ** (75)
- [ ] Straight Jacket (197)
- [ ] Supertoe (115)
- [ ] Teenage Warning (69)
- [ ] Terminator, Right * (45)
- [ ] The Thief ** (311)
- [ ] Twilight Zone ** (44)
- [ ] Vanishing Point ** (258)
- [ ] Void Continuation * R/X (45)
- [ ] W 'allnuts (86)
- [ ] Walk of LIfe * R (295)
- [ ] White Cloud (57)
- [ ] White Dike, The (237, 239)
- [ ] Wicked Arêtation (57)
- [ ] Wide Thing * (244)
- [ ] Ying-Yang ** (259)

5.11a

- [ ] 800 Club * (166)
- [ ] A la Moana (40)
- [ ] Alamo * R (335)
- [ ] Anchors Away *** (237)
- [ ] Astro Spam (174)
- [ ] Back in the Saddle (63)
- [ ] Bitches' Terror ** (167)
- [ ] Blasphemy (167)
- [ ] Blue Funk (237)
- [ ] Bluffer * (110)
- [ ] Bolt Adventures * (57)
- [ ] Book of Revelations ** (166)
- [ ] Buried Treasure * (262)
- [ ] Butterfinger ** (45)
- [ ] The Cafeteria Lieback * (243)
- [ ] Catchy Corner *** (45)
- [ ] Childhood's End ** (133)
- [ ] The Cobra * R (177)
- [ ] Controlled Burn ** (247)
- [ ] Cosmic Messenger * (35)
- [ ] Cosmic Ray (75)
- [ ] Cream ** (325)
- [ ] Critical Path (280)
- [ ] Days of Our Lives (135)
- [ ] Demon's Delight *** (115)
- [ ] Desperate Kneed, A (26)
- [ ] Destination Zero (201)
- [ ] Deviltry R (172)
- [ ] Drink and Drive * (148)
- [ ] DUI (119)
- [ ] Duncan Imperial (85)
- [ ] Ennui (296)
- [ ] Eraser Flake R (53)
- [ ] Fatal Mistake (344)
- [ ] Fist Puppet (36)
- [ ] Flagman (319)
- [ ] Flailing Dog * (53)
- [ ] Fly By (26)
- [ ] Free Bong (115)
- [ ] Galloping Consumption * (142)
- [ ] God Told Me To Skin You Alive (178)
- [ ] Grateful Pinheads * (63)
- [ ] The Happy Ending * (120)
- [ ] Here On The Inside * (119)
- [ ] High Profile * (37)
- [ ] The Hourglass, Left Side * R (93)
- [ ] Inch and a Quarter Blues * (328)
- [ ] Indubious Battle * (100)
- [ ] Jardine's Hand * (45)
- [ ] Jigsaw * R (295)
- [ ] Knuckle Buster ** (165)
- [ ] Koki Duck (146)

Rated Route Index

5.11a cont.

- ☐ Ladyfingers ★★ (45)
- ☐ Lagerhead ★ (118)
- ☐ Later (34)
- ☐ Law of Tools ★ (57)
- ☐ Lay Lady Lieback (247)
- ☐ Lean Years ★ (237)
- ☐ Left Rabbit Ear Route (291)
- ☐ Like a Hurricane (327)
- ☐ Look Before You Leap R/X (262)
- ☐ Malice Aforethought ★ (272)
- ☐ Maltese Falcon ★ (57)
- ☐ Master of Cylinders ★ (168)
- ☐ Megaforce ★ (311)
- ☐ Monster Boulder (342)
- ☐ Moon Age Daydream ★ (84)
- ☐ Mother of the Future (172)
- ☐ Motor Drive (81)
- ☐ New Dimensions ★★★ (32)
- ☐ North by Northwest R (304)
- ☐ Obscure Destiny ★ (49)
- ☐ Ochre Fields ★ R (232, 234)
- ☐ Overdrive (318)
- ☐ Plant Your Fingers (128)
- ☐ PMS (84)
- ☐ Power Failure ★★ (184)
- ☐ Precious Powder ★ (198)
- ☐ Pussy Licked (41)
- ☐ QED aka East of Eden (169)
- ☐ Radioactive (84)
- ☐ Rattlesnake Buttress (307)
- ☐ Ready or Not ★ (84)
- ☐ Return to the Stone Age ★ R (307)
- ☐ Right Mini-Meanie (182)
- ☐ Sacrilege (167)
- ☐ The Sceptor ★ (260)
- ☐ Seedy Leads (106)
- ☐ Shakey Flakes (181)
- ☐ Short but Thick ★ (36)
- ☐ Sidetrack (32)
- ☐ The Silent Freeway, Left Side ★ (120)
- ☐ Skid Row Messiah R (166)
- ☐ Smee's Come-on (100)
- ☐ South by Southwest ★★★ (269)
- ☐ Space Babble ★ R (283)
- ☐ Sparkling Give-away (105)
- ☐ Spring Chicken (65)
- ☐ Stacked Deck (176)
- ☐ Stand and Quiver ★ (53)
- ☐ Stealth Technology (35)
- ☐ Stinger ★ (53)
- ☐ Summary Judgement ★ (63)
- ☐ Sunset Strip (313)
- ☐ Super Nova ★ (330)
- ☐ Superstem (115)
- ☐ Sylvester's Meow (75)
- ☐ Texas Chain Saw Massacre (176)
- ☐ Thirsty Spire ★ (290)
- ☐ Thread of Life (106)
- ☐ Tidbit ★ (303)
- ☐ Trix (68)
- ☐ The Tube ★★ (53)
- ☐ Water Babies ★ (201)
- ☐ Whack and Dangle (78)
- ☐ Wind Chill (316)
- ☐ Windfall ★★ (314)

5.11b

- ☐ Aces and Eights ★ (176)
- ☐ Adrenaline ★ (172)
- ☐ Aftershock ★★ (44)
- ☐ Aid Route ★ (146)
- ☐ Anticipation ★★ (32)
- ☐ Ape Index ★ (229)
- ☐ Bark at the Moon (237)
- ☐ Basket Case (197)
- ☐ Bircheff-Williams ★★ (285)
- ☐ Black Heads (53)
- ☐ Black Primo ★ R (295)
- ☐ Burst of Brilliance ★ (65)
- ☐ Captain Hook, Right ★ (100)
- ☐ Carpet Bagger (244)
- ☐ Catch-U ★ R (86)
- ☐ Cherry Picker (119)
- ☐ Chester the Molester ★★ (118)
- ☐ The Chief ★ (207)
- ☐ Chiropodist Shop ★ (237)
- ☐ Circuit Breaker ★★ TR (243)
- ☐ Color Purple (70)
- ☐ Cosmic Charley (101)
- ☐ Crack the Whip ★★ (330)
- ☐ Crashline (344)
- ☐ Cristina (137)
- ☐ Cro-Magnon Capers ★ R (77)
- ☐ Dead Baby ★★ (232)
- ☐ Doctor of Gravity (196)
- ☐ Draw the Line ★ (174)
- ☐ Dwindling Energy ★★ (185)
- ☐ Elephant Talk ★★ (340)
- ☐ Emotional Wreckage ★ (327)
- ☐ End Game (116)
- ☐ The Enema ★★★ (45)
- ☐ Energizer ★★ (166)
- ☐ Ephemeral Clogdance ★ R (237)
- ☐ Essence ★★ (127)
- ☐ Exfoliator (305)
- ☐ Famous Potatoes (237)
- ☐ Fig Nuetron (42)
- ☐ Final Decision (132)
- ☐ Firefingers ★★ (172)
- ☐ Fish Fingers R (175)
- ☐ Free Clinic (201)

Rated Route Index

5.11b cont.

- [ ] G-Man R (53)
- [ ] Going Nowhere (303)
- [ ] Goldrush ★ (72)
- [ ] Green Dragon ★★★ (237)
- [ ] Grokin' ★ R (32)
- [ ] Groundhog (198)
- [ ] Guardian Angel R (53)
- [ ] Hairline (346)
- [ ] Hammerhead (118)
- [ ] Hardd ★★★ (44)
- [ ] Head Banger (118)
- [ ] High Pressure (322)
- [ ] Humdinger Continuation (63)
- [ ] The Hundredth Monkey (341)
- [ ] Inchworm R (32)
- [ ] Into the Fire ★ (260)
- [ ] Joe Palmer (141)
- [ ] The Knife (53)
- [ ] La Escuela ★★★ (104)
- [ ] Last in Line (45)
- [ ] Le Bachar ★ (334)
- [ ] Leanie Meanie ★★★ (32)
- [ ] Log Jam (118)
- [ ] Mad Pilot ★ (332)
- [ ] Magilla Gorilla ★★ (321)
- [ ] Maps and Legends ★★ (165)
- [ ] Mary's Tears ★★ (274)
- [ ] Micron (74)
- [ ] Monkey Hang (119)
- [ ] The Moratorium ★★ (116)
- [ ] Mouth To Perhaps (234)
- [ ] My-Toe-Sis ★ (53)
- [ ] Mystic Mint ★ (44)
- [ ] Never Say Dog ★★ (120)
- [ ] Nine Lives (53)
- [ ] No Rest for the Wicked ★ (167)
- [ ] On the Edge ★ R (214)
- [ ] Oranguatan Arch ★ (44)
- [ ] Out on a Limb (135)
- [ ] Pet Semetary ★ (337)
- [ ] Petty Larceny ★ (37)
- [ ] Pink Torpedo (133)
- [ ] Preface R/X (133)
- [ ] Pringles ★★ (45)
- [ ] The Promise ★ R (110)
- [ ] Psychic Energy (232)
- [ ] Pterodactyl Terrace, Right (106)
- [ ] The Right Profile (144)
- [ ] Rixon's Pinnacle, East Chimney, Final Decision (132)
- [ ] Rock Neurotic R (108)
- [ ] Savage Amusement ★ (258)
- [ ] Short but Thin ★ (104)
- [ ] Shortcake ★★★ (45)
- [ ] Skunk Crack ★ (49)
- [ ] Slamming Left ★ (63)
- [ ] Spinal Tap ★ (327)
- [ ] Spring Fever ★ (77)
- [ ] Stay Free ★ (144)
- [ ] Strange Energy (232)
- [ ] Stretch Mark (152)
- [ ] Submen ★ R (111)
- [ ] Terminator, Left ★ (45)
- [ ] This Ain't England (237)
- [ ] This Ain't England (239)
- [ ] Tightrope ★ R (232)
- [ ] Tooth or Consequences ★ (75)
- [ ] Total Way-ist ★★ (245)
- [ ] Turkey Vulture (185)
- [ ] Under Siege ★ (252)
- [ ] Uprising ★★★ (332)
- [ ] The Void ★ R (45)
- [ ] Wedge, The (53)
- [ ] What's Your Fnatasy (42)
- [ ] Yankee Clipper ★ (80)
- [ ] Yellow Peril ★ (80)
- [ ] Zoner ★★ (235)

5.11

- [ ] Absolute Vodka (129)
- [ ] Age of Industry (174)
- [ ] Astro Turf (174)
- [ ] Chouinard-Pratt (285)
- [ ] Dakshina ★ (195)
- [ ] Dead Souls (260)
- [ ] Deception (80)
- [ ] Deucey's Nose (115)
- [ ] Dirty Dancing (251)
- [ ] Dope Smoking Moron (250)
- [ ] Duck and Cover R/X (75)
- [ ] Facade (175)
- [ ] Far West (132)
- [ ] Fast As A Shark ★ (258)
- [ ] Fully BS or a Tree (152)
- [ ] GRE (34)
- [ ] Holy Diver (172)
- [ ] Hoppy's Creed (232)
- [ ] Ninja Flake (42)
- [ ] The Nose (99)
- [ ] The Odyssey (186)
- [ ] Penny Ante TR (78)
- [ ] Stumped Ray (63)
- [ ] Synchronicity (237)
- [ ] The Turret (291)
- [ ] Waste Not, Whip Not ★ (245)

Rated Route Index

5.11c

- [ ] 700 Club ★★ (167)
- [ ] Abazaba (116)
- [ ] Afterburner ★★★ (245)
- [ ] The Amoeba, Right Side (311)
- [ ] Animal Crackers (42)
- [ ] Astroman ★★★ (188)
- [ ] Bad Ass Baby TR (182)
- [ ] Beggar's Buttress ★★ (303)
- [ ] Blade Runner (161)
- [ ] Blockbuster (243)
- [ ] Boy and His Knob, A (57)
- [ ] Butterballs ★★★ (45)
- [ ] The Calf ★ (232)
- [ ] Chouinard-Herbert ★★ (255)
- [ ] Clan of the Big Hair (152)
- [ ] Cling Free ★ (247)
- [ ] Crack-a-Go-Go ★★★ (44)
- [ ] Dancin' Days (323)
- [ ] Dancing in the Dark ★ R (335)
- [ ] Deflowered (119)
- [ ] Delectable Pinnacle, Center Route ★ R (101)
- [ ] Delicate Delineate (247)
- [ ] Demimonde (172)
- [ ] Derelict's Delight (243)
- [ ] Disconnected (133)
- [ ] Edge-u-cator R (119)
- [ ] Escape From Freedom (204)
- [ ] False Prophets (247)
- [ ] Fistibule (228)
- [ ] Flakes Away (181)
- [ ] Floating Lama ★ (70)
- [ ] Follying (133)
- [ ] Fool's Finger ★ (168)
- [ ] Freaks of Nature (192)
- [ ] Freestone ★★★ (157)
- [ ] The Gauntlet TR (64)
- [ ] General Hospital R (135)
- [ ] Gorilla Grip (328)
- [ ] Gunks Revisited ★ R (87)
- [ ] Gunning For Buddha ★ (45)
- [ ] Hung Like a Manster ★ (178)
- [ ] Joe's Garage ★ (48)
- [ ] Kauk-ulator ★★★ (334)
- [ ] Klingon ★ (48)
- [ ] Machine Head (311)
- [ ] Mc D's Route ★★ (248)
- [ ] Mongoloid ★★ (247)
- [ ] Mother Earth ★★ (297)
- [ ] Neil Down (201)
- [ ] No Love-Chump Sucker ★ (135)
- [ ] Nothing on The Apron (237)
- [ ] Overhang Overpass ★★★ (306)
- [ ] Perfect Vision ★★★ (272)
- [ ] Pinky Paralysis ★★★ (37)
- [ ] Power Point ★★ R (275)
- [ ] Public Enema Number One ★ (176)
- [ ] Pulsing Pustules ★ (286)
- [ ] Pussy Whipped ★ (41)
- [ ] Realm of the Lizard King (263)
- [ ] Rest for the Wicked (72)
- [ ] Ribbon Candy ★★ (91)
- [ ] Rocket in My Pocket ★ (75)
- [ ] The Rostrum, The Regular North Face Route ★★★ (332)
- [ ] Rupto Pac (172)
- [ ] Showtime ★ R (53)
- [ ] Sky ★★ (341)
- [ ] Soul Sacrifice ★★ (302)
- [ ] Speed Racer R/X (243)
- [ ] Spiderman ★★ (258)
- [ ] Terminal Research (188)
- [ ] Thin Line R (90)
- [ ] Ticket to Nowhere ★★ R (295)
- [ ] Tidal Wave (153)
- [ ] TKO ★★ (32)
- [ ] Top Dope TR (293)
- [ ] Toxic Avenger (57)
- [ ] Ultimate Emotion (34)
- [ ] Valley Syndrome (201)
- [ ] The Viper ★★ (335)
- [ ] West Face ★ (97)

5.11d

- [ ] Absolutely Sweet Marie ★ (128)
- [ ] Abstract Corner ★★ (45)
- [ ] The Affliction ★★ R (277)
- [ ] Annette Funicello (114)
- [ ] The Anti-Christ ★★ (78)
- [ ] Autobahn ★★ R (219)
- [ ] Bad Ass Momma ★ TR (182)
- [ ] Bad Company (247)
- [ ] Battlescar (337)
- [ ] Big Easy ★★★ (245)
- [ ] Blind Faith (332)
- [ ] Bottom Line (136)
- [ ] Brass Knuckles (304)
- [ ] Bucket Brigade ★★★ (341)
- [ ] Candy-O ★ R (340)
- [ ] Catch a Wave (65)
- [ ] Champagne on Ice ★★ R (111)
- [ ] Cleaver (63)
- [ ] Colony of Slippermen (313)
- [ ] Constipation ★ (32)
- [ ] Crack a Brewski (154)
- [ ] Crazy ★★ (299)
- [ ] Desperado ★ (53)
- [ ] Dreamscape ★★ (218)
- [ ] Dynamo Hum ★ (137)
- [ ] Endorphine (172)
- [ ] Energy Crisis ★★★ (325)
- [ ] The Fast Lane ★★ R (219)
- [ ] Fire and Brimstone ★ (168)
- [ ] Freaky Styley ★ (250)

Rated Route Index

5.11d cont.

- ☐ Gait of Power ** (48)
- ☐ Goodhead (118)
- ☐ Gotham City * (63)
- ☐ Guillotine (49)
- ☐ Happy Days ** (36)
- ☐ Hat Pin * (53)
- ☐ The High Arc * (107)
- ☐ Hocus Pocus ** (341)
- ☐ Isotope (74)
- ☐ John's Ring Job * R/X (32)
- ☐ Jomo * (80)
- ☐ Karma (221)
- ☐ Lethal Weapon (172)
- ☐ Little Thing (87)
- ☐ Local Motion * (314)
- ☐ Lunar Lunacy * (237)
- ☐ Lunar Lunacy * (239)
- ☐ Lycra Virgin ** (118)
- ☐ Magic Carpet * R (77)
- ☐ Masquerade R (106)
- ☐ Max Deviator * (247)
- ☐ Min-Ne-Ah (156)
- ☐ Montgomery Cliff * (144)
- ☐ Moongerms (346)
- ☐ Mud Flats R (152)
- ☐ New Wave ** (246)
- ☐ Nightmare Continuation (346)
- ☐ Opposition * (36)
- ☐ The Panther * (185)
- ☐ Perfect Master * (237)
- ☐ Pimper's Paradise (69)
- ☐ The Premature Ejaculation (175)
- ☐ Pump Dummy * (319)
- ☐ Rainbow Bridge * (286)
- ☐ Red Zinger *** (44)
- ☐ River Boulder * TR (38)
- ☐ Rixon's Pinnacle, Direct South Face * (132)
- ☐ Rixon's Pinnacle, South Face (132)
- ☐ Rock Bottom * (136)
- ☐ Rocket Man (65)
- ☐ Samurai Crack (181)
- ☐ Season of the Bitch (250)
- ☐ Sentinel Rock, West Face ** (257)
- ☐ Short Circuit ** (30)
- ☐ Sink Like a Stone ** (118)
- ☐ Skindad The Scaler * (168)
- ☐ Slit Your Tires * (337)
- ☐ Smith-Crawford ** (298)
- ☐ Something for Nothing * (45)
- ☐ Spectacle ** (305)
- ☐ Sub Atomic (80)
- ☐ Thunderhead (237)
- ☐ Thunderhead (239)
- ☐ The Token ** R/X (237)
- ☐ Torque Converter * (35)
- ☐ Vibrator (81)
- ☐ The Wand * R (165)
- ☐ The Warbler ** (313)
- ☐ Whisker ** (262)
- ☐ White Owl (69)
- ☐ The White Zone (114)

5.12a

- ☐ Atomic Finger Crack * (84)
- ☐ Base Hits * (107)
- ☐ Believer * R (110)
- ☐ Cat's Squirrel * (53)
- ☐ Chump Change (78)
- ☐ Crimson Cringe *** (57)
- ☐ Digital Delight * (327)
- ☐ Don't Give Up the Ship * TR (41)
- ☐ Drive By Shooting *** (246)
- ☐ El Matador ** R (111)
- ☐ Fly Swatter * (341)
- ☐ Fun Terminal *** (341)
- ☐ Golden Shower * (80)
- ☐ Golden Years ** (121)
- ☐ Goldfinger ** (35)
- ☐ The Hidden * (250)
- ☐ Hookie * (176)
- ☐ Hotline (344)
- ☐ House of Pain ** (246)
- ☐ Index Eliminator (42)
- ☐ Jaws (342)
- ☐ Killing Yourself to Live * R (340)
- ☐ Landshark (323)
- ☐ Mirage * (70)
- ☐ New Generation (172)
- ☐ Oral Roberts ** (167)
- ☐ Pumping Hate (50)
- ☐ The Remnant, Center Route (74)
- ☐ Ride the Lightning ** (78)
- ☐ Road to Ruin ** (295)
- ☐ Roadside Attraction ** (38)
- ☐ Rock Horror Show ** (53)
- ☐ Sample the Dog (135)
- ☐ SAT (34)
- ☐ Scram *** (63)
- ☐ Scratch and Sniff * (80)
- ☐ Separate Reality *** (49)
- ☐ Slingshot * (154)
- ☐ Space Invader TR (182)
- ☐ Spike * (244)
- ☐ Stubs (63)
- ☐ Substance Abuse ** (245)
- ☐ Teacher's Pet * (296)
- ☐ That'll Teach You * (296)
- ☐ Tips ** (63)
- ☐ Tongue and Groove * (80)
- ☐ Underclingon * (53)
- ☐ Vulture Culture (232)
- ☐ Wings of Maybe (259)
- ☐ Wish You Were Here (244)
- ☐ Yellow Corner ** R (310)

Rated Route Index

5.12b

- ☐ Alien ★★★ (332)
- ☐ America's Cup ★ R (44)
- ☐ Bak to the Future (39)
- ☐ Berlin Wall ★ (246)
- ☐ Best Bet Arête ★ (244)
- ☐ The Big Juan ★★ (120)
- ☐ Burden of Dreams ★★ (116)
- ☐ Cat's Squirrel Continuation ★ (53)
- ☐ Changos Cabrones ★★ (50)
- ☐ Chips Ahoy ★★ (44)
- ☐ Collision Course (232)
- ☐ Colors ★★ (246)
- ☐ The Crucifix ★★★ R (275)
- ☐ Dog's Roof, A ★ (323)
- ☐ Double Dragon ★★ (246)
- ☐ Duty Now for the Future ★ R (107)
- ☐ Final Cut ★★★ (244)
- ☐ Fish Crack ★★ (57)
- ☐ Ginger Snap ★ (44)
- ☐ Journey to the East ★★ (264)
- ☐ Kryptonite ★ (87)
- ☐ Lighten Up ★★ (248)
- ☐ Lost Arrow Tip ★★ (160)
- ☐ Material Girl ★★ (118)
- ☐ Meteorite TR (101)
- ☐ Nutter Butter ★ (44)
- ☐ Omakara ★ (34)
- ☐ The Passage ★ (323)
- ☐ The Pointy Part ★★ (264)
- ☐ Police and Theives ★★ (154)
- ☐ Portside ★★ (50)
- ☐ Ray's Pin Job ★ (45)
- ☐ Roadside Infraction TR (38)
- ☐ Robin ★ (63)
- ☐ Stack o' Fun ★★ (154)
- ☐ Streamline ★ (229)
- ☐ Tales of Power ★★★ (49)
- ☐ Temple of Doom ★★ (245)
- ☐ Tiger By the Tail ★ (41)
- ☐ Tour de Force ★ R (284)
- ☐ Tucker's Proud Rock Climb ★★★ (245)

5.12

- ☐ Ain't That a Bitch (116)
- ☐ The Blade TR (64)
- ☐ Broken Circuit TR (243)
- ☐ Catholic Discipline R (167)
- ☐ Diminishing Standard (251)
- ☐ Hand Dog Flyer (181)
- ☐ Jack the Zipper ★ (232)
- ☐ King Snake (176)
- ☐ Master Lock (63)
- ☐ Notes From the Undergound ★★ (264)
- ☐ Old 5.11 ★ (81)
- ☐ Pegasus (108)
- ☐ Peter's Out (172)
- ☐ Pigs in Space (172)
- ☐ Pint-Sized (182)
- ☐ Pygmy Village (335)
- ☐ Razor's Edge ★★ (337)
- ☐ Remember Ribbon Falls (28)
- ☐ Scimitar ★ (237)
- ☐ Vortex (313)
- ☐ Walking on Mars (328)

5.12c

- ☐ 666 ★ (30)
- ☐ Follywood ★★ (133)
- ☐ Hall of Mirror ★★★ R (234)
- ☐ Hall of Mirrors ★★★ R (238)
- ☐ Highlander (65)
- ☐ Lost and Found ★ (260)
- ☐ Meltdown ★★ (50)
- ☐ Owl Roof (70)
- ☐ Psychological Warfare ★★ (57)
- ☐ Punchline ★★ (32)
- ☐ Satanic Mechanic R (44)
- ☐ The Shining ★★ R (178)
- ☐ Take Da Plunge ★ R (340)
- ☐ Wicked Gravity ★★★ (341)
- ☐ Zipperhead (45)

5.12d

- ☐ Isaiah 2:21 ★ (341)
- ☐ Jupiter ★ (79)
- ☐ Southern Belle (220)
- ☐ Tunnel Vision ★ (48)

Rated Route Index

5.13

- ☐ Dale's Pin 5.13 (39)
- ☐ The Stigma 5.13★★ (45)
- ☐ Title Fight 5.13 (63)
- ☐ Van Belle Syndrome 5.13★ (39)
- ☐ Atheist 5.13a★★ (166)
- ☐ Crossroads 5.13a★ (74)
- ☐ Dread and Freedom 5.13a★★ (264)
- ☐ General Dynamics 5.13a★★ R (107)
- ☐ Keepr of the Flame 5.13a★★★ (340)
- ☐ Phantom 5.13a★ R (74)
- ☐ The Phoenix 5.13a★★★ (58)
- ☐ Black Fly 5.13b★★ (244)
- ☐ Cookie Monster 5.13b★★★ (44)
- ☐ Cosmic Debris 5.13b★★★ (247)
- ☐ Cripps 5.13b★ (246)
- ☐ Fantasy Island 5.13b★★ (79)
- ☐ Keep the Muscle, Lose the Fat 5.13b★★ (50)
- ☐ Meat Grinder Arête 5.13b★★★ (44)
- ☐ Salathé Wall 5.13b (98)
- ☐ Shockwave 5.13b★★★ (250)
- ☐ Machine Gun 5.13c (87)
- ☐ Van Belle O Drome 5.13c★ (39)
- ☐ Whipcord 5.13c★★★ (328)

Route Index

10.96 (5.10d) 181
5.9 Grunt (5.9) 237
666 (5.12c) 30
700 Club (5.11c) 167
800 Club (5.11a) 166
A la Moana (5.11a) 40
A-5 Pinnacle (5.10a) 165
Abazaba (5.11c) 116
Absolute Vodka (5.11) 129
Absolutely Free, Center Route (5.9) 129
Absolutely Free, Left Side (5.9) 129
Absolutely Free, Right Side (5.10a) 129
Absolutely Sweet Marie (5.11d) 128
Abstract Corner (5.11d) 45
Aces and Eights (5.11b) 176
Adrenaline (5.11b) 172
Affliction, The (5.11d) 277
After Five (5.7) 126
After Seven (5.8) 124
After Six (5.6) 124
Afterburner (5.11c) 245
Afterglow (5.10d) 237
Aftershock (5.11b) 44
Age of Industry (5.11) 174
Agent Orange (5.10d) 63
Agricultural Manuvers in the Dark (5.8) 119
Ahwahnee Buttress (5.10d) 173
Aid Route (5.11b) 146
Aid Route 101
Aids Curve (5.10) 26
Ain't That a Bitch (5.12) 116
Air Bare (5.10c) 229
Alamo (5.11a) 335
Alien (5.12b) 332
Alley Cat (5.10a) 278
America's Cup (5.12b) 44
Amoeba, The, Left Side (5.8) 311
Amoeba, The, Right Side (5.11c) 311
Anal Tongue Darts (5.10c) 74
Anathema (5.10b) 45
Anchors Away (5.11a) 237
Andy Devine (5.7) 87
Angel's Approach (5.9) 237
Angelica (5.9) 234
Angelina (5.8) 87
Animal Crackers (5.11c) 42
Annette Funicello (5.11d) 114
Anti-Christ, The (5.11d) 78
Anti-Ego Crack (5.7) 66
Anticipation (5.11b) 32
Antique (5.7) 148
Apathy Buttress (5.9) 201
Ape Index (5.11b) 229

Apple Seeds (5.10a) 138
Application (5.9) 32
Apron Jam (5.9) 237
Arch Rock Pinnacle 34
Arches Terrace (5.8) 181
Arête Butler (5.10a) 175
Arlington Heights (5.9) 68
Armageddon (5.10d) 108
Armed & Dangerous (5.50a) 151
Arrowhead Spire (5.5) 164
As It Is (5.8) 166
Astro Spam (5.11a) 174
Astro Turf (5.11) 174
Astroman (5.11c) 188
Atheist (5.13a) 166
Atomic Finger Crack (5.12a) 84
Aunt Fanny's Pantry (5.4) 166
Autobahn (5.11d) 219
Avalon (5.10b) 142
Axis see Blotto
B & B (5.10a) 84
Babble On (5.10a) 53
Bacchigaloupe Wall (5.9) 150
Back in the Saddle (5.11a) 63
Back To The Slammer (5.10b) 201
Bad Acid (5.9) 237
Bad Ass Baby (5.11c) 182
Bad Ass Momma (5.11d) 182
Bad Company (5.11d) 247
Bad News Bombers (5.10a) 80
Bak to the Future (5.12b) 39
Banana Dreams (5.10a) 44
Barefoot Servants (5.10c) 311
Bark at the Moon (5.11b) 237
Barney Rubble (5.10d) 176
Base Hits (5.12a) 107
Basket Case (5.11b) 197
Battle-Ship (5.10) 334
Battlescar (5.11d) 337
Bay Bush, The (5.6) 258
Bear, The (5.10b) 232
Beat Around the Bush (5.10c) 148
Beat The Clock (5.10c) 311
Beer Pressure (5.10a) 124
Beggar's Buttress (5.11c) 303
Believer (5.12a) 110
Bench Warmer (5.10d) 152
Benzoin and Edges (5.10c) 181
Berlin Wall (5.12b) 246
Best Bet Arête (5.12b) 244
Betrayal (5.9) 252
Beverly's Tower (5.10a) 44
Beyond the Fringe (5.10c) 75

Route Index

Big Easy (5.11d) 245
Big Juan, The (5.12b) 120
Bijou (5.10c) 78
Bikini Beach Party (5.10a) 114
Bin, The (5.10d) 34
Bircheff-Williams (5.11b) 285
Birds of a Feather (5.7) 85
Bishop's Balcony (5.5) 167
Bishop's Terrace (5.8) 167
Bitches' Terror (5.11a) 167
Black Fly (5.13b) 244
Black Heads (5.11b) 53
Black is Brown (5.8) 166
Black Primo (5.11b) 295
Black Sunday (5.10a) 84
Blackballed (5.10b) 152
Blade Runner (5.11c) 161
Blade, The (5.12) 64
Blame it on 800 63
Blasphemy (5.11a) 167
Blazing Buckets (5.9) 74
Blazo (5.8) 108
Blind Alley (5.9) 272
Blind Faith (5.11d) 332
Blind Man's Bluff (5.9) 272
Block Horror Picture Show (5.9) 69
Blockbuster (5.11c) 243
Blotto (5.10d) 32
Bluballed (5.10b) 153
Blue Funk (5.11a) 237
Bluffer (5.11a) 110
Bolt Adventures (5.11a) 57
Bone Yard (5.10b) 327
Bongs Away, Center (5.10a) 74
Bongs Away, Left (5.8) 74
Bongs Away, Right (5.9) 74
Boogie with Stu (5.10d) 148
Book 'em Dano (5.10d) 53
Book End (5.9) 148
Book of Job (5.10b) 272
Book of Revelations (5.11a) 166
Bottom Feeder (5.10a) 295
Bottom Feeder (5.10a) 295
Bottom Line (5.11d) 136
Bourbon Street (5.10c) 245
Boy and His Knob, A (5.11c) 57
Braille Book, The (5.8) 272
Brainbucket (5.10d) 53
Brass Knuckles (5.11d) 304
Breast Fest (5.10c) 335
Breathalizer (5.10b) 198
Breezin' (5.10a) 314
Bridalveil East (5.10c) 307
Broken Circuit (5.12) 243
Brown Sugar (5.10a) 115
Brown-Eyed Girl (5.9) 119
Bryan's Crack (5.8) 252
Bucket Brigade (5.11d) 341
Building Blocks (5.8) 87
Bummer (5.10c) 152
Bunghole of the Universe (5.10a) 293
Burden of Dreams (5.12b) 116
Buried Treasure (5.11a) 262
Burst of Brilliance (5.11b) 65
Butterballs (5.11c) 45
Butterfinger (5.11a) 45
Butthole Climber (5.10c) 152
Buttocks, The (5.9) 136
By Way of the Flake (5.10c) 252
C.S. Concerto (5.8) 124
Cafeteria Lieback, The (5.11a) 243
Calf Continuation (5.10b) 232
Calf, The (5.11c) 232
Call of the Wild (5.10d) 222
Candy-O (5.11d) 340
Captain Hook, Left (5.7) 100
Captain Hook, Right (5.11b) 100
Carpet Bagger (5.11b) 244
Cartwheel (5.10a) 325
Castaways (5.10c) 314
Cat Dancing (5.10a) 295
Cat Fight (5.10b) 41
Cat's Squirrel (5.12a) 53
Cat's Squirrel Continuation (5.12b) 53
Catch a Wave (5.11d) 65
Catch-U (5.11b) 86
Catchy (5.10d) 45
Catchy Corner (5.11a) 45
Catholic Discipline (5.12) 167
Caverens, The (5.8) 148
Center Route (5.9) 26
Central Pillar of Frenzy (5.10d) 285
Cereal Killer (5.10a) 80
Chairman Ted Scraps the Time Machine (5.10a) 122
Champagne on Ice (5.11d) 111
Changos Cabrones (5.12b) 50
Chase, The (5.9) 26
Cheap Friction (5.10) 148
Cheek (5.10d) 136
Cherry Picker (5.11b) 119
Chester the Molester (5.11b) 118
Chicken Fever (5.10b) 53
Chicken Pie (5.9) 65
Chicken Pie see Turkey Pie
Chicken Pox (5.8) 65
Chicken's Choice (5.10b) 134
Chief, The (5.11b) 207
Childhood's End (5.11a) 133
Chimney for Two (5.6) 65
Chingando (5.10a) 74
Chips Ahoy (5.12b) 44
Chiropodist Shop (5.11b) 237
Chockblock Chimney (5.8) 248
Chockstone Chimney (5.9) 93
Chopper (5.10c) 135
Chosen Few, The (5.9) 311
Chouinard Crack (5.7) 235
Chouinard-Herbert (5.11c) 255
Chouinard-Pratt (5.11) 285
Chow Chow Chow (5.10c) 119
Chruch Bowl Chimney (5.6) 166
Chump Change (5.12a) 78
Church Bowl Lieback (5.8) 166

Route Index

Church Bowl Terrace (5.8) 166
Church Bowl Tree (5.10b) 166
Cid's Embrace (5.8) 137
Circuit Breaker (5.11b) 243
Clan of the Big Hair (5.11c) 152
Claude's Delight (5.7) 146
Cleaver (5.11d) 63
Cleft, The (5.9) 45
Cling Free (5.11c) 247
Cobra, The (5.11a) 177
Coffin Nail A3+) 44
Cold Fusion (5.10c) 237
Collision Course (5.12b) 232
Colony of Slippermen (5.11d) 313
Color Me Gone (5.9) 26
Color Purple (5.11b) 70
Colors (5.12b) 246
Combustable Knowledge (5.10d) 152
Commissioner Buttress (5.9) 126
Commitment (5.9) 148
Compass (5.10c) 40
Compass Rose (5.10a) 304
Concrete Jungle (5.10d) 335
Conductor Crack (5.10d) 64
Conquest of the Stud Monkey (5.10a) 119
Constipation (5.11d) 32
Controlled Burn (5.11a) 247
Cookie Cutter see Cookie Monster
Cookie Monster (5.13b) 44
Cookie, The, Center Route (5.9) 45
Cookie, The, Left Side (5.10a) 45
Cookie, The, Right Side (5.9) 45
Cool Cliff 170 (5.8) 26
Coonyard Pinnacle (5.9) 234
Coonyard to The Oasis (5.9) 234
Copper Penny (5.10a) 78
Cornball (5.7) 176
Cosmic Charley (5.11b) 101
Cosmic Comedy (5.7) 237
Cosmic Debris (5.13b) 247
Cosmic Messenger (5.11a) 35
Cosmic Ray (5.11a) 75
Cost of Living (5.10c) 134
Costa Rica (5.9) 26
Country Corner (5.9) 328
Cow, The, Center (5.5) 232
Cow, The, Left (5.8) 232
Cow, The, Right (5.7) 232
Crack 'n Face (5.10b) 78
Crack a Brewski (5.11d) 154
Crack of Deliverance (5.9) 346
Crack of Despair (5.10a) 346
Crack of Destiny (5.9) 341
Crack of Doom (5.10a) 346
Crack the Whip (5.11b) 330
Crack-a-Go-Go (5.11c) 44
Cracker, The 311
Cracker, The, Right Side (5.7) 311
Cramming (5.10d) 63
Crashline (5.11b) 344
Crazy (5.11d) 299
Crazy Train (5.10c) 74

Cream (5.11a) 325
Creeping Lethargy (5.10d) 201
Crest Jewel (5.10a) 194
Crimson Cringe (5.12a) 57
Cripps (5.13b) 246
Cristina (5.11b) 137
Critical Path (5.11a) 280
Cro-Magnon Capers (5.11b) 77
Cross-Country Crack (5.9) 34
Crossover (5.9) 26
Crossroads (5.13a) 74
Crotch Cricket (5.10a) 293
Crucifix, The (5.12b) 275
Cuthulu (5.10d) 100
Cynical Pinnacle, Right (5.10c) 229
Cynical Pinnacle, Wrong (5.10b) 229
Dakshina (5.11) 195
Dale's Pin (5.13) 39
Dancin' Days (5.11c) 323
Dancing in the Dark (5.11c) 335
Danger Will Robinson (5.10d) 74
Dark Shadows (5.10a) 228
Days of Our Lives (5.11a) 135
Dead Baby (5.11b) 232
Dead Souls (5.11) 260
Deaf, Dumb and Blind (5.10a) 148
Deception (5.11) 80
Deception Gully (5.9) 66
Deep Throat (5.10a) 234
Deflowered (5.11c) 119
Defoliation (5.10) 153
Deja Thorus (5.10a) 166
Delectable Pinnacle, Center Route (5.11c) 101
Delectable Pinnacle, Left Side (5.3) 101
Delectable Pinnacle, Right Side (5.7) 101
Delicate Delineate (5.11c) 247
Demimonde (5.11c) 172
Demon's Delight (5.11a) 115
Den, The (5.8) 250
Derelict's Delight (5.11c) 243
Derelict's Diagonal A4) 243
Desperado (5.11d) 53
Desperate for Doughnuts (5.8) 296
Desperate Kneed, A (5.11a) 26
Desperate Straights (5.10a) 53
Destination Zero (5.11a) 201
Deuceldike, The (5.9) 216
Deucey's Elbow (5.10d) 115
Deucey's Nose (5.11) 115
Deviltry (5.11a) 172
Dick Wrenching Classic (5.10b) 118
Digital Delight (5.12a) 327
Dihardral, The (5.10c) 120
Dime Bag (5.10c) 330
Diminishing Returns (5.10c) 198
Diminishing Standard (5.12) 251
Dinner Ledge (5.10a) 185
Dire Straights (5.10) 176
Dirty Dancing (5.11) 251
Dirty Little Secret (5.9) 32
Disconnected (5.11c) 133

Route Index

Distant Driver (5.10d) 175
DNB see Middle Cathedral Rock, Direct North Buttress
Doctor of Gravity (5.11b) 196
Dog's Roof, A (5.12b) 323
Doggie Deviations (5.9) 136
Doggie Diversion (5.9) 136
Doggie Do (5.10a) 136
Doggie Submission (5.10b) 243
Dolly Dagger (5.9) 87
Dome Polishers (5.9) 216
Domehead (5.10b) 53
Don't Give Up the Ship (5.12a) 41
Dope Smoking Moron (5.11) 250
Dorn's Crack (5.10c) 251
Double Dragon (5.12b) 246
Double Trouble (5.10b) 176
Dove, The (5.8) 85
Dr. Feel Good (5.10d) 237
Draw the Line (5.11b) 174
Dread and Freedom (5.13a) 264
Dreamscape (5.11d) 218
Dressed to Kill (5.10b) 26
Drink and Drive (5.11a) 148
Drive By Shooting (5.12a) 246
Dromedary (5.8d) 70
Dromedary Direct (5.10c) 70
Drop-out (5.10a) 311
Drunk Tank (5.10d) 119
Duck and Cover (5.11) 75
DUI (5.11a) 119
Duncan Imperial (5.11a) 85
Dust in the Wind (5.10a) 106
Duty Now for the Future (5.12b) 107
Dwindling Energy (5.11b) 185
Dwindling Stances (5.10c) 152
Dynamic Doubles (5.9) 124
Dynamite Crack (5.10) 42
Dynamo Hum (5.11d) 137
Eagle (5.10a) 337
Eagle Feather (5.10c) 85
Eagle's Eyrie (5.9) 26
Earth First (5.10) 251
East Arrow Chimney (5.10d) 164
East Buttress (5.10b) 113
East Buttress 280
Easy Wind (5.9) 124
Eat at Degnan's (5.10) 323
Edge of Night (5.10c) 135
Edge-u-cator (5.11c) 119
Ejesta (5.8) 75
El Matador (5.12a) 111
Electric Gully (5.7) 65
Elephant Guy (5.10) 337
Elephant Malt (5.9) 341
Elephant Rock, Right Side Route (5.10a) 346
Elephant Talk (5.11b) 340
Elephantiasis (5.10d) 341
Elevator Shaft (5.8) 44
Emotional Wreckage (5.11b) 327
End Game (5.11b) 116
End of the World (5.10d) 113
Endorphine (5.11d) 172
Enema, The (5.11b) 45
Energizer (5.11b) 166
Energy Crisis (5.11d) 325
English Breakfast Crack (5.10c) 32
Enigma, The (5.9) 45
Ennui (5.11a) 296
Entrance Exam (5.9) 32
Ephemeral Clogdance (5.11b) 237
Eraser Flake (5.11a) 53
Eraser Head (5.10d) 57
Eric's Book (5.9) 198
Escape (5.8) 45
Escape From Freedom (5.11c) 204
Essence (5.11b) 127
Euellogy (5.10a) 80
Exfoliator (5.11b) 305
Exit From The Notch (5.10d) 158
Exodus (5.10b) 295
Extra Credit (5.10d) 35
Eye in the Sky (5.10b) 216
Facade (5.11) 175
Face Card (5.10c) 176
Falcon (5.10b) 65
Fallen Arches (5.9) 181
Fallout (5.10c) 138
False Prophets (5.11c) 247
False Verde (5.9) 59
Famous Potatoes (5.11b) 237
Fang, The (5.10b) 184
Fantasy Island (5.13b) 79
Far East (5.8) 235
Far Right (5.10d) 198
Far West (5.11) 132
Farm Alarm (5.7) 26
Fast As A Shark (5.11) 258
Fast Lane, The (5.11d) 219
Fasten Your Seat Belts (5.10b) 77
Fatal Mistake (5.11a) 344
Fecophilia (5.9) 124
Feminine Protection (5.10d) 175
Fertile Attraction (5.10d) 153
Fifteen Seconds of Fame (5.9) 104
Fifty Crowded Variation (5.10a) 280
Fig Nuetron (5.11b) 42
Figment (5.8) 80
Filthy Rich (5.9) 57
Final Cut (5.12b) 244
Final Decision (5.11b) 132
Final Exam (5.10d) 212
Fine Line (5.10a) 174
Finger Lickin' (5.10d) 37
Fire and Brimstone (5.11d) 168
Fire Drill (5.10d) 239
Firefingers (5.11d) 172
Fish Crack (5.12b) 57
Fish Fingers (5.11b) 175
Fist Puppet (5.11a) 36
Fistibule (5.11c) 228
Five and Dime (5.10d) 78
Five o'Clock Shadow (5.9) 295

Route Index

Flagman (5.11a) 319
Flailing Dog (5.11a) 53
Flake, The (5.10b) 50
Flakes Away (5.11c) 181
Flakes, The (5.8) 300
Flakey Foont (5.9) 234
Flary Tales (5.10a) 57
Flatus (5.9) 75
Flexible Flyer (5.10d) 124
Flight Attendant (5.1oc) 335
Floating Lama (5.11c) 70
Fluke (5.9) 80
Fly By (5.11a) 26
Fly Swatter (5.12a) 341
Foaming at the Crotch (5.10a) 343
Folly, The, Left Side (5.9) 133
Follying (5.11c) 133
Follywood (5.12c) 133
Fool's Finger (5.11c) 168
Fool's Gold (5.10a) 90
Footstool, The, Left Side (5.8) 110
Footstool, The, Right Side (5.4) 110
Freaks of Nature (5.11c) 192
Freaky Styley (5.11d) 250
Free Bong (5.11a) 115
Free Clinic (5.11b) 201
Free Press (5.10a) 57
Free Ride (5.10a) 77
Freestone (5.11c) 157
Freewheelin' (5.10b) 295
Fresh Squeezed (5.10a) 229
Friday the 13th (5.10b) 181
Frosted Flakes (5.10d) 133
Fuddy Duddy (5.10a) 128
Fully BS or a Tree (5.11) 152
Fun (5.9) 72
Fun Flake (5.9) 37
Fun Terminal (5.12a) 341
G-Man (5.11b) 53
Gait of Power (5.11d) 48
Galloping Consumption (5.11a) 142
Gang Bang (5.10a) 72
Gardening At Night (5.10c) 166
Gash (5.10b) 305
Gauntlet, The (5.11c) 64
Gay Bob's (5.10b) 53
Geek Towers, Center Route (5.10a) 157
Geek Towers, Right Side (5.10a) 157
General Dynamics (5.13a) 107
General Hospital (5.11c) 135
Generator Crack (5.10c) 64
George's Secretary (5.8) 229
Gerbil Launcher, The (5.10d) 59
Gidget Goes to Yosemite (5.9) 114
Gillette (5.10) 138
Gilligan's Chicken (5.7) 53
Ginger Snap (5.12b) 44
Girl Next Door, The, Left Side (5.10) 141
Girl Next Door, The, Right Side (5.10a) 141
Goat For It (5.10a) 146
Goblet, The, Center (5.6) 234
Goblet, The, Left (5.4) 234

Goblet, The, Right (5.4) 234
God Told Me To Skin You Alive (5.11a) 178
God's Creation (5.9) 124
Going Nowhere (5.11b) 303
Gold Dust (5.10d) 246
Gold Leaf (5.9) 93
Gold Wall (5.10) 92
Golden Bough (5.10a) 89
Golden Dawn (5.10d) 205
Golden Needles (5.8) 57
Golden Shower (5.12a) 80
Golden Years (5.12a) 121
Goldfinger (5.12a) 35
Goldrush (5.11b) 72
Gollum, Left Side (5.10a) 108
Gollum, Right Side (5.8) 108
Good Book, The (5.10d) 133
Goodhead (5.11d) 118
Goodrich Pinnacle, Left Side (5.9) 234
Goodrich Pinnacle, Right Side (5.9) 234
Goosebumps (5.10c) 74
Gorilla Cookies (5.10d) 321
Gorilla Grip (5.11c) 328
Gotham City (5.11d) 63
Grack, The, Center Route (5.6) 232
Grack, The, Left Side (5.7) 232
Grack, The, Right Side (5.8) 232
Grape Nuts (5.9) 80
Grateful Pinheads (5.11a) 63
Gravity's Rainbow (5.10c) 225
Gray Bullet, The (5.8) 75
GRE (5.11) 34
Greasy but Groovy (5.10d) 181
Green Dragon (5.11b) 237
Gripper (5.10b) 32
Grokin' (5.11b) 32
Groundhog (5.11b) 198
Grove Route (5.8) 153
Guardian Angel (5.11b) 53
Guides Route (5.6) 153
Guillotine (5.11d) 49
Gunks Revisited (5.11c) 87
Gunning For Buddha (5.11c) 45
Guru Crack, Left (5.10c) 340
Guru Crack, Right (5.10a) 340
Hairline (5.11b) 346
Half Dome, Direct Northwest Face 213
Half Dome, North Ridge (5.10d) 210
Half Dome, Regular Northwest Face (5.9) 212
Hall of Mirror (5.12c) 234
Hall of Mirrors (5.12c) 238
Hammerhead (5.11b) 118
Hampton Estates (5.9) 68
Hand Dog Flyer (5.12) 181
Hand Job (5.10a) 72
Hand Me Down, The (5.10a) 258
Handshake (5.9) 150
Hanging Teeth, The (5.8) 148
Hangover Heights (5.10) 251
Happy Days (5.11d) 36
Happy Ending, The (5.11a) 120

Route Index

Happy Gully (5.8) 222
Happy's Favorite (5.10b) 119
Hardd (5.11b) 44
Hari-kiri (5.10a) 259
Harldy Pinnacle (5.10d) 105
Harry Daley Route (5.8) 235
Hat Pin (5.11d) 53
Hawaiian, The (5.10a) 26
Hawkman's Escape (5.9) 131
Hayley Anna (5.8) 26
He Can't Shout, Don't Hear You (5.7) 87
Head Banger (5.11b) 118
Health Insurance (5.10a) 37
Heathenistic Pursuit (5.10b) 246
Hell's Hollow (5.10a) 172
Henley Quits (5.10a) 137
Here On The Inside (5.11a) 119
Heretic (5.10c) 167
Hershey Highway (5.8) 181
Hidden, The (5.12a) 250
High Arc, The (5.11d) 107
High Pressure (5.11b) 322
High Profile (5.11a) 37
Higher Cathedral Rock, Northeast Buttress (5.9) 274
Higher Cathedral Spire, Regular (Southwest Face) Route (5.9) 270
Higher Cathedral Spire, Southeast Side, East Corner (5.10a) 271
Higher Cathedral Spire, Southeast Side, Southeast Face (5.10d) 271
Highlander (5.12c) 65
Highway Star (5.10a) 82
Ho Chi Minh Trail (5.10c) 290
Hocus Pocus (5.11d) 341
Holidays (5.8) 65
Holy Diver (5.11) 172
Home Run (5.10d) 295
Honor Thy Father (5.10c) 87
Hookie (5.12a) 176
Hoosier's Highway (5.10c) 234
Hoppy's Creed (5.11) 232
Hoppy's Favorite (5.10b) 232
Hot Tin Roof (5.9) 232
Hotline (5.12a) 344
Hourglass, The Left Side (5.11a) 93
Hourglass, The, Right Side (5.10a) 93
House of Pain (5.12a) 246
Humdinger (5.10d) 63
Humdinger Continuation (5.11b) 63
Hundredth Monkey, The (5.11b) 341
Hung Like a Manster (5.11c) 178
I Don't Know (5.10a) 324
I Don't Remember (5.9) 324
Icons of Filth (5.7) 251
Illusion, The (5.10d) 126
Ilsa She Wolf of the SS (5.10c) 175
Improbable Traverse (5.7) 320
Inch and a Quarter Blues (5.11a) 328
Inchworm (5.11b) 32
Independence Pinnacle 75

Independence Pinnacle, Center Route (5.10d) 75
Independent Route (5.10b) 75
Index Eliminator (5.12a) 42
Indica Point (5.10b) 150
Indisposed (5.10d) 245
Indubious Battle (5.11a) 100
Infraction (5.9) 45
Inner Reaches (5.7) 78
Into the Fire (5.11b) 260
Iota, The (5.4) 74
Isaiah 2:21 (5.12d) 341
Isotope (5.11d) 74
Jack Pinnacle, Left (5.9) 53
Jack Pinnacle, Right (5.7) 53
Jack the Zipper (5.12) 232
Jacob's Ladder (5.10c) 166
Jam Session (5.10b) 325
Jamcrack Route (5.9) 152
Jardine's Hand (5.11a) 45
Jaw Bone (5.10a) 37
Jaws (5.12a) 342
Jesu Joy (5.10c) 184
Jigsaw (5.11a) 295
Joe Palmer (5.11b) 141
Joe's Garage (5.11c) 48
John's Ring Job (5.11d) 32
Jojo (5.10b) 185
Joker, The (5.10b) 311
Jolly Green Giant (5.9) 138
Jomo (5.11d) 80
Jordi-Sattva (5.10b) 264
Journey to the East (5.12b) 264
Jug Monkey (5.9) 57
Jughead (5.8) 148
Jugs (5.8) 65
Juliette's Flake 35
Juliette's Flake, Left Side (5.8) 35
Juliette's Flake, Right Side IV) 35
Jump for Joy (5.9) 124
Jungle Book (5.15.10) 335
Jupiter (5.12d) 79
Just Do-D- It (5.10a) 124
Just Scraping By (5.8) 59
Karma (5.11d) 221
Katchup (5.10a) 40
Kauk-ulator (5.11c) 334
Keep the Muscle, Lose the Fat (5.13b) 50
Keepr of the Flame (5.13a) 340
Ken's Dream (5.10a) 201
Keystone Corner (5.8) 78
Kids are All Right, The (5.7) 181
Killing Yourself to Live (5.12a) 340
Kindergarten Crack (5.8) 34
King Cobra (5.10a) 63
King of Hearts (5.10d) 176
King Snake (5.12) 176
King Tut's Tomb (5.10b) 259
Klemens' Escape (5.9) 32
Kling Cobra (5.10d) 178
Klingon (5.11c) 48
Knife, The (5.11b) 53

Route Index

Knob Hill Rapist (5.8) 66
Knob Job (5.10b) 53
Knuckle Buster (5.11a) 165
Knuckleheads (5.10b) 53
Koki Duck (5.11a) 146
Kor0Beck (5.9) 282
Krovy Rookers (5.10b) 175
Kryptonite (5.12b) 87
Kung Pao Chicken (5.10b) 260
L.D. Getaway (5.8) 87
La Arista (5.10c) 105
La Cosita, Left (5.9) 105
La Cosita, Right (5.9) 105
La Escuela (5.11b) 104
La Escula Direct 104
Labor of Love (5.10b) 214
Ladyfingers (5.11a) 45
Lagerhead (5.11a) 118
Lancelot (5.9) 137
Landshark (5.12a) 323
Lap Lobster (5.10b) 293
Last in Line (5.11b) 45
Last Resort Pinnacle, The, Center (5.10a) 263
Last Resort Pinnacle, The, Left Side (5.9) 263
Later (5.11a) 34
Law of Tools (5.11a) 57
Lay Lady Lieback (5.11a) 247
Lazy Bum (5.10d) 152
Le Bachar (5.11b) 334
Lean Years (5.11a) 237
Leanie Meanie (5.11b) 32
Left Mini-Meanie (5.10b) 182
Left Rabbit Ear Route (5.11a) 291
Left Wing (5.10b) 148
Leisure Time (5.10b) 87
Lemon (5.9) 152
Lena's Lieback (5.9) 146
LeNocturne (5.10a) 119
Letdown, The (5.9) 237
Lethal Weapon (5.11d) 172
Level Two (5.10) 175
Lichen Madness (5.10a) 235
Lichen Nightmare (5.10a) 235
Lieback Route (5.8) 152
Lighten Up (5.12b) 248
Like a Hurricane (5.11a) 327
Lingering Lie (5.10d) 152
Lionheart, The (5.10b) 93
Little Girl's Route (5.10d) 250
Little John, Center (5.10d) 105
Little John, Left (5.8) 105
Little John, Right (5.8) 105
Little Thing (5.11d) 87
Little Wing (5.10d) 87
Local Motion (5.10d) 314
Log Jam (5.11b) 118
Loggerhead Ledge Route (5.7) 118
Lonely Dancer (5.10c) 237
Look Before You Leap (5.11a) 262
Looking for Lichen (5.10b) 235

Loose Tooth City (5.10a) 69
Lost and Found (5.12c) 260
Lost Arrow Chimney (5.10a) 158
Lost Arrow Tip (5.12b) 160
Lost Boys (5.9) 100
Lost Brother, Northwest Face Route (5.10c) 263
Lost Error (5.10a) 343
Lost Flake (5.6) 168
Lost on Venus (5.7) 322
Love Misslie F1-11 (5.10b) 252
Lower Cathedral Rock, East Buttress (5.10c) 302
Lower Cathedral Spire, Fredericks-Sacherer Variation (5.9) 268
Lower Cathedral Spire, Northeast Face (5.9) 268
Lower Cathedral Spire, Pratt-Faint Variation (5.9) 268
Lower Cathedral Spire, Regular Route (5.9) 269
Loyd's Lolly Pop (5.9) 335
Loyd's Return Trip (5.9) 334
Lucifer's Ledge (5.9) 237
Lucifer's to The Oasis (5.9) 237
Lunar Landscape (5.10b) 108
Lunar Lunacy (5.11d) 237
Lunar Lunacy (5.11d) 239
Lunatic Fringe (5.10c) 75
Lycra Virgin (5.11d) 118
Lynnea's Birthday Surprise (5.10a) 181
Machine Gun (5.13c) 87
Machine Head (5.11c) 311
Mad Pilot (5.11b) 332
Magic Carpet (5.11d) 77
Magical Mystery Tour (5.10a) 75
Magilla Gorilla (5.11b) 321
Mainliner (5.10c) 72
Malice Aforethought (5.11a) 272
Maltese Falcon (5.11a) 57
Manana (5.10d) 259
Maple Jam (5.10a) 128
Maps and Legends (5.11b) 165
Marginal (5.9) 232
Mark of Art, The (5.10d) 104
Marvin Gardens (5.10) 150
Mary's Tears (5.11b) 274
Masquerade (5.11d) 106
Mass Assault (5.9) 190
Master Lock (5.12) 63
Master of Cylinders (5.11a) 168
Material Girl (5.12b) 118
Max Deviator (5.11d) 247
Maxine's Wall (5.10c) 172
Mc D's Route (5.11c) 248
McPherson Struts (5.9) 234
Meat Grinder (5.10c) 44
Meat Grinder Arête (5.13b) 44
Meat Puppet (5.10) 63
Meatheads (5.10d) 50
Megaforce (5.11a) 311
Meltdown (5.12c) 50

Route Index

Mental Block (5.10c) 258
Metal Error (5.10d) 175
Meteorite (5.12b) 101
Micron (5.11b) 74
Middle Cathedral Rock, Direct North Buttress (5.10b) 289
Middle Catheral Rock, North Buttress (5.10a) 292
Midnight Rampest (5.10d) 75
Midterm (5.10b) 32
Mighty Crunchy (5.10d) 81
Milk Dud (5.10a) 232
Min-Ne-Ah (5.11d) 156
Mindahoonee Wall (5.10d) 143
Minor Kinda Unit (5.9) 335
Mirage (5.12a) 70
Miramonte (5.10c) 49
Mirror, Mirror Left (5.10b) 198
Mirror, Mirror Right (5.9) 198
Mischief (5.8) 150
Misty Beethoven (5.10d) 234
Moan Fest (5.10c) 173
Moby Dick, Ahab (5.10b) 106
Moby Dick, Center (5.10a) 106
Moby Dick, Left (5.9) 106
Moe, Larry, The Cheese (5.10c) 151
Mojo Tooth (5.8) 80
Monday Morning Slab, Left Side (5.2) 235
Monday Morning Slab, Right Side (5.1) 235
Monday Morning To Patio (5.9) 235
Mongolian Clusterfuck (5.10a) 72
Mongoloid (5.11c) 247
Monkey Do (5.10c) 325
Monkey Hang (5.11b) 119
Monster Boulder (5.11a) 342
Montgomery Cliff (5.11d) 144
Moon Age Daydream (5.11a) 84
Moonchild (5.10) 105
Moongerms (5.11d) 346
Morality Crack (5.10) 251
Moratorium, The (5.11b) 116
More Balls Than Brains A3) 166
Mothballed (5.1) 153
Mother Earth (5.11c) 297
Mother of the Future (5.11a) 172
Mother's Lament, A (5.10c) 232
Motor Drive (5.11a) 81
Mouse King, The (5.9) 124
Mouth To Perhaps (5.11b) 234
Mouth, The, Boche-Hennek Variation (5.9) 234
Mouth, The, Regular (5.9) 234
Movin' Like a Stud (5.10d) 181
Movin' to Montana (5.8) 66
Mr. Happy (5.10a) 119
Mr. Natural (5.10c) 237
Mud Flats (5.11d) 152
Mud Shark (5.8) 57
Mudflaps (5.10d) 138
Munginella (5.6) 148
My Left Foot (5.10b) 128

My Rhombus (5.10a) 169
My-Toe-Sis (5.11b) 53
Mystic Mint (5.11b) 44
Nagasaki My Love see East Arrow Chimney
Narrow Escape (5.10c) 28
Nautral End (5.9) 80
Negative Pinnacle, Center A4) 107
Negative Pinnacle, Left A3) 107
Neil Down (5.11c) 201
Nerf Test (5.8) 35
Neutron Escape (5.10a) 84
Never Say Dog (5.11b) 120
New Deviations (5.9) 65
New Dimensions (5.11a) 32
New Diversions (5.10a) 65
New Generation (5.12a) 172
New Testament (5.10d) 252
New Traditionalists (5.10b) 80
New Wave (5.11d) 246
Nightmare Continuation (5.11d) 346
Nine Lives (5.11b) 53
Ninja Flake (5.11) 42
No Butts About It (5.10b) 280
No Exit (5.10d) 37
No Falls Wall (5.10b) 84
No Love-Chump Sucker (5.11c) 135
No Rest for the Wicked (5.11b) 167
North by Northwest (5.11a) 304
North Dome, South Face Route (5.7) 190
North Dome, West Face Route (5.8) 190
Northwest Corner, Kat Pinnacle (5.7) 40
Nose, The (5.11) 99
Notably Knobular (5.8) 59
Notch Route (5.10b) 320
Notes From the Undergound (5.12) 264
Nothing Good Ever Lasts (5.10d) 77
Nothing on The Apron (5.11c) 237
Nottingham (5.10a) 93
Now (5.10a) 34
Nowhere Man (5.10c) 185
Nurdle (5.8) 53
Nutcracker (5.8) 124
Nutter Butter (5.12b) 44
Nutty Buddy (5.8) 128
NWR (Not Worth Repeating) (5.10b) 305
Obscure Destiny (5.11a) 49
Observation Point (5.9) 150
Ochre Fields (5.11a) 232, 234
Odyssey, The (5.11) 186
Old 5.11 (5.12) 81
Old Five Ten (5.10d) 75
Olga's Trick (5.10d) 74
Omakara (5.12b) 34
On Any Thursday (5.10b) 235
On the Edge (5.11b) 214
On The Loose (5.9) 248
On the Wedge (5.10a) 59
Open Trench (5.10a) 322
Opposite World (5.10) 57
Opposition (5.11d) 36
Oral Roberts (5.12a) 167
Orange Juice Avenue (5.10a) 118

Route Index

Orange Peel (5.10b) 295
Oranguatan Arch (5.11b) 44
Original Chips Ahoy (5.10c) 42
Original Route, Arch Rock Pinnacle (5.5) 34
Original Sin (5.10c) 320
Out on a Limb (5.11b) 135
Outer Limits (5.10c) 44
Overdrive (5.11a) 318
Overhang Bypass (5.7) 306
Overhang Overpass (5.11c) 306
Owl Bypass, The (5.9) 70
Owl Roof (5.12c) 70
Paddy Melt (5.10b) 335
Pandora's Box (5.10a) 37
Panther, The (5.11d) 185
Paradise Lost (5.10a) 288
Party Mix (5.10b) 107
Pass or Fail (5.9) 34
Passage, The (5.12b) 323
Pat Pinnacle (5.7) 53
Patio Pinnacle, Left Side (5.9) 234
Patio Pinnacle, Right Side (5.8) 234
Patio Pinnacle, Regular Route (5.8) 234
Patio To Coonyard (5.10a) 234
Pee Pee Pillar (5.10a) 288
Peeping Tom (5.10a) 174
Pegasus (5.12) 108
Penny Ante (5.11) 78
People's Court (5.10d) 53
Per-Spire-ation (5.10b) 34
Perfect Master (5.11d) 237
Perfect Vision (5.11c) 272
Perhaps (5.10d) 232
Permanent Waves (5.10b) 172
Perpetrator, The (5.10d) 26
Peruvian Flake (5.10a) 174
Pet Semetary (5.11b) 337
Peter Pan (5.9) 100
Peter's Out (5.12) 172
Petty Larceny (5.11b) 37
Phantom (5.13a) 74
Phantom Pinnacle, Left Side (5.9) 265
Phantom Pinnacle, Outside Face (5.10d) 265
Pharoah's Beard, Right Side (5.10d) 262
Pharoah's Beard, Regular Route (5.8) 262
Phoemix, The (5.13a) 58
Pieces of Eight (5.10c) 287
Pigs in Space (5.12) 172
Pimper's Paradise (5.11d) 69
Pine Line (5.7) 106
Pink Banana (5.10d) 63
Pink Dream (5.10a) 346
Pink Elephant (5.9) 341
Pink Pussycat A1) 36
Pink Torpedo (5.11b) 133
Pinky Paralysis (5.11c) 37
Pint-Sized (5.12) 182
Plane Fare (5.10b) 229
Plank, The (5.10b) 181
Plant Your Fingers (5.11a) 128
Plumb Line (5.10d) 343

Plumkin (5.10a) 84
PMS (5.11a) 84
Point Beyond (5.8) 237
Point Beyond, Direct (5.8) 237
Pointy Part, The (5.12b) 264
Poker Face (5.10b) 176
Pole Position (5.10a) 166
Police and Theives (5.12b) 154
Police State (5.10b) 165
Polymorphous Perverse (5.10c) 72
Poodle Bites see Concrete Jungle
Porcelain Pup (5.10b) 224
Porter's Pout (5.10a) 75
Portside (5.12b) 50
Positively 4th Street (5.9) 128
Pot Belly (5.7) 66
Powell-Reed (5.10c) 286
Power Failure (5.11a) 184
Power Point (5.11c) 275
Precious Powder (5.11a) 198
Preface (5.11b) 133
Premature Ejaculation, The (5.11d) 175
Priceless Friends (5.10a) 193
Prime Time (5.9) 50
Princess, The (5.9) 311
Pringles (5.11b) 45
Promise, The (5.11b) 110
Prow, The (5.10a) 185
Prude, The (5.9) 198
Prune (5.10a) 152
Psuedo Desperation (5.7) 63
Psychic Energy (5.11b) 232
Psycho Killer see Dakshina
Psychological Warfare (5.12c) 57
Pterodactyl Terrace, Left (5.1a) 106
Pterodactyl Terrace, Right (5.11b) 106
Public Enema Number One (5.11c) 176
Public Sanitation (5.10) 244
Pulpit Pooper (5.10b) 320
Pulpit Rock, East Face (5.7) 320
Pulsing Pustules (5.11c) 286
Pump Dummy (5.11d) 319
Pumping Hate (5.12a) 50
Punch Bowl, The (5.10a) 239
Punch Line, The (5.10d) 239
Punchline (5.12c) 32
Pussy Licked (5.11a) 41
Pussy Whipped (5.11c) 41
Pygmy Pillar (5.7) 154
Pygmy Sex Circus (5.10b) 71
Pygmy Village (5.12) 335
QED aka East of Eden (5.11a) 169
Quaker Flake (5.10b) 148
Quickie Quizzes (5.10b) 32
Quicksliver (5.9) 295
R and R (5.10a) 37
Radical Chic (5.9) 65
Radioactive (5.11a) 84
Rainbow Bridge (5.11d) 286
Raisin (5.9) 152
Rambler, The (5.10d) 181
Ramblin' Rose (5.10) 131

Route Index

Ramer (5.10c) 293
Ramp of Deception (5.9) 45
Rat's Tooth (5.10a) 258
Rattlesnake Buttress (5.11a) 307
Ray's Pin Job (5.12b) 45
Razor's Edge (5.12) 337
Ready or Not (5.11a) 84
Real Error (5.7) 343
Reality Check (5.10c) 343
Realm of the Lizard King (5.11c) 263
Reception, The (5.10a) 78
Rectum Ranch (5.8) 115
Red House (5.10a) 87
Red Zinger (5.11d) 44
Redtide (5.10d) 153
Reed's Leads (5.10b) 106
Reed's Pinnacle Direct (5.10a) 74
Reed's Pinnacle Regular Route (5.9) 74
Reed's Pinnacle, Left Side (5.10a) 74
Reefer Madness (5.10d) 181
Rehab Doll (5.10a) 81
Remember Ribbon Falls (5.12) 28
Remnant, The, Center Route (5.12a) 74
Remnant, The, Left Side (5.10b) 74
Remnant, The, Right Side (5.7) 74
Renegade, The see The Stigma
Renus Wrinkle (5.10a) 124
Rest for the Wicked (5.11c) 72
Resurrection (5.10a) 252
Return to the Stone Age (5.11a) 307
Revival (5.10a) 166
RF (5.8) 142
Ribald (5.9) 153
Ribbon Candy (5.11c) 91
Riddler, The (5.10a) 87
Ride the Lightning (5.12a) 78
Right Mini-Meanie (5.11a) 182
Right Profile, The (5.11b) 144
Right Side of The Folly see The Good Book
River Boulder (5.11d) 38
Rixon's Pinnacle, Direct South Face (5.11d) 132
Rixon's Pinnacle, East Chimney (5.10a) 132
Rixon's Pinnacle, East Chimney, Final Decision (5.11b) 132
Rixon's Pinnacle, East Chimney, Klemens Variation (5.10c) 132
Rixon's Pinnacle, South Face (5.11d) 132
Rixon's Pinnacle, West Face (5.10c) 132
Road to Ruin (5.12a) 295
Roadside Attraction (5.12a) 38
Roadside Infraction (5.12b) 38
Robin (5.12b) 63
Rock Bottom (5.11d) 136
Rock Horror Show (5.12a) 53
Rock Neurotic (5.11b) 108
Rocket in My Pocket (5.11c) 75
Rocket Man (5.11d) 65
Roger Stokes Route (5.8) 142
Roland's Hole Route see Portside
Romantic Tension (5.10d) 48
Rorp, The (5.7) 75

Rostrum, The, The Regular North Face Route (5.11c) 332
Rostrum, The, West Base Route (5.10c) 334
Roto Killer (5.10a) 229
Royal Arches Route (5.6) 174
Royal Arches Route (5.9) 177
Royal Prerogative (5.9) 175
Rum Sodomy in the Lash (5.10d) 175
Run With Me (5.10a) 239
Running Hummock (5.10) 148
Rupto Pac (5.11c) 172
Rurp Rape (5.10c) 198
Rycrisp (5.7) 311
Sacherer Cracker (5.10a) 104
Sacherer-Fredericks (5.10c) 281
Sacrilege (5.11a) 167
Said and Done (5.9) 63
Salami Ledge (5.10) 96
Salathé Route (5.10b) 215
Salathé Wall (5.13b) 98
Salin' Shoes (5.10d) 237
Sample the Dog (5.12a) 135
Samurai Crack (5.11d) 181
Sand Jam (5.9) 245
Sanitary Engineer (5.10d) 245
Santa Barbara (5.10d) 135
SAT (5.12a) 34
Satanic Mechanic (5.12c) 44
Savage Amusement (5.11b) 258
Sawyer Crack (5.9) 26
Say Mama, Say Daddy (5.10a) 108
Sceptor, The (5.11a) 260
Scimitar (5.12) 237
Scorpion Man (5.10d) 53
Scott-Child (5.10a) 197
Scram (5.12a) 63
Scratch and Sniff (5.12a) 80
Scratching Post (5.10b) 41
Scrooged (5.8) 153
Scrub Scouts (5.10c) 319
Scruv (5.9) 57
Scuz Ball (5.7) 87
Sea Cow (5.10) 174
Sea Hag (5.10) 174
Seaside (5.10c) 143
Season of the Bitch (5.11d) 250
Secret Agent (5.10c) 63
Secret Storm (5.10a) 135
Seedy Leads (5.11a) 106
Selaginella (5.8) 150
Sentinel Rock, West Face (5.11d) 257
Separate Reality (5.12a) 49
Sequel, The (5.8) 272
Serenity Crack (5.10d) 172
Sermon, The (5.10b) 321
Sex Farm (5.10c) 293
Sex, Drugs and Violence (5.10a) 84
Shaft, The (5.10d) 70
Shake and Bake (5.10a) 301
Shake, Rattle and Drop (5.10b) 65
Shakey Flakes (5.11a) 181
Shattered (5.10d) 84

Route Index

Sherrie's Crack (5.10c) 53
Shining, The (5.12c) 178
Shit on a Shingle (5.9) 72
Shiver-Me-Timers (5.8) 325
Shockwave (5.13b) 250
Short but Thick (5.11a) 36
Short but Thin (5.11b) 104
Short Circuit (5.11d) 30
Shortcake (5.11b) 45
Showtime (5.11c) 53
Shuttle Madness (5.9) 232
Siberian Swarm Screw (5.10a) 72
Side Kick (5.9) 84
Sidetrack (5.11a) 32
Silber Platter (5.10c) 225
Silent Freeway, The (5.10c) 120
Silent Freeway, The, Center Route (5.10b) 120
Silent Freeway, The, Left Side (5.11a) 120
Silent Majority (5.10b) 199
Simian Sex (5.10d) 118
Simulkrime (5.9) 108
Sink Like a Stone (5.11d) 118
Sixth Heaven (5.10b) 252
Skateaway (5.10a) 34
Skid Roper (5.10b) 81
Skid Row (5.8) 190
Skid Row Messiah (5.11a) 166
Skindad The Scaler (5.11d) 168
Skinheads (5.10d) 53
Skunk Crack (5.11b) 49
Sky (5.11c) 341
Sky Pilot (5.10c) 321
Slack, The, Center Route (5.10d) 104
Slack, The, Left Side (5.10b) 104
Slamming Left (5.11b) 63
Slamming Right (5.10d) 63
Slap that Bitch (5.10d) 63
Sleight of Hand (5.10b) 176
Slingshot (5.12a) 154
Slit Your Tires (5.11d) 337
Sloppy Seconds (5.5) 66
Sloth Wall (5.7) 66
Slumgullion (5.10) 84
Smee's Come-on (5.11a) 100
Smith-Crawford (5.11d) 298
Snake Dance (5.9) 216
Snake Dike (5.7) 216
Snake in the Grass (5.10b) 215
Snap, Crackle, and Pop (5.10c) 42
Snatch Power (5.10c) 37
Sober Up (5.10a) 119
Solid Waste (5.10d) 245
Solo Crack (5.9) 59
Soloist, The (5.10) 26
Something for Nothing (5.11d) 45
Son of Sam (5.9) 237
Sons of Yesterday (5.10a) 173
Sorry Poopsie (5.8) 119
Soul Sacrifice (5.11c) 302
South by Southwest (5.11a) 269
Southern Belle (5.12d) 220

Southwest Corner, Kat Pinnacle (5.7) 40
Sow Sow Sow (5.10a) 119
Space Babble (5.11a) 283
Space Case (5.10c) 184
Space Doubt (5.10c) 134
Space Invader (5.12a) 182
Spank Your Monkey (5.10b) 293
Sparkling Give-away (5.11a) 105
Spectacle (5.11d) 305
Speed Racer (5.11c) 243
Sphinxter, The (5.9) 259
Spiderman (5.11c) 258
Spike (5.12a) 244
Spinal Tap (5.11b) 327
Split Pinnacle, East Arête (5.10c) 127
Spooky Tooth (5.10a) 301
Spring Chicken (5.11a) 65
Spring Fever (5.11b) 77
Spuds McKenzie (5.10d) 42
Squeeze-n-Tease (5.8) 87
Stack o' Fun (5.12b) 154
Stacked Deck (5.11a) 176
Stand and Quiver (5.11a) 53
Starfire (5.10) 301
Start Me Up (5.4) 148
Static Clinb (5.10a) 334
Stay Free (5.11b) 144
Stay Lady Stay Back (5.10a) 119
Steal, The (5.10a) 84
Stealth Technology (5.11a) 35
Steck Route (5.9) 271
Steck-Salathé (5.9) 256
Stepahnie's Corner (5.8) 167
Steppin' Out (5.10d) 75
Stigma, The (5.13) 45
Stinger (5.11a) 53
Stone Groove (5.10b) 75
Stonequest (5.8) 26
Stoner's Highway (5.10c) 286
Straight Error (5.10c) 343
Straight In (5.10a) 90
Straight Jacket (5.10d) 197
Strange Energy (5.11b) 232
Strangers in the Night (5.10b) 65
Streamline (5.12b) 229
Stretch Mark (5.11b) 152
Stroke (My Erect Ear Tufts) (5.10c) 70
Stubs (5.12a) 63
Stumped Ray (5.11) 63
Stupid Pet Tricks (5.10b) 295
Sub Atomic (5.11d) 80
Sub-Mission (5.10c) 304
Submen (5.11b) 111
Substance Abuse (5.12a) 245
Sultans of Sling (5.10c) 152
Summary Judgement (5.11a) 63
Sunblast A3) 53
Sunday Driver (5.10b) 105
Sunnside Pinnacle (5.10) 152
Sunset Strip (5.11a) 313
Super Nova (5.11a) 330
Super Slab (5.9) 172

Route Index

Superstem (5.11a) 115
Supertoe (5.10d) 115
Supplication (5.10c) 32
Surplus Cheaper Hands (5.10c) 174
Surprise, The (5.8) 148
Sweet Pea (5.10c) 148
Swillar Pillar (5.10a) 119
Swollen Plecnode (5.9) 296
Syllable, The (5.8) 272
Sylvester's Meow (5.11a) 75
Symphony, The (5.9) 248
Synapse Collapse (5.1b) 232
Synchronicity (5.11) 237
Tail End 65
Take Da Plunge (5.12c) 340
Tales of Power (5.12b) 49
Tammy Fae (5.10c) 166
Tapestry (5.9) 295
TD's Dihedral (5.9) 142
Teacher's Pet (5.12a) 296
Tears of Joy (5.10a) 295
Teenage Abortion (5.10) 141
Teenage Mutant Blowjobs (5.10b) 119
Teenage Warning (5.10d) 69
Temple of Doom (5.12b) 245
Tennis Shoe Crack (5.6) 229
Terminal Research (5.11c) 188
Terminator 45
Terminator, Left (5.11b) 45
Terminator, Right (5.10d) 45
Texas Chain Saw Massacre (5.11a) 176
That'll Teach You (5.12a) 296
Thief, The (5.10d) 311
Thin Line (5.11c) 90
Thin Man (5.10c) 198
Thirsty Spire (5.11a) 290
This Ain't England (5.11b) 237
This Ain't England (5.11b) 239
This and That (5.10a) 63
Thread of Life (5.11a) 106
Through Bein' Cool (5.10c) 50
Thunderhead (5.11d) 237
Thunderhead (5.11d) 239
Ticket to Nowhere (5.11c) 295
Tidal Wave (5.11c) 153
Tidbit (5.11a) 303
Tiger By the Tail (5.12b) 41
Tiger's Paw (5.10a) 84
Tightrope (5.11b) 232
Tilted Mitten, Left Side (5.9) 258
Tilted Mitten, Right Side (5.8) 258
Tinkerbell, Left (5.7) 100
Tinkerbell, Right (5.9) 100
Tiny Tim (5.7) 153
Tips (5.12a) 63
Tithe (5.9) 248
Title Fight (5.13) 63
TKO (5.11c) 32
To Beer or Not To Be (5.10) 152
Token, The (5.11d) 237
Tom Cat (5.10b) 185
Tongue and Groove (5.12a) 80

Too High (5.6) 26
Too Much Paranoia (5.10b) 87
Tooth Fairy (5.10b) 81
Tooth or Consequences (5.11b) 75
Tooth, The (5.10a) 74
Top Dope (5.11c) 293
Torque Converter (5.11d) 35
Total Way-ist (5.11b) 245
Tour de Force (5.12b) 284
Toxic Avenger (5.11c) 57
Traffic Jam (5.9) 71
Transistor Sister (5.10c) 232
Tree Route (5.9) 320
Trial By Fire (5.8) 172
Trial by Jury (5.10a) 184
Tricky Fingers (5.10c) 53
Triscuit, The (5.9) 311
Trivial Pursuit (5.9) 178
Trix (5.11a) 68
Trough of Justice (5.10b) 53
Trowel, The (5.7) 178
Trundling Juan (5.10b) 343
Try Again Ledge (5.8) 148
Tube, The (5.11a) 53
Tucker's Proud Rock Climb (5.12b) 245
Tunnel Vision (5.12d) 48
Turkey Pie (5.7) 66
Turkey Vulture (5.11b) 185
Turning Point (5.10c) 84
Turning Yeller see Yellow Corner
Turret, The (5.11) 291
Tweedle Dee (5.8) 135
Twilight Zone (5.10d) 44
Twinkie (5.10c) 44
Twist of Fate (5.10a) 182
Two "D" (5.10c) 32
Udder Way, An (5.10a) 232
Ugly Duckling (5.10c) 146
Ultimate Emotion (5.11c) 34
Unagi (5.10c) 259
Uncertain Ending (5.10b) 49
Uncle Fanny (5.7) 166
Under Siege (5.11b) 252
Underclingon (5.12a) 53
Unemployment Line (5.9) 226
Uppity Women (5.10c) 199
Uprising (5.11b) 332
Valley Syndrome (5.11c) 201
Van Belle O Drome (5.13c) 39
Van Belle Syndrome (5.13) 39
Vanishing Point (5.10d) 258
Variation on a Themem (5.10b) 235
Vegetal Extraction (5.10) 153
Vendetta (5.10b) 45
Vibrator (5.11d) 81
Violent Bear It Away, The (5.10c) 178, 181
Viper, The (5.11c) 335
Void Continuation (5.10d) 45
Void, The (5.11b) 45
Vortex (5.12) 313
Voyage (5.10c) 32
Vulture Culture (5.12a) 232

Route Index

W'allnuts (5.10d) 86
Walk of LIfe (5.10d) 295
Walk on By (5.10a) 323
Walking on Mars (5.12) 328
Walrus (5.9) 71
Wand, The (5.11d) 165
Warbler, The (5.11d) 313
Wart Hog (5.8) 53
Wasp (5.9d) 65
Waste Not, Whip Not (5.11) 245
Waste of Time (5.10c) 321
Water Babies (5.11a) 201
Waterfall Route Start (5.10b) 111
Waverly Wafer (5.10c) 44
Way Lost (5.9) 229
Way-Homo Sperm Burpers from Fresno (5.10c) 175
Wedge, The (5.11b) 53
Weird Scenes in the Gold Mine (5.10a) 63
Wendy (5.9) 100
Werner's Ant Trees (5.10c) 148
Werner's Crack (5.8) 198
West Face (5.11c) 97
West Side Story (5.10b) 148
Whack and Dangle (5.11a) 78
What's Your Fantasy (5.11b) 42
Wheat Thin (5.10c) 45
Whim (5.9) 63
Whipcord (5.13c) 328
Whisker (5.11d) 262
White Cloud (5.10d) 57
White Dike, The (5.10d) 237, 239
White Owl (5.11d) 69
White Zone, The (5.11d) 114
Wicked Arêtation (5.10d) 57
Wicked Gravity (5.12c) 341
Wicked Jones Crusher (5.10b) 71
Wide Thing (5.10d) 244
Wild Child (5.9) 142
Wild Thing (5.10c) 133
Wild Turkey (5.10c) 85
William's Climb (5.10c) 72
Wind Chill (5.11a) 316
Windfall (5.11a) 314
Windjammer (5.10c) 314
Wing of Bat (5.1oc) 185
Wings of Maybe (5.12a) 259
Winter of Our Discontent (5.10) 148
Winterlewd (5.10b) 199
Wise Crack (5.10a) 176
Wish You Were Here (5.12a) 244
Woody Woodpecker (5.9) 26
Work Around the Skirt (5.10c) 148
Worst Error, Left Side (5.9) 344
Wrong Address (5.9) 68
Y Crack (5.10a) 175
Yankee Clipper (5.11b) 80
Yasoo Dome, South Face (5.9) 206
Yeast Infection (5.10c) 118
Yellow Corner (5.12a) 310
Yellow Peril (5.11b) 80
Ying-Yang (5.10d) 259
Yosemite Point Buttress, Direct Route (5.9) 162
Young and The Restless (5.10c) 134
Your Pizza is Ready (5.9) 323
Yuk (5.7) 81
Zipperhead (5.12c) 45
Zoner (5.11b) 235

BM 6259

24

19

Creek

Creek

6200

6000

30

Cascade

Falls

Falls

BM 5729

Fireplac

25

5400

5600

4600

ROAD

The Cascades

4600

4800

BM 3438

Wildcat Falls

TUNNEL

HIGHWAY

Powerhouse

PIPELINE

MERCED

Pulpit Rock

BM 3419

The Rostrum

4200

36

BM 4873

4600

WAWONA

BM 4622

Elephant Rock

Turtleback Dome

ROAD

Inspira Point

Relay Sta. 5267

5600

4921

Fort Monroe

GORGE

T 2 S
T 3 S

POHONO

ALLYEAR

ROAD

4000

WAWONA

5200

6000

R 20 E
R 21 E

1

5

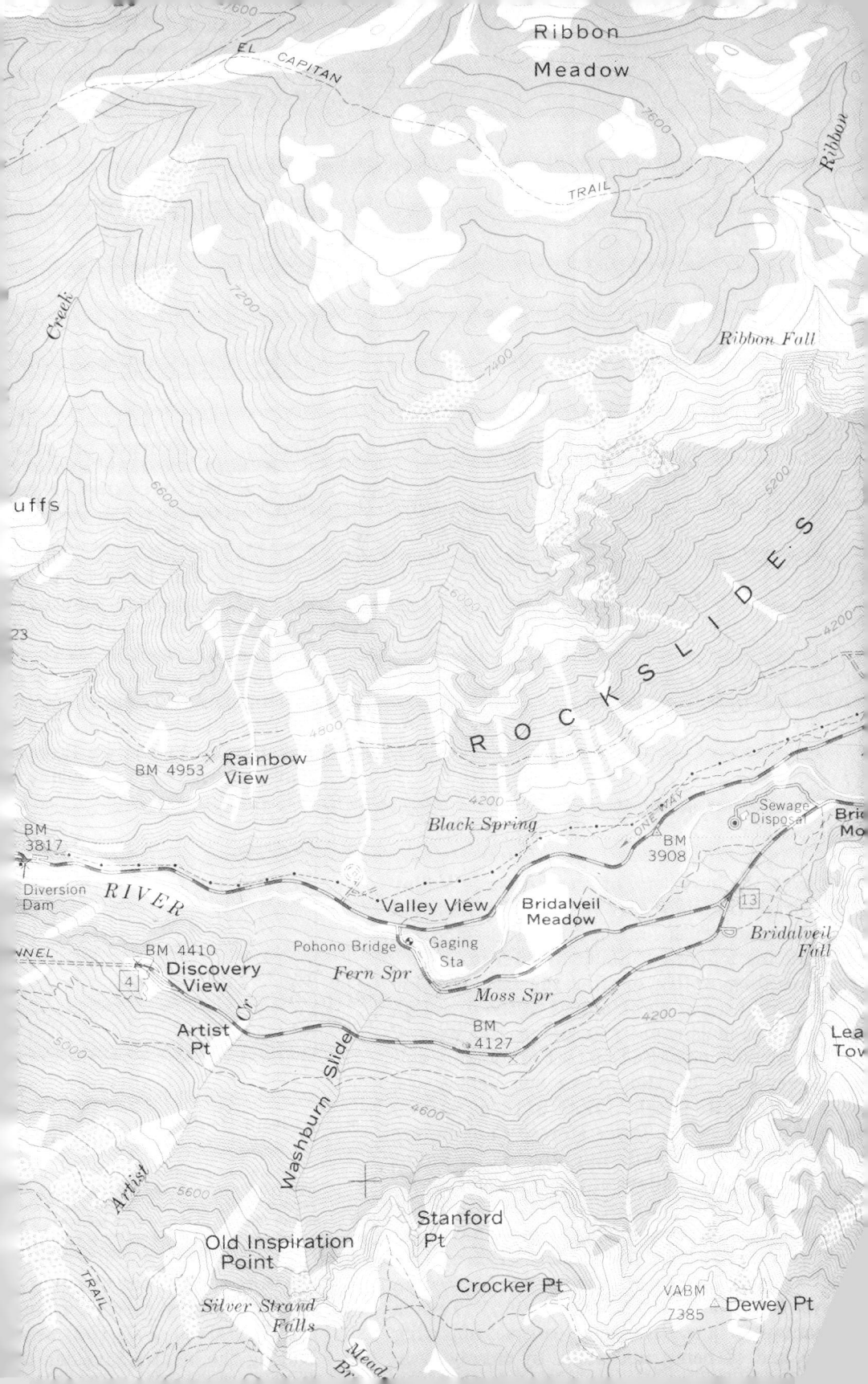

Ribbon Meadow
EL CAPITAN
TRAIL
Ribbon
Creek
Ribbon Fall
uffs
ROCKSLIDES
BM 4953 Rainbow View
Black Spring
Sewage Disposal
BM 3908
BM 3817
ONE WAY
13
Diversion Dam
RIVER
Valley View
Bridalveil Meadow
Bridalveil Fall
NNEL
BM 4410
Pohono Bridge
Gaging Sta
4
Discovery View
Fern Spr
Moss Spr
Lea Tow
Artist Pt
Cr
BM 4127
Washburn Slide
Artist
Old Inspiration Point
Stanford Pt
TRAIL
Silver Strand Falls
Crocker Pt
VABM 7385 Dewey Pt
Mead Br

Map labels

- Ribbon Creek
- 7925
- Three Brothers
- Eagle Creek
- Ribbon Fall
- El Capitan Gully
- K P Pinnacle 7569
- Split Pinnacle
- El Capitan 7042
- Y O
- 4144
- BM 3953
- ONE WAY
- 12
- BM 3976
- BM 3955
- El Capitan Bridge
- MERCED
- BM 3970
- BM 3954
- El Capitan Meadow
- ONE WAY
- BM 3971
- Sewage Disposal
- Bridalveil Moraine
- Cathedral Rocks
- 13
- Bridalveil Fall
- Gunsight
- 6545
- Church Tower
- 5907
- Cathedral Spires
- 6118
- Leaning Tower
- Bridalveil
- 5400
- 5200
- ley Pt
- Creek

Church Bowl
Royal A
Cascad
Visitor Center
Park Hdqrs
Water
Ahwahnee Hotel
Ahwahnee Bridge
ONE WAY
RESTRIC
Columbia Rock
BM 5031
YOSEMITE
10
BM 3967
Sentinel Bridge
6
BM 3990
Brother
Sunnyside Camp
Yosemite Lodge
Chapel
BM 3965
BM 3966
Riverside Camp
Housekeeping Camp
Stoneman Bridge
BM 3969
Leidig Meadow
ONE WAY
4000
4200
Curry Village
BM 3965
Foothbridge
Brother
RIVER
TRAIL
Union Pt
6314
Moran Pt
Staircas
S
E
M
I
GLACIER PT-FOURMILE
1
Water
VABM 7214
Sentinel Rock
7038
4600
Sentinel
Relay Sta
Water
BM 3973
Sentinel Fall
4000
Sentinel Dome
VABM 8122
RESTRICTED
Campground
Creek
ROAD
7600
Profile Cliff
Taft Pt
The Fissures
TRAIL
POINT
GLACIER
Ridge
POHONO
Pothole Meadows
7800
7400
Illilouette
7965

Mt Watkins
Watkins Pinnacles
6586
Creek
Snow
Snow Creek Falls
6700
TUOLUMNE
MEADOWS
TRAIL
Creek
LAKE
TENAYA
Basket Dome
7612
Indian
Ridge
8092
Creek
Creek
Arch
North Dome
Tenaya
TENAYA
C A
Quarter D
DOME
8200
8000
7400
7800
7000
7600
6200
4600
4400
5200
5400
6000
7000
5000
6400
6400
8000
7400
7000

Washington Column
Royal Arches
Lake
BM 4094
Bridge
BM 3980
Indian Cave
Footbridge
Group Camp
RESTRICTED
Iron Spring
BM 4002
Half Dome
8842
7000
Diving Board
JOHN
Stables
Tenaya Bridge
Clarks Bridge
Medial Moraine
6600
Pines Camp
ONE WAY
4400
5800
6400
Lost Lake
4000
E
Mt Broderick
6706
6200
Happy Isles Bridge
Gaging Sta
BM 4035
Trail Center
5
Happy Isles
Grizzly Peak
5400
TRAIL
LITTLE
Liberty Cap
7076
Emerald Pool
Vernal Fall
Sierra Pt
MERCED
LAKE
MIST
TR
Silver Apron
5305
MERCED
5910
Water
Clark Pt
5481
Nevada Fall
MUIR
JOHN
6500
Gorge
GLACIER
PT
PANORAMA
Panorama Cliff
7200
6000

Access: It's everybody's concern

THE ACCESS FUND, a national, non-profit climbers' organization, is working to keep you climbing. The Access Fund helps preserve access and protect the environment by providing funds for land acquisitions and climber support facilities, financing scientific studies, publishing educational materials promoting low-impact climbing, and providing start-up money, legal counsel and other resources to local climbers' coalitions.

Climbers can help preserve access by being responsible users of climbing areas. Here are some practical ways to support climbing:

- **COMMIT YOURSELF TO "LEAVING NO TRACE."** Pick up litter around campgrounds and the crags. Let your actions inspire others.
- **DISPOSE OF HUMAN WASTE PROPERLY.** Use toilets whenever possible. If none are available, choose a spot at least 50 meters from any water source. Dig a hole 6 inches (15 cm) deep, and bury your waste in it. *Always pack out toilet paper* in a "Zip-Lock"-type bag.
- **UTILIZE EXISTING TRAILS.** Avoid cutting switchbacks and trampling vegetation.
- **USE DISCRETION WHEN PLACING BOLTS AND OTHER "FIXED" PROTECTION.** Camouflage all anchors with rock-colored paint. Use chains for rappel stations, or leave rock-colored webbing.
- **RESPECT RESTRICTIONS THAT PROTECT NATURAL RESOURCES AND CULTURAL ARTIFACTS .** Appropriate restrictions can include prohibition of climbing around Indian rock art, pioneer inscriptions, and on certain formations during raptor nesting season. Power drills are illegal in wilderness areas. *Never chisel or sculpt holds in rock on public lands, unless it is expressly allowed* – no other practice so seriously threatens our sport.
- **PARK IN DESIGNATED AREAS,** not in undeveloped, vegetated areas. Carpool to the crags!
- **MAINTAIN A LOW PROFILE.** Other people have the same right to undisturbed enjoyment of natural areas as do you.
- **RESPECT PRIVATE PROPERTY.** Don't trespass in order to climb.
- **JOIN OR FORM A GROUP TO DEAL WITH ACCESS ISSUES IN YOUR AREA.** Consider clean-ups, trail building or maintenance, or other "goodwill" projects.
- **JOIN THE ACCESS FUND.** To become a member, *simply make a donation (tax-deductible) of any amount.* Only by working together can we preserve the diverse American climbing experience.

The Access Fund. Preserving America's diverse climbing resources.
The Access Fund • P.O. Box 17010 • Boulder, CO 80308